# Quantitative Methods for Business

Pearson
Education

We work with leading authors to develop the
strongest educational materials in business,
bringing cutting-edge thinking and best learning
practice to a global market.

Under a range of well-known imprints, including
Financial Times Prentice Hall imprint, we craft high quality
print and electronic publications which help
readers to understand and apply their content,
whether studying or at work.

To find out more about the complete range of our
publishing please visit us on the World Wide Web at:
www.pearsoneduc.com

# Quantitative Methods for Business

## Third Edition

## DONALD WATERS

FINANCIAL TIMES
Prentice Hall

*An imprint of* **Pearson Education**

Harlow, England · London · New York · Reading, Massachusetts · San Francisco
Toronto · Don Mills, Ontario · Sydney · Tokyo · Singapore · Hong Kong · Seoul
Taipei · Cape Town · Madrid · Mexico City · Amsterdam · Munich · Paris · Milan

**Pearson Education Limited**
Edinburgh Gate
Harlow
Essex CM20 2JE
England

and Associated Companies throughout the world

*Visit us on the World Wide Web at:*
http://www.pearsoneduc.com

First published 1993
Second edition published under the Addison-Wesley imprint 1997
**Third edition 2001**

ISBN 0 273 64694 X

*British Library Cataloguing-in-Publication Data*
A catalogue record for this book is available from the British Library.

10 9 8 7 6 5 4 3 2 1
05 04 03 02 01

Typeset by 32 in 10/12 Times
Produced by Pearson Education Asia Pte Ltd.
Printed in Malaysia

*Dedication:*

# To Charles

# Contents

Preface                                                                    xv


## PART ONE
## BACKGROUND TO QUANTITATIVE METHODS                                        1


### Chapter 1
### Numbers and managers                                                     3

Chapter outline                                                             3
1.1   Who needs numbers?                                                    4
1.2   Using models                                                          7
1.3   Stages in solving a problem                                           8
Chapter review                                                            10
Problems                                                                  10
Computer exercises                                                        11
Case study: Hamerson and Sons                                             11


### Chapter 2
### Tools for quantitative methods                                          13

Chapter outline                                                            13
2.1   Working with numbers                                                 14
2.2   Changing numbers to letters                                          21
2.3   Drawing graphs                                                       40
Chapter review                                                            52
Problems                                                                  53
Computer exercises                                                        54
Case study 1: The Crown and Anchor                                        56
Case study 2: Northern Feedstuffs                                         56

## PART TWO
## DATA COLLECTION AND DESCRIPTION 58

## Chapter 3
## Collecting data 60

Chapter outline 60
3.1   Introduction 61
3.2   Types of data 64
3.3   How to choose a sample 67
3.4   Ways of collecting data 74
3.5   Using the data 81
Chapter review 83
Problems 83
Computer exercises 85
Case study: Natural Biscuits 86

## Chapter 4
## Using diagrams to present data 88

Chapter outline 88
4.1   Summarizing data 89
4.2   Diagrams for presenting data 91
4.3   Frequency distributions 108
Chapter review 118
Problems 119
Computer exercises 121
Case study: High Acclaim Importers 123

## Chapter 5
## Using numbers to describe data 125

Chapter outline 125
5.1   Measures for business data 126
5.2   Finding the average 128
5.3   Measuring the spread of data 143
Chapter review 157
Problems 157
Computer exercises 159
Case study: Consumer advice office 161

## Chapter 6
## Describing changes with index numbers     **163**

Chapter outline     163
6.1   Index numbers for describing changes     164
6.2   Indices for more than one variable     172
Chapter review     180
Problems     180
Computer exercises     183
Case study 1: Macleod Engines     184
Case study 2: Retail sales in Europe     185

## PART THREE
## SOLVING BUSINESS PROBLEMS     **187**

## Chapter 7
## Calculations with money     **189**

Chapter outline     189
7.1   Financial ratios     190
7.2   Break-even point     193
7.3   Value of money over time     201
7.4   Mortgages, annuities and sinking funds     213
Chapter review     217
Problems     218
Computer exercises     219
Case study: Mrs Hamilton's retirement savings     222

## Chapter 8
## Relating variables by regression     **224**

Chapter outline     224
8.1   Measuring relationships     225
8.2   Linear relationships     230
8.3   Measuring the strength of a relationship     238
8.4   Extensions to linear regression     247
Chapter review     254
Problems     254
Computer exercises     256
Case study: Western General Hospital     259

**Chapter 9**
**Business forecasting** — 262

Chapter outline — 262
9.1 Forecasting in organizations — 263
9.2 Judgemental forecasting — 265
9.3 Projective forecasting — 267
9.4 Forecasting with seasonality and trend — 283
Chapter review — 294
Problems — 295
Computer exercises — 296
Case study: Workload planning — 298

**Chapter 10**
**Planning with linear programming** — 300

Chapter outline — 300
10.1 What is linear programming? — 301
10.2 Getting LP problems in the right form — 302
10.3 Using graphs to solve linear programmes — 308
10.4 Solving real problems — 315
Chapter review — 327
Problems — 327
Computer exercises — 330
Case study: Elemental Electronics — 332

**Chapter 11**
**Using calculus to describe changes** — 334

Chapter outline — 334
11.1 Differentiation — 335
11.2 Economic applications of differentiation — 346
Chapter review — 351
Problems — 351
Case study: Lundquist Transport — 351

**PART FOUR**
**BUSINESS STATISTICS** — 353

**Chapter 12**
**Uncertainty and probabilities** — 355

Chapter outline — 355
12.1 Measuring uncertainty — 356

12.2 Conditional probability for dependent events 365
Chapter review 375
Problems 376
Computer exercises 377
Case study: *The Gamblers' Press* 379


# Chapter 13
# Probability distributions 381

Chapter outline 381
13.1 What are probability distributions? 382
13.2 Combinations and permutations 384
13.3 Binomial distribution 388
13.4 Poisson distribution 396
13.5 Normal distribution 404
Chapter review 416
Problems 416
Computer exercises 418
Case study: Machined components 420


# Chapter 14
# Using samples in business 421

Chapter outline 421
14.1 Purpose of sampling 422
14.2 Estimating the population mean 423
14.3 Using small samples 438
14.4 Quality control 441
Chapter review 447
Problems 447
Computer exercises 449
Case study: Kings Fruit Farm 450


# Chapter 15
# Testing hypotheses 452

Chapter outline 452
15.1 Hypotheses about population means 453
15.2 Other tests 460
15.3 Non-parametric tests 471
Chapter review 483
Problems 483
Computer exercises 485
Case study: Willingham Consumer Protection Department 487

## PART FIVE
## BUSINESS PROBLEMS WITH UNCERTAINTY 488

### Chapter 16
### Analysing business decisions 490

Chapter outline 490
16.1 Giving structure to decisions 491
16.2 Decision-making under certainty 493
16.3 Decision-making under strict uncertainty 495
16.4 Decision-making under risk 501
16.5 Sequential decisions and decision trees 510
Chapter review 518
Problems 518
Computer exercises 521
Case study: The Newisham Reservoir 525

### Chapter 17
### Controlling stocks 526

Chapter outline 526
17.1 Background to stock control 527
17.2 The economic order quantity 530
17.3 Probabilistic demand 534
17.4 Periodic review systems 538
17.5 ABC analysis of stock 541
Chapter review 544
Problems 544
Computer exercises 545
Case study: Templar Manufacturing 546

### Chapter 18
### Planning projects with networks 548

Chapter outline 548
18.1 Project network analysis 549
18.2 Networks for projects 550
18.3 Timing of projects 557
18.4 Resource planning 563
Chapter review 568
Problems 568
Computer exercises 571
Case study: Westin Contractors 575

## Chapter 19
## Queues and simulation

|  |  | 576 |
| --- | --- | --- |
| Chapter outline |  | 576 |
| 19.1 | Background to queuing | 577 |
| 19.2 | Single-server queues | 578 |
| 19.3 | Simulation models | 583 |
| Chapter review |  | 590 |
| Problems |  | 590 |
| Computer exercises |  | 590 |
| Case study: The Palmer Centre for Alternative Therapy |  | 593 |

*Appendix A*
References for further reading — 594

*Appendix B*
Solutions to self-assessment questions — 599

*Appendix C*
Solutions to numerical problems — 607

*Appendix D*
Probabilities for the binomial distribution — 611

*Appendix E*
Probabilities for the Poisson distribution — 616

*Appendix F*
Probabilities for the Normal distribution — 619

*Appendix G*
Probabilities for the *t*-distribution (two-tail) — 620

*Appendix H*
Critical values for the $\chi^2$ distribution — 621

Index — 623

# Preface

## Introduction

This is a textbook on **quantitative methods for business**. It:

- is an introductory text and assumes no previous knowledge of management or quantitative methods
- takes a broad view and is useful for students doing a wide range of business courses, or people studying by themselves
- covers a lot of material, concentrating on methods that have proved useful in practice
- develops the contents in a logical order, starting with background material and moving through data, deterministic problems and statistics
- presents ideas in a straightforward way, avoiding abstract discussion, mathematical proofs and derivations
- illustrates principles by examples drawn from a range of real applications
- uses computer output – particularly spreadsheets – to illustrate calculations
- lists objectives for each chapter, and includes summaries, self-assessment questions, worked examples, reviews, additional problems, computer exercises and case studies

## Audience

A growing number of students take courses in management, and they all need some understanding of quantitative ideas. This book describes a range of quantitative methods that have proved useful to managers, and which are included in most business courses. It can be used widely as, for example, a source book for BTEC courses, in the early years of an undergraduate business studies course, for MBA students or in a short professional course. You will also find it useful if you are not attending a specific course but want to learn about quantitative ideas in business.

Management students have diverse backgrounds and interests, and so a textbook cannot assume much common knowledge. This book starts with the assumption that you have no previous knowledge of management or quantitative methods. It works from basic principles and develops ideas in a logical sequence.

Management students often find quantitative ideas difficult. Typically, you are not usually interested in mathematical proofs and derivations but are more concerned with how useful a result is and how you can apply it in your work. For this reason the contents of this book are practical rather than theoretical. A deliberate decision has been made to avoid rigorous (and often tedious) mathematics and concentrate on applications rather than theory. Wherever possible, the arithmetic is illustrated by computer printout – particularly spreadsheets.

# Format

Each chapter uses a consistent format which has:

- a list of contents for the chapter
- an outline of the material to be covered and list of things that you should be able to do by the end of the chapter
- the main material of the chapter divided into coherent sections
- worked examples to illustrate methods
- a summary of the main points at the end of each section
- self-assessment questions throughout the text to make sure you understand the material
- a review at the end of each chapter listing the material that has been covered
- additional problems
- computer exercises
- one or two case studies

Solutions to self-assessment questions and numerical problems are given in appendices, together with some suggestions for further reading. You can get more information from the author's web site which is at:

http://website.lineone.net/~donaldwaters

# Contents

Almost any topic in mathematics might be useful to managers in some circumstances. There is a wide range of material that we could put into a book of this type but, to keep it to a reasonable length, we have only included the most widely used methods. The book takes a balanced view and does not emphasize some topics at the expense of others. It takes a broad approach, describing many topics rather than concentrating on the details of a few.

The book is divided into five parts which develop the subject in a logical sequence:

- Part One gives an introduction to quantitative methods in business. The first chapter outlines the importance of quantitative methods to managers, says why they are used, describes quantitative data and so on. The second chapter gives a review of basic mathematical principles.

- Part Two describes the collection and description of data. All quantitative methods need reliable data, so these chapters show how such data are collected, presented and summarized.

- Part Three illustrates some applications of these quantitative ideas in finance, regression, forecasting, linear programming and calculus.

- Part Four describes some statistical methods, including calculation of probabilities, probability distributions and statistical inference.

- Part Five illustrates some applications of these ideas in decision analysis, inventory control, project network analysis, queues and simulation.

Students often find probabilistic ideas more difficult than deterministic ones. For this reason there is a clear separation of deterministic methods (described in Part Two with examples in Part Three) and probabilistic methods (described in Part Four with examples in Part Five).

The whole book gives you a solid foundation for understanding quantitative methods and their use in business.

# Third Edition

All textbooks evolve to meet changing demands and conditions. This edition contains many changes from the last edition, which was published in 1997. Some of these include:

- general updating and correction of any errors

- rewriting of material to make it clearer

- removal of some material that has become less relevant, particularly calculus and matrices

- introduction of new material that has become more popular, such as quality control

- increased use of computers, particularly spreadsheets (rather than use a specific spreadsheet, the book uses a generic one that has features available on every commercial package)

- more international examples

- more material for students and instructors on the author's web site (http://website.lineone.net/~donaldwaters) or via the Internet (donaldwaters@lineone.net)

# Companion Web Site

## A Companion Web Site accompanies
### *Quantitative Methods for Business*, 3E
### by Donald Waters

Visit the *Quantitative Methods for Business*, **3E** Companion Web site at
*www.booksites.net/waters* to find valuable teaching and learning material including:

**For students:**

- Study material designed to help you improve your results
- New case studies to demonstrate concepts covered in the book
- Suggested further reading to extend your knowledge

**For lecturers:**

- A secure, password protrected site with teaching material
- OHPs of key artwork from the book, to assist in lecturing
- Downloadable Instructor's manual including solutions to the exercises in the book

# PART ONE

# Background to quantitative methods

This book is divided into five parts, each of which covers a different aspect of quantitative methods in business. This first part gives the background and context for the rest of the book. The second part discusses data collection and description. The third part looks at ways of solving specific types of problem, and the last two parts describe various statistical analyses.

There are two chapters in this first part. Chapter 1 describes how we are surrounded by numbers. We use these in a variety of ways and must have some appreciation of quantitative ideas. This is particularly important in business, where managers use a range of numerical information to support their decisions.

Later chapters describe a number of quantitative models. Before we look at these in detail, you should be familiar with some basic mathematical tools. Chapter 2 looks at these tools, emphasizing:

- basic numerical skills
- drawing graphs
- use of algebra

## Ideas in Practice – RPF Global

Patrick Chua is the senior vice-president of RPF Global, a firm of financial consultants with offices in major cities around the Pacific Rim. He outlines his use of quantitative ideas as follows.

'Most of my work is communicating with managers in companies and government offices. I am certainly not a mathematician, and am often confused by figures – but I use quantitative ideas all the time. If I talk to a board of directors, they won't be impressed if I say, "This project is quite good; if all goes well you should make a profit at some point in the future". They want me to spell things out clearly and say, "You can expect a twenty per cent return over the next two years".

'My clients look for a competitive advantage in a fast-moving world. They make difficult decisions. Quantitative methods help us make better decisions – and they help explain and communicate these decisions. Quantitative methods allow us to:

- look logically and objectively at a problem;
- analyse a problem and look for practical solutions;
- compare alternative solutions and identify the best;
- compare performance across different operations, companies and times;
- explain the options and alternatives;
- support or defend a particular decision;
- overcome subjective and biased opinions.

'Quantitative methods are an essential part of any business. Without them, we just could not survive!'

# 1 Numbers and managers

| | | | | |
|---|---|---|---|---|
| Chapter outline | 3 | Chapter review | 10 |
| 1.1 Who needs numbers? | 4 | Problems | 10 |
| 1.2 Using models | 7 | Computer exercises | 11 |
| 1.3 Stages in solving a | | Case study: | |
| problem | 8 | Hamerson and Sons | 11 |

## CHAPTER OUTLINE

This chapter gives a general introduction to quantitative methods. It lays the foundation for the rest of the book by outlining the importance of numerical information to business. Then it describes the use of quantitative models for solving problems.

After reading this chapter and doing the exercises you should be able to:

- appreciate the importance of quantitative analyses
- say why these are particularly relevant to business
- understand the use of models
- describe a general approach to solving problems

## 1.1 | Who needs numbers?

We are surrounded by numbers. On a typical day we might find that the temperature is 17 °C, petrol costs 92 pence a litre, 1.3 million people are unemployed, a group of employees want a pay rise of £1.50 an hour, the local cricket team scored 274 runs in their last innings and 78% of people questioned want shops to open for longer on Sunday. Numbers are so common that we all need some appreciation of their use. Without this appreciation, a normal life would be almost impossible.

We use numbers in a variety of calculations. If you buy three bars of chocolate costing 30 pence each, you know that the total cost is 90 pence; if you pay for these with a £5 note you expect to get £4.10 in change. Often we do such calculations roughly to get an impression of the results. If, for example, you are going on a journey of 230 miles and travel at 50 miles an hour you know the journey will take around 5 hours. If you see a car being sold, you might not know exactly how much it costs to run, but a rough calculation shows if you can afford it; if you get a bill from a tradesman you can tell fairly quickly if it is reasonable. This kind of calculation is so common that we do it routinely without much thought. Such calculations, in one form or another, are a central part of our lives.

The main advantage of numbers is that they give an objective measure. When we can measure something and express it in numbers, we can describe it exactly: when we cannot measure it our understanding is much less clear. A bank manager, for example, can tell exactly how wealthy you are by counting your assets. But suppose you get a pain in your stomach and go to the doctor; it is very difficult to describe what kind of pain you have, how bad it is or how it makes you feel.

The use of numbers increases our understanding of a situation. This does not, of course, mean that we need to be expert mathematicians to live effectively. But it does mean that we should be able to appreciate quantitative arguments and do some numerical analyses. The following worked example shows how a simple calculation can make sure you get the best value for money.

## WORKED EXAMPLE 1.1

A jukebox has a notice which says, 'This machine only accepts 10p coins'. The number of plays given are:

10p – 1 play, 20p – 3 plays, 30p – 4 plays, 40p – 5 plays, 50p – 7 plays.

What is the best way for a customer to use the machine?

### Solution

Customers – we assume – want the lowest cost per play. The costs per play for each amount are:

10p: $10/1 = 10$p a play     20p: $20/3 = 6.7$p a play     30p: $30/4 = 7.5$p a play

40p: $40/5 = 8$p a play     50p: $50/7 = 7.1$p a play

The best option for customers is to buy 3 plays for 20p.

---

Unfortunately, we all make mistakes with even the simplest arithmetic. Thankfully, computers now do the calculations for us. Spreadsheets such as Excel, Lotus 123 and QuattroPro are particularly useful. Figure 1.1 shows a spreadsheet for the calculations in the last worked example.

|   | A | B | C | D |
|---|---|---|---|---|
| 1 | **Cost of jukebox** | | | |
| 2 | | | | |
| 3 | **Cost** | **Number of plays** | **Cost per play** | **Best option** |
| 4 | | | | |
| 5 | 10 | 1 | 10.00 | |
| 6 | 20 | 3 | 6.67 | ***** |
| 7 | 30 | 4 | 7.50 | |
| 8 | 40 | 5 | 8.00 | |
| 9 | 50 | 7 | 7.14 | |

**Figure 1.1** Example of a spreadsheet for doing calculations.

The ability to look at problems quantitatively is particularly important in business. Managers want to run their businesses as efficiently as possible, and to do this they make a series of decisions. Most of these decisions have a quantitative aspect which is phrased in terms of 'improving productivity', 'increasing return on investment', 'scheduling production', 'increasing numbers served', and so on. Taking a broader view, the overall performance of an organization is summarized by its accounts, which are largely numerical. This sets the tone for many decisions, and it is difficult to find a management decision that does not involve some quantitative analysis.

You should not be surprised that managers rely on quantitative analyses, as these are done routinely in many other jobs. Civil engineers, for example, are expected to do calculations when they design bridges; doctors prescribe measured quantities of drugs; accountants give quantitative views of a company's performance. In the past, many people took the view that managers did not need such formal analyses, but were expected to guess the right decisions using only their intuition. Here we are trying to overcome this rather strange view by showing the benefits of quantitative methods in a number of areas.

It is, of course, difficult to apply quantitative methods in some areas, such as industrial relations, negotiations, recruitment, identification of objectives, personal relations, or pattern recognition. These problems need experience, creative thinking or intuition. Usually, the best approach to decision-making is shown in Figure 1.2. Here both quantitative and qualitative analyses are done, but ultimately it is managers who make the decisions. They assess all available information, both quantitative and qualitative, and on the basis of their skills, knowledge and experience make final decisions.

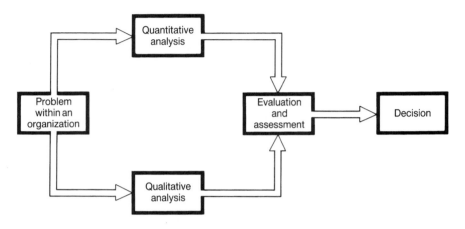

**Figure 1.2** Quantitative and qualitative aspects of decision-making.

## WORKED EXAMPLE 1.2

A firm of consultants aims to have 10 clients on its books for each consultant employed. Last month there were 125 clients on their books. How many consultants should they employ?

### Solution

A purely quantitative analysis would suggest employing 125/10 = 12.5 consultants. This could be rounded to either 12 or 13. Now a range of qualitative factors should be included (such as expected changes in business, attitudes of consultants, type of business, planned staff departures and arrivals, and so on). When all available information has been reviewed the management can make their final decision.

---

### IN SUMMARY

We are surrounded by numerical information and routinely use it in calculations. Problems in business often contain numerical elements, so it is important for managers to appreciate quantitative arguments.

## Self-assessment questions

**1.1** What are the benefits of quantitative methods?

**1.2** Are all management decisions based on mathematics?

**1.3** Do quantitative analyses make the best decisions?

**1.4** Why has the use of quantitative methods by managers increased in the past 20 years?

# 1.2 Using models

Most of this book looks at ways of solving particular types of problem. A common feature, however, is the use of **models**. Here we are defining a 'model' as any simplified representation of reality, and not its common meaning of a toy. Thus the main characteristics of a model are:

- it is a representation of reality
- it is simplified, with only relevant details included, and
- properties in reality are represented by other properties in the model

The most common models in business are **symbolic models**. These have real properties represented by some kind of symbol. A symbolic model may be a graph or chart but is more likely to be a series of equations. If a company makes a product for £200 a unit and sells it for £300 a unit, a symbolic model of the profit is:

$$\text{Profit} = \text{number made} \times (\text{selling price} - \text{cost})$$

or

$$P = N \times (300 - 200) = N \times 100$$

This gives a symbolic model with $P$ representing the profit and $N$ the number of units produced. You should not be intimidated by this use of symbols to represent real things: it is simply a useful notation which describes a situation accurately and concisely.

The main purpose of a model is to allow experiments without changing the real system. In the example above we looked at the relationship between profit and production. We could, of course, find the profit for various production levels by experimenting with the real system. In other words, we could change the production and measure the corresponding profit. This has obvious disadvantages: it is time-consuming, difficult to implement, expensive and could cause permanent damage to the company. It would be much easier to experiment with the symbolic model, $P = N \times 100$, substituting different values for $N$ and calculating the corresponding values for $P$.

Experimenting with real operations can be damaging, but it may also be impossible. A company could find the best location for a factory, by experimentally trying different locations and keeping the best – but this would be prohibitively expensive and disruptive. A company deciding which new product to make cannot start making all possible products and then scrapping those that it finds unsuitable. As experiments with reality are, at best, expensive the only feasible alternative is to build a model of the situation and experiment with this.

---

### IN SUMMARY

Quantitative analyses are based on symbolic models. These are simplified representations of reality where real features are depicted by symbols. In business the symbols used most commonly are variables in equations.

---

## Self-assessment questions

**1.5**   What is a model?

**1.6**   Why are models used in business?

**1.7**   What type of model will we use most frequently in this book?

# | 1.3 |   Stages in solving a problem

A wide variety of quantitative models are used in business. Some of these are very simple and easy to work with: others are very complex and take years to develop. Some situations are so complex that realistic models have not yet been built, and in other cases models have been built but they are too difficult to solve. Despite this diversity, we can describe a useful approach to most business problems. This has four distinct stages:

1   **observation stage**, where the problem is examined, data are collected, details of the problem are identified, objectives are set, context is considered, various ideas are discussed, and so on

2   **modelling stage**, where data are analysed, a model is built and tested, and initial solutions are obtained

3   **experimentation stage**, where solutions are tested to see if they match predictions, optimal solutions are searched for, movements away from optimal solutions are examined, alternative values for variables are considered, other data are collected, and recommendations are made

4 **implementation stage**, where final decisions are made, values for variables are set, these decisions are implemented, actual performance is monitored, feedback is given to management, and models are kept updated

The length and complexity of each stage depend on the type of problem tackled. An oil company with a complex production policy might take years to go through all this process, while a small company with a minor decision could finish it in a few minutes.

In business most decisions are not isolated, but are part of a continuing management process. Then it becomes important for the consequences of earlier decisions to be reviewed, so that good decisions are repeated, but poor ones are not. This is the basis of **feedback**. Feedback returns the consequences of decisions back to a manager who can use them to modify the model. This process is shown in Figure 1.3. This reinforces the view that management does not consist of a series of disconnected decisions, but is a continuous process which must be performed throughout the life of an organization.

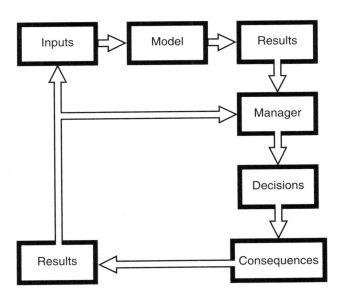

**Figure 1.3**  Feedback in decision-making.

## IN SUMMARY

Although models vary considerably, they share common features. Four distinct stages can be identified in the development of a model: observation, modelling, experimentation and implementation.

## Self-assessment questions

**1.8**  What are the major stages in developing a quantitative model?

**1.9**  Is there only one correct way to tackle a problem?

---

| CHAPTER REVIEW |

This chapter introduced the ideas of quantitative analysis. In particular it described:

- how we are surrounded by numerical information and constantly do calculations
- how quantitative analyses are particularly important in business
- the use of symbolic models
- an approach to solving business problems, based on observation, modelling, experimentation and implementation

---

## Problems

**1.1**  Last year at the Southern Florida Amateur Tennis Championships there were 1947 entries in the women's singles. If this was a standard knockout tournament, how many matches were needed to find the champion?

**1.2**  Sally was very pleased when her meal at the Golden Orient restaurant appeared to cost $14 for food and $8 for drinks. Unfortunately, her final bill added 12% federal tax, 6% state tax, 2% city tax, 15% alcohol duty and 10% service charge. How much did she pay in tax, and what was her final bill?

**1.3**  A family of three is having grilled steak for dinner. The steaks are grilled for 10 minutes on each side. Unfortunately, the family's grill pan is only big enough to grill one side of two steaks at a time. How long will it take to cook dinner?

**1.4**  A shopkeeper buys an article for £25. A customer buys it for £35 and pays with a £50 note. The shopkeeper does not have enough change, so he goes to a neighbour and changes the £50 note. A week later he is told that the £50 note was a forgery, so he immediately repays his neighbour the £50. How much does the shopkeeper lose in this transaction?

**1.5**  Design a scheme for doctors to see how bad a stomach pain is.

**1.6**  Describe a problem in business which has absolutely no quantitative elements.

**1.7**  Devise a fair system for electing parliamentary candidates.

---

# Computer exercises

**1.1** Computer programs can be used throughout this book. See what computers you have access to. Make sure you know how these work. Find out what programs there are and practise using these.

**1.2** Table 1.1 shows the number of units of a product sold each month by a shop, the amount the shop paid for each unit, and the selling price. Use a spreadsheet to find the total values of sales, costs, income and profit.

**Table 1.1**

| Month | Units sold | Cost to the shop | Selling price |
|-------|-----------|------------------|---------------|
| January | 56 | 120 | 135 |
| February | 58 | 122 | 138 |
| March | 55 | 121 | 145 |
| April | 60 | 117 | 145 |
| May | 54 | 110 | 140 |
| June | 62 | 106 | 135 |
| July | 70 | 98 | 130 |
| August | 72 | 110 | 132 |
| September | 43 | 119 | 149 |
| October | 36 | 127 | 155 |
| November | 21 | 133 | 161 |
| December | 22 | 130 | 161 |

Write a brief report on your finding, including graphs of the results.

# Case study

## Hamerson and Sons

Albert Hamerson is Managing Director of his family firm of builders' merchants. He is the third generation to run the company, and is keen for his daughter, Georgina, to have a job with him when she leaves university. Georgina is also keen to join the company, but she is not sure what kind of job she wants.

Hamerson and Sons is essentially a wholesaler. They buy 9000 different products from 1200 manufacturers and importers, and sell any kind of material needed by builders. The company works from five sites around Liverpool and employs over 300 people.

Georgina feels that the company is getting a bit behind the times. Whenever she goes into the office, for example, she is surprised at the amount of paperwork, when she assumed that computers would lead to a paperless office. When she walks around the stores, things still seem to be organized in the way they were 20 years ago. Georgina has some ideas for improvements, and wants the chance to develop these. She imagines herself as an 'internal consultant' looking around the company, finding areas that could be improved, and then doing projects to make operations more efficient.

The problem is that Georgina is studying for a degree in mathematics and business studies. Apart from reading reports written by the accountants, Albert has never had any contact with numerical ideas. He is not sure that Georgina's mathematical training will be of any practical value. After a lot of discussion, they agreed that Georgina will write a report giving some ideas of the type of problem where her mathematical training could be useful. Then she will spend some time in her next vacation looking in more detail at one of these problems.

If you were in Georgina's position, what would you discuss in your report?

# 2 | Tools for quantitative methods

| | | | |
|---|---|---|---|
| Chapter outline | 13 | Problems | 53 |
| 2.1 Working with numbers | 14 | Computer exercises | 54 |
| 2.2 Changing numbers to letters | 21 | Case study 1: The Crown and Anchor | 56 |
| 2.3 Drawing graphs | 40 | Case study 2: Northern Feedstuffs | 56 |
| Chapter review | 52 | | |

**CHAPTER OUTLINE**

Chapter 1 showed that managers need an appreciation of quantitative ideas. The rest of this book describes some quantitative methods which have proved particularly useful in business. Before we look at these methods in detail we need to revise some basic mathematics. You may find that these are all familiar, in which case the chapter will be fairly straightforward. Alternatively, some of the material may be new and you will need to spend more time on it. The tools lay the foundations for other chapters, so it is important that you understand them. If you have difficulties with any material it is worth spending the time to study it until you understand it thoroughly.

After reading this chapter and doing the exercises you should be able to:

- do arithmetic using integers, fractions, decimals and percentages
- appreciate the use of algebra to describe and solve problems
- solve simultaneous equations
- solve quadratic equations
- work with powers and roots
- draw graphs to show relationships between variables
- use graphs to solve simultaneous and quadratic equations

# ‖ 2.1 ‖ Working with numbers

## | 2.1.1 | Introduction

Chapter 1 showed that managers must be familiar with a range of quantitative ideas. The main argument was that managers are concerned with decisions about costs, profit, demand, productivity, output, and other factors, all of which are numerical. It follows that they can only make good decisions if they analyse the numerical aspects of a problem properly.

It is important to remember that this book describes the **use** of quantitative methods in business. Its approach is practical, and it describes methods which give valuable, and even essential, results. It is certainly not a book on pure mathematics; it does not describe ideas for their own sake, and does not get bogged down in the details of proofs, analyses or computation. Concepts are illustrated by examples rather than theoretical derivations.

Business students come from a variety of backgrounds, so it would be wrong to assume that you share a common body of mathematical knowledge. Some of you are strong mathematicians who are looking forward to applying your knowledge in a new area. Others will view the prospect of doing any mathematics with horror. Most of you are in between these extremes, can remember some quantitative ideas and have forgotten or are unsure about a lot more.

This chapter describes the basic tools of quantitative methods. You may find that these ideas are familiar, in which case the chapter will be fairly straightforward – so you can skip over sections and move to newer material. On the other hand, some of the material may be new and you need to spend more time over it. These tools lay the foundations for other chapters, so it is important that you understand them. If there is any part you find difficult, it is worth spending enough time working through the material until you understand it. You might also want to look at more detailed references, some of which are listed in Appendix A.

---

### IN SUMMARY

This book describes some quantitative methods which have proved useful in business. These methods do not rely on a high level of mathematical ability. Nonetheless, it is important to understand the basic tools that are described in this chapter.

## | 2.1.2 | Numbers and arithmetic

The main assumption in this book is that you are familiar with numbers and arithmetic operations. You can use these to do various calculations, and show that:

- if you buy 10 loaves of bread at 72 pence a loaf the bill will be £7.20
- if you drive at an average speed of 80 kilometres an hour it will take you 5 hours to complete a 400 kilometre journey

- if you spend £300 a month on housing, £100 a month on food and entertainment, and £200 a month on other things, your net income must be at least £600 a month, which is the same as £7,200 a year or £138.46 a week
- if a company has a gross income of $1 million a year and costs of $0.8 million a year, it makes a profit of $200,000 a year

In practice, you will do very few calculations by hand. Computers will do most calculations, while calculators can help with any straightforward arithmetic.

There are four basic operations in arithmetic: addition, subtraction, multiplication and division. To describe these we use the following notation:

- $+$  addition          e.g. $2 + 7 = 9$
- $-$  subtraction       e.g. $15 - 7 = 8$
- $\times$  multiplication    e.g. $4 \times 5 = 20$
- $/$  division          e.g. $12/4 = 3$

There are several variations on this notation. Division is sometimes shown as $12 \div 4 = 3$ or $\frac{12}{4} = 3$, while multiplication can be shown as $3 \times 2 = 6$, $3{\cdot}2 = 6$, $3.2 = 6$ or $3(2) = 6$.

We must be careful when describing arithmetic. Does $3 + 4 \times 5$, for example, mean $7 \times 5 = 35$ (with the addition done first) or $3 + 20 = 23$ (with the multiplication done first)? By convention, the second of these is correct and multiplication is done before addition. Whenever there is any doubt about the order of arithmetic, we can put brackets around parts of the calculation which are done together.

Then:

$$(3 + 4) \times 5 = 7 \times 5 = 35$$

while

$$3 + (4 \times 5) = 3 + 20 = 23$$

All calculations in brackets must be done first, so the general order of calculations becomes:

1 all operations inside brackets
2 raising to powers (which we mention later in the chapter)
3 multiplication and division in the order they appear
4 addition and subtraction in the order they appear

This means that we can use brackets to change the order in which calculations are done.

For example:

$$12 \times 2 + 4 + 2 = 24 + 4 + 2 = 30$$

while

$$12 \times (2 + 4 + 2) = 12 \times 8 = 96$$

and

$$12 \times (2 + 4) + 4 = 12 \times 6 + 4 = 72 + 4 = 76$$

Similarly:

$$4 \times 5 - 3 \times 4/4 - 2 = 20 - 3 - 2 = 15$$

while

$$(4 \times 5) - (3 \times 4)/(4 - 2) = 20 - 12/2 = 20 - 6 = 14$$

and

$$4 \times (5 - 3) \times (4/4) - 2 = 4 \times 2 \times 1 - 2 = 8 - 2 = 6$$

If one set of brackets is not enough, we can use several sets inside others. Then operations are done from the inside set of brackets and working outwards.

For example:

$$[(32/2) + (6/3)] - 1 = (16 + 2) - 1 = 17$$

while

$$[32/(2 + 6)]/(3 - 1) = (32/8)/2 = 4/2 = 2$$

Sometimes calculations with a lot of brackets appear rather messy, but you should have no difficulty in understanding them if you follow the order given above.

## WORKED EXAMPLE 2.1

Find the value of:

(a) 120/6    (b) –120/6    (c) –120/(–6)    (d) [(–2 × 4) × (15 – 17)] × (–2)
(e) (10+20) – (3×7)    (f) (15 – 5) + [(20 – 3) × 7)]

### Solution

Using the standard rules gives:

(a) 120/6 = 20

(b) –120/6 = –20

(c) –120/(–6) = 20 (Notice that the minus signs cancel each other.)

(d) [(–2 × 4) × (15 – 17)] × (–2) = [(–8) × (–2)] × (–2) = 16 × (–2) = –32

(Remember that multiplying two negative numbers together gives a positive number, while multiplying a positive number by a negative number gives a negative number.)

(e) $(10 + 20) - (3 \times 7) = 30 - 21 = 9$

(f) $(15 - 5) + [(20 - 3) \times 7)] = 10 + (17 \times 7) = 10 + 119 = 129$

---

The numbers used in Worked Example 2.1 are integers. In other words they are whole numbers, such as 20, 9 or 150. Integers can be positive (such as 3, 100, 257) or negative (such as −2, −157, −356). To improve clarity, long numbers are often divided into groups of three digits by commas (like 1,247,822), but some people prefer spaces (like 1 247 822).

Often we need to divide integers into smaller parts. When, for example, two people share a bar of chocolate they get $\frac{1}{2}$ each. Parts of integers are expressed either as **common fractions** (like $\frac{1}{2}$ or $\frac{3}{4}$) or **decimal fractions** (like 0.5 or 0.75). As metric units are replacing imperial units, and computers are used almost universally, decimal fractions have become more common. Nonetheless, common fractions (which are invariably abbreviated to 'fractions') are very important, particularly when dealing with ratios or probabilities. You should be familiar with the rules for manipulating these, which are illustrated in the following examples.

---

# WORKED EXAMPLE 2.2

Find the value of the following as decimal fractions:

(a) 6/8     (b) 36/8     (c) 1/2 + 4/5     (d) 3/4 − 1/6

(e) 1/4 × 2/3     (f) −1/4 × 2/3 × 1/2     (g) (3/5) ÷ (4/5)

## Solution

Common fractions can be transformed into decimal fractions by straightforward division.

(a) $6/8 = 0.75$

(b) $36/8 = 4.5$

For addition and subtraction of fractions, all numbers below the lines (called the **denominators**) are made the same, and then numbers above the line (called the **numerators**) are added or subtracted.

(c) $1/2 + 4/5 = 5/10 + 8/10 = 13/10 = 1.3$

(d) $3/4 - 1/6 = 9/12 - 2/12 = 7/12 = 0.583$

For multiplication of fractions, all the denominators are multiplied together, and all the numerators are multiplied together.

(e) $1/4 \times 2/3 = (1 \times 2)/(4 \times 3) = 2/12 = 1/6 = 0.167$

(f) $-1/4 \times 2/3 \times 1/2 = (-1 \times 2 \times 1)/(4 \times 3 \times 2) = -2/24 = -1/12 = -0.083$

For division of fractions, the fraction which is dividing is inverted and then used for multiplication.

(g) $(3/5) \div (4/5) = 3/5 \times 5/4 = (3 \times 5)/(5 \times 4) = 15/20 = 0.75$

## WORKED EXAMPLE 2.3

A Canadian visitor to Britain wants to change $250 into pounds. The exchange rate is $2.15 to the pound and banks charge a fee of £5 for the conversion. How many pounds does the visitor get?

### Solution

$250 is equivalent to 250/2.15 = £116.28. The bank then takes its fee of £5 to give the visitor £111.28.

## WORKED EXAMPLE 2.4

If 1 km is about 5/8 miles, how far is 2.4 miles in km?

### Solution

$$5/8 \text{ miles} = 1 \text{ km}$$

so

$$1 \text{ mile} = 8/5 \text{ km}$$

and

$$2.4 \text{ miles} = 2.4 \times 8/5 \text{ km} = (2.4 \times 8)/5 \text{ km} = 3.84 \text{ km}$$

An alternative way of describing fractions is to use **percentages**. These are fractions where the bottom line is 100, and the '/100' has been replaced by the abbreviation '%'. Then if we hear '20% of the electorate did not vote in the last election' we know that 20 people out of each 100 did not vote. This ratio can be represented as any of:

- common fraction: 20/100 = 1/5
- decimal fraction: 0.2
- percentage: 20%

If a company made a net profit of Kr12m last year and Kr3m of this came from overseas, we can make the equivalent statements:

- fraction of profit from overseas = 3/12 = 1/4
- decimal fraction of profit from overseas = 0.25
- percentage of profit from overseas = 25%

Calculations with percentages can be done in the same way as other fractions.

# WORKED EXAMPLE 2.5

(a) What is 17/20 as a percentage?

(b) What is 80% as a fraction?

(c) What is 35% as a decimal fraction?

(d) What is 40% of 120?

(e) If 20% of 50 is multiplied by $\frac{1}{2}$ of 60 and the result is divided by 0.25 of 60, what is the result?

## Solution

(a) $17/20 = 85/100 = 85\%$

(b) $80\% = 80/100 = 4/5$

(c) $35\% = 35/100 = 0.35$

(d) $40\%$ of $120 = 40/100 \times 120 = 0.4 \times 120 = 48$

(e) $20\%$ of $50 = 20/100 \times 50 = 0.2 \times 50 = 10$; $\frac{1}{2} \times 60 = 30$ ; $0.25 \times 60 = 15$

So the calculation is: $(10 \times 30)/15 = 300/15 = 20$

# WORKED EXAMPLE 2.6

A shop sells dining room tables for £400 each. At one time it was difficult to get supplies of the table, so the shop raised the price by 20%. When supplies returned to normal the shop reduced the higher price by 20%. What was the final selling price? What percentage reduction from the higher price would have returned the price to £400?

## Solution

- The normal price was £400. During the shortage the shop raised this by 20% to 120% of £400, which is $(120/100) \times 400 = 1.2 \times 400 = £480$.

- At the end of the shortage the shop reduced the higher price by 20% to give a final selling price of 80% of £480 which is $(80/100) \times 480 = 0.8 \times 480 = £384$.

- To return the price from £480 to £400 the price is reduced by a proportion 80/480, which equals 16.667/100 or 16.667%.

The last answer above was given as 16.667%. The exact answer is 16.666 6666...% (where ... signifies an unending row of sixes). We have rounded the answer to:

- three decimal places (showing only three digits after the decimal point) and

- five significant figures (showing only the five most important digits)

Rounding of this kind is widely used to ensure that we get enough information, but are not overwhelmed by too much detail. There is no general rule for the number of decimal places or significant figures that you should use, except the vague advice to use the number which best suits your purpose. We can give two more specific suggestions.

● Only give the number of decimal places or significant figures that is useful. Avoid answers like £120.347 826 59 and quote the figure as £120.35, or even £120.

● Results from calculation are only as accurate as the data used. When multiplying a forecast demand of 32.63 units by a unit cost of £17.19 we should not describe the projected total cost as $32.63 \times 17.19 = £560.9097$. A more reasonable answer would be £560.91 (or £561, £560 or £600 depending on the use of the data).

Remember the convention that when rounding to, say, two decimal places and the digit in the third decimal place is 0, 1, 2, 3 or 4 the result is rounded **down**, and when it is 5, 6, 7, 8 or 9 the result is rounded **up**. Then 11.111 become 11.11 to two decimal places, but 11.119 becomes 11.12; 1.364 becomes 1.36, while 1.365 becomes 1.37.

## WORKED EXAMPLE 2.7

What is 1374.341 481 2 to:
  (a) two decimal places      (b) four significant figures
  (c) two significant figures?

What is 3/7 as a decimal to three places?

### Solution

(a) 1374.341 481 2 is 1374.34 when rounded to two decimal places, and

(b) 1374 when rounded to four significant figures

(c) 1400 when rounded to two significant figures

  3/7 is 0.428 57... which is 0.429 when rounded to three decimal places.

IN SUMMARY

There are some standard rules for doing calculations. These can be used for integers, decimals and fractions. Percentages are a useful form of fraction. Results can be rounded to a specified number of decimal places or significant figures.

## Self-assessment questions

**2.1** Is it true that quantitative methods are widely used in business?

**2.2** What is the value of:
(a) $(-12)/(-3)$     (b) $(24/5) \div (3/7)$     (c) $[(2-4) \times (3-6)]/(7-5)$?

**2.3** What is the difference between 75%, 3/4, 15/20 and 0.75? Which of these gives the best representation?

**2.4** What is $1\,745\,800.362\,37$ rounded to three decimal places and three significant figures?

# 2.2 Changing numbers to letters

## 2.2.1 Forming equations

Suppose you want to find the cost of running a car. This is normally related to the distance travelled, so you might find during one period that you drove 6000 km and had total costs of £2400. Then you could say:

$$\text{cost per km} = \frac{2400}{6000} = £0.40 \text{ per km}$$

You calculated this specific result from the general equation:

$$\text{cost per km} = \frac{\text{total cost}}{\text{number of km travelled}}$$

Rather than writing this equation in full, we could save time by using some abbreviations. We could, for example, abbreviate the total cost to $T$, which is simple and easy to remember. Similarly, we could define:

$$C = \text{cost per km}$$

$$K = \text{number of km travelled}$$

Then we can write the cost per km as:

$$C = \frac{T}{K} = T/K$$

Now we have an equation that has the advantages of being general, concise and accurate. The only difference from the original equation is that we have used letters to represent numbers or quantities. This is the basis of algebra.

We chose the abbreviations $C$, $T$ and $K$ to remind us of what they stood for. We could equally have chosen other names. For example:

$$c = \frac{t}{k}$$

$$y = \frac{x}{z}$$

$$\text{COST} = \frac{\text{TOTAL}}{\text{KILOM}}$$

$$\text{COSTPERKM} = \frac{\text{TOTALCOST}}{\text{KILOMETRES}}$$

Provided that the meaning is clear, the names are not important. When choosing names you must remember that the multiplication sign in equations is often implicit, so that $4 \times a \times b \times c$ is written as $4abc$, and so on. This causes no problems when we use single-letter abbreviations, but can be confusing with longer names. If the total unit cost is abbreviated to $TUC$, it would make no sense to write an equation:

$$TUC = NTUC$$

when we really mean:

$$TUC = N \times T \times UC$$

Our basic equation:

$$C = T/K$$

can be rearranged to give two equivalent forms. If we multiply both sides of the equation by $K$, we get:

$$C \times K = \frac{T}{K} \times K \qquad \text{or} \qquad T = C \times K$$

Now if we divide both sides of this equation by $C$, we get:

$$T/C = C \times K/C \qquad \text{or} \qquad K = T/C$$

These three are different descriptions of the same situation. They are simple rearrangements of the first equation, and the equation remains true if we perform the same operations to both sides. Thus we could multiply both sides by 2 to get:

$$2C = 2T/K$$

and add 10 to get:

$$2C + 10 = 2T/K + 10$$

and divide by $3A$, where $A$ is a known constant, to give:

$$(2C + 10)/3A = (2T/K + 10)/3A$$

This kind of manipulation allows us to define some general laws of algebra. Because algebra simply replaces numbers by letters, these rules are the same as those used for calculations, so we can define the basic operations using two variables $a$ and $b$, as follows:

- \+  addition         e.g. $a + b$
- \−  subtraction      e.g. $a - b$
- ×  multiplication   e.g. $a \times b$
- /  division        e.g. $a/b$

One important point in algebra is that two adjacent variables are assumed to be multiplied together. Thus:

$a \times b$         is usually written as      $ab$

$l \times m \times n$       is usually written as      $lmn$

$a \times (b + c)$       is usually written as      $a(b + c)$

The order of evaluation remains the same, so we have:

1   all operations inside brackets
2   raising to powers (which we mention later in the chapter)
3   multiplication and division in the order they appear
4   addition and subtraction in the order they appear

## IN SUMMARY

Names can be used as abbreviations for general values, to replace numbers used for specific values. So £10 is a specific cost, while $C$ might be a general cost. These abbreviations can be used in a model, and manipulating the names is the basis of algebra.

## 2.2.2 | Solving simple equations

We saw above that the cost of running a car can be described by the equation $C = T/K$. Here the cost per km, $C$, is fixed and a driver cannot change it, so in any particular circumstances $C$ is a constant. The number of kilometres travelled, $K$, and the total cost, $T$, are both variables which are related through the equation. Thus we have:

- **constants**, which take fixed values
- **variables**, which can take any one of a range of values

The purpose of an equation is to show the relationship between constants and variables. Then we can find the value of a previously unknown constant or variable by relating it to other known constants and variables. This is called **solving an equation**.

The easiest way of solving an equation is to arrange it so that the unknown value is on one side of the equals sign, and all known values are on the other side.

Suppose, for example, a survey of managers finds that they spend an average of 15.2 hours a week attending meetings and that their time is valued at £22.40 an hour. The total cost of attending meetings a year for a typical manager is given by:

total annual cost = hours attending meetings a year × cost per hour

which we can abbreviate to:

$$T = H \times C$$
$$= (15.2 \times 52) \times 22.4$$
$$= £17,704.96 \text{ a year}$$

Here we have solved the equation by using the known values of $H$ and $C$ to find a previously unknown value, $T$.

This example highlights a number of points about equations.

- A single equation can only give the value of **one** unknown. If there are several unknowns, we must use more equations (as we shall see in the following section).

- We solve an equation by arranging it so that the unknown value is on one side of the equals sign and all the known values are on the other side.

- The units in the equation must be consistent. The equation above worked with hours and pounds for all values. Provided that the units are consistent, we can use any convenient ones.

- We have to round the answer to an appropriate number of significant figures. It is important to remember that results cannot be more accurate than the known values. In this case values are quoted to three significant figures, so we cannot reasonably say more than 'the annual cost of managers attending meetings is about £17,700'.

Now we can use these ideas to solve some problems. For this we have to take three steps:

> 1 define the relevant constants and variables
> 2 develop an equation to describe the relationship between the constants and variables, i.e. build a model
> 3 solve the equation

This approach – of defining the variables, building a model and finding a solution – is the most important part of quantitative methods. We meet it many times in later chapters but will give some examples here.

## WORKED EXAMPLE 2.8

The Belle Vue Hotel paid £1200 for heat and power in July. It found that heating costs were £200 short of three times the cost of power. How much did power cost?

### Solution

Let the cost of power in the month be $x$. Then the cost of heat is $3x - 200$. This gives a total cost for power and heat of $x + (3x - 200)$. But we know that the total cost was £1200, so:

$$x + (3x - 200) = 1200$$

Adding 200 to both sides of the equation gives:

$$x + 3x = 1400$$

or

$$4x = 1400$$

$$x = £350$$

## WORKED EXAMPLE 2.9

A company employing 10 people has total costs of £250,000 a year. These costs include a fixed cost of £50,000 for overheads and a variable cost for each person employed. What is this variable cost? What would be the total cost if the company expands to employ 45 people?

### Solution

Suppose we let:

$t$ = total cost

$o$ = overheads

$v$ = variable cost per employee

$n$ = number employed

The total cost is:

total cost = overheads + (variable cost × number employed)

or

$$t = o + nv$$

We know current values for $t$, $o$ and $n$, and so we can find the variable cost $v$ by rearranging the equation. If we subtract $o$ from both sides and divide by $n$ we get:

$$v = \frac{t - o}{n}$$

Substituting the known values gives:

$$v = \frac{250\,000 - 50\,000}{10} = £20,000 \text{ a year for each employee}$$

If the company expands we can find the new total cost $t$ by substituting known values for $v$, $o$ and $n$ in the original equation:

$$t = o + nv$$

$$= 50\,000 + 45 \times 20\,000$$

$$= £950,000 \text{ a year}$$

# WORKED EXAMPLE 2.10

1200 parts arrive from a manufacturer in two batches. Each unit of the first batch costs £35, while each unit of the second batch costs £37. If the total cost was £43,600 how many units were in each batch?

## Solution

Let $f$ be the number of units in the first batch and $(1200 - f)$ be the number in the second batch. Then the total cost is given by:

$$35f + 37(1200 - f) = 43\,600$$

so

$$35f + 44\,400 - 37f = 43\,600$$

$$35f - 37f = 43\,600 - 44\,400$$

$$-2f = -800$$

$$f = 400$$

So the first batch had 400 units while the second batch had 800 units.

---

## IN SUMMARY

Equations show the relationships between variables and constants. These equations can be solved to find previously unknown values. This is done by rearranging the equation until the unknown variable is on one side and all the known values are on the other side.

## 2.2.3 | Solving simultaneous equations

We can solve an equation to find one previously unknown value. If we want to find more than one unknown variable we must have more than one independent equation. In particular, to find $n$ values, we need $n$ independent equations relating them. With two unknowns, for example, we need two independent equations to find a solution. If we only knew that $x + y = 3$ it would be impossible to find values for both $x$ and $y$. If we also knew that $y - x = 1$ we have two independent equations and can find values for both $x$ and $y$ (in this case $x = 1$ and $y = 2$).

In this sense **independent** means the two equations are not simply different ways of saying the same thing. For example:

$$x + y = 10$$

and

$$x - 10 = y$$

are not independent as they are different forms of the same equation. Similarly:

$$x + y = 10$$

and

$$2x + 2y = 20$$

are not independent as, again, they are simply different forms of the same equation.

Sets of independent equations of this type are called **simultaneous equations**, and they are solved when values are found for all the unknowns.

We can start by considering two simultaneous equations with two unknown variables. The method of solving these is to multiply one equation by a number which allows the two equations to be added or subtracted to eliminate one of the variables. When one variable has been eliminated, we are left with a single equation with one variable. This process is best illustrated by an example.

## WORKED EXAMPLE 2.11

Two variables, $x$ and $y$, are related by the following equations. What are the values of the variables?

$$3y = 4x + 2 \tag{1}$$

$$y = -x + 10 \tag{2}$$

### Solution

If we multiply equation (2) by 3, we get the revised equations:

$$3y = 4x + 2 \text{ as before} \tag{1}$$

and

$$3y = -3x + 30 \tag{2}$$

Subtracting equation (2) from equation (1):

$$3y - 3y = (4x + 2) - (-3x + 30) = 4x - (-3x) + 2 - 30$$

or

$$0 = 7x - 28$$

so that

$$x = 4$$

This gives a value for one variable, which can be substituted in one of the original equations, say (1), to give the value for the other variable:

$$3y = 4x + 2$$

so

$$3y = 4 \times 4 + 2$$

or

$$y = 6$$

These answers can be checked in equation (2):

$$y = -x + 10$$

or

$$6 = -4 + 10$$

which is correct and confirms the solution.

This method of elimination can be used with any number of variables. If, for example, we have three variables, we can manipulate these until we get two equations with two variables, and then further manipulation gives one equation with one variable. We can solve this and substitute to find the other variables.

# WORKED EXAMPLE 2.12

Solve the simultaneous equations:

$$2x + y + 2z = 10 \tag{1}$$

$$x - 2y + 3z = 2 \tag{2}$$

$$-x + y + z = 0 \tag{3}$$

## Solution

We can start by using equations (2) and (3) to eliminate the variable $x$ from equation (1). Multiplying equation (2) by 2 gives:

$$2x - 4y + 6z = 4$$

Subtracting this from equation (1) gives:

$$5y - 4z = 6 \tag{4}$$

Multiplying equation (3) by 2 gives:

$$-2x + 2y + 2z = 0$$

Adding this to equation (1) gives:

$$3y + 4z = 10 \tag{5}$$

Now we have two equations, (4) and (5), with two unknowns, $y$ and $z$. Adding these together gives $8y = 16$ or $y = 2$.

Now we can substitute this value for $y$ in equation (4) to give $10 - 4z = 6$ or $z = 1$. The values for $y$ and $z$ can be substituted in equation (1) to give $2x + 2 + 2 = 10$ or $x = 3$.

These values can be confirmed by substitution in equations (2) and (3):

$$3 - 4 + 3 = 2 \tag{2}$$

$$-3 + 2 + 1 = 0 \tag{3}$$

---

There are two cases where this elimination method of solving simultaneous equations does not work. In the first, the equations are not independent. If, for example, we have the two equations:

$$2x + 3y = 6 \tag{1}$$

$$6x + 9y = 18 \tag{2}$$

multiplying equation (1) by 3 immediately gives equation (2), so we really have only one equation and cannot find the two unknowns.

In the second case where the method does not work there is a contradiction. Suppose we are told:

$$x + y = 7$$

$$2x + 2y = 12$$

Multiplying the first equation by 2 gives $2x + 2y = 14$ which contradicts the second equation. In these circumstances there is no feasible solution and we must assume there is a mistake in one of the equations.

We could use this approach to solve big sets of simultaneous equations, but it obviously makes more sense to use a computer. There are several ways of doing this, including spreadsheets with standard functions. Some of these are very easy to use, but others are a bit messy. One common approach in spreadsheets uses matrix arithmetic, where we have to:

1. describe the problem as a matrix and right-hand side
2. use a standard function to get the inverse of the matrix
3. multiply this inverse by the right-hand side to get the solution.

This seems a bit obscure, but is quite easy in practice, as you can see from the example in Figure 2.1.

| | A | B | C | D | E | F | G |
|---|---|---|---|---|---|---|---|
| 1 | **Solving simultaneous equations** | | | | | | |
| 2 | | | | | | | |
| 3 | **Equation** | **Original matrix** | | | | **Right-hand side** | |
| 4 | | **x** | **y** | **z** | | | |
| 5 | 1 | 2 | 2 | 4 | | 24 | |
| 6 | 2 | 6 | 3 | 0 | | 15 | |
| 7 | 3 | 0 | 1 | 2 | | 11 | |
| 8 | | | | | | | |
| 9 | | **Inverse matrix** | | | | **Results** | |
| 10 | | 0.50 | 0.00 | −1.00 | | x | 1 |
| 11 | | −1.00 | 0.33 | 2.00 | | y | 3 |
| 12 | | 0.50 | −0.17 | 0.50 | | z | 4 |

**Figure 2.1**  Using a spreadsheet to solve simultaneous equations.

Suppose you have three simultaneous equations:

1. $2x + 2y + 4z = 24$
2. $6x + 3y = 15$
3. $y + 2z = 11$

You can describe these as a matrix and right-hand side, as shown in rows 4–7 of Figure 2.1. A shorthand description of this says that you multiply a **matrix** by the variables to get the right-hand side:

$$\text{Matrix} \times \text{variables} = \text{right-hand side}$$

Then to find the variables you divide both sides by the matrix. In practice, rather than divide by the matrix we find the 'inverse matrix' and multiply both sides by this:

$$\text{Variables} = \text{inverse matrix} \times \text{right-hand side}$$

As you can see from Figure 2.1, the result is $x = 1$, $y = 3$ and $z = 4$.

# WORKED EXAMPLE 2.13

Mocha-to-Go blends two types of coffee beans, American and Brazilian, to make two kinds of coffee, Morning and Noon. The Morning blend uses 75% of the available American beans and 10% of the available Brazilian beans. The Noon blend uses 20% of available American beans and 60% of available Brazilian beans.

(a) If Mocha-to-Go buys 200 kg of American beans and 300 kg of Brazilian beans, how much of each blend can it make?

(b) If they want to make 400 kg of Morning blend and 600 kg of Noon blend, how many beans should they buy?

## Solution

If the amounts of American and Brazilian beans bought are $A$ and $B$ respectively, and the amounts of Morning and Noon blends made are $M$ and $N$ respectively, we know that:

1.  $0.75A + 0.1B = M$
2.  $0.2A + 0.6B = N$

(a) If $A = 200$ kg and $B = 300$ kg, then substitution shows that $M = 180$ kg and $N = 220$ kg.

(b) If $M = 400$ kg and $N = 600$ kg, we have to solve two simultaneous equations. The solutions are $A = 418$ kg and $B = 861$ kg, as shown in Figure 2.2.

| | A | B | C | D | E | F |
|---|---|---|---|---|---|---|
| | **Solving simultaneous equations** | | | | | |
| 1 | | | | | | |
| 2 | **Part (a)** | | | | | |
| 3 | **Equation** | **Original matrix** | | | **Right-hand side** | |
| 4 | | **A** | **B** | | | |
| 5 | | 200 | 300 | | | |
| 6 | **1 – Morning** | 0.75 | 0.1 | | 180 | |
| 7 | **2 – Noon** | 0.2 | 0.6 | | 220 | |
| 8 | | | | | | |
| 9 | **Part (b)** | | | | | |
| 10 | **Equation** | **Original matrix** | | | **Right-hand side** | |
| 11 | | **A** | **B** | | | |
| 12 | **1 – Morning** | 0.75 | 0.1 | | 400 | |
| 13 | **2 – Noon** | 0.2 | 0.6 | | 600 | |
| 14 | | | | | | |
| 15 | | **Inverse matrix** | | | **Results** | |
| 16 | – | 1.395 | –0.233 | | A | 418.6 |
| 17 | – | –0.465 | 1.744 | | B | 860.5 |

**Figure 2.2** Solution to Worked Example 2.13.

## IN SUMMARY

Values for $n$ unknown variables can be found using $n$ independent simultaneous equations. The equations can be solved by a process of elimination and substitution. For most problems this is done using a computer.

## 2.2.4 | **Powers and roots**

If a number is multiplied by itself several times the convention is to describe this by a superscript. Then if a variable $b$ is multiplied by itself the result is '$b$ to the power 2' or '$b$ squared', which is written as $b^2$. So if 3 is multiplied by itself the result is 3 squared, which is written as $3^2$ and this equals $3 \times 3$ or 9.

Similarly:

$$b \text{ squared} = b \times b = b^2$$

$$b \text{ cubed} = b \times b \times b = b^3$$

$$b \text{ to the fourth} = b \times b \times b \times b = b^4$$

and in general:

$$b \text{ to the power } n = b \times b \times b \times \dots (n \text{ times}) = b^n$$

If $b = 2$ we have:

$$2 \text{ squared} = 2 \times 2 = 2^2 = 4$$

$$2 \text{ cubed} = 2 \times 2 \times 2 = 2^3 = 8$$

$$2 \text{ to the fourth} = 2 \times 2 \times 2 \times 2 = 2^4 = 16$$

and in general:

$$2 \text{ to the power } n = 2 \times 2 \times 2 \times \dots (n \text{ times}) = 2^n$$

Suppose we want to multiply two variables which are raised to powers, perhaps multiplying $b^2$ by $b^3$. We can write this out in full as $b^2 \times b^3$ but this is $(b \times b) \times (b \times b \times b)$ or $b \times b \times b \times b \times b$ and is $b^5$. Thus $b^2 \times b^3 = b^5$. This illustrates the general rule that:

$$b^m \times b^n = b^{m+n}$$

Thus $3^2 \times 3^3 = 3^5$, which we can confirm by expanding the calculation to $3^2 \times 3^3 = 9 \times 27 = 243 = 3^5$. In passing we should note two common errors, and emphasize that:

$$b^m + b^n \text{ does } \textbf{not} \text{ equal } b^{m+n}$$

$$a^n + b^n \text{ does } \textbf{not} \text{ equal } (a + b)^n$$

You can check this by substituting any values such as $a = 1$, $b = 2$, $m = 1$ and $n = 3$.

Now we know how to multiply a variable raised to powers, we can extend this and look at division in the same way. If we want to divide $b^3$ by $b^2$ this can be written as:

$$\frac{b^3}{b^2} \qquad \text{which is} \qquad \frac{b \times b \times b}{b \times b} = b$$

We know that another way of writing $b$ is $b^1$, so we now have $b^3/b^2 = b^1$. This illustrates the general rule that:

$$\frac{b^m}{b^n} = b^{m-n}$$

Thus $5^4/5^2 = 5^{4-2} = 5^2$. We can check this by expanding the calculation to show that $5^4/5^2 = 625/25 = 25 = 5^2$. One interesting result from this comes when $m = n$. Suppose, for example, $m = n = 3$. Then with division we get:

$$\frac{b^3}{b^3} = \frac{b \times b \times b}{b \times b \times b} = 1$$

but

$$\frac{b^3}{b^3} = b^{3-3} = b^0$$

So $b^0 = 1$. This is a general result, that anything raised to the power 0 equals 1.

## WORKED EXAMPLE 2.14

What is the value of:   (a) $b^4 \times b^2$   (b) $b^6 \div b^2$   (c) $2^3 \times 2^2$
(d) $3^4 \div 3^2$   (e) $(1+b)^2$

### Solution

Using the rules above gives:

(a) $b^4 \times b^2 = b^{4+2} = b^6$
(b) $b^6 \div b^2 = b^{6-2} = b^4$
(c) $2^3 \times 2^2 = 2^{3+2} = 2^5 = 32$
(d) $3^4 \div 3^2 = 3^{4-2} = 3^2 = 9$

Values in brackets can be treated in the same way as other values.

(e) $(1 + b)^2 = (1 + b) \times (1 + b)$

We can expand this to:

$$1 \times (1 + b) + b \times (1 + b)$$
$$= (1 + b) + (b + b^2) = 1 + 2b + b^2$$

Suppose we apply the rule for division when $n$ is larger than $m$ with, say, $n = 3$ and $m = 2$. Then:

$$b^m/b^n = b^2/b^3 = b^{2-3} = b^{-1}$$

But how do we interpret a value raised to a negative power? We can find the answer by expanding the calculation:

$$\frac{b^2}{b^3} = \frac{b \times b}{b \times b \times b} = \frac{1}{b}$$

Then $b^{-1} = 1/b$, which illustrates the general rule:

$$b^{-n} = \frac{1}{b^n}$$

There is one other aspect of this notation that we need to consider – raising values to fractional powers. You can see the meaning of these from the work we have already done. Take, for example, $b^{0.5}$. If we square this, we know that:

$$b^{0.5} \times b^{0.5} = b^{0.5 + 0.5} = b^1 = b$$

Now the number which multiplied by itself gives $b$ is the square root of $b$, so we know that:

$$b^{0.5} = b^{1/2} = \sqrt{b}$$

Remember that $\sqrt{}$ is the standard sign for the square root, so $\sqrt{9} = 3$.

We could show similarly that:

$$b^{0.33} = b^{1/3} \text{ which is the cube root of } b$$

$$b^{0.25} = b^{1/4} \text{ which is the fourth root of } b$$

$$b^{0.2} = b^{1/5} \text{ which is the fifth root of } b$$

and so on.

We can extend this idea to other fractional powers. For example:

$$b^{1.5} = b^{3/2} = (b^{1/2})^3 = (\sqrt{b})^3$$

and

$$b^{2.5} = b^{5/2} = (b^{1/2})^5 = (\sqrt{b})^5$$

# WORKED EXAMPLE 2.15

What are the values of:  (a) $1/b^4$  (b) $b^5 \times b^{1/2}$  (c) $25^{1/2}$
(d) $9^{1.5}$  (e) $8^{0.67}$

## Solution

Using the rules defined above:

(a) $1/b^4 = b^{-4}$

(b) $b^5 \times b^{1/2} = b^{5+1/2} = b^{5.5} = (\sqrt{b})^{11}$

(c) $25^{1/2} = \sqrt{25} = 5$

(d) $9^{1.5} = 9^{3/2} = (\sqrt{9})^3 = 3^3 = 27$

(e) $8^{0.67} = 8^{2/3} = (8^{1/3})^2 = 2^2 = 4$

# WORKED EXAMPLE 2.16

If you leave £100 in the bank earning 6% interest, at the end of $n$ years you will have $100 \times 1.06^n$ (we shall talk about this result in more detail in Chapter 7). How much will you have at the end of each of the next ten years?

## Solution

We could do these calculations separately, starting with:

- at the end of the first year you have $100 \times 1.06^1 = £106$
- at the end of the second year you have $100 \times 1.06^2 = £112.36$

and so on. But it is much easier to use a spreadsheet, as shown in Figure 2.3.

| | A | B | C |
|---|---|---|---|
| 1 | **Calculation of money value** | | |
| 2 | | | |
| 3 | **Interest rate (%)** | | 6 |
| 4 | **Years** | | 10 |
| 5 | **Amount** | | 100 |
| 6 | | | |
| 7 | | | |
| 8 | **Year** | **Multiplier** | **Amount** |
| 9 | | | |
| 10 | 1 | 1.0600 | 106.00 |
| 11 | 2 | 1.1236 | 112.36 |
| 12 | 3 | 1.1910 | 119.10 |
| 13 | 4 | 1.2625 | 126.25 |
| 14 | 5 | 1.3382 | 133.82 |
| 15 | 6 | 1.4185 | 141.85 |
| 16 | 7 | 1.5036 | 150.36 |
| 17 | 8 | 1.5938 | 159.38 |
| 18 | 9 | 1.6895 | 168.95 |
| 19 | 10 | 1.7908 | 179.08 |

**Figure 2.3** Calculations for Worked Example 2.16.

This use of powers leads to a convenient notation for very large or very small numbers. **Scientific notation** is used to represent any number in the format:

$$a \times 10^b$$

where $a$ is a number between 0 and 10, and $b$ is the appropriate power of 10.

This notation is based on the fact that $10^1 = 10$, $10^2 = 100$, $10^3 = 1000$, and so on. Then:

- we can write 12 as $1.2 \times 10^1$ (that is, $1.2 \times 10$)
- 1200 is $1.2 \times 10^3$ (that is, $1.2 \times 1000$)
- 1 380 197.892 is about $1.38 \times 10^6$
- the United Kingdom's annual exports are about £$1.1 \times 10^{11}$

and so on.

Similarly, $10^{-1} = 0.1$, $10^{-3} = 0.001$ and $10^{-6} = 0.000\,001$, so:

- we can write 0.12 as $1.2 \times 10^{-1}$ (that is, $1.2 \times 0.1$)
- 0.0012 is $1.2 \times 10^{-3}$ (that is, $1.2 \times 0.001$)
- 0.000 004 29 is $4.29 \times 10^{-6}$

You can easily find the power that the 10 must be raised to by counting the number of places the decimal point must be moved. With, for example 15 762 the decimal point must be moved four places to the left, so 10 is raised to the power 4:

$$15\,762 = 1.5762 \times 10^4$$

With 0.0057 the decimal point must be moved three places to the right, so the 10 is raised to the power −3:

$$0.0057 = 5.7 \times 10^{-3}$$

Although we shall not use this format very often, it does give a useful way of describing very large or very small numbers.

---

### IN SUMMARY

Superscripts are used to show when values are raised to powers. There are several rules for manipulating powers, including:

- multiplication involves adding powers ($a^m \times a^n = a^{m+n}$)
- division involves subtracting powers ($a^m/a^n = a^{m-n}$)
- $a^{-n} = 1/a^n$

## 2.2.5 | Solving quadratic equations

In the last section we looked at variables raised to powers. Now we can try solving equations which contain such powers. Unfortunately, this is usually difficult and there are almost no general methods. One exception is an equation of the form:

$$ax^2 + bx + c = 0$$

where $a$, $b$ and $c$ are constants and $x$ is the variable to be found. This is called a **quadratic equation.**

If we look at a very simple quadratic equation, where $a = 1$, $b = 0$ and $c = -4$, we have:

$$x^2 - 4 = 0 \quad \text{or} \quad x^2 = 4$$

There are two solutions to this equation:

$$x = 2 \quad \text{and} \quad x = -2$$

and this illustrates the general rule, that a quadratic equation has two solutions. These are called the **roots**, which we can find from the standard formula:

$$x = \frac{-b \pm \sqrt{b^2 - 4ac}}{2a}$$

where $\pm$ means 'plus or minus'. In other words, the two roots of a quadratic equation are given by:

$$x = \frac{-b + \sqrt{b^2 - 4ac}}{2a} \quad \text{and} \quad x = \frac{-b - \sqrt{b^2 - 4ac}}{2a}$$

If we substitute the values used above, where $x^2 - 4 = 0$, we have $a = 1$, $b = 0$ and $c = -4$. Then the roots are:

$$x = \frac{-0 + \sqrt{0^2 - 4 \times 1 \times (-4)}}{2 \times 1} \quad \text{and} \quad x = \frac{-0 - \sqrt{0^2 - 4 \times 1 \times (-4)}}{2 \times 1}$$

$$= \ 4/2 \qquad\qquad\qquad\qquad = \ -4/2$$

$$= \ 2 \qquad\qquad\qquad\qquad\quad = \ -2$$

# WORKED EXAMPLE 2.17

What are the roots of the equation:

$$2x^2 + 3x - 2 = 0$$

## Solution

This is in the general form $ax^2 + bx + c = 0$, with $a = 2$, $b = 3$ and $c = -2$. The two roots are found by substitution in the equations:

$$x = \frac{-b + \sqrt{b^2 - 4ac}}{2a} \quad \text{and} \quad x = \frac{-b - \sqrt{b^2 - 4ac}}{2a}$$

to give

$$x = \frac{-3 + \sqrt{3^2 + 4 \times 2 \times 2}}{2 \times 2} \quad \text{and} \quad x = \frac{-3 - \sqrt{3^2 + 4 \times 2 \times 2}}{2 \times 2}$$

Notice that the calculation of $-4ac$ has been simplified from $-4 \times 2 \times (-2)$ to $+4 \times 2 \times 2$.

Then:

$$x = \frac{-3 + \sqrt{25}}{4} \quad \text{and} \quad x = \frac{-3 - \sqrt{25}}{4}$$

or

$$x = 2/4 \quad \text{and} \quad x = -8/4$$
$$= 0.5 \quad\quad\quad = -2$$

You can check these values by substitution in the original equation:

$$2 \times 0.5^2 + 3 \times 0.5 - 2 = 0 \quad \text{and} \quad 2 \times 2^2 - 3 \times 2 - 2 = 0$$

---

The only problem with this method comes when $4ac$ is greater than $b^2$. Then $b^2 - 4ac$ is negative and we have to find the square root of a negative number. This is not defined in real arithmetic, so we must conclude that there are no real roots and they are both imaginary.

One common example of quadratic equations in business occurs when the cost per unit varies with the number of units produced. Suppose, for example, that a workshop has fixed overheads of £2,000 a week, and the basic cost of making a unit of product is £200, but this declines by £5 for every unit of weekly production. Then the unit cost is $200 - 5x$, where $x$ is the weekly production. So:

total weekly cost = overheads + (unit cost × number made in week)

$$= 2000 + (200 - 5x) \times x$$
$$= 2000 + 200x - 5x^2$$

---

# WORKED EXAMPLE 2.18

The basic income from a product is £12 a unit, but this increases by £2 for every unit made. If there are fixed costs of £1,000 for the process, how many units must be sold to cover costs?

## Solution

The income from each unit is $12 + 2x$, where $x$ is the number of units sold. Therefore the total income is $12x + 2x^2$ and the profit is $2x^2 + 12x - 1000$. When this is equal to zero the income just covers costs. This happens when:

$$x = \frac{-b + \sqrt{b^2 - 4ac}}{2a} \quad \text{and} \quad x = \frac{-b - \sqrt{b^2 - 4ac}}{2a}$$

$$x = \frac{-12 + \sqrt{(12^2 + 4 \times 2 \times 1000)}}{4} \quad \text{and} \quad x = \frac{-12 - \sqrt{(12^2 + 4 \times 2 \times 1000)}}{4}$$

$$= 19.56 \qquad\qquad\qquad\qquad = -25.56$$

Obviously, the company cannot sell a negative number of units, so the answer must be 19.56 units.

---

## IN SUMMARY

Equations containing variables raised to powers are difficult to solve. The only equations of this type which are easy to solve are quadratic equations of the form:

$$ax^2 + bx + c = 0$$

---

# Self-assessment questions

**2.5**   Why is algebra useful in business?

**2.6**   Is the order of doing calculations in equations always the same?

**2.7**   Could you solve an equation of the form $y = 4x + 3$, where both $x$ and $y$ are unknown?

**2.8**   Would it be better to write an equation in the form:
   (a)   speed = distance/time
   (b)   $S = D/T$
   (c)   SPD = DST/TME
   (d)   $s = dt^{-1}$

**2.9**   What is the value of $((((1 + 3)/(4 - 2))/2) - 1)$?

**2.10**  If you knew values for $p$, $q$ and $r$, how would you solve the equations:
   (a)   $4r/(33 - 3x) = q/2p$      (b)      $(q - 4x)/2q - 7p/r = 0$

**2.11**  How many simultaneous equations would be needed to find values for seven unknown variables?

**2.12**  What is the value of $x^{1.5}/y^{2.5}$ when $x = 9$ and $y = 4$?

**2.13**  What is the value of $41.1635^\circ$?

**2.14**  Write $1\,230\,000\,000$ and $0.000\,000\,253$ in scientific notation.

**2.15**  What can you say about the roots of the equation $x^2 + 2x + 3 = 0$?

**2.16**  Having seen how to solve quadratic equations, why do we not describe formulae for solving other equations with variables raised to powers?

# 2.3 | Drawing graphs

## 2.3.1 | Cartesian coordinates

We can use algebra to describe many situations, but most people find it difficult to understand ideas from a set of equations. It is much easier to accept information which is presented in some form of diagram. We are going to discuss diagrams in Chapter 4, but will introduce one widely used type now. This is a **line graph**, which shows the relationship between two variables.

Graphs are usually drawn with two rectangular (or Cartesian) axes. The horizontal axis is traditionally labelled $x$ and the vertical axis is labelled $y$ (as shown in Figure 2.4). Then $x$ is the **independent variable**, which is the one that we can control, and $y$ is the **dependent variable**, whose value is set by $x$. Then $x$ might be the expenditure on advertising which we can control, while $y$ is the resulting sales which we cannot control; $x$ might be the interest rate for loans which can be fixed, while $y$ is the amount borrowed from banks; $x$ might be the price charged for a service and $y$ the resulting demand, and so on.

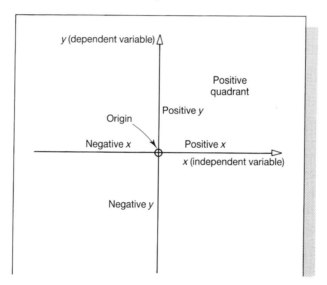

**Figure 2.4** Cartesian axes.

Although we are talking about dependent and independent variables we do not assume any cause and effect. There might be a clear relationship, but this is no evidence that a change in one variable actually **causes** changes in the other. A shopkeeper, for example, might find that when he reduces the price of overcoats the sales of ice cream increase. There might be a clear relationship between these two, but one does not cause the other, and they are both likely to be a result of hot weather. This theme is discussed in more detail in Chapter 8.

The point where the two axes cross is called the **origin** and corresponds to the point where both $x$ and $y$ have the value zero. At any point above the origin, $y$ is positive and, at any point below, *y* is negative: at any point to the left of the origin *x* is negative, while at any point to the right *x* is positive.

Having drawn the axes, we can specify any point on a graph by two numbers called **coordinates**. The first number specifies the distance along the *x* axis from the origin, while the second number specifies the distance up the *y* axis. The point $x = 3$, $y = 4$, for example, is three units along the *x* axis and four units up the *y* axis. A standard notation describes coordinates as $(x,y)$, so this point can be described as (3,4). The only thing we have to be careful about is that (3,4) is not the same as (4,3), as shown in Figure 2.5.

Points on the *x* axis have coordinates $(x,0)$ and points on the *y* axis have coordinates $(0,y)$. The origin is the point where the axes cross, which has coordinates (0,0). Many graphs are only concerned with areas where both the dependent and independent variables are positive (for example, a graph of income against sales) so they only show the positive quadrant.

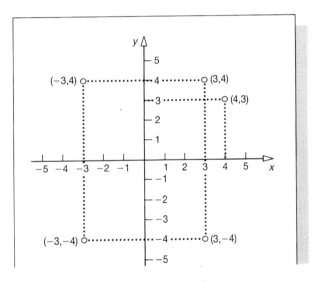

**Figure 2.5** Use of coordinates to locate points.

# WORKED EXAMPLE 2.19

Plot the following points on a graph.

| *x* | 2 | 5 | 7 | 10 | 15 |
|---|---|---|---|---|---|
| *y* | 7 | 18 | 22 | 30 | 46 |

Draw a line graph to emphasize the relationship between *x* and *y*.

## Solution

Only positive numbers are given so we need draw only the positive quadrant of the graph. Then the first point, (2,7), is 2 units along the $x$ axis and 7 units up the $y$ axis, and is shown as point A in Figure 2.6. The second point, (5,18), is 5 units along the $x$ axis and 18 units up the $y$ axis, and is shown by point B. The other points are plotted in the same way.

There seems to be a fairly strong relationship between $x$ and $y$, so we can emphasize this by joining the points by a line. Either this line can go through all the points to show detailed changes, or else it can ignore the details and show general trends. Figure 2.7 shows both the detailed line and a superimposed straight line of the general trend.

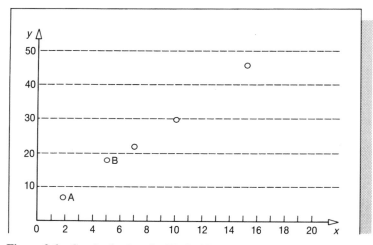

**Figure 2.6**   Graph of points for Worked Example 2.19.

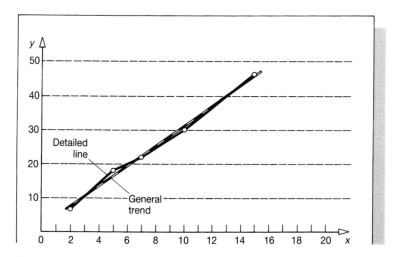

**Figure 2.7**   Line graph for Worked Example 2.19.

Graphs using rectangular coordinates give a useful means of showing a relationship between two variables; an independent one, $x$, and a dependent one, $y$.

## 2.3.2 | Drawing straight-line graphs

If two variables $x$ and $y$ are related, the relationship is described by an equation. We might find, for example, that $y = 4x + 10$. Then for every value of the independent variable $x$ there is a corresponding value of the dependent variable $y$. An alternative way of saying 'there is a relationship' is to describe **$y$ as a function of $x$**.

Now we can describe how to draw graphs, starting with a simple one, where $y$ does not vary with $x$. In other words, $y = c$, where $c$ is a constant. In this case we get a straight line which is parallel to the $x$ axis (see Figure 2.8). If, for example, $y = 10$, the graph of this is a straight line 10 units up the $y$ axis and parallel to the $x$ axis.

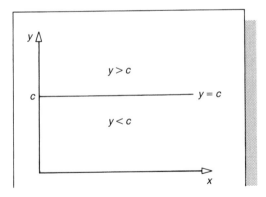

**Figure 2.8** Graph of $y = c$.

Such lines divide the area of the graph into three zones:

- at any point **on** the line $y$ is equal to $c$ (so we have $y = c$)
- at any point **above** the line $y$ is greater than $c$, which is written $y > c$
- at any point **below** the line $y$ is less than $c$, which is written $y < c$

We could equally say:

- at any point **on or above** the line $y$ is greater than or equal to $c$, which is written $y \geqslant c$
- at any point **on or below** the line $y$ is less than or equal to $c$, which is written $y \leqslant c$

The graph of $y = c$ is an example of a linear relationship, where the graph is a straight line. In general, such linear relationships have the form:

$$y = ax + b$$

where $x$ and $y$ are the independent and dependent variables, and $a$ and $b$ are constants.

One benefit of straight-line graphs is that we can draw them from only two points, as you can see in the following example.

## WORKED EXAMPLE 2.20

Draw a graph of $y = 10x + 50$.

### Solution

This is a straight-line graph of the standard form $y = ax + b$, with $a = 10$ and $b = 50$. We need only take two points to draw the line, so will take two convenient ones. We shall arbitrarily take $x = 0$ and $x = 20$.

Then:

- when $x = 0$, $y = 10x + 50 = 10 \times 0 + 50 = 50$, which defines the point $(0, 50)$
- when $x = 20$, $y = 10x + 50 = 10 \times 20 + 50 = 250$, which defines the point $(20, 250)$

Plotting these points and the connecting line gives the graph shown in Figure 2.9.

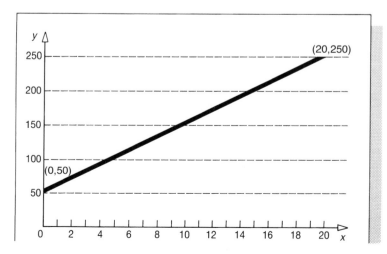

**Figure 2.9** Graph of $y = 10x + 50$ for Worked Example 2.20.

If you look at a straight-line graph, two features are obvious. These are:

- **intercept**, which shows where the line crosses the $y$ axis
- **gradient**, which shows how steep the line is

Now a line crosses the $y$ axis when $x$ has the value 0, so the intercept is the value of $y$ when $x = 0$. If we substitute $x = 0$ into the general equation $y = ax + b$, we find that this gives $y = b$. In other words, $b$ is the intercept of the line.

The gradient shows how quickly the line is rising, so it is the increase in $y$ for a unit increase in $x$. If you look at the graph of $y = 10x + 50$ shown in Figure 2.9 you can find the change in $y$ when $x$ rises between, say 10 and 11. (These numbers are chosen arbitrarily, as a straight line has the same gradient at any point.)

Substitution gives:

- when $x = 10$, $\ y = 10x + 50 = 10 \times 10 + 50 = 150$

and

- when $x = 11$, $\ y = 10x + 50 = 10 \times 11 + 50 = 160$

So the gradient is $(160 - 150) = 10$. But you can see that this is the value of $a$. This is no coincidence, and in general the gradient of a straight-line graph is always given by the value of $a$.

## WORKED EXAMPLE 2.21

Describe the graph of the equation $y = 4x + 20$.

### Solution

This is a straight-line graph with intercept of 20 and gradient of 4, as shown in Figure 2.10.

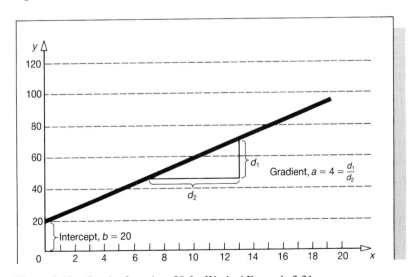

**Figure 2.10**   Graph of $y = 4x + 20$ for Worked Example 2.21.

## WORKED EXAMPLE 2.22

Plot the graph of $y = 100 - 5x$.

### Solution

This is a straight-line graph with $a = -5$ and $b = 100$. We only need to find two points to draw the line, so we shall take two convenient ones, such as $x = 0$ and $x = 10$. Then:

- when $x = 0$, $y = 100 - 5x = 100 - 5 \times 0 = 100$

  and

- when $x = 10$, $y = 100 - 5x = 100 - 5 \times 10 = 50$

Plotting the two points (0,100) and (10,50) and drawing the connecting line gives the result shown in Figure 2.11. In this example the gradient is negative, implying that $y$ decreases when $x$ increases.

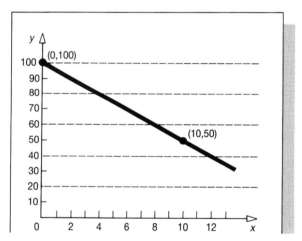

**Figure 2.11**   Graph of $y = 100 - 5x$ for Worked Example 2.22.

---

### IN SUMMARY

Line graphs are used to give a diagrammatic view of a function. Straight-line graphs have the form $y = ax + b$, where $a$ is the gradient and $b$ is the intercept. Such graphs can be drawn by plotting any two points and drawing the straight line through them.

## 2.3.3 | Drawing graphs of other equations

Now that we can draw straight-line graphs, we can extend these ideas to other functions. The easiest way of drawing a graph of a function is to take a series of convenient values for the independent variable $x$ and substitute these into the equation to find corresponding values for the dependent variable $y$. This gives a series of points for $(x,y)$. These points can be joined by a line to show the graph of the relationship. We can draw straight-line graphs from only two points, but we need more information to draw more complex functions.

## WORKED EXAMPLE 2.23

Draw the graph of the quadratic equation $y = 2x^2 + 3x - 3$, between $x = -6$ and $x = 5$ Where does this curve cross the $x$ axis?

### Solution

The shape of this graph is not obvious from the equation, but as we are interested in values of $y$ for $x$ between $-6$ and $+5$ we can calculate coordinates by substitution:

- when $x = -6$, $y = 2x^2 + 3x - 3 = 2 \times (-6)^2 + 3 \times (-6) - 3 = 51$
- when $x = -5$, $y = 2x^2 + 3x - 3 = 2 \times (-5)^2 + 3 \times (-5) - 3 = 32$

and so on, to give the following table:

| $x$ | $-6$ | $-5$ | $-4$ | $-3$ | $-2$ | $-1$ | 0 | 1 | 2 | 3 | 4 | 5 |
|---|---|---|---|---|---|---|---|---|---|---|---|---|
| $y$ | 51 | 32 | 17 | 6 | $-1$ | $-4$ | $-3$ | 2 | 11 | 24 | 41 | 62 |

Plotting these points on rectangular axes and joining them together gives the graph in Figure 2.12. You can see that the curve crosses the $x$ axis at roughly the points $x = -2$ and $x = 1$.

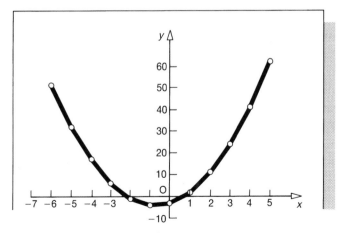

**Figure 2.12**   Graph of $y = 2x^2 + 3x - 3$ for Worked Example 2.23.

Quadratic equations always give this kind of U-shaped curve, which has one turning point (where the graph changes direction and the gradient changes sign). If the $x^2$ term in a quadratic equation is negative the graph is inverted, so it looks like a hill rather than a valley. Now we can relate this graph back to Section 2.2.5, which described the solution of quadratic equations. The two roots of a quadratic were defined as the points where $ax^2 + bx + c = 0$. In other words, they are the two points where $y = 0$ and the graph crosses the $x$ axis. For the worked example above, we can calculate the roots of the equation as:

$$x = \frac{-b + \sqrt{b^2 - 4ac}}{2a} \qquad \text{and} \qquad x = \frac{-b - \sqrt{b^2 - 4ac}}{2a}$$

$$= \frac{-3 + \sqrt{(9 + 24)}}{4} \qquad\qquad = \frac{-3 - \sqrt{(9 + 24)}}{4}$$

$$= 0.686 \qquad\qquad \text{and} \qquad = -2.186$$

These are more accurate values for our observations from the graph, and mean that the curve crosses the $x$ axis at the points $(0.686,0)$ and $(-2.186,0)$.

We have now drawn graphs of straight lines (where $y = ax + b$) and quadratic equations (where $y = ax^2 + bx + c$). These are two examples of **polynomials**, which are equations containing a variable, $x$, raised to some power (1 for straight lines and 2 for quadratics). Sometimes we need to look at polynomials where $x$ is raised to a higher power. Cubic equations, for example, contain $x$ raised to the power 3, with the form:

$$y = ax^3 + bx^2 + cx + d$$

These graphs are slightly more complex, but the method of drawing them is the same. Thankfully, spreadsheets and graphics packages make this very easy.

# WORKED EXAMPLE 2.24

Draw a graph of the function $y = x^3 - 1.5x^2 - 18x$ between $x = -5$ and $x = +6$.

## Solution

Taking values for $x$ and substituting to give corresponding values for $y$ gives the results shown in Figure 2.13. The spreadsheet automatically plots these as a graph.

| Drawing graphs | | | | | | | | | | | |
|---|---|---|---|---|---|---|---|---|---|---|---|
| | | | | | | | | | | | |
| **x** | −5 | −4 | −3 | −2 | −1 | 0 | 1 | 2 | 3 | 4 | 5 | 6 |
| **y** | −72.5 | −16 | 13.5 | 22 | 15.5 | 0 | −18.5 | −34 | −40.5 | −32 | −2.5 | 54 |

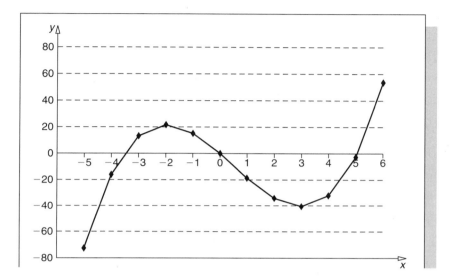

**Figure 2.13**   Using a spreadsheet to draw a more complex polynomial.

The graph in Figure 2.13 has two turning points where the gradient changes sign. These are located around $x = -2$ and $x = 3$. Most cubic equations have this general shape, but they vary a little in detail: some are the other way around, some have the two turning points merged into one, and so on. Figure 2.13 also illustrates the general point that more complex polynomials give more complex graphs. When drawing these we must be careful to:

- plot enough points to show the true shape of the curve and
- draw a smooth curve through the points.

We can extend this method of drawing graphs of polynomials to any other functions. Many functions are based on the exponential constant, e, which is defined as e = 2.718 281 8… Although this may seem a strange number, there are sound theoretical reasons for its use. It is particularly well suited to functions which rise at an accelerating rate, which is why you hear about 'exponential growth'. We shall return to exponential functions at several points in the book.

# WORKED EXAMPLE 2.25

Draw a graph of:
(a) $y = e^x$ for values of $x$ between 0 and 10
(b) $y = e^{-x}$ for values of $x$ between 0 and 8

## Solution

The easiest way of drawing these is to use a standard package. Figure 2.14 shows typical results from a spreadsheet. The first graph shows an exponential rise, while the second shows an exponential fall.

| Drawing graphs | | | | | | | | | | | |
|---|---|---|---|---|---|---|---|---|---|---|---|
| | | | | | | | | | | | |
| **x** | 0 | 1 | 2 | 3 | 4 | 5 | 6 | 7 | 8 | 9 | 10 |
| **y** | 1 | 2.718 | 7.389 | 20.09 | 54.6 | 148.4 | 403.4 | 1097 | 2981 | 8103 | 22026 |

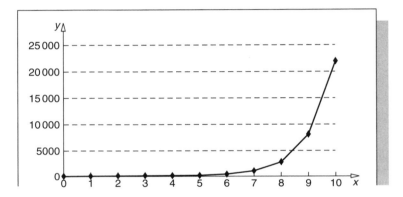

**Figure 2.14(a)** Graph of $y = e^x$.

| Drawing graphs | | | | | | | | | |
|---|---|---|---|---|---|---|---|---|---|
| | | | | | | | | | |
| **x** | 0 | 1 | 2 | 3 | 4 | 5 | 6 | 7 | 8 |
| **y** | 1 | 0.368 | 0.135 | 0.05 | 0.018 | 0.007 | 0.002 | 0.0009 | 0.00034 |

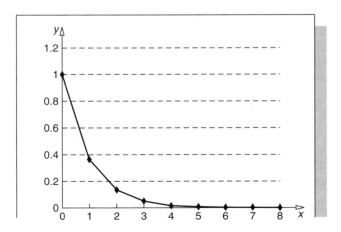

**Figure 2.14(b)** Graph of $y = e^{-x}$.

IN SUMMARY

Line graphs can be used to give a pictorial view of any function. They are drawn most easily by plotting a series of separate points $(x,y)$ and joining them with a line. This approach was illustrated using polynomials and exponential functions.

## 2.3.4 | Graphs of simultaneous equations

Earlier in the chapter we showed how to solve simultaneous equations algebraically. We can now show what these solutions mean on graphs. Suppose that we have two unknown variables $x$ and $y$ related by the simultaneous equations:

$$3y = 4x + 2 \tag{1}$$

$$y = -x + 10 \tag{2}$$

One way of finding a solution is to draw a graph of each equation. This gives a graph with two straight lines. The first equation is true at any point on the first line, and the second equation is true at any point on the second line. It follows that the point where the lines cross is the point where both equations are true. Figure 2.15 shows that the lines cross at about the point where $x = 4$ and $y = 6$.

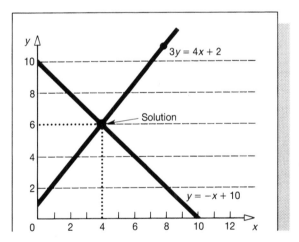

**Figure 2.15** Graphical solution of simultaneous equations.

We can check this result by tackling the problem algebraically:

$$3y = 4x + 2 \tag{1}$$

$$y = -x + 10 \tag{2}$$

Multiply equation (2) by 3 and subtract it from equation (1):

$$0 = 7x - 28$$

$$x = 4$$

Substituting in equation (1):

$$3y = 4 \times 4 + 2$$
$$y = 6$$

The main problem with using graphs to solve equations is accuracy. It is difficult to draw graphs exactly, and with complicated curves or small scales the results will not be very accurate. Graphs do, however, have the advantage of giving a clear picture of the problem.

---

> ## IN SUMMARY

Graphs can be used to solve simultaneous equations. In practice, the results are not very accurate, so it is better to draw graphs to get an overall view of the problem and then find the solutions algebraically.

---

## Self-assessment questions

**2.17** What is meant by a 'dependent variable'?

**2.18** What are the coordinates of the origin of a graph?

**2.19** Describe the graph of the equation $y = 2x + 4$.

**2.20** What are the gradients of the lines:
    (a)   $y = 10$        (b)   $y = x$       (c)   $x = 10$

**2.21** Where are the solutions of a quadratic equation found on a graph?

**2.22** What is a turning point of a graph?

**2.23** Why is it generally better to use algebraic rather than graphical methods to solve equations?

**2.24** What does it mean when two graphs cross each other?

---

> ## CHAPTER REVIEW

The remaining chapters in this book describe some quantitative analyses which are widely used in business. This chapter described the basic tools for these analyses. In particular, it described:

● the overall approach to quantitative methods

● calculations using integers, decimals, fractions and percentages

● the use of algebra

● the solution of simple, simultaneous and quadratic equations

● the use of powers and roots

- the drawing of graphs on Cartesian coordinates
- the use of graphs to solve equations

If you want more information about any point mentioned in this chapter it might be worth looking at a more detailed book on mathematics. Many of these are available and some useful ones are listed in Appendix A.

# Problems

**2.1** What are the values of:
  (a) $-12 \times 8$        (b) $-35/(-7)$        (c) $(24-8) \times (4+5)$
  (d) $(18-4)/(3+9-5)$    (e) $(22/11) \times (-18+3)/(12/4)$?

**2.2** Simplify the common fractions:
  (a) $3/5 + 1/2$        (b) $3/4 \times 1/6$        (c) $3/4 - 1/8$
  (d) $-18/5 \div 6/25$      (e) $(3/8 - 1/6) \div 4/7$

**2.3** What are the answers to Problem 2.2 as decimal fractions?

**2.4** (a) What is 23/40 as a percentage?    (b) What is 65% as a fraction?
  (c) What is 17% as a decimal?

**2.5** What is 1037/14 to:
  (a) three decimal places       (b) one decimal place
  (c) two significant figures     (d) one significant figure?

**2.6** In one exam 64 people passed and 23 failed; in a second exam 163 people passed and 43 failed. Which exam was the more difficult to pass?

**2.7** A car travels 180 miles in 3 hours. What is its average speed? What is the equation for the average speed of a car on any journey?

**2.8** A shopkeeper buys an item from a wholesaler and sells it to customers. If he sells $n$ units a day, what is his profit?

**2.9** A school has £1515 to spend on footballs. Match balls cost £35 each while practice balls cost £22 each. The school must buy 60 balls each year, so how many of each type should be bought to exactly match the budget?

**2.10** A company finds that 30% of its costs are direct labour. Each week raw materials cost £1000 more than twice this amount, and there is an overhead of 20% of direct labour costs. What are the weekly costs to the company?

**2.11** Solve the following simultaneous equations:
  (a) $a + b = 3$   and   $a - b = 5$
  (b) $2x + 3y = 27$   and   $3x + 2y = 23$
  (c) $x + y - 2z = -2$   and   $2x - y + z = 9$   and   $x + 3y + 2z = 4$
  (d) $4r - 2s + 3t = 12$   and   $r + 2s + t = -1$   and   $3r - s - t = -5$

**2.12** A company finds that one of its productivity measures is related to the number of employees $e$ and the production $n$ by the following equations:
$$10n + 3e = 45 \qquad \text{and} \qquad 2n + 5e = 31$$
What are the current values for $e$ and $n$?

**2.13** What are the values of:

(a) $x^{1/2} \times x^{1/4}$    (b) $(x^{1/3})^3$    (c) $9^{0.5}$

(d) $4^{2.5}$    (e) $7^{3.2}$    (f) $4^{1.5} \times 6^{3.7}/6^{1.7}$?

**2.14** What are the roots of:

(a) $x^2 - 6x + 8 = 0$    (b) $3x^2 - 2x - 5 = 0$    (c) $x^2 + x + 1 = 0$?

**2.15** The basic income generated by a product is £10 a unit, but this increases by £1 for every unit made. If there are fixed costs of £100 for the process how many units must be sold to cover costs?

**2.16** Draw a graph showing the following points: (2,12), (4,16), (7,22), (10,28), (15,38). How would you describe this function?

**2.17** The number of people employed in a chain of shops is related to the size (in consistent units) by the equation:

$$\text{employees} = \text{size}/1000 + 3$$

Draw a graph of this function and use it to find the number of employees in a shop of size 50 000 units.

**2.18** Draw a graph of:

(a) $y = 10$    (b) $y = x + 10$

(c) $y = x^2 + x + 10$    (d) $y = x^3 + x^2 + x + 10$

**2.19** Draw appropriate graphs to confirm the results of Problem 2.11.

**2.20** The output $y$ from an assembly line is related to one of the settings $x$ by the equation:

$$y = -5x^2 + 2500x - 12\ 500$$

What is the maximum output from the line, and the corresponding value for $x$?

**2.21** The unit cost of operating some production equipment is given by the equation:

$$\text{cost} = 1.5x^2 - 120x + 4000$$

where $x$ is the number of units produced. Draw a graph to find the minimum unit cost. What production level does this correspond to?

**2.22** Where does the line $y = 20x + 15$ cross the line $y = 2x^2 - 4x + 1$?

# Computer exercises

**2.1** Most calculations are done by computer. Spreadsheets (such as Excell, Lotus 1-2-3 and QuattroPro) are particularly useful in business. See what programs you have and make sure you know how to use them.

**2.2** Use a spreadsheet to calculate $x^3 - 3x^2 - 4x + 10$ for values of $x$ from 1 to 50. Draw a graph of this function.

**2.3** Use a suitable package to draw the graphs of $y = 22 - 3x$ and $y = x + 4$. Where do these lines cross?

**2.4** Use a suitable package to draw the functions $y = e^{2x}$ and $y = x^2 + 10$. Where do these lines cross?

**2.5** Over the past ten months Jefferson Young & Co. has collected information about their production, income and costs (Figure 2.16). Someone in the company has summarized these on the spreadsheet in Figure 2.17. Describe how the spreadsheet works and what it shows. What else could you do with the data?

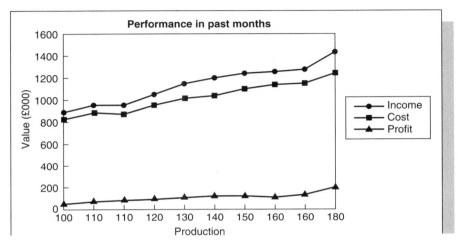

**Figure 2.16** Results prepared by Jefferson Young & Co.

|   | A | B | C | D | E | F | G | H | I |
|---|---|---|---|---|---|---|---|---|---|
| 1 | **Original data** | | | | | **Sorted data** | | | |
| 2 | | | | | | | | | |
| 3 | **Production** | **Income** | **Cost** | **Profit** | | **Production** | **Income** | **Cost** | **Profit** |
| 4 | 120 | 1070 | 960 | 110 | | 100 | 860 | 820 | 40 |
| 5 | 150 | 1270 | 1130 | 140 | | 110 | 950 | 890 | 60 |
| 6 | 180 | 1480 | 1280 | 200 | | 110 | 950 | 880 | 70 |
| 7 | 110 | 950 | 890 | 60 | | 120 | 1070 | 960 | 110 |
| 8 | 130 | 1150 | 1030 | 120 | | 130 | 1150 | 1030 | 120 |
| 9 | 160 | 1300 | 1170 | 130 | | 140 | 1210 | 1060 | 150 |
| 10 | 100 | 860 | 820 | 40 | | 150 | 1270 | 1130 | 140 |
| 11 | 110 | 950 | 880 | 70 | | 160 | 1300 | 1170 | 130 |
| 12 | 160 | 1320 | 1180 | 140 | | 160 | 1320 | 1180 | 140 |
| 13 | 140 | 1210 | 1060 | 150 | | 180 | 1480 | 1280 | 200 |

**Figure 2.17** Spreadsheet for Computer Exercise 2.5.

**2.6** Use a suitable package to plot the following points:

| $x$ | 1 | 3 | 6 | 8 | 9 | 10 | 13 | 14 | 17 | 18 | 21 | 25 | 26 | 29 |
|---|---|---|---|---|---|---|---|---|---|---|---|---|---|---|
| $y$ | 22 | 24 | 31 | 38 | 41 | 44 | 52 | 55 | 61 | 64 | 69 | 76 | 81 | 83 |

# Case study 1

## The Crown and Anchor

Tina Jones, along with her husband and staff of eight, runs the Crown and Anchor pub in Middleton. In recent years, Tina has found that serving meals has become an increasingly important source of income. Now she wants to improve the dining room and is hoping the bank will lend her some money to pay for this.

Tina is sure that the improvements will increase her profits and wants to make a good case to her bank manager. She has kept a record of the average number of meals served each day over the past 12 months, and the daily income from food (Table 2.1). Now she wants to do some figures and present this in a convincing way. What do you think she could do with the information she has collected? What other information should she get?

**Table 2.1**

|            | Dinners | Lunches | Income (£) |
|------------|---------|---------|------------|
| January    | 25      | 6       | 180        |
| February   | 23      | 6       | 178        |
| March      | 24      | 8       | 196        |
| April      | 26      | 9       | 216        |
| May        | 27      | 9       | 230        |
| June       | 42      | 32      | 525        |
| July       | 48      | 36      | 605        |
| August     | 48      | 37      | 603        |
| September  | 35      | 34      | 498        |
| October    | 31      | 30      | 451        |
| November   | 30      | 31      | 464        |
| December   | 37      | 38      | 592        |

# Case study 2

## Northern Feedstuffs

Northern Feedstuffs makes a range of different feeds which are used to supplement the diet of farm animals. In one mill they make four products (A, B, C and D) using four ingredients (w, x, y and z). Product A consists of 20% w, 30% x, 10% y and 40% z. Product B consists of 10% w, 60% x and 30% z. Product C consists of 30% w, 10% x, 50% y and 10% z. Product D consists of 50% w, 20% x, 10% y and 20% z.

Paul Gambol is the Production Manager in charge of this mill. Two years ago he set up a spreadsheet to help with planning. For example, next month Northern wants to make 100 tonnes of A, 50 tonnes of B, 40 tonnes of C and 60 tonnes of D, and Paul can use his spreadsheet to find the ingredients he must buy. Then he can simply adjust the figures to calculate the ingredients he needs for the following month's production of 120 tonnes of A, 60 tonnes of B, 30 tonnes of C and 50 tonnes of D. By adding the costs of ingredients Paul can also see how much he will spend on raw materials. At the moment the prices of ingredients are £100, £150, £200 and £160 respectively.

Another part of Paul's spreadsheet allows him to change production plans at short notice. Last month, for example, bad weather affected the harvesting in Canada and there were delays in getting ingredients. At the beginning of the month Paul estimated that he would get total deliveries of 60 tonnes of w, 80 tonnes of x, 50 tonnes of y and 90 tonnes of z. He was able to calculate the products he could make and the total weight he would have available for customers.

Now Northern wants to extend the use of Paul's system into other areas of the company. They would like you to write a report showing how the system works. They are particularly interested in ways of extending the system to more complicated products and different types of analysis.

# PART TWO

# Data collection
# and description

This book is divided into five parts, each of which covers a different aspect of quantitative methods in business. The first part gave the background and context for the rest of the book. This second part discusses data collection and description. The third part looks at methods of solving specific types of problem, while the last two parts describe various statistical analyses.

There are four chapters in this part. The first chapter discusses data collection, while the next three chapters cover aspects of data presentation and description.

Chapter 3 discusses data collection. Managers can only make good decisions if they have reliable information, and they get this by collecting data and processing them. Data collection and analysis are essential functions in every organization. The chapter describes different types of data and how they are collected, primarily through sampling.

The raw data collected often have too much detail, so they must be summarized and presented in forms that emphasize the important features. The purpose of data presentation is to show the main patterns of the data in a format that is both accurate and easy to understand. Chapter 4 describes how this can be done using diagrams.

Chapter 5 continues the theme of summarizing data by looking at numerical descriptions. In particular, it describes measures for the location and dispersion of data.

Chapter 6 looks at index numbers. A lot of analysis is concerned with the way that a variable changes over time, and one way of describing these changes is to use index numbers.

## Ideas in Practice – Mareco/Gallup International

For 50 years after the Second World War Poland had a centrally planned economy. During this time the government was responsible for most business decisions, and there was no role for market research. Then the economy was reformed in 1990, and newly privatized companies began to look directly at the demands of their customers.

The market research industry grew quickly, reaching $50 million a year by 1998.

There are nine major research companies, but Mareco is by far the largest with up to 90% of some markets. Mareco was founded in 1993 and joined Gallup International Association in 1994.

Many Polish companies have little interest in market research, as they maintain their traditional view that it is a waste of money. There are, however, many foreign companies investing in Poland who do not know the country well and want to learn about the new market. As a result, 80% of Mareco's clients are foreign companies starting operations in Poland.

Mareco aims to conduct research as quickly and accurately as possible, 'to provide the best insights into our clients' markets'. They organize operations from a head office in Warsaw, which has three separate departments.

- **Opinion Polls and Market Research Department.** This works at the start of a project, forming direct relations with customers, preparing research offers, scheduling work, designing questionnaires, selecting samples, and so on. Then it works on the final part, analysing the results of surveys and writing the reports for customers.

- **Field Research Department.** This runs the actual collection of data using a network of 24 co-ordinators and 200 interviewers throughout the whole of Poland.

- **Data Processing Department.** This takes the data collected in the field research, analyses them and creates databases.

The international link with Gallup allows Mareco to introduce new ideas to Poland, such as CATI (computer-assisted telephone interviews) and CAPI (computer-assisted personal interviews). It also allows them to use the experience of other Gallup companies to give a high quality service

Mareco's main problem is with its interviewers. Interviewing is not well paid, and it tends to attract students who want short-term employment. They can do simple data collection but lack the skills needed for in-depth interviews or some of the more demanding jobs. Unfortunately, the high staff turnover means that Mareco cannot train its interviewers as thoroughly as they would like. It also raises problems of reliability. The company runs checks and controls on the replies they receive, but it can be difficult to make sure that all replies come from genuine respondents.

# 3 Collecting data

| | | | | |
|---|---|---|---|---|
| Chapter outline | 60 | Chapter review | 83 |
| 3.1 Introduction | 61 | Problems | 83 |
| 3.2 Types of data | 64 | Computer exercises | 85 |
| 3.3 How to choose a sample | 67 | Case study: | |
| 3.4 Ways of collecting data | 74 | Natural Biscuits | 86 |
| 3.5 Using the data | 81 | | |

## CHAPTER OUTLINE

In Chapter 1 we said that managers should consider all available information before making their decisions. This information is gathered from a number of sources, and in this chapter we discuss the principles of data collection.

The chapter starts by outlining the importance of data collection and relating it to management decisions. There are several types of data and we describe some useful classifications. These are important, because data of different types are collected, presented and analysed in different ways.

Most data collection relies on sampling, where data are collected from only a proportion of possible suppliers. The chapter outlines available methods of selecting a sample. When an appropriate sample has been identified, actual data must be collected. This often uses questionnaires, and we give some guidelines for their design.

After reading the chapter and doing the exercises you should be able to:

- appreciate the importance of data collection

- discuss the timing and amount of data to be collected

- classify data in several ways

- appreciate the purpose of sampling

- select samples in different ways

- collect data in a number of ways

- design questionnaires

# 3.1 Introduction

## 3.1.1 Why collect data?

There is a difference between data and information. Essentially, data are the raw numbers or facts that must be processed to give useful information (see Figure 3.1). Thus 78, 64, 36, 70 and 52 are data which could be processed to give the information that the average mark of five students in an exam was 60%; data about new businesses could be collected as a large set of numbers, and this could be processed to give the information that two thirds of new companies cease trading within two years of opening; the ten-year government census has individual returns providing data, which are processed to give information about the population as a whole; entries in a company's transaction records give data which are consolidated into accounting information.

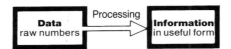

**Figure 3.1**  Relating data and information.

In this book we emphasize quantitative data, and these appear as sets of numbers. We should recognize, though, that data can be any collection of facts, observations, measurements, opinions, or anything else which gives details about a situation.

In business, data are collected and transformed into the information which allows managers to make their decisions. There are several implications in this statement:

● managers need information before they can make decisions

● they should examine all available information before making decisions

● they should have enough information to allow good decisions

● this information should be reliable

● the information is provided by data collection and analysis

It is clear, then, that data collection is an important, and even vital, function in any organization. Without data collection, managers do not have access to reliable information and cannot make reasoned decisions. The rest of this chapter discusses ways in which data can be collected.

> ## IN SUMMARY

Managers need reliable information to make decisions about the running of their organizations. This information is provided by data collection and processing.

## 3.1.2 | Timing and quantity of data collection

You can see that we are talking about the collection of data before discussing their presentation, which is covered in Chapter 4. This seems a sensible approach, as you have to collect data before presenting them. But data are collected for a specific purpose and the way they are used should have an effect on the way they are collected. If, for example, we want to decide how many beds a hospital should set aside for road accident victims, we could collect data from local accident statistics; if we want to know how retired people spend their leisure time, we could enclose a questionnaire with information which is routinely posted to pensioners; if we want to find how many people will buy a new product, we could run a market survey; if we want to see how many people wear car seat belts, we could stand by a road and observe passing cars. In other words, the way data will be used has an effect on the way they are collected. We should, therefore, design data collection to meet its specific purpose, and not the other way around.

> Data collection should be designed
> **after** deciding the use of the data.

One problem with data collection is knowing how much to collect. In many circumstances there is an almost limitless amount of data which could be collected and might be useful. We should resist the temptation to collect data simply because they are available, and limit ourselves to those which are relevant and useful. The reason for this is that data collection and processing inevitably costs money, and collecting unnecessary data is a waste.

In principle there is an optimal amount of data which should be collected for any purpose. If we consider the marginal cost of data as the cost of collecting the last 'unit', then the marginal cost increases with the amount of data collected. We could find some general data about, say, Canadian Pacific Railway very easily (it operates trains, employs staff, and so on); more detailed data would need a trip to a specialized library (to find exactly how many trains of different types are operated or staff of different grades employed); yet more detailed data would need a search of Canadian Pacific Railway's own records (to find the wage bill for each grade of employee in each region); yet more detailed data would need a special survey (to ask what each grade of employee felt about their conditions), and so on.

More detailed data are clearly more difficult and more expensive to collect. On the other hand, the marginal benefit of data (which is the benefit of the last 'unit' of data collected) is likely to fall. Using the above illustration, the fact that Canadian Pacific Railway runs a rail service is a very useful item of data, but most people would find the views of different grades of employees about their conditions less useful. We could use this observation to suggest the relationship shown in Figure 3.2.

An optimal amount of data collection can be defined by the point at which the marginal cost becomes greater than the marginal benefit. In other words, the cost of collecting another bit of data is greater than the benefit. Collecting more data would be wasteful, but collecting less would lose some potential benefit. In practice, of course, it is very difficult to define the costs and benefits of data so

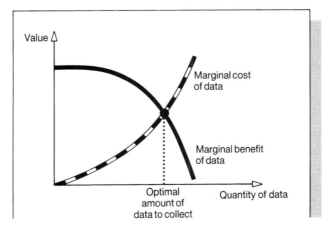

**Figure 3.2**   Finding the optimal quantity of data to collect.

organizations do not calculate the optimal amount, but simply collect the amount that their experience suggests is reasonable.

Another factor which is important in data collection is the time available. Some methods of collection, such as reviewing published statistics, can be done very quickly; others, such as running consumer surveys, need a lot of time. The time available can limit both the type of data that can be collected and the amount. If a company decides to launch a new product next year, this automatically sets a limit to the amount of consumer advice that can be collected.

A long period of data collection may also make the results either irrelevant or out of date before they can be properly analysed. It is often said that the 1851 census in America was not properly analysed before the 1861 census was taken. On a smaller scale it would be pointless to spend so long collecting data about the sales of a product that it was withdrawn from the market before the analysis could be completed.

If there are pressures on the time available for collecting data, or if proper planning is not done, then mistakes might be made. Many people say that some data, even if they are slightly inaccurate, are better than no data at all. In some circumstances this is a valid opinion. If we are buying a car it is better to ask a salesman for some details, even though we know that the replies may not be entirely accurate. But in many circumstances, wrong data can be worse than no data at all. A car salesman might mistakenly persuade us that an expensive car is cheap to run, and we might not be able to meet the payments. More broadly, inaccurate data may be so misleading that managers make the wrong decisions and actually harm an organization rather than give benefits. The obvious conclusion is that we must ensure data collected are as accurate as possible.

## IN SUMMARY

Data collection is expensive, so it is sensible to decide what the data will be used for before they are collected. In principle, there is an optimal amount of data which should be collected. These data should be as accurate as possible.

## Self-assessment questions

**3.1**   What is the difference between data and information?

**3.2**   Why is data collection important for an organization?

**3.3**   'It is always best to collect as much data as possible about a situation.' Is this statement true or false?

# 3.2 | Types of data

Data of different types are collected in different ways. The weights of packages coming off an assembly line can be measured directly; the number of customers in a shop can be found by observation; the efficiency of a service can be found by giving customers a questionnaire; the age of a population can be found in statistics published by the government; and so on. We should, then, start by describing different types of data.

Data can be classified in several ways. One classification we have already discussed defines data as either qualitative or quantitative. The collection, presentation and analysis of quantitative data is much easier and more precise so we should, wherever possible, use them in preference to qualitative data. Even data that are essentially qualitative can be given a quantitative form. For example, everybody has some opinion about a range of political questions, and although it is impossible to **measure** each of these opinions, we can say '70% of people generally agree with this policy' or '60% support the policies of this party'. Sometimes a scale can be added. Doctors, for example, may want to know how bad a patient's pain is. This is impossible to measure, but they can ask the patient to rank it on a scale of 0 to 10, where 0 corresponds to no pain at all and 10 is the worst pain it is possible to imagine.

Unfortunately, we have to be very careful when using numbers to express qualitative ideas. When we hear 'Eight out of ten dogs prefer' a particular kind of dog food we should think carefully about what this means and compare it with the less positive statement, 'In a limited test eight out of ten owners who expressed an opinion said their dog seemed to prefer this dog food to an alternative'.

Even so, not all data can be transformed into a convincing quantitative form. When we hear Browning ask, 'How do I love thee? Let me count the ways...' we know that this is more for effect than for realism.

An extension of this basic classification of data describes how well they can be measured. This describes data according to:

- nominal
- ordinal
- cardinal

## 3.2.1 | Nominal data

This is the kind of data which really cannot be quantified with any meaningful units. They are sometimes called categorical data. The fact that a company is a manufacturer, or a country operates a centrally planned economy, or a cake has cream in it, are examples of nominal data.

A common analysis for nominal data defines a number of different categories and says how many observations fall into each. Then a survey of companies in a particular area might show that there are seven manufacturers, 16 service companies and five in primary industries. This says nothing about companies' sizes, profits, owners and so on, and it does not matter in which order the categories are taken. A common example of nominal data comes from political polls, which typically show that 40% of respondents would vote for political party X, 35% for party Y, 20% for party Z, and 5% do not know.

## 3.2.2 | Ordinal data

Ordinal data are one step more quantitative, in that the categories into which observations are divided can be ranked in some order. Sweaters, for example, may be described as extra large, large, medium, small or extra small. Describing a sweater as 'medium' tells us something, but really gives little quantifiable information. In essence we are told, 'A medium sweater is smaller than a large one but larger than a small one'. Consumer surveys often collect ordinal data by asking questions like, 'Say how strongly you agree with this statement on a scale of 1 to 5 where 1 means strongly agree and 5 means strongly disagree'. Similarly, sociologists classify people according to A, B, C1, C2 and D. The essential characteristic is that data can be put into different categories, and that the order of these categories is important.

Sometimes, when there are few observations, they can all be ranked individually rather than put into ranked categories. So horses are ranked in a race, as are applicants for jobs, students' performance in courses, consumers' preferences between competing products, and so on.

## 3.2.3 | Cardinal data

Cardinal data have some attribute which can be directly measured. We can, for example, weigh a bag of chocolates, measure the time to finish a job and find the temperature in an office. These measures give a precise description of a particular feature. Cardinal data are generally the easiest to analyse and are the most relevant to quantitative methods.

Sometimes it is useful to group observations which are similar, and a common analysis for cardinal data defines different categories. A sample of basketball players might have 12 who are between 6 ft and 6 ft 2 in tall, eight who are 6 ft 2 in to 6 ft 4 in tall, and three who are 6 ft 4 in to 6 ft 6 in tall.

We can divide cardinal data into two types depending on whether they are discrete or continuous.

## Discrete data

Data are discrete if they can only take integer values. The number of children in families, for example, is 0, 1, 2 or some other integer number. Similarly, the number of cars owned, machines operated, shops opened and people employed are discrete data that can only come in integer quantities.

## Continuous data

Measures which can take any value and are not restricted to integers are continuous. The weight of a bag of biscuits is continuous as it can be any value, such as 256.312 grams. Similarly, the time taken to perform a task, the length of metal bars, the area covered by a carpet and the height of flagpoles are continuous data.

Sometimes there is a mismatch in data types. The circumferences of men's necks, for example, are continuous data, but shirt collars use a discrete measure; feet come in any size, but shoes come in a range of discrete sizes which are good enough for most needs; heights are continuous but most people describe their height to the nearest inch or centimetre. If the units of measurement are small, the distinction between discrete and continuous data begins to vanish. Salaries, for example, are really discrete as they must be multiples of a penny, but normally we would say that they are continuous because the units are small in comparison to the values measured.

There is one more classification of data which is directly related to the method of collection. If an organization wants to use some data for a particular purpose, it may use either primary or secondary data:

- **primary data** are collected by the organization itself for the particular purpose
- **secondary data** are collected by other organizations or for other purposes

Any data which are not collected by the organization for the specified purpose are secondary data. These may be published by other organizations, available from research studies, published by the government, and so on. They may also be collected by the organization itself for another purpose.

The benefits of primary data are that they fit the needs exactly, are up to date and are reliable. Secondary data have the advantages of being much cheaper and faster to collect. They also have the benefit of using sources which are not generally available: companies will, for example, respond to a survey by the government, the Confederation of British Industry, or a group of students, but they would not answer questions from another company.

If the secondary data are good enough, you should use them. Unfortunately, there are not usually enough appropriate, up-to-date secondary data for a particular purpose. Then a balance must be drawn between the benefits of primary data and the cost of obtaining them. If a company is about to launch a new product it will run a market survey to collect primary data and gauge customer reactions; if it wants to evaluate general economic activity in an area it will use secondary data prepared by the government. Sometimes a combination of primary and secondary data is used, perhaps using secondary data to give the overall picture, and then adding details from primary data. In any case, it is sensible to survey secondary data first, and then consider primary data for extensions and clarifications.

$\boxed{\textit{IN SUMMARY}}$

Data of different types can be collected in different ways. There are several classifications of data, including quantitative/qualitative, nominal/ordinal/ cardinal, discrete/continuous and primary/secondary.

## Self-assessment questions

**3.4**   Why is it useful to classify data?

**3.5**   How can you classify data?

**3.6**   What is the difference between discrete and continuous data?

**3.7**   Give examples of nominal, ordinal and cardinal data.

# 3.3 | How to choose a sample

## 3.3.1 | Purpose of sampling

If reasonable secondary data are not available, an organization must use primary data. Then there are several ways of collecting these, but most use some kind of sampling. In other words, data are collected from a representative sample of items or people, and these are used to infer characteristics about all items or people. Suppose, for example, a company is about to launch a new product and wants some data about likely sales. There are two ways of finding this:

- it could ask every person in the country who might buy the product whether they actually will buy it, and if so how much they will buy

- it could take a sample of people, ask them how much of the product they will buy, and then estimate the likely demand from the population as a whole

The first of these approaches (which is called a **census**) has the obvious disadvantage of being time consuming and expensive. The second approach (which uses **sampling**) has a number of advantages, the most obvious being the reduced cost and time. Another important point is that it may not be possible to collect data from an entire population. How, for example, could you find the views of everyone living in southeast England when at any time some people are sick, others are on holiday or travelling, some will refuse to answer questions, and so on?

The purpose of sampling is to get reliable results using only a sample of the whole population. Notice that we are using **population** in its statistical sense of a set of items which share some common characteristics. For data collection the population is the set of all items or people that could supply data. Suppose the

Post Office wants to find how long it takes to deliver first-class letters; then the population is all letters which are posted first class. A toy manufacturer getting reactions to a particular game might define the population of potential customers as all girls between the ages of 10 and 14; a consumer organization wanting to test the quality of a product would define the population as all units of the product that have been made; a bus company testing the reliability of a bus service would define the population as all journeys that their buses make.

When collecting data it is important to identify the proper population which could supply the data. This is not always as easy as it seems. The toy manufacturer above, for example, may find its population should also include boys aged 10 to 14. A survey of student opinion about a particular government policy would have a population which is clearly students – but does this mean full-time students only, or does it include part-time, day-release and distance-learning students? What about students doing block-release courses during their period of work, school students and those studying but not enrolled in courses? You must be careful to identify the correct population, because a mistake at this stage will make the remaining analysis useless.

Even when a population can be identified in principle there may be difficulties in practice. If you identify a population as all people who bought a foreign car within the last five years, or all people who use a particular supermarket, how could you actually find a list of such people? In some cases this is relatively straightforward. If the population is houses with telephones, they are easy to find from telephone directories. Such lists of the population are called **sampling frames**, and are often given by electoral registers, association membership lists (such as the Automobile Association), credit rating agencies, or specialized companies who prepare lists of people with specified characteristics. Unfortunately, sampling frames are often not available and then you have to use some other method of identifying a sample.

We have said that the purpose of sampling is to take a sample of units from the population, collect data about the desired feature and use these to estimate data for the population as a whole. Then the population is all items or people that **could** give data, while the sample is those items or people that **actually** give data. Now we need to discuss:

- a way of finding a suitable sample size (large enough to represent the population but small enough to be practical and cost effective)
- a method of selecting this sample

The problem of setting a sample size is considered in Chapter 14, but the next section describes some ways of choosing the sample.

### IN SUMMARY

Data collection often uses sampling, where data from a sample are used to estimate data for the population. This is done when data collection from the entire population would be too expensive, time-consuming or impractical.

## 3.3.2 | Types of sample

You can collect samples in several ways, such as:

- census
- random sample
- systematic sample
- quota sample
- stratified sample
- multi-stage sample
- cluster sample

### Census

If the population is small and the results are important it may be worth doing a census, where data are collected from every member of the population. Then the sample is the same as the population. The UK Government carries out a population census of this kind every ten years.

The benefit of a census is that it gives accurate data. Although the data may not be completely accurate (as there will still be errors and omissions), they are as accurate as possible. Unfortunately, a census is too expensive and time-consuming for most investigations and this means that a smaller sample is usually used.

### Random sample

If we do not take a census, we have to find a sample which accurately represents the population as a whole. The easiest way of arranging this is to take a **random sample**. The essential feature of a random sample is that every member of the population has exactly the same chance of being chosen for data collection. We have to emphasize that a random sample is not disorganized or haphazard. If we are collecting data about the contents of tinned soup, we could simply go to a supermarket and buy the first dozen tins of soup that we see. This would be haphazard, but it is certainly not random.

There are several ways of selecting random members of a population. A small club could ask each member to write their name on a piece of paper and put this in a hat. Then picking one piece of paper from the hat gives a random sample of one. Most random sampling is more complicated than this and needs a more formal approach, but this must still make sure that every member of the population has an equal chance of being picked. A common way of organizing this is to use random numbers.

Random numbers are simply a string of random digits, such as $4\,9\,3\,0\,1\,1\,4...$ Traditionally these have been prepared in tables but now they are almost invariably generated by computer, using a function such as RND or RAND. (Actually these give 'pseudo-random' numbers, but they are good enough for most purposes.)

Suppose we want to collect data from a random sample of people visiting an office. It might be too disruptive and impractical to take a census of visitors, so we could take a sample which is selected using random numbers. If we generate a series of random digits, 5 4 6 1 5 3 1, we could stand by the office door and interview the fifth person to pass, then the fourth person after that, then the sixth after that, then the first after that, and so on.

Random numbers can give totally random samples. This has a major benefit when using statistical analyses, most of which are only valid if the sample is genuinely random. Unfortunately, some samples which appear to be random are not. Suppose you decide to save time and simply write down a series of numbers which looks random. The series will probably not really be random, as most people have preferences – perhaps for even numbers, or for sequences which are easy to type on keyboards. Similarly, if interviewers are asked to choose people at random they will inevitably give a biased sample; they are more likely to approach people they find attractive, and to avoid people they find unattractive, or very tall people, people in an obvious hurry, or people in groups.

A well-organized random sample will ensure that, in the long run, the sample is representative of the population as a whole. If a sample does not exactly reflect the population, it is said to be **biased** in favour of one section. Unfortunately, random samples must be fairly large, as small samples can contain atypical results and show bias. We will see exactly how large a random sample should be in Chapter 14. Even so, a well-organized and relatively large sample could, by chance, give atypical data. This can be avoided by using some form of structured or non-random sample. These try to find results of equivalent accuracy but with a smaller sample.

# WORKED EXAMPLE 3.1

A company receives 10 000 invoices in a financial year. An auditor does not have time to examine each of these, so takes a random sample of 200. How might this sample be organized?

## Solution

The first thing to do is to form the sampling frame by listing the invoices and numbering them 0000 to 9999. Then we generate a set of 200 random numbers, each with four digits. One set starts:

4271 6845 2246 9715 4415 0330 8837 ...

Then we select invoices numbered 4271, 6845, 2246, and so on, as a completely random sample.

## Systematic sample

Perhaps the easiest way to organize a non-random sample is to collect data at regular intervals. For example, every tenth unit from a production line might be weighed, or every twentieth person that uses a service. The essence of a random sample is that every member of the population has the same chance of being chosen. If, say, every tenth member is chosen, this means that members 11, 12, 13 and so on have no chance of being selected and the sample is not random. In practice, a systematic sample is usually acceptable as being random, or at least pseudo-random. There are, however, occasions when the regularity introduces bias. Checking the contents of every twentieth bottle filled in a bottling plant may be invalid if every twentieth bottle is filled by the same head on the filling machine; collecting data from every thirtieth person leaving a bus station may introduce bias as buses hold an average of about 30 people, so we may always be interviewing the older and slower people who get off a bus last.

# WORKED EXAMPLE 3.2

A production line produces 5000 units a day. Quality control checks are needed on 2% of units. How could a systematic sample identify these?

## Solution

The number of samples a day is 2% of 5000, which is 100. A systematic sample to get 100 units a day would check every fiftieth unit (5000/100 = 50).

## Quota sample

An alternative way of giving some structure to samples is to make sure that the overall sample has the same characteristics as the population. Suppose, for example, we want to find how people would vote in an election. We could take a large random sample, and this would certainly reflect the views of the population. Unfortunately, the sample would have to be very large to ensure the right mix of people. An alternative is to look at population figures (where the population is those people who are eligible to vote) and see what proportions have various characteristics. Then the sample is chosen so that it contains the same proportions with these characteristics. If the population consists of 47% men and 32% who are over 50 years old, then the sample will also have 47% men and 32% over 50 years old. Political opinion polls are generally based on samples of around 1200 people, so 564 of the sample would be men and 384 would be over 50 years old.

This approach is known as quota sampling. Each interviewer is given a quota of people with different characteristics to interview: perhaps 12 women who are single, between 20 and 30 years old, have full-time professional jobs, and so on. Although each interviewer is given a quota of each type to fill, the actual choice of people is left to their discretion, so there is still a significant random element. The process is, however, not truly random, as an interviewer who has already filled the quota of one category of people does not interview any others in the category, so they have no chance of selection.

# WORKED EXAMPLE 3.3

56 300 people are eligible to vote in an electoral constituency. Census records suggest the following mix of features:

| Age | 18 to 25 | 16% |
|-----|----------|-----|
| | 26 to 35 | 27% |
| | 36 to 45 | 22% |
| | 46 to 55 | 18% |
| | 56 to 65 | 12% |
| | 66 and over | 5% |
| Sex | Female | 53% |
| | Male | 47% |
| Social class | A | 13% |
| | B | 27% |
| | C1 | 22% |
| | C2 | 15% |
| | D | 23% |

You want a poll of 1200 people to measure their probable voting behaviour. How many people should be in each category?

## Solution

The sample should contain exactly the same proportion in each category as the population. 16%, or 192 people, should be aged 18 to 25. Of these 192 people, 53% or 102, should be women. Of these 102 women, 13% or 13 should be in social class A. Similarly, 5%, or 60 people, should be over 66 years old, 47%, or 28 of these should be male, and 23% of these, or 6 people, should be in social class D. Repeating these calculations for all other combinations gives the quotas shown in Table 3.1.

The only problem with such calculations is that rounding to integers may sometimes cause small errors in the quotas. Provided the sample size is fairly large, these errors are small enough to ignore.

**Table 3.1**

|        |     | 18 to 25 | 26 to 35 | 36 to 45 | 46 to 55 | 56 to 65 | 66 and over |
|--------|-----|----------|----------|----------|----------|----------|-------------|
| Female | A   | 13       | 22       | 18       | 15       | 10       | 4           |
|        | B   | 27       | 46       | 38       | 31       | 21       | 9           |
|        | C1  | 22       | 38       | 31       | 25       | 17       | 7           |
|        | C2  | 15       | 26       | 21       | 17       | 11       | 5           |
|        | D   | 23       | 40       | 32       | 26       | 18       | 7           |
| Male   | A   | 12       | 20       | 16       | 13       | 9        | 4           |
|        | B   | 24       | 41       | 34       | 27       | 18       | 8           |
|        | C1  | 20       | 34       | 27       | 22       | 15       | 6           |
|        | C2  | 14       | 23       | 19       | 15       | 10       | 4           |
|        | D   | 21       | 35       | 29       | 23       | 16       | 6           |

## Stratified sample

We can use an extension to quota sampling when there are distinct groups or strata in the population. Then it may be a good idea to have some representatives from each stratum in the sample. Before any samples are taken, the population is divided into strata and a random sample is selected from each stratum. This randomness is the main difference from quota sampling. If, for example, we wanted to find the views of various companies, we might want views from manufacturers, transport operators, retailers, wholesalers, and so on. In a particular area there might not be many transport operators, but it would still be important to get their views. Then a stratified sample would specify that certain numbers of each type of company be approached, even if this means that small groups are over-represented. Any conclusions drawn from the results would, of course, have to bear this in mind.

## Multi-stage sample

Suppose an organization wants to take a sample of people who share certain characteristics – perhaps the fact that they subscribe to a certain magazine. The organization could simply take a random sample of the population (that is, the people who share this characteristic). Unfortunately, it would be expensive to travel and to meet these people and collect their views. A cheaper solution would be to use multi-stage sampling. In this, the country is divided into a number of geographical regions (independent television regions, for example). Some of these regions are chosen at random, and then subdivisions are considered, perhaps parliamentary constituencies or local authority areas. Some of these are again selected at random and then divided into smaller areas (perhaps towns or parliamentary wards). This process is continued until, say, streets are identified and then appropriate individuals in these streets are identified as the sample.

The benefit of this multi-stage approach is that samples are found which are concentrated in a few geographical areas. This dramatically reduces the amount of travelling needed by interviewers and obviously reduces the costs.

### Cluster sample

This chooses the items in a sample not individually, but in clusters. If, for example, we want views from people living in a town it would be easier to visit a sample which is clustered in a single area rather than visit a sample spread over the whole town. So the population is divided into a number of groups or clusters, and a number of these clusters are chosen at random to be the sample. Then one cluster might be everybody who lives in a particular road.

Cluster sampling has the benefits of reducing costs and being convenient to organize. It is especially useful when surveying people working in a particular industry. Then individual companies can form the clusters. In other words, companies are selected at random and the sample is made up of all people who work in these random companies. This method works best if the clusters are somewhat dissimilar so that the sample is more representative.

---

| *IN SUMMARY* |

There are several ways of sampling. These can be classified as census, random, systematic, quota, stratified, multi-stage and cluster samples. Each of these is best in different circumstances.

---

## Self-assessment questions

**3.8**  Why is sampling used to collect data?

**3.9**  Why is it important to identify the correct population for a survey?

**3.10**  What types of sampling can you use?

**3.11**  What is the key feature of random sampling?

**3.12**  What is the difference between quota sampling and stratified sampling?

**3.13**  Where could you find data about UK exports and imports?

# 3.4 Ways of collecting data

## 3.4.1 Types of survey

When an appropriate sample has been selected (and for simplicity we shall assume that this is a sample of people), the next stage is to approach them and actually collect data. In many cases data can be collected by observation (including measurement, counting, recording, and so on). In other cases data are collected by asking people relevant questions, in which case we can use a series of related questions presented in a questionnaire.

The Gallup organization suggests five possible objectives for a survey of this type:

- to find whether a respondent is aware of an issue ('Do you know of any plans to develop...')
- to get general feelings about an issue ('Do you think this development is beneficial...')
- to get views about specific points in an issue ('Do you think this development will affect...')
- to get reasons for a respondent's views ('Are you against this development because...')
- to find out how strongly these views are held ('On a scale of 1 to 5 how strong are your feelings about this development...')

There are other ways of collecting data, and the best one depends on a combination of use and type of sample. One classification of methods is as follows:

- observation
- personal interview
- telephone interview
- postal survey
- panel survey
- longitudinal survey

## Observation

If we want to take a sample from a population of machines, animals, files or other inanimate objects the only way we can collect data is by direct observation. Even when the population is people, the most reliable results often come from direct observation. This is because people often give the answer they feel they ought to give or the answer the interviewer wants, rather than the true answer. Studies have shown, for example, that more people say they use their car seat belts than are shown by direct observation. Similarly, more people say they wash their hands after going to the toilet than is found from observation.

The reliability of observation depends largely on the observer and the circumstances, so it is best for counting, but less good for data which need some judgement. This is particularly true when there is personal involvement. Asking people who are leaving a restaurant what they thought of the meal would get replies based on the whole experience (including who the people were with, how they felt, or what the weather was like) rather than a valid opinion of the food. Asking motorway police to give data on accidents would get biased results, because their personal involvement with accidents would lead to emotional. rather than factual replies.

## Personal interview

Personal interviews are the most reliable way of getting accurate information from people. They have the benefit of a high response rate, with only 10% of people generally refusing to answer questions. They also allow interviewers to help with questions which are unclear. In some situations, such as quota sampling, some assessment of people is needed before they are questioned, so personal interviews are the only feasible method.

In principle, collecting data by personal interviews is easy; it needs someone to pose questions and listen to the answers. The reality is more complicated, and interviewers need training to make sure they get reliable replies. Without training, some interviewers might, for example, explain the questions to people, or help those having trouble with an answer (hence introducing the interviewer's bias to the answer). Similarly, interviewers should be careful not to direct respondents to a particular answer by their expression, tone of voice or comments. If an interviewer listens to an answer and then says, 'How strange – not many people give that answer!' the person interviewed is likely to reconsider the answer and change it.

One of the main drawbacks of personal interviews is the cost. Each interviewer must be transported to the right place and given meals, accommodation, and so on. Typically, 40% of an interviewer's time is spent in travel, 25% is spent on preparation and administration, and only 35% is available for asking questions.

## Telephone interview

About 90% of people have a telephone, so this gives a popular way of organizing surveys. It has the advantages of being cheap and easy to organize, it involves no travel for interviewers, and it gets a high response rate. On the other hand, it has the disadvantages of introducing bias (as only those with telephones can be contacted), allowing no personal observation of respondents and annoying people who object to the intrusion of their homes.

The usual procedure for telephone interviews is for a computer to choose a telephone number at random from a directory listing. Then an interviewer asks the questions presented on a computer screen and types in the answers.

## Postal survey

Sending a printed questionnaire through the post has the advantage of being very cheap and easy to organize, so that very large samples can be used. Postal surveys work best when a series of short questions asks for factual (preferably numerical) data. Major drawbacks are the lack of opportunity to observe respondents and clarify points that they do not understand. Perhaps the main disadvantage of postal surveys is the low response. Generally, a survey can expect to get replies from about 20% of questionnaires. This response rate can be increased by ensuring the questionnaire is short and easy to complete, sending it to the correct, named individual, enclosing a pre-paid return envelope, promising anonymity of replies, using a follow-up letter or telephone call if replies are slow, promising a summary of results, or offering some reward for completion. Unfortunately, a reward for completion (which is typically a small gift or discount on a future purchase) introduces bias, since respondents feel more kindly towards the questionnaire.

One common problem with postal questionnaires is bias. When people are asked for their views on, say, a holiday more people who have had bad experiences will write to complain, than those who have had good experiences. This is an extension of the principle that book reviews are always written by 'critics' rather than by 'supporters'.

## Panel survey

Panel surveys are generally concerned with monitoring changes over time. A panel of respondents are selected, and they are asked a series of questions on different occasions. So the political views of a panel can be monitored during the lifetime of a government, or awareness of a product can be monitored during an advertising campaign. Panel surveys are expensive and difficult to administer, so they must rely on small samples.

One interesting problem with panel surveys is that respondents often become so involved in the issues raised that they change their views and behaviour. A panel which is looking at the effects of an anti-smoking advertising campaign might be encouraged to look more deeply into the question of smoking and change their own habits. Another problem is that panel members inevitably leave for some reason and the remainder of the panel become less representative of the population.

## Longitudinal survey

This is an extension of a panel survey that involves monitoring a group of respondents over a long period. One television company has, for example, been monitoring the progress of a group of children for the past 40 years. The obvious problem with this approach is that a lot of resources are needed to maintain an extended survey, and even then a small initial sample must be used. These small samples become vulnerable when some members leave during a long investigation. Longitudinal surveys are generally limited to studies of sociological, health and physical changes.

> ### IN SUMMARY

When a sample has been identified, data can be collected in several ways, including observation, personal interview, telephone interview, postal survey, panel survey or longitudinal survey.

## 3.4.2 | Design of questionnaires

Most data collection uses a questionnaire. Even observers are asked to record their observations on a sheet of questions. It is, therefore, important to design questionnaires carefully and after a great deal of thought. There are many examples of surveys which have failed because they asked the wrong questions, or asked the right questions in the wrong way.

Although it may seem easy, designing a good questionnaire is quite difficult. An enormous amount of work has been done on the design of questionnaires and this has led to some guidelines for good practice. The following comments are by no means complete, and, although most of them are common sense, they are often overlooked:

- A questionnaire should ask a series of related questions. These should be short, simple questions phrased in everyday terms, and should follow a logical sequence.

- Make questions simple and easy to understand; if people do not understand the question they will give any convenient answer rather than the true one.

- Make questions brief, unambiguous, and without too many conditional clauses.

- Be very careful with the phrasing of questions. Even simple changes in phrasing can give different results, so that, for example, a medical treatment which gives a 60% success rate is viewed differently from one which gives a 40% failure rate. Similarly, a phrase such as 'four out of five people' is viewed differently from '16 out of 20 people' or '80% of people'.

- Avoid leading questions such as 'Do you agree with the common view that BBC television programmes are of a higher quality than IBA television programmes?' Such questions encourage conformity rather than truthful answers.

- Use phrases which are as neutral as possible. Then, 'Do you like this cake?' would be rephrased as 'Say how you feel about the taste of this cake on a scale of 1 to 5'.

- Remember that respondents are not always objective, so the question 'Do you think prison sentences should be used to deter speeding drivers?' will get a different response from 'If you were caught speeding do you think you should go to prison?'

- Phrase all personal questions carefully. 'Have you retired from paid work?' might receive better responses and be just as useful as the more sensitive 'How old are you?'

- Do not start questions with warning clauses. A question which starts 'We hope you do not mind answering this question, but will understand if you do not want to...' will discourage everyone from answering.

- Avoid vague questions such as 'Do you usually buy more meat than vegetables?' This raises questions about 'What is usual?', 'What is more?', 'Should frozen meals be counted as meat or vegetables?' and so on.

- Ask positive questions such as 'Did you buy a Sunday newspaper last week?' rather than the less definite 'How has the number of Sunday newspapers you read changed in the past few years?'

- Avoid hypothetical questions such as 'How much would you spend on life insurance if you suddenly won £500,000 on the National Lottery?' This does not give useful data, because the answer is speculative and has probably not been thought out in any detail.

- Avoid asking two or more questions in one, such as 'Do you think this development should go ahead because it will increase employment in the area and improve facilities?' This will get confused answers from people who think the development should not go ahead, or those who think it will increase employment but not improve facilities.

- Make the questionnaire as short as possible, consistent with its purpose. People will often not answer a poorly presented questionnaire, or a long one.

- Do not ask irrelevant questions. There are a lot of data which could be collected and might be useful. It is always tempting to add an extra question or two, but this costs more to analyse and discourages people from completing the questionnaire.

- Open questions (such as 'Have you any other comments to make?') allow general comments, but they favour the articulate and quick-thinking. They are also difficult to analyse.

- Ask questions which allow precoded answers, so that respondents are offered a series of choices and have to select the most appropriate. There are many formats for these, some of which are illustrated in Figure 3.3.

1  Will you be joining an evening class this term?     YES/NO

2  How many children do you have? (please circle answer)

   0     1     2     3     4     more

3  Do you use a computer in your office? (please tick a box)

   Yes ☐          No ☐

4  Do you think the government should spend more on education? (please tick a box)

| Strongly agree | Agree | - Do not know | Disagree | Strongly disagree |
|---|---|---|---|---|
|  |  |  |  |  |

5  A proposal has been made to ban all traffic from the town centre. Please circle the number which most accurately reflects your view on this.

   Strongly approve   1     2     3     4 neutral    5     6     7   Strongly disapprove

6  Why are you taking this course? (please circle any appropriate answers)
   (a)  out of interest
   (b)  to get a qualification
   (c)  to help in work
   (d)  friends are taking it
   (e)  to resit a course failed last year
   (f)  other reason, please specify ...............................

7  How old are you? (please tick one answer)

   ☐ less than 18        ☐ 50 to 70

   ☐ 18 to 35            ☐ more than 70

   ☐ 35 to 50

**Figure 3.3**   Examples of precoded questions.

- Address postal surveys to a named person (or at least a title), enclose a covering letter to explain the purpose of the survey, benefits to the respondent, guarantee of anonymity, contact to discuss any difficulties, etc, and include a stamped, addressed return envelope.

- Be prepared for unexpected effects, such as sensitivity to the colour and format of the questionnaire, or different types of interviewer getting different responses.

- Always run a pilot survey before starting the whole survey. This will highlight any poor questions or other difficulties, and allow improvements to the questionnaire design.

## IN SUMMARY

Getting a good design for a questionnaire is difficult and needs a lot of thought. A number of guidelines can be given, but you should always run a pilot survey to sort out any problems.

## 3.4.3 | Non-responses

We have already mentioned that around 80% of questionnaires sent by post and 10% of personal interviews can expect to get no response. There are a number of reasons for non-response, including the following:

- people are unable to answer the questions (perhaps because of language difficulties or ill health)

- they were out when the interviewer called (this problem can be reduced by careful timing of calls and making revisits as necessary)

- they were away for some longer period (holiday or business commitments make surveys during summer more difficult)

- they have moved house and are no longer at the given address (it is rarely worth following up a new address)

- they refuse to answer (probably only 10% of people refuse to answer on principle, but nothing can be done about these)

To make things easy, we might be tempted simply to ignore non-responses and assume that the data collected are typical of the sample: in other words, that the respondents properly represent the sample which in turn properly represents the population. This is not necessarily true. In an extreme case a postal questionnaire might be used to see how fluently people can read and write (in the same way that people who have reading difficulties are told that they can pick up packages of information when they visit their local library, or can write to a central address for more information). Biased replies will also be found when, for example, a survey asks people how they use computers, with an initial question, 'Do you own a computer?' People who would answer 'No' to this question are unlikely to be interested enough to complete the rest of the questionnaire, so the responses are biased towards people which actually use computers.

To avoid this kind of bias, you should follow-up non-respondents, with another visit, telephone call or letter. Initially this should encourage non-respondents to reply, and surveys often increase their response rate by over 20% with a well-timed telephone call or letter. This does not always work and then you should examine non-respondents closely to make sure they do not share some common characteristic which is absent in respondents.

### IN SUMMARY

Most surveys can be expected to give some non-respondents. These should be carefully examined to make sure that they do not introduce bias to the data collected.

## 3.5 | Using the data

Chapter 1 described an approach to business problems with four stages – observation, modelling, experimentation and implementation. We could, of course, describe these stages in different ways. Some people suggest that modelling and experimentation really form one stage of analysis. Others add an extra stage at the end for monitoring and follow-up. Others start with a more detailed planning stage.

If you are starting a management investigation, it is certainly worth expanding the four basic stages into more detail. These might include the following steps:

1 **Observation**
   (a) Initial investigation – look at operations and recognize the problem
   (b) Define the problem – having recognized that there is a problem, carefully define it, set the objectives and measures of success
   (c) Plan the work – think how to tackle the problem, schedule necessary activities and check resources

2 **Modelling**
   (a) Show in detail how to tackle the problem
   (b) Build models to represent the problem
   (c) Collect data needed by the models
   (d) Test the models and data to make sure that they are accurate and describe the real operations

3 **Experimentation**
   (a) Analyse the operations, getting solutions to models
   (b) Generate alternative solutions to the problem
   (c) Compare these solutions, looking at all aspects of their expected performance
   (d) Identify the best overall solution

4 **Implementation**

    (a) Check that the proposed solution will really work and be an improvement

    (b) Plan all details of the implementation – such as training

    (c) Change the operations to introduce new ways of doing things

    (d) Monitor actual performance to make sure that the implementation goes well

    (e) Keep checking to make sure that the expected improvements actually occur

However we divide an investigation, and whatever we call the stages, you can see that data collection forms a central part. Moreover, the data collection and analysis must fit into the broader investigation. This does not happen by chance, but needs carefully planning. One useful approach has the following steps.

1 Define the purpose of the data and why they are being collected

2 Describe exactly what data are needed

3 Check available secondary data and see how useful they are

4 Define the relevant population to give primary data

5 Set the best sampling method and sample size

6 Identify an appropriate sample

7 Design a questionnaire or other method of collection

8 Train any interviewers, observers or experimenters needed

9 Run a pilot study and check for problems

10 Do the main study

11 Do any necessary follow-up, such as contacting non-respondents

12 Analyse and present the results

This may seem rather complicated, and you may be tempted to take short cuts. Remember, though, that decisions are based on available information. If this information is misleading, all the following analysis is wasted.

### IN SUMMARY

The collection of data must be carefully planned. All subsequent analyses depend on data, so it must be as reliable as possible.

## Self-assessment questions

**3.14** What method of data collection is most suitable for:

    (a) asking how different companies use computers?

    (b) asking colleagues for their views on a proposed change in working conditions?

(c) testing the effect of exercise on heart disease?

(d) testing the accuracy of invoices?

**3.15** What is wrong with the following questions in a survey?

(a) 'Most people want higher retirement pensions. Do you agree with them?'

(b) 'Does watching too much television affect children's school work?'

(c) 'Should the United Kingdom destroy its nuclear arms, reduce spending on conventional arms and increase expenditure on education?'

(d) 'What is the most likely effect of a single European currency on pensions?'

**3.16** What should be done about non-responses in a postal survey?

**3.17** Why are non-responses irrelevant for quota sampling?

**3.18** It is best to get some data quickly so that you can start thinking about useful analyses. Do you agree with this?

## CHAPTER REVIEW

This chapter considered the collection of data. In particular it:

- reviewed the need for information and explained how this relied on data collection
- considered the amount and timing of data collection
- classified data according to qualitative/quantitative, nominal/ordinal/cardinal, discrete/continuous and primary/secondary
- described how data collection relies on taking samples from appropriate populations
- discussed sampling methods, including census, random, systematic, quota, stratified, multi-stage and cluster samples
- classified alternative ways of collecting data from the sample, including observation, personal interview, telephone interview, postal survey, panel survey and longitudinal survey
- gave some guidelines for questionnaire design
- mentioned non-responses
- outlined the planning of data collection

# Problems

**3.1** How would you describe the following data:

(a) weights of books posted to a bookshop

(b) numbers of pages in books

(c) positions of football teams in the leagues

(d) opinions about a new novel?

**3.2** Use government statistics to find how the Gross National Product has changed over the past 20 years.

**3.3** What is the appropriate population to give data on:
(a) likely sales of a computer game
(b) problems facing small shopkeepers
(c) parking near a new shopping mall
(d) proposals to close a shopping area to all vehicles?

**3.4** Describe a sampling procedure to collect reliable data about house prices around the country.

**3.5** Auditors want to select a sample of 300 invoices from 9000 available. How could they do this?

**3.6** The readership of a Sunday newspaper has the following characteristics:

| | | |
|---|---|---|
| *Age* | 16 to 25 | 12% |
| | 26 to 35 | 22% |
| | 36 to 45 | 24% |
| | 46 to 55 | 18% |
| | 56 to 65 | 12% |
| | 66 to 75 | 8% |
| | 76 and over | 4% |
| *Sex* | Female | 38% |
| | Male | 62% |
| *Social class* | A | 24% |
| | B | 36% |
| | C1 | 24% |
| | C2 | 12% |
| | D | 4% |

What would be the quotas for a sample of 2000?

**3.7** Describe how you would collect data from a sample of shops selling postage stamps in a particular area.

**3.8** Give five examples of poor questions used in a survey.

**3.9** Give five examples where non-respondents could introduce bias to data.

**3.10** Run a survey to find the opinions of your colleagues on proposed restrictions on smoking in public places.

**3.11** Design a questionnaire to collect data on the closure of a shopping area to all vehicles.

**3.12** Find a copy of a recent survey by the Consumers' Association (or any equivalent organization). Describe the data collection used.

# Computer exercises

**3.1** Use a computer to generate a set of random numbers. Now use these numbers to design a sampling scheme for finding the views of passengers using a local bus service.

**3.2** Problem 3.6 gives some characteristics of the readers of a Sunday newspaper. Design a spreadsheet to find the quotas in each category for different sample sizes.

**3.3** Conduct a survey into the use of computers by companies operating in your area. How would you select a sample of companies for this? Now design a questionnaire to collect information from the companies. The combination of sample and questionnaire should be good enough to give a reliable view of computer use. Design a spreadsheet to record the data collected by your questionnaire. Now analyse the results and write a report on your findings.

**3.4** Design a questionnaire to find the views of a sample of your colleagues on a topical issue. Now use this questionnaire to collect actual data. Use a suitable package to record views and see how the results can be presented. Write a report on your findings.

**3.5** The spreadsheet shown in Figure 3.4 shows a way of choosing a random sample of ten from a population of 100. Make sure you understand how the spreadsheet works. How could you improve the format and results?

| | A | B | C | D | E | F | G |
|---|---|---|---|---|---|---|---|
| 1 | **Random sampling** | | | | | | |
| 2 | | | | | | | |
| 3 | **Sample size** | | 10 | | **Population** | 100 | |
| 4 | | | | | | | |
| 5 | **Number** | **Random numbers** | **Scaled sample numbers** | | **Sorted sample numbers** | | **Leave before next sample** |
| 6 | 1 | 0.97878 | 98 | | 11 | | 10 |
| 7 | 2 | 0.79543 | 80 | | 21 | | 9 |
| 8 | 3 | 0.21031 | 21 | | 40 | | 18 |
| 9 | 4 | 0.68597 | 69 | | 47 | | 6 |
| 10 | 5 | 0.3997 | 40 | | 52 | | 5 |
| 11 | 6 | 0.65158 | 65 | | 57 | | 4 |
| 12 | 7 | 0.52337 | 52 | | 65 | | 7 |
| 13 | 8 | 0.10796 | 11 | | 69 | | 2 |
| 14 | 9 | 0.76698 | 77 | | 77 | | 7 |
| 15 | 10 | 0.57474 | 57 | | 80 | | 2 |

**Figure 3.4** Spreadsheet for random sampling.

# Case study

## Natural Biscuits

Natural Biscuits makes a range of products which are sold to health food shops around the country. They divide the UK into 13 geographical regions based around major cities. The populations, number of shops stocking their goods and annual sales in each region last year are shown in Table 3.2.

Natural Biscuits are about to introduce a Vegan Veggie Bar which is made from a combination of nuts, seeds and dried fruit, and is guaranteed to contain no animal products. The company wants to find likely sales of the bar and is considering a market survey.

**Table 3.2**

| Region | Population ('000s) | Shops | Sales (£'000s) |
|---|---|---|---|
| Greater London | 8130 | 94 | 240 |
| Birmingham | 1205 | 18 | 51 |
| Glasgow | 870 | 8 | 24 |
| Leeds | 853 | 9 | 18 |
| Sheffield | 641 | 7 | 23 |
| Liverpool | 580 | 12 | 35 |
| Bradford | 556 | 8 | 17 |
| Manchester | 541 | 6 | 8 |
| Edinburgh | 526 | 5 | 4 |
| Bristol | 470 | 17 | 66 |
| Coventry | 372 | 8 | 32 |
| Belfast | 365 | 4 | 15 |
| Cardiff | 336 | 4 | 25 |

Natural Biscuits already sells 300 000 similar bars a year at an average price of 40 pence, and with an average profit of 7.5 pence. An initial survey of 120 customers in three shops earlier this year gave the characteristics of customers for these bars shown in Table 3.3.

Experience suggests that it costs £10 to interview a customer personally, while a postal or telephone survey costs £5 a response. The analysis of information can be done relatively cheaply by the Management Information Group at Natural Biscuits.

Natural Biscuits wants to collect more information about the potential sales of its Vegan Veggie Bar. They want as much information as possible, but obviously want to limit costs to reasonable levels.

Your problem is to design a data-collection project. Full details should be given of all aspects of the project, including timing and costs. You can use any relevant secondary information and make reasonable assumptions where necessary.

**Table 3.3**

| Sex | Female | 64% |
|---|---|---|
| | Male | 36% |
| | | |
| Age | Less than 20 | 16% |
| | 20 to 30 | 43% |
| | 30 to 40 | 28% |
| | 40 to 60 | 9% |
| | More than 60 | 4% |
| | | |
| Social class | A | 6% |
| | B | 48% |
| | C1 | 33% |
| | C2 | 10% |
| | D | 3% |
| | | |
| Vegetarian | Yes | 36% |
| | | (5% vegan) |
| | No | 60% |
| | Other response | 4% |
| | | |
| Reason for buying | Like the taste | 35% |
| | For fibre content | 17% |
| | Never tried before | 11% |
| | Help diet | 8% |
| | Other response | 29% |
| | | |
| Regular buyer of bar | Yes | 32% |
| | No | 31% |
| | Other response | 37% |

# 4 | Using diagrams to present data

| | | |
|---|---|---|
| Chapter outline | 88 | Chapter review | 118 |
| 4.1 Summarizing data | 89 | Problems | 119 |
| 4.2 Diagrams for | 91 | Computer exercises | 121 |
| presenting data | | Case study: | 123 |
| 4.3 Frequency distributions | 108 | High Acclaim Importers | |

**CHAPTER OUTLINE**

In the last chapter we saw how data could be collected. Now we are going to show how these data can be summarized and presented to an audience. There are essentially two ways of summarizing data, either using diagrams or numbers. This chapter discusses the use of diagrams, while Chapter 5 continues the theme by looking at numerical summaries.

Raw data often give so much detail that you cannot see the overall patterns. Data reduction clears away the detail and highlights the underlying patterns: it presents summarized results which are concise, but still give an accurate view of the original data. The reduction can be done in several ways, and in this chapter we describe alternative types of diagram.

After reading this chapter and doing the exercises you should be able to:

- outline the purpose of data reduction
- design tables of numerical data
- draw graphs to show the relationship between variables
- design pie charts
- draw a variety of bar charts
- draw pictograms and recognize their limitations
- use frequency distributions and tables
- draw histograms
- draw ogives and Lorenz curves for cumulative data

# | 4.1 || Summarizing data

## | 4.1.1 | Introduction

This chapter is based on the idea that there is a difference between data and information. Data are the raw numbers or facts that must be processed to give useful information. So 78, 64, 36, 70 and 52 are data which could be processed to give the information that the average mark of five students sitting an exam is 60%.

Imagine that you have spent a lot of effort collecting data and now want to communicate your findings to other people. This is done by **data presentation**. The purpose of data presentation is to show the characteristics of a set of data and highlight any important patterns. This can be done either numerically or by using diagrams. The remainder of this chapter describes presentations in diagrams, while the next chapter discusses numerical presentations.

If you look around, there are countless examples of information presented in diagrams. Newspaper articles often describe a situation, and then add summary diagrams. People are more likely to look at these diagrams than read the article (hence the saying, 'One picture is worth a thousand words'). The main benefit of diagrams is that people are good at recognizing patterns and can extract a lot of information in a short time.

In general, then, we can judge the success of a presentation by how easy it is to understand. A good presentation should make information clearer and allow us to see the overall picture. But good presentations do not happen by chance, and need careful planning. If you look at a diagram and cannot understand it, it is safe to assume that the presentation is poor; the fault is with the presenter rather than the viewer.

Sometimes, even when a presentation seems clear, you can look closer and see that it does not give a true picture of the data. This may be a result of poor presentation, but sometimes comes from a deliberate decision to present data in a form that is misleading or dishonest. Advertisements are notorious for presenting data in a way that gives the desired impression, rather than accurately reflecting a situation. Likewise, politicians may be concerned with appearance rather than truth. The problem is that diagrams are a powerful means of presenting data, but they only give a summary. This summary can easily be misleading, either intentionally or by mistake. In this chapter we shall demonstrate good practice in data presentation and shall be rigorous in presenting results that are fair and honest.

### IN SUMMARY

The aim of data presentation is to give an accurate summary of data. Here we concentrate on diagrammatic presentations. These have considerable impact, but need careful planning.

# 4.1.2 | Data reduction

Provided they come in small quantities, most people can deal with numerical data. We can happily say, 'This building is 60 metres tall', 'A car can travel 40 miles on a gallon of petrol', 'An opinion poll shows one political party has 6% more support than another', and so on. Problems begin when there are a lot of data and we are swamped with detail. Suppose, for example, we know that weekly sales of a product in a shop over the past year are:

> 51 60 58 56 62 69 58 76 80 82 68 90 72
>
> 84 91 82 78 76 75 66 57 78 65 50 61 54
>
> 49 44 41 45 38 28 37 40 42 22 25 26 21
>
> 30 32 30 32 31 29 30 41 45 44 47 53 54

If these data were given in a report, people would find it, at best, boring and would skip to more interesting material. They would ignore the figures, despite the fact that they could be important. To make the figures less daunting we could try including them in the text, but when there are a lot of numerical data this does not work. The figures above could only be described by saying, 'In the first week sales were 51 units, and then they rose by nine units in the second week, but in the third week they fell back to 58 units, and fell another two units in the fourth week...'. We need a more convenient way of presenting data.

The problem is that the raw data do not really tell us very much; we are simply swamped with detail and cannot see the wood for the trees. In most cases we are not interested in the small detail, but really want the overall picture. What we need, then, is a way of identifying general patterns in data and presenting a summary which allows these to be seen. This is the purpose of **data reduction**.

> The aim of data reduction is to give a simplified and accurate view of the data which shows the underlying patterns but does not overwhelm us with detail.

The usual sequence of activities for analysing data starts with data collection, then moves to data reduction, and finally to data presentation. In practice, there is no clear distinction between data reduction and data presentation, and they are combined into a single activity.

Data reduction has the clear advantages of having:

● results shown in a compact form
● results that are easy to understand
● graphical or pictorial representations
● clear overall patterns
● comparisons between different sets of data
● quantitative measures

On the other hand, it has the disadvantages that:

● details of the original data are lost
● the process is irreversible

| *IN SUMMARY* |
| --- |

The detail given in raw data can be overwhelming and can obscure overall patterns. Data reduction simplifies the data and presents them so that underlying patterns can be seen.

## Self-assessment questions

**4.1**  What is the difference between data and information?

**4.2**  Give five examples of misleading data presentation.

**4.3**  Why is data reduction necessary?

**4.4**  'Data reduction always gives a clear, detailed and accurate picture of the initial data.' Is this statement true?

# 4.1 | Diagrams for presenting data

## 4.2.1 | Introduction

There are several ways in which data can be summarized in diagrams, with the most important of these being:

- tables of numerical data
- graphs to show relationships between variables
- pie charts, bar charts and pictograms showing relative frequencies
- histograms which show relative frequencies of continuous data

The choice of best format is often a matter of personal judgement, but there are some guidelines. These are largely common sense and include, where appropriate:

- select the most suitable format for the purpose
- present data fairly and honestly
- make sure any diagram is clear and easy to understand
- give each diagram a title
- state the source of data
- use consistent units and say what these units are
- label axes clearly and accurately
- put clear scales on axes
- include totals, subtotals and any other useful summaries
- add notes to highlight reasons for unusual or atypical values.

It is worth mentioning that drawing diagrams for data presentation used to be quite time-consuming, but graphics packages (such as Harvard Graphics, Corel Draw, Perfect Presentation, Visio, Microsoft PowerPoint, and a whole range of equivalent packages) have made this task much easier.

### IN SUMMARY

Data can be presented in several ways, but the final choice is often a matter of opinion. We can give some guidelines for good practice.

## 4.2.2 | Tables

The easiest way of presenting numerical data is in a table. This is perhaps the most widely used method of data presentation – and has already been used several times in this book. Whenever you pick up a newspaper, magazine or report you are likely to see a number of tables. This is one of the easiest, and most effective, ways of presenting a lot of information.

The general features of a table can be seen in Table 4.1, which is a presentation of the data for sales given above.

This gives some idea of the overall patterns so we can see, for example, that demand is higher in the first two quarters and lower in the second two. In this format, though, the table is still really a presentation of the raw data and it is

**Table 4.1**

| Week | Quarter 1 | Quarter 2 | Quarter 3 | Quarter 4 | Total |
|---|---|---|---|---|---|
| 1 | 51 | 84 | 49 | 30 | 214 |
| 2 | 60 | 91 | 44 | 32 | 227 |
| 3 | 58 | 82 | 41 | 30 | 211 |
| 4 | 56 | 78 | 45 | 32 | 211 |
| 5 | 62 | 76 | 38 | 31 | 207 |
| 6 | 69 | 75 | 28 | 29 | 201 |
| 7 | 58 | 66 | 37 | 30 | 191 |
| 8 | 76 | 57 | 40 | 41 | 214 |
| 9 | 80 | 78 | 42 | 45 | 245 |
| 10 | 82 | 65 | 22 | 44 | 213 |
| 11 | 68 | 50 | 25 | 47 | 190 |
| 12 | 90 | 61 | 26 | 53 | 230 |
| 13 | 72 | 54 | 21 | 54 | 201 |
| Totals | 882 | 917 | 458 | 498 | 2755 |

difficult to get a feel for a typical week's sales; there is no indication of minimum or maximum sales; and so on. These defects would be even more noticeable if there were hundreds or thousands of observations. It would be useful to reduce the data and emphasize the patterns. The minimum sales are 21, so we might start by seeing how many weeks had sales in a range of, say, 20 to 29. If we count these, there are six weeks. Then we could count the number of observations in other ranges, as follows:

| Range of sales | Number of weeks |
|---|---|
| 20 to 29 | 6 |
| 30 to 39 | 8 |
| 40 to 49 | 10 |
| 50 to 59 | 9 |
| 60 to 69 | 7 |
| 70 to 79 | 6 |
| 80 to 89 | 4 |
| 90 to 99 | 2 |

This table shows how many values are in each range, and is called a **frequency table** (we shall return to these later in the chapter). The 'ranges' are usually referred to as **classes**. Then we can talk about the 'class of 20 to 29', where 20 is the lower class limit and 29 is the upper class limit and the class width is $29 - 20 = 9$. We arbitrarily chose classes of 20 to 29, 30 to 39, and so on, but could have used any reasonable classes. It might be useful, for example, to choose the classes 17 to 32, 33 to 48, or any other convenient ones. The only constraint is that there should be enough classes to make any patterns clear, but not so many to obscure them. If we felt that the eight classes used above were too many, we could redefine the classes to, say, the four shown in Table 4.2. This table has also been given a title and a statement about the source of data.

**Table 4.2**  Weekly sales of product

| Range | Number of weeks |
|---|---|
| 20 to 39 | 14 |
| 40 to 59 | 19 |
| 60 to 79 | 13 |
| 80 to 99 | 6 |

Source: Company weekly sales reports

These tables show one inevitable effect of data reduction: the more data are summarized, the more detail is lost. The last table, for example, shows the frequency of sales, but it gives no idea of the seasonal variations. Such loss of detail is acceptable if the table is easier to understand and still shows the information needed, but is not acceptable if we need to know more detail. Drawing tables needs a compromise between making them too long (where lots of details can be seen, but they are complicated with underlying patterns hidden) and too short (where underlying patterns are clear, but most details are lost). The number of classes, in particular, must be a subjective decision based on the use of the presentation, but a guideline would set a maximum number at about ten.

There is an almost limitless number of ways of drawing tables. Sometimes they are very simple, like a review of answers to the survey question, 'Did you read a Sunday newspaper last week?':

|  | *Percentage of replies* |
|---|---|
| Yes | 76% |
| No | 14% |
| Don't know | 10% |

Sometimes tables are very complex. They can show a lot of information and may be the only realistic means of presentation. The example in Table 4.3 shows figures for crops grown in the UK during the 1980s.

**Table 4.3**   Main cereal crops grown in the United Kingdom

|  | 1975–1977 average | 1984 | 1985 | 1986 |
|---|---|---|---|---|
| *Wheat* | | | | |
| Area ('000 hectares) | 1115 (30.6) | 1939 (48.2) | 1902 (47.5) | 1997 (49.8) |
| Harvest ('000 tonnes) | 4834 (33.3) | 14958 (56.4) | 12050 (53.8) | 13910 (56.9) |
| Yield (tonnes per hectare) | 4.32 | 7.71 | 6.33 | 6.96 |
| *Barley* | | | | |
| Area ('000 hectares) | 2313 (63.4) | 1979 (49.2) | 1966 (49.1) | 1917 (47.8) |
| Harvest ('000 tonnes) | 8897 (61.3) | 11064 (41.7) | 9740 (43.5) | 10010 (41.0) |
| Yield (tonnes per hectare) | 3.85 | 5.59 | 4.95 | 5.22 |
| *Oats* | | | | |
| Area ('000 hectares) | 221 (6.1) | 106 (2.6) | 134 (3.3) | 97 (2.4) |
| Harvest ('000 tonnes) | 783 (5.4) | 517 (1.9) | 615 (2.7) | 505 (2.1) |
| Yield (tonnes per hectare) | 3.54 | 4.89 | 4.59 | 5.16 |
| *Totals* | | | | |
| Area ('000 hectares) | 3649 | 4024 | 4002 | 4011 |
| Harvest ('000 tonnes) | 14514 | 26539 | 22405 | 24425 |

Source: adapted from *Annual Review of Agriculture*, HMSO
Notes:   Figures in brackets are percentages of annual totals
Rounding may make percentages not add to 100%
Droughts in the summers of 1975 and 1976 had an effect on yields in these years

In common with most tables there are several ways of presenting this information and the format given is only one suggestion. If you are repeatedly presenting data over some period, it is a good idea to keep the same format so that direct comparisons can be made. Useful examples of this are given in government publications, such as *Annual Abstract of Statistics*, *Monthly Digest of Statistics*, *Social Trends* and *Economic Trends* which are published by the Office of National Statistics.

---

IN SUMMARY

---

Tables are a widely used method of presenting numerical data. A well-designed table can show a lot of information and can be tailored to specific needs. A poorly designed table can obscure underlying patterns and lose details of the data.

## WORKED EXAMPLE 4.1

Carlson Industrial has collected the monthly performance indicators shown in Table 4.4 for the past five years. How would you summarize these?

**Table 4.4**

|           | Year |     |     |     |     |
|-----------|------|-----|-----|-----|-----|
|           | 1    | 2   | 3   | 4   | 5   |
| January   | 136  | 135 | 141 | 138 | 143 |
| February  | 109  | 112 | 121 | 117 | 118 |
| March     | 92   | 100 | 104 | 105 | 121 |
| April     | 107  | 116 | 116 | 121 | 135 |
| May       | 128  | 127 | 135 | 133 | 136 |
| June      | 145  | 132 | 138 | 154 | 147 |
| July      | 138  | 146 | 159 | 136 | 150 |
| August    | 127  | 130 | 131 | 135 | 144 |
| September | 135  | 127 | 129 | 140 | 140 |
| October   | 141  | 156 | 137 | 134 | 142 |
| November  | 147  | 136 | 149 | 148 | 147 |
| December  | 135  | 141 | 144 | 140 | 147 |

## Solution

There are many ways that we could summarize these data. Table 4.5 shows one possible solution from a spreadsheet.

**Table 4.5**

|   | A | B | C | D | E | F | G | H |
|---|---|---|---|---|---|---|---|---|
| 1 | **Range** | **Frequency** | | **Monthly averages** | | | **Annual averages** | |
| 2 | | | | | | | | |
| 3 | < 99 | 1 | | January | 138.6 | | Year 1 | 128.3 |
| 4 | 100–109 | 5 | | February | 115.4 | | Year 2 | 129.8 |
| 5 | 110–119 | 5 | | March | 104.4 | | Year 3 | 133.7 |
| 6 | 120–129 | 8 | | April | 119.0 | | Year 4 | 133.4 |
| 7 | 130–139 | 19 | | May | 131.8 | | Year 5 | 139.2 |
| 8 | 140–149 | 18 | | June | 143.2 | | | |
| 9 | > 150 | 4 | | July | 145.8 | | | |
| 10 | | | | August | 133.4 | | | |
| 11 | | | | September | 134.2 | | | |
| 12 | | | | October | 142.0 | | | |
| 13 | | | | November | 145.4 | | | |
| 14 | | | | December | 141.4 | | | |

# 4.2.3 │ Graphs

Tables are good at presenting a lot of information, but they do not necessarily highlight underlying patterns. We can see these more clearly with some form of pictorial representation. Perhaps the most widely used are graphs, which we described in Chapter 2.

In essence, a graph shows the relationship between two variables on a pair of rectangular (or Cartesian) axes, where:

● the horizontal or *x* axis shows the variable that is responsible for a change (the independent variable)

● the vertical or *y* axis shows the variable that we are trying to explain (the dependent variable)

In some cases it is not obvious which is the dependent and which the independent variable. If we are plotting sales of ice cream against temperature, then clearly there is an independent variable (temperature) and a dependent variable (sales of ice cream). But if we are plotting sales of ice cream against sales of sausages, there is no such clear relationship. Then it is a matter of choice as to which way round to plot the axes.

Graphs summarizing a set of raw data can be drawn in a number of ways. Returning to the weekly sales described earlier, we could start by plotting sales (the dependent variable that we are trying to explain) against the week (the independent variable that causes the changes). The simplest graph of this would just show the individual points in a **scatter diagram**, as illustrated in Figure 4.1.

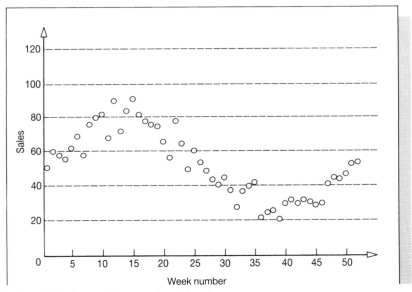

**Figure 4.1**   Scatter diagram of weekly sales.

This graph shows the general pattern, but this is made clearer if the points are joined, as shown in Figure 4.2. The sales clearly follow a seasonal cycle with peak sales around week 12 and lowest sales around week 38. There are small random variations away from this overall pattern, so the graph is not a smooth curve. Usually we are more interested in the smooth trend than the random variations, so we should emphasize this. Figure 4.3 shows individual points plotted around the smooth trend line.

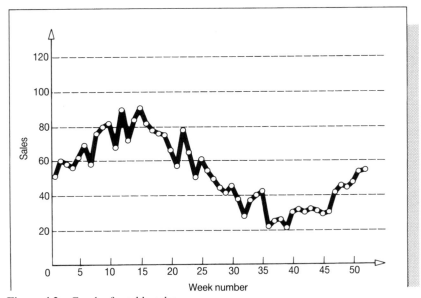

**Figure 4.2**   Graph of weekly sales.

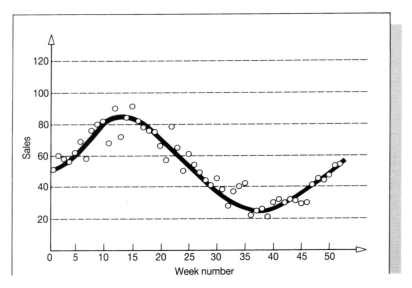

**Figure 4.3**   Smoothed graph of weekly sales.

The most common difficulty with graphs is the choice of scale for the *y* axis. We could redraw the graphs in Figures 4.1 – 4.3 with changed scales for the *y* axis, and the shape of the graph would vary considerably. Figure 4.4 shows a very stable pattern with only small variations from a low constant value. Figure 4.5 shows widely varying values, which are consistently high in the first half, and then almost zero in the second half.

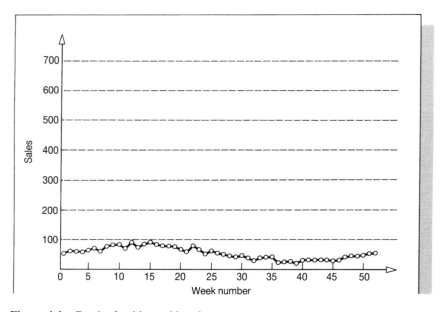

**Figure 4.4**   Graph of stable weekly sales.

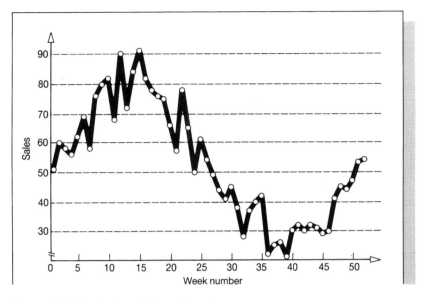

**Figure 4.5**   Graph of variable weekly sales.

Graphs give a very strong initial impact, so the choice of scale for the axes is important, with a bad choice giving a false view of the data. Although the choice of scale is largely subjective, some guidelines for good practice include:

- always label the axes clearly and accurately

- show the scales on both axes

- the maximum of the scale should be slightly above the maximum observation

- wherever possible the scale on axes should start at zero: if you cannot do this you must show the scale clearly, perhaps with a mark on the axis to indicate a break (see Figure 4.5)

- where appropriate, give the source of data

- where appropriate, give the graph a title

One of the benefits of graphs is their ability to compare data by plotting several graphs on the same axes. Figure 4.6, for example, shows how the unit price of a basic commodity has varied each month over the past five years. Notice that the price axis does not go down to zero. The price differences are small and are highlighted by using a narrower range for the y axis.

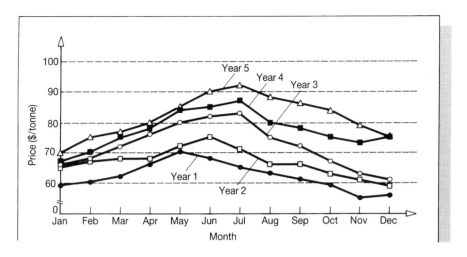

**Figure 4.6** Price in $ per tonne of commodity by month. (Source: UN Digest.)

## WORKED EXAMPLE 4.2

Table 4.6 shows the quarterly profit reported by a company and the corresponding average price of its shares quoted on the London Stock Exchange. Draw a graph of these data.

**Table 4.6**

| Year | 1 | | | | 2 | | | | 3 | | | |
|---|---|---|---|---|---|---|---|---|---|---|---|---|
| Quarter | 1 | 2 | 3 | 4 | 1 | 2 | 3 | 4 | 1 | 2 | 3 | 4 |
| Profit | 12.1 | 12.2 | 11.6 | 10.8 | 13.0 | 13.6 | 11.9 | 11.7 | 14.2 | 14.5 | 12.5 | 13.0 |
| Share price | 122 | 129 | 89 | 92 | 132 | 135 | 101 | 104 | 154 | 156 | 125 | 136 |

Source: company reports and the *Financial Times*
Note: profits are in millions of pounds and share prices are in pence

### Solution

The independent variable is the one that is responsible for changes; in this example it is the company profit. The dependent variable is the one that we are trying to explain; in this example it is the share price. A graph of these results is shown in Figure 4.7. The chosen scale highlights the linear relationship between profit and share price. As always, you should examine the information carefully, and in this case inflation might have a significant effect on the results. If it is important to show the cyclical nature of the data, we could also draw graphs of profit and share price against quarter.

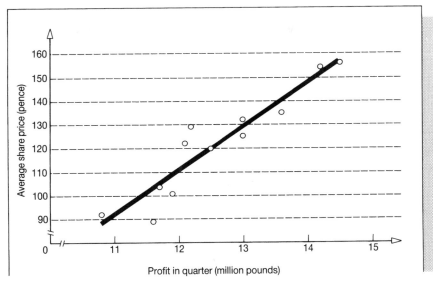

**Figure 4.7**  Graph of share price against sales for Worked Example 4.2.

## WORKED EXAMPLE 4.3

Draw a graph of the data described in Worked Example 4.1.

## Solution

There are several ways of drawing a graph of these data, with the simplest shown in Figure 4.8.

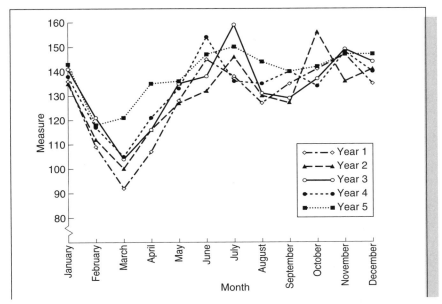

**Figure 4.8**  Graph for Worked Example 4.3.

> ## IN SUMMARY
>
> Graphs show clear relationships between two variables. We can easily see any underlying patterns and compare different sets of data. Care must be taken in choosing appropriate scales for the axes.

## 4.2.4 | Pie charts

Graphs are good at showing relationships between two variables, but other methods of presenting data make more use of pictures. Pie charts are simple diagrams that show comparisons of limited amounts of information.

To draw a pie chart the data are first classified into distinct categories. Then a circle is drawn (the pie) which is divided into sectors, each of which represents one category. The area of each sector (and so the angle at the centre of the circle) is proportional to the number of observations in the category.

## WORKED EXAMPLE 4.4

Sales in four regions are given in the following table. Draw a pie chart of these figures.

| Region | Sales |
|--------|-------|
| North | 25 |
| South | 10 |
| East | 45 |
| West | 25 |
| Total | 105 |

### Solution

There are 360° in a circle, and these represent 105 observations. So each observation is represented by an angle of 360°/105 = 3.4° at the centre of the circle. Then the sales in the North region are represented by a sector with an angle of $25 \times 3.4° = 86°$ at the centre of the circle; sales in the South region are represented by a sector with an angle of $10 \times 3.4° = 34°$ at the centre, and so on. In practice, of course, such diagrams are drawn by computer, and all these calculations are done automatically. A basic pie chart for this is shown in Figure 4.9(a). The appearance of pie charts can be improved in several ways, and Figure 4.9(b) shows the same results with slices in the pie sorted into order, percentages calculated and a three-dimensional effect added.

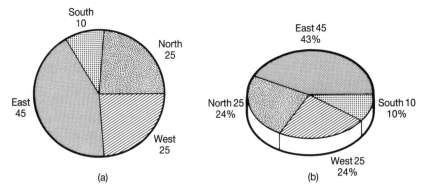

**Figure 4.9** (a) Basic pie chart of sales for Worked Example 4.4.
(b) Fuller pie chart of sales.

Pie charts compare the relative number of observations in different categories. They can be used for percentages, but really have little other use. When there are more than, say, four to eight categories, they become too complicated and lose their impact.

**IN SUMMARY**

Pie charts represent the relative frequency of observations by the sectors of a circle. They can give considerable impact, but are only useful for small amounts of data.

## 4.2.5 | Bar charts

Like pie charts, bar charts are diagrams that show the number of observations in different categories of data. This time, though, the numbers of observations are shown by lines or bars rather than sectors of a circle.

In a bar chart, each category of data is represented by a different bar, and the length of the bar is proportional to the number of observations. Bar charts are usually drawn vertically, but they can be horizontal, and there are many adjustments that improve their appearance. One constant rule, however, is that the scale must start at zero; you might be tempted to save space or expand the vertical scale by omitting the lower parts of bars but this is simply confusing.

## WORKED EXAMPLE 4.5

Draw a bar chart of the regional sales in Worked Example 4.4.

### Solution

Using a simple format, where the length of each bar corresponds to the number of sales in a region, gives the result shown in Figure 4.10.

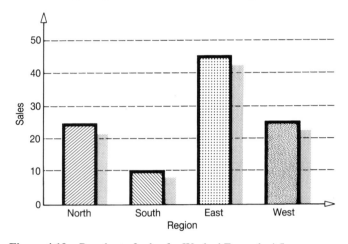

**Figure 4.10**  Bar chart of sales for Worked Example 4.5.

There are several different types of bar chart and the most appropriate is usually a matter of choice. But you should remember that the purpose of diagrams is to present the characteristics of the data clearly; it is not to draw the prettiest picture. One particularly useful type of bar chart compares several sets of data, as shown in the following example.

## WORKED EXAMPLE 4.6

South Middleton Health District has five hospitals, with the number of beds in each hospital as follows:

|  | Hospital | | | | |
|---|---|---|---|---|---|
|  | Foothills | General | Southern | Heathview | St John |
| Maternity | 24 | 38 | 6 | 0 | 0 |
| Surgical | 86 | 85 | 45 | 30 | 24 |
| Medical | 82 | 55 | 30 | 30 | 35 |
| Psychiatric | 25 | 22 | 30 | 65 | 76 |

Draw a bar chart to represent these data.

## Solution

There are many possible formats for bar charts. Figure 4.11 shows a simple vertical form. This chart emphasizes the number of beds of each type, but if we wanted to highlight the relative sizes of the hospitals, we could 'stack' the bars to give the single bars shown in Figure 4.12.

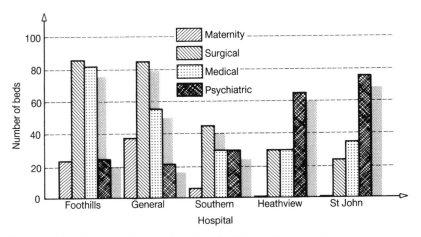

**Figure 4.11** Number of beds in hospitals for Worked Example 4.6.

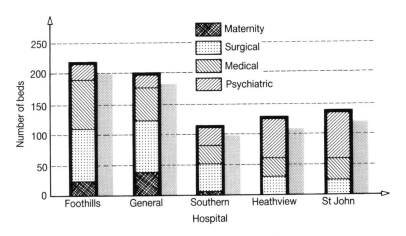

**Figure 4.12** Emphasizing the number of beds in each hospital.

We could also represent these as percentages, as shown in Figure 4.13. There is an almost limitless variety of bar charts, and the best one to use depends on the circumstances.

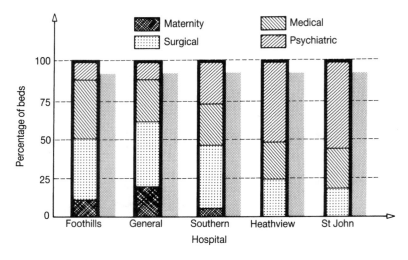

**Figure 4.13**   Percentage of beds.

*IN SUMMARY*

Bar charts can give flexible presentations. They use bars to represent categories, with the length of each bar proportional to the number of observations in the category.

## 4.2.6 | Pictograms

These are similar to bar charts, except the bars are replaced by sketches of the things being described. So the percentage of people owning cars might be represented as in Figure 4.14. In this pictogram, each 10% of people are represented by one car.

Pictograms are very eye-catching and are, therefore, widely used in newspapers and magazines. They are not very accurate, but they are effective in giving general impressions. One problem comes with fractional values, such as 53% of people owning cars. In Figure 4.14 this would have been shown by a stack of 5.3 cars, and the 0.3 of a car clearly has little meaning. Nonetheless, the diagram would give the general impression of 'just over 50%'.

Pictograms should show different numbers of observations by different numbers of sketches, as shown in Figure 4.14. The wrong way to draw them is to make a single sketch bigger, as shown in Figure 4.15. The problem here is that we should be concentrating on the height of the sketches, but it is the area that has the immediate impact. If the number of observations is doubled, the sketch is doubled

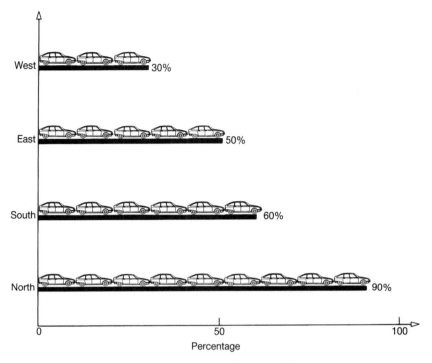

**Figure 4.14** Pictogram showing percentage of people with cars.

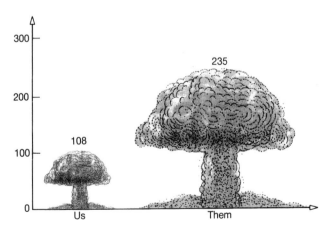

**Figure 4.15** Poor pictogram showing the number of nuclear missiles.

in height; unfortunately, this increases the area by a factor of four. Figure 4.15 shows (as nuclear bomb mushroom clouds) the number of nuclear missiles built by 'Us' and 'Them'. All the figures are put on the graph to show that 'They' have just over twice as many missiles as 'Us', but it is the area of the graph that makes the impact, and this suggests a much bigger difference.

---

**IN SUMMARY**

Pictograms replace the bars in bar charts by sketches. These can attract attention, but the results are not very accurate and need careful interpretation.

---

## Self-assessment questions

**4.5** What are the two main methods of presenting statistical data?

**4.6** What are the advantages of using tables of data?

**4.7** Why must you label the axes of graphs?

**4.8** If you had a large amount of numerical data what formats would you consider for their presentation?

**4.9** 'When using bar charts there is only one format that can be used for any set of data.' Is this statement true? Is it true of other methods of presenting data?

**4.10** What are the main problems with pictograms?

# 4.3 | Frequency distributions

Earlier in the chapter we showed that the number of observations in different classes could be drawn as a frequency table. In this section we are going to look at this idea in more detail.

## 4.3.1 | Frequency tables

We have already met a frequency table of the form shown below. This divides weekly sales into a number of distinct classes and shows the number of weeks where demand fell in each class. The result is called a **frequency distribution**.

| Class | Number of weeks |
|---------|-----------------|
| 20 to 39 | 14 |
| 40 to 59 | 19 |
| 60 to 79 | 13 |
| 80 to 99 | 6 |

There are six observations in the highest class of sales, 80 to 99. Sometimes it is better to be less specific when defining classes, particularly if there are odd outlying values. If, for example, the data had included one observation of 120 it would be better to include this in the highest class than create another class some distance from the others. Then we might define a class as '80 or more'. Similarly, it could be better to replace the precise '20 to 39' by the less precise '39 or fewer'.

When defining the boundaries between classes we must be sure that there is no doubt about which class an observation is in. We would not, for example, have adjacent classes of '20 to 30' and '30 to 40', as a value of 30 could be in either one. To overcome this, the classes are defined as '20 to 29' and '30 to 39'. This solution works if data are discrete (such as the number of sales) but is more difficult with continuous data. If, for example, we were classifying people by age we could not use classes '20 to 29' and '30 to 39', as this would leave no place for people who are 29.5. We must describe the classes clearly and unambiguously, and the age range might be '20 or more and less than 30'.

Most of the data described so far in this chapter have been discrete. This was largely for convenience, but now we can move on and discuss continuous data. This is not a major step, as all our previous comments apply equally to discrete and continuous data. We can show this by drawing a frequency table of continuous data.

## WORKED EXAMPLE 4.7

During a particular period the wages (in pounds) paid to 30 people have been recorded as follows:

202 457 310 176 480 277 87 391 325 120 554 94 362 221 274

145 240 437 404 398 361 144 429 216 282 153 470 303 338 209

Draw a frequency table of these data.

### Solution

Our first decision concerns the number of classes. Although this is largely a subjective decision, the number should be chosen carefully. Too few classes (say, three) would not show the patterns; too many classes (say, 20) is confusing and too detailed. Generally, you should look for about six classes.

Now we have to define ranges for our six classes. The range of wages is £87 to £554, and a reasonable set of classes is:

'Less than £100', '£100 or more and less than £200', '£200 or more and less than £300', and so on

Notice that we are careful **not** to say 'more than £100 and less than £200', as someone might earn exactly £100 and would not appear in any class.

Adding the number of observations in each class gives the following frequency table:

| Class | Frequency |
|---|---|
| less than £100 | 2 |
| £100 or more, but less than £200 | 5 |
| £200 or more, but less than £300 | 8 |
| £300 or more, but less than £400 | 9 |
| £400 or more, but less than £500 | 5 |
| £500 or more, but less than £600 | 1 |

This clearly shows the frequency distribution of wages. More than half of people earn between £200 and £400, and the biggest class is £300–£400.

Frequency distributions show the actual number of observations in each class. A useful extension is a **percentage frequency distribution**, which shows the percentage of observations in each class. The results are presented in exactly the same way as in standard frequency tables. The data in Worked Example 4.7 are shown in the following percentage frequency distribution:

| Class | Frequency | Percentage frequency |
|---|---|---|
| Less than £100 | 2 | 6.7 |
| £100 or more, but less than £200 | 5 | 16.7 |
| £200 or more, but less than £300 | 8 | 26.7 |
| £300 or more, but less than £400 | 9 | 30.0 |
| £400 or more, but less than £500 | 5 | 16.7 |
| £500 or more, but less than £600 | 1 | 3.3 |

Another useful extension of frequency distributions looks at **cumulative frequencies**. Instead of recording the number of observations in a class, cumulative frequency distributions add all observations in lower classes. In the last table there were 2 observations in the first class, 5 in the second class and 8 in the third. The cumulative frequency distribution shows 2 observations in the first class, 2 + 5 = 7 in the second class and 2 + 5 + 8 = 15 in the third. We can also extend this into a **cumulative percentage frequency distribution**, as shown in Table 4.7.

**Table 4.7**

| Class | Frequency | Cumulative frequency | Percentage frequency | Cumulative percentage frequency |
|---|---|---|---|---|
| Less than £100 | 2 | 2 | 6.7 | 6.7 |
| £100 or more, but less than £200 | 5 | 7 | 16.7 | 23.3 |
| £200 or more, but less than £300 | 8 | 15 | 26.7 | 50.0 |
| £300 or more, but less than £400 | 9 | 24 | 30.0 | 80.0 |
| £400 or more, but less than £500 | 5 | 29 | 16.7 | 96.7 |
| £500 or more, but less than £600 | 1 | 30 | 3.3 | 100.0 |

# WORKED EXAMPLE 4.8

Draw a table showing the frequency, cumulative frequency, percentage frequency and cumulative percentage frequency for the following discrete data:

150  141  158  147  132  153  176  162  180  165

174  133  129  119  103  188  190  165  157  146

161  130  122  169  159  152  173  148  154  171

## Solution

We start by defining suitable classes, and, as we do not know the purpose of the data, we can suggest any suitable ones. The data are discrete, so we can arbitrarily use 100 to 109, 110 to 119, 120 to 129, and so on. The results are shown in Table 4.8, where the calculations have been done on a spreadsheet.

**Table 4.8**

| | A | B | C | D | E |
|---|---|---|---|---|---|
| 1 | **Class** | **Frequency** | **Cumulative** | **Percentage** | **Cumulative** |
| 2 | | | **frequency** | **frequency** | **percentage** |
| 3 | | | | | **frequency** |
| 4 | | | | | |
| 5 | 100–109 | 1 | 1 | 3.33 | 3.33 |
| 6 | 110–119 | 1 | 2 | 3.33 | 6.67 |
| 7 | 120–129 | 2 | 4 | 6.67 | 13.33 |
| 8 | 130–139 | 3 | 7 | 10.00 | 23.33 |
| 9 | 140–149 | 4 | 11 | 13.33 | 36.67 |
| 10 | 150–159 | 7 | 18 | 23.33 | 60.00 |
| 11 | 160–169 | 5 | 23 | 16.67 | 76.67 |
| 12 | 170–179 | 4 | 27 | 13.33 | 90.00 |
| 13 | 180–189 | 2 | 29 | 6.67 | 96.67 |
| 14 | 190–199 | 1 | 30 | 3.33 | 100.00 |

IN SUMMARY

Frequency tables show the number of observations that fall into different classes. They can be used for both continuous and discrete data, and can be extended to show percentage frequency distributions and cumulative distributions.

## 4.3.2 | Histograms

**Histograms** are frequency distributions for continuous data. In appearance they are similar to bar charts, but there are some important differences. The most important difference is that histograms are only used for continuous data, so the horizontal axis has a continuous scale. Bars are drawn on this scale, so their width, as well as their height, has a definite meaning. This is an important point: in bar charts it is only the height of the bar that is important, but in histograms it is both the width and the height, or in effect the area. We can show this by drawing a histogram of the continuous data for wages shown above.

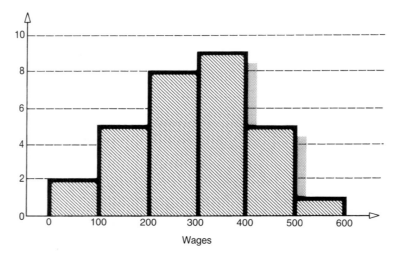

**Figure 4.16**   Histogram of wages.

In Figure 4.16 each class is the same width, so the areas are set by the height of the bars. In effect, this is the same as a bar chart. Suppose, though, that the classes are of different widths. If we doubled the width of one class, we would have to halve its height to keep the same area. This effect is shown in the following worked example.

# WORKED EXAMPLE 4.9

Draw a histogram of the following data:

| Class | Frequency |
|---|---|
| Less than 10 | 8 |
| 10 or more, but less than 20 | 10 |
| 20 or more, but less than 30 | 16 |
| 30 or more, but less than 40 | 15 |
| 40 or more, but less than 50 | 11 |
| 50 or more, but less than 60 | 4 |
| 60 or more, but less than 70 | 2 |
| 70 or more, but less than 80 | 1 |
| 80 or more, but less than 90 | 1 |

## Solution

Using the classes given, we can draw the histogram shown in Figure 4.17. Because this diagram has a long tail with only eight observations in the last four classes, we might be tempted to combine these into one class with eight observations and then draw the histogram in Figure 4.18. But this would be wrong. We cannot change the horizontal scale, so the single class would be four times as wide as the other classes. Making it four units wide and eight units high suggests that the last class represents 32 observations instead of eight. As the area represents the number of observations the single last box should be four units wide and, therefore, two units high, as shown in Figure 4.19.

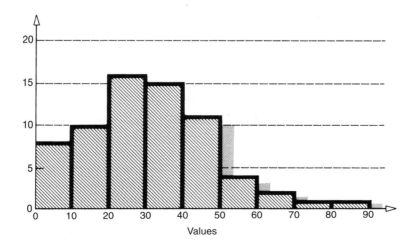

**Figure 4.17** Histogram of values for Worked Example 4.9.

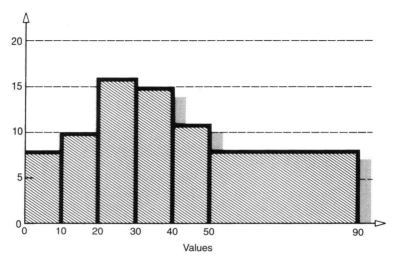

**Figure 4.18**  Incorrect histogram combining last few classes.

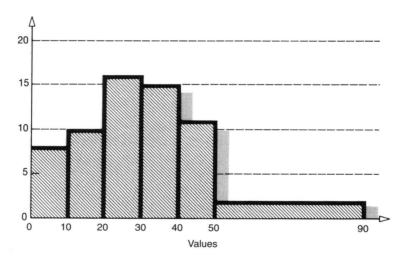

**Figure 4.19**  Correct histogram combining last few classes.

Another problem with histograms comes with open-ended categories. How, for example, do we deal with classes containing values 'greater than 20'? The answer (apart from avoiding such definitions wherever possible) is to make assumptions about the upper limit. By examining the data we can suggest an upper limit where 'greater than 20' might be interpreted as 'greater than 20 and less than 22'. Another consistent problem is that the shape of a histogram depends to a large extent on the way that classes are defined.

Overall, it can be quite difficult to use histograms properly. The less precise bar charts often give better-looking results with less effort, so there is some advantage in simply using these.

Histograms show frequency distributions for continuous data. They represent frequencies by areas and are useful in further analyses. It is sometimes difficult to draw a reasonable histogram.

## 4.3.3 | Summary charts

Earlier in this section we described tables of cumulative frequency distributions, like the one below:

| Class | Frequency | Cumulative frequency |
| --- | --- | --- |
| 100 or less | 22 | 22 |
| 150 or less, but more than 100 | 44 | 66 |
| 200 or less, but more than 150 | 79 | 145 |
| 250 or less, but more than 200 | 96 | 241 |
| 300 or less, but more than 250 | 44 | 285 |
| 350 or less, but more than 300 | 15 | 300 |

We can draw this kind of result on a graph relating cumulative frequency to class. The resulting curve has the scale of classes across the $x$ axis and the cumulative frequency up the $y$ axis and is called an **ogive.** We can start drawing an ogive of the data above by plotting the point (100,22) to show that 22 observations are in the class '100 or less'. The next point is (150,66) which shows that 66 observations are 150 or less, then the point (200,145) shows 145 observations are 200 or less, and so on. Plotting these points and joining them gives the result shown in Figure 4.20. Ogives are always drawn vertically, and they are usually elongated S shapes.

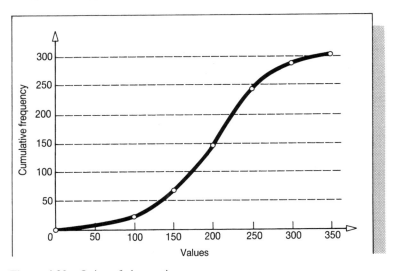

**Figure 4.20** Ogive of observations.

A specific extension to ogives is a **Lorenz curve**. This is primarily used in economics to describe the distribution of income or wealth among a population. It is a graph of cumulative percentage wealth, income or some other measure of wealth against cumulative percentage of the population.

## WORKED EXAMPLE 4.10

Annual tax returns suggest that the percentages of a country's total wealth owned by various percentages of the population are as shown in the following table:

| Percentage of population | Percentage of wealth before tax | Percentage of wealth after tax |
|---|---|---|
| 45 | 5 | 15 |
| 20 | 10 | 15 |
| 15 | 15 | 15 |
| 10 | 10 | 15 |
| 5 | 15 | 15 |
| 3 | 25 | 15 |
| 2 | 20 | 10 |

(a) Draw a Lorenz curve of the wealth before tax.

(b) Draw a Lorenz curve of the wealth after tax. What conclusion can you draw from these curves?

### Solution

(a) A Lorenz curve plots the cumulative percentage of population against the corresponding cumulative percentage of wealth, so we first have to find these values, as shown in the following table:

| Percentage of population | Cumulative percentage of population | Percentage of wealth before tax | Cumulative percentage of wealth |
|---|---|---|---|
| 45 | 45 | 5 | 5 |
| 20 | 65 | 10 | 15 |
| 15 | 80 | 15 | 30 |
| 10 | 90 | 10 | 40 |
| 5 | 95 | 15 | 55 |
| 3 | 98 | 25 | 80 |
| 2 | 100 | 20 | 100 |

Now we plot these cumulative figures on a graph. The first point is (45,5), the second point is (65,15) and so on, as shown in Figure 4.21. You can see that a diagonal line has also been added to emphasize the shape of the Lorenz curve.

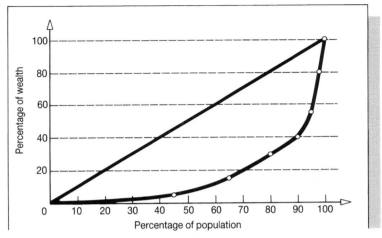

**Figure 4.21**  Lorenz curve for wealth before tax.

(b) Repeating the calculations for the after-tax wealth gives the following values, with the resulting Lorenz curve shown in Figure 4.22:

| Percentage of population | Cumulative percentage of population | Percentage of wealth after tax | Cumulative percentage of wealth |
|---|---|---|---|
| 45 | 45 | 15 | 15 |
| 20 | 65 | 15 | 30 |
| 15 | 80 | 15 | 45 |
| 10 | 90 | 15 | 60 |
| 5 | 95 | 15 | 75 |
| 3 | 98 | 15 | 90 |
| 2 | 100 | 10 | 100 |

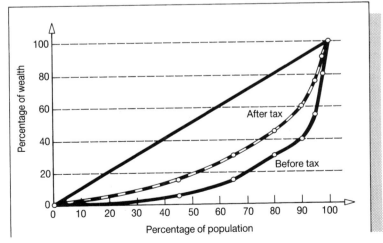

**Figure 4.22**  Lorenz curve for wealth after tax.

If the distribution of wealth is perfectly fair, we would get the diagonal straight line connecting the origin to the point (100,100). If the graph is significantly below this, the distribution of wealth is unequal, and the further from the straight line the less equal is the distribution. The Lorenz curve for after-tax wealth is closer to the straight line, and this shows that taxes have had an effect in redistributing wealth.

---

## IN SUMMARY

Ogives are graphs of cumulative frequency against class. One extension of these is the Lorenz curve, which shows the distribution of income or wealth among a population. It can also be used for related measures, such as the effect of taxation.

# Self-assessment questions

**4.11**  What is a frequency distribution?

**4.12**  What is the difference between a frequency distribution, a percentage frequency distribution, a cumulative frequency distribution and a cumulative percentage frequency distribution?

**4.13**  'In bar charts and histograms the height of the bar shows the number of observations in each class.' Is this statement correct?

**4.14**  If two classes of equal width are combined into one for a histogram, how high is the resulting bar?

**4.15**  What is the purpose of an ogive?

**4.16**  'A fair Lorenz curve should be a straight line connecting points (0,0) and (100,100).' Is this statement true?

---

## CHAPTER REVIEW

Once they have been collected, data must be processed to give useful information. This chapter considered one aspect of data processing, by describing how data can be summarized in diagrams. In particular it:

● discussed the purpose of data reduction as showing the overall pattern of data without getting bogged down in the details

● described alternative formats for data presentation, and suggested that the best depends on the purpose of the presentation – but it is largely a matter of personal judgement

- designed tables of numerical data (which can show a lot of information but do not emphasize overall patterns)
- drew graphs to show relationships between variables
- drew pie charts, bar charts and pictograms to show relative frequencies
- described frequency tables and distributions, including percentage and cumulative distributions
- drew histograms for continuous data
- drew ogives and Lorenz graphs

# Problems

**4.1** Find some recent trade statistics published by the government and present these in different ways to emphasize different features. Discuss which formats are fairest and which are most misleading.

**4.2** A question in a survey gets the answer 'Yes' from 47% of men and 38% of women, 'No' from 32% of men and 53% of women, and 'Do not know' from the remainder. How could you present this result effectively?

**4.3** The number of students taking a course in the past ten years is summarized in the following table:

| Year | 1 | 2 | 3 | 4 | 5 | 6 | 7 | 8 | 9 | 10 |
|---|---|---|---|---|---|---|---|---|---|---|
| Male | 21 | 22 | 20 | 18 | 28 | 26 | 29 | 30 | 32 | 29 |
| Female | 4 | 6 | 3 | 5 | 12 | 16 | 14 | 19 | 17 | 25 |

Use a selection of graphical methods to summarize these data. Which do you think is the best?

**4.4** Table 4.9 shows the quarterly profit reported by the Lebal Corporation and the corresponding average price of its shares quoted on the New York Stock Exchange. Design suitable formats for presenting these data.

**Table 4.9**

| Year | 1 | | | | 2 | | | | 3 | | | |
|---|---|---|---|---|---|---|---|---|---|---|---|---|
| Quarter | 1 | 2 | 3 | 4 | 1 | 2 | 3 | 4 | 1 | 2 | 3 | 4 |
| Profit | 36 | 45 | 56 | 55 | 48 | 55 | 62 | 68 | 65 | 65 | 69 | 74 |
| Share price | 137 | 145 | 160 | 162 | 160 | 163 | 166 | 172 | 165 | 170 | 175 | 182 |

Source: company reports and the *Wall Street Journal*
Note: profits are in millions of dollars and share prices are in dollars

**4.5** The number of people employed by Testel Electronics over the past ten years is as follows:

| Year | 1 | 2 | 3 | 4 | 5 | 6 | 7 | 8 | 9 | 10 |
|---|---|---|---|---|---|---|---|---|---|---|
| Number | 24 | 27 | 29 | 34 | 38 | 42 | 46 | 51 | 60 | 67 |

Design suitable ways of presenting these data.

**4.6** Four regions of Yorkshire classify companies according to primary, manufacturing, transport, retail and service. The number of companies operating in each region in each category is shown below. Draw a number of bar charts to represent these data. Are bar charts the most appropriate format here?

| | Industry type | | | | |
|---|---|---|---|---|---|
| | Primary | Manufacturing | Transport | Retail | Service |
| Daleside | 143 | 38 | 10 | 87 | 46 |
| Twendale | 134 | 89 | 15 | 73 | 39 |
| Underhill | 72 | 67 | 11 | 165 | 55 |
| Perithorp | 54 | 41 | 23 | 287 | 89 |

**4.7** The average wages of 45 people have been recorded as follows:

221 254 83 320 367 450 292 161 216 410 380 355 502 144 362
112 387 324 576 156 295 77 391 324 126 154 94 350 239 263
276 232 467 413 472 361 132 429 310 272 408 480 253 338 217

Draw a frequency table, percentage frequency and cumulative frequency table of these data. How could the data be presented in charts?

**4.8** Draw a histogram of the following data:

| Class | Frequency |
|---|---|
| Less than 100 | 120 |
| 100 or more, but less than 200 | 185 |
| 200 or more, but less than 300 | 285 |
| 300 or more, but less than 400 | 260 |
| 400 or more, but less than 500 | 205 |
| 500 or more, but less than 600 | 150 |
| 600 or more, but less than 700 | 75 |
| 700 or more, but less than 800 | 35 |
| 800 or more, but less than 900 | 15 |

How could the last   (a) two   (b) three classes be combined?

**4.9** Draw an ogive of the data in Problem 4.8.

**4.10** Present the following data in a number of appropriate formats:

| Class | Frequency |
|---|---|
| Less than 2.5 | 0 |
| 2.5 or more, but less than 4.5 | 26 |
| 4.5 or more, but less than 6.5 | 40 |
| 6.5 or more, but less than 8.5 | 61 |
| 8.5 or more, but less than 10.5 | 75 |
| 10.5 or more, but less than 12.5 | 69 |
| 12.5 or more, but less than 14.5 | 55 |
| 14.5 or more, but less than 16.5 | 38 |
| 16.5 or more, but less than 18.5 | 15 |
| 18.5 or more | 0 |

**4.11** The wealth of a population is described in the following frequency distribution. Draw Lorenz curves to represent this. Draw other appropriate graphs to represent the data.

| Percentage of people | 5 | 10 | 15 | 20 | 20 | 15 | 10 | 5 |
|---|---|---|---|---|---|---|---|---|
| Percentage of wealth before tax | 1 | 3 | 6 | 15 | 20 | 20 | 15 | 20 |
| Percentage of wealth after tax | 3 | 6 | 10 | 16 | 20 | 20 | 10 | 15 |

# Computer exercises

**4.1** The following table shows last year's total production and profits (in consistent units) from six factories:

| Factory | A | B | C | D | E | F |
|---|---|---|---|---|---|---|
| Production | 125 | 53 | 227 | 36 | 215 | 163 |
| Profit | 202 | 93 | 501 | 57 | 413 | 296 |

Use a suitable package to present these data in a number of formats.

**4.2** The following data have been collected by a company. Put them into a spreadsheet, and reduce, manipulate and present them.

245 487 123 012 159 751 222 035 487 655 197 655 458 766 123 453 493 444 123 537
254 514 324 215 367 557 330 204 506 804 941 354 226 870 652 458 425 248 560 510
234 542 671 874 710 702 701 540 360 654 323 410 405 531 489 695 409 375 521 624
357 678 809 901 567 481 246 027 310 679 548 227 150 600 845 521 777 304 286 220
667 111 485 266 472 700 705 466 591 398 367 331 458 466 571 489 257 100 874 577

Now describe them in suitable diagrams. Write a report on your findings.

**4.3** Jenny Oldroyde counted the number of customers entering her shop each morning for a month. Figure 4.23 shows the results on a spreadsheet. Check that her diagram is correct. How could she present the data more clearly? What other information would be useful?

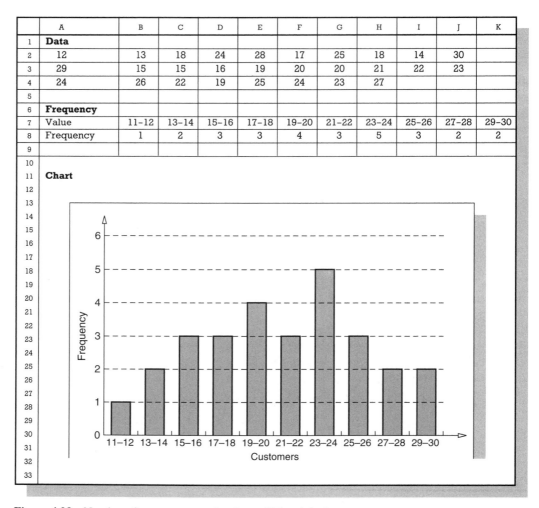

|   | A | B | C | D | E | F | G | H | I | J | K |
|---|---|---|---|---|---|---|---|---|---|---|---|
| 1 | **Data** | | | | | | | | | | |
| 2 | 12 | 13 | 18 | 24 | 28 | 17 | 25 | 18 | 14 | 30 | |
| 3 | 29 | 15 | 15 | 16 | 19 | 20 | 20 | 21 | 22 | 23 | |
| 4 | 24 | 26 | 22 | 19 | 25 | 24 | 23 | 27 | | | |
| 5 | | | | | | | | | | | |
| 6 | **Frequency** | | | | | | | | | | |
| 7 | Value | 11–12 | 13–14 | 15–16 | 17–18 | 19–20 | 21–22 | 23–24 | 25–26 | 27–28 | 29–30 |
| 8 | Frequency | 1 | 2 | 3 | 3 | 4 | 3 | 5 | 3 | 2 | 2 |
| 9 | | | | | | | | | | | |
| 10 | | | | | | | | | | | |
| 11 | **Chart** | | | | | | | | | | |

**Figure 4.23** Number of customers entering Jenny Oldroyde's shop.

**4.4** Figure 4.24 shows part of a spreadsheet. In this, a frequency table is drawn for a block of data. Use a spreadsheet to duplicate the results and extend the analysis.

|    | A    | B | C | D | E | F | G | H |
|----|------|---|---|---|---|---|---|---|
| 1  | **Data** |   |   |   |   |   |   |   |
| 2  | 5 | 4 | 1 | 2 |   |   |   |   |
| 3  | 4 | 5 | 5 | 2 |   |   |   |   |
| 4  | 6 | 7 | 6 | 4 |   |   |   |   |
| 5  | 7 | 1 | 4 | 8 |   |   |   |   |
| 6  | 1 | 5 | 3 | 7 |   |   |   |   |
| 7  | 1 | 4 | 8 | 6 |   |   |   |   |
| 8  | 2 | 8 | 7 | 6 |   |   |   |   |
| 9  | 4 | 2 | 4 | 3 |   |   |   |   |
| 10 | 5 | 4 | 2 | 4 |   |   |   |   |
| 11 | 7 | 8 | 6 | 4 |   |   |   |   |
| 12 | 8 | 6 | 4 | 5 |   |   |   |   |
| 13 | 8 | 4 | 3 | 1 |   |   |   |   |
| 14 | 9 | 8 | 7 | 2 |   |   |   |   |
| 15 | 4 | 1 | 9 | 9 |   | **Class frequency** | |   |
| 16 | 5 | 2 | 5 | 7 |   | 0 | 0 |   |
| 17 | 4 | 7 | 1 | 6 |   | 2 | 16 |   |
| 18 | 5 | 9 | 2 | 4 |   | 4 | 22 |   |
| 19 | 5 | 5 | 5 | 5 |   | 6 | 22 |   |
| 20 | 4 | 1 | 8 | 3 |   | 8 | 16 |   |
| 21 | 5 | 3 | 4 | 5 |   | 10 | 4 |   |

**Figure 4.24**   Frequency table drawn using a spreadsheet.

**4.5** You are asked to prepare a report on the distance that people travel to get to work. Design a questionnaire to collect expected travel times for a large group of people. Now use this questionnaire to collect a set of real data. Use appropriate software to reduce and analyse the data. Prepare your report in two formats:

- a written report
- overhead slides to accompany a presentation to clients

# Case study

## High Acclaim Importers

The finance director of High Acclaim Importers was giving a summary of company business to a group of shareholders. He asked Jim Bowlers to collect some data from company records for his presentation.

At first Jim had been worried by the amount of detail available. The company seemed to keep enormous amounts of data on all aspects of its operations. These data ranged from transaction records in the main database to subjective management views which were never written down. The finance director had told Jim to give him some concise figures that he could use on overhead slides.

Jim did a conscientious job of collecting data and he looked pleased as he approached the finance director. As he handed over the results (Table 4.10), Jim explained: 'Some of our most important trading results are shown in this table. We trade in four regions, so for movements between each of these I have recorded seven key facts. The following table shows the number of units shipped (in hundreds), the average income per unit (in pounds sterling), the percentage gross profit, the percentage return on investment, a measure (between 1 and 5) of trading difficulty, the number of finance administrators employed in each area, and the number of agents. I thought you could make a slide of this and use it as a focus during your presentation'.

**Table 4.10**

| From | To | | | |
|------|--------|---------|------|--------|
| | *Africa* | *America* | *Asia* | *Europe* |
| Africa | 105, 45, 12, 4, 4, 15, 4 | 85, 75, 14, 7, 3, 20, 3 | 25, 60, 15, 8, 3, 12, 2 | 160, 80, 13, 7, 2, 25, 4 |
| America | 45, 75, 12, 3, 4, 15, 3 | 255, 120, 15, 9, 1, 45, 5 | 60, 95, 8, 2, 2, 35, 6 | 345, 115, 10, 7, 1, 65, 5 |
| Asia | 85, 70, 8, 4, 5, 20, 4 | 334, 145, 10, 5, 2, 55, 6 | 265, 85, 8, 3, 2, 65, 7 | 405, 125, 8, 3, 2, 70, 8 |
| Europe | 100, 80, 10, 5, 4, 30, 3 | 425, 120, 12, 8, 1, 70, 7 | 380, 105, 9, 4, 2, 45, 5 | 555, 140, 10, 6, 1, 110, 8 |

The finance director looked at the figures for a few minutes and then asked for some details on how trade had changed over the past ten years. Jim replied that in general terms the volume of trade had risen by 1.5, 3, 2.5, 2.5, 1, 1, 2.5, 3.5, 3 and 2.5% respectively in each of the last ten years, while the average price had risen by 4, 4.5, 5.5, 7, 3.5, 4.5, 6, 5.5, 5 and 5% respectively.

The finance director looked up from his figures and said: 'I am not sure these figures will have much impact on our shareholders. I was hoping for something a bit briefer and with a bit more impact. Could you give me the figures in a revised format by this afternoon?'

Your problem is to help Jim Bowlers to put the figures into a suitable format for presentation to shareholders.

# 5 | Using numbers to describe data

| | | | | |
|---|---|---|---|---|
| Chapter outline | 125 | Chapter review | 157 |
| 5.1 Measures for business data | 126 | Problems | 157 |
| | | Computer exercises | 159 |
| 5.2 Finding the average | 128 | Case study: | 161 |
| 5.3 Measuring the spread of data | 143 | Consumer advice office | |

**CHAPTER OUTLINE**

Chapter 3 discussed data collection. Once a set of data has been collected it must be processed to give useful information. Chapter 4 discussed ways of summarizing data and presenting them in diagrams. This chapter continues the theme of data presentation by looking at numerical descriptions. The chapter concentrates on measures of average and spread.

After reading this chapter and doing the exercises you should be able to:

- appreciate the need for measures of data
- calculate arithmetic means for grouped and ungrouped data
- identify medians and modes for grouped and ungrouped data
- discuss the benefits and drawbacks of these measures
- calculate ranges and quartile deviations
- calculate mean absolute deviations
- calculate variances and standard deviations
- understand coefficients of variation and skewness

# 5.1 | Measures for business data

Chapter 3 discussed some aspects of data collection. Unfortunately, large quantities of raw data tend to overwhelm us with detail and obscure overall patterns: we cannot see the wood for the trees. This means that the data must be processed to give useful information. The process of summarizing data and highlighting general patterns is called **data reduction**. Chapter 4 discussed ways in which data could be reduced and presented in diagrams. In this chapter we are going to extend this idea by looking at numerical ways of summarizing data.

The benefit of diagrams is that they give powerful presentations which show patterns clearly. But they concentrate on overall impressions, giving a 'feel' for the data but not necessarily giving any objective measures. A pie chart, for example, shows patterns very clearly but relies on visual impact rather than accurate measures; a pictogram relies even more on impact. What we really need are some objective measures to describe data. These are given by the numerical measures described in this chapter.

Suppose we have the following data:

32 33 36 38 37 35 35 34 33 35 34 36 35 34 36 35 37 34 35 33

There are 20 observations, but what measures could we use to describe these data and differentiate them from the following set?

2 8 21 10 17 24 18 12 1 16 12 3 7 8 9 10 9 21 19 6

We could start by drawing frequency diagrams as shown in Figure 5.1. Although each set of data has 20 observations, there are two clear differences:

- the second set of data is lower than the first set, with its centre around 12 rather than around 35
- the second set of data is more spread out than the first set, ranging from 1 to 24 rather than 32 to 38

This suggests that we need two measures for data:

> - a **measure of location** to show where the centre of the data is: one suggestion for this is an average value
> - a **measure of spread** to show how spread out the data are around the centre: one suggestion for this is the range of values

If we take a histogram of observations, as shown in Figure 5.2, a measure of location would show where this histogram lies on the $x$ axis, while a measure of spread would show how dispersed the data are along the axis.

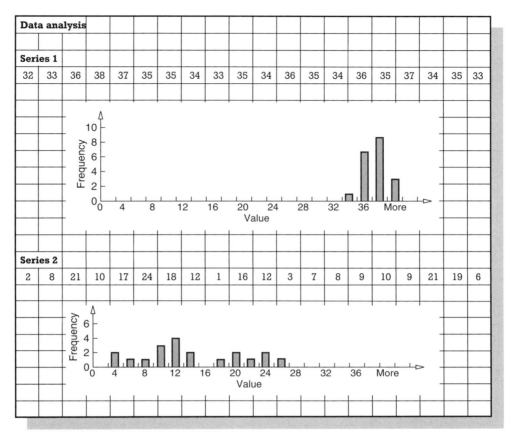

**Figure 5.1** Bar charts of data drawn with a spreadsheet.

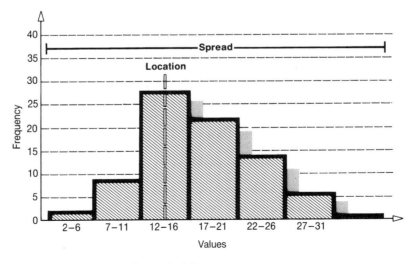

**Figure 5.2** Location and spread of data.

---

*IN SUMMARY*

Raw data must be summarized to give useful information. Diagrams are useful for this, but they emphasize the overall impression and do not give objective measures. Numerical measures are needed to describe data more accurately. Two important measures give the location and spread.

---

## Self-assessment questions

**5.1** What is the main problem with using diagrams to describe data?

**5.2** What is meant by the location of data?

**5.3** 'To fully describe a set of data we only need to measure its location and spread.' Do you think that this is true?

# 5.2 | Finding the average

## 5.2.1 | Introduction

Most people are familiar with the average as some sort of 'typical' value. If we know that the average age of students in a night class is 45, this gives some feel for what the class looks like; if the average income of a group of people is £60,000 a year we know they are prosperous; if houses in a village have an average of six bedrooms we know they are large; and so on. But these are largely intuitive feelings and we really need to discuss what we mean by an 'average' value. We can start by saying that it can be misleading. The group of people with an average income of £60,000 a year might consist of ten people, nine of whom have an income of £10,000 a year and one of whom has an income of £510,000 a year. The village where houses have an average of six bedrooms might have 99 houses with two bedrooms each, and a stately home with 402 bedrooms. In both of these cases the quoted average is accurate, but does not represent a typical value. To get around this problem, we can define different types of average for different purposes. The three most important for business are:

- **arithmetic mean**, or simple average
- **median**, which is the middle value
- **mode**, which is the most frequent value

Each of these is useful in different circumstances, as we shall see in the following sections.

IN SUMMARY

There are several measures for the location of data. We will concentrate on the most useful of these, being arithmetic mean, median and mode.

## 5.2.2 | Arithmetic mean

If you ask a group of people to find the average of 2, 4 and 6, they will usually say 4. This is the most widely used measure of location, which is called the **arithmetic mean**. It is usually abbreviated to the **mean**, and is sometimes called the arithmetic average, simple average, or average.

The method of calculating the (arithmetic) mean is:

1   add all observations together

2   divide this sum by the number of observations

In the illustration above we added all the observations to give $2 + 4 + 6 = 12$ and divided this by the number of observations, 3, to calculate the mean as $12/3 = 4$. We can make some general comments about means, but will first introduce a notation that describes the calculations more efficiently. This uses subscripts.

Suppose we have a set of observations. We could call them $a, b, c, d$ ... etc., but if we have more than 26 observations we run out of letters and have to start using other names. An easier notation is to call the set of data $x$, and identify each observation by a subscript. So $x_1$ is the first observation, $x_2$ is the second observation, $x_3$ is the third observation, and the $n$th observation is $x_n$.

One advantage of this notation is that we can refer to a general observation as $x_i$. Then when $i = 5$, $x_i$ is $x_5$. At first sight this may not seem very useful, but in practice it saves a lot of effort. Suppose, for example, we wanted to add $x_1, x_2, x_3$ and $x_4$. We could write an expression like:

$$y = x_1 + x_2 + x_3 + x_4$$

where $y$ is the sum we want. Alternatively we could write:

$$y = \text{sum of } x_i \text{ when } i = 1, 2, 3 \text{ and } 4$$

There is a standard abbreviation for this calculation which replaces 'sum of' by the Greek letter $\Sigma$, which is a capital sigma. Then we get:

$$y = \Sigma x_i \qquad \text{when } i = 1, 2, 3 \text{ and } 4$$

Ordinarily the values of $i$ are put on top of and below the $\Sigma$ to give:

$$y = \sum_{i=1}^{4} x_i$$

The '$i = 1$' below the $\Sigma$ gives the name of the variable, $i$, and the initial value, 1. The '4' above the $\Sigma$ gives the final value. The steps between the initial and final values are always assumed to be 1.

## WORKED EXAMPLE 5.1

(a) If you have a set of observations, $x$, how would you describe the sum of the first 10 observations?

(b) If you have a set of observations, $a$, how would you describe the sum of the observations numbered 18 to 35?

(c) With the following set of data, $p$, what is the value of:

$$\sum_{i=3}^{9} p_i$$

5 14 13 6 8 10 3 0 5 1 15 8 0

## Solution

(a) We want the sum of $x_i$ when $i = 1$ to 10. This is written as:

$$\sum_{i=1}^{10} x_i$$

(b) We want the sum of $a_i$ from $i = 18$ to 35. This is written as:

$$\sum_{i=18}^{35} a_i$$

(c) This calculates $p_3 + p_4 + p_5 + p_6 + p_7 + p_8 + p_9$. Reading the list of data you can see that $p_3$ is the third number, 13, $p_4$ is the fourth number, 6, and so on. Then the calculation becomes:

$$13 + 6 + 8 + 10 + 3 + 0 + 5 = 45$$

Now we can use this subscript notation to define the mean of a set of data. A common abbreviation is to call the mean $\bar{x}$ which is pronounced 'x bar'. Then the definition of the mean is:

$$\text{mean} = \bar{x} = \frac{x_1 + x_2 + x_3 + \ldots x_n}{n} = \frac{\sum\limits_{i=1}^{n} x_i}{n}$$

## WORKED EXAMPLE 5.2

The times taken to inspect five units coming from a production line are recorded as 3, 4, 1, 7 and 1 minutes. What is the mean?

### Solution

To find the mean we add the observations, $x_i$, and divide by the number of observations, $n$:

$$\text{mean} = \frac{\sum x}{n} = \frac{3 + 4 + 1 + 7 + 1}{5} = \frac{16}{5} = 3.2 \text{ minutes}$$

---

Notice that in this worked example we used the abbreviation $\sum x$ for the summation. When there can be no misunderstanding it is usual to replace the rather cumbersome:

$$\sum_{i=1}^{n} x_i$$

by the simpler

$$\sum x$$

where we assume that all values of $x_i$ are summed from $i = 1$ to $n$. The fuller notation is more precise, but it makes even simple equations seem rather daunting.

You will also notice that the mean of a set of integers is often a real number. This leads to the well known result that the average number of children in a family is 1.8. The mean clearly does not give a typical result, as no family can actually have 1.8 children, but it does give a calculated measure for the location of data.

Occasionally, the arithmetic mean does not even give a reasonable value. Suppose, for example, a company has three owner/directors who are voting on the percentage of profits which should be retained for future investment. If the directors suggest 5%, 7% and 9%, the mean is 7%, and this might be an acceptable value. Suppose, though, that the directors hold 10, 10 and 1000 shares respectively in the company. The views of the third director should carry more weight than the others. In such cases we can define a **weighted mean** where each observation is assigned a weight:

$$\text{weighted mean} = \frac{\sum w_i x_i}{\sum w_i}$$

where:

$$x_i = \text{observation } i$$
$$w_i = \text{weight given to observation } i$$

In the example above we could assign weights to opinions in proportion to the number of shares held. Then the weighted mean becomes:

$$\frac{\text{weighted}}{\text{mean}} = \frac{\sum w_i x_i}{\sum w_i} = \frac{\sum wx}{\sum w} = \frac{(10 \times 5) + (10 \times 7) + (1000 \times 9)}{(10 + 10 + 1000)} = \frac{9120}{1020} = 8.94$$

Often the weights are not this clear and they have to be agreed after discussions.

## WORKED EXAMPLE 5.3

Six observations, 12, 20, 17, 5, 9 and 22, are given the weights 10, 4, 6, 18, 16 and 3 respectively. What is the weighted mean?

### Solution

The weighted mean is:

$$\frac{\sum wx}{\sum w} = \frac{(10 \times 12) + (4 \times 20) + (6 \times 17) + (18 \times 5) + (16 \times 9) + (3 \times 22)}{(10 + 4 + 6 + 18 + 16 + 3)}$$

$$= \frac{602}{57} = 10.6$$

This compares with an arithmetic mean of $(12 + 20 + 17 + 5 + 9 + 22)/6 = 14.2$. The weighted mean clearly puts more emphasis on the lower observations.

We can extend this idea of weighted means to find the mean of data which have already had some processing. Suppose, for example, a set of raw data has been summarized in a frequency table. Then we have a set of **grouped data** where we do not know the actual observations, but we know the number of observations in each class. As we do not have the actual observations we cannot find the true mean, but we can find an approximate value. For this we assume that all observations in a class lie at the midpoint of the class. If, for example, we have ten observations in a class, 20 to 29, we assume that all ten observations have the value $(20 + 29)/2 = 24.5$. Then we calculate the mean in the usual way. The errors in this approximation should be reasonably small.

Suppose we have a frequency distribution for $n$ observations, with:

$$f_i \text{ as the number of observations in class } i$$

and

$$x_i \text{ as the midpoint of class } i$$

The sum of all observations is $\Sigma f_i x_i$, which is usually abbreviated to $\Sigma fx$. Then the mean of grouped data is:

$$\text{mean} = \bar{x} = \frac{\Sigma fx}{\Sigma f} = \frac{\Sigma fx}{n}$$

The top line in this equation is the sum of all observations, while the bottom line is the number of observations.

## WORKED EXAMPLE 5.4

Find the mean of the following discrete frequency distribution:

| Class | 1–3 | 4–6 | 7–9 | 10–12 | 13–15 | 16–18 |
|-------|-----|-----|-----|-------|-------|-------|
| Frequency | 1 | 4 | 8 | 6 | 3 | 1 |

### Solution

The important thing to remember is that the value of $x_i$ is taken as the midpoint of the class. The midpoint of the first class, $x_1$, is $(1 + 3)/2 = 2$, the midpoint of the second class, $x_2$, is $(4 + 6)/2 = 5$, and so on. Figure 5.3 shows the calculations in a

| | A | B | C | D |
|---|---|---|---|---|
| 1 | **Frequency distribution** | | | |
| 2 | | | | |
| 3 | **Class** | **Midpoint** | **Frequency** | |
| 4 | | **x** | **f** | **xf** |
| 5 | | | | |
| 6 | 1 – 3 | 2 | 1 | 2 |
| 7 | 4 – 6 | 5 | 4 | 20 |
| 8 | 7 – 9 | 8 | 8 | 64 |
| 9 | 10 – 12 | 11 | 6 | 66 |
| 10 | 13 – 15 | 14 | 3 | 42 |
| 11 | 16 – 18 | 17 | 1 | 17 |
| 12 | | | | |
| 13 | **Totals** | | 23 | 211 |
| 14 | **Mean** | | | 9.17 |

(a)

**Figure 5.3**  Calculation of the mean for discrete data: (a) values on a spreadsheet.

spreadsheet. Figure 5.3a shows the actual figures, while Figure 5.3b shows the calculations to get these results. The calculated mean value is 9.17.

|   | A | B | C | D |
|---|---|---|---|---|
| 1 | **Frequency distribution** | | | |
| 2 | | | | |
| 3 | **Class** | **Midpoint** | **Frequency** | |
| 4 | | **x** | **f** | **xf** |
| 5 | | | | |
| 6 | 1 – 3 | 2 | 1 | =+B6*C6 |
| 7 | 4 – 6 | 5 | 4 | =+B7*C7 |
| 8 | 7 – 9 | 8 | 8 | =+B8*C8 |
| 9 | 10 – 12 | 11 | 6 | =+B9*C9 |
| 10 | 13 – 15 | 14 | 3 | =+B10*C10 |
| 11 | 16 – 18 | 17 | 1 | =+B11*C11 |
| 12 | | | | |
| 13 | **Totals** | | =SUM(C6:C11) | =SUM(D6:D11) |
| 14 | **Mean** | | | =+D13/C13 |

(b)

**Figure 5.3**  Calculation of the mean for discrete data: (b) calculations.

# WORKED EXAMPLE 5.5

Find the mean of the following continuous frequency distribution:

| Class | 0–0.99 | 1.00–1.99 | 2.00–2.99 | 3.00–3.99 | 4.00–4.99 | 5.00–5.99 |
|---|---|---|---|---|---|---|
| Frequency | 1 | 4 | 8 | 6 | 3 | 1 |

## Solution

The midpoint of the first class, $x_1$, is $(0+0.99)/2 = 0.5$; the midpoint of the second class, $x_2$, is $(1.00+1.99)/2 = 1.50$, and so on, with the calculations shown in Figure 5.4.

| | A | B | C | D |
|---|---|---|---|---|
| 1 | **Frequency distribution** | | | |
| 2 | | | | |
| 3 | **Class** | **x** | **f** | **xf** |
| 4 | | | | |
| 5 | 0 – 0.99 | 0.5 | 1 | 0.5 |
| 6 | 1.00–1.99 | 1.5 | 4 | 6 |
| 7 | 2.00–2.99 | 2.5 | 8 | 20 |
| 8 | 3.00–3.99 | 3.5 | 6 | 21 |
| 9 | 4.00–4.99 | 4.5 | 3 | 13.5 |
| 10 | 5.00–5.99 | 5.5 | 1 | 5.5 |
| 11 | | | | |
| 12 | **Totals** | | 23 | 66.5 |
| 13 | **Mean** | | | 2.89 |

**Figure 5.4** Calculation of the mean for continuous data.

The arithmetic mean usually gives a reasonable measure for location and has the advantages of being:

● easy to calculate

● familiar and easy to understand

● able to use all the data

● useful in a number of other analyses

● objective

But it also has some weaknesses. Suppose seven people enter a shop during a 10 minute spell. The mean number of people entering each minute is 0.7, so we are left asking, 'What does 0.7 people mean?' The problem is that means can take any value, even when dealing with discrete data.

A further problem is that the mean can be misleading. If we know that five students get a mean mark of 50% in an exam, we would expect this to represent a typical value. But if the students' marks are 100%, 40%, 40%, 35% and 35%, four results are below the mean while only one is above.

A specific problem with grouped data comes with open classes such as 'more than 100'. For these we have to make some assumptions about the limits before doing the calculation. If, for example, we are running a survey of pupils in schools, we might have a distribution of age which has a class '5 and younger'. Then it would be reasonable to suggest a lower limit on this class of 4. The only guidance for finding suitable limits is to look at the data and use common sense.

In general, then, we can suggest that the mean has the following disadvantages. It:

- only works with cardinal data
- can be misleading
- may be some distance from the majority of observations
- is affected by outlying results
- can give fractional values, even for discrete data
- is approximated for grouped data

We really need some other measures for location to overcome these disadvantages, and the two most common alternatives are median and mode.

---

**IN SUMMARY**

The most commonly used measure of location is the arithmetic mean, which is calculated by $\sum x/n$ for ungrouped data and $\sum fx/\sum f$ for grouped data.

## 5.2.3 | Median

If a set of data is arranged in order of increasing size, the **median** is defined as the middle value. So the median of 10, 20 and 30 is 20. This measure does not really need any calculation, but we can find it by observation using the procedure:

1 arrange the observations in order of size
2 find the number of observations and hence the middle observation
3 identify the median as this middle value

With $n$ observations the median is the value of observation $(n + 1)/2$ when they are sorted into order.

---

## WORKED EXAMPLE 5.6

The times taken to inspect five units coming from a production line are recorded as 13, 14, 11, 17 and 11 minutes. What is the median?

### Solution

We find the median by arranging the values in order and selecting the middle one. There are five observations so the median is number $(5 + 1)/2 = 3$.

$$11, 11, \mathbf{13}, 14, 17 \qquad \text{median} = 13$$

---

There is an obvious problem with an even number of observations. Suppose the last worked example had one more observation of 16 minutes to give values of:

11, 11, 13, 14, 16, 17

With six observations the middle one is number $(6 + 1)/2 = 3.5$, so its value is somewhere between 13 and 14. The usual convention is to take the mean of these two values, to give the median as $(13 + 14)/2 = 13.5$. This gives a value which did not actually occur, but is the best estimate we can get.

If data are shown as a frequency distribution, finding the median is slightly more complicated. We have to start by seeing which class the median is in, and then find how far up this class it is. This is shown in the following worked example.

## WORKED EXAMPLE 5.7

Find the median of the following continuous frequency distribution:

| Class | 0–0.99 | 1.00–1.99 | 2.00–2.99 | 3.00–3.99 | 4.00–4.99 | 5.00–5.99 |
|---|---|---|---|---|---|---|
| Frequency | 1 | 4 | 8 | 6 | 3 | 1 |

## Solution

There are 23 observations, so when these are sorted into order the median is observation number $(n + 1)/2 = (23 + 1)/2 = 12$. There is one observation in the first class (0–0.99) and there are four in the second class (1.00–1.99), so the median is the seventh observation in the third class (2.00–2.99). As there are eight observations in this class, we can reasonably assume that the median is 7/8th of the way up the class. In other words:

$$\text{median} = \text{lower limit of third class} + \frac{7}{8} \times \text{width of third class}$$

$$= 2.00 + \frac{7}{8} \times (2.99 - 2.00) = 2.87$$

This calculation is equivalent to drawing an ogive (which plots cumulative number of observations against value) and finding the value on the $x$ axis which corresponds to the 12th point on the $y$ axis, as shown in Figure 5.5.

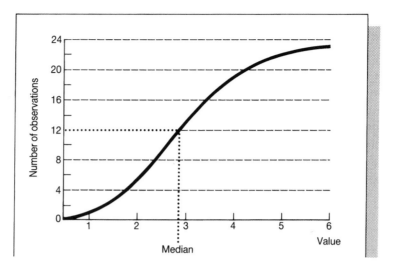

**Figure 5.5**  Finding the median from the ogive for Worked Example 5.7.

The median is quite widely used and understood. Its main advantages are that it:

- is easy to understand
- usually gives a value which actually occurred (except with grouped data)
- does not give fractional or impossible values (except with grouped data)
- can be used when the mean would be misleading
- is not affected by outlying values
- needs no calculation (for ungrouped data)

Conversely it has disadvantages, including that it:

- can only be used with cardinal data
- can give values which have not actually occurred (for grouped data)
- is not so easy to use in other analyses

IN SUMMARY

The median is the middle value, when observations are ranked in order of size. This sometimes gives a more typical result than the mean.

| 5.2.4 | Mode

The **mode** is the value which occurs most frequently. If we have four values 5, 7, 7 and 9, the value which occurs most frequently is 7, so this is the mode. Like the median, the mode relies more on observation than calculation. The way to find it is:

1   draw a frequency table for the data
2   identify the mode as the most frequent value

## WORKED EXAMPLE 5.8

The times taken to serve 12 customers in a shop have been recorded as 3, 4, 3, 1, 5, 2, 3, 3, 2, 4, 3 and 2 minutes. What is the mode of the times?

### Solution

Translating the data into a frequency table gives the following result:

| Class | Frequency |
|:-----:|:---------:|
| 1 | 1 |
| 2 | 3 |
| **3** | **5** |
| 4 | 2 |
| 5 | 1 |

The most frequent value is 3, so this is the mode. This compares with a mean of 2.7 minutes and a median of 3 minutes.

Sometimes there are several modes to a set of data. Consider the following observations:

$$3, 5, 3, 7, 6, 7, 4, 3, 7, 6, 7, 3, 2, 3, 2, 4, 6, 7, 8$$

A frequency table of these shows that the most frequent values are 3 and 7, which both appear five times. Then we say the data have two modes (they are bimodal) at 3 and 7, as illustrated in Figure 5.6. It is common for data to have several modes (being multimodal).

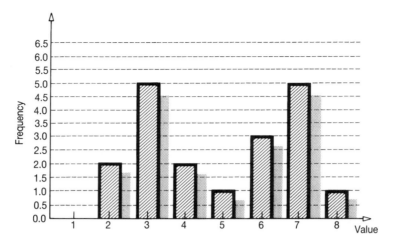

**Figure 5.6**  Frequency distribution for bimodal data.

When data are grouped in a frequency distribution, finding the mode is a bit more difficult. We have to start by identifying the modal class, which is the class with most observations. This gives the range within which the mode lies, but we still have to identify an actual value. The easiest way of finding this is to draw the two crossing lines, shown in the histogram in Figure 5.7. The point where these two lines cross is the mode. But this does not give a very useful analysis, and in practice the mode of grouped data is rarely used.

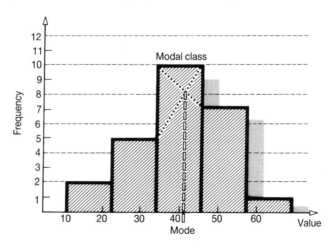

**Figure 5.7**  Calculating the mode for grouped data.

The mode has several advantages including that it:
- is an actual value (except for grouped data)
- shows the most frequent value
- needs no calculation (except for grouped data)
- can be used with non-numerical data

Conversely the disadvantages are:

- there can be several modes
- it cannot be used in further analyses
- it ignores all data that are not at the mode
- it is not very useful for grouped data

---

### IN SUMMARY

The mode is the most frequently occurring value in a set of data. Although useful in some circumstances, this is probably the least widely used measure of location.

## 5.2.5 | Choice of measure

We have now discussed three measures for the location of data, each of which describes a different aspect of the average:

- the mean gives the simple average of the data
- the median finds the middle observation
- the mode finds the most frequent value

Figure 5.8 shows a histogram of data and the typical relationship between mean, median and mode. If the histogram is symmetrical the three measures coincide, but if the histogram is asymmetrical the measures can differ by quite a lot. The best one to use depends on both the type of data and the purpose of the information. As with graphical summaries of data, the choice of best in any circumstances is often a matter of opinion.

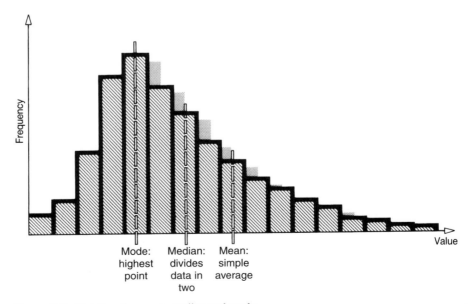

**Figure 5.8**   Relating the mean, median and mode.

Perhaps you can get more feel for the alternative measures of location from the following worked example.

## WORKED EXAMPLE 5.9

Two doctors and three receptionists work in a village health centre. Last year the gross annual salaries earned by these five were £52,000, £48,000, £14,000 £8000 and £8000. How could you describe the pay? Which is the most useful measure?

### Solution

The mean pay is £26,000 a year, the median is £14,000 and the mode is £8000. Here the mean gives a value which is not close to any observation, and the mode shows the lowest income. Although none is perfect, the median is probably the best measure.

Spreadsheets usually have a number of standard statistical functions, as shown in Figure 5.9.

| | A | B | C | D | E | F | G | H |
|---|---|---|---|---|---|---|---|---|
| 1 | **Descriptive statistics** | | | | | | | |
| 2 | | | | | | | | |
| 3 | **Number** | **Value** | | **Description** | | | **Sorted** | |
| 4 | | | | | | | | |
| 5 | 1 | 4 | | **Number** | 12 | | 1 | |
| 6 | 2 | 7 | | **Minimum** | 1 | | 2 | Mode |
| 7 | 3 | 6 | | **Maximum** | 9 | | 2 | |
| 8 | 4 | 9 | | **Range** | 8 | | 3 | |
| 9 | 5 | 1 | | | | | 3 | |
| 10 | 6 | 3 | | | | | 4 | Median |
| 11 | 7 | 2 | | **Mean** | 4.5 | | 4 | Mean + |
| 12 | 8 | 5 | | **Median** | 4 | | 5 | |
| 13 | 9 | 8 | | **Mode** | 2 | | 6 | |
| 14 | 10 | 3 | | | | | 7 | |
| 15 | 11 | 4 | | **Class** | **Frequency** | | 8 | |
| 16 | 12 | 2 | | 1 | 1 | | 9 | |
| 17 | | | | 2 | 2 | | | |
| 18 | | | | 3 | 2 | | | |
| 19 | | | | 4 | 2 | | | |
| 20 | | | | 5 | 1 | | | |
| 21 | | | | 6 | 1 | | | |
| 22 | | | | 7 | 1 | | | |
| 23 | | | | 8 | 1 | | | |
| 24 | | | | 9 | 1 | | | |

**Figure 5.9**   Description of data from a spreadsheet.

---

*IN SUMMARY*

The mean, median and mode all have distinct meanings and uses. You should be careful to use the most appropriate measure.

---

## Self-assessment questions

**5.4** 'The average of a set of data has a clear meaning which accurately describes the data.' Is this statement true?

**5.5** Define three measures for the average of a set of data.

**5.6** Why is the mean so widely used?

**5.7** If the mean of ten observations is 34, and the mean of an additional five observations is 37, what is the mean of all 15 observations?

**5.8** Why are we not concerned about the difficulty of calculating measures of location?

# 5.3 | Measuring the spread of data

## 5.3.1 | Initial measures

Averages give a measure for the location of a set of data, but they do not show the spread or dispersion. The average age of students in a night class might be 45 but this does not say if they are all around the same age, or if the ages range from 5 to 95. The dispersion is often important. A local authority may find that the mean number of people visiting a mobile library is 500 a week. This is useful information, but it would be even more useful if they knew how the numbers varied. There might be little variation from, say, 490 on quiet weeks to 510 on busy weeks; or there might be large variations between 0 and 2000. It is obviously easier to organize the library to deal with a steady demand than to cope with a widely fluctuating one.

The simplest measure of spread is the **range**, which is the difference between the largest and smallest values:

$$\text{range} = \text{maximum value} - \text{minimum value}$$

This calculation is easy for ungrouped data. It is more difficult for grouped data, because taking the range as the top of the largest class to the bottom of the smallest class gives a result that depends more on how the classes are defined than on the range of actual observations.

Another problem is that the range can be affected by one or two extreme values. A convenient way of overcoming any bias introduced by a few extreme results is to ignore outlying observations which are some distance from the mean. We can do this using **quartiles**. Quartiles are defined as values which are a quarter of the way through the data. Then we can define:

- $Q_1$ as the first quartile, which is the value below which 25% of observations lie
- $Q_2$ as the second quartile, which is halfway through the data and is, therefore, the median
- $Q_3$ as the third quartile, below which 75% of observations lie

We can use these quartiles to find a narrower range $Q_3$–$Q_1$ which contains 50% of observations. Then the **quartile deviation** or **semi-interquartile range** is calculated as:

$$\text{quartile deviation} = \frac{Q_3 - Q_1}{2}$$

It follows that data with a high quartile deviation are widely spread out, while data with a low quartile deviation are more compact. In practice, the quartile deviation is usually found for grouped data.

## WORKED EXAMPLE 5.10

Find the quartile deviation for the following data:

| Class | 0–9.9 | 10–19.9 | 20–29.9 | 30–39.9 | 40–49.9 | 50–59.9 | 60–69.9 |
|---|---|---|---|---|---|---|---|
| Observations | 5 | 19 | 38 | 43 | 34 | 17 | 4 |

### Solution

There are a total of 160 observations, or 40 in each quarter. When the observations are ranked, the first quartile, $Q_1$, is the 40th and the third quartile, $Q_3$, is the 120th.

- $Q_1$ is the 16th observation out of 38 in the class $20 - 29.9$, so a reasonable value is:

$$20 + (16/38) \times (29.9 - 20) = 24.2$$

- $Q_3$ is the 15th observation out of 34 in the class of $40 - 49.9$, so a reasonable value is:

$$40 + (15/34) \times (49.9 - 40) = 44.4$$

Then the quartile deviation is:

$$\frac{Q_3 - Q_1}{2} = \frac{44.4 - 24.2}{2} = 10.1$$

You can see these points in the ogive in Figure 5.10.

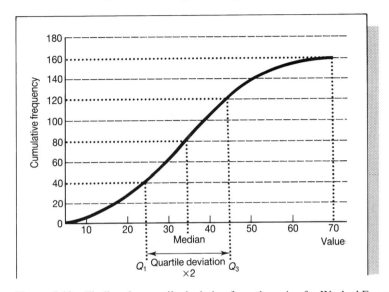

**Figure 5.10**    Finding the quartile deviation from the ogive for Worked Example 5.10.

There are several extensions to the calculation of quartile deviation which are usually based on various percentiles. The 5th percentile, for example, is defined as the value with 5% of observations below it, while the 95th percentile is defined as the value with 95% of observations below it. A frequent measure finds the range between the 5th and 95th percentile. This type of measure is useful for ignoring extreme values but it can ignore data which are very important.

---

IN SUMMARY

Two common measures of spread are range and quartile deviation. These are simple measures which describe the amount of dispersion in data.

## 5.3.2 | Mean absolute deviation

The quartile deviation is clearly related to the median. Other measures of spread are more closely related to the mean. In particular, they are based on the distance each observation is away from the mean, which is called the **deviation**:

$$\text{deviation} = (\text{value} - \text{mean value}) = (x_i - \bar{x})$$

Each observation has a deviation, so the mean of these deviations gives a measure of spread. The larger the mean deviation, the more dispersed the data. Unfortunately, the mean deviation has the major disadvantage of allowing positive and negative deviations to cancel. If we have observations of 3, 4 and 8, the mean is 5 and the mean deviation is:

$$\text{mean deviation} = \frac{(3 - 5) + (4 - 5) + (8 - 5)}{3} = 0$$

So a set of dispersed data can have a mean deviation of zero. The measure is clearly unreliable and is, therefore, rarely used. A more useful alternative is the **mean absolute deviation** (MAD), which simply takes the absolute values of deviations from the mean. In other words it ignores negative signs and adds all deviations as if they are positive. This gives a measure of the average distance of observations from the mean.

$$\text{mean absolute deviation} = \frac{\sum \text{ABS}(x - \bar{x})}{n}$$

$$\text{MAD} = \frac{\sum |x - \bar{x}|}{n}$$

where:

$x$ = the observations

$\bar{x}$ = mean value of observations

$n$ = number of observations

$\text{ABS}(x - \bar{x})$ = the absolute value of $x - \bar{x}$
(that is, ignoring sign): this is also written as $|x - \bar{x}|$

The steps in calculating the mean absolute deviation are:

1 calculate the mean value

2 find the deviation of each observation from this mean

3 take the absolute values of these deviations

4 add the absolute values

5 divide this sum by the number of observations to give the MAD

It is worth mentioning that many people refer to the mean absolute deviation as the mean deviation, so you should be careful to find exactly which measure is being used.

## WORKED EXAMPLE 5.11

What is the mean absolute deviation of 4, 7, 6, 10 and 8?

### Solution

The mean of the numbers is:

$$\bar{x} = \frac{4 + 7 + 6 + 10 + 8}{5} = 7$$

Then the mean absolute deviation is calculated as:

$$\text{MAD} = \frac{|4 - 7| + |7 - 7| + |6 - 7| + |10 - 7| + |8 - 7|}{5}$$

$$= \frac{|-3| + |0| + |-1| + |3| + |1|}{5} = \frac{3 + 0 + 1 + 3 + 1}{5} = 1.6$$

This tells us that on average the observations are 1.6 units away from the mean.

The calculation of MAD for grouped data is a little longer. We saw that the mean of a set of grouped data was found by taking the midpoint of each class and multiplying this by the number of observations in the class. We can use the same approach to calculate mean absolute deviations. The absolute deviation of each class is the difference between the midpoint of the class and the mean. So for grouped data the mean absolute deviation is defined as:

$$\text{mean absolute deviation} = \frac{\sum |x - \bar{x}|f}{\sum f} = \frac{\sum |x - \bar{x}|f}{n}$$

where:

$x$ = midpoint of a class

$f$ = number of observations in the class

$\bar{x}$ = mean value of all observations

$n$ = total number of observations

## WORKED EXAMPLE 5.12

Find the mean absolute deviation of the following data:

| Class | 0–4.9 | 5–9.9 | 10–14.9 | 15–19.9 | 20–24.9 |
|-------|-------|-------|---------|---------|---------|
| Frequency | 3 | 5 | 7 | 6 | 2 |

### Solution

Figure 5.11 shows this calculation on a spreadsheet. There are 23 observations with a mean of 12.28. This is used to find the deviation of each class. The calculated mean absolute deviation is 4.63, implying that observations are, on average, 4.63 from the mean.

| | A | B | C | D | E | F | G |
|---|---|---|---|---|---|---|---|
| 1 | | | | **Mean absolute deviation** | | | |
| 2 | | | | | | | |
| 3 | **Class** | **x** | **f** | **f*x** | **deviation** | **abs.dev.** | **f* abs. dev.** |
| 4 | | | | | | | |
| 5 | **0–4.9** | 2.5 | 3 | 7.5 | -9.78 | 9.78 | 29.35 |
| 6 | **5–9.9** | 7.5 | 5 | 37.5 | -4.78 | 4.78 | 23.91 |
| 7 | **10–14.9** | 12.5 | 7 | 87.5 | 0.22 | 0.22 | 1.52 |
| 8 | **15–19.9** | 17.5 | 6 | 105 | 5.22 | 5.22 | 31.30 |
| 9 | **20–24.9** | 22.5 | 2 | 45 | 10.22 | 10.22 | 20.43 |
| 10 | | | | | | | |
| 11 | **Sums** | | 23.00 | 282.50 | | | 106.52 |
| 12 | **Means** | | | 12.28 | | | 4.63 |

**Figure 5.11**    Spreadsheet for calculating the MAD in Worked Example 5.12.

By taking absolute values we make sure that positive and negative deviations do not cancel. The result is a measure which is easy to calculate and which is based on all observations. It also has a clear meaning: if the MAD is 2, observations are an average of 2 units away from the mean. It follows that larger MADs show a wider dispersion of data.

One drawback with the mean absolute deviation is that it can be affected by a few extreme values. But a more important problem is the difficulty of using it in any other statistical analyses. This tends to limit its use and an alternative, the variance, is more widely used.

IN SUMMARY

The absolute deviation is the difference between an observation and the mean. This can be used to calculate the mean absolute deviation for a set of data, which gives a clear measure of spread.

## 5.3.3 | Variance and standard deviation

The mean absolute deviation stopped positive and negative deviations from cancelling by taking absolute values. An alternative, which is equally simple, is to square the deviations. This is the basis of the **variance**, which finds the mean squared error. The variance has all the advantages of MAD, but overcomes some of its limitations.

$$\text{variance} = \frac{\sum (x - \bar{x})^2}{n}$$

An obvious problem with the variance is that the units are the square of the units of the original observations. If, for example, the observations are measured in tonnes the variance will have the meaningless units of tonnes$^2$. To return the units to normal, the square root of the variance can be taken. This gives the most widely used measure of spread, which is called the **standard deviation.**

$$\text{standard deviation} = s = \sqrt{\frac{\sum (x - \bar{x})^2}{n}} = \sqrt{\text{variance}}$$

The calculation of variance, and hence standard deviation, is very similar to the calculation of the mean absolute deviation. So the steps are:

1   calculate the mean value
2   find the deviation of each observation from this mean
3   take the square of these deviations
4   add the squares
5   divide this sum by the number of observations to give variance
6   take the square root of the variance to give the standard deviation

## WORKED EXAMPLE 5.13

Find the variance and standard deviation of 2, 3, 7, 8 and 10.

### Solution

The mean of these numbers is (2 + 3 + 7 + 8 + 10)/5 = 6.
 Then the deviations, defined as $(x - \bar{x})$, are:

$$2 - 6 = -4, \qquad 3 - 6 = -3, \qquad 7 - 6 = 1, \qquad 8 - 6 = 2 \qquad \text{and} \qquad 10 - 6 = 4$$

The variance is found by squaring these deviations, adding them and dividing by the number of observations to get the mean squared deviation:

$$\text{variance} = \frac{\Sigma(x - \bar{x})^2}{n}$$

$$= \frac{(-4)^2 + (-3)^2 + (1)^2 + (2)^2 + (4)^2}{5} = \frac{46}{5} = 9.2$$

Then the standard deviation is the square root of the variance:

$$\text{standard deviation} = s = \sqrt{9.2} = 3.03$$

The standard deviation is the most widely used measure of dispersion. Obviously, the bigger its value, the more spread out are the data. But its main strength is that a certain number of observations are almost always within, say, 2 standard deviations of the mean. This analysis was first done by Chebyshev, who found that for any sample:

● at least 3/4 of observations will fall within 2 standard deviations of the mean, i.e. in the range $(\bar{x} + 2s)$ to $(\bar{x} - 2s)$

● at least 8/9 of observations will fall within 3 standard deviations of the mean, i.e. in the range $(\bar{x} + 3s)$ to $(\bar{x} - 3s)$

● in general, if $k$ is any number greater than one, at least $(1 - 1/k^2)$ observations will fall within $k$ standard deviations of the mean, i.e. in the range $(\bar{x} + ks)$ to $(\bar{x} - ks)$

This rule is actually quite conservative, and observations suggest that for a frequency distribution with a single mode, 68% of observations will usually fall within 1 standard deviation of the mean, 95% of observations within 2 standard deviations and almost all observations within 3 standard deviations.

## WORKED EXAMPLE 5.14

Find the mean and standard deviation of the following 20 numbers. How many observations fall within 1, 2 and 3 standard deviations of the mean?

10.8  17.4  8.3  9.1  4.7  2.9  12.0  11.8  14.1  9.0

7.3  6.2  8.4  14.7  12.0  5.0  7.7  10.1  6.9  7.8

### Solution

The mean is $(\sum x)/n = 9.31$

The variance is:

$$\frac{\sum(x - \bar{x})^2}{n} = 12.30$$

so the standard deviation is $\sqrt{12.30} = 3.52$

- The range within one standard deviation of the mean is:

   $9.31 - 3.52$   to   $9.31 + 3.52$

   or:

   5.79   to   12.83

   There are 16 observations (80% of the total) within this range.

- The range within two standard deviations of the mean is:

   $9.31 - (2 \times 3.52)$   to   $9.31 + (2 \times 3.52)$

   or:

   2.27   to   16.35

   There are 19 observations (95% of the total) within this range.

- The range within three standard deviations of the mean is:

   $9.31 - (3 \times 3.52)$   to   $9.31 + (3 \times 3.52)$

   or:

   $-1.25$   to   19.87

   There are 20 observations (100% of the total) within this range.

We can now extend the calculations for variance and standard deviation to grouped data. As with the mean, the actual observations are approximated by the midpoint of the classes, giving:

$$\text{variance} = \frac{\sum (x - \bar{x})^2 f}{\sum f} = \frac{\sum (x - \bar{x})^2 f}{n}$$

$$\text{standard deviation} = \sqrt{\text{variance}}$$

$$s = \sqrt{\frac{\sum (x - \bar{x})^2 f}{\sum f}} = \sqrt{\frac{\sum (x - \bar{x})^2 f}{n}}$$

## WORKED EXAMPLE 5.15

Find the variance and standard deviation of the following data:

| *Class* | 0–4.9 | 5–9.9 | 10–14.9 | 15–19.9 | 20–24.9 |
|---------|-------|-------|---------|---------|---------|
| *Frequency* | 3 | 5 | 7 | 6 | 2 |

### Solution

Figure 5.12 shows the result on a spreadsheet. The mean of the 23 observations is 12.28 and this is used to find the deviations. Then the variance is calculated as 33.65, so the standard deviation is $\sqrt{33.65} = 5.8$.

| | A | B | C | D | E | F | G |
|---|---|---|---|---|---|---|---|
| 1 | **Variance** | | | | | | |
| 2 | | | | | | | |
| 3 | **Class** | **x** | **f** | **f*x** | **deviation** | **dev.sqrd.** | **f* dev.sqrd** |
| 4 | | | | | | | |
| 5 | **0–4.9** | 2.5 | 3 | 7.5 | –9.78 | 95.70 | 287.10 |
| 6 | **5–9.9** | 7.5 | 5 | 37.5 | –4.78 | 22.87 | 114.37 |
| 7 | **10–14.9** | 12.5 | 7 | 87.5 | 0.22 | 0.05 | 0.33 |
| 8 | **15–19.9** | 17.5 | 6 | 105 | 5.22 | 27.22 | 163.33 |
| 9 | **20–24.9** | 22.5 | 2 | 45 | 10.22 | 104.40 | 208.79 |
| 10 | | | | | | | |
| 11 | **Sums** | | 23.00 | 282.50 | | | 773.91 |
| 12 | **Means** | | | 12.28 | | | 33.65 |

**Figure 5.12**  Calculation of variance and standard deviation for grouped data.

One problem with variance and standard deviation is that they do not have a direct meaning like the mean absolute deviation. A large variance shows more spread than a smaller one, so we know that data with a variance of 22.5 are less spread out than equivalent data with a variance of 42.5. But the figures do not have any real meaning. Perhaps their most important property is that they can be used in a number of other analyses. Because of this they are the most widely used measures of dispersion.

One important feature of variances is that they can sometimes be added. Provided two sets of observations are completely unrelated (which is technically described as their covariance being zero) the variance of the sum of data is equal to the sum of the variances of each set. If, for example, the daily demand for an item has a variance of 4, while the daily demand for a second item has a variance of 5, the variance of total demand for both items is $4 + 5 = 9$. Standard deviations can never be added in this way.

# WORKED EXAMPLE 5.16

The mean weight and standard deviation of airline passengers are known to be 72 kg and 6 kg respectively. What is the mean weight and standard deviation of total passenger weight in a 200 seat aeroplane?

## Solution

The mean weight of 200 passengers is found by multiplying the mean weight of each passenger by the number of passengers:

$$\text{mean} = 200 \times 72 = 14\,400 \text{ kg}$$

Standard deviations cannot be added, but variances can. So the variance in weight of 200 passengers is found by multiplying the variance in weight of each passenger by the number of passengers:

$$\text{variance} = 200 \times 6^2 = 7200 \text{ kg}^2$$

The standard deviation in total weight is $\sqrt{7200} = 84.85$ kg

## IN SUMMARY

The most widely used measure of data spread is the variance, which is the mean squared deviation. The square root of this is the standard deviation.

# 5.3.4 | Other measures for data

In the last section we said that the standard deviation was important because it can be used for other analyses. Here we will mention two of these. The first calculates a coefficient of variation, while the second deals with the skewness of a frequency distribution.

The measures of dispersion described so far can describe a set of data, but they cannot compare different sets. The standard deviation, for example, calculates the dispersion of data around its mean, so unless two sets of data have the same mean we cannot really use the standard deviation to compare their relative dispersions. What we need is some means of relating dispersion and location. One measure for this is the **coefficient of variation**, which is defined as the ratio of standard deviation over mean.

$$\text{coefficient of variation} = \frac{\text{standard deviation}}{\text{mean}}$$

The higher the coefficient of variation, the more dispersed are the data. We might, for example, look at the costs of operating various facilities in one year and find a coefficient of variation of 0.8. If the coefficient rises to 0.9 in the following year it shows that there is more variation in costs, regardless of how these costs have changed in absolute terms.

A second measure based on the standard deviation is the **coefficient of skewness**. Frequency distributions may be symmetrical about their mean, or they may be skewed, as shown in Figure 5.13.

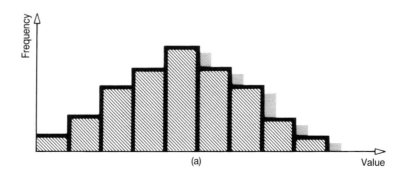

**Figure 5.13**   Various shapes of frequency distributions: (a) symmetrical.

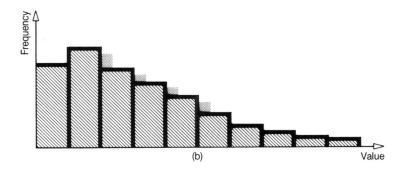

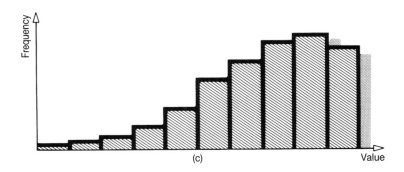

**Figure 5.13**   Various shapes of frequency distributions:
(b) positive skew;   (c) negative skew.

We really need some measure of skewness. Several measures are available for this, but a common one is Pearson's coefficient of skewness. This is defined as:

$$\text{coefficient of skewness} = \frac{3 \times (\text{mean} - \text{median})}{\text{standard deviation}}$$

This automatically gives the correct sign of the skew. Its precise interpretation is somewhat difficult, but values around +1 or –1 are generally considered highly skewed.

# WORKED EXAMPLE 5.17

Figure 5.14 shows a description of some data prepared by a spreadsheet. Can you say what the program has calculated?

| | A | B | C | D | E | F | G |
|---|---|---|---|---|---|---|---|
| 1 | **Data description** | | | | | | |
| 2 | | | | | | | |
| 3 | **Data** | | | | | **Description** | |
| 4 | | | | | | | |
| 5 | 15 | 38 | 26 | 42 | | Mean | 34.85 |
| 6 | 23 | 40 | 32 | 51 | | Median | 38 |
| 7 | 41 | 37 | 40 | 47 | | Mode | 40 |
| 8 | 16 | 52 | 50 | 51 | | Standard deviation | 12.73 |
| 9 | 32 | 20 | 18 | 30 | | Variance | 162.05 |
| 10 | 29 | 33 | 24 | 20 | | Kurtosis | −1.06 |
| 11 | 10 | 14 | 27 | 39 | | Skewness | −0.24 |
| 12 | 52 | 57 | 45 | 48 | | Range | 47 |
| 13 | 17 | 48 | 40 | 38 | | Minimum | 10 |
| 14 | 23 | 39 | 46 | 44 | | Maximum | 57 |
| 15 | | | | | | Sum | 1394 |
| 16 | | | | | | Count | 40 |

**Figure 5.14**  Description of data on a spreadsheet.

## Solution

After the headings, the first four columns, A – D, show the raw data. Then columns F and G show a number of measures describing these data. These include measure of location – the mean, median and mode; measures of dispersion – standard deviation, range, minimum and maximum; measures of shape – skewness and kurtosis (which is just another measure for the shape of a distribution); and general measures – number of observations and sum.

IN SUMMARY

The standard deviation can be used for other analyses, including the coefficients of variation and skewness.

# Self-assessment questions

**5.9** List four measures for data spread. Are there any other measures?

**5.10** Why is the mean deviation not used to measure data dispersion?

**5.11** If the mean of a set of observations is 10.37 metres, what are the units of the variance?

**5.12** Why is the standard deviation so widely used, when its practical meaning is unclear?

**5.13** Two sets of data have means of 10.2 and 33.4 and variances of 4.3 and 18.2. What does this tell you?

---

| CHAPTER REVIEW |

This chapter discussed ways in which sets of data can be described numerically. It concentrated on measures for location and spread. In particular it:

- talked about the need for numerical descriptions of data
- described measures for the location of data
- calculated the arithmetic mean, median and mode
- considered measures for the spread of data, starting with the range and quartile deviation
- calculated mean absolute deviation, variance and standard deviation
- mentioned the coefficients of variation and skewness

---

# Problems

**5.1** When Marcia Grosse was in hospital the number of visitors she received in five consecutive days were 4, 2, 1, 7 and 1. What are the mean, median and mode of numbers visiting?

**5.2** Find the mean, median and mode of the following numbers:

24 26 23 24 23 24 27 26 28 25 21 22 25 23 26 29 27 24 25 24 24 25

**5.3** Find the mean, median and mode of the following discrete frequency distribution:

| Class | 0–5 | 6–10 | 11–15 | 16–20 | 21–25 |
|---|---|---|---|---|---|
| Frequency | 1 | 5 | 10 | 8 | 2 |

**5.4** Find the mean, median and mode of the frequency distribution shown in the following table:

| Class | 1.00–2.99 | 3.00–4.99 | 5.00–6.99 | 7.00–8.99 | 9.00–10.99 | 11.00–12.99 |
|---|---|---|---|---|---|---|
| Frequency | 2 | 6 | 15 | 22 | 12 | 4 |

**5.5** Find the mean, median and mode of the frequency distribution shown in the following table:

| Class | 0–9.9 | 10–19.9 | 20–29.9 | 30–39.9 | 40–49.9 | 50–59.9 | 60–69.9 | 70–79.9 | 80–89.9 |
|---|---|---|---|---|---|---|---|---|---|
| Frequency | 2 | 15 | 27 | 32 | 25 | 19 | 12 | 7 | 1 |

**5.6** Find the mean absolute deviation, variance and standard deviation of 27, 32, 34, 28, 35, 30.

**5.7** Find the variance and standard deviation of the following data:

3   45   28   83   62   44   60   18   73   44   59   67   78   32   74   28
67   97   34   44   23   66   25   12   58   9   34   58   29   45   37   91
73   50   10   71   72   19   18   27   41   91   90   23   23   33

**5.8** Measure the spread of the ungrouped data described in Problems 5.1 and 5.2.

**5.9** Measure the spread of the grouped data described in Problems 5.3 to 5.5.

**5.10** How would you summarize the following data?

121 148 167 101 205 192 105 118 146  97 133 160 194 185 151

130 167 159 147 203  99 109 137 165 171 182 144 186 108 170

**5.11** The Langborne Hotel is concerned about the number of people who book rooms by telephone but do not actually turn up. Over the past few weeks it has kept records of the number of people who do this, as shown below. How can these data be summarized?

| Day | 1 | 2 | 3 | 4 | 5 | 6 | 7 | 8 | 9 | 10 | 11 | 12 | 13 | 14 | 15 |
|---|---|---|---|---|---|---|---|---|---|---|---|---|---|---|---|
| No-shows | 4 | 5 | 2 | 3 | 3 | 2 | 1 | 4 | 7 | 2 | 0 | 3 | 1 | 4 | 5 |
| Day | 16 | 17 | 18 | 19 | 20 | 21 | 22 | 23 | 24 | 25 | 26 | 27 | 28 | 29 | 30 |
| No-shows | 2 | 6 | 2 | 3 | 3 | 4 | 2 | 5 | 5 | 2 | 4 | 3 | 3 | 1 | 4 |
| Day | 31 | 32 | 33 | 34 | 35 | 36 | 37 | 38 | 39 | 40 | 41 | 42 | 43 | 44 | 45 |
| No-shows | 5 | 3 | 6 | 4 | 3 | 1 | 4 | 5 | 6 | 3 | 3 | 2 | 4 | 3 | 4 |

# Computer exercises

**5.1** Many programs describe data numerically. Figure 5.15 shows some results from a spreadsheet. Design your own spreadsheet to give a better version of these results. Compare these with standard functions.

|  | A | B | C | D | E | F | G |
|---|---|---|---|---|---|---|---|
| 1 |  |  | Measures of dispersion |  |  |  |  |
| 2 |  |  |  |  |  |  |  |
| 3 |  | Class |  |  |  | Sums | Means |
| 4 |  | 0–9.99 | 10–19.99 | 20–29.99 | 30–39.99 |  |  |
| 5 |  |  |  |  |  |  |  |
| 6 | x | 5 | 15 | 25 | 35 |  |  |
| 7 | f | 4 | 17 | 22 | 7 | 50 |  |
| 8 |  |  |  |  |  |  |  |
| 9 | f*x | 20 | 255 | 550 | 245 | 1070 | 21.4 |
| 10 |  |  |  |  |  |  |  |
| 11 | deviation | −16.4 | −6.4 | 3.6 | 13.6 |  |  |
| 12 |  |  |  |  |  |  |  |
| 13 | dev.sqrd | 268.96 | 40.96 | 12.96 | 184.96 |  |  |
| 14 | f*dev.sqrd | 1075.84 | 696.32 | 285.12 | 1294.72 | 3352 | 67.04 |
| 15 |  |  |  |  |  |  |  |
| 16 | abs.dev. | 16.4 | 6.4 | 3.6 | 13.6 |  |  |
| 17 | f*abs.dev. | 65.6 | 108.8 | 79.2 | 95.2 | 348.8 | 6.976 |

(a)

|  | A | B | C | D | E | F | G |
|---|---|---|---|---|---|---|---|
| 1 |  |  | Measures of dispersion |  |  |  |  |
| 2 |  |  |  |  |  |  |  |
| 3 |  | Class |  |  |  | Sums | Means |
| 4 |  | 0–9.99 | 10–19.99 | 20–29.99 | 30–39.99 |  |  |
| 5 |  |  |  |  |  |  |  |
| 6 | x | 5 | 15 | 25 | 35 |  |  |
| 7 | f | 4 | 17 | 22 | 7 | =SUM(B7:E7) |  |
| 8 |  |  |  |  |  |  |  |
| 9 | f*x | =+B7*B6 | =+C7*C6 | =+D7*D6 | =+E7*E6 | =SUM(B9:E9) | =+F9/F7 |
| 10 |  |  |  |  |  |  |  |
| 11 | deviation | =+B6–G9 | =+C6–G9 | =+D6–G9 | =+E6–G9 |  |  |
| 12 |  |  |  |  |  |  |  |
| 13 | dev.sqrd. | =+B11^2 | =+C11^2 | =+D11^2 | =+E11^2 |  |  |
| 14 | f*dev.sqrd. | =+B13*B7 | =+C13*C7 | =+D13*D7 | =+E13*E7 | =SUM(B14:E14) | =+F14/F7 |
| 15 |  |  |  |  |  |  |  |
| 16 | abs.dev. | =ABS(B11) | =ABS(C11) | =ABS(D11) | =ABS(E11) |  |  |
| 17 | f*abs.dev. | =+B16*B7 | =+C16*C7 | =+D16*D7 | =+E16*E7 | =SUM(B17:E17) | =+F17/F7 |

(b)

**Figure 5.15** Spreadsheet calculations for statistics: (a) values; (b) calculations.

**5.2** There are many specialized statistical packages. One of the best known is Minitab. In common with other statistical programs, this has several functions to describe a set of data. Figure 5.16 shows a printout from a typical session. Make sure you understand what is happening here. Use another package to get equivalent results, and extend the analysis. Two features are particularly interesting in Figure 5.16. The 'DESCRIBE' function includes a value TRMEAN, which is a 'trimmed mean' calculated by ignoring the largest and smallest 5% of observations. Second, the 'BOXPLOT' function draws a 'box and whisker' diagram. These are not widely used but give a concise picture of the spread of data. A box represents the middle half of the data, extended by lines to represent the largest and smallest 25% of values. The median is marked by a '+'.

```
MTB    > SET C1
DATA   > 25 32 27 29 30 28 31 29 30 26 30 29 31 30 28
DATA   > END
MTB    > HISTOGRAM OF C1

Histogram of C1    N = 15

Midpoint    Count
    25        1     *
    26        1     *
    27        1     *
    28        2     * *
    29        3     * * *
    30        4     * * * *
    31        2     * *
    32        1     *

MTB > DESCRIBE C1

           N     MEAN    MEDIAN    TRMEAN    STDEV    SEMEAN
C1        15    29.000   29.000    29.077    1.927    0.498

          MIN      MAX       Q1        Q3
C1      25.000   32.000   28.000    30.000

MTB > BOXPLOT C1
```

**Figure 5.16** Minitab listing to describe a set of data.

**5.3** Van den Hoof Corporation have collected the following data on sales (in thousands of dollars). See how you can reduce, manipulate and present them.

| | | | | | | | | | | | | |
|---|---|---|---|---|---|---|---|---|---|---|---|---|
| 245 | 487 | 123 | 012 | 159 | 751 | 222 | 035 | 487 | 655 | 197 | 655 | 458 |
| 766 | 123 | 453 | 493 | 444 | 123 | 537 | 254 | 514 | 324 | 215 | 367 | 557 |
| 330 | 204 | 506 | 804 | 941 | 354 | 226 | 870 | 652 | 458 | 425 | 248 | 560 |
| 510 | 234 | 542 | 671 | 874 | 710 | 702 | 701 | 540 | 360 | 654 | 323 | 410 |
| 405 | 531 | 489 | 695 | 409 | 375 | 521 | 624 | 357 | 678 | 809 | 901 | 567 |
| 481 | 246 | 027 | 310 | 679 | 548 | 227 | 150 | 600 | 845 | 521 | 777 | 304 |
| 286 | 220 | 667 | 111 | 485 | 266 | 472 | 700 | 705 | 466 | 591 | 398 | 367 |
| 331 | 458 | 466 | 571 | 489 | 257 | 100 | 874 | 577 | | | | |

Write a report about your findings.

**5.4**  Find a set of data about the performance of some sports teams (for example, last year's results from football leagues). Describe the performance of the teams, both numerically and graphically. Write a report about your findings.

**5.5**  Explain what is happening in the calculations shown in Figure 5.17. What other analyses could you do with the data?

|    | A | B | C | D | E | F | G | H |
|----|---|---|---|---|---|---|---|---|
| 1  | **Data description** | | | | | | | |
| 2  | **Data** | | | | | | **Description** | |
| 3  | | | | | | | | |
| 4  | 121 | 146 | 151 | 160 | 154 | | Mean | 83.52 |
| 5  | 130 | 132 | 140 | 150 | 145 | | Median | 78 |
| 6  | 144 | 155 | 160 | 157 | 150 | | Mode | 78 |
| 7  | 96 | 101 | 99 | 99 | 89 | | Standard deviation | 47.95 |
| 8  | 78 | 77 | 80 | 78 | 81 | | Variance | 2299.60 |
| 9  | 83 | 80 | 75 | 71 | 73 | | Kurtosis | −1.28 |
| 10 | 56 | 63 | 63 | 66 | 58 | | Skewness | 0.24 |
| 11 | 32 | 38 | 37 | 40 | 36 | | Range | 143 |
| 12 | 27 | 30 | 31 | 27 | 22 | | Minimum | 17 |
| 13 | 18 | 21 | 19 | 20 | 17 | | Maximum | 160 |
| 14 | | | | | | | Sum | 4176 |
| 15 | | | | | | | Count | 50 |

**Figure 5.17**  Calculations for Computer Exercise 5.5.

# Case study

## Consumer advice office

When people buy anything they have a number of statutory rights. A fundamental one is that the products should be of an adequate quality and fit for the purpose intended. When someone thinks these rights have been infringed they can do a number of things. One of the easiest and most effective is to contact their local authority's trading standards service.

Mary Smith has been working in Manchester as a consumer advice officer for the past 14 months. Her job is to advise people who have complaints against traders. She listens to the complaints, assesses the problem and then takes the follow-up action she thinks is needed. Often her clients can be dealt with quickly, but sometimes there is a lot of follow-up including legal work and appearances in court.

The local authority is always looking for ways to reduce costs and improve their service. So it is important for Mary to show that she is doing a good job. She is particularly keen to show that her increasing experience and response to pressures for improved efficiency have allowed her to deal with more clients.

Mary has kept records of the number of clients she dealt with during her first eight weeks at work, and during the same eight weeks this year.

- Number of customers dealt with each working day in the first eight weeks:

  | 6  | 18 | 22 | 9  | 10 | 14 | 22 | 15 | 28 | 9  | 30 | 26 | 17 | 9  | 11 |
  |----|----|----|----|----|----|----|----|----|----|----|----|----|----|----|
  | 25 | 31 | 17 | 25 | 30 | 32 | 17 | 27 | 34 | 15 | 9  | 7  | 10 | 28 | 10 |
  | 31 | 12 | 16 | 26 | 21 | 37 | 25 | 7  | 36 | 29 |    |    |    |    |    |

- Number of customers dealt with each working day in the last eight weeks:

  | 30 | 26 | 40 | 19 | 26 | 31 | 28 | 41 | 18 | 27 | 29 | 30 | 33 | 43 | 19 |
  |----|----|----|----|----|----|----|----|----|----|----|----|----|----|----|
  | 20 | 44 | 37 | 29 | 22 | 41 | 39 | 15 | 9  | 22 | 26 | 30 | 35 | 38 | 26 |
  | 19 | 25 | 33 | 39 | 31 | 30 | 20 | 34 | 43 | 45 |    |    |    |    |    |

During the past year she estimates that her working hours have increased by an average of two hours a week, which is unpaid overtime. Her wages increased by 3% after allowing for inflation. What she needs is a way of presenting these figures to her employers in a form that they will understand. How would you tackle this?

# 6 | Describing changes with index numbers

Chapter outline     163
6.1   Index numbers for     164
      describing changes
6.2   Indices for more than     172
      one variable
Chapter review     180

Problems     180
Computer exercises     183
Case study 1:     184
      Macleod Engines
Case study 2:     185
      Retail sales in Europe

## CHAPTER OUTLINE

Managers are often concerned with the way that a variable changes over time. Prices, for example, tend to increase with inflation; sales vary from month to month; the number of people employed changes each week. Index numbers give a means of monitoring these changes.

Index numbers measure the changing value of a variable over time in relation to its value at some fixed point. There are several different types of index, and the main ones are discussed in this chapter.

After reading this chapter and doing the exercises you should be able to:

- appreciate the use of index numbers
- calculate indices for changes in the value of a variable
- change the base of an index
- find simple aggregate and mean price relative indices
- calculate base weighting and current period weighting for aggregate indices
- appreciate the use of the Retail Price Index

# 6.1 | Index numbers for describing changes

## 6.1.1 | Introduction

The last two chapters have talked about graphical and numerical ways of describing data. These have taken a snapshot of data and have described the values at a specific time. But in business the values of most variables change over time. The prices paid for material, number of people employed, annual income and profit, company contributions to charities, number of customers, tax rates, and so on, all change over time. It would be useful to have a way of describing these changes. This chapter continues the theme of data presentation by using index numbers to describe the way that a variable changes over time.

Let us consider, as an example of changing values, the number of crimes committed in a particular area. Suppose there were 127 crimes of a particular type in one year, 142 crimes in the second year and 116 crimes in the third year. We could say that the number of crimes had risen by 11.8% between years 1 and 2, and had then declined by 18.3% between years 2 and 3. Although accurate, this is a rather messy description and has the disadvantage of not directly comparing the number of crimes in years 1 and 3. We could plot a graph of the number of crimes each year and this would certainly show any trends. But it would not give a **measure** for the changes. What we really need is a numerical measure for monitoring the changes, and this is given by an **index** or **index number**.

An index is a number which compares the value of a variable at any time with its value at another fixed time, called the **base period**. Then we can define:

$$\text{index for period} = \frac{\text{value in period}}{\text{value in base period}}$$

With the crime figures above we could use the first year as a base period. Then the index for the second year is 142/127 = 1.12, as shown in the following table:

| Year | Value | Calculation | Index |
|------|-------|-------------|-------|
| 1 | 127 | 127/127 | 1.00 |
| 2 | 142 | 142/127 | 1.12 |
| 3 | 116 | 116/127 | 0.91 |

The index in the base period will always be 1.00. The index of 1.12 in the second year tells us that crime is 12% higher than the **base value** (which is the value in the base period), while the index of 0.91 in the third period tells us that crime is 9% lower than the base value.

We chose the first year as the base period, but this was an arbitrary choice and we could have used any other year. The choice depends on the information needed. If a comparison of crimes in the third year is being made with previous years, we could take year 3 as the base year. Then the base value is 116, the index in year 1 is 127/116 = 1.09, and so on, as shown in the following table:

| Year | Value | Calculation | Index |
|------|-------|-------------|-------|
| 1    | 127   | 127/116     | 1.09  |
| 2    | 142   | 142/116     | 1.22  |
| 3    | 116   | 116/116     | 1.00  |

---

| IN SUMMARY |

In business, the value of most variables changes over time. An index can be used to measure these changes, by calculating the ratio of the current value over a base value.

## 6.1.1 | Price indices

One of the most important uses of indices is to show how the price of a product changes over time. This change might be caused by:

- changing costs of raw materials
- changes in the production process
- variable supply (such as seasonal vegetables)
- variable demand (such as holidays)
- changing financial objectives of suppliers (perhaps aiming for higher profits)
- general inflation which causes prices to drift upwards

The index we used above was based on a value of 1.00 in the base period. For convenience, indices are usually multiplied by 100 to define an index with a base figure of 100. Then subsequent price indices are defined as the ratio of the current price to the base price, multiplied by 100.

$$\text{price index in period } N = \frac{\text{price in period } N}{\text{base price}} \times 100$$

If the base price of a product is £5 and this rises to £7 the price index is 7/5 × 100 = 140. This immediately shows that the price has risen by 40% since the base period. If the price in the next period is £4 the index is 4/5 × 100 = 80, which is a decrease of 20% since the base period. As well as showing changes in one product's price, indices can be used for comparisons between different products. If the price indices of two products are 125 and 150 we know that the second product has risen in price twice as quickly as the first (assuming that the same base period is used).

## WORKED EXAMPLE 6.1

If the price of an item is £20 in January, £22 in February, £25 in March and £26 in April, what is the price index in each month using January as the base month?

### Solution

Taking January as the base month, the base price is £20. Then the price indices for each month are

January: $\dfrac{20}{20} \times 100 = 100$ (as expected in the base period)

February: $\dfrac{22}{20} \times 100 = 110$

March: $\dfrac{25}{20} \times 100 = 125$

April: $\dfrac{26}{20} \times 100 = 130$

In the last worked example, the index of 110 in February shows the price has risen by 10% over the base level, while an index of 125 in March shows a rise of 25% over the base level, and so on. Changes in indices between periods are referred to as **percentage point** changes. So between February and March the index shows an increase of $125 - 110 = 15$ percentage points. Be careful to note that a rise of 15 percentage points is not the same as a rise of 15%. In this case the percentage increase between February and March is $[(125-110)/110] \times 100 = 13.6\%$. Remember that percentage point changes refer back to the base price and not the current price.

# WORKED EXAMPLE 6.2

Amil Gupta's car showroom is giving a special offer on one type of car. The advertised price of this car in four consecutive quarters was £10,450, £10,800, £11,450 and £9,999. Find the price indices based on the final quarter's price. What are the quarterly changes in price in terms of percentage points and percentages?

## Solution

Taking indices based on the fourth quarter gives:

$$\text{price index in quarter} = \frac{\text{price in quarter}}{\text{price in fourth quarter}} \times 100$$

The percentage price rise in each quarter is found from:

$$\text{percentage price rise} = \frac{\text{price this quarter} - \text{price last quarter}}{\text{price last quarter}} \times 100$$

The percentage point rise is found from the indices as:

$$\text{percentage point price rise} = \text{index this quarter} - \text{index last quarter}$$

Doing these calculations on a spreadsheet gives the results shown in Figure 6.1.

| | A | B | C | D | E | F |
|---|---|---|---|---|---|---|
| 1 | **Price indices** | | | | | |
| 2 | | | | | | |
| 3 | **Period** | **Price** | **Index** | **Price rise** | **Percentage price rise** | **Percentage point price rise** |
| 4 | | | | | | |
| 5 | 1 | 10450 | 104.5 | 0.0 | 0.0 | 0.0 |
| 6 | 2 | 10800 | 108.0 | 350.0 | 3.3 | 3.5 |
| 7 | 3 | 11450 | 114.5 | 650.0 | 6.0 | 6.5 |
| 8 | 4 | 9999 | 100.0 | −1451.0 | −12.7 | −14.5 |

**Figure 6.1**  Indices for Worked Example 6.2.

So far we have talked about indices in terms of price indices, but we should make a number of general points:

- An index can be used to measure the way any variable changes over time, such as unemployment numbers, car registrations, or gross national product.
- We chose a base value of 100 for the index, but this is only for convenience and we could use any other value.

- The choice of base period can be any convenient time; it is usually a typical period when there are no unusual circumstances.

- The index can be calculated with any convenient frequency. Unemployment figures are updated monthly, stock market prices daily, GNP annually and so on.

## WORKED EXAMPLE 6.3

The following table shows the monthly price index for an item:

| Month | 1 | 2 | 3 | 4 | 5 | 6 | 7 | 8 | 9 | 10 | 11 | 12 |
|-------|-----|-----|----|----|----|----|----|-----|-----|-----|-----|-----|
| Index | 121 | 112 | 98 | 81 | 63 | 57 | 89 | 109 | 131 | 147 | 132 | 126 |

(a) If the price in month 3 is £240 what is the price in month 8?

(b) If the price in month 10 is £1200 what is the price in month 2?

### Solution

(a) In month 3 the price is £240 and the price index is 98, so:

$$\text{base price} = \frac{240}{98} \times 100 = £244.90$$

Then in month 8 the price index is 109 so:

$$\text{price} = 244.90 \times \frac{109}{100} = £266.94$$

We could have found this directly by taking the ratio of the price indices to give:

$$\text{price} = 240 \times \frac{109}{98} = £266.94$$

(b) The ratio of the price indices in periods 2 and 10 is 112/147, so in period 2:

$$\text{price} = 1200 \times \frac{112}{147} = £914.29$$

---

IN SUMMARY

Indices are often used to monitor price changes. They are commonly based on a value of 100, so that percentage point changes are easy to monitor.

## Changing the base period

When you calculate an index you can choose the base period as any convenient time. But rather than keep the same base period for a long time, it is usual to update it periodically. There are two reasons for this:

- **changing circumstances.** The index should be reset whenever there are significant changes in circumstances that would make comparisons with earlier periods meaningless. Manufacturers who calculate an index for production, for example, will return the base value to 100 whenever they change the product range.

- **an index becomes too large.** The index should be reset when its value becomes too high. If the index rises to, say, 1000 a 10% increase in a period will raise the index to 1100, and this seems a more significant change than, say, 100 to 110.

When the base period is changed, we must convert an existing, old index to a new one. Suppose we have an old index whose base value was set in period $N_1$. Then the old index for period $M$ is:

$$\text{old index} = \frac{\text{value in period } M}{\text{value in period } N_1} \times 100$$

If we want to reset the index to a base value set in period $N_2$ we have a new index defined by:

$$\text{new index} = \frac{\text{value in period } M}{\text{value in period } N_2} \times 100$$

Rearranging these equations gives the result:

$$\text{value in period } M \times 100 = \text{new index} \times \text{value in period } N_2$$

and

$$\text{value in period } M \times 100 = \text{old index} \times \text{value in period } N_1$$

So

$$\text{new index} = \text{old index} \times \frac{\text{value in period } N_1}{\text{value in period } N_2}$$

As the values in both periods $N_1$ and $N_2$ are fixed, we find the new index by multiplying the old index by a constant amount. If we know, for example, that the old index for a period is 250 and a new index is 100, the value of the constant is 100/250. Then we can find the new index for any period by multiplying the old index by 100/250; conversely, we can find the old index for any period by multiplying the new index by 250/100.

## WORKED EXAMPLE 6.4

The number of units produced each year in a factory is described by the following indices:

| Year | 1 | 2 | 3 | 4 | 5 | 6 | 7 | 8 |
|---|---|---|---|---|---|---|---|---|
| Index 1 | 100 | 138 | 162 | 196 | 220 | | | |
| Index 2 | | | | | 100 | 125 | 140 | 165 |

(a) What are the base years for the indices?

(b) If the factory had not changed to index 2, what values would index 1 have in years 6 to 8?

(c) What values would index 2 have in years 1 to 4?

(d) If the factory made 4860 units in year 3, how many did it make in year 7?

## Solution

(a) Indices take the value 100 in base periods, so index 1 uses the base year 1 and index 2 uses the base year 5.

(b) Index 1 is found by multiplying index 2 by a constant amount. We can find this constant from year 5 as 220/100. Then the values for index 1 are (see Figure 6.2)

$$year\ 6: \qquad 125 \times 220/100 = 275$$
$$year\ 7: \qquad 140 \times 220/100 = 308$$
$$year\ 8: \qquad 165 \times 220/100 = 363$$

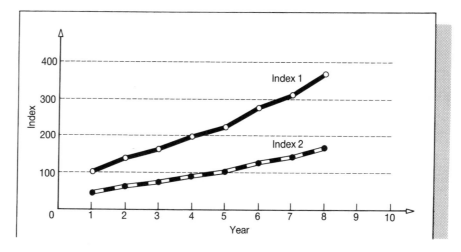

**Figure 6.2**  Graph of indices for production.

(c) Index 2 is found by multiplying index 1 by a constant amount. Again we can find this from year 5 as 100/220. Then the values for index 2 are

year 4:  $196 \times 100/220 = 89.09$

year 3:  $162 \times 100/220 = 73.64$

year 2:  $138 \times 100/220 = 62.73$

year 1:  $100 \times 100/220 = 45.45$

(d) If the factory made 4860 units in year 3 we can find the production in year 7 using either of the indices. Using index 1:

$$\frac{4860}{162} \times 308 = 9240 \text{ units}$$

This result can be confirmed using index 2:

$$\frac{4860}{73.64} \times 140 = 9240 \text{ units}$$

---

IN SUMMARY

Base periods for index numbers should be revised periodically. A new index number can be calculated by multiplying the old index by a constant.

# Self-assessment questions

**6.1** What is the purpose of an index number?

**6.2** 'Indices always use a base value of 100.' Is this true?

**6.3** When should the base period be changed?

**6.4** What is the difference between a percentage rise of 10% and a percentage point rise of 10?

**6.5** In one period the old price index for a product is 345 while the new price index is 125. In the following period the new price index is 132. What is the old index for this period?

# 6.2  Indices for more than one variable

## 6.2.1  Average indices

We have seen how an index can measure the changes in a variable over time. Sometimes we are not interested in the changes in a single variable but in a combination of different variables. The Retail Price Index, for example, shows how the aggregate price of a range of goods varies over time; a shop is interested in changes in sales of all items it sells rather than a single item; a local authority is interested in changes in the number of people of all types it employs. Indices which measure changes in a number of variables are called aggregate indices.

For simplicity we shall talk about price indices, but we can use the same reasoning for any other type of index.

Two obvious ways of defining an aggregate price index are:

- add all prices and calculate an index based on the total price. This is called the **simple aggregate index** or **simple composite index**:

$$\text{simple aggregate index for period } n = \frac{\text{sum of prices in period } n}{\text{sum of prices in base period}} \times 100$$

- calculate the mean value of separate indices for all items. The price of an item at any time divided by the base price is called the **price relative**, so the index based on mean values is called the **mean price relative index**:

$$\text{mean price relative index for period } n = \frac{\text{sum of all price relatives for period } n}{\text{number of indices}} \times 100$$

## WORKED EXAMPLE 6.5

Last year the prices of bread, milk and tea in a shop were 55 pence, 28 pence and 72 pence respectively. This year the same items cost 62 pence, 32 pence and 74 pence respectively. What are the simple aggregate index and the mean price relative index for this year, using last year as the base year?

### Solution

We can find the simple aggregate index by adding all prices and taking the ratio of total price:

$$\text{base price} = 55 + 28 + 72 = 155$$

$$\text{current price} = 62 + 32 + 74 = 168$$

So the simple aggregate index = $168/155 \times 100 = 108.4$.

To find the mean price relative index we calculate the price relative for each item and find the mean of these. The individual price relatives are

bread:     62/55 = 1.127

milk:      32/28 = 1.143

tea:       74/72 = 1.028

The mean price relative index is the mean of these multiplied by 100, which is:

$$100 \times \frac{1.127 + 1.143 + 1.028}{3} = 109.9$$

These two indices are easy to define and use, but they do not really give good measures. One obvious criticism, particularly of the simple aggregate index, is that it depends on the units used for each index. An aggregate index including the price of tea per kilogram would give a different index from one based on the price per pound. If the index used the price of tea per tonne, it would be so high as to swamp the other costs and effectively ignore them.

Another weakness of the two indices is that they do not consider the relative importance of each product. If people used more milk than tea, then the index should reflect this. Taking a broader example, a service company might have spent £1000 on raw materials and £1 million on wages in the base year, and this year it spends £2000 on raw materials and £1 million on wages. It would make little sense to say that the aggregate index of costs is 150, which is the mean price relative index calculated from the separate indices for raw materials (200) and wages (100). So a reasonable aggregate index must take into account two factors:

- the price paid for each unit of product

- the quantity of each product used

There are several ways of combining these into a weighted index, as we shall see.

## IN SUMMARY

An aggregate index shows changes in a combination of variables. A simple aggregate index or mean price relative index can be used, but these both have weaknesses.

## | 6.2.2 | Weighted indices

Weighted indices take into account the relative importance of each variable. If, for example, we are looking at the changing amount that a family pays for food, the easiest way of doing this is to look at each week's shopping basket and find the total cost. This total cost depends both on the price of each item and on the number of items bought, so we could define a weighted price index as:

$$\text{weighted price index} = \frac{\text{current cost of week's shopping basket}}{\text{cost of shopping basket in base period}}$$

This seems reasonable, but there is an immediate problem. If some prices change, the amount that a family buys will also change. Suppose, for example, the price of cake rises relative to the price of biscuits; then a family may reduce the number of cakes they buy and increase the number of biscuits. The index we use should take such changes into account, but still emphasize changes in price. In practice, there are two widely used methods of doing this:

- **base-period weighted index** assumes that the quantities purchased do not change from the base period
- **current-period weighted index** assumes that the current shopping basket was used in the base period

### Base-period weighted index

Suppose that in the base period the shopping basket contained quantities $Q_0$ at prices $P_0$; then the total cost is the sum of all quantities multiplied by the prices:

$$\text{total cost in base period} = \text{sum of quantities} \times \text{price}$$
$$= \Sigma Q_0 P_0$$

In another period, $n$, the prices changed to $P_n$, but we assume that the quantities bought remained unchanged, so the total cost is $\Sigma Q_0 P_n$. Then we can calculate a base-period weighted index as the ratio of these two costs:

> base-period weighted index
>
> $$= \frac{\text{cost of base-period quantities at current prices}}{\text{cost of base-period quantities at base-period prices}}$$

This index is usually multiplied by 100, giving:

> $$\text{base-period weighted index} = \frac{\Sigma Q_0 P_n}{\Sigma Q_0 P_0} \times 100$$

This is sometimes called the Laspeyre index, after its inventor. It has the advantage of giving a direct comparison of costs and reacting to actual price rises. On the other hand, it has the disadvantage of assuming that amounts bought do not change over time. In practice, purchases do change and, in particular, the quantities are affected by price; a product with rapidly increasing price may well be replaced by one with lower price. The result is that base-period weighted indices tend to give values which are too high. But updating the base period at suitable intervals (and particularly by adjusting the list of purchases) can keep the errors small.

## Current-period weighted index

If prices in a period $n$ are $P_n$, and a family buys a shopping basket with quantities $Q_n$, the total cost is $\sum Q_n P_n$. A reasonable price index would compare this cost with the cost of the same products in the base period, which would have been $\sum Q_n P_0$. Then the current-period weighted index is the ratio of these costs:

$$
\begin{aligned}
&\text{current-period weighted index} \\
&= \frac{\text{cost of current quantities at current prices}}{\text{cost of current quantities at base-period prices}}
\end{aligned}
$$

Again, this index is usually multiplied by 100, giving:

$$
\text{current-period weighted index} = \frac{\sum Q_n P_n}{\sum Q_n P_0} \times 100
$$

This index is sometimes called the Paasche index. It has the advantage of giving an accurate measure of changes in the costs of current purchases. On the other hand, it has the disadvantage of changing the basis of calculation each period, so that it does not give a direct comparison of prices over time. Moreover, by allowing substitution of products which are relatively cheaper than they were in the base period, it gives an index which tends to be too low. This index also takes more effort to update, primarily because of the data collection needed to monitor continually changing quantities purchased. For these reasons, current-period weighting is less widely used than base-period weighting.

## WORKED EXAMPLE 6.6

A company buys four products with the following characteristics:

| Items | Number of units bought | | Price paid per unit | |
|---|---|---|---|---|
| | Year 1 | Year 2 | Year 1 | Year 2 |
| A | 20 | 24 | 10 | 11 |
| B | 55 | 51 | 23 | 25 |
| C | 63 | 84 | 17 | 17 |
| D | 28 | 34 | 19 | 20 |

(a) Find the price indices for each product in year 2 using year 1 as the base year.

(b) Calculate a base-weighted index for the products.

(c) Calculate a current-period weighted index.

## Solution

(a) Simple price indices do not take into account usage of a product, so we have

$$\text{Product A:} \quad 11/10 \times 100 = 110$$
$$\text{Product B:} \quad 25/23 \times 100 = 108.7$$
$$\text{Product C:} \quad 17/17 \times 100 = 100$$
$$\text{Product D:} \quad 20/19 \times 100 = 105.3$$

(b) A base-weighted index shows the price that would be paid later for the basket of items bought in the base period:

$$\text{base-weighted index} = \frac{\Sigma Q_0 P_n}{\Sigma Q_0 P_0} \times 100$$

$$= \frac{(20 \times 11) + (55 \times 25) + (63 \times 17) + (28 \times 20)}{(20 \times 10) + (55 \times 23) + (63 \times 17) + (28 \times 19)} = \frac{3226}{3068} \times 100$$

$$= 105.15$$

(c) A current-period weighted index shows how the price of the basket of items bought in a later period has changed since the base period:

$$\text{current-period weighted index} = \frac{\Sigma Q_n P_n}{\Sigma Q_n P_0} \times 100$$

$$= \frac{(24 \times 11) + (51 \times 25) + (84 \times 17) + (34 \times 20)}{(24 \times 10) + (51 \times 23) + (84 \times 17) + (34 \times 19)} = \frac{3647}{3487} \times 100$$

$$= 104.59$$

# WORKED EXAMPLE 6.7

Figure 6.3 shows some calculations in a spreadsheet. Explain what is happening.

| | A | B | C | D | E | F | G | H | I |
|---|---|---|---|---|---|---|---|---|---|
| 1 | Index calculation | | | | | | | | |
| 2 | | | | | | | | | |
| 3 | Values | | | | | | | | |
| 4 | | Year 1 | | Year 2 | | Year 3 | | Year 4 | |
| 5 | Product | Quantity | Cost | Quantity | Cost | Quantity | Cost | Quantity | Cost |
| 6 | 1 | 24 | 16 | 26 | 16 | 30 | 15 | 35 | 15 |
| 7 | 2 | 3 | 21 | 5 | 21 | 8 | 21 | 10 | 21 |
| 8 | 3 | 11 | 20 | 11 | 21 | 10 | 22 | 8 | 24 |
| 9 | 4 | 15 | 9 | 10 | 11 | 5 | 14 | 2 | 16 |
| 10 | 5 | 8 | 22 | 12 | 21 | 14 | 21 | 16 | 20 |
| 11 | 6 | 2 | 40 | 2 | 41 | 2 | 40 | 2 | 40 |
| 12 | 7 | 1 | 36 | 1 | 37 | 1 | 37 | 1 | 37 |
| 13 | 8 | 1 | 5 | 2 | 7 | 1 | 8 | 1 | 10 |
| 14 | 9 | 8 | 16 | 6 | 17 | 4 | 19 | 2 | 19 |
| 15 | 10 | 20 | 12 | 19 | 13 | 15 | 14 | 10 | 15 |
| 16 | | | | | | | | | |
| 17 | Simple indices | | | | | | | | |
| 18 | | Year 1 | | Year 2 | | Year 3 | | Year 4 | |
| 19 | Product | Quantity | Cost | Quantity | Cost | Quantity | Cost | Quantity | Cost |
| 20 | 1 | 100.0 | 100.0 | 108.3 | 100.0 | 125.0 | 93.8 | 145.8 | 93.8 |
| 21 | 2 | 100.0 | 100.0 | 166.7 | 100.0 | 266.7 | 100.0 | 333.3 | 100.0 |
| 22 | 3 | 100.0 | 100.0 | 100.0 | 105.0 | 90.9 | 110.0 | 72.7 | 120.0 |
| 23 | 4 | 100.0 | 100.0 | 66.7 | 122.2 | 33.3 | 155.6 | 13.3 | 177.8 |
| 24 | 5 | 100.0 | 100.0 | 150.0 | 95.5 | 175.0 | 95.5 | 200.0 | 90.9 |
| 25 | 6 | 100.0 | 100.0 | 100.0 | 102.5 | 100.0 | 100.0 | 100.0 | 100.0 |
| 26 | 7 | 100.0 | 100.0 | 100.0 | 102.8 | 100.0 | 102.8 | 100.0 | 102.8 |
| 27 | 8 | 100.0 | 100.0 | 200.0 | 140.0 | 100.0 | 160.0 | 100.0 | 200.0 |
| 28 | 9 | 100.0 | 100.0 | 75.0 | 106.3 | 50.0 | 118.8 | 25.0 | 118.8 |
| 29 | 10 | 100.0 | 100.0 | 95.0 | 108.3 | 75.0 | 116.7 | 50.0 | 125.0 |
| 30 | | | | | | | | | |
| 31 | Aggregate indices | | | | | | | | |
| 32 | | | Year 1 | Year 2 | Year 3 | Year 4 | | | |
| 33 | Simple aggregate | | 100.0 | 104.1 | 107.1 | 110.2 | | | |
| 34 | Mean price relative | | 100.0 | 108.3 | 115.3 | 122.9 | | | |
| 35 | | | | | | | | | |
| 36 | Base-weighted | | 100.0 | 104.5 | 109.1 | 113.6 | | | |
| 37 | Current-weighted | | 100.0 | 103.3 | 103.0 | 101.3 | | | |

**Figure 6.3**  Spreadsheet calculations for indices.

## Solution

The spreadsheet is calculating a number of indices for a set of data. These raw data are given at the top of the table as a set of quantities and costs for ten products over four years. The spreadsheet calculates individual indices for each quantity and cost using year 1 as the base year. Then it calculates the four aggregate indices we discussed. You can see that these aggregate indices give quite different results. The first two simple indices give general impressions but are not very reliable. The second two indices are more reliable, but the base-weighted index tends to be high, while the current-period weighted index tends to be low.

---

### IN SUMMARY

Aggregate price indices should reflect changes in both price and quantities bought. The two most common aggregate indices use base-period weighting and current-period weighting.

## 6.2.3 | Retail price indices

Each month the government publishes figures for the annual rate of inflation. Several indices are used to monitor this, but the most important is the Retail Price Index (RPI). This shows changes in the amount spent by a typical household. It is an aggregate index based on the price of a representative selection of 350 products and services in 14 main groups (listed in Problem 6.10). Details of current prices are collected on the Tuesday nearest the middle of the month, with a total of 150 000 prices collected. Some of these are collected centrally, but accurate figures need to reflect price variations around the country, so prices are also collected by visits to representative shops.

The index is used for a number of purposes, including wage bargaining, calculating index-linked benefits, and raising insurance values. But it can be criticized for not properly representing the inflation felt by certain groups of people. People who do not have a mortgage, for example, are not affected when mortgage interest rates change. The government does try to take into account some of these factors, by publishing special indices for households which consist of, for example, only one or two pensioners. It also publishes specific indices for each group of items (such as food or transport). In practice, these effects are surprisingly small, and the RPI is widely accepted as giving a reasonable measure of changing prices.

The RPI has important practical uses, particularly when considering inflation. If someone's pay doubled between 1974 and 1979 they would expect to be much better off. Unfortunately, this was a period of high inflation and the index of prices in 1979, with 1974 as the base year, was 206. So wages would have to more than double just to keep up with prices.

## WORKED EXAMPLE 6.8

Table 6.1 shows the price index of manufactured products from 1970 to 1998.

(a) How could you find the approximate rate of inflation in each year?

(b) If an item cost £1400 in 1970 how much would you expect it to cost in 1998?

(c) Which is the cheapest real price of £1000 in 1970, £1500 in 1980 or £2000 in 1990?

**Table 6.1**

| Year | Index | Year | Index | Year | Index | Year | Index |
|------|-------|------|-------|------|-------|------|-------|
| 1970 | 120   | 1978 | 339   | 1986 | 623   | 1994 | 916   |
| 1971 | 131   | 1979 | 376   | 1987 | 646   | 1995 | 935   |
| 1972 | 138   | 1980 | 428   | 1988 | 676   | 1996 | 954   |
| 1973 | 149   | 1981 | 469   | 1989 | 710   | 1997 | 974   |
| 1974 | 181   | 1982 | 505   | 1990 | 752   | 1998 | 992   |
| 1975 | 223   | 1983 | 533   | 1991 | 798   |      |       |
| 1976 | 260   | 1984 | 566   | 1992 | 862   |      |       |
| 1977 | 310   | 1985 | 597   | 1993 | 888   |      |       |

## Solution

(a) The annual rate of inflation shows the percentage increase in prices. This can be found directly from the price index.

Between 1970 and 1971 the price index rose by:

$$\frac{131 - 120}{120} \times 100 = 9.2\%$$

which is the annual rate of inflation.

Between 1971 and 1972 the price index rose by:

$$\frac{138 - 131}{131} \times 100 = 5.3\%$$

and so on.

(b) The price would be raised by the ratio of the indices in 1998 and 1970 to give:

price in 1998 = 1400 × 992/120 = £11,573.33

(c) We can compare the prices by finding their values in the base year – that is dividing the amounts by the price index:

£1000 in 1970 is worth 1000/120 × 100 in the base year = £833.33

£1500 in 1980 is worth 1500/428 × 100 in the base year = £350.47

£2000 in 1990 is worth 2000/752 × 100 in the base year = £265.96

So inflation makes the highest **actual** price of £2000 in 1990, the cheapest **real** price.

### IN SUMMARY

The Retail Price Index is a widely used measure of price increase based on the expenditure of a typical family.

## Self-assessment questions

**6.6** How are the mean price relative index and the simple aggregate index defined?

**6.7** What are the weaknesses of the mean price relative index and the simple aggregate index?

**6.8** What is the difference between base-period weighting and current-period weighting for aggregate indices?

**6.9** Base-period weighting often gives a higher index than current-period weighting. Why?

**6.10** Is it possible to use a weighting other than base period or current period?

**6.11** 'The Retail Price Index gives an accurate measure of the cost of living.' Is this statement true?

### CHAPTER REVIEW

This chapter discussed the use of index numbers to describe changing values over time. In particular it:

- talked about the need to monitor changing values
- calculated index numbers for prices and other variables
- changed the base of indices
- described the use of aggregate indices including base-period weighting and current-period weighting
- commented on the Retail Price Index

## Problems

**6.1** The price of an item in consecutive months has been £106, £108, £111, £112, £118, £125, £130 and £132. Use an index based on the first month to describe these changes. How would this compare with an index based on the last month?

**6.2** The number of fishing boats operating from Port Newpier over the past ten years has been recorded as follows:

325 321 316 294 263 241 197 148 102 70

Describe these changes by indices based on the first and last year's observations.

**6.3** The number of people employed by Westbury Cladding over the past 12 months is as follows. Use an index to describe these figures.

| Month | 1 | 2 | 3 | 4 | 5 | 6 | 7 | 8 | 9 | 10 | 11 | 12 |
|---|---|---|---|---|---|---|---|---|---|---|---|---|
| Number | 121 | 115 | 97 | 112 | 127 | 135 | 152 | 155 | 161 | 147 | 133 | 131 |

**6.4** The annual output of a company is described by the following indices:

| Year | 1 | 2 | 3 | 4 | 5 | 6 | 7 | 8 |
|---|---|---|---|---|---|---|---|---|
| Index 1 | 100 | 125 | 153 | 167 | | | | |
| Index 2 | | | | 100 | 109 | 125 | 140 | 165 |

If the factory made 23 850 units in year 2, how many did it make in the other years? What is the percentage increase in output each year?

**6.5** ARP Insurance uses an index to describe the number of agents working for it. This index was revised five years ago, and had the following values over the past ten years:

| Year | 1 | 2 | 3 | 4 | 5 | 6 | 7 | 8 | 9 | 10 |
|---|---|---|---|---|---|---|---|---|---|---|
| Index 1 | 106 | 129 | 154 | 173 | 195 | 231 | | | | |
| Index 2 | | | | | | 100 | 113 | 126 | 153 | 172 |

If ARP had not changed to index 2, what values would index 1 have in years 7 to 10? What values would index 2 have in years 1 to 5? If the company had 645 agents in year 4, how many did it have in each other year?

**6.6** Employees in a company are put into four wage groups. During a three-year period the number employed in each group and the average weekly wage are as follows:

| Group | Year 1 | | Year 2 | | Year 3 | |
|---|---|---|---|---|---|---|
| | Number | Wage | Number | Wage | Number | Wage |
| 1 | 45 | 125 | 55 | 133 | 60 | 143 |
| 2 | 122 | 205 | 125 | 211 | 132 | 224 |
| 3 | 63 | 245 | 66 | 268 | 71 | 293 |
| 4 | 7 | 408 | 9 | 473 | 13 | 521 |

Use different indices to describe changes in wages paid and numbers employed.

**6.7** The following table shows the price of drinks served in The Lion Inn. Find the simple aggregate index and mean price relative index for each year.

|        | Beer | Lager | Cider | Soft drinks |
|--------|------|-------|-------|-------------|
| Year 1 | 91   | 95    | 78    | 35          |
| Year 2 | 97   | 105   | 85    | 39          |
| Year 3 | 102  | 112   | 88    | 42          |
| Year 4 | 107  | 125   | 93    | 47          |

**6.8** A company buys four products with the following characteristics:

| Products | Number of units bought | | Price paid per unit | |
|----------|--------|--------|--------|--------|
|          | Year 1 | Year 2 | Year 1 | Year 2 |
| A        | 121    | 141    | 9      | 10     |
| B        | 149    | 163    | 21     | 23     |
| C        | 173    | 182    | 26     | 27     |
| D        | 194    | 103    | 31     | 33     |

Calculate a base-period weighted index and a current-period weighted index for the products.

**6.9** The average prices for four items over four years are as follows:

| Item | Year 1 | Year 2 | Year 3 | Year 4 |
|------|--------|--------|--------|--------|
| A    | 25     | 26     | 30     | 32     |
| B    | 56     | 61     | 67     | 74     |
| C    | 20     | 25     | 30     | 36     |
| D    | 110    | 115    | 130    | 150    |

The number of units of each item bought by one company are approximately 400, 300, 800 and 200 respectively. Calculate weighted price indices for years 2 to 4, taking year 1 as the base year.

**6.10** The Retail Price Index currently uses the following weights:

| | | | |
|--------|-----|--------|-----|
| Food                 | 158 | Household goods              | 71 |
| Catering             | 47  | Household services           | 40 |
| Alcoholic drink      | 77  | Clothing and footwear        | 69 |
| Tobacco              | 34  | Personal goods and services  | 39 |
| Housing              | 185 | Fares and travel costs       | 21 |
| Fuel and light       | 50  | Leisure goods                | 48 |
| Motoring expenditure | 131 | Leisure services             | 30 |

How are these weights used in calculating the RPI? What are the most important categories of expenditure? What would be the effect on the RPI of a 10% increase in the cost of housing? What would be the effect of a 10% increase in fares and travel costs?

# Computer exercises

**6.1** Figure 6.4 shows part of a spreadsheet for calculating aggregate indices. Analyse the results and make sure they are correct. Design a spreadsheet to do these calculations. Extend the analysis to calculate other indices.

| | A | B | C | D | E | F | G |
|---|---|---|---|---|---|---|---|
| 1 | | | | Calculation of indices | | | |
| 2 | | | | | | | |
| 3 | | Year 0 | | Year n | | | |
| 4 | Item | Quantity | Price | Quantity | Price | PoQo | PnQo |
| 5 | Shoes | 4 | 25 | 5 | 28 | 100 | 112 |
| 6 | Shirts | 10 | 8 | 8 | 10 | 80 | 100 |
| 7 | Trousers | 5 | 28 | 4 | 32 | 140 | 160 |
| 8 | Dresses | 8 | 45 | 8 | 48 | 360 | 384 |
| 9 | Gloves | 4 | 5 | 6 | 6 | 20 | 24 |
| 10 | Hats | 3 | 12 | 3 | 12 | 36 | 36 |
| 11 | Coats | 2 | 95 | 3 | 120 | 190 | 240 |
| 12 | | | | | | | |
| 13 | Sums | | | | | 926 | 1056 |
| 14 | | | | | | | |
| 15 | | | | Ratio | | Index | |
| 16 | Base-weighted | | | 1.14 | | 114.04 | |
| 17 | | | | | | | |

**Figure 6.4** Spreadsheet calculating aggregate indices.

**6.2** Use a spreadsheet to calculate indices for the data in Table 6.2.

**Table 6.2**

| Item | Year 1 | | Year 2 | | Year 3 | | Year 4 | |
|---|---|---|---|---|---|---|---|---|
| | Price | Quantity | Price | Quantity | Price | Quantity | Price | Quantity |
| AL403 | 142 | 27 | 147 | 26 | 155 | 32 | 165 | 32 |
| ML127 | 54 | 284 | 58 | 295 | 65 | 306 | 75 | 285 |
| FE872 | 1026 | 5 | 1026 | 8 | 1250 | 2 | 1250 | 3 |
| KP332 | 687 | 25 | 699 | 25 | 749 | 20 | 735 | 55 |
| KP333 | 29 | 1045 | 31 | 1024 | 32 | 1125 | 36 | 1254 |
| CG196 | 58 | 754 | 64 | 788 | 72 | 798 | 81 | 801 |
| CG197 | 529 | 102 | 599 | 110 | 675 | 120 | 750 | 108 |
| CG404 | 254 | 306 | 275 | 310 | 289 | 305 | 329 | 299 |
| CG405 | 109 | 58 | 115 | 62 | 130 | 59 | 140 | 57 |
| NA112 | 86 | 257 | 83 | 350 | 85 | 366 | 90 | 360 |
| QF016 | 220 | 86 | 220 | 86 | 225 | 86 | 225 | 86 |
| QT195 | 850 | 10 | 899 | 9 | 949 | 12 | 999 | 16 |
| LJ878 | 336 | 29 | 359 | 38 | 499 | 11 | 499 | 25 |

**6.3** The government publishes many statistics in its *Monthly Digest of Statistics*. Take an appropriate set of figures (such as the annual inflation rate) and see how indices have been used to monitor changes over the past 20 years. Use a spreadsheet to check the published indices.

**6.4** Run a survey to find the contents of a typical week's purchases for a sample of people. Find the cost of these purchases. Now find government figures for inflation over the past 30 years. Find the cost of the purchases at different times. Write a report about your findings, being sure to mention any specific problems, the generality of results, and so on.

# Case study 1

## Macleod Engines

In the 1980s Macleod Engines had a poor record of industrial relations. In the early 1990s it tried hard to overcome these and made a series of major changes in the way employees were rewarded and involved in decision-making. Some of these changes included profit sharing, reducing the number of layers of management from 13 to 6, introducing more flexible working practices, improved communications between different grades of employees, and using the same basic pay rise for all grades of employees.

As part of these changes the company negotiated an annual basic pay rise for all employees. This pay rise was proposed by a committee with representatives from all parts of the company and a number of independent members. The purpose of the independent members was to give a disinterested view in a process which, by its nature, generates strong feelings from those involved. John Burns was one of these independent members. This meant that he could not work for Macleod Engines, be a shareholder or be connected in any other way with the company operations. John was an accountant working at the head office of a major building society, and his employers had no connection at all with Macleod or with engineering work.

John was preparing for the first meeting to set this year's annual wage rise. His aim was to make suggestions about a fair settlement and he was collecting initial ideas. He already had some data about Macleod for the past ten years, as shown in Table 6.3. Unfortunately, John did not know how well the company was doing at the moment or how well it was likely to do next year. He had to work out some initial ideas, based only on the limited data he had. How would you suggest he tackle this problem?

**Table 6.3**

| Year | Average weekly earnings | Average hours worked | Company revenue (£ million) | Gross company profit (£000) | Index of industry wages | Retail Price Index |
|---|---|---|---|---|---|---|
| 1 | 80.45 | 44 | 12.0 | 1210 | 85.5 | 84.5 |
| 2 | 104.32 | 43 | 15.1 | 1450 | 100.0 | 100.0 |
| 3 | 124.21 | 45 | 17.3 | 1650 | 115.6 | 113.5 |
| 4 | 140.56 | 46 | 20.8 | 1920 | 130.2 | 126.4 |
| 5 | 152.80 | 46 | 21.6 | 2150 | 141.1 | 139.8 |
| 6 | 182.90 | 45 | 22.3 | 2290 | 158.3 | 156.2 |
| 7 | 214.33 | 44 | 29.3 | 2950 | 168.1 | 168.8 |
| 8 | 242.75 | 43 | 34.5 | 2210 | 182.5 | 185.6 |
| 9 | 254.16 | 43 | 42.6 | 2890 | 190.7 | 198.9 |
| 10 | 264.34 | 42 | 44.5 | 3870 | 201.3 | 218.4 |

# Case study 2

## Retail Sales in Europe

In 1998 the American Retail Consortium sponsored an investigation into the main trends in retail purchasing. McAuley and Associates did most of the investigation, with help from other companies around the country. As part of this study, they included a breakdown of retail sales by major geographic region, as shown in Table 6.4.

In 2000, McAuley were asked to do an equivalent study in Europe, concentrating on countries within the European Union. This was a major undertaking with co-operation between many bodies over several years.

The definition of the study was left deliberately vague so that the report could move in the most productive directions. The sponsors were more interested in long-term strategic directions than details of operations. The question is, what kind of analysis can McAulay do? What information can they collect? How can they collect it? How should they present the results? What kinds of analysis will they do? Put yourself in their shoes, and start preparing some ideas for the direction and scope of the study.

**Table 6.4**  Retail sales by region in billion US$

| Year | US | NE | Midwest | South | West |
|------|------|-----|---------|-------|------|
| 1970 | 375 | 94 | 108 | 107 | 67 |
| 1971 | 414 | 99 | 117 | 119 | 73 |
| 1972 | 459 | 105 | 128 | 133 | 83 |
| 1973 | 512 | 114 | 145 | 153 | 92 |
| 1974 | 542 | 119 | 157 | 163 | 98 |
| 1975 | 588 | 126 | 171 | 177 | 110 |
| 1976 | 656 | 136 | 191 | 199 | 125 |
| 1977 | 722 | 152 | 196 | 228 | 137 |
| 1978 | 804 | 165 | 223 | 252 | 164 |
| 1979 | 897 | 181 | 243 | 285 | 188 |
| 1980 | 957 | 195 | 247 | 312 | 203 |
| 1981 | 1039 | 209 | 263 | 345 | 221 |
| 1982 | 1069 | 219 | 269 | 356 | 225 |
| 1983 | 1170 | 241 | 290 | 394 | 246 |
| 1984 | 1287 | 266 | 320 | 434 | 267 |
| 1985 | 1375 | 286 | 342 | 461 | 287 |
| 1986 | 1450 | 313 | 354 | 482 | 300 |
| 1987 | 1541 | 333 | 369 | 516 | 322 |
| 1988 | 1656 | 366 | 395 | 547 | 347 |
| 1989 | 1759 | 381 | 418 | 577 | 383 |
| 1990 | 1845 | 386 | 437 | 610 | 412 |
| 1991 | 1856 | 379 | 447 | 619 | 410 |
| 1992 | 1952 | 389 | 472 | 663 | 427 |
| 1993 | 2074 | 407 | 503 | 716 | 447 |
| 1994 | 2230 | 427 | 539 | 783 | 482 |
| 1995 | 2329 | 438 | 567 | 822 | 502 |
| 1996 | 2461 | 463 | 598 | 870 | 530 |
| 1997 | 2566 | 485 | 624 | 902 | 552 |

# PART THREE

# Solving business problems

This book is divided into five parts, each of which covers a different aspect of quantitative methods in business. The first part gave the background and context for the rest of the book. The second part discussed data collection and description. This is the third part, which looks at methods of solving specific types of business problem. The problems tackled here are essentially deterministic, which means that they do not involve any probabilities. The next part introduces probabilities and statistical methods. The final part shows how these ideas can be applied in probabilistic models.

There are five chapters in this part.

Chapter 7 describes some financial calculations, including break-even points and economies of scale. Then it looks at the changing value of money over time. These calculations are based on compound interest rates, with applications including investment decisions, project comparison, depreciation and mortgages.

Chapter 8 describes linear regression. This is a method of relating variables so that the value of one can be predicted from the value of another. The demand for a product may, for example, be predicted from the price charged. Linear regression can be used for forecasting, and this theme is continued in the following chapter.

Chapter 9 describes some standard methods of forecasting. Perhaps the most common type of forecast is based on judgement. A more reliable method is projective forecasting, which examines past patterns of observations and projects these into the future.

Chapter 10 describes linear programming. This is a method of solving problems where an optimal solution is needed, but there are constraints on the values that can be used. Linear programming is widely used in business and has proved particularly useful for planning decisions.

Chapter 11 looks at some uses of calculus. This is used to describe situations of change and can again find optimal solutions to certain types of problem.

## Ideas in Practice – Survey into use of quantitative methods

For many years Peder Kristensen has been looking at the way that managers actually use quantitative methods. In 1998 he sent a questionnaire to 241 managers asking them how much they used standard quantitative analyses. Some of these results were quite disappointing. He said, 'Some methods were widely used – such as break-even analyses, basic statistics and inventory control. On the other hand, some common methods – such as linear programming and regression analysis – were used surprisingly little. My survey did contain a lot of small companies which are less likely to use sophisticated methods, but the results were still a little disappointing'.

It did not take Peder long to recognize the fault in his data collection. He explained, 'It was the most basic and embarrassing mistake. I assumed that most managers would be familiar with a range of quantitative methods. I simply asked questions like, "Do you use break-even analyses in your work?" Actually, relatively few of the managers had any formal training in quantitative methods, and so were unlikely to use them'.

Peder repeated the survey in 1999. This time he asked more appropriate questions, such as, 'Do you know about break-even analyses? If the answer is "yes" do you ever use them in your work?'

This time the results were more interesting. The following table shows some typical results.

| Topic | Per cent aware of | Per cent of these using |
|---|---|---|
| Descriptive statistics | 90 | 95 |
| Discounted cash flow | 77 | 86 |
| Inventory control | 71 | 81 |
| Forecasting | 65 | 72 |
| Regression | 62 | 75 |
| Project planning | 53 | 61 |
| Linear programming | 51 | 55 |
| Queuing models | 35 | 30 |
| Integer programming | 20 | 35 |

Many people believe that managers do not use quantitative methods because they do not trust them, or they believe the analyses are too difficult or inappropriate. Peder began to show that the real reason that managers do not use quantitative methods is simply that they do not know about them.

# 7 Calculations with money

| | | |
|---|---|---|
| Chapter outline | 189 | Chapter review | 217 |
| 7.1 Financial ratios | 190 | Problems | 218 |
| 7.2 Break-even point | 193 | Computer exercises | 219 |
| 7.3 Value of money over time | 201 | Case study: Mrs Hamilton's retirement savings | 222 |
| 7.4 Mortgages, annuities and sinking funds | 213 | | |

## CHAPTER OUTLINE

Every organization is concerned with its finances. For this reason, many quantitative models have been developed to help managers make financial decisions. This chapter looks at some of the most important of these analyses. It starts by looking at financial ratios and then calculates a break-even point, which ensures that an organization makes enough products to cover its fixed costs.

The rest of the chapter looks at the value of money over time. Money invested earns interest, so its value increases over time. This has important consequences for many business decisions, such as the comparison of alternative investments, project funding, depreciation allowances, and mortgage repayments.

After reading the chapter and doing the exercises you should be able to:

- consider financial ratios
- calculate break-even points
- appreciate the reasons for economies of scale
- calculate investment values with simple and compound interest
- calculate present values and internal rates of return
- depreciate the value of assets
- calculate payments for sinking funds, mortgages and annuities

# 7.1 | Financial ratios

The performance of every organization is measured by its finances. This is true of companies wanting to make a profit, charities wanting to collect and disperse as much money as possible, hospitals wanting to treat all patients at acceptable cost, local authorities wanting to provide services within a fixed budget, or schools wanting to provide education from limited resources.

Most decisions in finance are based on quantitative analyses. An organization will typically prepare a set of annual accounts which describe performance over the past year and outline future plans. These give a quantitative view of the organisation, emphasizing:

- **profit and loss account** – which shows the overall profit (or loss) from normal operations
- **balance sheet** – which gives a snapshot of the company's assets and liabilities
- **cash flow statement** – which records the actual, rather than notional, receipts and payments.

A key figure coming from these accounts is the organization's profit. If you subtract all the costs of running a business from the income generated by sales, you are left with the profit. If the total income is less than the costs, the organization makes a loss. This seems straightforward, but you have to remember that the profit relies on accounting conventions, definitions and internal decisions and does not necessarily give an objective view. You also have to consider the point where profit is calculated:

- **profit before interest and tax** = sales – operating costs
- **profit before tax** = profit before interest and tax – interest paid to lenders
- **profit after tax** = profit before tax – tax paid to the government
- **retained earnings** = profit after tax – dividends paid to shareholders

Unfortunately, such figures do not really say much about a company. If Bill's Car Repairs makes a million pounds profit after tax, it would be a miracle – but if Vodafone makes a profit of a million pounds, it would be a disaster. It makes more sense to relate the profit to the size of the company. There are several ways of doing this:

- **Profit margin** – gives the profit before tax as a percentage of sales:

$$\text{profit margin} = \frac{\text{profit before tax}}{\text{sales}} \times 100$$

- **Return on total assets** – relates the profit to the organization's assets:

$$\text{return on total assets} = \frac{\text{profit before interest and tax}}{\text{fixed assets} + \text{current assets}} \times 100$$

This is arguably the most comprehensive measure of business performance, but you have to remember that different types of company need very different amounts of assets. An advertising agency needs few assets and should have a much higher return on assets than a car manufacturer.

Another way of looking at the return on total assets is to say that:

$$\text{return on total assets} = \frac{\text{income}}{\text{sales}} \times \frac{\text{sales}}{\text{assets}}$$

$$= \text{profit margin} \times \text{asset turn}$$

- **Return on equity.** An organization gets money from selling shares to get equity capital, borrowing through loans and retaining profits to plough back into the business. The return on equity shows the profit that could be returned to shareholders:

$$\text{return on equity} = \frac{\text{profit after tax}}{\text{shareholders' money}} \times 100$$

As you can see, many financial analyses use ratios to compare different things. There are literally hundreds of possible ratios, each of which is useful in different circumstances. Two common measures, for example, look at the assets and liabilities.:

- $$\text{acid test} = \frac{\text{liquid assets (cash and readily saleable assets)}}{\text{current liabilities}}$$

- $$\text{gearing} = \frac{\text{borrowed money}}{\text{shareholders' money}} \times 100$$

Some other measures that are particularly important for investors include:

- $$\text{earnings per share} = \frac{\text{profit after tax}}{\text{number of shares}}$$

- $$\text{dividends per share} = \frac{\text{amount distributed as dividends}}{\text{number of shares}}$$

- $$\text{price-earnings ratio} = \frac{\text{share price}}{\text{earnings per share}}$$

- $$\text{dividend cover} = \frac{\text{profit after tax}}{\text{profit distributed to shareholders}}$$

- $$\text{yield} = \frac{\text{dividend}}{\text{share price}} \times 100$$

The analyses and interpretation of such ratios can be a very specialized area, but they reinforce the importance of quantitative ideas. Such quantitative arguments are at the heart of every organization.

# WORKED EXAMPLE 7.1

How could you measure the performance of a major company such as AstraZeneca?

## Solution

There are hundreds of measures that you could use for AstraZeneca. The following table shows a handful that you can find in their annual report.

|  |  |  | $ million |
|---|---|---|---|
| Profit before interest and tax |  |  | 1963 |
| interest paid | 4 |  |  |
| Profit before tax | 1963 – 4 | = | 1959 |
| tax paid | 815 |  |  |
| Profit after tax | 1959 – 815 | = | 1144 |
| other items | 1 |  |  |
| Earnings | 1144 – 1 | = | 1143 |
| dividends paid | 1242 |  |  |
| Retained earnings | 1143 – 1242 | = | –99 |

| | | |
|---|---|---|
| Number of shares | 1775 million | |
| Share price | £25.68 | |
| Total assets | $19,816 million | |
| Earnings per share | $0.64 | ($1143 million / 1775 million) |
| Dividend per share | $0.70 | ($1242 million / 1775 million) |
| Return on assets | 9.9% | ($1963 million / $19,816 million) |

---

## IN SUMMARY

Finances are important for all organizations. Many quantitative models have been developed to help with financial decisions. This chapter concentrates on break-even points and the changing value of money over time.

# 7.2 Break-even point

## 7.2.1 Making enough for a profit

Organizations usually aim at making a profit, where **profit** is defined as the difference between revenue and total cost:

$$\text{profit} = \text{revenue} - \text{total cost}$$

Most organizations sell a range of different products (both services and goods) and it is important to know how much profit or loss each one makes. An important calculation for this finds the break-even point.

When a company sells a product for a fixed price, the revenue is found from:

$$\text{revenue} = \text{price per unit} \times \text{number of units sold}$$
$$= PN$$

where:

$$P = \text{price charged for unit}$$
$$N = \text{number of units sold}$$

The costs associated with the product are a little more awkward as some are fixed regardless of the number of units made, while others vary with the output. If, for example, a machine is leased to make a certain product, the cost of leasing may be fixed regardless of the number of units made, but the cost of raw materials will vary. Another example of this is the cost of running a car, which can be divided into a fixed cost (repayment of purchase loan, road tax, insurance, etc) and a variable cost for each mile travelled (petrol, oil, tyres, depreciation, etc). So, in general, we have:

$$\text{total cost} = \text{fixed cost} + \text{variable cost}$$
$$= \text{fixed cost} + (\text{cost per unit} \times \text{number of units made})$$
$$= F + CN$$

where:

$$F = \text{fixed cost}$$
$$C = \text{cost per unit}$$
$$N = \text{number of units made}$$

Comparing the total cost of producing $N$ units of a product with the revenue generated from selling them leads to the important idea of a **break-even point**. This is the number of units that must be sold before a profit is made. Suppose a new product needs £200,000 spent on research, development, equipment and other preparations before production can start. During normal production each unit costs £20 to make and sells for £30. The company only starts to make a profit when the original £200,000 has been recovered. The point when this happens is the break-even point. In this example each unit sold contributes £30 – £20 = £10 to the company, so 200 000/10 = 20 000 units must be sold to cover the original investment. After this point the excess of revenue over expenditure is profit.

The break-even point is defined as the point where:

$$\text{revenue} = \text{total cost}$$

$$\frac{\text{price per}}{\text{unit}} \times \frac{\text{number of}}{\text{units sold}} = \text{fixed cost} + \frac{\text{cost per}}{\text{unit}} \times \frac{\text{number of}}{\text{units made}}$$

Assuming that all production is sold, this gives:

$$PN = F + CN$$

so:

$$N(P - C) = F$$

or:

$$\text{break-even point} = N = \frac{F}{P - C}$$

Both the revenue and total cost rise linearly with the number of units, so we can plot the relationships on the graph in Figure 7.1.

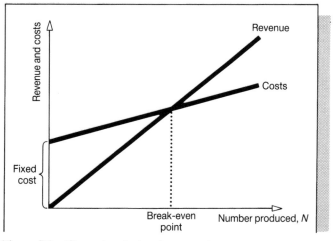

**Figure 7.1**   Illustrating the break-even point.

You can see from Figure 7.2 that:

- if the number of units sold is higher than the break-even point, revenue is higher than costs and there is a profit:

$$\text{profit} = N(P - C) - F$$

- if the number of units sold is equal to the break-even point, revenue equals total cost:

$$N(P - C) = F$$

- if the number of units sold is less than the break-even point, costs are higher than revenue and there is a loss:

$$\text{loss} = F - N(P - C)$$

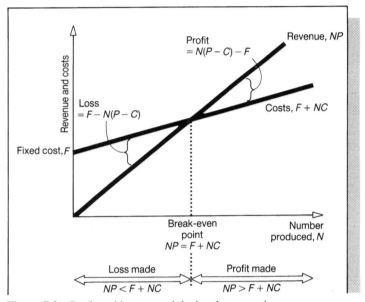

**Figure 7.2** Profit and loss around the break-even point.

# WORKED EXAMPLE 7.2

A company makes and sells 200 units of a product every week; the fixed costs for buildings, machines and employees are $12,000 a week, while raw material and other variable costs are $50 a unit.

(a) What is the profit if the selling price is $130 a unit?

(b) What is the profit if the selling price is $80 a unit?

(c) What is the profit if the selling price is fixed at $80 but sales rise to 450 units a week?

## Solution

(a) We know that:

$$N = 200 \text{ units} = \text{number of units sold each week}$$

$$F = \$12{,}000 \text{ a week} = \text{fixed cost each week}$$

$$C = \$50 \text{ a unit} = \text{variable cost per unit}$$

If the selling price $P$ is set at $130, the break-even point is:

$$N = \frac{F}{P - C} = \frac{12\,000}{130 - 50} = 150 \text{ units}$$

Actual sales are more than this, so the product makes a profit of:

$$\text{profit} = N(P - C) - F = 200 \times (130 - 50) - 12\,000$$

$$= \$4000 \text{ a week}$$

(b) If the selling price $P$ is set at $80, the break-even point is:

$$N = \frac{F}{P - C} = \frac{12\,000}{80 - 50} = 400 \text{ units}$$

Actual sales are less than this, so the product makes a loss of:

$$\text{loss} = F - N(P - C) = 12\,000 - 200 \times (80 - 50)$$

$$= \$6000 \text{ a week}$$

(c) With the selling price set at $80 a unit, the break-even point is 400 units. If sales increase to 450 units a week the product makes a profit of:

$$\text{profit} = N(P - C) - F = 450 \times (80 - 50) - 12\,000$$

$$= \$1500 \text{ a week}$$

This shows that a profit can still be made with a low selling price provided that sales are high enough.

# WORKED EXAMPLE 7.3

NorElec offers two prices for domestic customers. The normal rate has standing charges of £18.20 a quarter, with each unit of electricity used costing £0.142. A special economy rate has standing charges of £22.70 a quarter, with each unit of electricity during the day costing £0.162, but each unit used during the night costing only £0.082. What consumption pattern would make it cheaper to use the economy rate?

## Solution

If a consumer uses an average of $D$ units per quarter during the day and $N$ units a quarter during the night, their costs are:

normal rate: $18.20 + 0.142 \times (D + N)$

economy rate: $22.70 + 0.162 \times D + 0.082 \times N$

It is cheaper to use the economy rate when:

$$22.7 + 0.162 \times D + 0.082 \times N < 18.2 + 0.142 \times (D + N)$$
$$4.5 < 0.06 \times N - 0.02 \times D$$

or

$$D < 3 \times N - 225$$

If consumption during the day is less than three times consumption during the night minus 225 units, it is cheaper to use the economy rate; otherwise it is cheaper to use the standard rate. This is illustrated in Figure 7.3.

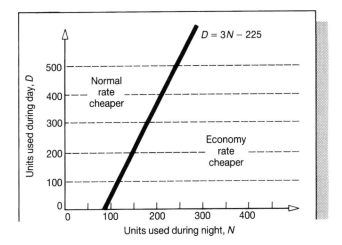

**Figure 7.3** Cost of electricity for Worked Example 7.3.

A break-even analysis is useful for the obvious purpose of seeing how many units must be sold to make a profit, but it also helps with other types of decision, such as the choice between buying or leasing equipment, making sure there is enough capacity when buying new equipment, whether to buy an item or make it within the company, or the choice of competitive tenders for services.

It is also worth mentioning the most common difficulty in calculating break-even points, which is assigning a reasonable proportion of overheads to the fixed cost of each product. This depends on the accounting conventions used within the organization. The problem is made worse if the product mix is constantly changing. Then accounting practices will allocate a changing amount of overheads to each product. In other words, the costs of making a particular product, and hence its profit, can change even though there has been no change in the product itself or the way it is made.

IN SUMMARY

Costs can be classified as either fixed or variable and revenue must cover both of these before a profit is made. The number of units at which revenue equals total cost is called the break-even point.

## 7.2.2 | Economies of scale

The break-even analysis shows one reason why organizations can get **economies of scale**, where the average unit cost falls as the number of units sold increases. We know that:

$$\text{total cost} = \text{fixed cost} + \text{variable cost}$$

$$T = F + NC$$

Now we can find the average cost per unit by dividing the total cost by the number of units, $N$:

$$\text{average total cost per unit} = T/N = F/N + C$$

As $N$ increases, the average cost per unit will fall, because the proportion of fixed cost to be recovered by each unit sold is reduced, as shown in Figure 7.4.

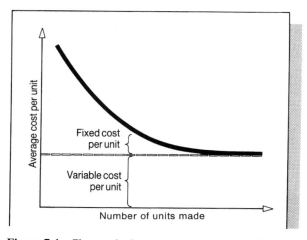

**Figure 7.4** Changes in the average cost per unit with production quantity.

## WORKED EXAMPLE 7.4

Jane's Seafood Diner serves 200 meals a day at an average price of €20. The variable cost of each meal is €10 and there are fixed costs of running the restaurant of €1750 a day.

(a) What profit does the restaurant make?

(b) What is the average total cost of a meal?

(c) By how much would the average cost of a meal fall if the number served rose to 250 a day?

## Solution

(a) The break-even point is:

$$N = \frac{F}{P - C} = \frac{1750}{20 - 10} = 175$$

Actual sales are above this so the profit is:

$$\text{profit} = N(P - C) - F = 200 \times (20 - 10) - 1750$$
$$= €250 \text{ a day}$$

(b) The average total cost of a meal is:

$$\text{average cost} = \text{total cost} / \text{number of meals}$$

$$= \frac{1750 + 200 \times 10}{200}$$

$$= €18.75 \text{ a meal}$$

(c) Serving 250 meals a day would give:

$$\text{average cost} = \frac{1750 + 250 \times 10}{250}$$

$$= €17 \text{ a meal}$$

The distribution of fixed costs to more units is only one reason for economies of scale. In many situations there are economies of scale even when the fixed costs are ignored. These cost reductions occur because people become more familiar with the operations and take less time, machine operators become more practised, problems are sorted out, or disruptions are eliminated.

Economies of scale are often suggested as a reason for making facilities as large as possible. This is certainly the reason why, say, oil tankers have become so big, but there can also be **diseconomies of scale**. Here the advantage of reduced fixed cost per unit is more than offset by increased bureaucracy, difficulties of communication, more complex management hierarchies, increased costs of supervision, and perceived reduction in the importance of individuals. These effects usually lead to economies of scale up to an optimal size, and then diseconomies of scale, as shown in Figure 7.5.

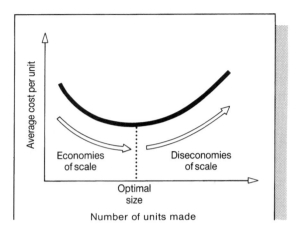

**Figure 7.5** Economies and diseconomies of scale.

## IN SUMMARY

Organizations can get economies of scale, partly by spreading fixed costs over a larger number of units made. There may also be diseconomies of scale.

# Self-assessment questions

**7.1** 'Only companies aiming to make a profit are interested in financial analyses.' Is this statement true?

**7.2** What is meant by the 'return on assets'?

**7.3** What does the 'variable cost' vary with?

**7.4** What is the 'break-even point'?

**7.5** The break-even point for a product is calculated as 1500 units a week. If actual sales are 1200 units a week, what does this mean?

**7.6** 'Because of economies of scale it is always better to have a single large factory than a number of smaller ones.' Do you think this is true?

# 7.3 | Value of money over time

If you want to buy a house, there are several ways of paying for it. One option is to save enough money and then pay cash. Unfortunately, experience suggests that house prices rise faster than our savings, so a better option is to save a deposit and then borrow the rest of the money as a mortgage. This is repaid over a long period, and even though the total repayments are two or three times the original amount borrowed, it is still considered a good investment.

Anyone borrowing money must pay the lender **interest**. The amount borrowed is called the **principal** and the time for which it is borrowed is called the **duration of the loan**. The amount of interest is usually quoted as an annual percentage of the principal, so a typical interest rate is 10% a year.

## 7.3.1 | Interest rates

If you put money into a bank account it earns interest. If you leave £1000 in an account offering interest of 10% a year it will earn $1000 \times 10/100 = £100$ interest at the end of the year. If you take the interest earned from the account, the initial deposit stays unchanged at £1000. This is the principle of **simple interest**, where interest is only paid on the initial deposit. Each year the same amount of interest is paid. If the original amount invested is $A_0$ and the interest rate is $I$, the amount of interest paid each year is $A_0I$. Then after $n$ periods:

● total interest paid is:

$$\frac{A_0 In}{100}$$

● value of investment:

$$A_n = A_0 + \frac{A_0 In}{100} = A_0 \times \left(1 + \frac{In}{100}\right)$$

where: $A_0$ = original amount invested

$A_n$ = amount of money after $n$ periods

$I$ = percentage interest rate earned each period

$n$ = number of periods considered

It is easier to consider the interest rate as a decimal fraction or proportion, $i$, rather than as a percentage, $I$. This means that an interest rate of 10% is shown as $i = 0.1$, an interest rate of 15% by $i = 0.15$, and so on. Then with simple interest, the interest paid is:

amount of principal × interest rate × duration = $A_0 in$

and the value of $A_0$ after $n$ periods is:

for simple interest     $A_n = A_0 \times (1 + in)$

Simple interest assumes that no additional interest is paid on interest that has already been earned. In practice, most loans are based on **compound interest**, which pays interest both on the original investment and on interest earned previously and left in the account.

If you put an amount of money $A_0$ into a bank account and leave it untouched for a year earning interest at an annual rate $i$, at the end of the year there will be an amount $A_1$, where:

$$A_1 = A_0 \times (1 + i)$$

If you leave the amount $A_1$ untouched for a second year it will earn interest not only on the initial amount deposited, but also on the interest earned in the first year. This comes to:

$$A_2 = A_1 \times (1 + i)$$

or, substituting the value of $A_1$:

$$A_2 = [A_0 \times (1 + i)] \times (1 + i)$$
$$= A_0 \times (1 + i)^2$$

The amount of money will increase in this compound way, so that at the end of three years there will be $A_0 \times (1 + i)^3$ in the account, and at any time $n$ years in the future the account will contain $A_n$, where:

> for compound interest $\quad A_n = A_0 \times (1 + i)^n$

The change in $A_n$ over time is shown in Figure 7.6. This shows how an initial investment of £1 increases with different interest rates between 3% and 25%.

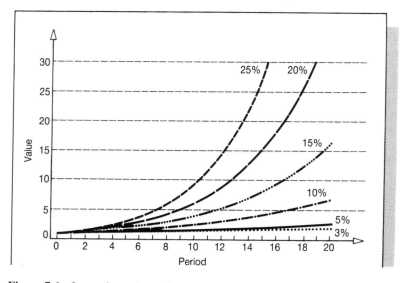

**Figure 7.6** Increasing value with varying interest rates.

# WORKED EXAMPLE 7.5

If £1000 is left in a bank account earning 5% compound interest a year, how much will be in the account at the end of 5 years? How much will there be at the end of 20 years?

## Solution

We know that:

$$A_0 = £1000$$
$$i = 0.05$$

With compound interest the amount in the account is:

$$A_n = A_0 \times (1 + i)^n$$

At the end of five years there will be:

$$A_5 = 1000 \times (1 + 0.05)^5 = 1000 \times 1.2763 = £1276$$

At the end of 20 years there will be:

$$A_{20} = 1000 \times (1 + 0.05)^{20} = 1000 \times 2.6533 = £2653$$

Interest rates are usually quoted annually, but any consistent units can be used, such as 1% a month or 0.03% a day. There are several ways of calculating interest, and to avoid confusion, there is often a legal requirement to quote an APR, or **annual percentage rate**. This is the true cost of borrowing. Suppose you borrow £100 with interest payable of 2% at the end of each month. You might do a quick calculation to suggest that this is equal to $2 \times 12 = 24\%$ a year. In fact, this is the **notional interest rate**, but it is not the APR. We can show this as follows:

- Borrowing £100 at 24% APR would raise the debt to $100 \times (1 + 0.24) = £124$ by the end of the year.

- Borrowing £100 at 2% a month, and using compound interest to calculate the debt at the end of 12 months gives:

$$A_n = A_0 \times (1 + i)^n = 100 \times (1 + 0.02)^{12} = £126.82$$

This means that interest of £26.82 will be charged, giving an APR of 26.82%.

## IN SUMMARY

The value of money varies over time, and a given amount at present can generate a larger amount in the future. Any money invested with compound interest increases over time, so that $A_n = A_0 \times (1 + i)^n$.

# Present value of money

In the last section we saw that an amount of money $A_0$ invested now will have a value of $A_0(1 + i)^n$ at a time $n$ periods in the future. Turning this the other way round, we could say that an amount $A_n$, $n$ periods in the future, has a present value of $A_0$, where:

$$A_0 = \frac{A_n}{(1 + i)^n}$$

$$= A_n \times (1 + i)^{-n}$$

The process of calculating the present value of an amount in the future is called **discounting to present value** or finding the discounted value. We can use this to compare amounts of money that become available at different times.

## WORKED EXAMPLE 7.6

A company is thinking about introducing a new product. There are two alternatives available. The profits from these are phased over many years, but they can be summarized as:

- product 1 gives a profit of £300,000 in five years' time
- product 2 gives a profit of £500,000 in ten years' time.

Which product should the company introduce if it uses a discounting rate of 20% a year for future profits?

### Solution

This problem needs a comparison of money earned at different times. The way to make such comparisons is to find the value of both amounts at the same time. Any convenient time can be used, but the obvious one is to reduce amounts to their present value.

- Product 1: $A_n = £300,000$ and $n = 5$ years:
$$A_0 = A_n \times (1 + i)^{-n}$$
$$= 300\,000 \times (1 + 0.2)^{-5}$$
$$= £120,563$$

- Product 2: $A_n = £500,000$ and $n = 10$ years:
$$A_0 = A_n \times (1 + i)^{-n}$$
$$= 500\,000 \times (1 + 0.2)^{-10}$$
$$= £80,753$$

Now we have the present values of both products, and the better clearly has the higher value. Based on this information, product 1 is the better alternative.

Using a simple interest rate for discounting is often an over-simplification, as it ignores the effects of inflation, opportunity costs, taxes and other factors. There is also the problem that interest rates vary over time. It is clearly difficult to set a discount rate that takes all these factors into account. One step towards this calculates a real interest rate from:

$$\text{real interest rate} = \text{actual interest rate} - \text{inflation}$$

If the rate of inflation is low, the real interest rate is positive and the value of money invested will grow; if the rate of inflation is high, the real interest rate is negative and any money invested will decrease in value.

Discounting to present values is particularly useful for large projects that have payments and incomes spread over varying time periods. Then we can discount all amounts to their present values, and subtracting the present value of all costs from the present value of all revenues gives a **net present value**:

$$\begin{array}{c}\text{net present} \\ \text{value}\end{array} = \begin{array}{c}\text{sum of discounted} \\ \text{revenues}\end{array} - \begin{array}{c}\text{sum of discounted} \\ \text{costs}\end{array}$$

If the net present value is negative, a project will make a loss and we should not undertake it. If alternative projects have positive net present values, the best is the one with the highest net present value.

## WORKED EXAMPLE 7.7

Three alternative projects have initial costs and revenues (each in thousands of pounds) for the next five years as shown below:

| Project | Initial cost | *Net revenue in each year* | | | | |
| --- | --- | --- | --- | --- | --- | --- |
| | | *1* | *2* | *3* | *4* | *5* |
| A | 1000 | 500 | 400 | 300 | 200 | 100 |
| B | 1000 | 200 | 200 | 300 | 400 | 400 |
| C | 500 | 50 | 200 | 200 | 100 | 50 |

If the company has enough resources to start only one project, use a discounting rate of 10% to suggest the best.

## Solution

Conventional accounting often takes an **average rate of return**, which is the average annual revenue as a percentage of initial investment. In this example the average rates of return are:

|  | *Project A* | *Project B* | *Project C* |
|---|---|---|---|
| Initial cost | 1000 | 1000 | 500 |
| Total revenue | 1500 | 1500 | 600 |
| Average annual revenue | 300 | 300 | 120 |
| Average rate of return | 30% | 30% | 24% |

Projects A and B have the same average rate of return, but project C has a lower rate and would only be considered if the company could not afford the initial investment of £1 million, if 24% were considered an acceptable rate of return, or if some other factor made projects A and B less acceptable.

Looking in more detail at the money flows for projects A and B, you can see that the revenues vary over time and, in particular, A offers more in early years while B offers more in later years. To give a valid comparison between these we can transform all amounts to present values and compare the net present value of each project. So, for project A:

- 500 in year 1 has a present value of $500/1.1^1 = 454.55$
- 400 in year 2 has a present value of $400/1.1^2 = 330.58$
- 300 in year 3 has a present value of $300/1.1^3 = 225.39$

and so on. These calculations are shown in Figure 7.7. Adding the present values of revenues and then subtracting the present values of costs (in this case the single initial project costs) gives the net present values.

|  | A | B | C | D | E | F | G | H |
|---|---|---|---|---|---|---|---|---|
| 1 | **Net present values** | | | | | | | |
| 2 | | | | | | | | |
| 3 | | | **Project A** | | **Project B** | | **Project C** | |
| 4 | **Year** | **Discount factor** | **Revenue** | **Present value** | **Revenue** | **Present value** | **Revenue** | **Present value** |
| 5 | 1 | 1.1 | 500 | 454.55 | 200 | 181.82 | 50 | 45.45 |
| 6 | 2 | 1.21 | 400 | 330.58 | 200 | 165.29 | 200 | 165.29 |
| 7 | 3 | 1.331 | 300 | 225.39 | 300 | 225.39 | 200 | 150.26 |
| 8 | 4 | 1.4641 | 200 | 136.60 | 400 | 273.21 | 100 | 68.30 |
| 9 | 5 | 1.61051 | 100 | 62.09 | 400 | 248.37 | 50 | 31.05 |
| 10 | **Totals** | | **1500** | **1209.21** | **1500** | **1094.08** | **600** | **460.35** |
| 11 | | | | | | | | |
| 12 | **Present values** | | | | | | | |
| 13 | | **Revenues** | | 1209.21 | | 1094.08 | | 460.35 |
| 14 | | **Costs** | | 1000 | | 1000 | | 500 |
| 15 | | | | | | | | |
| 16 | **Net present values** | | | **209.21** | | **94.08** | | **–39.65** |

**Figure 7.7**   Net present values for Worked Example 7.7.

Project A has the highest net present value and should, all other things being equal, be the one adopted. Project C has a negative net present value, showing a loss, and this alternative should clearly be avoided. One other consideration is that the revenues from A are declining, suggesting the project has a limited life span of around five years, while revenues from project B are rising, implying a longer life. Factors of this kind must be taken into account before making any final decisions.

---

### IN SUMMARY

Discounting amounts to present values allows direct comparison of revenues and payments at different times. The difference between these is the net present value.

## 7.3.3 | Internal rate of return

To compare the three projects in Worked Example 7.7 we assumed that the discounting rate was fixed, and calculated three net present values. It is often difficult to find a suitable discounting rate that takes into account interest rates, inflation, taxes, opportunity costs, exchange rates, risk and everything else. An alternative is to find the discounting rate that leads to a specified net present value: in other words, keep the same net present value for each project and calculate three different discounting rates. The usual approach is to calculate the discounting rate that leads to a net present value of zero; this is called the **internal rate of return**:

> The internal rate of return is the discounting rate
> that leads to a net present value of zero

Projects with higher internal rates of return have better financial performances – so we can compare different projects by calculating the internal rate of return (IRR) for each, and adopting the one with the highest value. We should add one note of caution here: if the internal rate of return is less than the current discounting rate, a project should not be started, as it will generate a net loss. In other words, we choose the project with the highest IRR, provided this is greater than the current discounting rate.

One small difficulty with internal rates of return is that there is no straightforward formula for calculating them. This means that we have to use iterative calculations, getting closer to the IRR at each step.

In project B of Worked Example 7.7 a discounting rate of 10% gave a net present value of £94,080. If we use a discounting rate of 15%, the net present value is – £50,030. In other words, a discounting rate of 10% gives a positive net present value while a discounting rate of 15% gives a negative value, so the internal rate of return (which gives a net present value of zero) must lie between these two. By doing more calculations we can narrow the range of the internal rate of return. The actual value is between 13.1% and 13.2%.

Thankfully, such calculations are usually done by standard functions, and Figure 7.8 shows the results from a typical spreadsheet. The data are from Project B in Worked Example 7.7, with the initial expenditure shown as a negative profit in year zero. The calculation is done automatically, and there is a check to make sure the net present value is actually zero (the 0.04 is simply a rounding error).

|    | A | B | C | D | E |
|----|---|---|---|---|---|
| 1  | **Internal rate of return** | | | | |
| 2  | | | | | |
| 3  | **Calculation** | | | **Check** | |
| 4  | | | | | |
| 5  | **Year** | **Revenue** | | **Discount rate** | **Discounted revenue** |
| 6  | 0 | −1000 | | 1 | −1000.00 |
| 7  | 1 | 200 | | 1.1314 | 176.77 |
| 8  | 2 | 200 | | 1.2801 | 156.24 |
| 9  | 3 | 300 | | 1.4483 | 207.14 |
| 10 | 4 | 400 | | 1.6386 | 244.12 |
| 11 | 5 | 400 | | 1.8539 | 215.76 |
| 12 | | | | | |
| 13 | **IRR** | **13.14%** | | | **0.04** |

**Figure 7.8** Internal rate of return calculation.

# WORKED EXAMPLE 7.8

Five projects have the annual revenues shown in Table 7.1 (in thousands of dollars). Which gives the best internal rate of return?

**Table 7.1**

| Year | Project 1 | Project 2 | Project 3 | Project 4 | Project 5 |
|------|-----------|-----------|-----------|-----------|-----------|
| 1 | −80 | −100 | −40 | −25 | 100 |
| 2 | −30 | −20 | −30 | −5 | 80 |
| 3 | 15 | 6 | −5 | 20 | 60 |
| 4 | 35 | 10 | 20 | 20 | −10 |
| 5 | 60 | 30 | 50 | 15 | −40 |
| 6 | 50 | 50 | 70 | −5 | −50 |
| 7 | 40 | 80 | 80 | −15 | −60 |

## Solution

The calculations for this are shown in the spreadsheet in Figure 7.9. You can see the internal rates of return are between –9% and 28%. The project with the highest IRR is best, and this is Project 3.

| | A | B | C | D | E | F | G |
|---|---|---|---|---|---|---|---|
| 1 | **Internal rate of return** | | | | | | |
| 2 | | | | | | | |
| 3 | **Year** | | **Project 1** | **Project 2** | **Project 3** | **Project 4** | **Project 5** |
| 4 | 1 | | –80 | –100 | –40 | –25 | 100 |
| 5 | 2 | | –30 | –20 | –30 | –5 | 80 |
| 6 | 3 | | 15 | 6 | –5 | 20 | 60 |
| 7 | 4 | | 35 | 10 | 20 | 20 | –10 |
| 8 | 5 | | 60 | 30 | 50 | 15 | –40 |
| 9 | 6 | | 50 | 50 | 70 | –5 | –50 |
| 10 | 7 | | 40 | 80 | 80 | –15 | –60 |
| 11 | | | | | | | |
| 12 | **IRR** | | 16% | 8% | 28% | 12% | –9% |

**Figure 7.9**   Comparison of internal rates of return for Worked Example 7.8.

---

IN SUMMARY

The internal rate of return is the discounting rate that gives a net present value of zero. The best investment is the one with the highest internal rate of return.

## 7.3.4 | Depreciation

When people buy a car, they expect to drive it for a few years and then replace it. This is because maintenance and repair costs rise, the car breaks down more often, new cars are more efficient and comfortable, and so on. Clearly the value of a car decreases as it gets older. In the same way, when a company buys a piece of equipment, it is used for some period and then replaced. But one problem for companies is that equipment forms part of the assets, and they must have an accurate valuation at any time. The value will obviously reduce over time, and the allowance for this is known as **depreciation**.

Most organizations **write down** the value of their assets each year. This means that they reduce the book value that they put on assets. Depreciation is then recorded as a loss that can be counted against profits, so the company can replace equipment when necessary.

There are several ways of calculating depreciation, but the two most widely used are:

- straight-line method
- reducing-balance method

Both of these assume that equipment is bought, operated for its expected life, and then sold for a scrap value. This scrap value is normally the resale value and does not mean that the equipment is actually scrapped. Perhaps a better term is residual value.

## Straight-line method

This reduces the equipment's value by the same amount every year. Then:

$$\text{annual depreciation} = \frac{\text{cost of equipment} - \text{scrap value}}{\text{estimated life of equipment}}$$

A machine costing £20,000 with an estimated scrap value of £5000 and a useful life of 10 years has an annual depreciation of:

$$\text{annual depreciation} = \frac{20\,000 - 5000}{10} = £1500$$

Straight-line depreciation is easy to calculate, but it does not reflect actual values. Most equipment loses a lot of value in the first year of operation, and will actually be worth less than its depreciated value.

## Reducing-balance method

In the reducing-balance method, a fixed percentage of the value of equipment is written off each year. Typically, equipment has its book value reduced by 20% a year. This has the benefit of giving more depreciation in the first few years, and gives a more accurate estimate of the real value of equipment.

With the reducing-balance method, the calculation of an asset's value is a simple extension of compound interest. We know that an amount $A_0$ which increases at a fixed percentage, $i$, in each period has a value after $n$ periods of:

$$A_n = A_0 \times (1 + i)^n$$

If the amount is decreasing at a fixed percentage, as it does with depreciation, we simply subtract $i$ instead of adding it. Then for a depreciation rate of $i$, equipment whose initial cost is $A_0$ has a depreciated value after $n$ periods of:

$$A_n = A_0 \times (1 - i)^n$$

## WORKED EXAMPLE 7.9

David Krishnan bought a machine for £10,000 and now has to consider its depreciation.

(a) Use the straight-line method to find the annual depreciation if the machine has an expected life of five years and a scrap value of £1000.

(b) If the reducing-balance method is used with a depreciation rate of 30%, what is the value of the machine after five years?

(c) With the reducing-balance method, what depreciation rate would reduce the machine's value to £2000 after three years?

### Solution

(a) For straight-line depreciation we know that:

$$\text{annual depreciation} = \frac{\text{cost of equipment} - \text{scrap value}}{\text{estimated life of equipment}}$$

so:

$$\text{annual depreciation} = \frac{10\,000 - 1000}{5} = £1800$$

(b) For reducing-balance depreciation:

$$A_n = A_o \times (1 - i)^n$$

or:

$$A_5 = 10\,000 \times (1 - 0.3)^5 = £1681$$

(c) We want $A_n$ to be £2000 when $n$ is 3, so:

$$A_n = A_o \times (1 - i)^n$$

or:

$$2000 = 10\,000 \times (1 - i)^3$$
$$0.2 = (1 - i)^3$$
$$0.585 = 1 - i$$

or:

$$i = 0.415$$

giving a depreciation rate of 41.5%.

## WORKED EXAMPLE 7.10

Hamil Leasing buys vans for $50,000 and expects to use them for five years. Then the suppliers will buy them back for $10,000 and offer a replacement. If Hamil uses straight-line depreciation, what is the book value of the machine each year? What depreciation rate should the company use with the reducing-balance method, and what is the van's book value each year? If Hamil discounts future amounts by 10% a year, what are the current values of all these amounts?

## Solution

Straight-line depreciation would reduce the book value of the machine by $(50\,000 - 10\,000)/5 = £8000$ a year. For the reducing-balance method $50\,000 \times (1 - i)^5 = 10\,000$, so $i = 0.2752$ (calculated by the computer). Now we can use these depreciation rates to calculate the book value of the machine each year, and then discount these amounts to present values. These calculations are shown in the spreadsheet in Figure 7.10.

|  | A | B | C | D | E | F | G |
|---|---|---|---|---|---|---|---|
| 1 | **Depreciation** | | | | | | |
| 2 | | | | | | | |
| 3 | | | **Straight-line** | | | **Reducing-balance** | |
| 4 | **Rate** | | 8000 | | | 0.2752 | |
| 5 | | | | | | | |
| 6 | **Year** | **Discount factor** | **Amount** | **Present value** | | **Amount** | **Present value** |
| 7 | 0 | 1 | 50000 | 50000 | | 50000 | 50000 |
| 8 | 1 | 1.1 | 42000 | 38182 | | 36239 | 32945 |
| 9 | 2 | 1.21 | 34000 | 28099 | | 26265 | 21707 |
| 10 | 3 | 1.331 | 26000 | 19534 | | 19037 | 14302 |
| 11 | 4 | 1.464 | 18000 | 12294 | | 13797 | 9424 |
| 12 | 5 | 1.611 | 10000 | 6209 | | 10000 | 6209 |

**Figure 7.10** Calculations for depreciation in Worked Example 7.10.

---

## IN SUMMARY

The value of equipment decreases with its age. There are several methods for calculating depreciated values, with the straight-line and reducing-balance methods being widely used.

## Self-assessment questions

**7.7** Is £1000 now worth

(a) more than £1000 in five years' time

(b) less than £1000 in five years' time

(c) the same as £1000 in five years' time?

**7.8** Is an interest rate of 12% a year the same as 1% a month?

**7.9** How could you compare the net benefits of two projects, one of which lasts for five years and the other for seven years?

**7.10** What is a discounting rate?

**7.11** What is the difference between the straight-line and the reducing-balance methods of calculating depreciation?

# ∥ 7.4 ∥ Mortgages, annuities and sinking funds

In the last section we saw how the value of money changes over time, and in particular how it can earn interest and grow at a compound rate. In this section we shall look at an extension to this, where regular savings are also added. This happens in a variety of circumstances including mortgages, annuities and sinking funds.

Suppose you have an initial amount to invest, $A_0$, which earns interest at a rate $i$, and you add an additional investment $F$ at the end of each period. It is fairly easy to show that the amount invested after $n$ periods is:

$$A_n = A_0 \times (1 + i)^n + \frac{F \times (1 + i)^n - F}{i}$$

The first part of this equation shows the income generated by the original investment, while the second part shows the amount accumulated by regular payments.

## WORKED EXAMPLE 7.11

An investor puts £1000 into a building society account that earns 10% interest a year. If the investor adds another £500 at the end of each year, how much will be in the account at the end of five years?

### Solution

The values we are given are:

$$A_0 = £1000$$
$$i = 0.1$$
$$F = £500$$
$$n = 5$$

and we want the value of $A_5$, which we can find from substitution as:

$$A_n = A_0 \times (1 + i)^n + \frac{F \times (1 + i)^n - F}{i}$$

so:

$$A_5 = 1000 \times 1.1^5 + \frac{500 \times 1.1^5 - 500}{0.1} = £4663$$

This kind of calculation is used by businesses that want to set aside regular payments to accumulate a certain amount of money at the end of some period. This is called a **sinking fund** and is typically set up to allow for replacement of equipment or vehicles. Sinking funds usually do not have an initial payment (so $A_0 = 0$), but have equal payments in every period.

## WORKED EXAMPLE 7.12

How much should be invested each year to give a sinking fund with £20,000 at the end of ten years, when expected interest rates are 15%?

### Solution

The variables are:

$$A_n = £20,000$$
$$A_0 = £0$$
$$i = 0.15$$
$$n = 10$$

So we can substitute into:

$$A_n = A_0 \times (1 + i)^n + \frac{F \times (1 + i)^n - F}{i}$$

to give:

$$20\,000 = 0 + \frac{F \times (1 + 0.15)^{10} - F}{0.15}$$

$$3000 = F \times 4.046 - F$$

or:

$$F = £985.04$$

The company should put £985.04 into the fund each year.

Many people do not like debts, but they can have benefits. Given a choice between £100 now or £100 in a year's time we should take the money now because it has a higher value. This reasoning can be used to justify some debts: they allow us to borrow money now and then make repayments in the future using money that has a lower value. From a financial point of view, whether debts are beneficial or not depends on the purpose to which the money is put, real interest rates, the inflation rate, and so on. The most widely used purpose of private borrowing is to buy a house. This is usually financed by a mortgage, which uses the kind of regular payments described above. The initial investment $A_0$ is then negative, and the investment after $n$ periods must be zero, showing that the debt has been repaid.

# WORKED EXAMPLE 7.13

A mortgage of £30,000 is borrowed over 25 years at 12% interest. This loan is repaid by regular instalments at the end of every year. How much should each instalment be?

## Solution

We know that:

$$A_0 = -£30,000$$

$$A_{25} = £0$$

$$i = 0.12$$

$$n = 25$$

and we want to find $F$. Substituting these values gives:

$$A_n = A_o \times (1 + i)^n + \frac{F \times (1 + i)^n - F}{i}$$

$$0 = -30\,000 \times 1.12^{25} + \frac{F \times 1.12^{25} - F}{0.12}$$

Then:

$$30\,000 \times 17 \times 0.12 = F \times 17 - F$$

or:

$$F = £3825$$

After 25 payments of £3825 the original debt will be repaid. Notice that the total payment here is $25 \times 3825 = £95,625$. It is quite common for total mortgage repayments to be several times the original loan, especially when interest rates are high.

An annuity is the reverse of a mortgage. In other words, someone who has a lump sum can invest it and in return get regular payments for some period in the future. This scheme is usually run by finance companies and appeals to retired people who can convert their savings into a regular income.

## WORKED EXAMPLE 7.14

If interest rates are 12%, how much would an annuity cost that gave £10,000 a year for the next 10 years?

### Solution

If we take the position of the person paying the annuity, we get the same pattern as a mortgage, with:

$$A_n = 0$$

$$F = £10,000$$

$$n = 10$$

$$i = 0.12$$

and we want to find $A_0$.

Now:

$$A_n = A_o \times (1 + i)^n + \frac{F \times (1 + i)^n - F}{i}$$

so:

$$0 = A_0 \times (1 + 0.12)^{10} + \frac{10\,000 \times (1 + 0.12)^{10} - 10\,000}{0.12}$$

$$= A_0 \times 3.11 + 175\,487.35$$

or:

$$A_0 = -\pounds 56{,}502$$

The negative sign here shows that the original payment is made to the borrower.

---

## IN SUMMARY

The value of an investment with regular additional payments is given by:

$$A_n = A_0(1 + i)^n + \frac{F(1 + i)^n - F}{i}$$

This equation has several applications in finance.

---

# Self-assessment questions

**7.12** What is a sinking fund?

**7.13** How would you calculate the payment worth making for an annuity?

**7.14** 'The value of $i$ is always the current interest rate.' Is this true?

## CHAPTER REVIEW

Every organization is concerned with its finances. Many quantitative models are available to help with these, and this chapter has described some of the most important. In particular it described:

- some common ratios
- calculation of break-even points and the reason for economies of scale
- the value of money over time with simple and compound interest
- discounting to present values and internal rates of return
- depreciation of assets
- payments of sinking funds, mortgages and annuities

# Problems

**7.1** A firm of taxi operators has an average fixed cost of £4500 a year for each car. Each kilometre driven costs 20 pence with fares averaging 30 pence. How many kilometres a year does each car need to travel before making a profit? Last year each car drove 160 000 kilometres. What were the total and net incomes?

**7.2** Air Atlantic is considering a new service between Aberdeen and Calgary. Its existing aeroplanes, each of which has a capacity of 240 passengers, could be used for one flight a week with fixed costs of £30,000 and variable costs amounting to 50% of ticket price. If the airline plans to sell tickets at £200 each, how many passengers will be needed to break even on the proposed route? Does this seem a reasonable number?

**7.3** A company is planning the introduction of a new product. It must choose one product from three available and has estimated the following data:

|  | Product A | Product B | Product C |
|---|---|---|---|
| Annual sales | 600 | 900 | 1200 |
| Unit cost | 680 | 900 | 1200 |
| Fixed cost | 200 000 | 350 000 | 500 000 |
| Product life | 3 years | 5 years | 8 years |
| Selling price | 760 | 1000 | 1290 |

Which product would you recommend?

**7.4** How much will an initial investment of £1000 earning interest of 8% a year be worth at the end of 20 years?

**7.5** Several years ago a couple bought an endowment insurance policy that has recently matured. They have the option of receiving £20,000 now or £40,000 in ten years' time. Because they have retired and pay no income tax, they could invest the money with a real interest rate expected to remain at 10% a year for the foreseeable future. Which option should they take?

**7.6** Given the cash flows for three projects shown in Table 7.2, calculate the net present values using a discounting rate of 12% a year.

**Table 7.2**

|  | Project A | | Project B | | Project C | |
|---|---|---|---|---|---|---|
| Year | Income | Expenditure | Income | Expenditure | Income | Expenditure |
| 0 | 0 | 18 000 | 0 | 24 000 | 0 | 21 000 |
| 1 | 2500 | 0 | 2000 | 10 000 | 0 | 12 000 |
| 2 | 13 500 | 6000 | 10 000 | 6000 | 20 000 | 5000 |
| 3 | 18 000 | 0 | 20 000 | 2000 | 20 000 | 1000 |
| 4 | 6000 | 2000 | 30 000 | 2000 | 30 000 | 0 |
| 5 | 1000 | 0 | 30 000 | 2000 | 30 000 | 0 |

**7.7** What is the internal rate of return for the data in Problem 7.6?

**7.8** What is the internal rate of return for a product that gives the following net cash flow?

| Year | 1 | 2 | 3 | 4 | 5 | 6 | 7 | 8 | 9 |
|---|---|---|---|---|---|---|---|---|---|
| Net cash flow | − 6000 | − 1500 | − 500 | 600 | 1800 | 2000 | 1400 | 300 | 100 |

**7.9** Hamilton Car Hire buys new vehicles for £15,000. If these have an expected life of six years, and a scrap value of £2000, use a straight-line method to find annual depreciation. If the reducing-balance method is used with a depreciation rate of 25%, what is the value of the vehicles after six years? What depreciation rate would reduce the vehicles' value to £1000 after four years?

**7.10** A company makes fixed annual payments to a sinking fund to replace equipment in five years' time. The equipment is valued at £100,000 and interest rates are 12%. How much should each payment be?

**7.11** How much are monthly payments on a mortgage of £25,000 taken out for 25 years at an interest rate of 1% a month?

**7.12** Suppose that you are about to buy a new car. You have decided on the model, which costs £12,000. The supplier gives you an option of either a five-year car loan at a reduced APR of 7%, or £1250 in cash and a five-year car loan with an APR of 10%. Which choice is the better? If you depreciate the car at 20% a year, what will its value be in ten years' time?

# Computer exercises

**7.1** Use a suitable package to check the calculations in Worked Examples 7.8 and 7.10.

**7.2** The fixed cost of a product is £100,000 and the variable cost is £50. If the product sells for £100, use a spreadsheet to calculate the break-even point. Use the figures to draw a graph of the profit and loss. Extend the spreadsheet to deal with other values.

**7.3** Figure 7.11 shows the printout from a package that calculates the net present value for a project, taking into account a number of features such as depreciation and tax. The investment, revenue and expenses are given for each year. Make sure you understand what is happening in this printout. See what packages you have to do financial calculations. Use them to confirm the results given.

Financial Analysis – Net Present Value
Straight Line Depreciation

Data Entered

| | |
|---|---|
| Number of time periods : | 4 |
| Initial investment : | 20000 |
| Estimated salvage value : | 2000 |
| Tax rate : | 0.3000 |
| Discount rate : | 0.2000 |
| Investment threshold : | 0 |

Financial Analysis – Net Present Value
Straight Line Depreciation

Solution

| | Year0 | Year1 | Year2 | Year3 | Year4 |
|---|---|---|---|---|---|
| Investment | 20000 | 10000 | 2000 | 0 | 0 |
| Revenue | 0 | 5000 | 10000 | 20000 | 20000 |
| Expenses | 0 | 5000 | 5000 | 5000 | 5000 |
| Before tax cash flow | 0 | 0 | 5000 | 15000 | 15000 |
| Depreciation | 0 | 4500 | 7833.3330 | 8833.3330 | 8833.3330 |
| Taxable cash flow | 0 | −4500 | −7333.3330 | −1166.6660 | 5000.0010 |
| Taxes | 0 | 0 | 0 | 0 | 1500.0004 |
| After tax cash flow | 0 | 0 | 5000 | 15000 | 13500 |
| PV cash flow | 0 | 0 | 3472.2222 | 8680.5547 | 6510.4160 |

Salvage

| | |
|---|---|
| Investment | 0 |
| Revenue | 2000 |
| Expenses | 0 |
| Before tax cash flow | 2000 |
| Depreciation | 0 |
| Taxable cash flow | 2000 |
| Taxes | 0 |
| After tax cash flow | 2000 |
| PV cash flow | 964.5062 |

Financial Summary

| | |
|---|---|
| NPV of total investment : | 29722.2227 |
| Total PV cash flows : | 19627.6992 |
| Investment threshold : | 0 |
| Discount rate : | 0.2000 |
| Project NVP : | −10094.5225 |

**Conclusion = DO NOT FUND PROJECT**

**Figure 7.11** A package for calculating net present value.

**7.4** Figure 7.12 shows (a) some iterative calculations used by a spreadsheet to calculate the internal rate of return and (b) the results drawn on a graph. Look at the spreadsheet and make sure you understand how it works. Then design your own spreadsheet for doing such calculations (without using the standard IRR function). Draw a graph of results and confirm the values in Figure 7.12.

|   | A | B | C | D | E | F | G | H |
|---|---|---|---|---|---|---|---|---|
| 1 |   |   | **Calculation of internal rate of return** | | | | | |
| 2 |   |   |   |   |   |   |   |   |
| 3 | **Discount rate step** | | **0.001** |   |   |   |   |   |
| 4 |   |   |   |   |   |   |   |   |
| 5 |   |   |   | ------- | **Discount rates** | | ------- | ------- |
| 6 | **Year** | **Revenue** | **Costs** | **0.137** | **0.138** | **0.139** | **0.14** | **0.141** |
| 7 |   |   |   |   |   |   |   |   |
| 8 | 0 | 0 | 5000 | −4397.54 | −4393.67 | −4389.82 | −4385.96 | −4382.12 |
| 9 | 1 | 1000 | 3000 | −1759.01 | −1757.47 | −1755.93 | −1754.39 | −1752.85 |
| 10 | 2 | 2000 | 1000 | 773.5334 | 772.1745 | 770.8912 | 769.4675 | 768.1194 |
| 11 | 3 | 4000 | 1000 | 2040.985 | 2035.609 | 2030.253 | 2024.915 | 2019.595 |
| 12 | 4 | 4000 | 1000 | 1795.062 | 1788.761 | 1782.487 | 1776.241 | 1770.022 |
| 13 | 5 | 4000 | 1000 | 1578.77 | 1571.846 | 1564.958 | 1558.106 | 1551.29 |
| 14 | **Totals** | **15000** | **12000** | **31.7983** | **17.24804** | **2.774764** | **−11.622** | **−25.9426** |

(a)

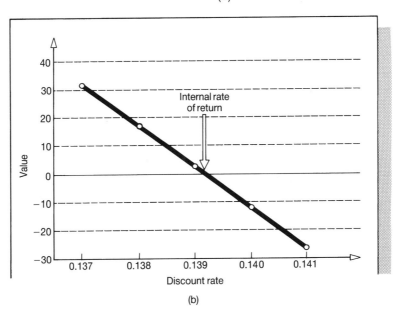

(b)

**Figure 7.12** Spreadsheet for calculating the internal rate of return: (a) table of results; (b) graph of results.

**7.5** Imagine that you are about to take out a mortgage. Find the current interest rates quoted by a number of financial institutions. Use a suitable program to calculate the monthly payments. Then find the payments, interest, principal repaid and debt outstanding at the end of each month. Prepare a report of your findings.

**7.6** Five projects generate the incomes shown in Table 7.3 (in thousands of pounds) over the next ten years. Analyse these figures and discuss the characteristics of each. Write a report about your findings.

**Table 7.3**

| Project | A | B | C | D | E |
|---------|------|------|------|------|------|
| Year 1 | – 120 | – 200 | – 60 | 0 | – 500 |
| Year 2 | – 60 | 0 | 30 | 10 | – 200 |
| Year 3 | 5 | 100 | 30 | 20 | – 100 |
| Year 4 | 30 | 80 | 30 | 30 | 50 |
| Year 5 | 45 | 60 | 30 | 30 | 100 |
| Year 6 | 55 | 50 | – 40 | 20 | 200 |
| Year 7 | 65 | 40 | 30 | – 100 | 300 |
| Year 8 | 65 | 40 | 30 | 50 | 350 |
| Year 9 | 60 | 35 | 30 | 40 | 400 |
| Year 10 | 50 | 35 | 30 | 30 | 450 |

# Case study

## Mrs Hamilton's retirement savings

Mrs Hamilton has just had her 55th birthday. For many years she has been investing in endowment insurance policies and some of these have now matured to give her a lump sum of around £50,000. She is self-employed and plans to continue working until she is 65. This means that Mrs Hamilton is looking for an investment that will increase in value over the next ten years.

Mrs Hamilton went to her bank manager for some advice. When she said that she could add another £2000 a year to her savings the manager did some sums, and made several suggestions:

- a Saving Account that would give a return of 7.5% a year

- a Gold Account for the fixed sum. This would give a return of 9% but would leave the money tied up for at least a year. The additional savings could go into a Saving Account

- a Personal Accumulator that gives 5% interest on a minimum of £30,000, but 15% on any savings above this.

Mrs Hamilton also visited a building society manager who gave her similar advice, but gave an additional option: 'The most secure investment is to put the money in our Inflation Fighter. This has an interest rate that is linked to the Retail Price Index, and is guaranteed to give a return that is 1% above inflation'.

The building society manager also discussed the possibility of buying a house as an investment: 'The housing market has been very unsettled lately. If you take a long-term view, house prices have risen by an average of 10% to 15% a year for the past decade. During this time inflation has averaged 3.5%, so houses have been a good investment. They can also generate income from rent. Usually you could expect to get about 0.5% of the value of the house a month. Something like a quarter of this is needed for repairs and maintenance. Some of my customers take out a mortgage with interest of 9% a year to add to their savings and buy a bigger house'.

Mrs Hamilton went home and did some thinking. She could calculate how much each of the investments would be worth at the end of ten years. Perhaps, though, she should decide how much she wants to have when she retires, and add to her savings to achieve this amount. She thought that £150,000 would be enough, but perhaps she should aim for more. She wants a reasonable income over the next 20 years, even when taking inflation into account. She thought that perhaps an annuity would suit her.

Mrs Hamilton has to decide what to do with her savings. She would like some advice on the schemes she has considered, and any other alternatives.

# 8 Relating variables by regression

Chapter outline 224
8.1 Measuring relationships 225
8.2 Linear relationships 230
8.3 Measuring the strength 238
of a relationship
8.4 Extensions to 247
linear regression

Chapter review 254
Problems 254
Computer exercises 256
Case study: Western 259
General Hospital

## CHAPTER OUTLINE

Chapter 2 showed how the relationship between two variables can be plotted as a graph. In this chapter we look in more detail at such relationships and their use in business. The chapter begins by suggesting that observations often follow an underlying pattern, but with some unpredictable variations. The size of these variations can be used to measure the strength of a relationship.

The chapter then describes linear regression, which draws the straight line of best fit through a set of data. The closeness of this fit is measured by the coefficients of determination and correlation. Extensions to linear regression include multiple regression and non-linear regression.

After reading this chapter and doing the exercises you should be able to:

- appreciate the need for measuring the strength of a relationship
- calculate mean errors, mean absolute deviations and mean squared errors
- find the straight line of best fit using linear regression
- use linear regression to forecast values
- calculate coefficients of determination and correlation
- understand the methods of multiple and non-linear regression

# 8.1 | Measuring relationships

## 8.1.1 | Noise and errors

Chapter 2 showed how we can plot the relationship between two variables as a graph. At the time, we said that any relationship will be shown clearly on a graph, but we made no attempt to **measure** the strength of a relationship. In this chapter we are going to develop a measure for this. We shall approach this in two stages:

- find the best relationship (which is called **regression**)
- see how well this relationship fits the data

Both these calculations are based on the errors that are found in actual observations. We have already discussed these in connection with data spread in Chapter 5, so this section starts by revising some important results.

Suppose we have collected data about the consumption of electricity in a region and the corresponding average daily temperature. We might get the data shown below (where some consistent units are used):

| Observation | 1 | 2 | 3 | 4 | 5 | 6 |
|---|---|---|---|---|---|---|
| Temperature | 5 | 7 | 10 | 12 | 15 | 17 |
| Electricity | 15 | 19 | 25 | 29 | 35 | 39 |

Generally, if you have a set of data like this, the first step in analysing it is to draw a graph. A scatter diagram shows any underlying pattern, and in this case there is a linear relationship, as shown in Figure 8.1. This shows a perfect relationship, with the dependent variable being set exactly by the independent variable. In fact:

$$\text{consumption of electricity} = 2 \times \text{average temperature} + 5$$

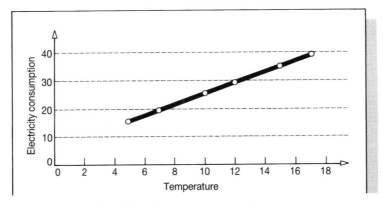

**Figure 8.1** Graph of electricity consumption against temperature.

The relationship between variables is rarely this exact, and there is usually some fluctuation about expected values. It would, for example, be more common to find figures relating electricity consumption to average daily temperature like the following:

| Observation | 1 | 2 | 3 | 4 | 5 | 6 |
|---|---|---|---|---|---|---|
| Temperature | 5 | 7 | 10 | 12 | 15 | 17 |
| Electricity | 17 | 22 | 26 | 24 | 30 | 42 |

There is still a clear linear relationship, but superimposed on this underlying pattern is a random variation called **noise.** Then the relationship becomes:

> actual value = underlying pattern + random noise

There might be even more noise, and Figure 8.2 shows three sets of figures with varying amounts.

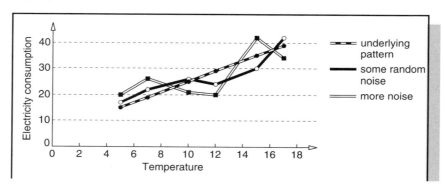

**Figure 8.2**    Graphs of electricity consumption with noise.

The amount of random noise shows how strong a relationship is:

● If there is no noise, as in the first set of figures above, the relationship is perfect.
● If there is some noise, the relationship is weaker.
● If there is a lot of noise, the relationship becomes even weaker until it hardly exists.

What we need is a way of measuring the noise and hence the strength of the relationship.

You can think of the noise in an observation as an error, $E_i$, which is the difference between the value expected from the relationship and the actual value:

> $E_i$ = actual value of observation $i$
> − value predicted by relationship

Now we need to combine all the errors from separate observations into a single measure for the strength of the relationship.

| IN SUMMARY |

In practice there is usually some noise in the relationship between two variables. The amount of noise determines the strength of a relationship. We need some measure of the strength, and this should be based on individual errors.

## 8.1.2 | Combining individual errors

Suppose two variables have a linear relationship, but there is superimposed noise. A graph of observations will show variations about a straight line, as shown in Figure 8.3. Each observation has an error, which is the vertical distance from the line. The error in observation $i$ is defined as $E_i$, where:

$$E_i = y_i - \hat{y}_i$$

where:

$y_i$ = actual value

$\hat{y}_i$ (which is pronounced 'y hat') = value suggested by the underlying relationship

This error is often called the **residual**. If we repeat the calculation for each observation we can find a mean error, where:

$$\text{mean error} = \frac{\sum E_i}{n} = \frac{\sum (y_i - \hat{y}_i)}{n}$$

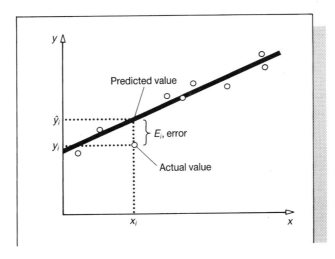

**Figure 8.3** Showing noise as an error in $y_i$.

The mean error has a major drawback, which we have already met in Chapter 5. It allows positive and negative errors to cancel each other, and data with very large errors can have zero mean error. We really need an alternative measure, and the two most common ones take the absolute values of errors (and calculate the **mean absolute deviation**) and the squares of errors (and calculate the **mean squared error**):

$$\text{mean absolute deviation} = \frac{\sum |E_i|}{n} = \frac{\sum |y_i - \hat{y}_i|}{n}$$

$$\text{mean squared error} = \frac{\sum (E_i)^2}{n} = \frac{\sum (y_i - \hat{y}_i)^2}{n}$$

The mean absolute deviation has an obvious meaning; when it takes a value of 1.5 the actual value is on average 1.5 away from the predicted value. The mean squared error has a less clear meaning but is useful for other analyses. Whichever measure we use, smaller values show that there is less noise in the observations and therefore a stronger relationship between variables.

## WORKED EXAMPLE 8.1

Six sets of values have been recorded for an independent variable $x$ and dependent variable $y$. These are thought to be related by the equation $y = 3x + 3$. What are the errors in the actual observations?

| Observation | 1 | 2 | 3 | 4 | 5 | 6 |
|---|---|---|---|---|---|---|
| $x$ | 3 | 6 | 10 | 8 | 4 | 1 |
| $y$ | 10 | 24 | 29 | 25 | 12 | 5 |

### Solution

To measure the errors, we first have to find the calculated values of $y$. We find these by substituting values for $x$ into $y = 3x + 3$. Then the error for each observation is found from:

$$E_i = \text{actual } y_i - \text{calculated } y_i = y_i - \hat{y}_i$$

These calculations are shown in Figure 8.4.

|   | A | B | C | D | E | F | G |
|---|---|---|---|---|---|---|---|
| 1 | **Calculating errors** | | | | | | |
| 2 | | | | | | | |
| 3 | **Observation** | **x** | **Actual y** $= y_i$ | **Calculated y** $= \hat{y}_i$ | **Error** | **Absolute error** | **Squared error** |
| 4 | 1 | 3 | 10 | 9 | 1 | 1 | 1 |
| 5 | 2 | 6 | 24 | 21 | 3 | 3 | 9 |
| 6 | 3 | 10 | 29 | 33 | −4 | 4 | 16 |
| 7 | 4 | 8 | 25 | 27 | −2 | 2 | 4 |
| 8 | 5 | 4 | 12 | 15 | −3 | 3 | 9 |
| 9 | 6 | 1 | 5 | 6 | −1 | 1 | 1 |
| 10 | | | | | | | |
| 11 | **Sums** | | | | −6 | 14 | 40 |
| 12 | **Means** | | | | −1 | 2.33 | 6.67 |

**Figure 8.4**  Calculation of errors.

---

| IN SUMMARY |
| :--- |

The noise found in most relationships can be considered as errors or deviations from expected values. These can be measured by the mean error, mean absolute deviation and mean squared error. The mean squared error is particularly useful for other analyses.

---

# Self-assessment questions

**8.1**  What is meant by the 'noise' in a relationship?

**8.2**  Why do almost all relationships contain errors?

**8.3**  What is the mean error and why is it of limited value?

**8.4**  Define two other measures of error.

**8.5**  Two people suggest different equations to fit a set of data. How can you tell which gives the stronger relationship?

# 8.2 | Linear relationships

## 8.2.1 | Finding the line of best fit

In the last section we said that many relationships could be viewed as an underlying pattern with superimposed noise. In this section we are going to continue this theme, concentrating on examples where the underlying pattern is a straight line. The sales of a product, for example, might rise linearly with the price being charged, demand for a service might depend on advertising expenditure, productivity might depend on bonus payments, borrowings might depend on interest rates, crop size might depend on the amount of fertilizer used. These are examples of causal relationships where changes in the first (dependent) variable are actually caused by changes in the second (independent) variable. But relationships between variables need not be causal. Sales of ice cream are directly related to sales of sunglasses, but there is no cause and effect here, and the way to increase sales of ice cream is not to increase the sales of sunglasses. Obviously, both variables are affected by a third factor – the weather.

People commonly assume that because a relationship exists there must be some cause and effect. But this is not true, and it is easy to spot ridiculous examples. The number of lamp posts is related to prosecutions for drunken driving; the number of storks nesting in Sweden is related to the birth rate in the United Kingdom; the number of people in higher education is related to life expectancy; and in the nineteenth century there was a direct link between the number of asses and the number of PhD graduates in America. Unfortunately, not all mistakes of this kind are as easy to spot. The productivity of a coalmine, for example, may decline while investment increases (because of the age of the mine and the increasing difficulty of extracting coal); some economists say that price inflation is caused by high wages (ignoring the fact that countries with the highest wage rates often have the lowest inflation); and the income generated by a bus company is directly related to the fares charged (but increasing fares deter passengers and will reduce long-term income).

In this section, then, we shall look at relationships between variables without suggesting any cause and effect. In particular, we shall use available data to find a linear relationship between two variables; in other words, we are looking for the straight line that best fits the data. This process is called **linear regression**, and we can illustrate the overall approach by the following example.

## WORKED EXAMPLE 8.2

Van Hofen Inc. records the number of shifts worked each month and the resulting output, as shown in the following table. If 30 shifts are planned for next month, what is their expected output?

| Month | 1 | 2 | 3 | 4 | 5 | 6 | 7 | 8 | 9 |
|---|---|---|---|---|---|---|---|---|---|
| Shifts worked | 50 | 70 | 25 | 55 | 20 | 60 | 40 | 25 | 35 |
| Output | 352 | 555 | 207 | 508 | 48 | 498 | 310 | 153 | 264 |

## Solution

The best thing to do with a set of data is to draw a graph of it. A scatter diagram of shifts worked (the independent variable, $x$) and output (the dependent variable, $y$) shows a clear linear relationship (Figure 8.5). We can draw by eye a reasonable straight line through the data. This line shows that with 30 shifts worked, the output will be around 200 units.

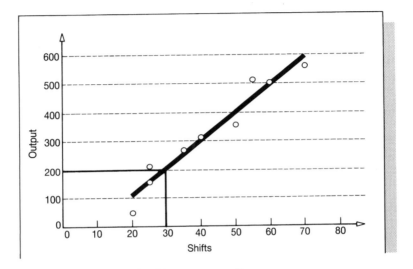

**Figure 8.5**   Linear relationship on a scatter diagram.

In the worked example above we drew a scatter diagram, noticed a linear relationship and then drew a line of best fit by eye. Although this informal approach can work quite well, it is not very reliable. It would be useful to have a more formal way of defining a **line of best fit** through the data. This is the purpose of linear regression.

As we saw in Chapter 2, the equation of a straight line is:

$$y = a + b \times x$$

where:

$x$ = independent variable

$y$ = dependent variable

$a$ = point where the line intersects the $y$ axis

$b$ = gradient of the line

Linear regression looks for the values of the constants $a$ and $b$ that define the line of best fit through a set of points. We can approach this by looking at the errors. Even the best line will not usually fit the data perfectly, so there will be an error at each point, $x_i$. In other words, at each point $i$:

$$y_i = a + bx_i + E_i$$

The line of best fit is defined as the line that minimizes some measure of this error. We saw earlier that simply adding the errors and finding the mean allows positive and negative errors to cancel. Better alternatives would be to minimize the mean absolute deviation or the mean squared error. Because it allows other statistical analyses, the mean squared error is used for regression. Then the equation for the line of best fit is given by the following standard result:

$$b = \frac{n \sum xy - \sum x \sum y}{n \sum x^2 - (\sum x)^2}$$

$$a = \bar{y} - b\bar{x}$$

where $n$ is the number of observations, $\bar{x}$ is the mean value of the independent variable and $\bar{y}$ is the mean value of the dependent variable.

## WORKED EXAMPLE 8.3

Find the line of best fit through the following data for advertising budget (in thousands of Euros) and units sold. Then forecast the number of units sold if the advertising budget is €30,000.

| Month | 1 | 2 | 3 | 4 |
|---|---|---|---|---|
| Advertising budget | 20 | 40 | 60 | 80 |
| Units sold | 120 | 170 | 210 | 230 |

### Solution

There is a clear linear relationship here, as shown in Figure 8.6, with:

units sold, $y = a + b \times$ advertising budget, $x$

We can do the calculations in a number of ways. As you can see, the equations are fairly messy, so you should always use a computer. The top part of Figure 8.7 shows the calculations done on a spreadsheet, where the computer automatically finds:

$$n = 4$$

$$b = \frac{n \sum (xy) - \sum x \sum y}{n \sum x^2 - (\sum x)^2}$$

$$= \frac{4 \times 40\,200 - 200 \times 730}{4 \times 12\,000 - 200 \times 200}$$

$$= 1.85$$

$$a = \bar{y} - b\bar{x}$$

$$= 182.5 - 1.85 \times 50$$

$$= 90$$

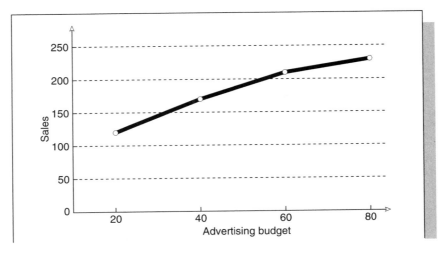

**Figure 8.6**  Scatter diagram for Worked Example 8.3.

The line of best fit is:

$$y = a + bx$$

units sold = 90 + 1.85 × advertising budget

With an advertising budget of £30,000, $x = 30$, so

$$\text{units sold} = 90 + 1.85 \times 30$$

$$= 145.5$$

Spreadsheets have a standard function for doing regression, as illustrated in the second part of Figure 8.7. We have given these results in full, and they show a common problem with computer printouts – they often give so much information that you can hardly see the result you are looking for. Here the computer calculates some regression statistics based on $r$ (the coefficient of correlation which we will talk about in the next section), then it prints a table of results for ANOVA (analysis of variance) which see how good the relationship is, then it prints a table of results for the 'intercept' and 'X variable 1'. The first two entries in this, 90 and 1.85, are the two figures we want, and the other figures give more information for statistical tests. We will talk about some of these later, but in the meantime will only print the results that we want and will ignore the others.

Linear regression is one of the most widely used analyses in business. It is fairly simple to do using good software, many people understand the principles, and the results can be used in a wide range of applications. But it is often used badly. People look at the results and suggest false cause-and-effect relationships and they see linear trends in random patterns. This is, of course, the fault of the people doing the analysis and not the method itself.

|  | A | B | C | D | E | F | G |
|---|---|---|---|---|---|---|---|
| 1 | **Linear regression** | | | | | | |
| 2 | | | | | | | |
| 3 | **Calculation** | | | | | | |
| 4 | | **Data** | | | **Calculations** | | |
| 5 | **Month** | **x** | **y** | | **xy** | **x$^2$** | |
| 6 | 1 | 20 | 120 | | 2400 | 400 | |
| 7 | 2 | 40 | 170 | | 6800 | 1600 | |
| 8 | 3 | 60 | 210 | | 12600 | 3600 | |
| 9 | 4 | 80 | 230 | | 18400 | 6400 | |
| 10 | **Sums** | 200 | 730 | | 40200 | 12000 | |
| 11 | **Means** | 50 | 182.5 | | | | |
| 12 | **Substitution** | | **b** | 1.85 | **a** | 90 | |
| 13 | | | | | | | |
| 14 | **Function** | | | | | | |
| 15 | *Regression statistics* | | | | | | |
| 16 | Multiple r | 0.984 | | | | | |
| 17 | r$^2$ | 0.967 | | | | | |
| 18 | Adjusted r$^2$ | 0.951 | | | | | |
| 19 | Standard error | 10.724 | | | | | |
| 20 | Observations | 4 | | | | | |
| 21 | | | | | | | |
| 22 | *ANOVA* | | | | | | |
| 23 | | *df* | *SS* | *MS* | *F* | *Significance F* | |
| 24 | Regression | 1 | 6845 | 6845 | 59.522 | 0.016 | |
| 25 | Residual | 2 | 230 | 115 | | | |
| 26 | Total | 3 | 7075 | | | | |
| 27 | | | | | | | |
| 28 | | *Coefficients* | *Standard error* | *t stat* | *P-value* | *Lower 95%* | *Upper 95%* |
| 29 | Intercept | **90** | **13.134** | **6.852** | **0.021** | **33.489** | **146.511** |
| 30 | X variable 1 | **1.85** | **0.240** | **7.715** | **0.016** | **0.818** | **2.882** |

**Figure 8.7**   Using a spreadsheet to do regression.

IN SUMMARY

Linear regression can be used to find the line of best fit through a set of data. Standard calculations find the line of best fit, which is defined as the line which minimizes the sum of squared errors.

## 8.2.2 | Using linear regression to forecast

The main purpose of linear regression is to predict the value of a dependent variable for a known value of the independent variable. In Worked Example 8.3 we found a relationship between advertising budget and sales. Now we can use this relationship to forecast expected sales when the advertising budget is set at any particular value. Similarly, in the following worked example the expected number of defects can be forecast when the number of inspections is set at a particular value. This approach is known as **causal forecasting**, even though changes in the independent variable may not actually cause changes in the dependent variable.

# WORKED EXAMPLE 8.4

A cereal farmer finds that his profit per acre is affected by the amount he spends on fertiliser as follows. How much profit should he expect if he spends £4000 on fertiliser?

| Cost of fertiliser | 500 | 1000 | 1500 | 2000 | 2500 | 3000 | 3500 | 4000 | 4500 | 5000 | 5500 | 6000 |
|---|---|---|---|---|---|---|---|---|---|---|---|---|
| Profit per acre | 35 | 70 | 110 | 160 | 200 | 220 | 260 | 310 | 350 | 380 | 430 | 460 |

## Solution

The calculations for this are shown in Figure 8.8. In this spreadsheet the original data are listed, and the values of $a$ and $b$ are calculated as $-4.091$ and $0.078$ respectively. These values are used to forecast expected profits for various spending on fertilisers. As you can see, if the farmer spends £4000 on fertiliser he should expect a profit of £307.91 an acre.

|   | A | B | C | D | E | F |
|---|---|---|---|---|---|---|
| 1 | **Linear regression** | | | | | |
| 2 | | | | | | |
| 3 | | | | | | |
| 4 | **Cost of fertiliser** | **Profit per acre** | | | | |
| 5 | | **Actual** | **Forecast** | | | |
| 6 | 500 | 35 | 34.91 | | **Intercept, a** | −4.091 |
| 7 | 1000 | 70 | 73.91 | | **Gradient, b** | 0.078 |
| 8 | 1500 | 110 | 112.91 | | | |
| 9 | 2000 | 160 | 151.91 | | | |
| 10 | 2500 | 200 | 190.91 | | | |
| 11 | 3000 | 220 | 229.91 | | | |
| 12 | 3500 | 260 | 268.91 | | | |
| 13 | 4000 | 310 | 307.91 | | | |
| 14 | 4500 | 350 | 346.91 | | | |
| 15 | 5000 | 380 | 385.91 | | | |
| 16 | 5500 | 430 | 424.91 | | | |
| 17 | 6000 | 460 | 463.91 | | | |

**Figure 8.8** Calculations for Worked Example 8.4.

## WORKED EXAMPLE 8.5

A company is about to change the way it inspects a product. Experiments were done with differing numbers of inspections, and figures are now available to show how the average number of defects varies with the number of inspections:

| Inspections | 0 | 1 | 2 | 3 | 4 | 5 | 6 | 7 | 8 | 9 | 10 |
|---|---|---|---|---|---|---|---|---|---|---|---|
| Defects | 92 | 86 | 81 | 72 | 67 | 59 | 53 | 43 | 32 | 24 | 12 |

If the company does six inspections, how many defects would they expect? What is the effect of doing 20 inspections?

## Solution

The independent variable $x$ is the number of inspections, and the dependent variable $y$ is the consequent number of defects. There is a clear linear relationship between these, as shown in Figure 8.9. Then we can find the values $n = 11$, $\Sigma x = 55$, $\Sigma y = 621$, $\Sigma(xy) = 2238$ and $\Sigma x^2 = 385$, and substitution gives:

$$b = \frac{n\,\Sigma\,(xy) - \Sigma\,x\,\Sigma\,y}{n\,\Sigma\,x^2 - (\Sigma\,x)^2}$$

$$= \frac{11 \times 2238 - 55 \times 621}{11 \times 385 - 55 \times 55} = -7.88$$

$$a = \bar{y} - b\,\bar{x} = 621/11 + 7.88 \times 55/11 = 95.85$$

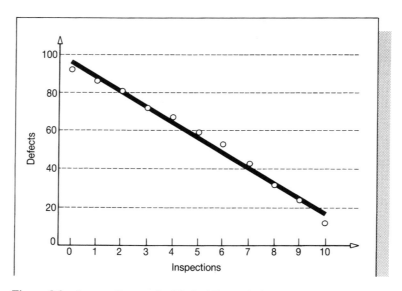

**Figure 8.9**  Scatter diagram for Worked Example 8.5.

The line of best fit is:

$$y = 95.85 - 7.88x$$

or

$$\text{defects} = 95.85 - 7.88 \times \text{number of inspections}$$

With six inspections the company could forecast

$$95.85 - 7.88 \times 6 = 48.57 \text{ defects}$$

With 20 inspections we have to be a little more careful, as substitution gives $95.85 - 7.88 \times 20 = -61.75$. It is clearly impossible to have a negative number of defects, so we would simply forecast zero defects.

The last example shows how the line of best fit is only really valid within the range of $x$ used to find it. A value of $x$ within this range can be substituted into the regression equation to find a corresponding value of $y$; this is known as **interpolation**. But there is no evidence that the same relationship holds outside the range of $x$. Using a value of $x$ outside the specified range to find a corresponding value of $y$ is called **extrapolation**, and we cannot be sure of the results. In practice, of course, we often need to extrapolate values, and provided the values of $x$ are not too far outside the range, the errors should not be too large. But you should use these results with caution.

It is also worth emphasizing that we are finding the regression of $y$ on $x$: then $x$ is the independent variable which is used to find a dependent variable $y$. This equation cannot be used to set a value for $y$ and predict the corresponding value for $x$. In the last worked example we found that the number of defects was given by:

$$\text{defects} = 95.85 - 7.88 \times \text{number of inspections}$$

Then we can substitute a number of inspections to find the number of defects. But we **cannot** substitute a number of defects and expect this to give the corresponding number of inspections.

An important use of regression is to forecast future values by setting time periods as the independent variable, as shown in the following worked example.

# WORKED EXAMPLE 8.6

Demand for a product in each of the last eight weeks has been 17, 23, 41, 38, 42, 47, 51 and 56. Use linear regression to forecast demand for next week.

## Solution

In this example we can use time (that is, week number) as the independent variable and demand as the dependent variable. Then we get:

| Week, $x$ | 1 | 2 | 3 | 4 | 5 | 6 | 7 | 8 |
|---|---|---|---|---|---|---|---|---|
| Demand, $y$ | 17 | 23 | 41 | 38 | 42 | 47 | 51 | 56 |

Using regression in the usual way gives the line of best fit as:

$$\text{demand} = 16.07 + 5.18 \times \text{week}$$

Substituting week = 9 gives the demand as $16.07 + 5.18 \times 9 = 62.69$. This has, of course, used extrapolation, but the figures suggest that the results will be reasonably good.

---

IN SUMMARY

The main purpose of linear regression is to predict the value of a dependent variable for a known value of an independent variable. Care should be taken when interpreting the results.

---

## Self-assessment questions

**8.6**  What is the main purpose of linear regression?

**8.7**  Define each of the terms in the linear regression equation $y_i = a + b \times x_i + E_i$.

**8.8**  If you want to forecast future values, what is the most common meaning of $x_i$?

# 8.3 Measuring the strength of a relationship

## 8.3.1 Coefficient of determination

Now we can find the line of best fit through a set of data, but still need some way of measuring how good this line is. If the errors are small the line is a good fit, but if the errors are large even the best line is not very good. To measure the goodness of fit we shall use the **coefficient of determination**.

We defined the line of best fit as the one that minimizes the sum of squared errors. If we look carefully at the errors, we can separate this sum of squared errors (SSE) into different components. Suppose we take a number of observations of $y_i$ and calculate the mean, $\bar{y}$. Actual values will vary around this mean, and we can define the total sum of squared errors as:

$$\text{total SSE} = \Sigma\,(y_i - \bar{y})^2$$

When we build a regression model, we estimate values, $\hat{y}_i$, which show what the observations would be if all noise is eliminated. So the regression model explains some of the variation from the mean:

$$\text{explained SSE} = \Sigma\,(\hat{y}_i - \bar{y})^2$$

Because of random noise, the regression model does not explain all the variation, and there is some residual left unexplained:

$$\text{unexplained SSE} = \Sigma\,(y_i - \hat{y}_i)^2$$

With a little algebra we can show that:

$$\text{total SSE} = \text{explained SSE} + \text{unexplained SSE}$$

as shown in Figure 8.10. The coefficient of determination is defined as the proportion of total SSE explained by the regression model:

$$\text{coefficient of determination} = \frac{\text{explained SSE}}{\text{total SSE}}$$

This measure has a value between zero and one. If it is near to one, most of the variation is explained by the regression and the line is a good fit for the data. If the value is near to zero, most of the variation is unexplained and the line is not a good fit.

The coefficient of determination is found from the messy-looking equation:

$$\text{coefficient of determination} =$$

$$\left[ \frac{n\,\Sigma\,xy - \Sigma\,x\,\Sigma\,y}{\sqrt{[n\,\Sigma\,x^2 - (\Sigma\,x)^2] \times [n\,\Sigma\,y^2 - (\Sigma\,y)^2]}} \right]^2$$

The coefficient of determination is usually called $r^2$. If you look back to the spreadsheet in Figure 8.7 you will see that this is one of the figures it calculates. There $r^2$ was 0.967, which is high and shows a very strong linear relationship. 96.7% of the variation from the mean is explained by the relationship, while only 3.3% is due to random noise.

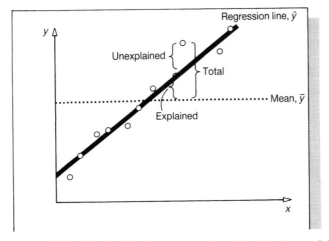

**Figure 8.10**  Relationships between total, explained and unexplained variations.

## WORKED EXAMPLE 8.7

Calculate the coefficient of determination for the data in Worked Example 8.5.

### Solution

We have already done the regression for these figures and found that $n = 11$, $\Sigma x = 55$, $\Sigma y = 621$, $\Sigma (xy) = 2238$ and $\Sigma x^2 = 385$, and the line of best fit is $y = 95.85 - 7.88x$. Now we could also find that $\Sigma y^2 = 41\ 977$ and substitute this to get:

$$\text{coefficient of determination} = \left[ \frac{n \Sigma xy - \Sigma x \Sigma y}{\sqrt{[n \Sigma x^2 - (\Sigma x)^2] \times [n \Sigma y^2 - (\Sigma y)^2]}} \right]^2$$

$$= \left[ \frac{11 \times 2238 - 55 \times 621}{\sqrt{[11 \times 385 - 55 \times 55] \times [11 \times 41\ 977 - 621 \times 621]}} \right]^2$$

$$= [-0.9938]^2$$

$$= 0.9877$$

This shows that 99% of the variation can be explained by the regression model and only 1% is unexplained and is due to random noise. The line is a very good fit.

If a coefficient of determination had a value of 0.9, we would know that 90% of the variation from the mean is explained by the regression, and 10% is unexplained (and due to random effects or other explanations). Normally any value for the coefficient of determination above about 0.5 is considered a good fit. If the coefficient of determination is low at, say, 0.2, then 80% of the variation is not explained by the regression and some other factors should be considered.

### IN SUMMARY

The coefficient of determination measures the proportion of the total variation explained by the regression line. A value close to 1 shows a good fit of the regression line, while a value close to 0 shows a poor fit.

## 8.3.2 | Coefficient of correlation

A second useful measure in regression is the coefficient of correlation which answers the basic question 'are $x$ and $y$ linearly related?' The coefficients of correlation and determination answer very similar questions, and a straightforward calculation shows:

$$\text{coefficient of correlation} = \sqrt{\text{coefficient of determination}}$$

As the coefficient of determination is usually called $r^2$, the coefficient of correlation is $r$.

This correlation coefficient is often called Pearson's coefficient and, as you can see, has a value between +1 and −1:

- a value of $r = 1$ shows that the two variables have a perfect linear relationship with no noise at all, and as one increases so does the other

- a lower positive value of $r$ shows that the linear relationship is getting weaker

- a value of $r = 0$ shows that there is no correlation at all between the two variables and no linear relationship

- a lower negative value of $r$ shows that the linear relationship is getting stronger

- a value of $r = -1$ shows that the two variables have a perfect linear relationship and as one increases the other decreases

With a correlation coefficient, $r$, near to +1 or −1 there is a strong linear relationship between the two variables. When $r$ is between 0.7 and −0.7 the coefficient of determination, $r^2$, is less than 0.49 and less than half the sum of squared errors is explained by the regression model. So values of $r$ between 0.7 and −0.7 suggest that a linear regression line is not very reliable. These results are shown in the graphs in Figure 8.11.

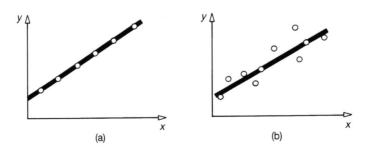

**Figure 8.11** Variation in coefficient of correlation:
(a) $r = +1$ (perfect positive correlation);    (b) $r$ is close to +1 (line is good fit);

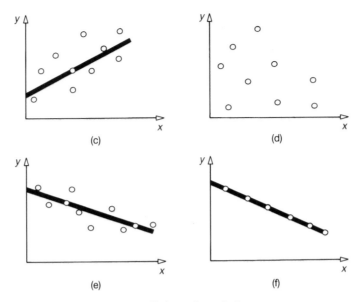

**Figure 8.11** Variation in coefficient of correlation:
(c) $r$ is decreasing (line is poor fit); (d) $r = 0$ (random points);
(e) $r$ is close to $-1$ (line is good fit); (f) $r = -1$ (perfect negative correlation).

## WORKED EXAMPLE 8.8

Calculate the coefficients of correlation and determination for the following data. What conclusions can you draw from these? What is the line of best fit?

| $x$ | 4 | 17 | 3 | 21 | 10 | 8 | 4 | 9 | 13 | 12 | 2 | 6 | 15 | 8 | 19 |
|---|---|---|---|---|---|---|---|---|---|---|---|---|---|---|---|
| $y$ | 13 | 47 | 24 | 41 | 29 | 33 | 28 | 38 | 46 | 32 | 14 | 22 | 26 | 21 | 50 |

### Solution

Figure 8.12 shows the calculations done on a spreadsheet.

You can see that $n = 15$, $\Sigma x = 151$, $\Sigma y = 464$, $\Sigma xy = 5442$, $\Sigma x^2 = 2019$ and $\Sigma y^2 = 16\,230$. You can check the calculations as:

$$r = \left[ \frac{n\,\Sigma\,(xy) - \Sigma\,x\,\Sigma\,y}{\sqrt{[n\,\Sigma\,x^2 - (\Sigma\,x)^2] \times [n\,\Sigma\,y^2 - (\Sigma\,y)^2]}} \right]$$

$$= \left[ \frac{15 \times 5442 - 151 \times 464}{\sqrt{[15 \times 2019 - 151 \times 151] \times [15 \times 16\,230 - 464 \times 464]}} \right]$$

$$= 0.797$$

This indicates quite a strong linear relationship. If we square this we get the coefficient of determination:

$$r^2 = 0.635$$

This shows that 63.5% of the variation is explained by the linear relationship, and only 36.5% is unexplained.

As there is a fairly strong linear relationship, the line of best fit will be fairly reliable:

$$y = 15.376 + 1.545x$$

As you already know, we do not actually have to do all the calculations shown in the spreadsheet, as we can get the results from standard functions. Results from these are shown in the bottom part of Figure 8.12. Here we have done only the full calculations to show what the spreadsheet is doing.

| | A | B | C | D | E | F | G |
|---|---|---|---|---|---|---|---|
| 1 | **Linear regression** | | | | | | |
| 2 | | | | | | | |
| 3 | **Calculation** | | | | | | |
| 4 | **Data** | | | | **Calculation** | | |
| 5 | Observation | **x** | **y** | | **xy** | **$x^2$** | **$y^2$** |
| 6 | 1 | 4 | 13 | | 52 | 16 | 169 |
| 7 | 2 | 17 | 47 | | 799 | 289 | 2209 |
| 8 | 3 | 3 | 24 | | 72 | 9 | 576 |
| 9 | 4 | 21 | 41 | | 861 | 441 | 1681 |
| 10 | 5 | 10 | 29 | | 290 | 100 | 841 |
| 11 | 6 | 8 | 33 | | 264 | 64 | 1089 |
| 12 | 7 | 4 | 28 | | 112 | 16 | 784 |
| 13 | 8 | 9 | 38 | | 342 | 81 | 1444 |
| 14 | 9 | 13 | 46 | | 598 | 169 | 2116 |
| 15 | 10 | 12 | 32 | | 384 | 144 | 1024 |
| 16 | 11 | 2 | 14 | | 28 | 4 | 196 |
| 17 | 12 | 6 | 22 | | 132 | 36 | 484 |
| 18 | 13 | 15 | 26 | | 390 | 225 | 676 |
| 19 | 14 | 8 | 21 | | 168 | 64 | 441 |
| 20 | 15 | 19 | 50 | | 950 | 361 | 2500 |
| 21 | **Sums** | 151 | 464 | | 5442 | 2019 | 16230 |
| 22 | **Means** | 10.067 | 30.933 | | | | |
| 23 | | | | | | | |
| 24 | **Substitution** | | **a** | 15.376 | **b** | 1.545 | |
| 25 | | | **r** | 0.797 | **$r^2$** | 0.635 | |
| 26 | | | | | | | |
| 27 | **Standard function** | | | | | | |
| 28 | *Regression statistics* | | | | | | |
| 29 | Multiple r | 0.797 | | | | | |
| 30 | $r^2$ | 0.635 | | | | | |
| 31 | Observations | 15 | | | | | |
| 32 | | | | | | | |
| 33 | | | *Coefficients* | | | | |
| 34 | Intercept | 15.376 | | | | | |
| 35 | X variable 1 | 1.545 | | | | | |

**Figure 8.12**  Calculation of coefficients of correlation and determination.

Now we can combine the discussions so far, and suggest a general way of tackling linear regression problems. This has the steps:

1  Collect and check the relevant data.

2  Draw a graph of the data and see whether it suggests a linear relationship.

3  Find the line of best fit through the data.

4  Calculate the coefficients of correlation and determination to see how well this line fits the data.

5  If there is a good fit, we can substitute appropriate values for the independent variable to find corresponding values for the dependent variable.

6  If there is not a good fit, or there is some other problem, we cannot use the equations and have to refine the model or look for some other approach.

---

## IN SUMMARY

The correlation coefficient shows how strong the linear relationship is between two variables. A value close to 1 or −1 shows a strong relationship, while a value close to zero shows a weak one.

---

## 8.3.3 | Rank correlation

Although it is the most widely used measure of correlation, Pearson's coefficient can only be used for cardinal data (that is, data that have known, numerical values). Sometimes we need to measure the strength of a relationship between ordinal data (that is data that are ranked, but the values are not known). This is common with market surveys, where a questionnaire might ask respondents to put their choices into an order of preference. If we have two sets of ranked data it would be useful to see whether there is a linear relationship between them. We could then see, for example, whether people who prefer one newspaper also prefer a particular type of television programme. The way of doing this is to use a correlation coefficient based on rankings, which is called **Spearman's coefficient of rank correlation**.

Suppose we have five products (V to Z) which are ranked in some order of preference, 1 to 5, according to two characteristics, *a* and *b*. We might get the following results:

| Characteristic for ranking | Product | | | | |
|---|---|---|---|---|---|
| | *V* | *W* | *X* | *Y* | *Z* |
| *a* | 2 | 5 | 1 | 3 | 4 |
| *b* | 1 | 3 | 2 | 4 | 5 |

We can see if there is a linear relationship between the ranks of $a$ and $b$ by using Spearman's rank correlation coefficient. This is based on the differences between ranking, so we define:

$$D = \text{ranking of } a - \text{ranking of } b$$

Then Spearman's coefficient, which is usually called $r_s$, is calculated as:

$$\text{Spearman's coefficient} = r_s = 1 - \frac{6 \sum D^2}{n(n^2 - 1)}$$

where $n$ is the number of pairs of observations.

In this case there are five rankings, so $n = 5$. The sum of $D^2$ is:

$$(2 - 1)^2 + (5 - 3)^2 + (1 - 2)^2 + (3 - 4)^2 + (4 - 5)^2 = 1 + 4 + 1 + 1 + 1 = 8$$

So Spearman's coefficient of correlation is:

$$r_s = 1 - \frac{6 \times 8}{5 \times (25 - 1)} = 1 - \frac{48}{120} = 0.6$$

This suggests quite a strong linear relationship.

Spearman's coefficient is not really a separate measure, but is derived from Pearson's coefficient. This means that the interpretation of values is exactly the same. The only difference is that Spearman's coefficient is based on ranks, and the calculation is easier.

It is worth remembering that ordinal data are less precise than cardinal, so an item ranked first may be slightly better than the item ranked second, or it may be much better. It follows that the results of rank regressions are also less precise and we must interpret them carefully. Wherever possible you should use Pearson's coefficient.

# WORKED EXAMPLE 8.9

Seven trainees are employed by Hoggart & Co. Their performance is judged by a combination of interviews and job performance. In the last year they have been ranked as follows:

| Trainee | A | B | C | D | E | F | G |
|---|---|---|---|---|---|---|---|
| Interview | 3 | 2 | 6 | 4 | 1 | 7 | 5 |
| Job performance | 1 | 3 | 5 | 2 | 4 | 6 | 7 |

Calculate Spearman's coefficient for these data.

## Solution

There are seven rankings, so $n = 7$. The differences are:

| Trainee | A | B | C | D | E | F | G |
|---|---|---|---|---|---|---|---|
| *Interview* | 3 | 2 | 6 | 4 | 1 | 7 | 5 |
| *Job performance* | 1 | 3 | 5 | 2 | 4 | 6 | 7 |
| *Difference* | 2 | − 1 | 1 | 2 | − 3 | 1 | − 2 |
| *Difference²* | 4 | 1 | 1 | 4 | 9 | 1 | 4 |

The sum of squared differences is $4 + 1 + 1 + 4 + 9 + 1 + 4 = 24$. Then Spearman's coefficient is:

$$r_s = 1 - \frac{6 \Sigma D^2}{n(n^2 - 1)} = 1 - \frac{6 \times 24}{7(49 - 1)} = 0.57$$

This shows a reasonably strong relationship between interview and job performance.

---

IN SUMMARY

Spearman's coefficient of correlation can be used for ranked data. It is based on Pearson's coefficient of correlation, and is interpreted in the same way.

---

# Self-assessment questions

**8.9** What is measured by the coefficient of determination?

**8.10** What values can be taken by the coefficient of correlation, and how is it related to the coefficient of determination?

**8.11** What is the difference between Pearson's and Spearman's coefficients of correlation?

**8.12** 'A coefficient of determination of 0.9 shows that 90% of variation in the dependent variable is caused by change in the independent variable.' Is this statement true?

# 8.4 | Extensions to linear regression

## 8.4.1 | Multiple regression

There are several extensions to the basic linear regression model. Here we are going to mention two of these: multiple regression and non-linear regression.

For linear regression we looked at problems where $y = a + bx$, so, for example, sales of a product were related to the amount spent on advertising:

$$\text{sales} = a + b \times \text{advertising}$$

But suppose the sales were also related to price, unemployment rates, average incomes, competition, and so on. In other words, the dependent variable, $y$, is not set by a single independent variable, $x$, but by a number of separate independent variables $x_i$. Then we could write:

$$y = a + b_1 x_1 + b_2 x_2 + b_3 x_3 + b_4 x_4 + b_5 x_5 \ldots$$

or in our example:

$$\text{sales} = a + b_1 \times \text{advertising} + b_2 \times \text{price} + b_3 \times \text{unemployment}$$
$$\text{rate} + b_4 \times \text{income} + b_5 \times \text{competition}$$

By adding more independent variables we are aiming to get a better model for describing sales. We might find that advertising explains 60% of the variation in sales, but if we add another term for price this explains 75% of the variation, and adding another term for unemployment explains 85% of the variation, and so on.

Because we are looking for a linear relationship between a dependent variable and a set of independent ones, this approach should really be called **multiple linear regression** – but it is always abbreviated to **multiple regression**. Now we need a way of calculating the variables $a$ and $b_i$, so that when we have a set of independent variables $x_i$ we can find a value for the independent variable $y$. After looking at the calculations in simple linear regression, you can imagine that the calculations for multiple regression are rather complicated. They are never tackled by hand. As usual, though, a lot of software includes multiple regression as a standard function.

## WORKED EXAMPLE 8.10

Figures for sales, advertising costs and prices for one of Causehead Trader's products are shown in the data section of Figure 8.13. The rest of this figure shows some results for multiple regression given by a spreadsheet. Describe the important points in these results.

|   | A | B | C | D | E | F |
|---|---|---|---|---|---|---|
| 1 | **Multiple regression** | | | | | |
| 2 | | | | | | |
| 3 | **Data** | | | | | |
| 4 | **Sales** | **Advertising** | **Price** | | | |
| 5 | 2450 | 100 | 50 | | | |
| 6 | 3010 | 130 | 56 | | | |
| 7 | 3090 | 160 | 45 | | | |
| 8 | 3700 | 190 | 63 | | | |
| 9 | 3550 | 210 | 48 | | | |
| 10 | 4280 | 240 | 70 | | | |
| 11 | | | | | | |
| 12 | **Summary output** | | | | | |
| 13 | *Regression statistics* | | | | | |
| 14 | Multiple r | 0.9958 | | | | |
| 15 | $r^2$ | 0.9916 | | | | |
| 16 | Adjusted $r^2$ | 0.9861 | | | | |
| 17 | Standard error | 75.0553 | | | | |
| 18 | Observations | 6 | | | | |
| 19 | | | | | | |
| 20 | *ANOVA* | | | | | |
| 21 | | *df* | *SS* | *MS* | *F* | *Significance F* |
| 22 | Regression | 2 | 2003633.452 | 1001816.726 | 177.839 | 0.000765 |
| 23 | Residual | 3 | 16899.882 | 5633.294 | | |
| 24 | Total | 5 | 2020533.333 | | | |
| 25 | | | | | | |
| 26 | | *Coefficients* | *Standard error* | *t stat* | *P-value* | |
| 27 | Intercept | 585.965 | 195.574 | 2.996 | 0.058 | |
| 28 | X variable 1 | 9.923 | 0.765 | 12.972 | 0.000 | |
| 29 | X variable 2 | 19.107 | 4.127 | 4.630 | 0.019 | |

**Figure 8.13**   Results for multiple regression in Worked Example 8.10.

## Solution

We are given data for two independent variables – advertising and price – and one dependent variable – sales. So we are looking for a relationship of the form:

$$\text{sales} = a + b_1 \times \text{advertising} + b_2 \times \text{price}$$

From lines 27–29 of Figure 8.13, you can see that the line of best fit is:

$$\text{sales} = 585.965 + 9.923 \times \text{advertising} + 19.107 \times \text{price}$$

The coefficient of correlation, $r$, equals 0.9958. This shows a very strong linear relationship, which is confirmed by the coefficient of determination, $r^2$, which shows that 99.16% of the variation is explained by the relationship. You can see on line 16 a reference to the 'adjusted $r^2$'. This is because the normal value is sometimes a bit optimistic, especially when there are only a few data points. To overcome this bias, the computer calculates an adjusted value. The rest of the figures are given for statistical tests, some of which we shall describe later in the book.

When dealing with multiple regression there are a few precautions we need to take. For example, the method only works properly if there is no significant linear relationship between the independent variables. So in the last worked example there should be no relationship between the advertising costs and price. But these relationships often exist in the real world, and we should accept the results if the relationships are not too strong. So now we have to find how strong the relationships are between the independent variables, and we can again use the coefficient of correlation for this. Taking the data from Worked Example 8.10, we can get a spreadsheet to calculate the coefficients of correlation shown in Figure 8.14. This table shows, not surprisingly, a perfect correlation between each variable and itself. We would like a very high correlation between sales and each of the independent variables. So it is good that there is a correlation of 0.9653 between sales and advertising, and 0.7228 between sales and price. Not so good, though, is the relatively high correlation of 0.5348 between advertising and price. Ideally we would like this to be lower, but the result is not too bad. The technical term for such a relationship between the independent variables is **multicollinearity**.

| | A | B | C | D |
|---|---|---|---|---|
| 1 | **Correlation** | | | |
| 2 | **Data** | | | |
| 3 | **Sales** | **Advertising** | **Price** | |
| 4 | 2450 | 100 | 50 | |
| 5 | 3010 | 130 | 56 | |
| 6 | 3090 | 160 | 45 | |
| 7 | 3700 | 190 | 63 | |
| 8 | 3550 | 210 | 48 | |
| 9 | 4280 | 240 | 70 | |
| 10 | | | | |
| 11 | **Correlation** | | | |
| 12 | | *Sales* | *Advertising* | *Price* |
| 13 | Sales | 1 | | |
| 14 | Advertising | 0.9653 | 1 | |
| 15 | Price | 0.7228 | 0.5348 | 1 |

**Figure 8.14** Coefficients of correlation for variables in Worked Example 8.10.

This table of coefficients of correlation shows that a simple linear regression model relating sales to advertising would explain 93.2% of the variation in sales (coming from the value of $r^2$ when $r = 0.9653$). But when we added price as a second variable, we increased this to 99.2% (from Figure 8.13) which shows an even better model.

Apart from multicollinearity, there is another common problem in multiple regression when the error terms are not independent. Multiple regression only really works when the errors are independent, but in practice the errors may not be so random. If we collect monthly data there may be a regular seasonal variation, and this gives a correlation between the error terms – a low value in November might always be followed by a high value in December. When there is a relationship between the errors, this is called **autocorrelation**.

## WORKED EXAMPLE 8.11

Elsom Service Corporation is trying to see how the number of shifts worked, bonus rates paid to employees, average hours of overtime and staff morale affect production. They have collected the following data, using some consistent units. What conclusions can Elsom reach from these data?

| *Production* | 2810 | 2620 | 3080 | 4200 | 1500 | 3160 | 4680 | 2330 | 1780 | 3910 |
|---|---|---|---|---|---|---|---|---|---|---|
| *Shifts* | 6 | 3 | 3 | 4 | 1 | 2 | 2 | 7 | 1 | 8 |
| *Bonus* | 15 | 20 | 5 | 5 | 7 | 12 | 25 | 10 | 12 | 3 |
| *Overtime* | 8 | 10 | 22 | 31 | 9 | 22 | 30 | 5 | 7 | 20 |
| *Morale* | 5 | 6 | 3 | 2 | 8 | 10 | 7 | 7 | 5 | 3 |

### Solution

Some of the calculations for this problem are shown in Figure 8.15. Here the line of best fit is:

$$\text{production} = 346.331 + 181.805 \times \text{shifts} + 50.132 \times \text{bonus}$$
$$+ 96.172 \times \text{overtime} - 28.705 \times \text{morale}$$

This model fits the data very well, with a coefficient of correlation of 0.997, which means that 99.5% of the variation in production is explained, and only 0.5% is unexplained. The separate coefficients of correlation between each pair of independent variables are low, so Elsom does not need to worry about multicollinearity. But we would like higher coefficients of correlation between production and the independent variables. Apart from the correlation between production and overtime, these values are very low, and there is a surprising slight negative correlation between production and morale. Elsom should look at its data carefully and see whether it can improve the model. Some of the statistical analyses we will describe later in the book can give guidance for this.

|   | A | B | C | D | E | F |
|---|---|---|---|---|---|---|
| 1 | **Multiple regression** | | | | | |
| 2 | | | | | | |
| 3 | **Data** | | | | | |
| 4 | **Production** | **Shifts** | **Bonus** | **Overtime** | **Morale** | |
| 5 | 2810 | 6 | 15 | 8 | 5 | |
| 6 | 2620 | 3 | 20 | 10 | 6 | |
| 7 | 3080 | 3 | 5 | 22 | 3 | |
| 8 | 4200 | 4 | 5 | 31 | 2 | |
| 9 | 1500 | 1 | 7 | 9 | 8 | |
| 10 | 3160 | 2 | 12 | 22 | 10 | |
| 11 | 4680 | 2 | 25 | 30 | 7 | |
| 12 | 2330 | 7 | 10 | 5 | 7 | |
| 13 | 1780 | 1 | 12 | 7 | 5 | |
| 14 | 3910 | 8 | 3 | 20 | 3 | |
| 15 | | | | | | |
| 16 | **Correlation** | | | | | |
| 17 | | *Production* | *Shifts* | *Bonus* | *Overtime* | *Morale* |
| 18 | Production | 1 | | | | |
| 19 | Shifts | 0.2623 | 1 | | | |
| 20 | Bonus | 0.1531 | –0.3147 | 1 | | |
| 21 | Overtime | 0.8778 | –0.1085 | –0.0220 | 1 | |
| 22 | Morale | –0.3321 | –0.3947 | 0.4512 | –0.2654 | 1 |
| 23 | | | | | | |
| 24 | **Regression** | | | | | |
| 25 | *Regression statistics* | | | *Coefficients* | | |
| 26 | Multiple r | 0.997 | | Intercept | 346.331 | |
| 27 | $r^2$ | 0.995 | | X variable **1** | 181.805 | |
| 28 | Adjusted $r^2$ | 0.990 | | X variable **2** | 50.132 | |
| 29 | Standard error | 100.807 | | X variable **3** | 96.172 | |
| 30 | Observations | 10 | | X variable **4** | – 28.705 | |

**Figure 8.15**   Multiple regression calculations for Worked Example 8.11.

---

*IN SUMMARY*

Sometimes a dependent variable is related to a number of independent variables. Then instead of using simple linear regression, we can use multiple regression. For this we need to find the values of $a$ and $b_i$ which define the best relationship. Many packages have standard functions for multiple regression. Coefficients of correlation are important for these analyses.

## 8.4.2 | Non-linear regression

Linear regression finds the straight line of best fit through a set of data, but sometimes there is a clear pattern that is not linear. There might, for example, be a clear quadratic relationship, or a constant rate of growth. In these cases we want to fit other functions to data. This is generally called **non-linear regression**. This is exactly the same in principle as linear regression, but as you can imagine, the arithmetic is more complicated.

## WORKED EXAMPLE 8.12

Helen Stanmore is convinced that her accountant has raised his prices more than the cost of inflation. Over the past 11 years Helen has noticed that the cost of doing her accounts (in thousands of pounds) is as follows. What can she do with these data?

| Year | 1 | 2 | 3 | 4 | 5 | 6 | 7 | 8 | 9 | 10 | 11 |
|------|-----|-----|-----|-----|-----|-----|-----|-----|-----|-----|-----|
| Cost | 0.8 | 1.0 | 1.3 | 1.7 | 2.0 | 2.4 | 2.9 | 3.8 | 4.7 | 6.2 | 7.5 |

### Solution

The first thing Helen can do is find the line of best fit for the data. You can see, without bothering to draw a graph or calculate the correlation, that the data are not a straight line. One option is to draw a 'growth' curve through the data, which has the standard form, $y = bm^x$ where $x$ and $y$ are the independent and dependent variables, and $b$ and $m$ are constants. Many packages will do this kind of curve fitting automatically, as shown in the spreadsheet of Figure 8.16a.

In this figure, the spreadsheet has calculated the line of best fit as:

$$y = bm^x \qquad y = 0.6541 \times 1.2475^x$$

and then it has used this equation to find the trend in prices charged by the accountant over the past 11 years. The value of 1.2475 for $m$ suggests that the accountant's charges are rising by almost 25% a year, which is certainly more than current inflation.

A slight variation on these calculations forces the value of $b$ to 1, to find the slightly simpler growth curve, $y = m^x$. The spreadsheet results for this calculation are shown in Figure 8.16b. You can see here that the line does not seem to be quite such a good fit, and we could confirm this by calculating the coefficients of correlation.

Spreadsheets – and other packages – can normally fit a number of curves to data, including:

- linear models $\qquad y = a + bx$
- multiple linear $\qquad y = a + b_1x_1 + b_2x_2 + b_3x_3 + \ldots$
- polynomials $\qquad y = a + bx + cx^2 + dx^3 + \ldots$
- exponential $\qquad y = ax^b$
- growth $\qquad y = ab^x$

|   | A | B | C | D | E | F | G |
|---|---|---|---|---|---|---|---|
| 1 | **Non-linear regression** | | | | | | |
| 2 | | | | | | | |
| 3 | **Data** | | | **Results** | | **Line of fit** | |
| 4 | **Year** | **Price** | | **Predicted price** | | **y=bm^x** | |
| 5 | 1 | 0.8 | | 0.8160 | | **b =** | 0.6541 |
| 6 | 2 | 1 | | 1.0179 | | **m =** | 1.2475 |
| 7 | 3 | 1.3 | | 1.2699 | | | |
| 8 | 4 | 1.7 | | 1.5842 | | | |
| 9 | 5 | 2 | | 1.9763 | | | |
| 10 | 6 | 2.4 | | 2.4654 | | | |
| 11 | 7 | 2.9 | | 3.0756 | | | |
| 12 | 8 | 3.8 | | 3.8368 | | | |
| 13 | 9 | 4.7 | | 4.7864 | | | |
| 14 | 10 | 6.2 | | 5.9710 | | | |
| 15 | 11 | 7.5 | | 7.4489 | | | |

**Figure 8.16a**   Example of non-linear regression.

|   | A | B | C | D | E | F | G |
|---|---|---|---|---|---|---|---|
| 1 | **Non-linear regression** | | | | | | |
| 2 | | | | | | | |
| 3 | **Data** | | | **Results** | | **Line of fit** | |
| 4 | **Year** | **Price** | | **Predicted price** | | **y=bm^x** | |
| 5 | 1 | 0.8 | | 1.1803 | | **b =** | 1.0000 |
| 6 | 2 | 1 | | 1.3931 | | **m =** | 1.1803 |
| 7 | 3 | 1.3 | | 1.6443 | | | |
| 8 | 4 | 1.7 | | 1.9408 | | | |
| 9 | 5 | 2 | | 2.2907 | | | |
| 10 | 6 | 2.4 | | 2.7037 | | | |
| 11 | 7 | 2.9 | | 3.1911 | | | |
| 12 | 8 | 3.8 | | 3.7665 | | | |
| 13 | 9 | 4.7 | | 4.4456 | | | |
| 14 | 10 | 6.2 | | 5.2472 | | | |
| 15 | 11 | 7.5 | | 6.1932 | | | |

**Figure 8.16b**   Repeating the calculations when *b* is forced to equal 1.

---

## IN SUMMARY

Sometimes we look for the line of best fit through non-linear data. We can find this line automatically using similar analyses to linear regression.

## Self-assessment questions

**8.13** What are the most common extensions to linear regression?

**8.14** 'Multiple regression always considers linear relationships.' Is this statement true?

**8.15** How can you tell whether multiple regression will find a better fit to a set of data than simple linear regression?

**8.16** What is multicollinearity?

---

CHAPTER REVIEW

This chapter described the relationship between variables. It concentrated on linear regression, which finds the straight line of best fit through a set of data. The goodness of fit is judged by the coefficients of determination and correlation. In particular the chapter:

- outlined the need to measure the strength of relationships
- measured errors, including mean error, mean absolute deviation and mean squared error
- used linear regression to find the line of best fit through data
- showed how to use linear regression for forecasting
- used the coefficients of determination and correlation to measure the goodness of fit
- described multiple regression
- mentioned non-linear regression

---

## Problems

**8.1** The productivity of a factory has been recorded over ten months, together with forecasts made the previous month by the production manager, the foreman and the management services department (Table 8.1). Compare the three sets of forecasts in terms of bias and accuracy.

**Table 8.1**

| Month | 1 | 2 | 3 | 4 | 5 | 6 | 7 | 8 | 9 | 10 |
|---|---|---|---|---|---|---|---|---|---|---|
| Productivity | 22 | 24 | 28 | 27 | 23 | 24 | 20 | 18 | 20 | 23 |
| Production manager | 23 | 26 | 32 | 28 | 20 | 26 | 24 | 16 | 21 | 23 |
| Foreman | 22 | 28 | 29 | 29 | 24 | 26 | 21 | 21 | 24 | 25 |
| Management services | 21 | 25 | 26 | 27 | 24 | 23 | 20 | 20 | 19 | 24 |

**8.2**  Find the line of best fit through the following data. How good is this fit?

| x | 10 | 19 | 29 | 42 | 51 | 60 | 73 | 79 | 90 | 101 |
|---|----|----|----|----|----|----|----|----|----|-----|
| y | 69 | 114 | 163 | 231 | 272 | 299 | 361 | 411 | 483 | 522 |

**8.3**  A local amateur dramatic society is staging a play and wants to know how much to spend on advertising. It wants to attract as many people as possible, up to the hall capacity. For the past 11 productions the spending on advertising (in hundreds of pounds) and audience is shown in the following table. If the hall capacity is now 300 people how much should it spend on advertising?

| Spending | 3 | 5 | 1 | 7 | 2 | 4 | 4 | 2 | 6 | 6 | 4 |
|----------|---|---|---|---|---|---|---|---|---|---|---|
| Audience | 200 | 250 | 75 | 425 | 125 | 300 | 225 | 200 | 300 | 400 | 275 |

**8.4**  Ten experiments were done to assess the effects of bonus rates paid to salesmen on sales, with the following results:

| % Bonus | 0 | 1 | 2 | 3 | 4 | 5 | 6 | 7 | 8 | 9 |
|---------|---|---|---|---|---|---|---|---|---|---|
| Sales ('00s) | 3 | 4 | 8 | 10 | 15 | 18 | 20 | 22 | 27 | 28 |

What is the line of best fit through these data? How good is this line?

**8.5**  Sales of a product for the past ten months are shown below. Use linear regression to forecast sales for the next six months. How reliable are these figures?

| Month | 1 | 2 | 3 | 4 | 5 | 6 | 7 | 8 | 9 | 10 |
|-------|---|---|---|---|---|---|---|---|---|----|
| Sales | 6 | 21 | 41 | 75 | 98 | 132 | 153 | 189 | 211 | 243 |

**8.6**  A company records sales of four products for a ten-month period. What can you say about these figures?

| Month | 1 | 2 | 3 | 4 | 5 | 6 | 7 | 8 | 9 | 10 |
|-------|---|---|---|---|---|---|---|---|---|----|
| p | 24 | 36 | 45 | 52 | 61 | 72 | 80 | 94 | 105 | 110 |
| q | 2500 | 2437 | 2301 | 2290 | 2101 | 2001 | 1995 | 1847 | 1732 | 1695 |
| r | 150 | 204 | 167 | 254 | 167 | 241 | 203 | 224 | 167 | 219 |
| s | 102 | 168 | 205 | 221 | 301 | 302 | 310 | 459 | 519 | 527 |

**8.7**  A company's staff appraisal scheme uses the views of two managers. In one department the two managers rank staff as follows. How reliable does this scheme seem?

| Person | A | B | C | D | E | F | G | H | I | J | K | L |
|--------|---|---|---|---|---|---|---|---|---|---|---|---|
| Rank 1 | 5 | 10 | 12 | 4 | 9 | 1 | 3 | 7 | 2 | 11 | 8 | 6 |
| Rank 2 | 8 | 7 | 10 | 1 | 12 | 2 | 4 | 6 | 5 | 9 | 11 | 3 |

**8.8**  A panel of tasters ranked eight foods as follows:

| Food | A | B | C | D | E | F | G | H |
|------|---|---|---|---|---|---|---|---|
| Rank | 3 | 2 | 8 | 5 | 7 | 1 | 4 | 6 |

The amount of a taste enhancer added to each food was also known:

| Food | A | B | C | D | E | F | G | H |
|------|---|---|---|---|---|---|---|---|
| Amount | 22 | 17 | 67 | 35 | 68 | 10 | 37 | 50 |

Use a ranking method to see whether the flavour enhancer works.

**8.9**  What is the line of best fit through the following data?

| y | 420 | 520 | 860 | 740 | 510 | 630 | 650 | 760 | 590 | 680 |
|---|-----|-----|-----|-----|-----|-----|-----|-----|-----|-----|
| a | 1 | 2 | 3 | 4 | 5 | 6 | 7 | 8 | 9 | 10 |
| b | 3 | 7 | 9 | 3 | 1 | 6 | 2 | 9 | 6 | 6 |
| c | 23 | 15 | 64 | 52 | 13 | 40 | 36 | 20 | 19 | 24 |
| d | 109 | 121 | 160 | 155 | 175 | 90 | 132 | 145 | 97 | 107 |

**8.10**  What is the best line through the following data?

| x | 1 | 2 | 3 | 4 | 5 | 6 | 7 | 8 | 9 | 10 |
|---|---|---|---|---|---|---|---|---|---|----|
| y | 9 | 14 | 20 | 28 | 40 | 60 | 90 | 130 | 180 | 250 |

# Computer exercises

**8.1**  Figure 8.17 shows the printout from a session using Minitab. Make sure you can understand the basic functions here, but do not worry about the statistical details. Use a suitable package to check the results.

```
MTB    > set c2
DATA   > 17 23 41 38 42 47 51 56
DATA   > end
MTB    > set c1
DATA   > 8 7 6 5 4 3 2 1
DATA   > end
MTB    > correlate c2 c1
```

Correlation of C2 and C1 $= -0.949$

```
MTB    > regress c2 1 c1 c20 c21;
SUBC   > coefficients c22;
SUBC   > residuals c23.
```

The regression equation is
C2 $= 62.7 - 5.18$ C1

| Predictor | Coef | Stdev | t-ratio | p |
|---|---|---|---|---|
| Constant | 62.679 | 3.536 | 17.73 | 0.000 |
| C1 | $-5.1786$ | 0.7002 | $-7.40$ | 0.000 |

$s = 4.538$      R-sq $= 90.1\%$      R-sq(adj) $= 88.5\%$

Analysis of Variance

| SOURCE | DF | SS | MS | F | p |
|---|---|---|---|---|---|
| Regression | 1 | 1126.3 | 1126.3 | 54.71 | 0.000 |
| Error | 6 | 123.5 | 20.6 | | |
| Total | 7 | 1249.9 | | | |

Unusual Observations

| Obs. | C1 | C2 | Fit | Stdev.Fit | Residual | St.Resid |
|---|---|---|---|---|---|---|
| 3 | 6.00 | 41.00 | 31.61 | 1.92 | 9.39 | 2.28R |

R denotes an obs. with a large st. resid.

```
MTB    > print c1 c2 c20-c23
```

| ROW | C1 | C2 | C20 | C21 | C22 | C23 |
|---|---|---|---|---|---|---|
| 1 | 8 | 17 | $-1.22634$ | 21.2500 | 62.6786 | $-4.25000$ |
| 2 | 7 | 23 | $-0.88668$ | 26.4286 | $-5.1786$ | $-3.42857$ |
| 3 | 6 | 41 | 2.28398 | 31.6071 | | 9.39286 |
| 4 | 5 | 38 | 0.28706 | 36.7857 | | 1.21429 |
| 5 | 4 | 42 | 0.00844 | 41.9643 | | 0.03571 |
| 6 | 3 | 47 | $-0.03474$ | 47.1429 | | $-0.14286$ |
| 7 | 2 | 51 | $-0.34174$ | 52.3214 | | $-1.32143$ |
| 8 | 1 | 56 | $-0.43282$ | 57.5000 | | $-1.50000$ |

**Figure 8.17**  Printout from a Minitab session.

**8.2**  Figure 8.18 shows a spreadsheet that has been used for regression. Design a spreadsheet that will do linear regression and check these results. How could you improve the spreadsheet's presentation of results?

**8.3**  The average number of flights from a small airport has been recorded over a typical period as follows:

24 23 25 24 27 29 32 30 35 34 34 39 41 40
38 46 41 51 48 46 41 57 56 62 61 62 68

Analyse these figures and forecast future numbers of flights. Present your results in a report, including graphs of the figures.

|   | A | B | C | D | E | F | G |
|---|---|---|---|---|---|---|---|
| 1 | **x** | **y** | | | **Regression output** | | |
| 2 | 10 | 89 | | | Constant | | 5.745961 |
| 3 | 19 | 201 | | | St err of Y est | | 19.08293 |
| 4 | 29 | 294 | | | R squared | | 0.991783 |
| 5 | 42 | 389 | | | No. of observations | | 6 |
| 6 | 55 | 512 | | | Degress of freedom | | 4 |
| 7 | 59 | 587 | | | | | |
| 8 | | | | **X coefficient(s)** | | 9.521141 | |
| 9 | | | | **Std err of coef.** | | 0.43333 | |
| 10 | | | | | | | |
| 11 | | | | **x** | **y** | **Predictions** | **Residuals** |
| 12 | | | | 10 | 89 | 100.96 | −11.96 |
| 13 | | | | 19 | 201 | 186.65 | 14.35 |
| 14 | | | | 29 | 294 | 281.86 | 12.14 |
| 15 | | | | 42 | 389 | 405.63 | −16.63 |
| 16 | | | | 55 | 512 | 529.41 | −17.41 |
| 17 | | | | 59 | 587 | 567.49 | 19.51 |
| 18 | | | | | | | |

**Figure 8.18**   Using a spreadsheet for regression.

**8.4**   A manufacturing company, Emilio Gaspin, records the data in Table 8.2. Use appropriate packages to analyse these data. Write a report about your findings.

**Table 8.2**

| Period | Output | Shifts | Advertising | Bonuses | Faults |
|--------|--------|--------|-------------|---------|--------|
| 1 | 1120 | 10 | 1056 | 0 | 241 |
| 2 | 131 | 10 | 1050 | 0 | 236 |
| 3 | 144 | 11 | 1200 | 0 | 233 |
| 4 | 152 | 11 | 1250 | 10 | 228 |
| 5 | 166 | 11 | 1290 | 15 | 210 |
| 6 | 174 | 12 | 1400 | 20 | 209 |
| 7 | 180 | 12 | 1510 | 20 | 225 |
| 8 | 189 | 12 | 1690 | 20 | 167 |
| 9 | 201 | 12 | 1610 | 25 | 210 |
| 10 | 225 | 12 | 1802 | 30 | 128 |
| 11 | 236 | 13 | 1806 | 35 | 201 |
| 12 | 245 | 13 | 1988 | 40 | 165 |
| 13 | 261 | 13 | 1968 | 40 | 132 |
| 14 | 266 | 13 | 2045 | 40 | 108 |
| 15 | 270 | 14 | 2163 | 45 | 98 |
| 16 | 289 | 15 | 2138 | 50 | 134 |
| 17 | 291 | 16 | 2431 | 50 | 158 |
| 18 | 300 | 16 | 2560 | 55 | 109 |
| 19 | 314 | 16 | 2570 | 55 | 65 |

8.5 A tourist agency has been looking at the prices charged for hotel rooms in a major seaside resort. They have collected the data in Table 8.3 from a sample of hotels. What information can you get from these data?

**Table 8.3**

| Cost | Rating | Rooms | Location | Facilities | Meals | Staff |
|------|--------|-------|----------|------------|-------|-------|
| 45 | 1 | 45 | 2 | 4 | 10 | 70 |
| 85 | 3 | 90 | 4 | 6 | 8 | 70 |
| 40 | 2 | 120 | 1 | 5 | 6 | 120 |
| 65 | 4 | 30 | 1 | 2 | 4 | 8 |
| 35 | 3 | 40 | 5 | 9 | 5 | 8 |
| 120 | 5 | 240 | 3 | 12 | 12 | 140 |
| 15 | 1 | 8 | 5 | 2 | 2 | 4 |
| 16 | 1 | 12 | 4 | 2 | 2 | 5 |
| 28 | 2 | 40 | 2 | 6 | 6 | 18 |
| 60 | 4 | 100 | 1 | 8 | 10 | 45 |
| 120 | 5 | 60 | 3 | 12 | 12 | 100 |
| 95 | 3 | 80 | 3 | 8 | 8 | 30 |
| 55 | 2 | 50 | 4 | 2 | 10 | 20 |
| 60 | 2 | 45 | 1 | 2 | 8 | 15 |
| 18 | 1 | 40 | 1 | 12 | 2 | 30 |
| 28 | 3 | 30 | 4 | 4 | 6 | 8 |

8.6 Find a set of government figures for variables that you think should be related. You might start with, say, inflation and unemployment over the past 25 years. See whether there is a strong relationship between these. Extend your analysis to related figures, such as gross national product and interest rates. What conclusions can you reach from these results?

# Case study

## Western General Hospital

Each term the Western General Hospital accepts a batch of 50 new student nurses. Their training lasts for several years before they become state registered or state enrolled.

It is very expensive to train nurses and hospital administrators want to make sure that the training is cost-effective. A continuing problem is the number of nurses who fail exams and do not complete their training. If the hospital could reduce the number of these nurses leaving they could save a lot of money.

It has been suggested that the recruitment procedure could be improved, and administrators should take more care in selecting students who are likely to complete the course. One way of doing this could be to relate the nurses' likely performance in exams to their performance in school exams. Unfortunately, nurses come from a variety of backgrounds and start training at different ages, so their performance at school may not be relevant. Other possible factors are age and number of previous jobs.

Table 8.4 shows results for last term's nurses. Grades in exams have been converted to numbers (A = 5, B = 4 and so on), and average marks are given.

**Table 8.4**

| Nurse | Year of birth | Nursing grade | School grade | Number of jobs | Nurse | Year of birth | Nursing grade | School grade | Number of jobs |
|-------|------|------|------|------|----|----|-----|-----|----|
| 1 | 82 | 2.3 | 3.2 | 0 | 26 | 70 | 4.1 | 3.7 | 4 |
| 2 | 75 | 3.2 | 4.5 | 1 | 27 | 84 | 2.6 | 2.3 | 1 |
| 3 | 82 | 2.8 | 2.1 | 1 | 28 | 84 | 2.3 | 2.7 | 1 |
| 4 | 72 | 4.1 | 1.6 | 4 | 29 | 82 | 1.8 | 1.9 | 2 |
| 5 | 80 | 4.0 | 3.7 | 2 | 30 | 81 | 3.1 | 1.0 | 0 |
| 6 | 83 | 3.7 | 2.0 | 1 | 31 | 72 | 4.8 | 1.2 | 3 |
| 7 | 75 | 3.5 | 1.5 | 0 | 32 | 78 | 2.3 | 3.0 | 1 |
| 8 | 73 | 4.8 | 3.6 | 0 | 33 | 80 | 3.1 | 2.1 | 5 |
| 9 | 83 | 2.8 | 3.4 | 2 | 34 | 81 | 2.2 | 4.0 | 2 |
| 10 | 84 | 1.9 | 1.2 | 1 | 35 | 82 | 3.0 | 4.5 | 3 |
| 11 | 79 | 2.3 | 4.8 | 2 | 36 | 72 | 4.3 | 3.3 | 0 |
| 12 | 83 | 2.5 | 4.5 | 0 | 37 | 82 | 2.4 | 3.1 | 1 |
| 13 | 76 | 2.8 | 1.0 | 0 | 38 | 78 | 3.2 | 2.9 | 0 |
| 14 | 69 | 4.5 | 2.2 | 3 | 39 | 84 | 1.1 | 2.5 | 0 |
| 15 | 84 | 2.0 | 3.0 | 1 | 40 | 69 | 4.2 | 1.9 | 2 |
| 16 | 80 | 3.4 | 4.0 | 0 | 41 | 78 | 2.0 | 1.2 | 1 |
| 17 | 78 | 3.0 | 3.9 | 2 | 42 | 84 | 1.0 | 4.1 | 0 |
| 18 | 78 | 2.5 | 2.9 | 2 | 43 | 77 | 3.0 | 3.0 | 0 |
| 19 | 79 | 2.8 | 2.0 | 1 | 44 | 80 | 2.0 | 2.2 | 0 |
| 20 | 81 | 2.8 | 2.1 | 1 | 45 | 76 | 2.3 | 2.0 | 2 |
| 21 | 78 | 2.7 | 3.8 | 0 | 46 | 76 | 3.7 | 3.7 | 4 |
| 22 | 71 | 4.5 | 1.4 | 3 | 47 | 68 | 4.7 | 4.0 | 5 |
| 23 | 75 | 3.7 | 1.8 | 2 | 48 | 75 | 4.0 | 1.9 | 2 |
| 24 | 80 | 3.0 | 2.4 | 6 | 49 | 75 | 3.8 | 3.1 | 0 |
| 25 | 81 | 2.9 | 3.0 | 0 | 50 | 79 | 2.5 | 4.6 | 1 |

When the hospital collected data on the number of nurses who did not finish training in the past ten terms, they got the following results:

| Term | 1 | 2 | 3 | 4 | 5 | 6 | 7 | 8 | 9 | 10 |
|---|---|---|---|---|---|---|---|---|---|---|
| Number | 4 | 7 | 3 | 6 | 9 | 11 | 10 | 15 | 13 | 17 |

The hospital is looking for three things:

- a presentation of the data in a form that is easy to understand
- a discussion of which, if any, of the factors listed can be used to predict nurses' grades
- a discussion of other factors to consider in future analyses

# 9 | Business forecasting

Chapter outline      262
9.1 Forecasting      263
     in organizations
9.2 Judgemental forecasting      265
9.3 Projective forecasting      267
9.4 Forecasting with      283
     seasonality and trend

Chapter review      294
Problems      295
Computer exercises      296
Case study:      298
     Workload planning

## CHAPTER OUTLINE

All decisions become effective at some point in the future. Managers should, therefore, base their decisions not on present circumstances, but on circumstances as they will be when the decisions become effective. These circumstances must be forecast, so forecasting becomes a central part of any organization.

Despite the importance of forecasting, progress in many areas has been disappointing. There are many methods of forecasting, but even the best are not entirely accurate. There are differences between forecast and actual observations, which is why we cannot rely on weather forecasts, predict the winner of a horse race, become rich by speculating on the price of shares or buy the right amount of food for a dinner party. There are, however, many circumstances in which we can make good forecasts. This chapter looks at some of the most widely used methods.

After reading this chapter and doing the exercises you should be able to:

- appreciate the importance of forecasting in organizations
- list different types of forecasting
- describe different types of judgemental forecasting
- discuss the characteristics of projective forecasting
- appreciate the importance of time series
- calculate errors in forecasts
- forecast using simple averages, moving averages and exponential smoothing
- forecast for time series with seasonality and trend

# 9.1 | Forecasting in organizations

In Chapter 7 we described a break-even analysis. This finds the number of units of a product that must be sold to recover fixed costs and begin making a profit. If a company considers a new product, but its sales are unlikely to reach the break-even point, the product will make a loss and it should not be introduced. This analysis clearly depends on forecast demand. We could give many similar examples that show the importance of forecasting. In practice, all decisions become effective at some point in the future, so they should be based on circumstances not as they are at present, but as they will be when the decision becomes effective. It is clear, then, that any decision depends on forecasts of future circumstances. This means that forecasting is very important to all organizations. If you have any doubts about this you might try to think of a decision that does not involve some form of forecasting.

We should say that a lot of the following discussion talks of 'forecasting demand'. But this is only for convenience and in practice, forecasting is used for almost anything from opening a new university to gambling on horse races.

It would be convenient to say that 'a lot of work has been done on forecasting and the best method is...'. Unfortunately, we cannot do this. Because of the wide range of things to be forecast and the different situations in which forecasts are needed, there is no single best method. In this chapter we shall describe a variety of methods and suggest the circumstances in which each can be used.

We can start by classifying the different methods of forecasting, and can do this in several ways. One classification concerns the time in the future covered by forecasts. In particular:

- **long-term forecasts** look ahead several years (the time typically needed to build a new factory)

- **medium-term forecasts** look ahead between three months and two years (the time typically needed to replace an old product by a new one)

- **short-term forecasts** cover the next few weeks (describing the continuing demand for a product)

The time horizon affects the choice of forecasting method because of the availability and relevance of historical data, time available to make the forecast, cost involved, effects of errors, effort considered worthwhile, and so on.

Another classification of forecasting methods draws a distinction between qualitative and quantitative approaches (as shown in Figure 9.1).

If a company is already making a product, it will probably have records of past demand and know the factors that affect this. Then it could use a quantitative method to forecast future demand. There are two alternatives for this:

- **projective methods**, which examine the pattern of past demand and extend this into the future. If demand in the past four weeks has been 100, 120, 140 and 160, it would be reasonable to project this pattern and suggest that demand in the following week will be around 180

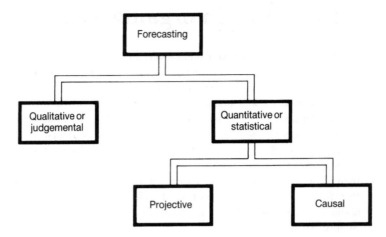

**Figure 9.1**  Classification of forecasting methods.

- **causal methods**, which analyse the effects of outside influences and use these to produce forecasts. Productivity of an office might depend on the bonus rates paid to employees, so it would be sensible to use the current bonus rate to forecast productivity. This approach has been described by linear regression in Chapter 8

Both of these approaches rely on the availability of accurate, quantified data. Suppose, though, that a company is introducing an entirely new product. There are no past demand figures that can be projected forwards, and the company does not know the factors that affect demand. In such circumstances there are no quantitative data and it must use a qualitative method. Such methods are called **judgemental**, and they rely on subjective assessments and opinions.

We have described causal forecasting using linear regression in the last chapter, so the rest of this chapter looks at other forecasting methods, starting with qualitative or judgemental methods.

---

> ### IN SUMMARY

Forecasting is an essential part of all planning and decision-making. There are several ways of classifying forecasts, with two useful ones describing the time they look ahead and the overall approach used.

---

# Self-assessment questions

**9.1**  Why is forecasting used in organizations?

**9.2**  'Forecasting is a specialized function that uses mathematical techniques to project historical data.' Do you think this statement is true?

**9.3** List three fundamentally different approaches to forecasting.

**9.4** What factors should be considered when choosing a forecasting method?

# 9.2 Judgemental forecasting

Suppose a company is about to market an entirely new product, or a medical team is considering a new organ transplant, or a board of directors is considering plans for 25 years in the future. In these circumstances, there are no appropriate historical data they can use for a quantitative forecast. Sometimes there is a complete absence of data, and at other times the available data are unreliable or irrelevant to the future. As quantitative forecasts cannot be used, a judgemental method is the only alternative. These methods use subjective assessments from various informed sources. Five widely used methods are:

- personal insight
- panel consensus
- market surveys
- historical analogy
- Delphi method

## 9.2.1 Personal insight

This has a single expert who is familiar with the situation and produces a forecast based on their own judgement. This is the most widely used forecasting method, and is the one that managers should try to avoid. It relies entirely on one person's judgement (their opinions, as well as prejudices and ignorance). It can give good forecasts, but often gives very bad ones, and there are countless examples of experts being totally wrong. Perhaps the major weakness of the method is its unreliability. This may not matter for minor decisions, but when there are serious consequences of errors some more reliable method should be used.

Comparisons of forecasting methods clearly show that someone who is familiar with a situation, using experience and subjective opinions to forecast, will consistently produce **worse** forecasts than someone who knows nothing about the situation but uses a more formal method.

## 9.2.2 Panel consensus

A single expert can easily make a mistake, but collecting together several experts and allowing them to talk freely to each other should lead to a consensus that is more reliable. If there is no secrecy and the panel are encouraged to talk openly, a genuine consensus may be found. On the other hand, there may be difficulties in combining the views of different experts when a consensus cannot be found.

Although it is more reliable than one person's insight, panel consensus still has the major weakness that all experts can make mistakes. There are also problems of group working, where 'he who shouts loudest gets his way', everyone tries to please the boss, some people do not speak well in groups, and so on. Overall, panel consensus is an improvement on personal insight, but you should view results from either method with caution.

### 9.2.3 | Market surveys

Sometimes, even groups of experts do not have enough knowledge to make a reasonable forecast. This frequently happens with the launch of a new product. Experts may give their views, but more useful information is found by talking directly to potential customers. Market surveys collect data from a representative sample of customers. Their views are analysed, with inferences drawn about the population at large (as described in Chapter 3).

Market surveys can give useful information, but they tend to be expensive and time-consuming. They are also prone to errors as they rely on:

- a sample of customers that fairly represents the population

- useful, unbiased questions

- accurate analyses of the replies

- valid conclusions drawn from the analyses

### 9.2.4 | Historical analogy

If a new product is being introduced, it may be possible to find a similar product that was launched recently, and assume that demand for the new product will follow the same pattern. If, for example, a publisher is introducing a new book, it could forecast likely demand from the actual demand for the last, similar book it published.

Historical analogy relies on the availability of similar products that were introduced in the recent past. In practice, it is often difficult to find products that are similar enough to give reliable results.

### 9.2.5 | Delphi method

This is the most formal of the judgemental methods and has a well-defined procedure. A number of experts are contacted by post and each is given a questionnaire to complete. The replies from these questionnaires are analysed and summaries are passed back to the experts. Each expert is then asked to reconsider their original reply in the light of the summarized replies from others. Each reply is anonymous so there is no undue influences of status, or pressures of face-to-face discussions. This process of modifying responses in the light of replies made by the rest of the group is repeated several times (usually between three and six). By this time, the range of opinions should have narrowed enough to help with decisions.

We can illustrate this process by an example from offshore oil fields. A company may want to know when underwater inspections on platforms will be done entirely by robots rather than by divers. A number of experts would be contacted to start the Delphi forecast. These experts would come from various backgrounds, including divers, technical staff from oil companies, ships' captains, maintenance engineers and robot designers. The overall problem would then be explained, and each of the experts would be asked when they thought robots would replace divers. The initial returns would probably give a wide range of dates from, say, 2005 to 2050 and these would be summarized and passed back. Each person would then be asked if they would like to reassess their answer in the light of other replies. After repeating this several times, views might converge so that 80% of replies suggest a date between 2010 and 2015, and this would be enough to help planning.

---

### IN SUMMARY

Judgemental forecasts are typically used when there are no relevant historical data. They rely on subjective views and opinions, as demonstrated by personal insight, panel consensus, market surveys, historical analogy and the Delphi method.

---

## Self-assessment questions

**9.5** What are judgemental forecasts?

**9.6** List five types of judgemental forecast.

**9.7** What are the main problems with judgemental forecasts?

# 9.3 | Projective forecasting

Projective forecasting takes historical observations and uses these to forecast future values. It ignores any external influences and only looks at past values of, say, demand to suggest future demand. We are going to describe four methods of this type:

- simple averages
- moving averages
- exponential smoothing
- models for seasonality and trend

These methods are most commonly used with time series, which are described in the following section.

## 9.3.1 | Time series

A lot of data occur as **time series**, which are series of observations taken at regular intervals of time. Monthly unemployment figures, daily rainfall, weekly demand, and annual population statistics are examples of time series.

Like many other sets of data, if you have a time series the first step in analysing it is to draw a graph, and a simple scatter diagram can show any underlying patterns. The three most common patterns in time series are:

- **constant series**, in which observations take roughly the same value over time, such as annual rainfall
- **series with a trend**, which either rise or fall steadily, such as the gross national product per capita
- **seasonal series**, which have a cyclical component, such as the weekly sales of soft drinks

These three patterns are shown in Figure 9.2.

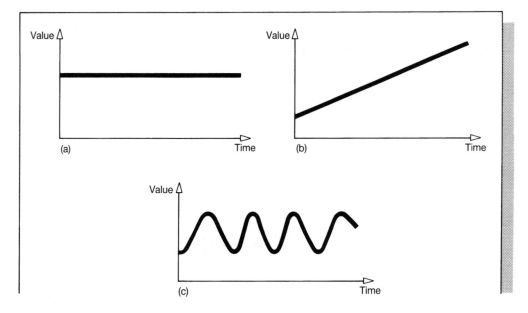

**Figure 9.2**  Common patterns in time series:
(a) constant series;   (b) series with a trend;   (c) seasonal series.

If observations followed such simple patterns we would have no problems with forecasting. Unfortunately, there are nearly always differences between actual observations and the underlying pattern. A random noise is superimposed on the underlying pattern so that a constant series, for example, does not always take exactly the same value, but is somewhere close. So:

200  205  194  195  208  203  200  193  201 198

is a constant series of 200 with superimposed noise (see Figure 9.3).

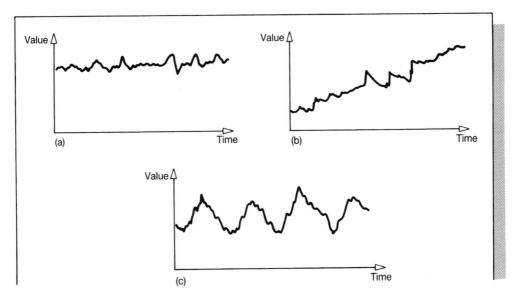

**Figure 9.3**  Common patterns in time series including noise:
(a) constant series;   (b) series with a trend;   (c) seasonal series.

We met this idea of noise when talking about regression in the last chapter. It is this random noise that makes forecasting so difficult. If the noise is relatively small it is easy to get good forecasts, but if there is a lot of noise it hides the underlying pattern and forecasting becomes more difficult:

actual value = underlying pattern + random noise

In Chapter 8, we showed that the difference between an actual observation and the value predicted by the underlying pattern can be seen as an error. If, for example, the underlying pattern in a set of data is a linear trend, a graph of observations will show variations about a straight line, as shown in Figure 9.4. Each observation has an error, which is its vertical distance from the line. Then the error in period $t$ is defined as $E_t$:

$$E_t = \text{observation in period } t$$
$$\quad - \text{value forecast from underlying pattern}$$
$$= y_t - F_t$$

where:

$$y_t = \text{the actual observation}$$

$$F_t = \text{the value forecast from the underlying pattern}$$

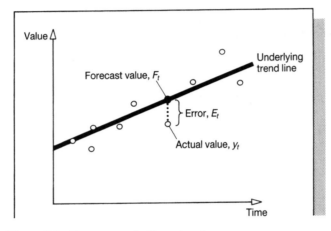

**Figure 9.4** Errors around a linear trend.

This error is the **residual.** If we repeat this calculation for each period we can find a mean error, where:

$$\text{mean error} = \frac{\Sigma E_t}{n} = \frac{\Sigma (y_t - F_t)}{n}$$

As we have seen before, the mean error has the major drawback of allowing positive and negative errors to cancel each other, and data with very large errors can have zero mean error. Consider, for example, the following values for demand and forecast:

| $t$ | 1 | 2 | 3 | 4 |
|---|---|---|---|---|
| $y_t$ | 100 | 200 | 300 | 400 |
| $F_t$ | 0 | 0 | 0 | 1000 |

The demand pattern is clear and forecasting should be easy. The forecasts are obviously very poor, but the mean error is zero. This shows that the mean error is not a reliable measure of forecast accuracy, but measures bias. If the mean error has a positive value, the forecast is consistently too low; if the mean error has a negative value, the forecast is consistently too high.

The two most common alternatives to the mean error are the mean absolute deviation (MAD) and the mean squared error (MSE):

$$\text{mean absolute deviation} = \frac{\sum |E_t|}{n} = \frac{\sum |y_t - F_t|}{n}$$

$$\text{mean squared error} = \frac{\sum (E_t)^2}{n} = \frac{\sum (y_t - F_t)^2}{n}$$

# WORKED EXAMPLE 9.1

Two forecasting methods have been used to give the following results for a time series. Which method is better?

| $t$ | 1 | 2 | 3 | 4 | 5 |
|---|---|---|---|---|---|
| $y_t$ | 20 | 22 | 26 | 19 | 14 |
| $F_t$ with method 1 | 17 | 23 | 24 | 22 | 17 |
| $F_t$ with method 2 | 15 | 20 | 22 | 24 | 19 |

## Solution

Method 1 gives forecasts that are always nearer to actual demand than method 2, so in this case the decision is easy. We can confirm this by calculating the errors.

*Method 1*

| $t$ | 1 | 2 | 3 | 4 | 5 |
|---|---|---|---|---|---|
| $y_t$ | 20 | 22 | 26 | 19 | 14 |
| $F_t$ with method 1 | 17 | 23 | 24 | 22 | 17 |
| $E_t$ | 3 | $-1$ | 2 | $-3$ | $-3$ |
| $|E_t|$ | 3 | 1 | 2 | 3 | 3 |
| $(E_t)^2$ | 9 | 1 | 4 | 9 | 9 |

- mean error = $(3 - 1 + 2 - 3 - 3)/5 = -0.4$ (so each forecast is slightly biased, being an average of 0.4 too high)
- mean absolute deviation = $(3 + 1 + 2 + 3 + 3)/5 = 2.4$ (so each forecast is, on average, 2.4 away from actual demand)
- mean squared error = $(9 + 1 + 4 + 9 + 9)/5 = 6.4$

*Method 2*

| $t$ | 1 | 2 | 3 | 4 | 5 |
|---|---|---|---|---|---|
| $y_t$ | 20 | 22 | 26 | 19 | 14 |
| $F_t$ with method 2 | 15 | 20 | 22 | 24 | 19 |
| $E_t$ | 5 | 2 | 4 | – 5 | – 5 |
| $\lvert E_t \rvert$ | 5 | 2 | 4 | 5 | 5 |
| $(E_t)^2$ | 25 | 4 | 16 | 25 | 25 |

- mean error = (5 + 2 + 4 – 5 – 5)/5 = 0.2 (so each forecast is slightly biased, being an average of 0.2 too low)
- mean absolute deviation = (5 + 2 + 4 + 5 + 5)/5 = 4.2 (so each forecast is, on average, 4.2 away from actual demand)
- mean squared error = (25 + 4 + 16 + 25 + 25)/5 = 19.0

The first forecasting method has lower mean absolute deviation and mean squared error, and is the better choice. The second method has slightly less bias, measured by the mean error.

---

| IN SUMMARY |
|---|

Projective forecasts only look at historical observations to forecast future values. There are several methods of projective forecasting. These are commonly used for time series, which are observations taken at regular intervals. Time series generally follow an underlying pattern with superimposed noise.

## 9.3.2 | Simple averages

Suppose you are going away on holiday and want to know the expected temperature at your destination. The easiest way of finding this is to look up records for past years and take an average. With a holiday due to start on 1st July you could find the average temperature on 1st July over, say, the past 20 years. This is an example of forecasting using simple averages:

$$\text{for simple averages forecast, } F_{t+1} = \frac{\Sigma y_t}{n}$$

where:

$n$ = number of periods of historical data

$t$ = time period

$y_t$ = observation at time $t$

$F_{t+1}$ = forecast for time $t + 1$

## WORKED EXAMPLE 9.2

John Butler runs two dental surgeries. He has recorded the number of patients visiting each over the past five weeks. Use simple averages to forecast the numbers of patients visiting in week 6. How accurate are the forecasts? What are the forecasts for week 24?

| Week | 1 | 2 | 3 | 4 | 5 |
|------|-----|-----|-----|-----|-----|
| Surgery 1 | 98 | 100 | 98 | 104 | 100 |
| Surgery 2 | 140 | 66 | 152 | 58 | 84 |

### Solution

Surgery 1: $F_6 = 1/n \times \sum y_t = 1/5 \times 500 = 100$

Surgery 2: $F_6 = 1/5 \times 500 = 100$

Although the forecasts are the same, there is clearly less noise for surgery 1 than for surgery 2. So we would be more confident in the first forecast.

Simple averages assume that the underlying pattern is constant. So the forecasts for week 24 are the same as the forecasts for week 6 – that is 100.

Using simple averages to forecast is easy and can work well for constant values. Unfortunately, it does not work so well if the pattern changes. Older data tend to swamp the latest figures and the forecast is very unresponsive to the change. Suppose, for example, demand for an item has been constant at 100 units a week for the past two years. Simple averages give a forecast demand for week 105 of 100 units. If the actual demand in week 105 suddenly rises to 200 units, simple averages give a forecast for week 106 of:

$$F_{106} = \frac{104 \times 100 + 200}{105} = 100.95$$

A rise in demand of 100 gives an increase of 0.95 in the forecast. If demand continues at 200 units a week following forecasts are:

$$F_{107} = 101.89 \qquad F_{108} = 102.80 \qquad F_{109} = 103.70, \text{ and so on}$$

The forecasts are rising but the response is very slow.

Very few time series are stable over long periods, and the restriction that simple averages only work for constant series means that they are not used very much in practice. The problem is that old data, which may be out of date, tend to swamp newer, more relevant data. One way round this is to ignore old data and only use a number of the most recent observations. This is the principle of **moving averages**, which is described in the following section.

> ## IN SUMMARY
>
> Using simple averages can give reasonable results for constant time series. For any other patterns some other method should be used.

## 9.3.3 | Moving averages

The patterns in observations often vary over time, and only a certain quantity of historical data are relevant to future forecasts. This suggests that all observations older than some specified time can be ignored. Then we can design a forecasting method which uses the average demand over, say, the past six weeks and ignores any data older than this. This is the basis of moving averages. Instead of taking the average of all historical data, we only use the latest $n$ periods. As new data become available we ignore the oldest data. Then $n$-period moving average forecasts are found from:

$$
\begin{aligned}
F_{t+1} &= \text{average of } n \text{ most recent pieces of data} \\
&= \frac{\text{latest demand + next latest} + \dots \text{ } n\text{th latest}}{n} \\
&= \frac{y_t + y_{t-1} + \dots y_{t-n+1}}{n}
\end{aligned}
$$

## WORKED EXAMPLE 9.3

The number of employee grievances dealt with by Epsilan Court & Co. has been recorded each month as follows:

| Month, $t$ | 1 | 2 | 3 | 4 | 5 | 6 |
|---|---|---|---|---|---|---|
| Grievances, $y_t$ | 135 | 130 | 125 | 135 | 115 | 80 |

Continuously changing conditions within the company mean that any data over three months old are no longer valid. Use a moving average to forecast the number of grievances in the future.

### Solution

Only data more recent than three months are valid, so we can use a three-month moving average for the forecast. If we consider the situation at the end of period 3, the forecast for period 4 is:

$$F_4 = \frac{y_1 + y_2 + y_3}{3} = \frac{135 + 130 + 125}{3} = 130$$

At the end of period 4, when actual numbers are known to be 135, this forecast can be updated to give:

$$F_5 = \frac{y_2 + y_3 + y_4}{3} = \frac{130 + 125 + 135}{3} = 130$$

Similarly:

$$F_6 = \frac{y_3 + y_4 + y_5}{3} = \frac{125 + 135 + 115}{3} = 125$$

$$F_7 = \frac{y_4 + y_5 + y_6}{3} = \frac{135 + 115 + 80}{3} = 110$$

In this example, the forecast is clearly responding to changes, with a high number of grievances moving the forecast upwards and vice versa. This ability of a forecast to respond to changing demand is important, and most forecasting methods allow the speed of response, or sensitivity, to be adjusted. We can adjust the sensitivity of a moving average by altering the period, which means changing the value of $n$. A large value of $n$ takes the average of a large number of observations and the forecast is unresponsive: the forecast will smooth out random variations, but may not follow genuine changes in patterns. On the other hand, a small value for $n$ gives a responsive forecast that will follow genuine changes, but may be too sensitive to random fluctuations. You should use a compromise value of $n$ that gives reasonable results and typically this is around six periods.

# WORKED EXAMPLE 9.4

The following table shows monthly demand for a product over the past year. Use moving averages with $n = 3$, $n = 6$ and $n = 9$ to get one-period-ahead forecasts.

| Month | 1 | 2 | 3 | 4 | 5 | 6 | 7 | 8 | 9 | 10 | 11 | 12 |
|--------|----|----|----|----|----|----|----|----|----|----|----|----|
| Demand | 16 | 14 | 12 | 15 | 18 | 21 | 23 | 24 | 25 | 26 | 37 | 38 |

## Solution

The earliest forecast we can make using a three-period moving average (i.e. $n = 3$) is:

$$F_4 = \frac{y_1 + y_2 + y_3}{3}$$

Similarly, the earliest forecasts for a six- and nine-period moving average are $F_7$ and $F_{10}$ respectively. Then the forecasts are as shown in Figure 9.5. Plotting a graph of these forecasts shows a rising trend, which the three-month moving average is following quite quickly, while the nine-month moving average is less responsive (Figure 9.6).

| | A | B | C | D | E |
|---|---|---|---|---|---|
| 1 | **Moving averages** | | | | |
| 2 | | | | | |
| 3 | | | **Forecasts** | | |
| 4 | **Month** | **Demand** | **n=3** | **n=6** | **n=9** |
| 5 | 1 | 16 | | | |
| 6 | 2 | 14 | | | |
| 7 | 3 | 12 | | | |
| 8 | 4 | 15 | 14.00 | | |
| 9 | 5 | 18 | 13.67 | | |
| 10 | 6 | 21 | 15.00 | | |
| 11 | 7 | 23 | 18.00 | 16.00 | |
| 12 | 8 | 24 | 20.67 | 17.17 | |
| 13 | 9 | 25 | 22.67 | 18.83 | |
| 14 | 10 | 26 | 24.00 | 21.00 | 18.67 |
| 15 | 11 | 37 | 25.00 | 22.83 | 19.78 |
| 16 | 12 | 38 | 29.33 | 26.00 | 22.33 |
| 17 | 13 | | 33.67 | 28.83 | 25.22 |

**Figure 9.5**   Calculating moving averages in a spreadsheet.

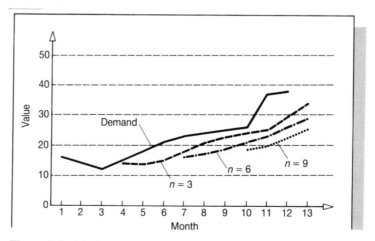

**Figure 9.6**   Moving averages for Worked Example 9.4.

Moving averages are particularly useful for data that have strong seasonal variations. If $n$ is chosen to equal the number of periods in a season, a moving average will completely deseasonalize the data, as you can see in the following example.

## WORKED EXAMPLE 9.5

Use a moving average with two, four and six periods to calculate the one-month-ahead forecasts for the following data:

| Month | 1 | 2 | 3 | 4 | 5 | 6 | 7 | 8 | 9 | 10 | 11 | 12 |
|---|---|---|---|---|---|---|---|---|---|---|---|---|
| Demand | 100 | 50 | 20 | 150 | 110 | 55 | 25 | 140 | 95 | 45 | 30 | 145 |

### Solution

These data have a clear seasonal pattern, with a peak every fourth month. Calculating the moving averages gives the results shown in Figure 9.7, and you can clearly see the patterns in the graph in Figure 9.8. The moving averages with both $n$ = 2 and $n$ = 6 have responded to the peaks and troughs of demand, but neither has got the timing right: both forecasts lag behind demand. As expected, the two-period moving average is much more responsive than the six-period one. The most interesting result is the four-period moving average which has completely deseasonalized the data.

| | A | B | C | D | E |
|---|---|---|---|---|---|
| 1 | **Moving averages** | | | | |
| 2 | | | | | |
| 3 | | | **Forecasts** | | |
| 4 | **Month** | **Demand** | **n=2** | **n=4** | **n=6** |
| 5 | 1 | 100 | | | |
| 6 | 2 | 50 | | | |
| 7 | 3 | 20 | 75 | | |
| 8 | 4 | 150 | 35 | | |
| 9 | 5 | 110 | 85 | 80.00 | |
| 10 | 6 | 55 | 130 | 82.50 | |
| 11 | 7 | 25 | 82.5 | 83.75 | 80.83 |
| 12 | 8 | 140 | 40 | 85.00 | 68.33 |
| 13 | 9 | 95 | 82.5 | 82.50 | 83.33 |
| 14 | 10 | 45 | 117.5 | 78.75 | 95.83 |
| 15 | 11 | 30 | 70 | 76.25 | 78.33 |
| 16 | 12 | 145 | 37.5 | 77.50 | 65.00 |
| 17 | 13 | | 87.5 | 78.75 | 80.00 |

**Figure 9.7**  Removing seasonal variations with moving averages.

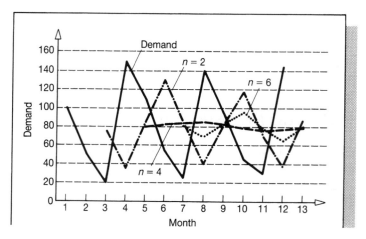

**Figure 9.8** Moving averages for Worked Example 9.5.

Although moving averages overcome some of the problems with simple averages, the method still has a number of defects, including:

- all observations are given the same weight

- the method only works well with constant time series (as we have seen, it either removes seasonal factors or gets the timing wrong)

- a large amount of historical data must be stored to update forecasts

- the choice of $n$ is often arbitrary.

We can overcome the first of these defects by giving different weights to observations. A three-period moving average, for example, gives equal weight to the last three observations, so each is given a weight of 0.33. We could change these weights to put more emphasis on later results, perhaps using:

$$F_4 = 0.2 \times y_1 + 0.3 \times y_2 + 0.5 \times y_3$$

In practice, a more convenient way of changing the weights is to use exponential smoothing, which is described in the next section.

## IN SUMMARY

Moving averages give forecasts based on the latest $n$ observations and ignore all older values. The sensitivity can be changed by altering the value of $n$. Time series can be deseasonalized by setting $n$ to the number of periods in the season.

## 9.3.4 | Exponential smoothing

Exponential smoothing is the most widely used forecasting method. It is based on the idea that as data get older they become less important and should be given less weight. In particular, exponential smoothing gives a declining weight to observations, as shown in Figure 9.9. This declining weight is achieved using only the latest observation and the previous forecast. In particular, a new forecast is calculated by taking a proportion, $\alpha$, of the latest observation and adding a proportion, $1 - \alpha$, of the previous forecast:

> new forecast = $\alpha \times$ latest observation + $(1 - \alpha) \times$ last forecast
>
> or
>
> $$F_{t+1} = \alpha y_t + (1 - \alpha)F_t$$

In this equation, $\alpha$ is the **smoothing constant**, which usually takes a value between 0.1 and 0.2.

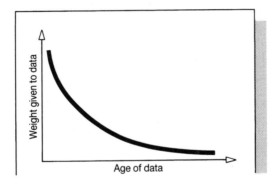

**Figure 9.9**  Weight given to data with exponential smoothing.

We can show how exponential smoothing adapts to changes in observations with a simple example. Suppose a forecast is optimistic and suggests a value of 200 for an observation that actually turns out to be 180. Taking a value of $\alpha = 0.2$, the forecast for the next period is:

$$F_{t+1} = \alpha y_t + (1 - \alpha)F_t$$
$$= 0.2 \times 180 + (1 - 0.2) \times 200$$
$$= 196$$

The optimistic forecast is noted and the value for the next period is adjusted downwards. You can see the reason for this adjustment if we rearrange the exponential smoothing formula:

$$F_{t+1} = \alpha y_t + (1 - \alpha)F_t$$
$$= F_t + \alpha(y_t - F_t)$$

but the error is:

$$E_t = y_t - F_t$$

so

$$F_{t+1} = F_t + \alpha E_t$$

The error in each forecast is noted and a proportion is added to adjust the next forecast. The larger the error in the last forecast, the greater is the adjustment for the next forecast.

## WORKED EXAMPLE 9.6

Use exponential smoothing with $\alpha = 0.2$ and an initial value of $F_1 = 170$ to get one-period-ahead forecasts for the following time series:

| Month | 1 | 2 | 3 | 4 | 5 | 6 | 7 | 8 |
|---|---|---|---|---|---|---|---|---|
| Demand | 178 | 180 | 156 | 150 | 162 | 158 | 154 | 132 |

### Solution

We know that $F_1 = 170$ and $\alpha = 0.2$. Substitution then gives:

$$F_2 = \alpha y_1 + (1 - \alpha)F_1 = 0.2 \times 178 + 0.8 \times 170 = 171.6$$

$$F_3 = \alpha y_2 + (1 - \alpha)F_2 = 0.2 \times 180 + 0.8 \times 171.6 = 173.3$$

$$F_4 = \alpha y_3 + (1 - \alpha)F_3 = 0.2 \times 156 + 0.8 \times 173.3 = 169.8$$

and so on, as shown in the spreadsheet in Figure 9.10.

| | A | B | C |
|---|---|---|---|
| 1 | Exponential smoothing | | |
| 2 | | | |
| 3 | Month | Demand | Forecast |
| 4 | 1 | 178 | 170.00 |
| 5 | 2 | 180 | 171.60 |
| 6 | 3 | 156 | 173.28 |
| 7 | 4 | 150 | 169.82 |
| 8 | 5 | 162 | 165.86 |
| 9 | 6 | 158 | 165.09 |
| 10 | 7 | 154 | 163.67 |
| 11 | 8 | 132 | 161.74 |
| 12 | 9 | | 155.79 |

**Figure 9.10**   Calculations for Worked Example 9.6.

The value given to the smoothing constant $\alpha$ is important in setting the sensitivity of the forecasts. $\alpha$ sets the balance between the last forecast and the latest observation. To give responsive forecasts, we use a high value of $\alpha$ (say 0.3 to 0.35): to give less responsive forecasts we use a lower value (say 0.05 to 0.1). Again, we need a compromise between having a responsive forecast (which might follow random fluctuations) and an unresponsive one (which might not follow real patterns).

## WORKED EXAMPLE 9.7

The following time series has a clear step upwards in demand in month 3. Use an initial forecast of 500 to compare exponential smoothing forecasts with different values of $\alpha$.

| Month | 1 | 2 | 3 | 4 | 5 | 6 | 7 | 8 | 9 | 10 | 11 |
|-------|-----|-----|------|------|------|------|------|------|------|------|------|
| Demand | 480 | 500 | 1500 | 1450 | 1550 | 1500 | 1480 | 1520 | 1500 | 1490 | 1500 |

### Solution

Taking values of $\alpha = 0.1$, 0.2, 0.3 and 0.4 gives the results shown in Figure 9.11. All these forecasts would eventually follow the sharp step and raise forecasts to around 1500. Higher values of $\alpha$ make this adjustment more quickly and give a more responsive forecast, as shown in Figure 9.12.

|  | A | B | C | D | E | F |
|----|----|----|----|----|----|----|
| 1 | **Exponential smoothing** | | | | | |
| 2 | | | | | | |
| 3 | | | Forecast | | | |
| 4 | **Month** | **Demand** | $\alpha = 0.1$ | $\alpha = 0.2$ | $\alpha = 0.3$ | $\alpha = 0.4$ |
| 5 | 1 | 480 | 500.00 | 500.00 | 500.00 | 500.00 |
| 6 | 2 | 500 | 498.00 | 496.00 | 494.00 | 492.00 |
| 7 | 3 | 1500 | 498.20 | 496.80 | 495.80 | 495.20 |
| 8 | 4 | 1450 | 598.38 | 697.44 | 797.06 | 897.12 |
| 9 | 5 | 1550 | 683.54 | 847.95 | 992.94 | 1118.27 |
| 10 | 6 | 1500 | 770.19 | 988.36 | 1160.06 | 1290.96 |
| 11 | 7 | 1480 | 843.17 | 1090.69 | 1262.04 | 1374.58 |
| 12 | 8 | 1520 | 906.85 | 1168.55 | 1327.43 | 1416.75 |
| 13 | 9 | 1500 | 968.17 | 1238.84 | 1385.20 | 1458.05 |
| 14 | 10 | 1490 | 1021.35 | 1291.07 | 1419.64 | 1474.83 |
| 15 | 11 | 1500 | 1068.22 | 1330.86 | 1440.75 | 1480.90 |
| 16 | 12 | | 1111.39 | 1364.69 | 1458.52 | 1488.54 |

**Figure 9.11** Varying forecast sensitivity with different values of $\alpha$.

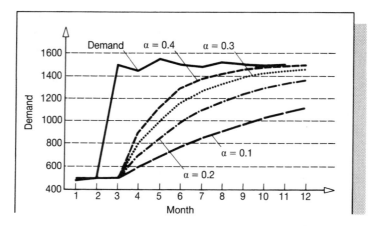

**Figure 9.12** Exponential smoothing with different smoothing constants.

Although higher values of $\alpha$ give more responsive forecasts, they do not necessarily give more accurate ones. Observations always contain noise, and very sensitive forecasts tend to follow these random fluctuations. One way of choosing a suitable value for $\alpha$ is to test several values over a trial period, and use the one that gives the smallest errors.

> **IN SUMMARY**

Exponential smoothing gives forecasts by adding portions of the last forecast and the latest observation. This reduces the weight given to data as their age increases. The smoothing constant sets the sensitivity of the forecast.

# Self-assessment questions

**9.8** 'All time series follow a simple pattern.' Do you think this is true?

**9.9** Why do almost all forecasts contain errors?

**9.10** How would you compare the results from two forecasting methods?

**9.11** Why are simple averages not widely used for forecasting?

**9.12** How can you make a moving average forecast more responsive?

**9.13** What is the drawback with a responsive forecast?

**9.14** How can you deseasonalize data?

**9.15** Why do we call the forecasting method 'exponential smoothing'?

**9.16** How can you make exponential smoothing more responsive?

# 9.4 | **Forecasting with seasonality and trend**

## 9.4.1 | Overall approach

The methods described so far give good results for constant time series, but they need adjusting to deal with other patterns. There are several ways of doing this, but the easiest is to split observations into separate components, and then forecast each component separately. Then we get the final forecast by recombining the separate components. For this we shall assume that an observation is made up of four components:

- **trend** $(T)$ is the long-term direction of a time series. It is typically a steady upward or downward movement

- **seasonal factor** $(S)$ is the regular variation around the trend. Typically this shows a variation in demand over a year

- **cyclical factor** $(C)$ is a longer-term variation that occurs over several seasons. Typically these are business cycles over many years

- **residual** $(R)$ is the random noise whose effects we cannot explain.

Depending on how we define these four components, we can use two different approaches to forecasting. First, we can define them in an **additive model**, so that the observation $y$ is:

$$y = T + S + C + R$$

In this model, all the variables are numbers, so the seasonal factor $S$ is an amount added to the trend to allow for the season. Observations in summer may, for example, be 100 units higher than the trend (so $S$ takes a value of 100), while observations in winter are 100 units lower (so $S$ takes a value of $-100$).

Sometimes, particularly when the trend is changing quickly, it is better to use indices for seasonal and cyclical variations. Summer sales might be say, 50% higher than the trend, while winter sales are 50% lower than the trend. These indices are used in a **multiplicative model** so that:

$$y = T \times S \times C \times R$$

Here $T$ is a number, while $S$, $C$ and $R$ are ratios.

In general, of course, $R$ is unknown, so we cannot include this in forecasts, which are found from:

additive model: $\quad F = T + S + C$

multiplicative model: $\quad F = T \times S \times C$

## WORKED EXAMPLE 9.8

(a) What is the forecast value for an additive model if the trend is 20, seasonal factor is 5 and cyclical factor is 2?

(b) What is the forecast value for a multiplicative model if the trend is 20, seasonal factor is 1.25 and cyclical factor is 1.08?

### Solution

(a) With the additive model, $T = 20$, $S = 5$ and $C = 2$, so the forecast is:

$$F = T + S + C = 20 + 5 + 2 = 27$$

(b) With the multiplicative model, $T = 20$, $S = 1.25$ and $C = 1.08$, so the forecast is:

$$F = T \times S \times C = 20 \times 1.25 \times 1.08 = 27$$

Because it is used more widely, and gives better results for observations with a trend, we shall concentrate on the multiplicative model. The additive model is very similar and the analysis only varies in detail.

In most circumstances there are not really enough data to include cycles in the analysis. Business cycles, for example, may have an effect on an organization's performance, but they are not regular enough to include in a forecasting model. In the following analyses we shall assume that there are no usable cyclical factors, so $C$ is fixed at 1.

Now we can start forecasting. The procedure uses historical data to:

1 deseasonalize the data and find the underlying trend, $T$
2 find the seasonal indices, $S$
3 use the calculated trend and seasonal indices to forecast $F = T \times S$

The details are described in the following sections.

### IN SUMMARY

There are many ways of forecasting more complex time series. The easiest is to consider separate components and combine them into a final forecast. We shall use a multiplicative model for this.

## 9.4.2 | Finding the trend

There are two ways of finding the trend $T$, both of which we have already met:

- linear regression with time as the independent variable
- moving averages with a period equal to the length of a season

Both of these give generally good results. If the trend is clearly linear, regression is probably better, as it gives more information and we have a definite equation for the trend. If the trend is not clearly linear, moving averages are better. The choice is often a matter of personal preference.

## WORKED EXAMPLE 9.9

Suppose you are asked to forecast future values for the following set of observations which has been recorded over the past 12 periods:

| Period | 1 | 2 | 3 | 4 | 5 | 6 | 7 | 8 | 9 | 10 | 11 | 12 |
|---|---|---|---|---|---|---|---|---|---|---|---|---|
| Observation | 291 | 320 | 142 | 198 | 389 | 412 | 271 | 305 | 492 | 518 | 363 | 388 |

(a) Use linear regression to find the deseasonalized trend.

(b) Use moving averages to find the deseasonalized trend.

### Solution

(a) With the values given:

$$n = 12 \qquad \Sigma x = 78 \qquad \Sigma y = 4089 \qquad \Sigma x^2 = 650 \qquad \Sigma (xy) = 29\ 160$$

Substituting these in the standard linear regression equations gives:

$$b = \frac{n\Sigma (xy) - \Sigma x\Sigma y}{n\Sigma x^2 - (\Sigma x)^2} = \frac{12 \times 29\ 160 - 78 \times 4089}{12 \times 650 - 78 \times 78}$$

$$= 18.05$$

$$a = \bar{y} - b \times \bar{x} = 4089/12 - 18.05 \times 78/12$$

$$= 223.41$$

The line of best fit gives the trend as:

$$observation = 223.41 + 18.05 \times period$$

The deseasonalized trend value for period 1 is $223.41 \times 18.05 \times 1 = 241.46$.

As always, we could have done these calculations on a spreadsheet to get the deseasonalized trend values shown in Figure 9.13, and plotted in Figure 9.14. One point about this regression line is that the coefficient of determination is low at 0.349. The reason is obviously that a lot of the variation is explained not by the trend, but by the seasonality. When we use linear regression to deseasonalize data, a low coefficient of determination does not necessarily mean that the results are going to be poor.

|   | A | B | C | D |
|---|---|---|---|---|
| 1 | **Seasonal trend** | | | |
| 2 | | | | |
| 3 | **Period** | **Observation** | | **Deseasonalized** |
| 4 | | | | **trend value** |
| 5 | 1 | 291 | | 241.46 |
| 6 | 2 | 320 | | 259.51 |
| 7 | 3 | 142 | | 277.57 |
| 8 | 4 | 198 | | 295.62 |
| 9 | 5 | 389 | | 313.67 |
| 10 | 6 | 412 | | 331.72 |
| 11 | 7 | 271 | | 349.78 |
| 12 | 8 | 305 | | 367.83 |
| 13 | 9 | 492 | | 385.88 |
| 14 | 10 | 518 | | 403.93 |
| 15 | 11 | 363 | | 421.99 |
| 16 | 12 | 388 | | 440.04 |
| 17 | | | | |
| 18 | **Summary output** | | | |
| 19 | | | | |
| 20 | *Regression statistics* | | | |
| 21 | Multiple r | 0.591 | | |
| 22 | $r^2$ | 0.349 | | |
| 23 | Adjusted $r^2$ | 0.284 | | |
| 24 | Observations | 12 | | |
| 25 | | | | |
| 26 | | *Coefficients* | | |
| 27 | Intercept | 223.409 | | |
| 28 | X variable 1 | 18.052 | | |

**Figure 9.13** Using linear regression to deseasonalize the observations.

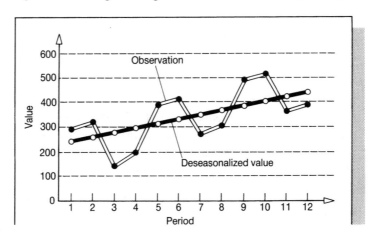

**Figure 9.14** Using linear regression to deseasonalize data for Worked Example 9.9.

(b) Figure 9.14 shows that the values have a clear season of four periods. Then we can deseasonalize the data by taking a four-period moving average, as shown in Figure 9.15. In this spreadsheet you can see an obvious problem with the data. When deseasonalizing data we are suggesting that average values occur at average times. If we take the first four periods, the average value of (291 + 320 + 142 + 198)/4 = 237.75 occurs at the average time of (1 + 2 + 3 + 4)/4 = 2.5. In other words, it occurs halfway through a period. This is the reason why the entry in the spreadsheet is shown at period 2.5. We meet this problem whenever a season has an even number of periods (but obviously not when the season has an odd number of periods).

| | A | B | C | D | E |
|---|---|---|---|---|---|
| 1 | **Seasonal trend** | | | | |
| 2 | | | | | |
| 3 | **Period** | **Observation** | | **Four-period** | **Deseasonalized** |
| 4 | | | | **moving average** | **values** |
| 5 | 1 | 291 | | | |
| 6 | 1.5 | | | | |
| 7 | 2 | 320 | | | |
| 8 | 2.5 | | | 237.75 | |
| 9 | 3 | 142 | | | 250.00 |
| 10 | 3.5 | | | 262.25 | |
| 11 | 4 | 198 | | | 273.75 |
| 12 | 4.5 | | | 285.25 | |
| 13 | 5 | 389 | | | 301.38 |
| 14 | 5.5 | | | 317.50 | |
| 15 | 6 | 412 | | | 330.88 |
| 16 | 6.5 | | | 344.25 | |
| 17 | 7 | 271 | | | 357.13 |
| 18 | 7.5 | | | 370.00 | |
| 19 | 8 | 305 | | | 383.25 |
| 20 | 8.5 | | | 396.50 | |
| 21 | 9 | 492 | | | 408.00 |
| 22 | 9.5 | | | 419.50 | |
| 23 | 10 | 518 | | | 429.88 |
| 24 | 10.5 | | | 440.25 | |
| 25 | 11 | 363 | | | |
| 26 | 11.5 | | | | |
| 27 | 12 | 388 | | | |

**Figure 9.15**  Using moving averages to find deseasonalized values.

Then the easiest way to find the deseasonalized value at each period is to take the average of the two values on either side of it. The deseasonalized value for period 3 is the average of the deseasonalized values at times 2.5 and 3.5. This is (237.75 + 262.25)/2 = 250. This calculation is repeated to give the values shown in Figure 9.15, and plotted in Figure 9.16.

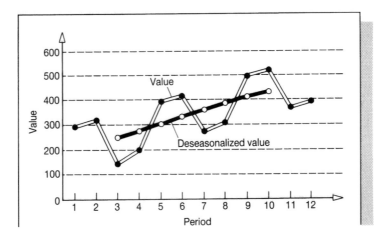

**Figure 9.16**   Using moving averages to deseasonalize data for Worked Example 9.9.

Another problem with moving averages is that we now only have deseasonalized data for eight periods, rather than the original 12 periods. Here there are just about enough data to find the patterns, but this gives another reason why it is generally better to use regression. You can see from this example that the two approaches give similar, but not identical, results.

---

*IN SUMMARY*

Both linear regression and moving averages can be used to find the deseasonalized trend of a set of data. These methods give similar results, but regression is usually better.

## 9.4.3 | Finding the seasonal indices

In multiplicative models, seasonal variations are measured by seasonal indices (which we have already met in Chapter 6). These are defined as the amounts by which deseasonalized values must be multiplied to get seasonal values:

$$\text{seasonal index} = \frac{\text{seasonal value}}{\text{deseasonalized value}}$$

Suppose a newspaper has average daily sales of 1000 copies in a particular area, but this rises to 2000 copies on Saturday and falls to 500 copies on Monday and Tuesday. The deseasonalized value is 1000; the seasonal index for Saturday is 2000/1000 = 2.0; the seasonal indices for Monday and Tuesday are 500/1000 = 0.5; and seasonal indices for other days are 1000/1000 = 1.0.

In the last section we deseasonalized data and found the trend. Now for every period we have the actual observation and the deseasonalized trend value. If we divide the actual observation by the trend value, we get a value for the seasonal index. This index is affected by noise in the data, so it is only an approximation, but if we take several complete seasons we can find average indices that are more reliable.

# WORKED EXAMPLE 9.10

In Worked Example 9.9, data were deseasonalized using linear regression. Find the seasonal indices.

## Solution

Taking a single period, say 4, we have an actual observation of 198. The deseasonalized value using linear regression is 295.62, so the seasonal index is 198/295.62 = 0.67. Repeating this calculation for other periods gives the results shown in Figure 9.17.

| | A | B | C | D |
|---|---|---|---|---|
| 1 | **Seasonal indices** | | | |
| 2 | | | | |
| 3 | | | **Linear regression** | |
| 4 | **Period** | **Observation** | **Deseasonalized** | **Seasonal** |
| 5 | | | **trend value** | **index** |
| 6 | 1 | 291 | 241.46 | 1.21 |
| 7 | 2 | 320 | 259.51 | 1.23 |
| 8 | 3 | 142 | 277.57 | 0.51 |
| 9 | 4 | 198 | 295.62 | 0.67 |
| 10 | 5 | 389 | 313.67 | 1.24 |
| 11 | 6 | 412 | 331.72 | 1.24 |
| 12 | 7 | 271 | 349.78 | 0.77 |
| 13 | 8 | 305 | 367.83 | 0.83 |
| 14 | 9 | 492 | 385.88 | 1.28 |
| 15 | 10 | 518 | 403.93 | 1.28 |
| 16 | 11 | 363 | 421.99 | 0.86 |
| 17 | 12 | 388 | 440.04 | 0.88 |

**Figure 9.17** Calculation of seasonal indices for Worked Example 9.10.

Now we have a seasonal index for each period, and we can take averages to find more accurate values. We know from the graphs in Figures 9.14 and 9.16 that there are four periods in a season, so we need to calculate four seasonal indices.

Taking periods 1, 5 and 9 as the first periods in consecutive seasons, we can find an average seasonal index for the first period in a season as $(1.21 + 1.24 + 1.28)/3 = 1.24$. Similarly, the average indices for other periods in a season are:

- first period in season $(1.21 + 1.24 + 1.28)/3 = 1.24$
- second period in season $(1.23 + 1.24 + 1.28)/3 = 1.24$
- third period in season $(0.51 + 0.77 + 0.86)/3 = 0.71$
- fourth period in season $(0.67 + 0.83 + 0.88)/3 = 0.79$

Now that we have found both the trend and seasonal index, we can start forecasting for the future. The procedure for forecasting is:

1 find the deseasonalized value in the future
2 multiply this by the appropriate seasonal index

## WORKED EXAMPLE 9.11

Forecast values for periods 13 to 17 for the time series in Worked Example 9.9.

### Solution

We found the trend by linear regression (in Worked Example 9.9) to be:

$$\text{value} = 223.41 + 18.05 \times \text{period}$$

Now we can substitute 13 to 17 for the period and find the deseasonalized trend for these times. Then we multiply these by the appropriate seasonal index (which we found in Worked Example 9.10) to get the forecasts:

*Period 13*

deseasonalized trend $= 223.41 + 18.05 \times 13 = 458.06$

seasonal index $= 1.24$ (first period in season)

forecast $= 458.06 \times 1.24 = 568$

*Period 14*

deseasonalized trend $= 223.41 + 18.05 \times 14 = 476.11$

seasonal index $= 1.24$ (second period in season)

forecast $= 476.11 \times 1.24 = 590$

*Period 15*

deseasonalized trend = 223.41 + 18.05 × 15 = 494.16

seasonal index = 0.71 (third period in season)

forecast = 494.16 × 0.71 = 351

*Period 16*

deseasonalized trend = 223.41 + 18.05 × 16 = 512.21

seasonal index = 0.79 (fourth period in season)

forecast = 512.21 × 0.79 = 405

*Period 17*

deseasonalized trend = 223.41 + 18.05 × 17 = 530.26

seasonal index = 1.24 (first period in season)

forecast = 530.26 × 1.24 = 658

## WORKED EXAMPLE 9.12

Use a multiplicative model to forecast values for the next four periods of the following time series:

| $t$ | 1 | 2 | 3 | 4 | 5 | 6 | 7 | 8 |
|---|---|---|---|---|---|---|---|---|
| $y$ | 986 | 1245 | 902 | 704 | 812 | 1048 | 706 | 514 |

### Solution

Looking at the data, you can see that there is a linear trend with a season of four periods. You could confirm this by drawing a graph, but the pattern is already clear enough. We can use linear regression to deseasonalize the data, and then calculate four seasonal indices. These calculations are shown on the spreadsheet in Figure 9.18, which finds:

- linear regression equation:    $y = 1156.75 - 64.92t$
- average seasonal indices:    0.94, 1.29, 0.97 and 0.80

We can use these to give a forecast for period 9 of:

$(1156.75 - 64.92 \times 9) \times 0.94 = 537.82$     (allowing for rounding errors)

Similarly the forecasts for periods 10, 11 and 12 are:

$(1156.75 - 64.92 \times 10) \times 1.29 = 654.35$

$(1156.75 - 64.92 \times 11) \times 0.97 = 430.02$

$(1156.75 - 64.92 \times 12) \times 0.80 = 300.53$

| | A | B | C | D | E |
|---|---|---|---|---|---|
| 1 | Forecasting | | | | |
| 2 | | | | | |
| 3 | Period | Observation | Regression | Seasonal | Period |
| 4 | | | value | index | in season |
| 5 | 1 | 986 | 1091.83 | 0.90 | 1 |
| 6 | 2 | 1245 | 1026.92 | 1.21 | 2 |
| 7 | 3 | 902 | 962.00 | 0.94 | 3 |
| 8 | 4 | 704 | 897.08 | 0.78 | 4 |
| 9 | 5 | 812 | 832.17 | 0.98 | 1 |
| 10 | 6 | 1048 | 767.25 | 1.37 | 2 |
| 11 | 7 | 706 | 702.33 | 1.01 | 3 |
| 12 | 8 | 514 | 637.42 | 0.81 | 4 |
| 13 | | | | | |
| 14 | Summary output | | | | |
| 15 | | | | | |
| 16 | Regression statistics | | | Seasonal indices | |
| 17 | Multiple r | 0.691 | | 1 | 0.94 |
| 18 | $r^2$ | 0.477 | | 2 | 1.29 |
| 19 | Adjusted $r^2$ | 0.390 | | 3 | 0.97 |
| 20 | Observations | 8 | | 4 | 0.8 |
| 21 | | | | | |
| 22 | | Coefficients | | | |
| 23 | Intercept | 1156.75 | | | |
| 24 | X variable 1 | −64.92 | | | |
| 25 | | | | | |
| 26 | Forecasts | | | | |
| 27 | | | | | |
| 28 | Period | Value | | | |
| 29 | 9 | 537.82 | | | |
| 30 | 10 | 654.35 | | | |
| 31 | 11 | 430.02 | | | |
| 32 | 12 | 300.53 | | | |

Figure 9.18   Spreadsheet showing multiplicative forecasting.

# WORKED EXAMPLE 9.13

Use an additive model to forecast demand for the time series in Worked Example 9.12.

## Solution

The approach of additive models is exactly the same as multiplicative models, except that the seasonal variations are amounts to be added rather than an index to be multiplied. The spreadsheet in Figure 9.19 shows the analysis for this.

|   | A | B | C | D | E |
|---|---|---|---|---|---|
| 1 | **Forecasting** | | | | |
| 2 | | | | | |
| 3 | **Period** | **Observation** | **Regression** | **Seasonal** | **Period** |
| 4 | | | **value** | **adjustment** | **in season** |
| 5 | 1 | 986 | 1091.83 | –105.83 | 1 |
| 6 | 2 | 1245 | 1026.92 | 218.08 | 2 |
| 7 | 3 | 902 | 962.00 | –60.00 | 3 |
| 8 | 4 | 704 | 897.08 | –193.08 | 4 |
| 9 | 5 | 812 | 832.17 | –20.17 | 1 |
| 10 | 6 | 1048 | 767.25 | 280.75 | 2 |
| 11 | 7 | 706 | 702.33 | 3.67 | 3 |
| 12 | 8 | 514 | 637.42 | –123.42 | 4 |
| 13 | | | | | |
| 14 | **Summary output** | | | | |
| 15 | | | | | |
| 16 | *Regression statistics* | | | *Seasonal adjustment* | |
| 17 | Multiple r | 0.691 | | 1 | –63.00 |
| 18 | $r^2$ | 0.477 | | 2 | 249.42 |
| 19 | Adjusted $r^2$ | 0.390 | | 3 | –28.17 |
| 20 | Observations | 8 | | 4 | –158.25 |
| 21 | | | | | |
| 22 | | *Coefficients* | | | |
| 23 | Intercept | 1156.75 | | | |
| 24 | X variable 1 | –64.92 | | | |
| 25 | | | | | |
| 26 | | | | | |
| 27 | **Forecasts** | | | | |
| 28 | | | | | |
| 29 | **Period** | **Value** | | | |
| 30 | 9 | 509.5 | | | |
| 31 | 10 | 757.0 | | | |
| 32 | 11 | 414.5 | | | |
| 33 | 12 | 219.5 | | | |

**Figure 9.19** Forecasting with an additive model.

The regression equation is $1156.75 - 64.92 \times t$ and the average seasonal adjustments are $-63.00, 249.42, -28.17$ and $-158.25$. The forecast for period 9 is:

$(1156.75 - 64.92 \times 9) - 63.00 = 509.5$     (allowing for rounding errors)

Similarly, the forecasts for periods 10, 11 and 12 are:

$(1156.75 - 64.92 \times 10) + 249.42 = 757.0$

$(1156.75 - 64.92 \times 11) - 28.17 = 414.5$

$(1156.75 - 64.92 \times 12) - 158.25 = 219.5$

As there is a clear trend in the data, the multiplicative model is likely to be more reliable than the additive one.

---

### IN SUMMARY

Seasonal indices are defined as:

$$\text{seasonal index} = \frac{\text{actual value}}{\text{deseasonalized value}}$$

These can be used to adjust the trend and forecast values for any period in the future.

---

## Self-assessment questions

**9.17** What is the difference between an additive and a multiplicative forecasting model?

**9.18** Why are cyclical data not usually included in forecasting models?

**9.19** Does the moving average of deseasonalized data always occur in the middle of a period?

**9.20** Would you prefer to use regression or moving averages to deseasonalize a set of data?

### CHAPTER REVIEW

This chapter has discussed various aspects of forecasting. It started by discussing the need to forecast and then described the different ways in which organizations can make forecasts. In particular it:

- outlined the importance of forecasting in all organizations
- described three basic approaches to forecasting as causal (which we illustrated by linear regression in Chapter 8), judgemental and projective
- discussed the use of judgemental or qualitative methods when there are no relevant quantitative data
- outlined the use of time series, which can be described by an underlying pattern with superimposed random noise
- forecast using simple and moving averages
- forecast using exponential smoothing
- produced forecasts for time series with seasonality and trend

# Problems

**9.1** Use linear regression to forecast values for periods 11 to 13 with the following time series:

| Period | 1 | 2 | 3 | 4 | 5 | 6 | 7 | 8 | 9 | 10 |
|---|---|---|---|---|---|---|---|---|---|---|
| Observation | 121 | 133 | 142 | 150 | 159 | 167 | 185 | 187 | 192 | 208 |

**9.2** Use simple averages to forecast values for the data in Problem 9.1. Which method gives the better results?

**9.3** Use a four-period moving average to forecast values for the data in Problem 9.1.

**9.4** Find the two-, three- and four-period moving average for the following time series, and, by calculating the errors, say which gives the best results:

| t | 1 | 2 | 3 | 4 | 5 | 6 | 7 | 8 |
|---|---|---|---|---|---|---|---|---|
| y | 280 | 240 | 360 | 340 | 300 | 220 | 200 | 360 |

**9.5** Use exponential smoothing with $\alpha = 0.1$ and 0.2 to forecast values for the data in Problem 9.4. Which smoothing constant gives better forecasts?

**9.6** Use exponential smoothing with smoothing constant equal to 0.1, 0.2, 0.3 and 0.4 to produce one-period-ahead forecasts for the following time series. Use an initial value of $F_1 = 208$ and say which value of $\alpha$ is best.

| t | 1 | 2 | 3 | 4 | 5 | 6 | 7 | 8 |
|---|---|---|---|---|---|---|---|---|
| y | 212 | 216 | 424 | 486 | 212 | 208 | 208 | 204 |

**9.7** Baliol.com recorded their opening share price for ten consecutive weeks. Find deseasonalized forecasts and identify the underlying trend:

| t | 1 | 2 | 3 | 4 | 5 | 6 | 7 | 8 | 9 | 10 |
|---|---|---|---|---|---|---|---|---|---|---|
| y | 75 | 30 | 52 | 88 | 32 | 53 | 90 | 30 | 56 | 96 |

**9.8** Forecast values for the next six periods in Problem 9.7.

**9.9** Use an appropriate multiplicative model to forecast values for the next three periods of the following time series:

| t | 1 | 2 | 3 | 4 | 5 | 6 |
|---|---|---|---|---|---|---|
| y | 100 | 160 | 95 | 140 | 115 | 170 |

**9.10** Use an appropriate multiplicative model to forecast values for the next eight periods of the following time series:

| t | 1 | 2 | 3 | 4 | 5 | 6 | 7 | 8 | 9 | 10 |
|---|---|---|---|---|---|---|---|---|---|---|
| y | 101 | 125 | 121 | 110 | 145 | 165 | 160 | 154 | 186 | 210 |

**9.11** Use additive models to forecast values for the time series in Problems 9.9 and 9.10.

# Computer exercises

**9.1** Figure 9.20 shows a printout from a spreadsheet used for forecasting. Make sure you understand what is happening in this printout. Use another program to check the results.

| | A | B | C | D | E |
|---|---|---|---|---|---|
| 1 | **Hatherall Holdings** | **Weekly performance** | | | |
| 2 | | | | | |
| 3 | **Week** | **Demand** | **Actual averages** | **Moving averages** | **Exponential smoothing** |
| 4 | | | | **Period 4** | **alpha=0.2** |
| 5 | 1 | 126 | | | |
| 6 | 2 | 85 | | | |
| 7 | 3 | 128 | 105.50 | | 126.00 |
| 8 | 4 | 159 | 113.00 | | 97.30 |
| 9 | 5 | 138 | 124.50 | 124.50 | 118.79 |
| 10 | 6 | 97 | 127.20 | 127.50 | 146.94 |
| 11 | 7 | 145 | 122.17 | 130.50 | 140.68 |
| 12 | 8 | 160 | 125.43 | 134.75 | 110.10 |
| 13 | | | 129.75 | 135.00 | 134.53 |
| 14 | | | | | |
| 15 | Mean | | 129.75 | | |
| 16 | Standard Error | | 9.60 | | |
| 17 | Median | | 144 | | |
| 18 | Standard Deviation | | 27.16 | | |
| 19 | Sample Variance | | 737.64 | | |
| 20 | Kurtosis | | −0.62 | | |
| 21 | Skewness | | −0.65 | | |
| 22 | Range | | 75 | | |
| 23 | Minimum | | 85 | | |
| 24 | Maximum | | 160 | | |
| 25 | Sum | | 1038 | | |
| 26 | Count | | 8 | | |

**Figure 9.20** Sample printout from a spreadsheet.

**9.2** Figure 9.21 shows a printout from a specialized forecasting program using exponential smoothing. Make sure you understand what is happening in this printout. Use another program to check the results.

**9.3** In Section 9.4 we showed how forecasting with seasonality and trend can be done on a spreadsheet. Design a spreadsheet to check the results, and give improved formats.

Forecasting with simple exponential smoothing

Data entered

Number of time periods    :    8
Data smoothing coefficient  :    0.1000
Initial data value       :  54

Value

P1    55
P2    53
P3    60
P4    61
P5    58
P6    56
P7    62
P8    59

Solution

| Period | Y1 (Yp) | Computed (Sp − 1) | Difference (Yp − Sp − 1) |
|--------|---------|-------------------|--------------------------|
| P0 | 54 | 0 | 0 |
| P1 | 55 | 54 | 1 |
| P2 | 53 | 54.1000 | −1.1000 |
| P3 | 60 | 53.9900 | 6.0100 |
| P4 | 61 | 54.5910 | 6.4090 |
| P5 | 58 | 55.2319 | 2.7681 |
| P6 | 56 | 55.5087 | 0.4931 |
| P7 | 62 | 55.5578 | 6.4422 |
| P8 | 59 | 56.2020 | 2.7980 |

Average Y1          :   57.5556
Mean square error      :   17.0799
Mean absolute deviation  :    3.3773
Forecast value        :   56.4818

a

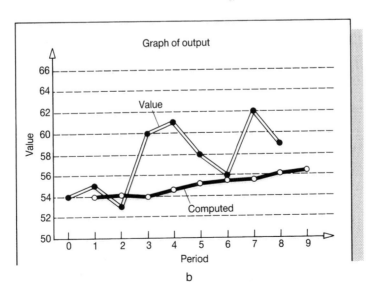

b

**Figure 9.21**   Printout from a forecasting program for exponential smoothing.

**9.4** Most spreadsheets have a number of standard functions for forecasting, typically including exponential smoothing, simple averages, moving averages, and regression. Look at the programs you have and see how these functions work.

**9.5** Design a spreadsheet which produces forecasts in a number of different ways. Test your program with the following set of data. These figures show the gross national product (in thousand million pounds) of the United Kingdom between 1949 and 1989 at factor cost:

| | | | | | | | | |
|------|------|------|------|------|------|------|------|------|
| 11.1 | 11.7 | 12.9 | 14.0 | 15.0 | 15.9 | 16.9 | 18.4 | 19.5 |
| 20.3 | 21.3 | 22.8 | 24.3 | 25.4 | 27.1 | 29.2 | 31.5 | 33.4 |
| 35.2 | 37.7 | 39.9 | 43.6 | 49.5 | 55.4 | 64.5 | 74.7 | 94.4 |
| 115.0 | 129.2 | 149.5 | 172.3 | 199.0 | 219.0 | 238.7 | 262.6 | 283.5 |
| 307.5 | 327.3 | 357.8 | 388.3 | 411.6 | | | | |

Use these figures to forecast the GNP for the following ten years. How accurate are your results? Write a report about your findings, including suitable graphs and charts.

**9.6** Find figures published by the government for the total consumption of electricity in Europe over a suitable historic period. Hence forecast the future demand for electricity. Write a report about your findings, emphasizing the methods used and problems met. Assume that your report is to be presented to a group of people for discussion, and that the quality of presentation is important.

# Case study

## Workload planning

Mary James worked in the purchasing department of Ambrosiana Merceti, a medium-sized construction company. One morning she walked into the office and said, 'The problem with this office is lack of planning. I have been reading a few articles about planning, and it seems to me that forecasting is the key to an efficient business. We have never done any forecasting, but simply rely on experience to guess our future workload. I think we should start using exponential smoothing to do some forecasting. Then we can foresee problems and schedule our time more efficiently'.

As Mary was in charge of the office, she soon persuaded the others to follow her advice. Unfortunately, they were going through a busy period and nobody in the office had time to develop any plans. A month later nothing had actually happened. Mary was not very pleased and said that their current high workload would be reduced if they did some forecasting and organized their time more effectively. In particular, they would not be overwhelmed by periodic surges in work.

To make some progress with the forecasting, Mary seconded a management trainee to work on some figures. The trainee examined their work, and divided it into seven categories, including searching for business, preparing estimates, submitting tenders and finding suppliers. For each of these categories he added the number of distinct pieces of work that the office had completed in each quarter of the past three years. He took six weeks to collect these figures, and summarized them as shown in Table 9.1.

Now the trainee wanted to forecast likely workload for the next two years. He knew a little about forecasting, and felt that exponential smoothing might not be the answer. He was not sure whether the results would be reliable enough. He also wanted to link the forecasts to planning, so he converted the different types of work into 'standard work units'. These could be used to determine the office's overall workload. After some discussion he devised a comparison with each piece of work allocated the following work units:

| | | |
|---|---|---|
| Work 1    2 units | Work 2    1.5 units | Work 3    1 unit |
| Work 4    0.7 units | Work 5    0.4 units | Work 6    3 units |
| Work 7    2.5 units | | |

**Table 9.1**

| Quarter | Work 1 | Work 2 | Work 3 | Work 4 | Work 5 | Work 6 | Work 7 |
|---|---|---|---|---|---|---|---|
| 1,1 | 129 | 74 | 1000 | 755 | 1210 | 204 | 24 |
| 2,1 | 138 | 68 | 1230 | 455 | 1520 | 110 | 53 |
| 3,1 | 110 | 99 | 890 | 810 | 1390 | 105 | 42 |
| 4,1 | 118 | 119 | 700 | 475 | 1170 | 185 | 21 |
| 1,2 | 121 | 75 | 790 | 785 | 1640 | 154 | 67 |
| 2,2 | 137 | 93 | 1040 | 460 | 1900 | 127 | 83 |
| 3,2 | 121 | 123 | 710 | 805 | 1860 | 187 | 80 |
| 4,2 | 131 | 182 | 490 | 475 | 1620 | 133 | 59 |
| 1,3 | 115 | 103 | 610 | 775 | 2010 | 166 | 105 |
| 2,3 | 126 | 147 | 840 | 500 | 2340 | 140 | 128 |
| 3,3 | 131 | 141 | 520 | 810 | 2210 | 179 | 126 |
| 4,3 | 131 | 112 | 290 | 450 | 1990 | 197 | 101 |

Your job is to prepare a report on the results found by the trainee. This should contain forecasts of future workload, a description of the forecasting methods used, discussion of the reliability of results, patterns of workload in the office, implications for work scheduling and further work to be done.

# 10 | Planning with linear programming

| | | | |
|---|---|---|---|
| Chapter outline | 300 | 10.4 Solving real problems | 315 |
| 10.1 What is linear programming? | 301 | Chapter review | 327 |
| | | Problems | 327 |
| 10.2 Getting LP problems in the right form | 302 | Computer exercises | 330 |
| | | Case study: Elemental Electronics | 332 |
| 10.3 Using graphs to solve linear programmes | 308 | | |

## CHAPTER OUTLINE

Managers often have to allocate scarce resources in the best possible way. There are always constraints on their options, so these problems are described as 'constrained optimization'. This chapter describes linear programming, which is a widely used method of solving problems of constrained optimization. Here 'programming' is used in its broad sense of 'planning', and has nothing to do with computer programming.

Linear programming can appear complicated, but this is mainly due to the cumbersome arithmetic. For this reason we shall demonstrate some principles with a simple example, and assume that real problems are always solved by a computer.

After reading this chapter and doing the exercises you should be able to:

- appreciate the ideas of constrained optimization
- formulate linear programmes and recognize the assumptions made
- use graphical methods to solve linear programmes
- calculate the effect of changes in the objective function
- calculate marginal values and the ranges over which these apply
- understand printouts from computer packages for linear programming

# 10.1 | What is linear programming?

Managers often have to achieve some objective when there are constraints on the resources available. An operations manager wants to make as many units as possible with limited production facilities; a marketing manager wants to maximize the impact of an advertising campaign without going over a specified budget; a finance manager wants to maximize the return on investment of a limited amount of funds; a construction manager wants to minimize the cost of a project without exceeding the time available. Such problems have:

- an aim of optimizing (i.e. maximizing or minimizing) some objective

- a set of constraints which limit the possible solutions

For this reason they are called problems of **constrained optimization.**

**Linear programming** (LP) is a widely used method of solving problems of constrained optimization. We should say straight away that linear programming was developed in the 1950s, when 'programming' was not used to mean 'computer programming'. The name comes from the more general meaning of 'planning'.

Linear programming needs three stages to solve a problem. These stages are:

- **formulation** – getting the problem in the right form

- **solution** – finding an optimal solution to the problem

- **sensitivity analysis** – seeing what happens when the problem is changed slightly

Linear programmes can be quite difficult to formulate, and in practice this is the most difficult stage. They need a lot of data (so there can be problems getting reliable information for objectives and constraints) and the formulation is quite unwieldy. But when a problem is in the right form, getting a solution is straightforward because this is **always** done by a computer. The approach we use here, then, is to demonstrate formulations with simple examples, and show how computers can get optimal solutions.

---

### IN SUMMARY

Many problems in business can be described as constrained optimization. Linear programming is a widely used method of tackling such problems.

---

## Self-assessment questions

**10.1** What is constrained optimization?

**10.2** What is linear programming?

# 10.2 | Getting LP problems in the right form

Linear programming finds optimal solutions to some problems of constrained optimization. Before it can be used, however, we have to describe the problem in a standard format. It is easiest to describe this formulation stage with an example and for this we shall use production planning.

Suppose a small factory makes two types of liquid fertilizer, Growbig and Thrive. These are made by similar processes, using the same equipment for blending raw materials, distilling the mix and finishing (bottling, testing, weighing, etc). Because the factory has a limited amount of equipment, there are constraints on the total time available for each process. In particular, no more than 40 hours of blending are available in a week, 40 hours of distilling and 25 hours of finishing. We shall assume that these are the only constraints and that there are none on, say, sales or availability of raw materials.

The fertilizers are made in batches, and each batch needs the following number of hours on each process:

| Process | Growbig | Thrive |
| --- | --- | --- |
| Blending | 1 | 2 |
| Distilling | 2 | 1 |
| Finishing | 1 | 1 |

If the factory makes a net profit of £30 on each batch of Growbig and £20 on each batch of Thrive, how many batches of each should it make a week?

This problem is clearly one of optimizing an objective (maximizing profit) subject to constraints (production capacity) as shown in Figure 10.1. Common sense would suggest that the profit on Growbig is higher than the profit on Thrive, so we should make as much of this as possible. The factory can make 20 batches of Growbig before all the available distilling time is used, with a profit of £600. As we shall see, this is not the best solution, and linear programming will suggest an alternative which gives the maximum profit as £650.

In this example we want to find the optimal number of batches of Growbig and Thrive, so these are the **decision variables**, which we can define as follows:

- Let $G$ be the number of batches of Growbig made in a week
- Let $T$ be the number of batches of Thrive made in a week

Now consider the time available for blending. Each batch of Growbig uses 1 hour of blending, so $G$ batches use $G$ hours. Similarly, each batch of Thrive uses 2 hours of blending, so $T$ batches use $2T$ hours. Adding these together gives the total amount of blending time used as $G + 2T$. The maximum amount of blending time available is 40 hours, so the time used must be less than, or at worst equal to, this. Now we have the first constraint:

$$G + 2T \leqslant 40 \qquad \text{blending constraint}$$

(Remember that $\leqslant$ means 'less than or equal to'.)

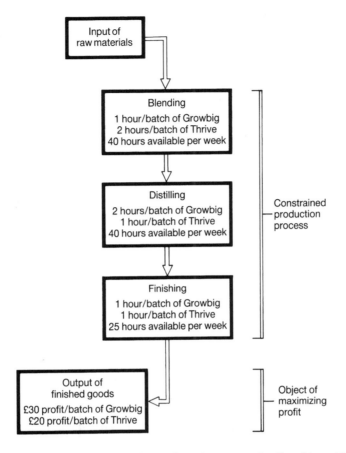

**Figure 10.1**  Constrained manufacturing process for Growbig and Thrive.

Turning to the distilling constraint, each batch of Growbig uses 2 hours of distilling, so $G$ batches use $2G$ hours. Each batch of Thrive uses 1 hour of distilling, so $T$ batches use $T$ hours. Adding these together gives the total amount of distilling used and this must be less than, or at worst equal to, the amount of distilling time available (40 hours). This gives the second constraint:

$$2G + T \leqslant 40 \qquad \text{distilling constraint}$$

Now the finishing constraint has the total time used for finishing ($G$ for batches of Growbig plus $T$ for batches of Thrive) less than or equal to the time available (25 hours) to give:

$$G + T \leqslant 25 \qquad \text{finishing constraint}$$

These are the three constraints for the process, but there is another implicit constraint. The company cannot make a negative number of batches, so both $G$ and $T$ must be positive. This **non-negativity constraint** is a standard feature of linear programmes:

$$G \geqslant 0 \qquad \text{and} \qquad T \geqslant 0 \qquad \text{non-negativity constraints}$$

Now we have all the constraints, and can turn to the objective. In this case the objective is to maximize profit. £30 is made on each batch of Growbig, and $G$ batches are made, so the profit is $30G$; £20 is made on each batch of Thrive, and $T$ batches are made, so the profit is $20T$. Adding these gives the total profit, which is to be maximized. This is called the **objective function**:

$$\text{Maximize} \qquad 30G + 20T \qquad \text{objective function}$$

We have now completed the linear programming formulation for this problem, with descriptions of:

- decision variables
- an objective function
- a set of constraints
- a non-negativity constraint

In this example we have:

Maximize:      $30G + 20T$      objective function

subject to:

$$G + 2T \leqslant 40$$
$$2G + T \leqslant 40 \qquad \} \quad \text{constraints}$$
$$G + T \leqslant 25$$

with

$$G \geqslant 0 \text{ and } T \geqslant 0 \qquad \text{non-negativity constraints}$$

This formulation has made a number of assumptions that are implicit in all LP. Most importantly, the objective function and constraints must all be linear functions of the variables. This means that the use of resources is proportional to the quantity being produced: if production is doubled the use of resources is doubled. This is usually a reasonable assumption, but it is not always valid. Increased production may, for example, use longer production runs which reduce set-up times and running-in problems. On the other hand, higher production can mean faster throughput with more units having faults and being scrapped.

A second assumption is that adding the resources used for each product gives the total amount of resources used. Again, this assumption may not always be valid. A craft manufacturer, for example, will use the most skilled craftsmen for more complex jobs. If there are no complex jobs in one period the skilled craftsmen will work on less complex jobs, which will then be done better or faster than usual.

## WORKED EXAMPLE 10.1

A political campaign wants to hire photocopying machines to make leaflets for a local election. There are two suitable machines:

- ACTO costs $120 a week to rent, occupies 2.5 square metres of floor space and can make 15 000 copies a day
- ZENMAT costs $150 a week to rent, occupies 1.8 square metres of floor space and can make 18 500 copies a day

The campaign has allowed up to $1200 a week for copying machines, which will be put in a room of 19.2 square metres. What are the problem variables, objective function and constraints for this problem?

### Solution

The problem variables are the things we can vary, which are the number of ACTO and ZENMAT machines rented. Let $A$ be the number of ACTO machines rented, and let $Z$ be the number of ZENMAT machines rented.

The objective is to make as many copies as possible.

Maximize:

$$15\,000A + 18\,500Z \qquad \text{objective function}$$

There are constraints on floor space and costs.

Subject to:

$$120A + 150Z \leqslant 1200 \qquad \text{cost constraint}$$

$$2.5A + 1.8Z \leqslant 19.2 \qquad \text{space constraint}$$

with

$$A \geqslant 0 \text{ and } Z \geqslant 0 \qquad \text{non-negativity constraint}$$

## WORKED EXAMPLE 10.2

Lorentzian Investment Trust has £1 million to invest. After consulting its financial advisers it decides that there are six possible investments with the following characteristics:

| Investment | % risk | % dividend | % growth | Rating |
|:---:|:---:|:---:|:---:|:---:|
| 1 | 18 | 4 | 22 | 4 |
| 2 | 6 | 5 | 7 | 10 |
| 3 | 10 | 9 | 12 | 2 |
| 4 | 4 | 7 | 8 | 10 |
| 5 | 12 | 6 | 15 | 4 |
| 6 | 8 | 8 | 8 | 6 |

The trust wants to invest the £1 million with minimum risk, but with a dividend of at least £70,000 a year, average growth of at least 12% and average rating of at least 7. Formulate this problem as a linear programme.

## Solution

The decision variables are the amount of money put into each investment:

Let $X_1$ be the amount of money put into investment 1

Let $X_2$ be the amount of money put into investment 2

etc, so $X_i$ is the amount of money put into investment $i$.

The objective is to minimize risk.

Minimize:

$$0.18X_1 + 0.06X_2 + 0.10X_3 + 0.04X_4 + 0.12X_5 + 0.08X_6$$

There are constraints on the amount of:

- money (the total invested must equal £1 million):

$$X_1 + X_2 + X_3 + X_4 + X_5 + X_6 = 1\,000\,000$$

- dividend (which must be at least 7% of £1 million):

$$0.04X_1 + 0.05X_2 + 0.09X_3 + 0.07X_4 + 0.06X_5 + 0.08X_6 \geq 70\,000$$

- average growth (which must be at least 12% of £1 million):

$$0.22X_1 + 0.07X_2 + 0.12X_3 + 0.08X_4 + 0.15X_5 + 0.08X_6 \geq 120\,000$$

- rating (the average, weighted by the amount invested, must be at least 7):

$$4X_1 + 10X_2 + 2X_3 + 10X_4 + 4X_5 + 6X_6 \geq 7\,000\,000$$

The non-negativity constraints $X_1$, $X_2$, $X_3$, $X_4$, $X_5$ and $X_6 \geq 0$ complete the formulation.

# WORKED EXAMPLE 10.3

An oil company makes two blends of fuel by mixing three oils. The costs and daily availability of the oils are:

| Oil | Cost (£/litre) | Amount available (litres) |
|-----|----------------|---------------------------|
| A | 0.25 | 10 000 |
| B | 0.28 | 15 000 |
| C | 0.35 | 20 000 |

The blends of fuel contain:

| | |
|---|---|
| *Blend 1* | At most 25% of A |
| | At least 30% of B |
| | At most 40% of C |
| *Blend 2* | At least 20% of A |
| | At most 50% of B |
| | At least 30% of C |

Each litre of blend 1 sells for £0.60 and each litre of blend 2 sells for £0.70. Long-term contracts need at least 10 000 litres of each blend. Formulate this blending problem as a linear programme.

## Solution

The decision variables are the amount of each type of crude oil which is put into each blend:

Let $A_1$ be the amount of oil A put into blend 1

Let $A_2$ be the amount of oil A put into blend 2

Let $B_1$ be the amount of oil B put into blend 1

and so on.

The total amounts of blend 1 and blend 2 made are:

blend 1: $A_1 + B_1 + C_1$

blend 2: $A_2 + B_2 + C_2$

Similarly, the quantities of each oil used are:

oil A: $A_1 + A_2$

oil B: $B_1 + B_2$

oil C: $C_1 + C_2$

The objective is to maximize profit. The income from selling blends is:

$$0.6 \times (A_1 + B_1 + C_1) + 0.7 \times (A_2 + B_2 + C_2)$$

while the cost of buying oil is:

$$0.25 \times (A_1 + A_2) + 0.28 \times (B_1 + B_2) + 0.35 \times (C_1 + C_2)$$

The profit is the difference between the income and the cost, which can be rearranged as the objective function:

Maximize:

$$0.35A_1 + 0.45A_2 + 0.32B_1 + 0.42B_2 + 0.25C_1 + 0.35C_2$$

There are constraints on the availability of oils:

$$A_1 + A_2 \leqslant 10\ 000$$

$$B_1 + B_2 \leqslant 15\ 000$$

$$C_1 + C_2 \leqslant 20\ 000$$

There are also six blending constraints. The first of these says that blend 1 must be at most 25% of oil A. In other words:

$$A_1 \leq 0.25 \times (A_1 + B_1 + C_1) \qquad \text{or} \qquad 0.75A_1 - 0.25B_1 - 0.25C_1 \leq 0$$

Similarly for the other blends:

$$B_1 \geq 0.3 \times (A_1 + B_1 + C_1) \qquad \text{or} \qquad 0.3A_1 - 0.7B_1 + 0.3C_1 \leq 0$$

$$C_1 \leq 0.4 \times (A_1 + B_1 + C_1) \qquad \text{or} \qquad -0.4A_1 - 0.4B_1 + 0.6C_1 \leq 0$$

$$A_2 \geq 0.2 \times (A_2 + B_2 + C_2) \qquad \text{or} \qquad -0.8A_2 + 0.2B_2 + 0.2C_2 \leq 0$$

$$B_2 \leq 0.5 \times (A_2 + B_2 + C_2) \qquad \text{or} \qquad -0.5A_2 + 0.5B_2 - 0.5C_2 \leq 0$$

$$C_2 \geq 0.3 \times (A_2 + B_2 + C_2) \qquad \text{or} \qquad 0.3A_2 + 0.3B_2 - 0.7C_2 \leq 0$$

The long-term contracts adds the conditions that:

$$A_1 + B_1 + C_1 \geq 10\,000$$

$$A_2 + B_2 + C_2 \geq 10\,000$$

The non-negativity conditions that all variables, $A_1$, $A_2$, $B_1$, etc are greater than or equal to 0 completes the formulation.

---

## IN SUMMARY

Before linear programming can be used to find an optimal solution, a problem must be put into a standard form. The resulting formulation has decision variables, an objective function and constraints.

---

## Self-assessment questions

**10.3** What are the main assumptions behind linear programming?

**10.4** What happens when you formulate a linear programme?

**10.5** What are the components that make up an LP formulation?

# 10.3 | Using graphs to solve linear programmes

For most real problems the formulation stage is the most difficult. Actually finding the solution to a problem is relatively straightforward because real linear programmes are always solved by computer. We shall not go into the details of how these programs work, but will illustrate the general principles. For this we can use the previous Growbig and Thrive example.

Returning to the example, the blending constraint is $G + 2T \leq 40$. But we know that the equation $G + 2T = 40$ can be drawn as a straight line on a graph of $G$ against $T$ as shown in Figure 10.2. If you are not sure about this have another look at Chapter 2. Remember that the easiest way to draw lines of this type is to take two convenient points and draw a straight line through them. Here setting $G = 0$ gives $2T = 40$ or $T = 20$: then setting $T = 0$ gives $G = 40$. So we can draw the line through the points $G = 0$, $T = 20$ and $G = 40$, $T = 0$.

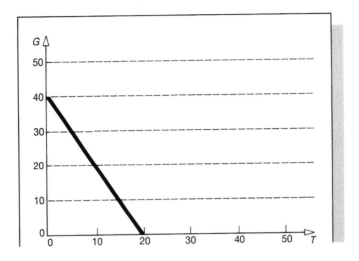

**Figure 10.2**   Graph of blending constraint.

It is important to realize that any point above this line will break the blending constraint, while for any point on or below the line the blending constraint will hold. You can check this by taking any points at random. The point $G = 10$, $T = 10$, for example, is below the line and substituting into the constraint gives:

$$1 \times 10 + 2 \times 10 \leq 40$$

which is true and the constraint is not broken. On the other hand, the point $G = 20$, $T = 20$ is above the line and substitution gives:

$$1 \times 20 + 2 \times 20 \leq 40$$

which is not true and the constraint is broken. Points that are actually on the line satisfy the equality. For example, the point $G = 20$, $T = 10$ is on the line, and substitution gives:

$$1 \times 20 + 2 \times 10 \leq 40$$

which is true and represents the extreme values allowed by the constraint. So the line divides the graph into two areas: all points above the line break the constraint while all points on or below the line do not break the constraint (as shown in Figure 10.3).

We can add the other two constraints in the same way. The distilling constraint ($2G + T \leq 40$) is the straight line through $G = 20$, $T = 0$ and $G = 0$, $T = 40$. As before, any point above the line breaks the constraint while any point on

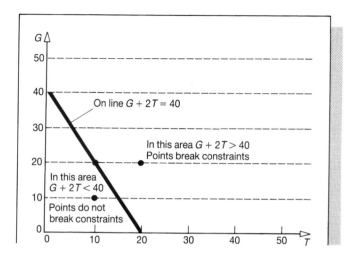

**Figure 10.3** Blending constraint divides graph into two areas.

or below it does not break the constraint and can be in the solution. The finishing constraint $(G + T \leq 25)$ is the straight line through the points $G = 0$, $T = 25$ to $G = 25$, $T = 0$ and, again, any point above the line will break the constraint and be unacceptable (as shown in Figure 10.4).

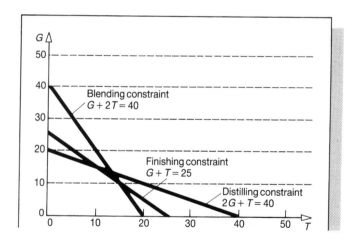

**Figure 10.4** Three constraints added to graph.

Any point that is above any of the lines will break at least one of the constraints and cannot represent a feasible solution. Adding the non-negativity constraints limits feasible solutions to the positive quadrant of the graph and defines a **feasible region**. This is the area in which all feasible solutions must lie. Any point inside the feasible region represents a valid solution to the problem while any point outside breaks at least one of the constraints (as shown in Figure 10.5).

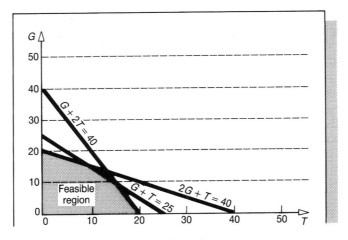

**Figure 10.5** Defining the feasible region.

Now we know the area in which feasible solutions lie, so the next stage is to examine all feasible solutions and identify the best or optimal one. This is where we use the objective function. For this problem the objective function to be maximized is:

$$\text{profit} = 30G + 20T$$

We can plot this line on the graph of $G$ against $T$ in the same way as the constraints. Although we do not know the optimal value of the profit, we can start looking at an arbitrary, trial value of, say, £600. Then we can draw the graph of $30G + 20T = 600$ through two convenient points, say $G = 0$, $T = 30$ and $G = 20$, $T = 0$. In the same way, we can draw lines for a number of other arbitrary values for profit, with the results shown in Figure 10.6.

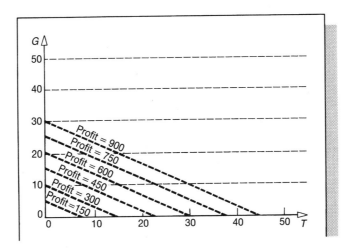

**Figure 10.6** Objective function lines for different profits.

The lines for different profits are all parallel and the further they are from the origin the higher is the value of the objective function. This observation shows how we can find an optimal solution for the problem. We can superimpose an objective function line on the graph of constraints so that it passes through the feasible region (as shown in Figure 10.7). Then we can move this line away from the origin and the further it moves the higher is the profit. As the objective function line is moved further out there comes a point where it only just passes through the feasible region and eventually just passes through a single point (as shown in Figure 10.8). This single point is the optimal solution.

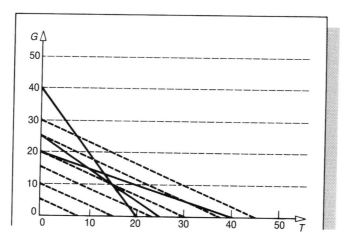

**Figure 10.7**  Superimposing objective function on constraint lines.

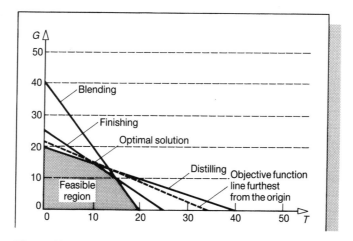

**Figure 10.8**  Identifying the optimal solution.

You can see from the graph that the optimal solution is about the point $G = 15$, $T = 10$. This is the point where the distilling constraint crosses the finishing constraint and these are the active constraints that limit production. There must be spare capacity in blending and this constraint does not limit production. We can find the optimal solution more accurately by solving the simultaneous equations of the limiting constraints.

Limiting constraints are:

$$2G + T = 40 \qquad \text{distilling}$$

$$G + T = 25 \qquad \text{finishing}$$

which we can solve to confirm that the optimal solution is:

$$G = 15 \qquad \text{and} \qquad T = 10$$

Substituting these values into the objective function gives the maximum profit:

$$30G + 20T = 30 \times 15 + 20 \times 10 = £650$$

Substituting $G = 15$ and $T = 12$ into the constraints gives:

Blending:

        time available = 40 hours

        time used = $G + 2T = 15 + 2 \times 10 = 35$

        spare capacity = 5 hours

Distilling:

        time available = 40 hours

        time used = $2G + T = 2 \times 15 + 10 = 40$

        spare capacity = 0

Finishing:

        time available = 25 hours

        time used = $G + T = 1 \times 15 + 1 \times 10 = 25$

        spare capacity = 0

This gives us the final solution for the linear programme and defines the optimal production plan for the company.

# WORKED EXAMPLE 10.4

Find the optimal solution to the following linear programme.

Minimize:

$$2X + Y$$

Subject to:

| | |
|---|---|
| $X + Y \leq 10$ | (1) |
| $X - Y \leq 2$ | (2) |
| $X \geq 4$ | (3) |
| $Y \leq 5$ | (4) |

with $X$ and $Y$ greater than or equal to zero.

## Solution

The formulation for this problem is already done, so we can immediately draw a graph of the problem, as shown in Figure 10.9. Sometimes it may not be obvious if a constraint limits solutions to points above the line or below it (constraint 2, for example). In these cases you can take random points on either side of the line and see which ones break the constraint.

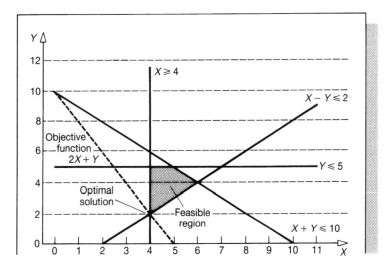

**Figure 10.9**   Solution for Worked Example 10.4.

This time we want to minimize the objective function, so instead of pushing it as far as possible away from the origin, we pull it as close as possible. As the line moves towards the origin the last point it passes through in the feasible region is the point where constraints (2) and (3) cross. Here:

$$X - Y = 2 \tag{2}$$

and

$$X = 4 \tag{3}$$

These can be solved to give the optimal solution of $X = 4$ and $Y = 2$. Substituting these values into the objective function gives a minimum value of $2 \times 4 + 1 \times 2 = 10$.

You can see from these examples that the feasible region is always a polygon without any indentations and the optimal solution is always at a corner or **extreme point**. This is not a coincidence but is a fundamental property of all linear programmes.

> If an optimal solution exists for a linear programme
> it will be at an extreme point of the feasible region.

This is a very useful property as it shows how computers can tackle large problems. Essentially, they search extreme points around the feasible region until they find an optimal.

---

### IN SUMMARY

Constraints can be drawn on a graph to find a feasible region. An objective function line can be superimposed on this graph. Moving the objective function line away from the origin increases its value, and the maximum value is the last point in the feasible region which the objective function line passes through. An optimal solution is always at an extreme point of the feasible region.

---

## Self-assessment questions

**10.6** What is the feasible region for a problem?

**10.7** What is the role of the objective function in a LP model?

**10.8** What are the extreme points of a feasible region and what is their significance?

**10.9** How can you identify the optimal solution on a graph?

# 10.4 | Solving real problems

## 10.4.1 | Computer solutions

We have seen how to solve problems with two variables using a graph. If you are good at drawing, you can extend this approach to problems with three variables. But this is still far too small for any realistic problem and we need to find some other methods. These use a lot of arithmetic, so computers are always used to solve real LP problems.

We have already suggested a method that computers could use, based on the fact that the feasible region for linear programmes is always convex and that an optimal solution lies at one of the extreme points of the feasible region. The solution procedure is simply to look at all the extreme points and choose the best. A formal procedure for this is called the 'simplex method'.

Earlier in the chapter we looked at the production planning of Growbig and Thrive. It would be interesting to confirm our results by looking at a computer solution to this problem. The formulation is:

> Maximize:     $30 \times G + 20 \times T$
>
> subject to:
>
> $$1 \times G + 2 \times T \leqslant 40$$
>
> $$2 \times G + 1 \times T \leqslant 40$$
>
> $$1 \times G + 1 \times T \leqslant 25$$
>
> with
>
> $$G \geqslant 0 \text{ and } T \geqslant 0$$

For most packages the data are presented as a matrix, so we have to rewrite this problem as:

|  | G | T |  |  |
|---|---|---|---|---|
| Maximize: | 30 | 20 |  |  |
| subject to: | 1 | 2 | $\leqslant$ | 40 |
|  | 2 | 1 | $\leqslant$ | 40 |
|  | 1 | 1 | $\leqslant$ | 25 |

Spreadsheets usually have functions for linear programming, such as 'solver' in Excel. Figure 10.10 shows a typical example of a spreadsheet used to solve a linear programme. The first part of this lists the data to make sure the problem was entered properly. Then the computer calculates and prints the results. As you can see, the results here confirm that the optimal values are $G = 15$ and $T = 10$, with a profit of £650, and they show the spare resources in constraint 1.

|    | A | B | C | D | E | F |
|----|---|---|---|---|---|---|
| 1 | **Linear programming** | | | | | |
| 2 | | | | | | |
| 3 | **Problem** | | | | | |
| 4 | | | | | | |
| 5 | **Variables** | | G | T | | |
| 6 | **Maximize** | | 30 | 20 | | |
| 7 | **s.t.** | 1 | 1 | 2 | ≤ | 40 |
| 8 | | 2 | 2 | 1 | ≤ | 40 |
| 9 | | 3 | 1 | 1 | ≤ | 25 |
| 10 | | | | | | |
| 11 | **Solution** | | | | | |
| 12 | | | | | | |
| 13 | **Variables** | | 15 | 10 | | |
| 14 | **Objective** | 650 | | | | |
| 15 | **Constraints** | 1 | 35 | **Spare** | 5 | |
| 16 | | 2 | 40 | | 0 | |
| 17 | | 3 | 25 | | 0 | |

**Figure 10.10**  Example of a spreadsheet for solving linear programmes.

If you have a more complicated linear programming problem, it is easier to use specialized software rather than a spreadsheet. There are many packages around, with LINDO being one of the best known. The data for this problem were put into a linear programming package, with the results shown in Figure 10.11. Again, the program starts by listing the problem to make sure the data were entered properly. Then it gives the results in two parts. The first shows the optimal values we have already found, including the values for $G$ and $T$, profit per unit of $G$ and $T$ (labelled 'original coefficients'), spare resources (labelled 'slack or surplus') and objective function value. There are several other figures that show the sensitivity of the solution to changes. The 'shadow price', for example, shows how much the profit would rise if we had one more unit of the resource. We will look at this sensitivity analysis in more detail in the next section.

-=*=- INFORMATION ENTERED -=*=-

| NUMBER OF VARIABLES | : | 2 |
|---|---|---|
| NUMBER OF <= CONSTRAINTS | : | 3 |
| NUMBER OF = CONSTRAINTS | : | 0 |
| NUMBER OF >= CONSTRAINTS | : | 0 |

MAXIMIZE Profit = 30 G + 20 T

SUBJECT TO:

| Blending | 1 G + 2 T | <= | 40 |
|---|---|---|---|
| Distilling | 2 G + 1 T | <= | 40 |
| Finishing | 1 G + 1 T | <= | 25 |

-=*=- RESULTS -=*=-

| VARIABLE | VARIABLE VALUE | ORIGINAL COEFFICIENT | COEFFICIENT SENSITIVITY |
|---|---|---|---|
| G | 15 | 30 | 0 |
| T | 10 | 20 | 0 |

| CONSTRAINT | ORIGINAL RIGHT-HAND VALUE | SLACK OR SURPLUS | SHADOW PRICE |
|---|---|---|---|
| Blending | 40 | 5 | 0 |
| Distilling | 40 | 0 | 10 |
| Finishing | 25 | 0 | 10 |

OBJECTIVE FUNCTION VALUE: 650

— SENSITIVITY ANALYSIS —

OBJECTIVE FUNCTION COEFFICIENTS

| VARIABLE | LOWER LIMIT | ORIGINAL COEFFICIENT | UPPER LIMIT |
|---|---|---|---|
| G | 20 | 30 | 40 |
| T | 15 | 20 | 30 |

RIGHT-HAND-SIDE VALUES

| CONSTRAINT | LOWER LIMIT | ORIGINAL VALUE | UPPER LIMIT |
|---|---|---|---|
| Blending | 35 | 40 | NO LIMIT |
| Distilling | 35 | 40 | 50 |
| Finishing | 20 | 25 | 26.667 |

———— E N D O F A N A L Y S I S ————

**Figure 10.11** Printout from LP package for Growbig–Thrive problem.

---

## IN SUMMARY

Graphs can only solve linear programmes with two – or at most three – variables. For any realistic problem we must use some other methods of solution. These involve a lot of arithmetic and always use computers.

# 10.4.2 | Sensitivity of solutions to changes

Linear programming can find an optimal solution to a problem. But managers might want to use a slightly different solution. They may, for example, take into account future changes in conditions, or they might have related experience from the past, or there might be factors which could not be quantified or put into an LP formulation, or the assumptions in the model might not be completely accurate, and so on. You will also see that linear programmes use a lot of data and these might include approximations or even errors. So it is important to know how sensitive the optimal solution is to changes. If, for example, a linear programming solution suggests a production quantity of 200 units but a manager feels that 300 units would be better, we want to know how this will affect the profits. The solution to a linear programme shows some resources are limiting and it would be useful to know if we could make more profit by buying more resources. This kind of **sensitivity analysis** is done automatically by LP programs.

There are two important questions in sensitivity analysis:

- What happens when the amount of resources change?
- What happens when the profit on a product changes?

We will look at each of these questions separately.

## What happens when the amount of resources change?

If you look again at the printout in Figure 10.11, you will see a column headed 'SHADOW PRICE'. This shows how much the profit will rise if one extra unit of the resource is available. This is also the amount the profit will fall if one unit less of the resource is available. So in our example the constraints are on blending, distilling and finishing, with shadow prices 0, 10 and 10 respectively. As there is already spare capacity in blending, it is not surprising that the shadow price is zero. Another unit of blending would not increase the profit but would simply give another spare, unused unit. But if we had another unit of either distilling or finishing the profit would rise by £10 (it is just coincidence that both shadow prices are the same here – they are usually different). You can see how this shadow price is calculated by looking at the limiting constraints again. These were:

$$2G + T = 40 \quad \text{distilling constraint}$$

$$G + T = 25 \quad \text{finishing constraint}$$

But if one extra hour of distilling is available the limiting constraints become:

$$2G + T = 41 \quad \text{new distilling constraint}$$

$$G + T = 25 \quad \text{unchanged finishing constraint}$$

Solving these equations gives the answer $G = 16$ and $T = 9$. Then substituting these values into the objective function gives a profit of $30 \times 16 + 20 \times 9 = £660$. In other words, one extra unit of distilling raises the profit from £650 to £660. This confirms the value of the shadow price for distilling of £10. Another way of looking at this, is to say that £10 is the most you would pay to buy an extra hour of distilling. Or you could say that if production is disrupted and you lost an hour of distilling it would reduce your profits by £10.

The shadow price is only valid for small changes in capacity. We found that one extra hour of distilling is worth £10, but there are limits on this and an extra 1000 hours would certainly not be worth £10,000. The other two constraints would become active long before this, and they would limit production and give spare capacity in distilling. So how can we tell the ranges within which the shadow prices are valid? The answer is shown in the 'RIGHT-HAND-SIDE VALUES' part of the printout of Figure 10.11. If you look at distilling you can see that the original amount is 40 hours (in 'ORIGINAL VALUE') and the shadow price is valid between the lower limit of 35 hours and the upper limit of 50 hours. Outside this range we do not know what will happen. So if you could get another 10 hours of distilling (raising the amount to 50 hours), it is worth paying up to $10 \times 10 = £100$. But you can not tell how much to pay for another 20 hours (raising the amount beyond the limit of 50 hours). In the same way, the shadow price of £10 on finishing is valid between the lower limit of 20 hours and the upper limit of 26.667 hours.

These calculations have assumed that one resource is changed at a time. But supposing both resources change at the same time – perhaps giving an extra hour of both distilling and finishing. We can find the effect of this by solving:

$$2G + T = 41 \quad \text{new distilling constraint}$$

$$G + T = 26 \quad \text{new finishing constraint}$$

The solution to these equations is $G = 15$ and $T = 11$ and substitution into the objective function gives a profit of £670. This is £20 more than the original optimal solution – and is the sum of the two shadow prices when the increases were made separately. So for small changes in resources, the total benefit is the sum of the benefits of increasing each resource separately.

## What happens when the profit on a product changes?

Suppose the profit on each batch of Growbig or Thrive changes. How much would this affect the optimal solution? Provided the changes are small, the optimal solution – that is the number of batches of Growbig and Thrive made – does not change. If, say, the profit on each batch of Growbig rises from £30 to £31 the optimal solution still has 15 batches of Growbig – so the profit simply rises by £15. But what exactly is a small change, and what change is big enough to give another optimal solution? The answer to this is the 'OBJECTIVE FUNCTION COEFFICIENTS' in Figure 10.11. This shows the ranges over which the optimal solution does not change. So the profit on a batch of Growbig can change between £20 and £40 and not change the optimal solution. We would calculate the new profit by simply substituting the new value in the objective function. Beyond these limits we do not know what will happen. Similarly, the profit on a batch of Thrive can vary between £15 and £30 and not change the optimal solution.

Now the only figures we have not explained in Figure 10.11 are the 'COEFFICIENT SENSITIVITY'. Normally in an LP solution some variables have positive values while others are at zero. Suppose our production plan had another type of fertiliser, but the optimal solution said that none of it should be made. The coefficient sensitivity shows how much the profit on this other fertiliser would have to rise before it becomes part of the optimal solution – that is, before we make any of it. You could also look at this as the amount the total profit would fall if a batch of this other fertiliser is actually made.

# WORKED EXAMPLE 10.5

Look again at our standard fertiliser example. Suppose a new fertiliser, Vegup, can be made in addition to Growbig and Thrive. Vegup uses 2 hours of blending, 2 hours of distilling and 2 hours of finishing for each batch, and makes a profit of £50. Would you make this new product?

## Solution

If you make one batch of Vegup you must make less Growbig and Thrive, as the total production is still limited by the available resources. Now we can use the shadow prices to see how much the profit will fall from making less Growbig and Thrive. A batch of Vegup uses 2 hours of distilling with a shadow price of £10, so this reduces profit by £20. The batch of Vegup also uses 2 hours of finishing with a shadow price of £10, so this also reduces profit by £20. Finally, the batch of Vegup uses 2 hours of blending, but as this has a shadow price of zero it does not cost anything. So making a batch of Vegup will reduce profits by a total of £40. But it actually earns a profit of £50 – so you should certainly make some batches of Vegup. Unfortunately you can not find the number of batches to make from the original solution, so you have to add this to the model and solve the new linear programme.

# WORKED EXAMPLE 10.6

Amalgamated Engineering makes two kinds of gear box, manual and automatic. There are four stages in the production of these, with details of times needed and weekly availabilities given below. The company makes a profit of £64 on each manual sold and £100 on each automatic.

| Stages in manufacture | Time needed (hours per unit) | | Time available (hours a week) |
|---|---|---|---|
| | *Manual* | *Automatic* | |
| Foundry | 3 | 5 | 7500 |
| Machine shop | 5 | 4 | 10 000 |
| Assembly | 2 | 1 | 3500 |
| Testing | 1 | 1 | 2000 |

(a) Formulate this problem as a linear programme.

(b) Find an optimal solution to the problem.

(c) Amalgamated Engineering could start making a new semi-automatic gear box which needs 4, 4, and 1 hour respectively in each manufacturing stage and gives a profit of £80 a unit. Should they make this new gear box?

## Solution

(a) Let $M$ be the number of manual gear boxes made a week and let $A$ be the number of automatic gear boxes made. The formulation becomes:

Maximize:

$$64M + 100A$$

Subject to :

$$3M + 5A \leqslant 7500 \quad \text{foundry constraint}$$

$$5M + 4A \leqslant 10\,000 \quad \text{machine shop constraint}$$

$$2M + A \leqslant 3500 \quad \text{assembly constraint}$$

$$M + A \leqslant 2000 \quad \text{testing constraint}$$

$$M, A \geqslant 0 \quad \text{non-negativity constraint}$$

(b) We can find a solution to this problem using any LP package. Figure 10.12 shows a typical result. To show that all LP packages give similar information we have used a different one for this problem. Although this printout is in a slightly different form, you can see that the differences between packages are often quite small. Here the optimal solution is to make 1250 manual gear boxes and 750 automatic ones, with a profit of £155,000. All the foundry time is used and the shadow price is £18, which is valid between 7000 and 10000 (the current value of the right-hand side minus the allowable decrease, to the current value plus the allowable increase). There is spare capacity of 750 hours and 250 hours respectively in the machine shop and assembly. All testing time is used and this has a shadow price of £10 which is valid from 1500 to 2071.43. The optimal solution will not change provided the profit on manual gear boxes stays between £60 and £100, and the profit on automatic gear boxes stays between £64 and £106.67.

(c) The new semi-automatic gear box needs:

4 hours of foundry costing £18 an hour = £72
4 hours of machine shop costing £0 an hour = £0
1 hour of assembly costing £0 an hour = £0
1 hour of testing costing £10 an hour = £10

So the total cost of making a unit is £82, while the profit is £80. This means that there would be a loss of £2 on every unit made, and Amalgamated Engineering should not start making the semi-automatic gear box.

```
LINEAR PROGRAMMING SOLVER
VARIABLES              A        M
PROBLEM ENTERED
MAX
64 M + 100 A
ST
1)      FOUNDRY          3 M + 5 A ≤ 7500
2)      MACHINE SHOP     5 M + 4 A ≤ 10000
3)      ASSEMBLY         2 M + 1 A ≤ 3500
4)      TESTING          1 M + 1 A ≤ 2000
LP OPTIMUM FOUND AT STEP              2
```

OBJECTIVE FUNCTION VALUE
1)   155000.00

| VARIABLE | VALUE | REDUCED COST |
|----------|-------|--------------|
| M | 1250.00 | .00 |
| A | 750.00 | .00 |

| ROW | | SLACK OR SURPLUS | SHADOW PRICES |
|-----|--|------------------|---------------|
| 1) | FOUNDRY | .00 | 18.00 |
| 2) | MACHINE SHOP | 750.00 | .00 |
| 3) | ASSEMBLY | 250.00 | .00 |
| 4) | TESTING | .00 | 10.00 |

NO. ITERATIONS= 2

RANGES IN WHICH THE BASIS IS UNCHANGED:

OBJ COEFFICIENT RANGES

| VARIABLE | CURRENT COEF | ALLOWABLE INCREASE | ALLOWABLE DECREASE |
|----------|--------------|--------------------|--------------------|
| M | 64.00 | 36.00 | 4.00 |
| A | 100.00 | 6.67 | 36.00 |

RIGHT-HAND-SIDE RANGES

| ROW | CURRENT RHS | ALLOWABLE INCREASE | ALLOWABLE DECREASE |
|-----|-------------|--------------------|--------------------|
| 1) | 7500.00 | 2500.00 | 500.00 |
| 2) | 10000.00 | INFINITY | 750.00 |
| 3) | 3500.00 | INFINITY | 250.00 |
| 4) | 2000.00 | 71.43 | 500.00 |

**Figure 10.12**  Output from an LP package for Worked Example 10.6.

# WORKED EXAMPLE 10.7

West Coast Wood Products Ltd makes four types of pressed panel from pine and spruce. Each sheet of panel must be cut and pressed. The following table shows the hours needed to produce a batch of each type of panel and the hours available each week:

| Panel type | Hours of cutting | Hours of pressing |
|---|---|---|
| Classic | 1 | 1 |
| Western | 1 | 4 |
| Nouveau | 2 | 3 |
| East Coast | 2 | 2 |
| Available | 80 | 100 |

There is a limited amount of suitable wood available. The amounts needed for a batch of each type of panel and the amount available each week are given in the following table:

| | Classic | Western | Nouveau | East Coast | Available |
|---|---|---|---|---|---|
| Pine | 50 | 40 | 30 | 40 | 2500 |
| Spruce | 20 | 30 | 50 | 20 | 2000 |

The profit on each batch of panels is $40 for Classic, $110 for Western, $75 for Nouveau and $35 for East Coast.

(a) Formulate this as a linear programme.

(b) A computer program gave the results for this problem shown in Figure 10.13. What do these results show?

## Solution

(a) We start by defining the decision variables as the number of batches of each type of panelling made a week ($CLS$, $WST$, $NOU$ and $EST$). Then the formulation is given by the following matrix:

| | CLS | WST | NOU | EST | | | |
|---|---|---|---|---|---|---|---|
| Maximize: | 40 | 110 | 75 | 35 | | | |
| Subject to: | 50 | 40 | 30 | 40 | $\leqslant$ | 2500 | pine |
| | 20 | 30 | 50 | 20 | $\leqslant$ | 2000 | spruce |
| | 1 | 1 | 2 | 2 | $\leqslant$ | 80 | cutting |
| | 1 | 4 | 3 | 2 | $\leqslant$ | 100 | pressing |

with $CLS$, $WST$, $NOU$ and $EST \geqslant 0$

(b) Putting these figures into a linear programming package gives the results in Figure 10.13. The results show that the optimal solution is to make 37.5 batches of Classic a week, 15.625 batches of Western and none of the others.

$- = * = -$    INFORMATION ENTERED    $- = * = -$

NUMBER OF VARIABLES          : 4
NUMBER OF $<=$ CONSTRAINTS : 4
NUMBER OF  $=$ CONSTRAINTS : 0
NUMBER OF $>=$ CONSTRAINTS : 0

MAXIMIZE Profit =    40    CLS +    110    WST +    75    NOU +    35    EST

SUBJECT TO:

| 50 | CLS + | 40 | WST + | 30 | NOU + | 40 | EST | $<=$ | 2500 |
| 20 | CLS + | 30 | WST + | 50 | NOU + | 20 | EST | $<=$ | 2000 |
| 1 | CLS + | 1 | WST + | 2 | NOU + | 2 | EST | $<=$ | 80 |
| 1 | CLS + | 4 | WST + | 3 | NOU + | 2 | EST | $<=$ | 100 |

$- = * = -$    RESULTS    $- = * = -$

| VARIABLE | VARIABLE VALUE | ORIGINAL COEFFICIENT | COEFFICIENT SENSITIVITY |
|---|---|---|---|
| CLS | 37.5 | 40 | 0 |
| WST | 15.625 | 110 | 0 |
| NOU | 0 | 75 | 7.5 |
| EST | 0 | 35 | 26.25 |

| CONSTRAINT NUMBER | ORIGINAL RIGHT-HAND VALUE | SLACK OR SURPLUS | SHADOW PRICE |
|---|---|---|---|
| 1 | 2500 | 0 | 0.312 |
| 2 | 2000 | 781.25 | 0 |
| 3 | 80 | 26.875 | 0 |
| 4 | 100 | 0 | 24.375 |

OBJECTIVE FUNCTION VALUE:          3218.75

$- -$    SENSITIVITY ANALYSIS    $- -$

OBJECTIVE FUNCTION COEFFICIENTS

| VARIABLE | LOWER LIMIT | ORIGINAL COEFFICIENT | UPPER LIMIT |
|---|---|---|---|
| CLS | 27.5 | 40 | 137.5 |
| WST | 100 | 110 | 160 |
| NOU | NO LIMIT | 75 | 82.5 |
| EST | NO LIMIT | 35 | 61.25 |

RIGHT-HAND-SIDE VALUES

| CONSTRAINT NUMBER | LOWER LIMIT | ORIGINAL VALUE | UPPER LIMIT |
|---|---|---|---|
| 1 | 1000 | 2500 | 3933.333 |
| 2 | 1218.75 | 2000 | NO LIMIT |
| 3 | 53.125 | 80 | NO LIMIT |
| 4 | 50 | 100 | 250 |

$- - - - - - - -$    END OF ANALYSIS    $- - - - - - -$

**Figure 10.13**    Printout for Worked Example 10.7.

This gives a profit of $3218.75. If a batch of Nouveau is made it would reduce profit by $7.50 while making a batch of East Coast would reduce profit by $26.25.

The limiting constraints are pine and pressing (numbers 1 and 4), with spare capacity in spruce (781.25) and cutting (26.875 hours). This will remain true while the constraint on spruce remains over 1218.75 and the amount of cutting remains above 53.13 hours. The shadow price of pine is $0.312 (valid for amounts between 1000 and 3933.333) and of pressing is $24.375 (valid for between 50 and 250 hours).

The profit for each batch of Classic could vary between $27.50 and $137.50 without changing the optimal solution. Similarly the ranges over which profit can vary on Western, Nouveau and East Coast without affecting the optimal solution are $100.00 and $160.00, below $82.50 and below $61.25 respectively.

In practice LP formulations can be very large and complex, and it is common to have tens of thousands of constraints. Such large problems need a lot of effort to make sure that there are no errors. Two particular problems found in computer printouts are:

- **unbound solution**, which means that the constraints do not limit the solution, and the feasible region effectively extends to infinity
- **infeasible solution**, which means the constraints have left no feasible region

If you get these you have to check the input data carefully and make sure they are accurate.

### IN SUMMARY

Sensitivity analyses find how the optimal solution changes when there are small alterations to the problem. These alterations might be to the amount of resources available, or profits on each product. LP packages do these calculations automatically.

## Self-assessment questions

10.10  Why are computers always used to solve linear programmes?

10.11  What information might be given in a computer printout for the solution of a linear programme?

10.12  What is meant by 'sensitivity analysis' in LP problems?

10.13  What are 'shadow prices' in linear programming?

10.14  Within what limits are the shadow prices valid?

## CHAPTER REVIEW

Many problems in business are types of constrained optimization. This chapter has discussed linear programming, which is a method of tackling such problems. In particular it:

- outlined the characteristics of constrained optimization and linear programmes
- formulated problems as linear programmes
- used a graph to solve linear programmes
- looked at computer solutions to larger problems
- looked at the sensitivity of solutions to changes in the objective function and constraints

# Problems

**10.1** Two additives, X1 and X2, can be used to increase the octane number of petrol. One kg of X1 in 5000 litres of petrol will increase the octane number by 10, while one kg of X2 in 5000 litres will increase the octane number by 20. The total additives must increase the octane number by at least 5, but a total of no more than 500 g can be added to 5000 litres, and the amount of X2 plus twice the amount of X1 must be at least 500 g. If X1 costs £30 a kg and X2 costs £40 a kg, formulate this problem as a linear programme.

**10.2** Use a graphical method to solve the formulation in Problem 10.1.

**10.3** A housing association is planning a number of blocks of flats. Five types of block have been designed, containing flats of four categories (senior citizens, single person, small family and large family). The number of flats in each block, and other relevant information, is given in Table 10.1. The association wants to build a total of 500 flats with at least 40 in category 1 and 125 in each of the other categories. In the past, high-rise flats have proved unpopular and the association wants to limit the number of storeys in the development. In particular, the average number of storeys must be at

**Table 10.1**

| Type of block | No. of flats in each category | | | | No. of storeys | Plan area | Cost per block (£'000) |
|---|---|---|---|---|---|---|---|
| | 1 | 2 | 3 | 4 | | | |
| A | 1 | 2 | 4 | 0 | 3 | 5 | 208 |
| B | 0 | 3 | 6 | 0 | 6 | 5 | 320 |
| C | 2 | 2 | 2 | 4 | 2 | 8 | 300 |
| D | 0 | 6 | 0 | 8 | 8 | 6 | 480 |
| E | 0 | 0 | 10 | 5 | 3 | 4 | 480 |

most five and at least half the flats must be in blocks of three or fewer storeys. An area of 300 units has been set aside for the development and any spare land will be used as a park. Formulate this problem as a linear programme.

**10.4** Weekly production schedules are needed for the manufacture of two products X and Y. Each unit of X uses one component made in the factory, while each unit of Y uses two of the components, and the factory has a maximum output of 80 components a week. Each unit of X and Y needs 10 hours of subcontracted work and agreements have been signed with subcontractors for a weekly minimum of 200 hours and a maximum of 600 hours. The marketing department says that it can sell all production of Y but there is a maximum demand of 50 units of X, despite a long-term contract to supply 10 units of X to one customer. The net profit on each unit of X and Y is £200 and £300 respectively.

(a) Formulate this problem as a linear programme.

(b) Use a graphical method to find an optimal solution. Confirm this result using a suitable program.

**10.5** Novacook Ltd makes two types of cooker, one electric and one gas. There are four stages in the production of each of these, with details given in Table 10.2. The electric cooker has variable costs of £200 a unit and a selling price of £300 while the gas cooker has variable costs of £160 and a selling price of £240 a unit. Fixed overheads are £60,000 a week and the company works a 50-week year. The marketing department suggest maximum sales of 800 electric and 1250 gas cookers a week.

**Table 10.2**

| Manufacturing stage | Time required (hours per unit) | | Total time available (hours a week) |
|---|---|---|---|
| | Electric | Gas | |
| Forming | 4 | 2 | 3600 |
| Machine shop | 10 | 8 | 12 000 |
| Assembly | 6 | 4 | 6000 |
| Testing | 2 | 2 | 2800 |

(a) Formulate this as a profit-maximizing linear programme.

(b) Find an optimal product mix for the company. What is the expected annual profit?

(c) Find the use and spare capacity of each manufacturing stage.

(d) What are the shadow prices of each manufacturing stage?

(e) An outside consultant offers his testing services to the company. What price should Novacook be willing to pay for this service and how many hours should they buy a week?

(f) A new cooker is planned, which would use the manufacturing stages for 4, 6, 6 and 2 hours respectively. At what selling price should Novacook consider making this cooker if the other variable costs are £168 a unit?

**10.6** Warsaw Woda produces two types of circuit tester, Standard and Normal. The production time, in hours, for each type and the capacity of each production process are given below. All testers made can be sold and the profits on each unit of Standard and Normal are 600 zl and 800 zl respectively.

| Process | Standard | Normal | Capacity (hours per month) |
| --- | --- | --- | --- |
| Pressing | 2 | 4 | 160 |
| Wiring | 6 | 2 | 240 |
| Assembly | 4 | 4 | 200 |

(a) Formulate the problem of maximizing monthly profit as a linear programme.
(b) Find the optimal solution to this problem.
(c) What are the spare capacities in production facilities?
(d) Calculate the shadow prices of production facilities.
(e) The selling price of the Standard tester could be raised. To what level could it be raised without changing the optimal pattern of production?
(f) A new tester is planned, which could go through pressing, wiring and assembly at a rate of 2 units an hour on each process. What profit is needed before this new tester is made?

**10.7** An oil company makes two blends of fuel by mixing three oils. The costs and daily availability of the oils are:

| Oil | Cost (£/litre) | Amount available (litres) |
| --- | --- | --- |
| A | 0.33 | 5000 |
| B | 0.40 | 10 000 |
| C | 0.48 | 15 000 |

The requirements of the blends of fuel are:

| | |
| --- | --- |
| Blend 1 | at least 30% of A |
| | at most 45% of B |
| | at least 25% of C |
| Blend 2 | at most 35% of A |
| | at least 30% of B |
| | at most 40% of C |

Each litre of blend 1 can be sold for £1.00 and each litre of blend 2 can be sold for £1.20. Long-term contracts require at least 10 000 litres of each blend to be produced. Formulate this blending problem as a linear programme. What can you say about the optimal solution?

# Computer exercises

**10.1** Figure 10.14 shows a printout from a linear programming package. Make sure you can understand all of this and can explain the results. Use a suitable package to check the results.

**10.2** The printouts from LP packages are often difficult to interpret. Figure 10.15 shows the printout from one package. Describe the results given here and say how the printout could be improved.

**10.3** Some spreadsheets can solve linear programmes automatically. See whether you have access to one of these and find how to use it. Use it to test some of the previous results. Would it be easy to design a spreadsheet for solving linear programmes?

**10.4** Use a linear programming package to check the solutions to the problems in Worked Examples 10.1 to 10.7.

**10.5** Leo Hamlich has forecast the numbers of a component that his company will need each month. Unfortunately, the cost of the component is rising fairly quickly. Table 10.3 shows the forecast requirement and cost. Leo can purchase components ahead of time to avoid the price increases, but there is a cost of £2 a unit for carrying stock from one period to the next. Formulate a linear programme that will find the best pattern for ordering the component. Use a suitable program to find the optimal solution to this problem.

**Table 10.3**

| Month | Jan | Feb | Mar | Apr | May | Jun | Jul | Aug | Sep | Oct | Nov | Dec |
|---|---|---|---|---|---|---|---|---|---|---|---|---|
| Demand | 100 | 90 | 80 | 60 | 50 | 50 | 70 | 90 | 100 | 100 | 110 | 110 |
| Cost (£) | 200 | 200 | 205 | 205 | 210 | 210 | 210 | 220 | 220 | 230 | 230 | 240 |

$-=*=-$     INFORMATION ENTERED     $-=*=-$

NUMBER OF VARIABLES      : 3
NUMBER OF <= CONSTRAINTS : 1
NUMBER OF   = CONSTRAINTS : 0
NUMBER OF >= CONSTRAINTS : 2

MINIMIZE Costs =      10    PrA +    5    PrB +    3    PrC

SUBJECT TO:

    120    PrA +    23    PrB +   10    PrC <=   1545

    150    PrA +    35    PrB +   10    PrC >=    550

    100    PrA +    15    PrB +   55    PrC >=    675

$-=*=-$     RESULTS     $-=*=-$

| VARIABLE | VARIABLE VALUE | ORIGINAL COEFFICIENT | COEFFICIENT SENSITIVITY |
|---|---|---|---|
| PrA | 3.241 | 10 | 0 |
| PrB | 0 | 5 | 3.069 |
| PrC | 6.379 | 3 | 0 |

| CONSTRAINT NUMBER | ORIGINAL RIGHT-HAND VALUE | SLACK OR SURPLUS | SHADOW PRICE |
|---|---|---|---|
| 1 | 1545 | 1092.241 | 0 |
| 2 | 550 | 0 | 0.034 |
| 3 | 675 | 0 | 0.048 |

OBJECTIVE FUNCTION VALUE:      51.552

$--$     SENSITIVITY ANALYSIS     $--$

OBJECTIVE FUNCTION COEFFICIENTS

| VARIABLE | LOWER LIMIT | ORIGINAL COEFFICIENT | UPPER LIMIT |
|---|---|---|---|
| PrA | 5.455 | 10 | 22.535 |
| PrB | 1.931 | 5 | NO LIMIT |
| PrC | 0.667 | 3 | 5.5 |

RIGHT-HAND-SIDE VALUES

| CONSTRAINT NUMBER | LOWER LIMIT | ORIGINAL VALUE | UPPER LIMIT |
|---|---|---|---|
| 1 | 452.759 | 1545 | NO LIMIT |
| 2 | 122.727 | 550 | 1012.5 |
| 3 | 366.667 | 675 | 3025 |

$----$ END OF ANALYSIS $----$

**Figure 10.14**    Printout from a linear programming package.

LINEAR PROGRAMMING SOLUTION

LP OPTIMUM FOUND AT STEP       2

OBJECTIVE FUNCTION VALUE

1)                    417.50000

| VARIABLE | VALUE | REDUCED COST |
|---|---|---|
| X | 27.500000 | .000000 |
| Y | 15.000000 | .000000 |

| ROW | SLACK OR SURPLUS | DUAL PRICES |
|---|---|---|
| 2) | 2.500000 | .000000 |
| 3) | .000000 | 4.500000 |
| 4) | .000000 | 3.500000 |

NO. ITERATIONS =       2

RANGES IN WHICH THE BASIS IS UNCHANGED:

OBJ COEFFICIENT RANGES

| VARIABLE | CURRENT COEF | ALLOWABLE INCREASE | ALLOWABLE DECREASE |
|---|---|---|---|
| X | 7.000000 | 3.000000 | 7.000000 |
| Y | 15.000000 | INFINITY | 4.500000 |

RIGHT-HAND-SIDE RANGES

| ROW | CURRENT RHS | ALLOWABLE INCREASE | ALLOWABLE DECREASE |
|---|---|---|---|
| 2 | 30.000000 | INFINITY | 2.500000 |
| 3 | 15.000000 | 18.333330 | 1.666667 |
| 4 | 100.000000 | 5.000000 | 55.000000 |

**Figure 10.15**   Printout from a linear programming package.

# Case study

## Elemental Electronics

Elemental Electronics assembles microcomputers and acts as wholesalers for some components. For the manufacturing business, they buy components from a number of suppliers and assemble them in a well-tried design. They do virtually no research and development, and are happy to use designs that have been tested by other manufacturers. They also spend little on advertising, preferring to sell computers through a few specialized retailers. As a result they have very low overheads, and can sell their machines at a much lower price than major competitors.

a)  One component that Elemental buys is a standard board. There are at least six suppliers of this board in America, Europe and the Far East. Elemental acts as a wholesaler for two of these suppliers, one in the Far East and one in South America. These boards are delivered in bulk and Elemental tests and repackages them to sell to a number of small manufacturers. Each board from the Far East takes 2 hours to test and 2 hours to repackage, while each board from South America takes 3 hours to test and 1 hour to repackage. Elemental has enough facilities for up to 8000 hours a week for testing and 4000 hours a week for repackaging. There are maximum sales of 1500 a week for the board from the Far East and each board gives a profit of £10 when sold.

- What is the optimal mix of these boards for Elemental?
- How does this optimal mix vary with changing profits on each board?
- What are the shadow prices on each resource and over what ranges are these valid?
- If another version of the board becomes available from Europe, which takes 2 hours of testing, 1 hour of repackaging and gives a profit of £10, should this new board be imported?

b)  Elemental manufactures four models of computer. Each of these has four stages in manufacturing: sub-assembly, main assembly, final assembly and finishing. The times needed for each stage are known approximately, as are the total availabilities each week (Table 10.4).

**Table 10.4**

| Manufacturing stage | Hours needed per unit | | | | Number of machines | Hours available per machine per week |
|---|---|---|---|---|---|---|
| | Model A | Model B | Model C | Model D | | |
| Sub-assembly | 2 | 3 | 4 | 4 | 10 | 40 |
| Main assembly | 1 | 2 | 2 | 3 | 6 | 36 |
| Final assembly | 3 | 3 | 2 | 4 | 12 | 38 |
| Finishing | 2 | 3 | 3 | 3 | 8 | 40 |

Fixed costs of production are £3 million a year. Selling prices are £2,500, £2,800, £3,400 and £4,000 for the four models, with direct costs of £1,600, £1,800, £2,200 and £2,500 respectively. On average the sub-assembly machines need 10% of their total time for maintenance, main assembly machines need 16.667%, final assembly machines 25% and finishing machines 10%. The company works a standard 48-hour week.

- Formulate a linear programme describing the assembly.
- What is the best mix of models?
- Write a report explaining your results, highlighting any particularly interesting points.

# 11 Using calculus to describe changes

| | | | | |
|---|---|---|---|---|
| Chapter outline | 334 | Chapter review | 351 |
| 11.1 Differentiation | 335 | Problems | 351 |
| 11.2 Economic applications of differentiation | 346 | Case study: Lundquist Transport | 351 |

## CHAPTER OUTLINE

The average speed of a car is defined as the distance travelled divided by the time taken: any change in speed is described as either acceleration or deceleration. Calculus was originally developed to describe this kind of physical change, but is now used for problems which involve any kind of change. This chapter will discuss some applications of calculus to business problems, looking at the way costs change with production quantities, sales change with price, revenues change with output, and so on.

After reading this chapter and doing the exercises you should be able to:

- understand the concept of differentiation
- differentiate functions of the form $y = ax^n$
- calculate optimal values for continuous functions
- use differentiation for marginal analyses and price elasticity of demand

# 11.1 Differentiation

## 11.1.1 Basis of differentiation

The equation of a straight line is $y = ax + b$, where $b$ is the point where the line crosses the $y$ axis and $a$ is the gradient. The gradient is defined as the rate of change of $y$ with respect to $x$, so it is the amount that $y$ changes for every unit change in $x$.

## WORKED EXAMPLE 11.1

The cost of running a family car is £400 a year for fixed costs (road tax, insurance, depreciation, etc) plus a variable cost of 30 pence for every mile travelled (for petrol, oil, maintenance, etc). What is the equation for total annual cost? What is the gradient of this line and what does this mean?

### Solution

With $y$ as the total annual cost (in pounds) of running the car, and $x$ as the distance travelled (in miles) in a year, we have:

$$y = 0.30x + 400$$

This is in the form $y = ax + b$, and the gradient is clearly the variable cost – every unit increase in $x$ causes an increase of 0.3 units in $y$ (see Figure 11.1). The total cost $y$ is linear with respect to $x$, so the gradient is constant and every mile has the same variable cost, whether it is the fifth mile or the five thousandth.

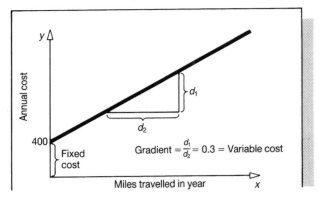

**Figure 11.1**  Constant gradient of a straight line (for Worked Example 11.1).

Suppose the family in Worked Example 11.1 look at the costs of their car in more detail. They might find that higher annual mileage increases depreciation and insurance costs, so that the variable cost per mile actually rises with distance travelled. Then they have the total cost shown in Figure 11.2. Now it is more difficult to calculate the cost of travelling a mile at any particular point. Suppose the car has already travelled 5000 miles this year; what is the cost of travelling the next mile?

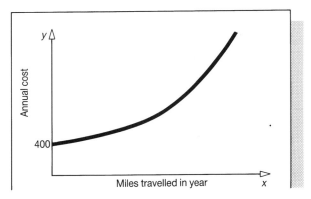

**Figure 11.2**   Variable cost rising with distance travelled.

Worked Example 11.1 reminded us that the graph of total cost against distance travelled has the variable cost equal to the gradient. So to find the variable cost at any point in Figure 11.2 we need to find the gradient of the line at that point. Unfortunately, the gradient now varies with $x$. So to find the cost of travelling the 5000th mile we specifically need the gradient of the line when $x = 5000$. We could draw a graph and simply measure the gradient, but this is time-consuming and not very accurate. A more useful approach is to calculate the gradient.

We can start this calculation by approximating the gradient when $x = 5000$ to the average gradient near that point. In general, to find the gradient at a point $x$, we can take two points, say $(x_1, y_1)$ and $(x_2, y_2)$, so that one point is on either side of $x$, as shown in Figure 11.3. Then:

$$\text{gradient at point } x \text{ is approximately} = \frac{y_2 - y_1}{x_2 - x_1}$$

This gives the average gradient around $x$, but it is not the gradient **exactly at** $x$. In other words we have the average gradient, but not the **instantaneous gradient**. If we move $x_1$ and $x_2$ closer together we can get closer to the instantaneous gradient. Then, if we make $x_1$ and $x_2$ very, very close to $x$, we can get a value that is very, very close to the instantaneous gradient. In other words, as the distance between $x_1$ and $x_2$ approaches zero, we find the instantaneous gradient as the tangent to the curve at $x$ (Figure 11.4).

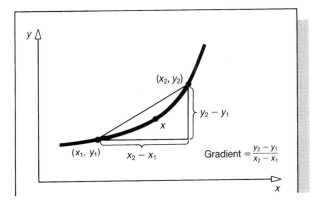

**Figure 11.3** Approximate gradient at point $x$.

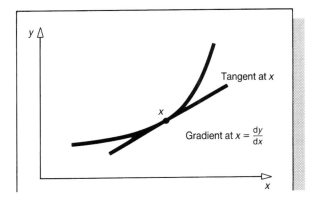

**Figure 11.4** The tangent at $x$ gives the instantaneous gradient.

We still need an easy way of calculating the gradient of the tangent at $x$, and this is where we use **differentiation**. This calculates the instantaneous rate of change of $y$ with respect to $x$. This instantaneous gradient is referred to as $dy/dx$ (pronounced 'dee $y$ by dee $x$'), and details of the calculation are described in the following section.

---

### IN SUMMARY

Differentiation finds the instantaneous gradient of a function. This gradient is called $dy/dx$, and is the rate of change of $y$ with respect to $x$.

## 11.1.2 | Rules for differentiation

A lot of differentiation can be done using two simple rules.

### Differentiation rule 1

If:
$$y = ax^n$$
where $a$ and $n$ can take any values, then:
$$\frac{dy}{dx} = anx^{n-1}$$

## WORKED EXAMPLE 11.2

Differentiate $y = 2x^3$. How quickly is $y$ increasing when $x = 5$?

### Solution

This has the general form $y = ax^n$ with $a = 2$ and $n = 3$. Substitution into the equation of rule 1 gives:

$$\frac{dy}{dx} = anx^{n-1} = 2 \times 3 \times x^{3-1} = 6x^2$$

The instantaneous gradient of $2x^3$ is $6x^2$. When $x = 5$, the gradient is $6 \times 5^2 = 150$.

## WORKED EXAMPLE 11.3

The total cost $y$ of a process is related to the daily output $x$ by the equation $y = 7x^2$. How quickly does the cost change when 100 units a day are being made?

### Solution

We can find the rate of change of cost by differentiating the total cost. Substituting $a = 7$ and $n = 2$ into the equation of rule 1 gives:

$$\frac{dy}{dx} = anx^{n-1} = 7 \times 2 \times x^{2-1} = 14x$$

When $x = 100$ the rate of change of cost is $14 \times 100 = 1400$. In other words, increasing daily output by one unit (to 101 units) will increase processing costs by 1400. (Actually it will increase costs by a bit more than 1400 because the gradient of the line changes slightly between 100 and 101.)

There is one important result when $y = a$, and $a$ is any constant:

$$\frac{dy}{dx} = 0$$

This result is obvious if you realize that the line $y = a$ is a straight line parallel to the $x$ axis, and therefore has a gradient of zero.

A second rule allows us to extend the use of differentiation.

## Differentiation rule 2

If:

$$y = u + v$$

then:

$$\frac{dy}{dx} = \frac{du}{dx} + \frac{dv}{dx}$$

This means that we can differentiate a function consisting of several parts by applying the first rule to each part separately.

# WORKED EXAMPLE 11.4

Differentiate $y = 3x^3 + 14x^2 - x - 12$ with respect to $x$.

## Solution

Rule 2 allows us to apply rule 1 to each part of the equation in turn:

- differentiating the first term, $3x^3$, gives $3 \times 3 \times x^{3-1} = 9x^2$
- differentiating the second term, $14x^2$, gives $14 \times 2 \times x^{2-1} = 28x$
- differentiating the third term, $-x$, gives $-1 \times x^{1-1} = -1$
- differentiating the fourth term, $-12$, gives zero.

Then adding the separate terms gives the solution as:

$$\frac{dy}{dx} = 9x^2 + 28x - 1$$

## WORKED EXAMPLE 11.5

The output $y$ from a process over time $x$ is described by $y = 2x^3 - 3x$. How fast is the output changing when (a) $x = 1$, (b) $x = 4$?

### Solution

The rate of change of the output is given by the gradient. Differentiating $y = 2x^3 - 3x$ gives the gradient at any point:

$$\frac{dy}{dx} = 3 \times 2 \times x^{3-1} - 1 \times 3 \times x^{1-1} = 6x^2 - 3$$

(a) Substituting $x = 1$ gives the instantaneous gradient when $x = 1$ as:

$$6x^2 - 3 = 6 \times 1^2 - 3 = 3$$

So the output is rising by 3 units in each time period.

(b) Substituting $x = 4$ gives the instantaneous gradient when $x = 4$ as:

$$6 \times 4^2 - 3 = 93$$

So the output is now rising much faster.

---

### IN SUMMARY

The two basic rules of differentiation are:

- if $y = ax^n$ then $dy/dx = anx^{n-1}$, for any values of $a$ and $n$
- if $y = u + v$, then $dy/dx = du/dx + dv/dx$

## 11.1.3 | Maximum and minimum values

In Chapter 10 we saw how linear programming tackled problems of constrained optimization. Differentiation can also be used to find optimal values for certain problems. Specifically, it can find the maximum and minimum values of a continuous function.

Figure 11.5 shows a graph of the equation $y = ax^2 + bx + c$. This has a clear minimum. If you look at the gradient at point A, it is clearly negative, showing that $y$ is falling in value as $x$ increases. At point B the gradient is positive, showing that $y$ is increasing in value as $x$ increases. The most interesting point comes between these at point C, where the gradient is zero; in other words the tangent to the curve is parallel to the $x$ axis. This only happens at one specific point and this is the minimum value of the graph.

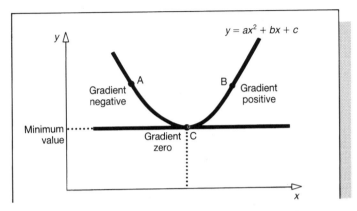

**Figure 11.5**   The minimum of a function has a gradient of zero.

# WORKED EXAMPLE 11.6

What can you say about the minimum of $y = 2x^2 - 4x + 10$?

## Solution

We can differentiate $y = 2x^2 - 4x + 10$ to find the gradient at any point. Then:

$$\frac{dy}{dx} = 2 \times 2 \times x - 4 = 4x - 4$$

For a minimum value of $y$ this gradient is equal to zero. In other words:

$$4x - 4 = 0 \quad \text{or} \quad x = 1$$

Substituting $x = 1$ into the equation for $y$ gives the minimum value:

$$y = 2x^2 - 4x + 10 = 2 \times 1^2 - 4 \times 1 + 10 = 8$$

So the minimum value of the graph is $y = 8$, which occurs when $x = 1$.

In the worked example above, the point where the gradient was zero was identified as a minimum. But, if you look at Figure 11.6, you can see that maximum values also have gradients of zero.

Points on a graph where the gradient is zero are called **turning points**. They identify optimal values, which may be either maxima or minima. A related problem is that the optimal value may be a **local optimum** rather than a real one, as shown in Figure 11.7. We clearly need to find more information about the shape of the curve, and in particular we need to find if a turning point is a minimum or a maximum. We could do this by drawing a graph of the function, but we can find more information from calculations.

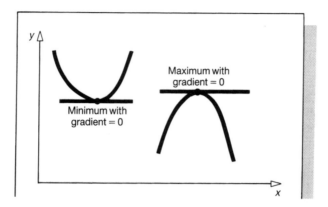

**Figure 11.6**  Both minima and maxima have gradients of zero.

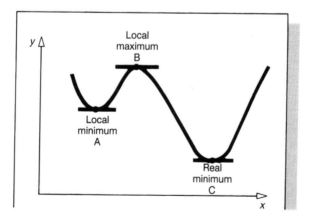

**Figure 11.7**  Illustrating local and real minima (points A, B and C are turning points).

The top part of Figure 11.8 shows a curve with a minimum at point A and a maximum at point B. The gradient is clearly zero at these two points, but if we follow the curve we can see some interesting points. At the left-hand side of the graph the gradient $dy/dx$ is negative. Then at point A it goes through zero and becomes positive. Then at point B it goes through zero and becomes negative again. So we can draw the graph of $dy/dx$ corresponding to the graph of $y$, as shown in the bottom part of Figure 11.8.

This graph shows clearly that:

- for a minimum value of the function $y$, the derivative $dy/dx$ has the value 0 and is increasing
- for a maximum value of the function $y$, the derivative $dy/dx$ has the value 0 and is decreasing

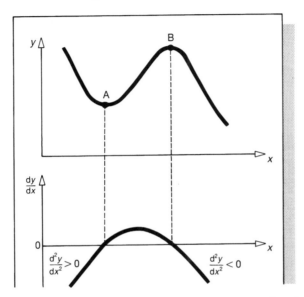

**Figure 11.8**   For optimal values of $y$, $dy/dx = 0$, and $d^2y/dx^2$ identifies maxima and minima.

These observations show how we can identify a turning point as either a maximum or a minimum, without actually drawing the graph. All we need to do is find the rate of change of $dy/dx$ and see whether this is positive (showing that $dy/dx$ is increasing and we have a minimum) or negative (showing that $dy/dx$ is decreasing and we have a maximum).

If we have a function $y$, its rate of change is found by differentiation to be $dy/dx$. Now if we have a function $dy/dx$, its rate of change can be found by differentiation in exactly the same way. In other words, we differentiate $dy/dx$ and the result is the second derivative which is called $d^2y/dx^2$ (pronounced  'dee two $y$ by dee $x$ squared'). If this is negative the gradient is decreasing and the function has a maximum value; if this is positive the gradient is increasing and the function has a minimum value.

We can consolidate these results into the general rule:

- The maximum of a function occurs when $dy/dx = 0$
  and $d^2y/dx^2 < 0$
- The minimum of a function occurs when $dy/dx = 0$
  and $d^2y/dx^2 > 0$

## WORKED EXAMPLE 11.7

If $y = 4x^2 + 3x - 2$, what are (a) $dy/dx$, (b) $d^2y/dx^2$?

### Solution

(a) If $y = 4x^2 + 3x - 2$ then differentiating in the usual way gives:

$$\frac{dy}{dx} = 8x + 3$$

(b) If $dy/dx = 8x + 3$ then differentiating in the usual way gives:

$$\frac{d^2y}{dx^2} = 8$$

## WORKED EXAMPLE 11.8

The total cost of a manufacturing process is $3x^2 - 12x + 30$, where $x$ is the number of units produced each week. What production level minimizes this total cost?

### Solution

We know that $y = 3x^2 - 12x + 30$. This has a gradient given by $dy/dx = 6x - 12$. There is a turning point when this gradient has a value 0; that is, $6x - 12 = 0$, or $x = 2$. At this point the function has the value:

$$y = 3x^2 - 12x + 30 = 3 \times 2^2 - 12 \times 2 + 30 = 18.$$

We also know that $d^2y/dx^2 = 6$. This is positive, so the turning point is a minimum. Then the total cost of production is a minimium of 18 when production is 2 units a week.

## WORKED EXAMPLE 11.9

The duration of a project can be altered by using varying amounts of resources. Using an amount $x$ gives a net revenue of:

$$\text{net revenue} = x^3 - 3x^2$$

This result is only valid in the range $x = 0$ to $x = 5$. What does the revenue function look like? What value of $x$ gives the highest net revenue?

## Solution

We can differentiate the revenue to find the turning points. As the equation is a cubic there will be two turning points, one a maximum and the other a minimum. Then:

$$y = x^3 - 3x^2 \qquad \text{so} \qquad \frac{dy}{dx} = 3x^2 - 6x$$

The turning points occur when this is equal to zero, so:

$$3x^2 - 6x = 0 \qquad 3x(x - 2) = 0$$

giving:

$$x = 0 \qquad \text{and} \qquad x = 2$$

Taking the second derivative:

$$\frac{d^2y}{dx^2} = 6x - 6$$

When $x = 0$, $d^2y/dx^2 = 6x - 6 = -6$, so this point is a maximum, and when $x = 2$, $d^2y/dx^2 = 6x - 6 = 6$, so this point is a minimum.

From this information, you might think that the revenue is maximized when $x = 0$. But if you draw a graph of the revenue, as shown in Figure 11.9, you can see that this is only a local maximum. In the valid range of $x = 0$ to $x = 5$ the net revenue is essentially U-shaped and it has a maximum value when $x = 5$, so revenue $= 5^3 - 3 \times 5^2 = 50$.

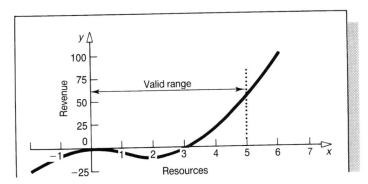

**Figure 11.9**  Graph of revenue for Worked Example 11.9.

## IN SUMMARY

The optimal value of a function occurs at the point where the gradient is zero, so $dy/dx = 0$. The function has a minimum value when $d^2y/dx^2 > 0$ and a maximum value when $d^2y/dx^2 < 0$.

## Self-assessment questions

**11.1** What is the purpose of differentiation?

**11.2** What is meant by $dy/dx$?

**11.3** What conditions must be satisfied to identify the minimum point of a curve?

**11.4** If $p = q + r$, how could you find $dp/dc$?

**11.5** Explain in words what is meant by $d^2y/dx^2$.

# ▌ 11.2 ▌ Economic applications of differentiation

## ▌ 11.2.1 ▌ Marginal analyses

Calculus was originally developed to solve problems in the physical sciences, but it can be used for many management problems. It is particularly useful for calculating the cost of various processes. Suppose, for example, we know the total cost of making a number of units of a product. We can divide this total cost by the number of units to get an average cost. But it is often more useful to look at the **marginal cost**, which is defined as the cost of making one extra unit. Suppose we have already made 100 units at a total cost of £50,000. The average cost is £50,000/100 = £500. But the marginal cost is the cost of making the 101st unit. Because all investment in equipment may already have been recovered, and we have a lot of experience in making the product, this marginal cost might be considerably lower than the average cost.

The marginal cost, MC, of a product is the additional cost of making one extra unit. In making this extra unit the total cost will increase by MC, so the marginal cost is the rate at which the total cost is changing; in other words it is the gradient of the total cost curve. Now, if we know the equation for the total cost curve, we can differentiate it to get the marginal cost.

> If:
> $$\text{total cost, TC} = y$$
> then
> $$\text{marginal cost, MC} = \frac{dy}{dx}$$

The same argument holds for revenues. If we have a total revenue TR, then the marginal revenue is the additional revenue from the next unit, and this is the amount by which the total revenue increases. Then the marginal revenue is the rate of change of total revenue, so we can say:

> If:
> $$\text{total revenue, TR} = y$$
>
> then
> $$\text{marginal revenue, MR} = \frac{dy}{dx}$$

# WORKED EXAMPLE 11.10

The total cost of serving $x$ customers is TC $= 2x^2 + 4x + 500$. What are the expressions for total, fixed, variable, marginal and average costs? What are these costs if 500 customers are served?

## Solution

- Total cost TC is given as TC $= 2x^2 + 4x + 500$.
- Fixed cost is the cost that is incurred regardless of the number of customers, $x$, so this is 500.
- Variable cost is the cost that changes with the number of customers served, so this is $2x^2 + 4x$.
- Marginal cost MC is found by differentiating TC, so MC $= 4x + 4$.
- Average cost is found from:
  $$\text{TC}/x = (2x^2 + 4x + 500)/x = 2x + 4 + 500/x$$
  If $x$ is 500, then:
- Total cost, TC $= 2 \times 500^2 + 4 \times 500 + 500 = 502\,500$
- Fixed cost remains unchanged at 500
- Variable cost is $2 \times 500^2 + 4 \times 500 = 502\,000$
- Marginal cost $= 4 \times 500 + 4 = 2004$
- Average cost $= 2 \times 500 + 4 + 500/500 = 1005$

We can do similar calculations to find marginal and average revenues. The total profit is the difference between total revenue and total cost, so we can use differentiation to find the point of maximum profit. With a little thought, you can see that profit will be a maximum when the marginal revenue is equal to the marginal cost. The reasoning behind this is:

- if marginal cost is higher than marginal revenue, each additional unit makes a net loss, so fewer units should be made

- if marginal revenue is higher than marginal cost, each additional unit makes a net profit, so more units should made
- only when marginal cost is the same as marginal revenue do we have a point of stability which maximizes profit

## WORKED EXAMPLE 11.11

The total cost and total revenue for a product are related to production, $x$, by:

$$TC = x^3 - 15x^2 + 1000$$

$$TR = 14x - x^2 + 2000$$

How many units should the company make to (a) maximize total revenue, (b) minimize total cost, (c) maximize profit?

### Solution

(a) We can find the rate of change of total revenue by differentiating TR with respect to $x$. This gives the marginal revenue MR $= 14 - 2x$. A turning point occurs when this is equal to zero, i.e $14 - 2x = 0$ or $x = 7$. Differentiation again gives $-2$, which is negative, confirming that the turning point is a maximum. At this point the total revenue is $14 \times 7 - 7^2 + 2000 = 2049$.

(b) We can find the rate of change of total cost by differentiating TC with respect to $x$. This gives the marginal cost MC $= 3x^2 - 30x$. Turning points occur when this is equal to zero, i.e. $3x^2 - 30x = 0$, $3x(x - 10) = 0$, so $x = 0$ or $10$. Differentiating again gives $6x - 30$. This is negative when $x = 0$, indicating a maximum, and positive when $x = 10$, indicating a minimum. So the total costs are minimized by making 10 units. At this point the total cost is $10^3 - 15 \times 10^2 + 1000 = 500$. As we have seen before, this may be a local minimum, so a graph should be drawn to check these results.

(c) Total profit    TP = total revenue – total cost

$$= TR - TC$$

$$= 14x - x^2 + 2000 - (x^3 - 15x^2 + 1000)$$

$$= -x^3 + 14x^2 + 14x + 1000$$

Differentiating this gives turning points when:

$$-3x^2 + 28x + 14 = 0$$

The positive root of this is 9.8. Differentiating again gives $-6x + 28$, which is negative when $x = 9.8$, confirming a maximum.

Then the total profit is:

$$-x^3 + 14x^2 + 14x + 1000$$

$$= -9.8^3 + 14 \times 9.8^2 + 14 \times 9.8 + 1000 = 1540.6$$

IN SUMMARY

If the equation for the total cost (or revenue) is known, it can be differentiated to give the marginal cost (or revenue). This can be used in a number of associated calculations.

## 11.2.2 | Price elasticity of demand

Differentiation can also be used to find the **price elasticity of demand**. This is defined as the change in demand for a product when there is a change in price. A formal definition has:

$$\text{elasticity of demand} = \frac{\text{proportional change in demand}}{\text{proportional change in price}}$$

If the quantity sold is $q$ and the price charged is $p$, then the definition gives:

$$\text{elasticity of demand} = \frac{\text{change in } q/\text{original } q}{\text{change in } p/\text{ original } p}$$

$$= \frac{\text{original } p}{\text{original } q} \times \frac{\text{change in } q}{\text{change in } p}$$

If there are very small changes in price $p$ and quantity $q$ (so small that they approach zero), then (change in $q$)/(change in $p$) is the rate of change of $q$ with respect to $p$, which is $dq/dp$.

$$\frac{\text{change in } q}{\text{change in } p} = \text{instantaneous gradient} = \frac{dq}{dp}$$

So:

$$\text{elasticity of demand} = \frac{p}{q} \times \frac{dq}{dp}$$

## WORKED EXAMPLE 11.12

Experience suggests that the price, $p$, and demand, $q$, for a product are related by:
$$p = 200 - q^2$$
What is the price elasticity of demand? What is the value of this when $q$ is equal to 10?

### Solution

Differentiating $p$ with respect to $q$ gives:

$$\frac{dp}{dq} = -2q$$

We want $dq/dp$, and can find this from:

$$\frac{dq}{dp} = \frac{1}{dp/dq} = -\frac{1}{2q}$$

Then substitution gives:

$$\text{elasticity of demand} = \frac{p}{q} \times \frac{dq}{dp}$$

$$= \frac{200 - q^2}{q} \times \frac{(-1)}{2q} = -\frac{(200/q - q)}{2q}$$

When $q = 10$:

$$\text{elasticity of demand} = -\frac{(200/q - q)}{2q} = -\frac{(200/10 - 10)}{2 \times 10} = -0.5$$

A negative elasticity of demand is the most common result and implies that an increase in price will decrease demand. In this case, every unit increase in price will decrease demand by 0.5 units.

---

### IN SUMMARY

The price elasticity of demand can be calculated from:

$$\text{elasticity of demand} = \frac{p}{q} \times \frac{dq}{dp}$$

---

## Self-assessment questions

**11.6** How would you define the marginal cost of production?

**11.7** Given the total revenue function for a product, how could you find the average revenue and the marginal revenue?

**11.8** Explain what is meant by elasticity of demand.

**11.9** What would a positive elasticity of demand mean?

CHAPTER REVIEW

This chapter has introduced the methods of calculus for describing the way a function changes. In particular it:

- showed how differentiation finds the equation for the instantaneous rate of change of a function at any point
- described two basic rules for differentiation:

    if $y = ax^n$ then $dy/dx = anx^{n-1}$, for any values of $a$ and $n$

    if $y = u + v$ then $dy/dx = du/dx + dv/dx$

- showed how optimal values can be found when $dy/dx = 0$
- outlined the use of differentiation for marginal analysis and price elasticity of demand

## Problems

**11.1**  Differentiate $y = 12x^7$ with respect to $x$.

**11.2**  Differentiate $y = 6.2x^4 + 3.3x^3 - 7.1x^2 - 11.9x + 14.3$ with respect to $x$ and find the turning points. What are the maximum and minimum values?

**11.3**  Differentiate $x = 2y^2 - 3y + 7$ with respect to $y$.

**11.4**  A certain product sells for £10 a unit. The total cost of making and selling $x$ units of the product is given by:

$$\text{cost} = x^2 - 20x + 30$$

What is the fixed cost of production? How is the profit related to the number of units produced? What level of production will maximize profit?

**11.5**  Does the function $y = 2x^2 + 5x + 10$ have a turning point? Is this a minimum or a maximum? How does this compare with $y = x^3 + 6x^2 - 15x$?

**11.6**  The total cost TC and total revenue TR associated with a product are:

$$\text{TR} = 12x - 2x^2 + 5000 \qquad \text{and} \qquad \text{TC} = x^3 - 10x^2 + 3000$$

How many units should the company produce to (a) maximize total revenue, (b) minimize total cost, (c) maximize profit?

# Case study

## Lundquist Transport

Lundquist Transport provides a specialist service, designing logistics systems for companies around Scandinavia. It also runs a fleet of long-distance trucks based outside Copenhagen. This is a very competitive business, and the company is constantly looking for ways to improve operations.

One current problem for Lundquist concerns deliveries between Scandinavia and Eastern Europe. The quantity of goods moving to eastern Germany, Poland, Hungary and beyond is increasing rapidly and Lundquist wants to get a share of this important market.

Lundquist recently examined its revenues and costs. Costs do not rise linearly with demand, as the company can get economies of scale and can adjust operations to meet demand in different ways. Revenues are also not linear, as they give discounts for larger orders and longer distances. The actual figures are highly confidential, so Lundquist transformed them into 'standard' values for comparisons and discussion, as shown in the following table:

| Volume of business | Revenues | Costs |
| --- | --- | --- |
| 0.25 | 3250 | 3375 |
| 0.5 | 4500 | 3000 |
| 0.75 | 4750 | 2875 |
| 0.85 | 4570 | 2895 |
| 1.0 | 4000 | 3000 |
| 1.1 | 3420 | 3120 |
| 1.25 | 2250 | 3375 |

The current volume of business is described as '1.0' and the operations managers think that this is putting too much pressure on them. If Lundquist wants to expand, it will have to make some major changes in the way that it works – particularly buying new facilities and employing more people. This does, of course, involve some risk.

In the short term, it may be better to maintain current operations and change the volume of business. It is fairly easy to change the volume of business in such a competitive market, simply by changing the price structure. Lundquist has done no detailed calculations on this, but the commonly accepted rule is that a 5% increase in price reduces demand by 10%. However, this approach also involves risk, as it might encourage competitors to develop their own operations.

Your job is to write a report for the senior managers of Lundquist. This should include a description of the situation, analysis of available information, discussion of alternative policies and your recommendation for the company's best options.

# PART FOUR

# Business statistics

This book is divided into five parts, each of which covers a different aspect of quantitative methods in business. The first part gave the background and context for the rest of the book. The second part discussed data collection and description. The third part looked at methods of solving specific types of business problem. The problems tackled there were deterministic, which means that they do not involve any probabilities. This is the fourth part, which gives an introduction to probabilities and statistical methods. The final part shows how these ideas can be applied to probabilistic models.

There are four chapters in this part.

Chapter 12 introduces the ideas of probability. In many situations the values taken by variables are not known exactly; there is some uncertainty. Probabilities measure this uncertainty and allow related analyses.

Chapter 13 describes how probability distributions can be used to describe data that contain uncertainty. Many probability distributions follow a standard pattern, and the chapter discusses the most important of these.

We have already shown how samples are used for collecting data, and this theme is expanded in Chapter 14. The essence of sampling is that we infer some characteristic of a population from the characteristics of a sample. Here we discuss how confident we are in making such inferences, and how this confidence is related to the sample size.

Chapter 15 introduces the ideas of statistical testing. In particular, it discusses hypothesis testing, which sees whether a belief about a population is supported by the evidence from a sample.

## Ideas in Practice – CIS Personal Pensions

Investing in the stock market is risky. Sometimes share prices rise quickly and lucky investors make a fortune; at other times, share prices plummet and unlucky investors lose their shirt. Unfortunately, there seems little underlying logic behind these variations. The 'value' of a company can collapse one day, and then soar the next day. One Market Commentary by the Royal Bank of Canada looked at wild fluctuations in the stock market and said that 'Market volatility continued in the second quarter of

2000 due to concerns about strong economic growth, inflationary pressures, currency fluctuations and valuations in general'.

Investors can spread their risk by putting money into a wide range of shares. One way of organizing this over the long term is with a personal pension, probably arranged through an insurance company.

The problem is that the company providing your pension has no idea how its investments will perform over time. Companies such as CIS can only quote returns that you will get if they achieve annual growth of 5%, 7% or 9%. Then they have to add cautionary notes:

- 'These figures are only examples and are not guaranteed – they are not minimum or maximum amounts. What you get back depends on how your investment works.'

- 'You could get back more or less than this.'

- 'All insurance companies use the same rates of growth for illustrations but their charges vary.'

- 'Do not forget that inflation would reduce what you could buy in the future with the amounts shown.'

Unfortunately, all organizations have to work with uncertainty when making their decisions. They do not know exactly what will happen in the future and have to allow for some unknown variation. To help with this, they use a range of statistical analyses. The purpose of statistics is to help us describe, and work with, situations of uncertainty.

# 12 | Uncertainty and probabilities

Chapter outline 355
12.1 Measuring uncertainty 356
12.2 Conditional probability 365
    for dependent events
Chapter review 375

Problems 376
Computer exercises 377
Case study: 379
    *The Gamblers' Press*

## CHAPTER OUTLINE

Previous chapters in this book have assumed that we know the value of variables with certainty. When considering sales, for example, we could say that, 'Acme will sell 1000 units next year'. In this chapter we are looking at situations where this is not true, and there is some uncertainty. We know roughly what future sales will be, but cannot give exact numbers. This kind of uncertainty is measured by probabilities.

The probability of an event can be viewed as its likelihood or relative frequency. The probability of rolling a six on a die is 1/6, the probability that Christmas Day is a Monday is 1/7, and so on.

After reviewing some results for independent probabilities, the chapter looks at conditional probabilities. These happen when the probability of one event occurring is influenced by other events.

The material in this chapter lays the foundations for the following chapters. It is important that you thoroughly understand probabilities before moving on.

After reading this chapter and doing the exercises you should be able to:

- appreciate the difference between deterministic and stochastic problems
- calculate probabilities and appreciate their meaning
- know the rules for multiplying and adding probabilities for independent events
- understand dependent events
- use Bayes' theorem to calculate conditional probabilities
- draw probability trees

# 12.1 | Measuring uncertainty

## 12.1.1 | Introduction

So far in this book we have assumed that the value of any variable is fixed and can be found with certainty. When we look at sales we assume that the number of sales and the prices charged are known with certainty, so we can say, 'A company sells 1000 units a year at £20 a unit'. When we look at production, the output and costs are known with certainty; when we look at employees, the number of people employed and their hours of work are known with certainty; when we look at a service, we know how many customers there will be and how much each will spend. Such situations are called **deterministic**.

In reality, information about most situations is not so well known. When we spin a coin we do not know whether it will come down heads or tails; a company launching a new product does not know exactly how many sales it will make; someone selling a house does not know exactly how much it will fetch; a manufacturer does not know exactly how many units it will make in a period. Each of these has some uncertainty. Such situations are called **stochastic** or **probabilistic**.

Although stochastic problems contain uncertainty, this is not the same as ignorance. When we spin a coin we know that it will come down either heads or tails, and we know that each of these outcomes is equally likely. When a company launches a new product it will normally do some market research to find that likely sales are, say, around 2000 units a year. Then the company has some information and knows roughly what level of sales to expect, but there is some uncertainty and it does not know the exact figure. In this chapter we are going to discuss ways of measuring this uncertainty. This is done by **probabilities**.

---

### IN SUMMARY

Many situations are not deterministic (when all values are known exactly) but stochastic (when there is uncertainty). Probabilities are a way of measuring this uncertainty.

## 12.1.2 | Defining probability

Probabilities give a way of measuring uncertainty. To be more precise, the probability of an event is a measure of its likelihood or relative frequency.

Experience leads us to believe that when a fair coin is tossed it will come down heads half the time and tails half the time. From this observation we can say, 'The probability of a fair coin coming down heads is 0.5'. This statement uses a definition of the probability of an event as the proportion of times the event occurs:

probability of an event =

$$\frac{\text{number of ways that the event can occur}}{\text{number of possible outcomes}}$$

When we spin a coin there are two possible outcomes (heads and tails) and one of these is a head, so the probability of a head is 1/2. Similarly, there are 52 cards in a pack of cards and one ace of hearts, so a card chosen at random has a probability of 1/52 of being the ace of hearts. In the last 500 days the train to work has broken down 10 times, so the probability of it breaking down on any day is 10/500, or 0.02. For 200 of the last 240 trading days the Toronto Stock Exchange has had more advances than declines, so there is a probability of 200/240, or 0.83, that the Stock Exchange advances on a particular day.

As probability measures the proportion of times that an event occurs, its values can only be defined in the range 0 to 1:

- probability = 0 means that the event will **never** occur
- probability = 1 means that the event will **always** occur
- probability between 0 and 1 gives relative frequency
- probabilities outside the range 0 to 1 have no meaning

An event with a probability of 0.8 is quite likely (it will happen eight times out of ten); an event with a probability of 0.5 is equally likely to happen as not; an event with a probability of 0.2 is quite unlikely (it will happen two times out of ten).

Rather than keep saying 'the probability of an event is 0.8' we can abbreviate this to $P(\text{event}) = 0.8$. Then spinning a coin has $P(\text{head}) = 0.5$.

# WORKED EXAMPLE 12.1

A magazine advertises a prize draw with one first prize, five second prizes, 100 third prizes and 1000 fourth prizes. The prizes are drawn at random from entries for the competition and after each draw the winning ticket is returned to the draw. By the closing date there are 10 000 entries and at the draw no entry won more than one prize. What is the probability that a given ticket won first prize or that it won any prize?

## Solution

There are 10 000 entries and one first prize, so the probability of a given ticket winning first prize is 1/10 000.

Similarly, there are five second prizes, so the probability of winning one of these is 5/10 000. The probabilities of winning third or fourth prizes are 100/10 000 and 1000/10 000 respectively.

There are a total of 1106 prizes so the probability of winning one of these is 1106/10 000 = 0.1106. On the other hand, the probability of not winning a prize is 8894/10 000 = 0.8894.

## WORKED EXAMPLE 12.2

An office has the following types of employee:

|                | Female | Male |
| -------------- | ------ | ---- |
| Administrative | 25     | 15   |
| Operational    | 35     | 25   |

If one person from the office is selected at random, what is the probability that the person is (a) a male administrator, (b) a female operator, (c) male, (d) an operator?

## Solution

(a) There are 100 people working in the office. Of these 15 are male administrators, so:

$$P(\text{male administrator}) = 15/100 = 0.15$$

(b) 35 people in the office are female operators, so:

$$P(\text{female operator}) = 35/100 = 0.35$$

(c) A total of 40 people in the office are male, so:

$$P(\text{male}) = 40/100 = 0.4$$

(d) A total of 60 people in the office are operators, so:

$$P(\text{operator}) = 60/100 = 0.6$$

In the worked examples above, we calculated the probabilities from observations. Generally, there are two ways of finding probabilities:

● Theoretical argument can be used to give *a priori* probabilities:

$$\text{probability of an event} = \frac{\text{number of ways that the event can occur}}{\text{number of possible outcomes}}$$

The probability that a husband and wife share the same birthday is 1/365 (ignoring leap years). This is an *a priori* probability, calculated by saying that there are 365 days on which the second partner can have a birthday and only one of these corresponds to the birthday of the first partner.

● Historical data can be used to give **empirical** values:

$$\text{probability of an event} = \frac{\text{number of times that the event occurred}}{\text{number of observations}}$$

The last 100 times that a football team has played at home, it had a crowd of more than 20 000 for 62 matches. This gives an empirical probability of 62/100 = 0.62 that next week's game will have a crowd of more than 20 000 (all other things being equal).

One problem with using empirical values is that the historical data may not be typical. If a coin is tossed five times and comes down heads each time, this does not mean that it will always come down heads. Empirical values must be based on typical values, collected over a long period.

There is another method of getting probabilities, which is not generally recommended. This asks people to give their subjective views about likely probabilities. We might, for example, ask knowledgeable people to suggest a probability that a company will make a profit of more than a million pounds next year. This is equivalent to judgemental forecasting, and has the same drawbacks. In particular, subjective probabilities are often little more than guesses and are generally unreliable.

---

### IN SUMMARY

The probability of an event is the likelihood that the event will occur, or its relative frequency. This is measured on a scale of 0 to 1 with:

probability = 0   meaning that there is no chance of the event happening

probability = 1   meaning that the event is certain to happen

---

## 12.1.3 | Calculations with probabilities

An important idea for probabilities is **mutually exclusive** events. Two events are mutually exclusive if one event's happening means that the second event cannot happen. When a coin is tossed, having it come down heads is mutually exclusive with having it come down tails; the event that a company makes a profit in a year is mutually exclusive with the event that it makes a loss in the year; the event that sales increase is mutually exclusive with the event that sales decrease.

With this definition we can do some calculations of probabilities. For mutually exclusive events we find the probabilities of one **or** another happening by adding the separate probabilities:

---

For mutually exclusive events:
OR means ADD probabilities:

$$P(a \text{ OR } b) = P(a) + P(b)$$

$$P(a \text{ OR } b \text{ OR } c) = P(a) + P(b) + P(c)$$

$$P(a \text{ OR } b \text{ OR } c \text{ OR } d) = P(a) + P(b) + P(c) + P(d)$$

and so on

---

An illustration of this was given in Worked Example 12.1, where the probability that a particular ticket won a magazine prize draw was calculated as 1106/10 000. The probability that it did not win was 8894/10 000. Each ticket must either win or lose, and these two events are mutually exclusive, so:

$$P(\text{win OR lose}) = 1$$

$$P(\text{win}) + P(\text{lose}) = 0.1106 + 0.8894 = 1$$

or

$$P(\text{lose}) = 1 - P(\text{win})$$

# WORKED EXAMPLE 12.3

A company makes 40 000 washing machines a year. Of these, 10 000 are for the home market, 8000 are exported to North America, 7000 to Europe, 5000 to South America, 4000 to the Far East, 3000 to Australasia and 3000 to other markets.

(a) What is the probability that a particular machine is sold on the home market?
(b) What is the probability that a machine is exported?
(c) What is the probability that a machine is exported to either North or South America?
(d) What is the probability that a machine is sold in either the home market or Europe?

## Solution

(a) The probability that a machine is sold on the home market is:

$$P(\text{home}) = \frac{\text{number sold on home market}}{\text{number sold}} = \frac{10\,000}{40\,000} = 0.25$$

(b) All events (that is, areas of sales) are mutually exclusive, so the probability that a machine is exported is found by adding the total number of machines which are exported and dividing this by the total number of machines made:

$$P(\text{exported}) = 30\ 000/40\ 000 = 0.75$$

Alternatively, we could say that all machines are sold somewhere, so the probability that a machine is sold is 1.0. It is either sold on the home market or exported, so:

$$P(\text{sold}) = 1 = P(\text{exported}) + P(\text{home})$$

Then:

$$P(\text{exported}) = 1 - P(\text{home}) = 1 - 0.25 = 0.75$$

(c) $P(\text{North America OR South America}) = P(\text{North America}) + P(\text{South America})$

$$= 8000/40\ 000 + 5000/40\ 000 = 0.2 + 0.125 = 0.325$$

(d) $P(\text{home OR Europe}) = P(\text{home}) + P(\text{Europe})$

$$= 10\ 000/40\ 000 + 7000/40\ 000 = 0.25 + 0.175 = 0.425$$

---

A useful way of presenting probabilities is given by **Venn diagrams**, which use circles to represent the probabilities of events. If two events are mutually exclusive, the Venn diagram has separate circles as shown in Figure 12.1.

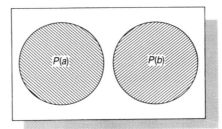

$P(a \text{ OR } b) = P(a) + P(b)$

**Figure 12.1**   Venn diagram for mutually exclusive events.

If two events are **not** mutually exclusive, there is a probability that they can both occur, as shown in the Venn diagram of Figure 12.2. The circles now overlap, with the overlap representing the probability that both events occur. If we simply add the probabilities of each event, we effectively add the overlap twice, and to correct this we must subtract the probability of both events.

> For events that are not mutually exclusive:
>
> $$P(a \text{ OR } b) = P(a) + P(b) - P(a \text{ AND } b)$$

Suppose we pick a single card from a pack. What is the probability that it is an ace or a heart? These are not mutually exclusive events, so we say:

$$P(\text{ace OR heart}) = P(\text{ace}) + P(\text{heart}) - P(\text{ace AND heart})$$

$$= 4/52 + 13/52 - 1/52 = 16/52 = 0.31$$

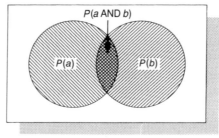

$P(a \text{ OR } b) = P(a) + P(b) - P(a \text{ AND } b)$

**Figure 12.2** Venn diagram for non-mutually-exclusive events.

Another important idea for events is independence. If the occurrence of one event does not affect the occurrence of a second event, the two events are said to be **independent.** The fact that a person works in a bank is independent of the fact that they are left-handed. The fact that a factory has a shipment of raw materials delayed is independent of the fact that they had problems with machine reliability last year. Using the notation:

$P(a)$ = the probability of event $a$

$P(a/b)$ = the probability of event $a$ given that $b$ has already occurred

$P(a/\underline{b})$ = the probability of event $a$ given that $b$ has **not** occurred

the two events, $a$ and $b$, are independent if:

$P(a) = P(a/b) = P(a/\underline{b})$

The probability that a person buys a particular newspaper is independent of the probability that they suffer from hay fever. Then:

$P(\text{buys } \textit{Times}) = P(\text{buys } \textit{Times}/\text{suffers from hay fever})$

$= P(\text{buys } \textit{Times}/\text{does not suffer from hay fever})$

We use a second rule for probabilities when a number of separate events all occur. For independent events we find the probability of one **and** another happening by multiplying the probabilities of the separate events:

---

For independent events:
AND means MULTIPLY probabilities:

$P(a \text{ AND } b)$ $\qquad\qquad = P(a) \times P(b)$

$P(a \text{ AND } b \text{ AND } c)$ $\qquad = P(a) \times P(b) \times P(c)$

$P(a \text{ AND } b \text{ AND } c \text{ AND } d) = P(a) \times P(b) \times P(c) \times P(d)$

and so on

---

## WORKED EXAMPLE 12.4

A mail-order company combines two parts, products and invoices, into a box for delivery. An average of 10% of products are defective and 5% of invoices. If defects in products and invoices are independent, what is the probability that a final delivery has both products and invoices defective?

### Solution

For independent events:

$$P(\text{products defective AND invoices defective}) = P(\text{products defective})$$
$$\times P(\text{invoices defective})$$
$$= 0.1 \times 0.05$$
$$= 0.005$$

Similarly:

$$P(\text{products defective AND invoices not defective}) = 0.1 \times 0.95 = 0.095$$

$$P(\text{products not defective AND invoices defective}) = 0.9 \times 0.05 = 0.045$$

$$P(\text{products not defective AND invoices not defective}) = 0.9 \times 0.95 = 0.855$$

These are the only four possible combinations, so it is not surprising that the probabilities add to 1.

## WORKED EXAMPLE 12.5

A warehouse classifies its stock into three categories: A, B and C. On all category A items it promises a service level of 97% (in other words, there is a probability of 0.97 that the warehouse can meet demand immediately from stock). On category B and C items it promises service levels of 94% and 90% respectively. If service levels are independent, what are the probabilities that the warehouse can immediately supply an order for:

(a) one item of category A and one item of category B

(b) one item from each category

(c) two different items from A, one from B and three from C

(d) three different items from each category?

### Solution

(a) As the events are independent we can multiply the probabilities to give:

$$P(\text{one A AND one B}) = P(\text{one A}) \times P(\text{one B}) = 0.97 \times 0.94 = 0.912$$

(b) $P(\text{one A AND one B AND one C}) = P(\text{one A}) \times P(\text{one B}) \times P(\text{one C})$
$$= 0.97 \times 0.94 \times 0.90 = 0.821$$

(c) $P$(two A AND one B AND three C) = $P$(two A) $\times$ $P$(one B) $\times$ $P$(three C)

We have to break this down a bit further by noting that the probability of two items of category A is the probability that the first is there AND the second is there. In other words:

$$P(\text{two A}) = P(\text{one A AND one A}) = P(\text{one A}) \times P(\text{one A}) = P(\text{one A})^2$$

Similarly:

$$P(\text{three C}) = P(\text{one C})^3$$

Then the answer becomes:

$$P(\text{one A})^2 \times P(\text{one B}) \times P(\text{one C})^3 = 0.97^2 \times 0.94 \times 0.9^3$$

$$= 0.645$$

(d) $P$(three A AND three B AND three C) = $P$(one A)$^3$ $\times$ $P$(one B)$^3$ $\times$ $P$(one C)$^3$

$$= 0.97^3 \times 0.94^3 \times 0.9^3$$

$$= 0.553$$

## WORKED EXAMPLE 12.6

Every year a company bids for an annual contract. The probability that it will win the contract is 0.75. What is the probability that the company will win the contract either this year or next year?

### Solution

One thing we **cannot** do with this problem is say:

$P$(win this year) = 0.75

$P$(win next year) = 0.75

Then:

$$P(\text{win this year OR win next year}) = P(\text{win this year}) + P(\text{win next year})$$

$$= 0.75 + 0.75 = 1.5$$

The addition rule only works if the two events are mutually exclusive. In this case, the events (winning the contract this year and winning it next year) are not mutually exclusive, and the company could win the contract in both years. A proper analysis gives:

$P$(win this year AND win next year) = $0.75 \times 0.75 = 0.5625$

$P$(win this year AND lose next year) = $0.75 \times 0.25 = 0.1875$

$P$(lose this year AND win next year) = $0.25 \times 0.75 = 0.1875$

$P$(lose this year AND lose next year) = $0.25 \times 0.25 = 0.0625$

The probability that the company wins the contract in at least one year is $1 - 0.0625 = 0.9375$. The probability that the company wins the contract in only one year is $0.1875 + 0.1875 = 0.3750$.

> ## IN SUMMARY
>
> For mutually exclusive events:
>
> OR means ADD probabilities, so $P(a \text{ OR } b) = P(a) + P(b)$
>
> For independent events:
>
> AND means MULTIPLY probabilities, so $P(a \text{ AND } b) = P(a) \times P(b)$

## Self-assessment questions

**12.1** What is the probability of an event?

**12.2** What are independent events?

**12.3** What are mutually exclusive events?

**12.4** How could you find the probability that one of several mutually exclusive events occur?

**12.5** How could you find the probability of all of several independent events occurring?

**12.6** If one of events A, B and C is certain to happen, what is $P(A)$?

# | 12.2 || Conditional probability for dependent events

## | 12.2.1 | Bayes' theorem

In the last section we assumed that events are independent. But this is often not true and we should now look at events where the occurrence of one directly effects the occurrence of the other. For example, the fact that a person is employed in one of the professions is not independent of their having higher education; the probability that a machine will break down this week is not independent of its age; the probability that there is a mistake on an invoice is not independent of the company submitting the invoice, and so on.

For dependent events, the fact that one event has occurred or not changes the probability that a second event will occur. Then, if:

$P(a)$ = the probability of event $a$

$P(a/b)$ = the probability of event $a$ given that $b$ has already occurred

$P(a/\underline{b})$ = the probability of event $a$ given that $b$ has **not** occurred

the two events, $a$ and $b$, are dependent if:

$$P(a) \neq P(a/b) \neq P(a/\underline{b})$$

(Remember that the symbol $\neq$ means 'is not equal to'.)

The probability that the price of a company's shares rises is dependent on whether the company announces a profit or a loss. Then:

$$P(\text{share price rises}) \neq P(\text{share price rises}/\text{announce profit})$$

$$\neq P(\text{share price rises}/\text{announce loss})$$

Probabilities in the form $P(a/b)$ are called **conditional** probabilities. There is one important result that you must understand about conditional probabilities: this is the general rule that the probability of two dependent events occurring is the probability of the first, multiplied by the conditional probability that the second occurs given that the first has already occurred. This rather clumsy statement can be written as:

$$P(a \text{ AND } b) = P(a) \times P(b/a)$$

where:

$P(a \text{ AND } b) = $ probability that both $a$ and $b$ occur

$P(a) = $ probability that $a$ occurs

$P(b/a) = $ probability that $b$ occurs given that $a$ has already occurred

With a little thought we can extend this to give the obvious result:

$$P(a \text{ AND } b) = P(a) \times P(b/a) = P(b) \times P(a/b)$$

Taking the second two terms and rearranging them gives:

$$P(a/b) = \frac{P(b/a) \times P(a)}{P(b)}$$

This result is known as **Bayes' theorem**, and is used in most calculations of conditional probabilities.

# WORKED EXAMPLE 12.7

The following table describes the students in a particular class:

|        | Home | Overseas |
|--------|------|----------|
| Male   | 66   | 29       |
| Female | 102  | 3        |

(a) If you select a student at random from the class, what is the probability that the student is from overseas?

(b) If the student selected is female, what is the probability that she is from overseas?

(c) If the student is from overseas, what is the probability that he or she is female?

## Solution

(a) $P$(overseas) = number from overseas/number of students

$$= 32/200 = 0.16$$

(b) We can find this by considering only the 105 female students, to give:

$$P(\text{overseas/female}) = \text{number of overseas females/number of females}$$

$$= 3/105 = 0.029$$

We can find the same result using:

$$P(\text{overseas/female}) = \frac{P(\text{overseas AND female})}{P(\text{female})}$$

Now:

$$P(\text{overseas AND female}) = 3/200 = 0.015$$

$$P(\text{female}) = 105/200 = 0.525$$

So:

$$P(\text{overseas/female}) = \frac{P(\text{overseas AND female})}{P(\text{female})}$$

$$= 0.015/0.525 = 0.029$$

(c) Now we want $P$(female/overseas). We can tackle this in several ways. To start with we can look directly at the 32 overseas students and say:

$$P(\text{female/overseas}) = 3/32 = 0.094$$

We can find the same result using:

$$P(\text{female/overseas}) = \frac{P(\text{female AND overseas})}{P(\text{overseas})}$$

Now:

$$P(\text{female AND overseas}) = 3/200 = 0.15$$

$$P(\text{overseas}) = 32/200 = 0.16$$

So:

$$P(\text{female/overseas}) = 0.15/0.16 = 0.094$$

We can also use Bayes' theorem to check this result. This shows that:

$$P(\text{female/overseas}) = \frac{P(\text{overseas/female}) \times P(\text{female})}{P(\text{overseas})}$$

In part (a) we found that $P$(overseas/female) = 0.029, and we know that $P$(female) = 0.525 and $P$(overseas) = 0.16. So:

$$P(\text{female/overseas}) = 0.029 \times 0.525/0.16 = 0.094$$

We have found this result from three different routes – which are really different versions of the same calculation. In practice we normally only have data for one type of calculation.

## WORKED EXAMPLE 12.8

Two machines make identical parts, which are combined on a production line. The older machine makes 40% of the units, of which 85% are of satisfactory quality. The newer machine makes 60% of the units, of which 92% are of satisfactory quality. A random check further down the production line shows an unusual fault, which shows that the machine which made the unit needs adjusting. What is the probability that the older machine made the unit?

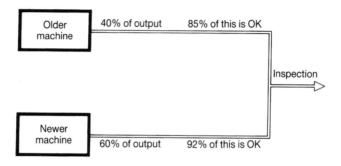

**Figure 12.3**   Process for Worked Example 12.8.

## Solution

This problem is shown in Figure 12.3. Using the abbreviations O for the older machine, N for the newer machine, OK for good units and F for faulty ones, we want $P(O/F)$, and can find this using Bayes' theorem:

$$P(a/b) = \frac{P(b/a) \times P(a)}{P(b)} \qquad \text{so} \qquad P(O/F) = \frac{P(F/O) \times P(O)}{P(F)}$$

We know that $P(O) = 0.4$ and $P(F/O) = 0.15$, so the remaining value we need is $P(F)$, the probability that a unit is faulty. With a little thought you can see that:

probability that a unit is faulty = probability that it is faulty from the old machine OR that it is faulty from the new machine

So:

$$P(F) = P(F \text{ AND } O) + P(F \text{ AND } N)$$

or

$$P(F) = P(F/O) \times P(O) + P(F/N) \times P(N)$$
$$= 0.15 \times 0.4 + 0.08 \times 0.6 = 0.108$$

Substitution then gives:

$$P(O/F) = \frac{P(F/O) \times P(O)}{P(F)} = \frac{0.15 \times 0.4}{0.108} = \frac{0.06}{0.108} = 0.556$$

To check this result we can also calculate:

$$P(N/F) = \frac{P(F/N) \times P(N)}{P(F)} = \frac{0.08 \times 0.6}{0.108} = 0.444$$

As the faulty unit must have come from either the older or the newer machine, the fact that $P(O/F) + P(N/F) = 1$ confirms the result.

---

IN SUMMARY

Conditional probabilities occur when two events are dependent. Associated calculations can be done using Bayes' theorem.

# 12.2.2 | Calculations for Bayes' theorem

The arithmetic for Bayes' theorem is quite straightforward, but it gets tedious for larger problems. An obvious solution is to use a computer, and Figure 12.4 shows a printout of the results for Worked Example 12.8. In this printout you can see a number of values that we calculated, and some others that we shall explain now. For this we shall use an easy mechanical procedure. This mechanical procedure starts by putting the data in a table:

|  | *Faulty* | *OK* |  |
|---|---|---|---|
| Older machine | 0.15 | 0.85 | 0.4 |
| Newer machine | 0.08 | 0.92 | 0.6 |

The left-hand box gives the conditional probabilities. So $0.15 = P(F/O)$, $0.08 = P(F/N)$ etc. The box to the right gives the values of $P(O)$ and $P(N)$, which are called the prior probabilities.

BAYESIAN ANALYSIS MODEL

−=*=−   DATA ENTERED   −=*=−

| | |
|---|---|
| NUMBER OF STATES | : 2 |
| NUMBER OF ALTERNATIVES | : 2 |

PRIOR PROBABILITIES

| | |
|---|---|
| 1 Older machine | 0.4000 |
| 2 Newer machine | 0.6000 |

CONDITIONAL PROBABILITIES

| | 1 Faulty | 2 OK |
|---|---|---|
| 1 Older machine | 0.1500 | 0.8500 |
| 2 Newer machine | 0.0800 | 0.9200 |

−=*=−   RESULTS   −=*=−

PREDICTIONS − JOINT PROBABILITIES

| | 1 Faulty | 2 OK |
|---|---|---|
| 1 Older Machine | 0.0600 | 0.3400 |
| 2 Newer machine | 0.0480 | 0.5520 |

PREDICTIONS − MARGINAL PROBABILITIES

| | |
|---|---|
| 1 Faulty | 0.1080 |
| 2 OK | 0.8920 |

PREDICTIONS − REVISED PROBABILITIES

| | 1 Faulty | 2 OK |
|---|---|---|
| 1 Older machine | 0.5556 | 0.4444 |
| 2 Newer machine | 0.3812 | 0.6188 |

−−−−−−−−−−   END OF ANALYSIS   −−−−−−−−−−

**Figure 12.4**   Computer printout for Bayesian analysis.

Now we form a third box by multiplying each conditional probability in the left-hand box by the prior probability on the same line. So $0.15 \times 0.4 = 0.060$, $0.08 \times 0.6 = 0.048$, etc. These results are called **joint** probabilities.

| | *Faulty* | *OK* | | *Faulty* | *OK* |
|---|---|---|---|---|---|
| Older machine | 0.15 | 0.85 | 0.4 | 0.060 | 0.340 |
| Newer machine | 0.08 | 0.92 | 0.6 | 0.048 | 0.552 |
| | | | | 0.108 | 0.892 |

Adding each column of joint probabilities gives a marginal probability. Then:

$0.060 + 0.048 = 0.108$, which is the probability that a unit is faulty

$0.340 + 0.552 = 0.892$, which is the probability that a unit is OK

Finally, dividing each of the joint probabilities by the marginal probability in the same column gives the revised probabilities, shown in the bottom box. So:

$$0.060/0.108 = 0.556, 0.340/0.892 = 0.381, \text{etc.}$$

These revised probabilities give $P(O/F)$, $P(N/OK)$, and so on:

|  | Faulty | OK |  | Faulty | OK |
|---|---|---|---|---|---|
| Older machine | 0.15 | 0.85 | 0.4 | 0.060 | 0.340 |
| Newer machine | 0.08 | 0.92 | 0.6 | 0.048 | 0.552 |
|  |  |  |  | 0.108 | 0.892 |
| Older machine |  |  |  | 0.556 | 0.381 |
| Newer machine |  |  |  | 0.444 | 0.619 |

Although the description of this procedure may seem a bit strange, if you look at the equation for Bayes' theorem you can see that we are simply repeating the calculations described there. The results of this calculation are illustrated in Figure 12.5.

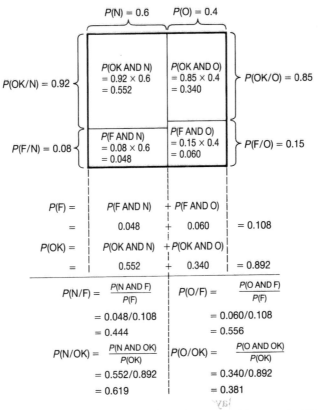

**Figure 12.5** Illustrating the calculation of conditional probabilities.

## WORKED EXAMPLE 12.9

The probabilities of X and Y are 0.3 and 0.7 respectively. There are three events that can follow X and Y, with conditional probabilities given in the following table. Use Bayes' theorem on these figures.

|   | A | B | C |
|---|---|---|---|
| X | 0.1 | 0.5 | 0.4 |
| Y | 0.7 | 0.2 | 0.1 |

### Solution

The table gives the conditional probabilities of $P(A/X)$, $P(B/X)$, etc. We know that the prior probabilities of $P(X) = 0.3$ and $P(Y) = 0.7$. Then the mechanical procedure for Bayes' theorem is shown in the spreadsheet in Figure 12.6.

|   | A | B | C | D | E | F | G | H |
|---|---|---|---|---|---|---|---|---|
| 1 | **Bayes theory** | | | | | | | |
| 2 | | | | | | | | |
| 3 | | **Conditional probabilities** | | | **Priors** | **Joint probabilities** | | |
| 4 | | **A** | **B** | **C** | | **A** | **B** | **C** |
| 5 | **X** | 0.1 | 0.5 | 0.4 | 0.3 | 0.03 | 0.15 | 0.12 |
| 6 | **Y** | 0.7 | 0.2 | 0.1 | 0.7 | 0.49 | 0.14 | 0.07 |
| 7 | | | | | | 0.52 | 0.29 | 0.19 |
| 8 | | | | | **X** | 0.06 | 0.52 | 0.63 |
| 9 | | | | | **Y** | 0.94 | 0.48 | 0.37 |

**Figure 12.6** Calculating conditional probabilities on a spreadsheet.

The marginal probabilities have $P(A) = 0.52$, $P(B) = 0.29$ and $P(C) = 0.19$. The predictions in the bottom boxes show that $P(X/A) = 0.06$, $P(X/B) = 0.52$, and so on.

---

IN SUMMARY

The calculations for Bayes' theorem are quite straightforward but are best done on a spreadsheet or specialized program.

## Probability trees

It is sometimes easier to visualize conditional probabilities on a **probability tree**. These diagrams are drawn from left to right with branches representing a series of possible events. Figure 12.7 shows a probability tree for the previous data for faults on two machines. Each branch represents a possible event, and they emerge from nodes, which are shown as circles. Node 1 is the starting point. From here there are two alternatives for a part:

- it comes from the older machine
- it comes from the newer machine

Then at both nodes 2 and 3 there are two possibilities:

- the part is faulty
- the part is all right

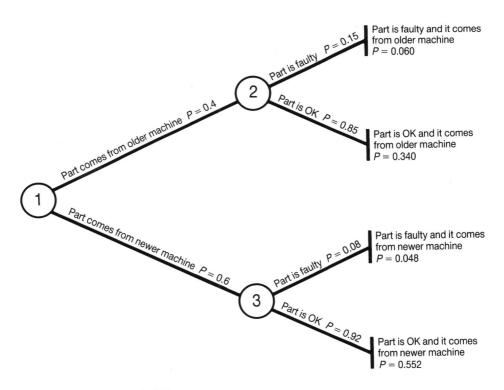

**Figure 12.7**   A probability tree.

Each branch is labelled with its probability, and as we include all possible events, the sum of probabilities on branches leaving any node should be 1. At the right of the tree are the terminal values, which show the probabilities of reaching the terminal points. Terminal values are found by multiplying the probabilities on all branches taken to reach that point. So the first terminal node shows the probability that a part is faulty and that it comes from the older machine, which is $0.4 \times 0.15 = 0.060$. The second terminal node shows the probability that a part is all right and that it comes from the older machine which is $0.4 \times 0.85 = 0.340$. Again, the sum of all terminal values should be 1.

# WORKED EXAMPLE 12.10

Second-hand cars can be classified as either good buys or bad buys. Among good buys, 70% have low oil consumption and 20% have medium oil consumption. Among bad buys, 50% have high oil consumption and 30% have medium oil consumption. A test was done on a second-hand car and showed a low oil consumption. If 60% of second-hand cars are good buys, what is the probability that this car is a good buy?

## Solution

We can start by defining the abbreviations GB and BB for good buy and bad buy; HOC, MOC and LOC for high, medium and low oil consumption. Then we can substitute the known values into the equation for Bayes' theorem. Using the mechanical format we get the following results:

|      | HOC | MOC | LOC |     | HOC  | MOC  | LOC  |
|------|-----|-----|-----|-----|------|------|------|
| GB   | 0.1 | 0.2 | 0.7 | 0.6 | 0.06 | 0.12 | 0.42 |
| BB   | 0.5 | 0.3 | 0.2 | 0.4 | 0.20 | 0.12 | 0.08 |
|      |     |     |     |     | 0.26 | 0.24 | 0.50 |
|      |     |     |     | GB  | 0.23 | 0.5  | 0.84 |
|      |     |     |     | BB  | 0.77 | 0.5  | 0.16 |

From this table, the probability that a car is a good buy, given that it has a low oil consumption, is 0.84. The table also shows that the probability of a low oil consumption is 0.5 (compared with 0.26 for a high oil consumption). The problem is also shown in the probability tree in Figure 12.8.

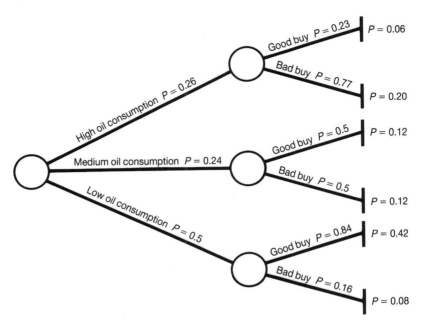

**Figure 12.8** Probability tree for Worked Example 12.10.

Sometimes it is easier to visualize a problem with a probability tree. These represent alternative events by branches.

## Self-assessment questions

**12.7**  What are dependent events?

**12.8**  What are conditional probabilities?

**12.9**  What is Bayes' theorem and when is it used?

**12.10**  What is the benefit of a probability tree?

*CHAPTER REVIEW*

This chapter introduced the ideas of uncertainty and probability. The probability of an event is a measure of its likelihood or relative frequency. The chapter:

● discussed uncertainty and stochastic problems

● defined probabilities and their use

- developed rules for calculating probabilities for independent and mutually exclusive events
- discussed conditional probabilities and calculations using Bayes' theorem
- drew probability trees

The ideas developed in the chapter will be used to build probabilistic models in the following chapters.

# Problems

**12.1**   An office has the following types of employee:

|               | Female | Male |
|---------------|--------|------|
| Administrative | 20     | 21   |
| Managerial     | 12     | 10   |
| Operational    | 42     | 38   |

If one person from the office is selected at random what is the probability that the person is:  (a) a male administrator,  (b) a female manager, (c) male,  (d) an operator,  (e) either a manager or an administrator, (f) either a female administrator or a female manager?

**12.2**   A quality control test has five equally likely outcomes, A, B, C, D and E:
(a) What is the probability of C occurring?
(b) What is the probability of A or B or C occurring?
(c) What is the probability that neither A nor B occurs?

**12.3**   Four mutually exclusive events A, B, C and D have probabilities of 0.1, 0.2, 0.3 and 0.4 respectively. What are the probabilities of: (a)  A and B occurring,  (b) A or B,  (c) neither A nor B,  (d) A and B and C, (e) A or B or C,   (f) none of A, B or C?

**12.4**   If a card is picked from a deck of cards, what is the probability that it is:
(a) an ace,  (b) a heart,   (c) an ace and a heart,   (d) an ace or a heart?

**12.5**   A salesman schedules three calls for a particular day, and each call has a probability of 0.5 of making a sale. What is the probability of making:
(a) 3 sales,   (b) 2 or more sales,   (c) no sales?

**12.6**   There are 20 people in a room. What is the probability that they all have different birthdays?

**12.7**   If $P(a) = 0.4$ and $P(b/a) = 0.3$, what is $P(a$ AND $b)$? If $P(b) = 0.6$, what is $P(a/b)$?

**12.8** The probabilities of two events X and Y are 0.4 and 0.6 respectively. The conditional probabilities of three other events A, B and C occurring, given that X or Y has already occurred, are given in the following table:

|   | A | B | C |
|---|---|---|---|
| X | 0.2 | 0.5 | 0.3 |
| Y | 0.6 | 0.1 | 0.3 |

What are the conditional probabilities of X and Y occurring given that A, B or C has already occurred?

**12.9** A manufacturer uses three suppliers for a component. X supplies 35% of the component, Y supplies 25% and Z supplies the rest. The quality of each component is described as 'good', 'acceptable' or 'poor', with the proportions from each supplier given below:

|   | Good | Acceptable | Poor |
|---|---|---|---|
| X | 0.2 | 0.7 | 0.1 |
| Y | 0.3 | 0.65 | 0.05 |
| Z | 0.1 | 0.8 | 0.1 |

What information can you find using Bayes' theorem on these figures?

**12.10** Draw probability trees for Worked Examples 12.7 and 12.8.

**12.11** Data collected from Cape Town show that 60% of drivers are above 30 years old. Five per cent of all the drivers over 30 will be prosecuted for a driving offence during a year, compared with 10% of drivers 30 or younger. If a driver has been prosecuted, what is the probability they are 30 or younger?

**12.12** A family have two children. If one of these is a girl, what is the probability the other is a boy?

**12.13** It is estimated that 0.5% of the population have a certain type of cancer. A new test for detecting this cancer is said to be 98% accurate. If 10 000 people are tested, how many of them will give a positive response, and how many of these will actually have cancer?

# Computer exercises

**12.1** Figure 12.9 shows the printout from a computer program that does Bayesian analysis. Make sure you understand what is happening here. Use an equivalent program to check the results.

**12.2** Figure 12.10 shows a printout from a spreadsheet that has been used to do a Bayesian analysis. Design a spreadsheet to check these results and improve the format.

BAYESIAN ANALYSIS MODEL

−=＊=−     DATA ENTERED     −=＊=−

NUMBER OF STATES          :   4
NUMBER OF ALTERNATIVES  :   4

PRIOR PROBABILITIES

|   |      |
|---|------|
| 1 | 0.15 |
| 2 | 0.25 |
| 3 | 0.3  |
| 4 | 0.3  |

CONDITIONAL PROBABILITIES

|   | 1 | 2 | 3 | 4 |
|---|------|------|------|------|
| 1 | 0.1000 | 0.4000 | 0.2000 | 0.3000 |
| 2 | 0.2000 | 0.3000 | 0.3000 | 0.2000 |
| 3 | 0.3000 | 0.3000 | 0.4000 | 0.0000 |
| 4 | 0.4000 | 0.3000 | 0.2000 | 0.1000 |

−=＊=−     RESULTS     −=＊=−

PREDICTIONS–JOINT PROBABILITIES

|   | 1 | 2 | 3 | 4 |
|---|------|------|------|------|
| 1 | 0.0150 | 0.0600 | 0.0300 | 0.0450 |
| 2 | 0.0500 | 0.0750 | 0.0750 | 0.0500 |
| 3 | 0.0900 | 0.0900 | 0.1200 | 0.0000 |
| 4 | 0.1200 | 0.0900 | 0.0600 | 0.0300 |

PREDICTIONS – MARGINAL PROBABILITIES

|   |        |
|---|--------|
| 1 | 0.2750 |
| 2 | 0.3150 |
| 3 | 0.2850 |
| 4 | 0.1250 |

PREDICTIONS – REVISED PROBABILITIES

|   | 1 | 2 | 3 | 4 |
|---|------|------|------|------|
| 1 | 0.0545 | 0.1905 | 0.1053 | 0.3600 |
| 2 | 0.1818 | 0.2381 | 0.2632 | 0.4000 |
| 3 | 0.3273 | 0.2857 | 0.4211 | 0.0000 |
| 4 | 0.4364 | 0.2857 | 0.2105 | 0.2400 |

−−−−−−−     END OF ANALYSIS     −−−−−−−

**Figure 12.9**  Computer printout for Bayesian analysis.

**12.3**  How could you improve the presentation of the results in Figure 12.10? Design a spreadsheet that will give a better and more general presentation.

**12.4**  The number of absentees each day from a factory during a typical period has been recorded as follows:

13 16 24 21 15 23 15 26 25 11 10 24 27 30 15 31 25 19 15 27

A new scheme for payments was introduced without any discussion with the workforce, and the numbers of absentees were recorded as follows:

31 29 27 30 26 28 38 34 40 25 29 34 33 30 28 26 41 45 30 28

After some negotiations, a new, agreed incentive scheme was introduced and the numbers of absentees each day were:

09 12 16 08 24 09 15 16 20 21 09 11 10 10 25 17 16 18 09 08

What do you think these figures suggest?

| | A | B | C | D | E | F | G | H |
|---|---|---|---|---|---|---|---|---|
| 1 | **Bayes' theory** | | | | | | | |
| 2 | | | | | | | | |
| 3 | | | Conditional | | Priors | | Joint | |
| 4 | | **A** | **B** | **C** | | **A** | **B** | **C** |
| 5 | **P** | 0.5 | 0.3 | 0.2 | 0.2 | 0.1 | 0.06 | 0.04 |
| 6 | **Q** | 0.3 | 0.4 | 0.3 | 0.3 | 0.09 | 0.12 | 0.09 |
| 7 | **R** | 0.2 | 0.5 | 0.3 | 0.5 | 0.1 | 0.25 | 0.15 |
| 8 | | | | | **Marginal** | 0.29 | 0.43 | 0.28 |
| 9 | | | | | **P** | 0.344 828 | 0.139 535 | 0.142 857 |
| 10 | | | Prediction | | **Q** | 0.310 345 | 0.279 07 | 0.321 429 |
| 11 | | | | | **R** | 0.344 828 | 0.581 395 | 0.535 714 |

**Figure 12.10**   Spreadsheet for Bayes' theorem.

# Case study

## The Gamblers' Press

*The Gamblers' Press* is a weekly paper that publishes large amounts of information that is used by gamblers. Its main contents are detailed sections on horse racing, greyhound racing, football, and other major sporting activities. It also runs regular features on card games, casino games and any other areas that gamblers may find interesting.

*The Gamblers' Press* was founded in 1897 and now has a regular circulation of around 50 000 copies. It is considered a highly respectable paper and has a strict policy of only giving factual information. It never gives tips or advice.

Last year *The Gamblers' Press* decided to run a special feature on misleading or dishonest practices. This idea was suggested when four unconnected reports were passed to the editors.

The first of these reports concerned an 'infallible' way of winning at roulette. Customers were charged $500 for the details of the scheme, which was based on a record of all the numbers that won on the roulette wheel during an evening. Then the customers were advised to bet on two sets of numbers:

- those that had come up more often, because the wheel might be biased in their favour

- those that had come up least often, because the laws of probability say that numbers which appear less frequently on one night, must appear more frequently on another night

The second report showed that a number of illegal chain letters were circulating in Germany. These letters contained a list of eight names. Individuals were asked to send a pound to the name at the top of the list. Then they should delete the name at the top, insert their own name at the bottom, and send a copy of the letter to eight of their friends. As each name moved to the top of the list they would receive payments from people who joined the chain later. The advertising sent with these letters guaranteed to make respondents millionaires, with frequent claims of 'you cannot lose!!!' It also said that people not responding would be letting down their friends and would inevitably be plagued by bad luck.

The third report was from a 'horse racing consultant'. This person sent a letter saying which horse would win a race the following week. A week later he sent a second letter saying that the selected horse had won, and giving another tip for the following week. This was repeated for a third week. Then after three wins the consultant said he would send the name of another horse that was guaranteed to win next week, but this time there would be a cost of £1000. This seemed a reasonable price as the horse was certain to win and gamblers could place bets of any size. Unfortunately, this scheme had a drawback. It was thought that the consultant sent out 10 000 copies of the original letter and randomly tipped each horse in a five-horse race. The second letter was only sent to those people who had been given the winning horse. The next two letters followed the same pattern, with follow-up letters only sent to those who had been given the winning horse.

The fourth report concerned a North American lottery. Here people selected six numbers in the range 00 to 99, and bought a lottery ticket for $1. At the end of a week a computer randomly generated a set of six numbers. Anyone with the same six numbers won several million dollars, and people with four or five matching numbers won smaller prizes. A magazine reported a way of dramatically increasing the chances of winning. This suggested taking your eight favourite numbers and then betting on all possible combinations of six numbers from these eight. The advertisement explained the benefit of this by saying: 'Suppose there is a chance of one in a million of winning the first prize. If one of your lucky numbers is chosen by the computer, you will have this number in over a hundred entries, so your chances of winning are raised by 100 to only one in 10 000'.

*The Gamblers' Press* was aware of many schemes like these four, and they decided to write a major article on them. Your job is to write this article. You should start by explaining why the four schemes mentioned above do not work, and then expand the study to include other examples of this kind of scheme.

# 13 | Probability distributions

Chapter outline                              381
13.1 What are probability                    382
     distributions?
13.2 Combinations and                        384
     permutations
13.3 Binomial distribution                   388
13.4 Poisson distribution                    396

13.5 Normal distribution                     404
Chapter review                               416
Problems                                     416
Computer exercises                           418
Case study: Machined                         420
     components

## CHAPTER OUTLINE

The last chapter introduced the idea of probabilities. In this chapter we are going to extend this by looking at probability distributions. These are a type of relative frequency distribution.

Empirical distributions can be drawn for specific problems, but there are a number of widely used standard distributions. In this chapter we shall describe the binomial, Poisson and Normal distributions.

The binomial distribution calculates the probability of a number of successes in a series of trials. The Poisson distribution finds the probability of a number of successes in a continuous background of failures. Both the binomial and Poisson distributions are used for discrete data.

The Normal distribution is the most widely used probability distribution. It describes continuous data and can be used in many situations.

After reading this chapter and doing the exercises you should be able to:

- understand the purpose of probability distributions
- draw empirical probability distributions from data
- do calculations with combinations and permutations
- understand when and how to use the binomial distribution
- understand when and how to use the Poisson distribution
- understand when and how to use the Normal distribution

# 13.1 | What are probability distributions?

In Chapter 4 we looked at ways of presenting data in diagrams. One useful diagram was a relative frequency distribution, which showed the proportion of observations in different classes. In the last chapter we said that probabilities could be viewed as relative frequencies. Now we are going to combine these two ideas and show how a set of data can be described by a **probability distribution**.

We shall start by building a probability distribution for a set of discrete values. There are three steps in this:

1  list all possible events

2  calculate the probability of each event

3  present these probabilities in a suitable table or diagram

## WORKED EXAMPLE 13.1

Every night a hotel has a number of people who book rooms by telephone, but do not actually turn up. The number of no-shows was recorded over a typical period as follows:

2 4 6 7 1 3 3 5 4 1 2 3 4 3 5 6 2 4 3 2 5 5

0 3 3 2 1 4 4 4 3 1 3 6 3 4 2 5 3 2 4 2 5 3 4

Draw a probability distribution of these data. What is the probability that there are more than four no-shows?

## Solution

Adding the number of nights with various numbers of no-shows gives the following frequency distribution:

| No-shows | 0 | 1 | 2 | 3 | 4 | 5 | 6 | 7 |
|----------|---|---|---|----|----|---|---|---|
| Frequency | 1 | 4 | 8 | 12 | 10 | 6 | 3 | 1 |

If we divide each of the frequencies by the total number of observations (45), we get the following relative frequency or probability distribution:

| No-shows | 0 | 1 | 2 | 3 | 4 | 5 | 6 | 7 |
|----------|------|------|------|------|------|------|------|------|
| Probability | 0.02 | 0.09 | 0.18 | 0.27 | 0.22 | 0.13 | 0.07 | 0.02 |

We can draw a histogram of this probability distribution, as shown in Figure 13.1. Remember that the **area** of each rectangle in this histogram represents the probability, so the total area under the histogram must equal 1. The probability of more than four no-shows is:

$$P(5) + P(6) + P(7) = 0.13 + 0.07 + 0.02 = 0.22$$

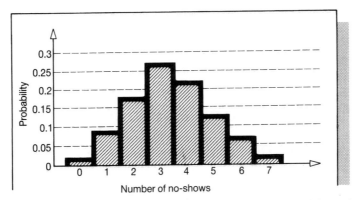

**Figure 13.1** Probability distribution for no-shows in Worked Example 13.1.

The probability distribution drawn above is **empirical**, which means that it came from actual observations. You can use this approach for any problem where observations are made, but the resulting distribution is specific to that particular problem. It has been found, however, that empirical probability distributions often follow standard patterns. In the rest of this chapter we shall look at three of the most common patterns:

- binomial distribution
- Poisson distribution
- Normal (or Gaussian) distribution

The first two describe discrete data, while the Normal distribution describes continuous data.

### IN SUMMARY

A probability distribution is a description of the relative frequency of events or classes of observations. Empirical distributions describe specific situations, but several standard distributions are widely used.

## Self-assessment questions

**13.1**   What is the purpose of a probability distribution?

**13.2**   What is the difference between empirical and *a priori* data?

**13.3**   What is the total area in the histogram of a probability distribution?

# 13.2 | Combinations and permutations

The first of the standard probability distributions is the binomial distribution. But before we talk about this we need to look at some aspects of sequencing. In particular, we must describe combinations and permutations.

Sequencing problems occur when a number of activities can be performed in different orders. Then the order in which activities are taken can affect the overall performance. The time taken for a bus to travel between a suburb and a city centre, for example, depends on the order in which it visits stops; the time taken to process a number of jobs on a machine depends on the order in which the jobs are taken; the number of people needed to work in a restaurant depends on the order in which they are assigned to shifts, days off and holidays.

The objective with a sequencing problem is to examine all the possible orders in which activities can be taken, and select the best. Although this appears simple it is notoriously difficult, primarily because of the large number of possible sequences that have to be considered. If we look at the sequencing of $n$ activities we can choose the first as any one of the $n$. We can choose the second activity as any one of the remaining $(n-1)$, so there are $n(n-1)$ possible sequences for the first two activities. The third activity can be any one of the remaining $(n-2)$, the fourth any of $(n-3)$, and so on. Then the total number of sequences for $n$ activities is:

$$\text{number of sequences} = n(n-1)(n-2)(n-3) \ldots 3 \times 2 \times 1 = n!$$

This means that even a small problem with 15 activities has $15! = 1.3 \times 10^{12}$ possible sequences. Remember that $n!$ (pronounced '$n$ factorial') is an abbreviation for $n(n-1)(n-2) \ldots \times 3 \times 2 \times 1$.

Instead of finding the best sequence of $n$ activities, suppose we only want to find the best sequence of $r$ of the $n$ activities. There are two important calculations for this, which are called **combinations and permutations**.

Suppose we have $n$ things that are distinct (that is, we can tell the difference between them) and we want to choose $r$ of these. In how many ways can this be done? If we are not interested in the order in which the $r$ things are chosen, the answer is the **combination** of $r$ things from $n$, which is written as $^nC_r$:

> The number of ways in which $r$ things can be chosen from
> $n$, regardless of the order of selection, is given by:
>
> $$^nC_r = \frac{n!}{r!(n-r)!}$$

If there is a pool of ten cars, and three customers arrive to use them, there are $^{10}C_3$ ways of allocating cars to customers:

$$^{10}C_3 = \frac{10!}{3! \times (10-3)!} = 120$$

If we have $n$ things that are distinct and want to choose $r$ of these, but this time we are concerned with the order of selection, then we are interested in the **permutation** of $r$ things from $n$, which is written as $^nP_r$:

> The number of ways in which $r$ things can be chosen from
> $n$, when the order of selection is important, is given by:
>
> $$^nP_r = \frac{n!}{(n-r)!}$$

Suppose there are ten applicants for a social club's committee, consisting of a chairman, deputy chairman, secretary and treasurer. We are interested in choosing a group of four from ten, but the order in which they are selected is important (corresponding to the different jobs). Then the number of ways in which we can choose the committee of four is:

$$^nP_r = \frac{n!}{(n-r)!} = \frac{10!}{(10-4)!} = 5040$$

If we want to choose four ordinary committee members (that is, with no different job description and so no importance to the order in which they are chosen), we are interested in the combinations of four from ten. The number of ways of selecting ordinary members is:

$$^nC_r = \frac{n!}{r!(n-r)!} = \frac{10!}{4!(10-4)!} = 210$$

Permutations depend on order of selection and combinations do not, so there are always a lot more permutations than combinations. The number of combinations of four letters of the alphabet is $26!/(4! \times 22!) = 14\,950$. One combination is the letters A, B, C and D, but these can be arranged in 24 different ways (ABCD, ABDC, ACBD, etc.). The number of permutations of four letters from the alphabet is $26!/22! = 358\,800$, which is 4! times the number of combinations.

## WORKED EXAMPLE 13.2

(a) Last summer ALM Holdings had eight applicants to fill eight different jobs. In how many different ways can it assign applicants to jobs?

(b) There is a sudden reorganization in ALM and the number of available jobs falls to six. In how many different ways can the jobs be filled with the eight applicants?

(c) Suppose the reorganization leads to a reclassification of jobs and the six jobs are now identical. In how many different ways can they be filled?

### Solution

(a) This essentially asks, 'How many different sequences of eight things are there?' and the answer is 8!. The applicants can be assigned to jobs in $8! = 40\,320$ different ways.

(b) This asks the number of ways in which six things can be chosen from eight. As the jobs are different we are interested in the order of selection and so the permutation. The number of ways that six different jobs can be filled from eight applicants is:

$$^{n}P_{r} = \frac{n!}{(n-r)!} = \frac{8!}{(8-6)!} = 20\,160$$

(c) This again asks the number of ways in which six things can be chosen from eight, but now the jobs are identical, so the order of selection is not important. The number of ways in which six identical jobs can be filled from eight applicants is:

$$^{n}C_{r} = \frac{n!}{r!(n-r)!} = \frac{8!}{6!(8-6)!} = 28$$

We could look at this last problem from another viewpoint, of finding how many ways two applicants can be rejected from eight. Then with $r = 2$ we have:

$$^{n}C_{r} = \frac{n!}{r!(n-r)!} = \frac{8!}{2!(8-2)!} = 28$$

## WORKED EXAMPLE 13.3

Twelve areas in the North Sea become available for oil exploration, and government policy of encouraging competition limits the allocation of these to at most one area for any exploration company.

(a) If 12 exploration companies bid for the areas, in how many ways can the areas be allocated?

(b) Initial forecasts show that each area is equally likely to produce oil, so they can be considered equally attractive. If 20 exploration companies put in bids for areas, how many ways are there of allocating areas to companies?

(c) A last-minute report shows the probabilities of major oil discoveries in each area. Based on this, four companies withdraw their bid. If the areas are now allocated randomly, in how many ways can this allocation be done?

## Solution

(a) There are 12 companies receiving one area each, so the companies can be sequenced in 12! possible ways, or $4.79 \times 10^8$.

(b) There are 20 companies, only 12 of whom will be selected. As each area is equally attractive, it does not matter in which order the companies are selected, so the number of possible combinations is:

$$^nC_r = \frac{n!}{r!(n-r)!} = \frac{20!}{12!(20-12)!} = 125\,970$$

(c) Now the areas are different, and we are interested in the orders in which the remaining 16 companies can be selected. This is given by:

$$^nP_r = \frac{n!}{(n-r)!} = \frac{16!}{(16-12)!}$$

$$= 8.72 \times 10^{11}$$

---

## IN SUMMARY

- There are $n!$ possible sequences of $n$ different things.
- If the order of selection is **not** important, $r$ things can be selected from $n$ in $^nC_r$ different ways (these are combinations).
- If the order of selection **is** important, $r$ things can be selected from $n$ in $^nP_r$ different ways (these are permutations).

$$^nC_r = \frac{n!}{r!(n-r)!} \quad \text{and} \quad ^nP_r = \frac{n!}{(n-r)!}$$

---

# Self-assessment questions

**13.4** In how many ways can $n$ different activities be sequenced?

**13.5** What is the difference between a permutation and a combination?

**13.6** When selecting $r$ things from $n$ are there more combinations than permutations or vice versa?

# 13.3 | Binomial distribution

Now that we have done the background work, we can return to probability distributions. The first of these is the binomial distribution. This is used when a series of **trials** have the following characteristics:

- each trial has two possible outcomes (conventionally called success and failure)
- the two outcomes are mutually exclusive
- there are constant probabilities of success, $p$, and failure, $q = 1 - p$
- the outcomes of successive trials are independent

Tossing a coin is a standard example of a binomial process. Each toss is a trial; each head, say, is a success with a constant probability of 0.5 and each tail is a failure. Another example of a binomial process occurs when inspecting a batch of a product for defects. Each inspection of a unit is a trial; each fault is a success and each good unit is a failure. Then the binomial distribution gives the probability of any number of faults in the batch. More generally, it considers $n$ trials and finds the probability of $r$ successes. We can find this probability through the following argument.

Suppose the number of trials is $n$, and we want the probability of $r$ successes. In each trial the probability of a success is constant at $p$. Then for independent trials the probability of the first $r$ being successes is $p^r$. Similarly, the probability of the next $n - r$ trials being failures is $q^{n-r}$. Then the probability of the first $r$ trials being successes **and** the next $n - r$ trials being failures is $p^r q^{n-r}$.

But the sequence of $r$ successes followed by $n - r$ failures is only one way of getting $r$ successes in $n$ trials. We must find how many other possible sequences there are. In the last section we found that the number of sequences of $r$ things chosen from a population of $n$, when the order of selection does not matter, is $^nC_r = n!/r!(n - r)!$. There must, therefore, be $^nC_r$ possible sequences of $r$ successes and $n - r$ failures, each with probability $p^r q^{n-r}$. We can find the overall probability of $r$ successes by multiplying the number of sequences with $r$ successes by the probability of each sequence. This gives the probability of $r$ successes in $n$ trials as:

$$P(r \text{ successes in } n \text{ trials}) = {}^nC_r\, p^r q^{n-r}$$

$$= \frac{n!}{r!(n-r)!}\, p^r q^{n-r}$$

This is the calculation for the binomial probability distribution.

## WORKED EXAMPLE 13.4

Jenny Albright knows that in the long term she has a 50% chance of making a sale when calling on a customer. One morning she arranges six calls.

(a) What is the probability of making exactly three sales?

(b) What are the probabilities of making other numbers of sales?

(c) What is the probability of making fewer than three sales?

## Solution

The problem has a binomial process with the probability of success (that is, of making a sale) of $p = 0.5$, the probability of failure (not making a sale) $q = 1 - p = 0.5$, and the number of trials $n = 6$.

(a) The probability of making exactly three sales (so $r = 3$) is:

$$P(r \text{ successes in } n \text{ trials}) = {}^{n}C_{r}\, p^{r} q^{n-r}$$

$$P(3 \text{ successes in 6 trials}) = {}^{6}C_{3} \times 0.5^{3} \times 0.5^{(6-3)}$$

$$= \frac{6!}{3!3!} \times 0.125 \times 0.125 = 0.3125$$

(b) Substituting other values for $r$ (or using standard functions in spreadsheets) gives the values:

| $r$ | 0 | 1 | 2 | 3 | 4 | 5 | 6 |
|---|---|---|---|---|---|---|---|
| $P(r$ successes in 6 trials) | 0.0156 | 0.0938 | 0.2344 | 0.3125 | 0.2344 | 0.0938 | 0.0156 |

Figure 13.2 shows these values in a probability distribution.

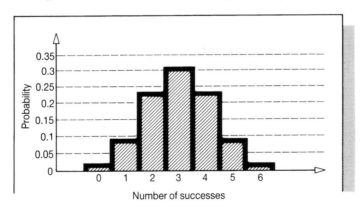

**Figure 13.2**  Probability distribution for binomial process with $n = 6$ and $p = 0.5$.

(c) The probability of making fewer than three sales is the sum of the probabilities of making 0, 1 and 2 sales:

$$P(\text{fewer than 3 sales}) = P(0 \text{ sales}) + P(1 \text{ sale}) + P(2 \text{ sales})$$

$$= 0.0156 + 0.0938 + 0.2344$$

$$= 0.3438$$

The shape of the binomial distribution varies with $p$ and $n$. For small values of $p$, the distribution is asymmetrical and the peak is to the left of centre. As $p$ increases the peak moves to the centre of the distribution, and with $p = 0.5$ the distribution is symmetrical. As $p$ increases further the distribution again becomes asymmetrical but this time the peak is to the right of centre. For larger values of $n$ the distribution is flatter and broader. Some typical binomial distributions are shown in Figure 13.3.

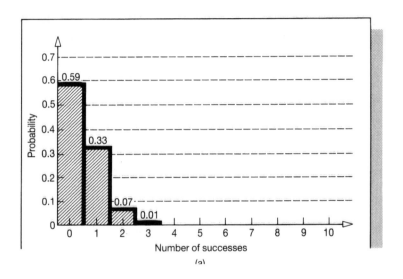

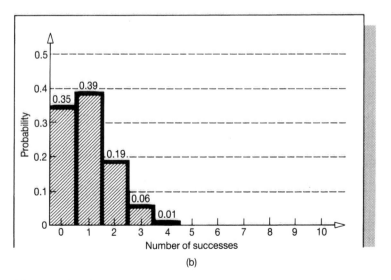

**Figure 13.3**  Typical binomial distributions for varying values of $n$ and $p$: (a) $n = 5, p = 0.1$; (b) $n = 10, p = 0.1$.

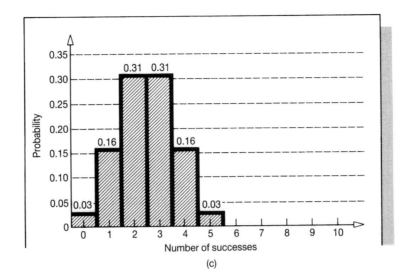

(c)

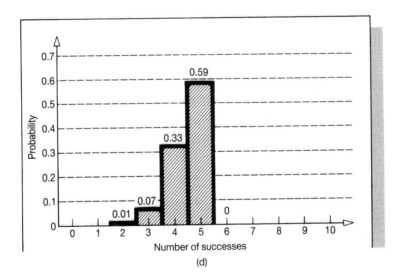

(d)

**Figure 13.3**  Typical binomial distributions for varying values of $n$ and $p$:
(c) $n = 5$, $p = 0.5$; (d) $n = 5$, $p = 0.9$.

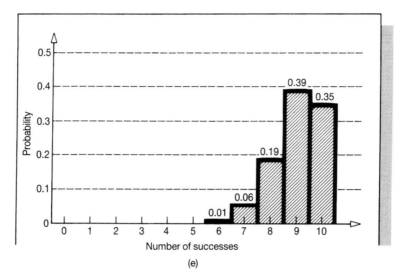

**Figure 13.3** Typical binomial distributions for varying values of *n* and *p*:
(e) *n* = 10, *p* = 0.9.

Whatever the values of *n* and *p*, the mean, variance and standard deviation of a binomial distribution are calculated as follows:

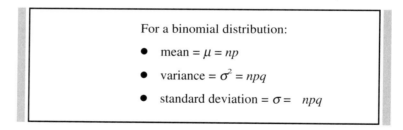

For a binomial distribution:

● mean = $\mu = np$

● variance = $\sigma^2 = npq$

● standard deviation = $\sigma = \sqrt{npq}$

Notice that in these definitions we have used the Greek letter $\mu$ (mu) for the mean rather than $\bar{x}$ and the Greek letter $\sigma$ (sigma) for the standard deviation rather than *s*. This follows a standard notation, where:

● the mean and standard deviation of a sample are called $\bar{x}$ and *s* respectively

● the mean and standard deviation of a population are called $\mu$ and $\sigma$ respectively

The calculations of probabilities with the binomial distribution are straightforward, and standard functions are readily available. Appendix D contains a table of some values which you can use to confirm the results that we found above.

## WORKED EXAMPLE 13.5

A company makes a particularly sensitive electronic component, and 10% of the output is defective. Twenty units of the component are packed into boxes and tested.

(a) Describe the number of defective units in each box.

(b) What is the probability of no defects in a box?

### Solution

(a) This is a binomial process, with success being a faulty unit. In each box $n = 20$ and $p = 0.1$. The mean number of faulty units in a box is:

$$np = 20 \times 0.1 = 2$$

The variance is:

$$npq = 20 \times 0.1 \times 0.9 = 1.8$$

so the standard deviation is:

$$\sqrt{1.8} = 1.34$$

(b) The probability of no defects is:

$$P(0) = 0.9^{20} = 0.12$$

## WORKED EXAMPLE 13.6

Peter Black is a market researcher who has to visit 12 houses in a given area between 7.30 and 9.30 one evening. Previous calls suggest that there will be someone at home in 85% of houses.

(a) Describe the probability distribution of the number of houses with people at home.

(b) What is the probability that Peter will find someone at home in exactly nine houses?

(c) What is the probability that there will be someone at home in exactly seven houses?

(d) What is the probability that there will be someone at home in at least ten houses?

### Solution

(a) The process is binomial, with visiting a house as a trial and finding someone at home a success. Then we have $n = 12$, $p = 0.85$ and $q = 0.15$. Substituting in the standard values gives:

$$\text{mean number of houses with someone at home} = np = 12 \times 0.85 = 10.2$$

$$\text{variance} = npq = 12 \times 0.85 \times 0.15 = 1.53$$

$$\text{standard deviation} = \sqrt{1.53} = 1.24$$

(b) Let $P(9)$ be the probability that there is someone at home in exactly nine houses. Then:

$$P(9) = {}^{12}C_9 \times 0.85^9 \times 0.15^3 = 220 \times 0.231\,617 \times 0.003\,375 = 0.172$$

(c) Similarly:

$$P(7) = {}^{12}C_7 \times 0.85^7 \times 0.15^5 = 792 \times 0.320\,577 \times 0.000\,076 = 0.0193$$

You can check these figures in Appendix D. Values are only given for $p$ up to 0.5, so to use the tables we must redefine 'success' as finding a house with no one at home. Then $p = 0.15$ and $r = 5$. Looking at the entry for $n = 12$, $p = 0.15$ and $r = 3$ (finding nine houses with someone at home is the same as finding three houses with no one at home) confirms the value 0.1720, while $r = 5$ confirms the value 0.0193.

(d) We want:

$$P(\text{at least } 10) = P(10) + P(11) + P(12)$$

If we want to use tables, 'success' must again be defined as finding no one at home. Then:

$$P(\text{at least } 10) = 0.2924 + 0.3012 + 0.1422 = 0.7358$$

---

It is always easier to use a computer to calculate a probability distribution. Figure 13.4 (a) shows a typical result when a statistics package is asked to calculate the binomial probabilities for $n = 20$ and $p = 0.3$. The first command in this Minitab printout asks for the probability distribution function (pdf) and the subcommand specifies the distribution. Figure 13.4 (b) shows the same results in a spreadsheet.

In some circumstances the arithmetic for calculating binomial probabilities becomes difficult, even using computers. In the following situation, $n$ is very large while $p$ is very small. The accounts department of a company sends out 10 000 invoices a month and on average five of these are returned with some error. What is the probability that exactly four invoices will be returned in a given month?

This is a typical application for the binomial distribution, where a trial is sending out an invoice, and a success is having an error. Unfortunately, as soon as we try to do the arithmetic we run into difficulties. Substituting known values gives:

$$n = 10\,000 \qquad r = 4 \qquad p = 5/10\,000 \qquad q = 9995/10\,000$$

so:

$$P(r \text{ returns}) = \frac{n!}{r!(n-r)!}\, p^r q^{n-r}$$

$$= \frac{10\,000!}{4! \times 9996!} \times (5/10\,000)^4 \times (9995/10\,000)^{9996}$$

Although we can do this calculation, it does not seem reasonable to raise figures to the power of 9996 or to contemplate 10 000 factorial. Fortunately, there is an alternative. When $n$, the number of trials, is large and $p$, the probability of success, is small we can approximate the binomial distribution by a Poisson distribution. This is described in the following section.

```
MTB  > pdf;
SUBC > binomial n = 20 p = 0.3.

BINOMIAL WITH N = 20 P = 0.300000

    K              P(X = K)
    0              0.0008
    1              0.0068
    2              0.0278
    3              0.0716
    4              0.1304
    5              0.1789
    6              0.1916
    7              0.1643
    8              0.1144
    9              0.0654
   10              0.0308
   11              0.0120
   12              0.0039
   13              0.0010
   14              0.0002
   15              0.0000

MTB > stop
```

(a)

|    | A | B | C |
|----|---|---|---|
| 1 | **Binomial probabilities** | | |
| 2 | | | |
| 3 | n | 20 | |
| 4 | p | **0.3000** | |
| 5 | | | |
| 6 | r | P[r] | Cum prob |
| 7 | 0 | 0.0008 | 0.0008 |
| 8 | 1 | 0.0068 | 0.0076 |
| 9 | 2 | 0.0278 | 0.0355 |
| 10 | 3 | 0.0716 | 0.1071 |
| 11 | 4 | 0.1304 | 0.2375 |
| 12 | 5 | 0.1789 | 0.4164 |
| 13 | 6 | 0.1916 | 0.6080 |
| 14 | 7 | 0.1643 | 0.7723 |
| 15 | 8 | 0.1144 | 0.8867 |
| 16 | 9 | 0.0654 | 0.9520 |
| 17 | 10 | 0.0308 | 0.9829 |
| 18 | 11 | 0.0120 | 0.9949 |
| 19 | 12 | 0.0039 | 0.9987 |
| 20 | 13 | 0.0010 | 0.9997 |
| 21 | 14 | 0.0002 | 1.0000 |
| 22 | 15 | 0.0000 | 1.0000 |

(b)

**Figure 13.4**  Binomial probabilities from (a) a typical statistics package and (b) a spreadsheet.

IN SUMMARY

The binomial distribution is used when an event has two mutually exclusive outcomes, called success and failure. It calculates the probability of $r$ successes in $n$ trials as:

$$P(r \text{ successes in } n \text{ trials}) = {}^{n}C_{r}\, p^{r} q^{n-r}$$

## Self-assessment questions

**13.7**  In what circumstances can you use a binomial distribution?

**13.8**  Define all the terms in the equation $P(r) = {}^{n}C_{r}\, p^{r} q^{n-r}$

**13.9**  How are the mean, variance and standard deviation of a binomial distribution calculated?

**13.10**  Find, from the tables in Appendix D, the probability of two successes from seven trials, when the probability of success is 0.2.

# | 13.4 || Poisson distribution

The Poisson distribution is a close relative of the binomial distribution and can be used to approximate it when:

- the number of trials, $n$, is large (say, greater than 20)
- the probability of success, $p$, is small (so that $np$ is less than 5)

As $n$ gets larger and $p$ gets smaller the approximation becomes better.

The Poisson distribution is also useful in its own right for solving problems where events occur at random. The number of accidents each month in a factory, the number of defects in a metre of cloth and the number of phone calls received each hour in an office follow Poisson distributions.

The main difference between the binomial and Poisson distributions is that the binomial distribution uses the probabilities of both success and failure, while the Poisson uses only the probability of success. The reason is that the probability of success is very small, so the number of failures is very large: effectively we are looking for a few successes in a continuous background of failures. When looking at the number of spelling mistakes in a long report, the number of faults in a pipeline, or the number of accidents in a month, we are only interested in the number of successes and are not bothered by the large number of events that are failures.

A Poisson distribution is described by the equation:

$$P(r \text{ successes}) = \frac{e^{-\mu} \mu^r}{r!}$$

where:

$$e = \text{exponential constant} = 2.7183$$

$$\mu = \text{mean number of successes}$$

We can show how the Poisson distribution deals with the binomial example we did not finish above. The accounts department of a company sends out 10 000 invoices a month and on average five of these are returned with some error. What is the probability that exactly four invoices will be returned in a given month?

Here $n$ is large and $np = 5$ (fairly high but the result should still be reasonable), so we can use the Poisson approximation to the binomial. The variables are $r = 4$ and $\mu = 5$:

$$P(r \text{ successes}) = \frac{e^{-\mu} \mu^r}{r!}$$

so:

$$P(5 \text{ successes}) = \frac{e^{-5} 5^4}{4!} = \frac{0.0067 \times 625}{24}$$

$$= 0.1755$$

# WORKED EXAMPLE 13.7

On a North Sea oil rig there have been 40 accidents that were serious enough to report in the past 50 weeks. In what proportion of weeks would you expect 0, 1, 2, 3, 4 and more than 4 accidents?

## Solution

A small number of accidents occur, presumably at random, over time. We are not interested in the number of accidents that did **not** occur, so the process follows a Poisson distribution:

$$P(r \text{ successes}) = \frac{e^{-\mu} \mu^r}{r!}$$

The mean number of accidents a week is 40/50 = 0.8, so substituting $\mu = 0.8$ and $r = 0$ gives:

$$P(0) = \frac{e^{-0.8} \times 0.8^0}{0!} = 0.4493$$

Similar substitution of $r = 1$ etc gives:

$$P(1) = \frac{e^{-0.8} \times 0.8^1}{1!} = 0.3595$$

$$P(2) = \frac{e^{-0.8} \times 0.8^2}{2!} = 0.1438$$

$$P(3) = \frac{e^{-0.8} \times 0.8^3}{3!} = 0.0383$$

$$P(4) = \frac{e^{-0.8} \times 0.8^4}{4!} = 0.0077$$

Then:

$$P(>4) = 1 - P(\leq 4)$$
$$= 1 - P(0) - P(1) - P(2) - P(3) - P(4)$$
$$= 1 - 0.4493 - 0.3595 - 0.1438 - 0.0383 - 0.0077$$
$$= 0.0014$$

When events occur at random, we can usually use a Poisson distribution, but strictly speaking there are a number of other requirements. In particular a Poisson process needs:

- events that are independent
- the probability of an event happening in an interval is proportional to the length of the interval
- in theory, an infinite number of events should be possible in an interval

Then:

For a Poisson distribution:

- mean, $\mu = np$
- variance, $\sigma^2 = np$
- standard deviation, $\sigma = \sqrt{np}$

The shape and position of the Poisson distribution are set by the single parameter, $\mu$. For small $\mu$ the distribution is asymmetrical with a peak to the left of centre. As $\mu$ increases, the distribution becomes more symmetrical. This is illustrated for some typical values in Figure 13.5

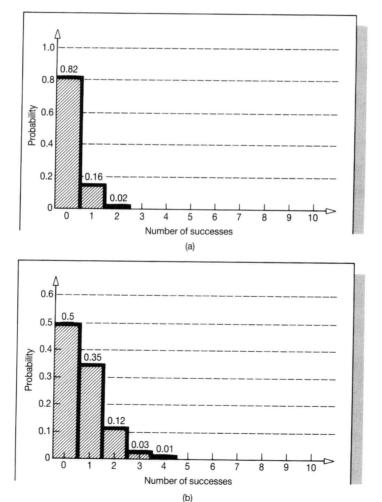

**Figure 13.5** Typical Poisson distribution for varying values of $\mu$: (a) $\mu = 0.2$; (b) $\mu = 0.7$.

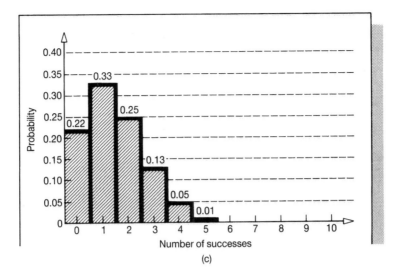

(c)

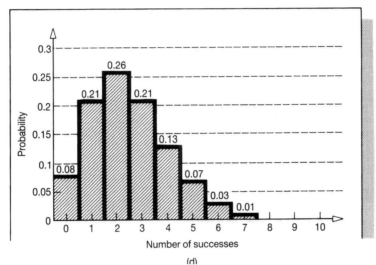

(d)

**Figure 13.5**  Typical Poisson distribution for varying values of $\mu$:
(c) $\mu = 1.5$; (d) $\mu = 2.5$.

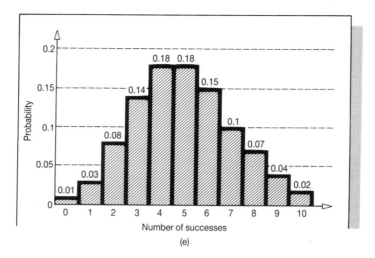

**Figure 13.5** Typical Poisson distribution for varying values of $\mu$: (e) $\mu = 5.0$.

Figure 13.6 shows typical printouts from a statistics package and spreadsheet calculating Poisson probabilities. Standard tables are also available, and you can use the Poisson tables in Appendix E to check the probabilities calculated in this section.

```
MTB  > pdf;
SUBC > poisson mu = 6.

POISSON WITH MEAN = 6.000

    K            P(X = K)
    0            0.0025
    1            0.0149
    2            0.0446
    3            0.0892
    4            0.1339
    5            0.1606
    6            0.1606
    7            0.1377
    8            0.1033
    9            0.0688
   10            0.0413
   11            0.0225
   12            0.0113
   13            0.0052
   14            0.0022
   15            0.0009
   16            0.0003
   17            0.0001
   18            0.0000
MTB > stop

              (a)
```

|    | A | B | C |
|----|---|---|---|
| 1 | **Poisson probabilities** | | |
| 2 | | | |
| 3 | **mean** | **6** | |
| 4 | | | |
| 5 | **k** | **Prob (k)** | **Cum prob** |
| 6 | 0 | 0.0025 | 0.0025 |
| 7 | 1 | 0.0149 | 0.0174 |
| 8 | 2 | 0.0446 | 0.0620 |
| 9 | 3 | 0.0892 | 0.1512 |
| 10 | 4 | 0.1339 | 0.2851 |
| 11 | 5 | 0.1606 | 0.4457 |
| 12 | 6 | 0.1606 | 0.6063 |
| 13 | 7 | 0.1377 | 0.7440 |
| 14 | 8 | 0.1033 | 0.8472 |
| 15 | 9 | 0.0688 | 0.9161 |
| 16 | 10 | 0.0413 | 0.9574 |
| 17 | 11 | 0.0225 | 0.9799 |
| 18 | 12 | 0.0113 | 0.9912 |
| 19 | 13 | 0.0052 | 0.9964 |
| 20 | 14 | 0.0022 | 0.9986 |
| 21 | 15 | 0.0009 | 0.9995 |
| 22 | 16 | 0.0003 | 0.9998 |
| 23 | 17 | 0.0001 | 0.9999 |
| 24 | 18 | 0.0000 | 1.0000 |

(b)

**Figure 13.6** Poisson probabilities from (a) a typical statistics package and (b) a spreadsheet.

# WORKED EXAMPLE 13.8

A Poisson process has a mean of five events in a period of time.

(a) Describe the distribution of events in a period.

(b) What is the probability of two events?

## Solution

(a) In this case the mean number of events, $\mu$, is 5. This is also the variance, and the standard deviation is $\sqrt{5} = 2.236$.

(b) The probability of $r$ events is:

$$P(r) = \frac{e^{-\mu}\mu^r}{r!} \quad \text{so } P(2) = \frac{e^{-5} \times 5^2}{2!} = 0.0842$$

# WORKED EXAMPLE 13.9

Hellier council ran a test to see whether a road junction should be improved. During this test it was found that cars arrive randomly at the intersection at an average rate of five cars every ten minutes.

(a) What is the probability that during a ten-minute period exactly three cars arrive?

(b) What is the probability that more than five cars arrive in a ten-minute period?

## Solution

(a) Random arrivals over time give a Poisson process. The mean number of successes (that is, cars arriving at the junction in ten minutes) is $\mu = 5$. Then we can find the probability of exactly three cars arriving from:

$$P(r) = \frac{e^{-\mu}\mu^r}{r!} \quad \text{so} \quad P(3) = \frac{e^{-5} \times 5^3}{3!} = 0.1404$$

You can check this value in the tables in Appendix E. Looking up the value for $\mu = 5$ and $r = 3$ also gives 0.1404.

(b) To find the probability that more than five cars arrive at the junction in a ten-minute period we need to calculate:

$$P(>5) = 1 - P(5 \text{ or less})$$
$$= 1 - P(0) - P(1) - P(2) - P(3) - P(4) - P(5)$$

We can either calculate these values or look them up in tables to give:

$$P(>5) = 1 - 0.0067 - 0.0337 - 0.0842 - 0.1404 - 0.1755 - 0.1755$$

$$= 0.384$$

The probability distribution for this problem is shown in Figure 13.7.

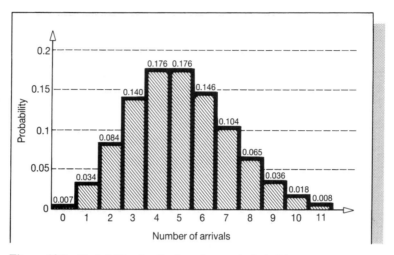

**Figure 13.7**   Probability distribution of car arrivals in Worked Example 13.9.

# WORKED EXAMPLE 13.10

Last year LMP Industries bought a network of oil pipelines in Eastern Europe. LMP knew the network was not in good condition, and they were told that 40% of the oil pumping stations along an important section had faults, and there was an average of one fault in the pipeline every 10 km. If there are 20 pumping stations along the 50 km of pipeline, how many faults should LMP expect in this part of the system?

## Solution

You can look at this problem in two parts. Firstly there are the faults in pumping stations, and secondly there are the faults along the actual pipeline.

Faults in the pumping station follow a binomial distribution – they are either faulty or not faulty. Then the number of trials is the number of stations along the length of pipeline, which gives $n = 20$. The probability of success (which is a faulty station) $p = 0.4$ and the probability of failure (which is no fault in the station) $q = 0.6$. So the mean number of faults in the pumping stations = $np = 20 \times 0.4 = 8$.

Assuming faults along the pipeline are random, they follow a Poisson distribution. So the mean number of successes is 0.1, which is the average number of faults in a kilometre of pipeline. In 50 km the mean number of faults is $50 \times 0.1 = 5$.

This means that LMP should expect an average of 13 faults in this part of the system – eight in the pumping stations and five in the pipeline. But we can calculate some more probabilities, as shown in the spreadsheet of Figure 13.8. With these figures LMP can do some more detailed analyses of likely faults and costs.

| | A | B | C | D | E |
|---|---|---|---|---|---|
| 1 | **Pipeline faults** | | | | |
| 2 | | | | | |
| 3 | **Pumping stations** | | | | **Pipeline** |
| 4 | | | | | |
| 5 | **Mean faults** | 8.00 | | **Mean faults** | 5.00 |
| 6 | **Stand dev** | 2.19 | | **Stand dev** | 2.24 |
| 7 | | | | | |
| 8 | **Faults** | **Probability** | | **Faults** | **Probability** |
| 9 | 0 | 0.0000 | | 0 | 0.0067 |
| 10 | 1 | 0.0005 | | 1 | 0.0337 |
| 11 | 2 | 0.0031 | | 2 | 0.0842 |
| 12 | 3 | 0.0123 | | 3 | 0.1404 |
| 13 | 4 | 0.0350 | | 4 | 0.1755 |
| 14 | 5 | 0.0746 | | 5 | 0.1755 |
| 15 | 6 | 0.1244 | | 6 | 0.1462 |
| 16 | 7 | 0.1659 | | 7 | 0.1044 |
| 17 | 8 | 0.1797 | | 8 | 0.0653 |
| 18 | 9 | 0.1597 | | 9 | 0.0363 |
| 19 | 10 | 0.1171 | | 10 | 0.0181 |
| 20 | 11 | 0.0710 | | 11 | 0.0082 |
| 21 | 12 | 0.0355 | | 12 | 0.0034 |
| 22 | 13 | 0.0146 | | 13 | 0.0013 |
| 23 | 14 | 0.0049 | | 14 | 0.0005 |
| 24 | 15 | 0.0013 | | 15 | 0.0002 |
| 25 | 16 | 0.0003 | | 16 | 0.0000 |

**Figure 13.8**   Calculations for faults in pipeline.

Sometimes it is difficult to use a Poisson distribution. This happens particularly when $p$ is high and $r$ is large. Consider the following example. A motor insurance policy is only sold to drivers with low risk of accidents. One hundred drivers holding the policy in a certain area expect an average of 0.2 accidents each a year. What is the probability that less than 15 drivers have accidents in one year?

You will recognize this as a binomial process with mean $= np = 100 \times 0.2 = 20$. So the probability that exactly $r$ drivers have accidents in the year is:

$$^{20}C_r \times 0.2^r \times 0.8^{100-r}$$

We can find the probability that less than 15 drivers will have accidents in the year by adding this calculation for all values of $r$ from 0 to 14:

$$\sum_{r=0}^{14} (^{20}C_r \times 0.2^r \times 0.8^{100-r})$$

This is a messy calculation, so we should look for a Poisson approximation. Unfortunately $np$ (= $100 \times 0.2$) = 20, which does not meet the requirement that $np$ be less than 5. We need to look for another approach, and this time we shall use the most common probability distribution of all. When $n$ is large and $np$ is greater than 5 the binomial distribution can be approximated by the Normal distribution. This is described in the following section.

---

### IN SUMMARY

The Poisson distribution can be used as an approximation to the binomial distribution when the probability of success is small. It can also be used to describe infrequent, random events:

$$P(r \text{ successes}) = \frac{e^{-\mu} \mu^r}{r!}$$

---

## Self-assessment questions

**13.11** In what circumstances can a Poisson distribution be used?

**13.12** How are the mean and variance of a Poisson distribution calculated?

**13.13** The average number of defects per square yard of material is 0.8. Use the tables in Appendix E to find the probability that a square yard has exactly two defects.

**13.14** In what circumstances can a Poisson distribution be used as an approximation for a binomial distribution?

# 13.5 | Normal distribution

Both the binomial and Poisson distributions are used with discrete data. Often, though, we want a probability distribution to describe continuous data. Although these two are very similar in principle, there is one fundamental difference. With discrete probabilities we can find the probability of, say, five successes in ten trials. But with continuous data we cannot find the probability that, say, a person weighs exactly 80.456 456 456 kg. If the measurement is made precise enough, the probability of this happening will always be zero. What we really need is the probability that a person weighs, say, between 80.4 kg and 80.5 kg. So continuous probability distributions find the probability that a value is within a specified range.

There are several distributions for continuous data, including the most widely used distribution of all. The **Normal distribution** (sometimes called Gaussian) is a bell-shaped curve that is used in a wide variety of circumstances. Many natural phenomena, such as the heights of trees, harvest from an acre of land, weight of horses and daily temperature, follow this distribution. It also describes many business functions, such as daily takings in a shop, number of customers a week, number of employees in particular types of industry, and production in a factory. The distribution is so common that we can certainly defend the rule of thumb 'For large numbers of observations use the Normal distribution'.

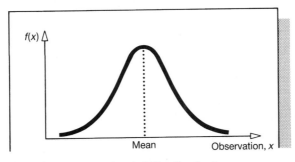

**Figure 13.9**   Normal probability distribution.

The Normal distribution is illustrated in Figure 13.9 and has the following properties:

> The Normal distribution:
>
> - is continuous
>
> - is symmetrical about the mean value, $\mu$
>
> - has mean, median and mode all equal
>
> - has the total area under the curve equal to 1
>
> - in theory, the curve extends to plus and minus infinity on the $x$ axis.

The equation for the Normal distribution is rather complicated but you do not have to worry about this, as it is hardly ever used. With continuous data the height of the curve at any specific point does not have much meaning, and probabilities are calculated from the area under the curve.

Suppose a factory makes boxes of chocolates with a mean weight of 1000 g. There will be small variations in the weight of each box, and if a large number of boxes are made the weights will follow a Normal distribution. Managers in the factory will not be interested in the number of boxes that weigh, say, exactly 1005.0000 g, but they may be interested in the number of boxes that weigh more than 1005 g. This is represented by the area under the right-hand tail of the distribution, as shown in Figure 13.10.

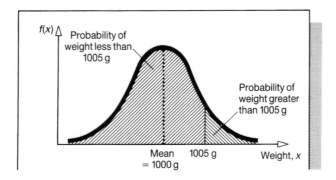

**Figure 13.10**  Distribution of weights of chocolate boxes.

There are two reasonable ways of finding the area under the tail of the distribution. We can:

- look up values in standard tables
- get a computer to do the calculation

Normal distribution tables are based on a value, Z, which is calculated from the mean of a distribution and its standard deviation. To be precise, Z is the number of standard deviations a point is away from the mean, and Normal tables show the probability of a value greater than this. With the boxes of chocolates mentioned above, the mean weight is 1000 g, and we shall assume that the standard deviation is 3 g. To find the probability that a box has a weight greater than 1005 g, we need the area in the tail of the probability distribution, as shown in Figure 13.10. To find this we calculate the number of standard deviations that the point of interest (1005 g) is away from the mean, and tables give the corresponding probability:

$$Z = \text{number of standard deviations from the mean}$$

$$= \frac{\text{value} - \text{mean}}{\text{standard deviation}} = \frac{x - \mu}{\sigma}$$

$$= \frac{1005 - 1000}{3}$$

$$= 1.67$$

Appendix F gives a table of areas under the Normal curve, and looking up 1.67 in these gives a value of 0.0475. This is the probability that a box will weigh more than 1005 g.

Tables of Normal curves have slight differences, so you must be careful when using them. The tables given in Appendix F show the area under the tail of the distribution.

Because the Normal distribution curve is symmetrical about the mean, we can do some other calculations. For example, the probability that a box of chocolates weighs less than 995 g is the same as the probability that it weighs more than 1005 g and has been calculated as 0.0475 (as shown in Figure 13.11).

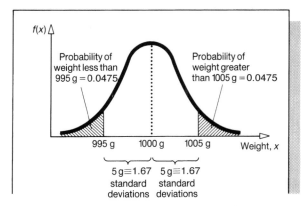

**Figure 13.11** Symmetrical distribution of weights of chocolate boxes.

The two factors that affect the position and shape of the Normal curve are the mean and the standard deviation. The distribution is always symmetrical, so these only affect its height and position. The larger the standard deviation the greater is the spread, while the mean sets the position of the distribution on the $x$ axis (as illustrated in Figure 13.12).

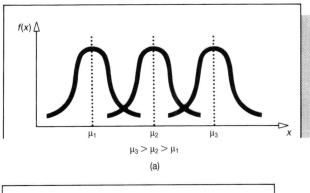

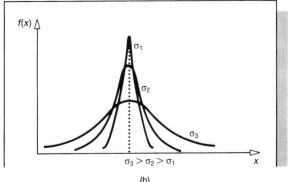

**Figure 13.12** Differences in mean and standard deviation for Normal distributions:
    (a) Normal distributions with same standard deviations but different means;
    (b) Normal distributions with same means but different standard deviations.

In a Normal distribution, about 68% of observations are within one standard deviation of the mean, 95% are within two standard deviations and 99.7% are within three standard deviations (see Figure 13.13).

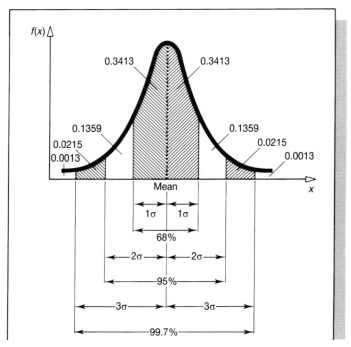

**Figure 13.13**   Areas under the Normal distribution.

## WORKED EXAMPLE 13.11

Figures kept by McClure and Hanover Auctioneers, for the past five years, show that the weight of beef cattle brought to their market has a mean of 950 kg and a standard deviation of 150 kg. What proportion of these have weights:

(a) more than 1250 kg

(b) less than 850 kg

(c) between 1100 kg and 1250 kg

(d) between 800 kg and 1300 kg?

### Solution

In this example there are presumably a large number of cattle brought to market, so we can assume a Normal distribution with $\mu = 950$ and $\sigma = 150$.

(a) The probability of weight greater than 1250 kg is found as follows:

$$Z = \text{number of standard deviations from the mean}$$

$$= \frac{1250 - 950}{150}$$

$$= 2.0$$

Looking this up in the Normal tables in Appendix F gives a value of 0.0228, which is the required probability (see Figure 13.14).

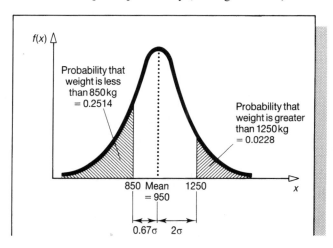

**Figure 13.14**   Calculations for Worked Example 13.11.

(b) The probability of weight less than 850 kg is found in the same way:

$$Z = \frac{850 - 950}{150}$$

$$= -0.67$$

The table only shows positive values, but as the distribution is symmetrical we can use the value for +0.67, which is 0.2514. This is the area under the tail of the curve and is the required probability.

Because the tables only show probabilities under the tail of the distribution, we often need to do some juggling of the values. There are several different ways of doing the following calculations, all of which give the same results.

(c) The calculation that the weight is between 1100 kg and 1250 kg relies on the relationship (see Figure 13.15):

$$P(\text{between } 1100 \text{ kg and } 1250 \text{ kg})$$

$$= P(\text{greater than } 1100 \text{ kg}) - P(\text{greater than } 1250 \text{ kg})$$

For weight above 1100 kg:

$$Z = \frac{1100 - 950}{150} = 1 \quad \text{probability} = 0.1587$$

For weight above 1250 kg:

$$Z = \frac{1250 - 950}{150} = 2 \quad \text{probability} = 0.0228$$

So the probability that the weight is between these two is:

$$0.1587 - 0.0228 = 0.1359.$$

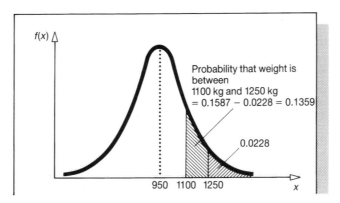

**Figure 13.15** Calculations for Worked Example 13.11.

(d) The calculation that the weight is between 800 kg and 1300 kg relies on the relationship (see Figure 13.16):

$$P(\text{between 800 kg and 1300 kg})$$

$$= 1 - P(\text{less than 800 kg}) - P(\text{greater than 1300 kg})$$

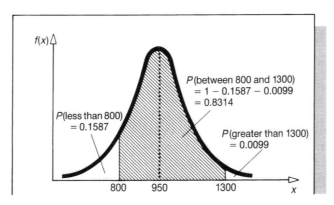

**Figure 13.16** Calculations for Worked Example 13.11.

For weight below 800 kg:

$$Z = \frac{800 - 950}{150} = -1 \quad \text{probability} = 0.1587$$

For weight above 1300 kg:

$$Z = \frac{1300 - 950}{150} = 2.33 \quad \text{probability} = 0.0099$$

So the probability that the weight is between these two is:

$$1 - 0.1587 - 0.0099 = 0.8314$$

# WORKED EXAMPLE 13.12

We could not use the Poisson distribution for the example of motor insurance described above, where a policy is only sold to drivers with low risk of accidents. One hundred drivers holding the insurance policy in a certain area expect an average of 0.2 accidents each a year. Use a Normal distribution to find the probability that less than 15 drivers will have accidents in a year. How could you take into account the integer number of accidents?

## Solution

This is a binomial process with $n = 100$ and $p = 0.2$, so the mean $= np = 100 \times 0.2 = 20$. The standard deviation of a binomial distribution is $\sqrt{npq} = \sqrt{16} = 4$. We cannot use a Poisson approximation for the binomial, but we can use a Normal approximation. Then to find the probability of less than 15 drivers having an accident:

$$Z = \frac{15 - 20}{4} = -1.25$$

and this gives a probability $= 0.1056$

Because the number of accidents is discrete, a 'continuity correction' is sometimes used. We are looking for the probability of less than 15 accidents but it is clearly impossible to have **between** 14 and 15 accidents. We can add an allowance to interpret 'less than 15' as 'less than 14.5' (Figure 13.17).

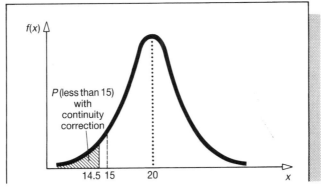

**Figure 13.17**   Normal distribution with continuity correction for Worked Example 13.12.

This continuity correction for integer values then gives:

$$Z = \frac{14.5 - 20}{4} = -1.375 \quad \text{probability} = 0.0846$$

If the question had asked for '15 or less' accidents the continuity correction might have been applied to interpret this as 'less than 15.5'. Then:

$$Z = \frac{15.5 - 20}{4} = -1.125 \quad \text{probability} = 0.1303$$

# WORKED EXAMPLE 13.13

A manufacturer of electric cable finds an average of 20 faults in a week's production. What is the probability of more than 30 faults in a week?

## Solution

As this problem looks at random events over time, it is a Poisson process. But the calculations for the Poisson distribution are somewhat tedious, as shown in Figure 13.18. Here a spreadsheet calculated the cumulative probabilities of up to 30 faults a week as 0.9865. So the probability of more than 30 faults is $1 - 0.9865 = 0.0135$.

|  | A | B | C | D | E | F | G | H |
|---|---|---|---|---|---|---|---|---|
| 1 | **Poisson probabilities** | | | | | | | |
| 2 | | | | | | | | |
| 3 | **r** | **Cum prob** | | **r** | **Cum prob** | | **r** | **Cum prob** |
| 4 | 0 | 2.06E–08 | | | | | | |
| 5 | 1 | 4.33E–07 | | 11 | 0.0214 | | 21 | 0.6437 |
| 6 | 2 | 4.56E–06 | | 12 | 0.0390 | | 22 | 0.7206 |
| 7 | 3 | 3.20E–05 | | 13 | 0.0661 | | 23 | 0.7875 |
| 8 | 4 | 1.69E–04 | | 14 | 0.1049 | | 24 | 0.8432 |
| 9 | 5 | 7.19E–04 | | 15 | 0.1565 | | 25 | 0.8878 |
| 10 | 6 | 2.55E–03 | | 16 | 0.2211 | | 26 | 0.9221 |
| 11 | 7 | 7.79E–03 | | 17 | 0.2970 | | 27 | 0.9475 |
| 12 | 8 | 2.09E–02 | | 18 | 0.3814 | | 28 | 0.9657 |
| 13 | 9 | 5.00E–02 | | 19 | 0.4703 | | 29 | 0.9782 |
| 14 | 10 | 1.08E–01 | | 20 | 0.5591 | | 30 | 0.9865 |

**Figure 13.18** Cumulative probabilities for Worked Example 13.13.

In these circumstances it is much easier to use a Normal approximation. We know that for the Poisson distribution:

$$\mu = 20 = \text{variance}$$

so:

$$\sigma = \sqrt{20} = 4.47$$

We shall use a continuity correction and interpret 'more than 30 faults' as '30.5 and more'.

Then:

$$Z = \frac{x - \mu}{\sigma} = \frac{30.5 - 20}{4.47} = 2.35$$

Looking this up in Normal tables gives:

probability = 0.0094

You may think that the approximation 0.0094 is not very close to the actual value of 0.0135. The difference is because the numbers we are dealing with are not really big enough for the Normal distribution to work properly. Even so, the difference is quite small, and amounts to a probability of only 0.0041 – or four chances in a thousand.

# WORKED EXAMPLE 13.14

On average a supermarket sells 500 pints of milk a day with a standard deviation of 50 pints.

(a) If the supermarket has 600 pints in stock at the beginning of a day, what is the probability that it will sell out of milk?

(b) What is the probability that demand is between 450 and 600 pints in a day?

(c) How many pints should the supermarket stock if it wants the probability of running out to be 0.05?

(d) How many should it stock if it wants the probability of running out to be 0.01?

## Solution

(a) The probability of running out of stock with 600 pints (see Figure 13.19) is:

$$Z = \frac{600 - 500}{50} = 2.0 \quad \text{probability} = 0.0228$$

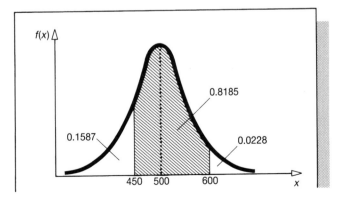

**Figure 13.19** Probabilities for Worked Example 13.14.

(b) The probability of demand greater than 600 is 0.0228. The probability of demand less than 450 pints is:

$$Z = \frac{450 - 500}{50} = -1.0 \quad \text{probability} = 0.1587$$

Then the probability of demand between 450 and 600 is:

$$1 - 0.0228 - 0.1587 = 0.8185$$

(c) For this problem we know the probability and want to find how far away from the mean this is. For probability = 0.05, $Z = 1.645$ (look up 0.05 in the body of the table and this is midway between 1.64 and 1.65). So the point we are interested in is 1.645 standard deviations away from the mean. 1.645 standard deviations is $1.645 \times 50 = 82.25$ pints from the mean. Therefore, the supermarket needs $500 + 83 = 583$ pints at the beginning of the day (rounding up to make sure there is a maximum probability of stockouts of 0.05).

(d) For probability 0.01, $Z = 2.33$. This is $2.33 \times 50 = 116.5$ pints from the mean. Therefore, the supermarket needs $500 + 117 = 617$ pints at the beginning of the day (see Figure 13.20).

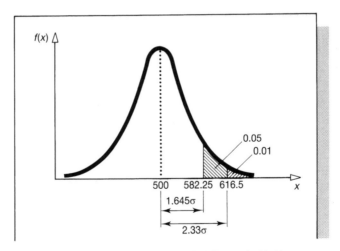

**Figure 13.20**  Calculations for Worked Example 13.14.

Of course, we could have done these calculations on a computer. Figure 13.21 shows the calculations done using a spreadsheet. This also lists the commands – in this case using the standard functions NORMDIST and NORMINV which come with Excel.

| | A | B | C | D | E | F |
|---|---|---|---|---|---|---|
| 1 | **Normal probabilities** | | | | | |
| 2 | | | | | | |
| 3 | **Mean** | 500 | | | | |
| 4 | **Stand dev** | 50 | | | | |
| 5 | | | | | | |
| 6 | a) Prob | > 600 | | 0.0228 | | =1-NORMDIST(600,$B$3,$B$4,1) |
| 7 | | | | | | |
| 8 | b) Prob | 450 to 600 | | 0.8185 | | =NORMDIST(600,$B$3,$B$4,1)-<br>NORMDIST(450,$B$3,$B$4,1) |
| 9 | | | | | | |
| 10 | c) Number | 0.05 | | 582.243 | | =NORMINV(1-$B$10,$B$3,$B$4) |
| 11 | | | | | | |
| 12 | d) Number | 0.01 | | 616.317 | | =NORMINV(1-$B$12,$B$3,$B$4) |

**Figure 13.21**  Using a spreadsheet for calculations with the Normal distribution.

---

## IN SUMMARY

Large numbers of observations often follow a Normal probability distribution. This is a continuous distribution, which gives the probability of observations being within given ranges. These probabilities are found from standard tables or computers.

---

# Self-assessment questions

**13.15**  In what circumstances can you use a Normal distribution?

**13.16**  What is the most obvious difference between a Normal distribution and a binomial or Poisson distribution?

**13.17**  What two factors affect the location and shape of a Normal distribution?

**13.18**  In what circumstances can a Normal distribution be used as an approximation to a binomial distribution?

**13.19**  If the mean of a set of observations is 100 and the standard deviation is 10, what proportion of observations will be between 90 and 110?

**13.20**  What is a 'continuity correction' for discrete data?

This chapter has described the use of probability distributions. Empirical distributions can be found for particular problems, but a number of standard probability distributions can be used in many situations. These were illustrated by the binomial, Poisson and Normal distributions. In particular the chapter:

● discussed probability distributions in terms of relative frequencies

● discussed sequencing by reference to combinations and permutations

● described the binomial distribution for trials that end in either success or failure

● described the Poisson distribution for random occurrences

● described the Normal distribution for a large number of observations

The ideas developed here will be used to build probabilistic models in the following chapters.

# Problems

**13.1** Find the probability distribution of the following set of observations:

10 14 13 15 16 12 14 15 11 13 17 15 16 14 12 13 11 15 15 14

12 16 14 13 13 14 13 12 14 15 16 14 11 14 12 15 14 16 13 14

**13.2** A company calculates its likely profit for next year with the following probabilities:

| Profit | – 100 000 | – 50 000 | 0 | 50 000 | 100 000 | 150 000 |
|---|---|---|---|---|---|---|
| Probability | 0.05 | 0.15 | 0.3 | 0.3 | 0.15 | 0.05 |

What is the probability that the company will make a profit next year? What is the probability that the profit will be at least 100 000?

**13.3** Find the value of $^nC_r$ and $^nP_r$ when (a) $r = 5$ and $n = 15$, (b) $r = 2$ and $n = 10$, (c) $r = 8$ and $n = 10$.

**13.4** An open-plan office has ten desks. If ten clerks work in the area, how many different seating arrangements are there? If two clerks leave, how many seating arrangements are there?

**13.5** A salesman wants to visit 12 customers. In how many different ways can he visit them? One day the salesman is only able to visit eight customers. In how many different ways can he choose the eight? As the salesman has to travel between customers, the order in which his visits are scheduled is important. How many different schedules are there for eight customers?

**13.6** A binomial process has a probability of success of 0.15. If eight trials are run, what is the mean number of successes and the standard deviation? What is the probability of: (a) two successes, (b) seven successes, (c) at least six successes?

**13.7** In a town, 60% of families are known to drive British cars. If a sample of ten families is chosen, what is the probability that at least eight will drive British cars? If a sample of 1000 families is chosen, what is the probability that at least 800 will drive British cars?

**13.8** Norfisk Oil is drilling some exploratory wells on the mainland of Norway. The results are described as either a dry well or a producer well. Past experience suggests that 10% of such exploratory wells can be classified as producer wells. If 12 wells are drilled, what is the probability that all 12 wells will be producer wells? What is the probability that all 12 wells will be dry wells? What is the probability that exactly one well will be a producer? What is the probability that at least three wells will be producers?

**13.9** One hundred trials are run for a Poisson process. If the probability of a success is 0.02, what is the mean number of successes and the standard deviation? What is the probability of: (a) exactly two successes, (b) exactly seven successes, (c) at least six successes?

**13.10** During a typical hour an office receives 13 phone calls. What is the expected number of calls in a five-minute period?

**13.11** During a busy period at an airport, planes arrive at an average rate of ten an hour. What is the probability that 15 or more planes will arrive in an hour?

**13.12** A machine makes a product, with 5% of units having faults. If a sample of 20 units is taken, what is the probability that at least one is defective? If a sample of 200 units is taken, what is the probability that at least ten are defective?

**13.13** Some observations follow a Normal distribution with mean 40 and standard deviation 4. What proportion of observations have values: (a) greater than 46, (b) less than 34, (c) between 34 and 46, (d) between 30 and 44, (e) between 43 and 47?

**13.14** A large number of observations have a mean of 120 and variance of 100. What proportion of observations is: (a) below 100, (b) above 130, (c) between 100 and 130, (d) between 130 and 140, (e) between 115 and 135?

**13.15** Cath's Cafe & Burger Bar finds that the number of meals it serves in a week is Normally distributed with a mean of 6000 and a standard deviation of 600.

(a) What is the probability that in a given week the number of meals served is less than 5000?

(b) What is the probability that more than 7500 are served?

(c) What is the probability that between 5500 and 6500 are served?

(d) There is a 90% chance that the number of meals served in a week exceeds what value?

**13.16** A service consists of two parts. The first part takes an average of 10 minutes with a standard deviation of 2 minutes. The second part takes an average of 5 minutes with a standard deviation of 1 minute. Describe how long it will take to complete the service. What is the probability that a customer can be served in less than 12 minutes? What is the probability that a customer will take more than 20 minutes?

# Computer exercises

**13.1** Figure 13.22 shows the printout from a statistical package. In this printout the probability distribution function is found for a binomial and Poisson distribution. Then 100 random points are taken from a Poisson distribution with a mean of 6 and are plotted and described. Make sure you can understand what is happening in this printout. Use another package to check the results.

**13.2** Use a spreadsheet to compile your own set of binomial probabilities.

**13.3** Use a spreadsheet to compile your own set of Poisson probabilities.

**13.4** Plane, bus and train timetables show expected arrival times. Choose a convenient service and collect data to show how actual arrival times compare with expected times. Write a report about your results, including analyses and diagrams.

**13.5** The number of people visiting a shop each working hour for the past week has been recorded as follows:

12 23 45 09 16 74 58 21 31 07 26 22 14 24 50
23 30 35 68 47 17 08 54 11 24 33 55 16 57 27
02 97 54 23 61 82 15 34 46 44 37 26 28 21 07
64 38 71 79 18 24 16 10 60 50 55 34 44 42 47

Use a package to analyse these figures. What conclusions can you draw? Write a report about your findings.

**13.6** Different countries within the European Union report different levels of telephone ownership and use. How could you use frequency distributions to show the likely effects on e-commerce?.

```
COMMAND      > pdf;
SUBCOMMAND > binomial n = 15 p = 0.3.
```

BINOMIAL WITH N = 15  P = 0.300000

| K | P(X = K) |
|---|----------|
| 0 | 0.0047 |
| 1 | 0.0305 |
| 2 | 0.0916 |
| 3 | 0.1700 |
| 4 | 0.2186 |
| 5 | 0.2061 |
| 6 | 0.1472 |
| 7 | 0.0811 |
| 8 | 0.0348 |
| 9 | 0.0116 |
| 10 | 0.0030 |
| 11 | 0.0006 |
| 12 | 0.0001 |
| 13 | 0.0000 |

```
COMMAND      > pdf;
SUBCOMMAND > Poisson mu = 4.
```

POISSON WITH MEAN = 4.000

| K | P(X = K) |
|---|----------|
| 0 | 0.0183 |
| 1 | 0.0733 |
| 2 | 0.1465 |
| 3 | 0.1954 |
| 4 | 0.1954 |
| 5 | 0.1563 |
| 6 | 0.1042 |
| 7 | 0.0595 |
| 8 | 0.0298 |
| 9 | 0.0132 |
| 10 | 0.0053 |
| 11 | 0.0019 |
| 12 | 0.0006 |
| 13 | 0.0002 |
| 14 | 0.0001 |
| 15 | 0.0000 |

```
COMMAND      > random 100 cl;
SUBCOMMAND > poisson mu = 6.
COMMAND      > dotplot cl
```

```
COMMAND > describe cl
```

| | N | MEAN | MEDIAN | TRMEAN | STDEV | SEMEAN |
|---|---|------|--------|--------|-------|--------|
| Cl | 100 | 5.990 | 6.000 | 5.967 | 2.423 | 0.242 |

| | MIN | MAX | Q1 | Q3 |
|---|-----|-----|-----|-----|
| Cl | 1.000 | 13.000 | 4.000 | 8.000 |

**Figure 13.22**  Sample printout from a statistical package.

# Case study

## Machined components

The operations manager was speaking calmly to the marketing manager: 'I said it usually takes 70 days to make a batch of these components. We have to buy parts and materials, make sub-assemblies, set up machines, schedule operations, make sure everything is ready to start production, then actually make the components, check them and shift them to the finished goods stores, and so on. Actually making the components involves 187 distinct steps taking a total of 20 days. The whole process usually takes 70 days, but there is a lot of variability. This batch you are shouting about is going to take about 95 days because we were busy working on other jobs, and an important machine broke down so we had to wait for parts to be flown in from Tokyo and that took another five days, and so on. It is your fault: you heard my estimate and then assumed I was exaggerating so you promised the customer delivery in 65 days'.

The marketing manager looked worried. 'Why didn't you rush through this important job?' he asked. 'Why is there such variation in time? Why did the breakdown of one machine disrupt production by so much? What am I going to say to our customer?'

The reply was, 'Let me answer your questions in order. Because I was rushing through other important jobs. The variation isn't really that much; our estimates are usually within ten days. It is a central machine that affects the capacity of the whole plant. I can only suggest you apologize and say that you will listen to the operations manager more carefully in the future'.

Despite his apparent calmness, the operations manager was concerned about the variability in production times. He could see why there was some variability, but the total amount for the component they were considering did seem a lot. As an experiment he had once tried to match capacity exactly with expected throughput. Then he found that those operations near the beginning of the process were performing reasonably well, but at the end of the process the variability seemed to be magnified and the output times seemed to be out of control. At one point he had eight machines in a line, each of which processed a part for 10 minutes before passing it to the next machine. Although this arrangement seemed perfectly balanced, he found that stocks of work-in-progress built up dramatically. Some people suggested that this was because the actual processing time could vary between 5 and 15 minutes. Whatever the reason, the experiment was stopped.

What the operations really need is a study to see why there is variability, how much variability should be expected, what are the effects of this, how can it be reduced, what benefits will reduced variability bring, and so on. Such a study will need some funding, and a proposal will have to be passed by the relevant department. Your job is to write an initial report to this department including a detailed proposal for a larger study.

# 14 | Using samples in business

Chapter outline | 421
14.1 Purpose of sampling | 422
14.2 Estimating the population mean | 423
14.3 Using small samples | 438
14.4 Quality control | 441

Chapter review | 447
Problems | 447
Computer exercises | 449
Case study:
    Kings Fruit Farm | 450

## CHAPTER OUTLINE

The last two chapters developed some ideas about statistics. In particular, Chapter 12 talked about probabilities, while Chapter 13 described probability distributions. In this chapter we are going to apply these ideas to sampling.

The purpose of sampling is to draw a representative sample from a population. Then you analyse the sample, so that you can estimate the properties of the population from the properties of the sample. This is the basis of statistical inference.

Most statistical inference uses sampling distributions, which show the distribution of values expected in samples. In this chapter we shall use these to estimate the population mean, and do associated calculations.

After reading this chapter and doing the exercises you should be able to:

- understand how and why sampling is used
- appreciate the aims of statistical inference
- use sampling distributions
- find point estimates for population values
- calculate confidence intervals with one- and two-sided distributions
- use t-distributions for small samples
- appreciate the aims of quality control

# 14.1 Purpose of sampling

All quantitative models need reliable data, and in Chapter 3 we described how these could be collected. We also showed that data collection is often based on sampling. In this chapter we are going to see how statistical analyses can help in choosing and analysing appropriate samples.

The aim of sampling is to get reliable data by looking at a few observations rather than all possible observations; then we estimate the properties of a population by looking at the properties of the sample. Suppose, for example, we want to do a final check on the quality of goods leaving a factory. We might run a test on 10% of the output rather than examine all of it, and then we judge the quality of the total output by the quality of the sample.

This approach is used in public opinion polls. A political party that runs an election campaign will want to know how many votes it can expect in a forthcoming election. There are two ways of finding this:

- it can ask every person eligible to vote in the constituency what their intentions are (this is a census)
- it can take a sample of eligible people, ask them their intentions and use these to estimate the voting intentions of the population as a whole

The second approach has a number of advantages. Information is expensive to collect and analyse, so the more people who are surveyed the more it costs; using a sample significantly reduces costs. It also reduces the time needed to collect and analyse data. Another important point concerns the amount of effort worth putting into data collection. Even if an entire population of people is surveyed it is unlikely that they will all answer the questions, or that they will tell the truth, or that their views will stay constant over time. So it is impossible to get completely accurate responses, and we have to accept that even the results from a census are approximations. It is difficult to justify the cost of a census, when we can get results that are just as accurate from a sample.

Sometimes it is simply impossible to test all of a population. It would make no sense, for example, to find the average life of light bulbs made in a factory by testing the entire output until they failed.

Despite these obvious advantages, sampling has a number of drawbacks. Perhaps the most important is the need to define a reliable sample that represents the whole population fairly. Notice that we are again using the term **population** to refer to all things that could be examined rather than its more general use for populations of people:

> - A **population** is all the things that could be tested.
> - A **sample** is those that actually are tested.

The purpose of sampling, then, is to:

- take a sample of units from the population
- measure the desired property (quality, weight, length, etc)
- estimate the value of the property for the population as a whole

This process is called **statistical inference**.

The sample must accurately represent the population. One way of making sure this happens is to take a random sample. We saw in Chapter 3 how these could be organized, commonly using random numbers. Suppose, for example, that we are interested in the number of people travelling in each car on a particular stretch of road. The cars might be travelling too quickly to count the number of occupants in each, so we would select a sample using a set of random numbers, such as 836351847101. Then we could look at the eighth car, the third after that, the sixth after that, and so on.

The essence of random sampling is that each member of the population has an equal probability of being chosen. This is an important point for statistical analyses. In the following discussion, it is assumed that any sample is a simple random sample drawn from the population. If this condition is not met, many of the analyses are no longer valid.

---

## IN SUMMARY

Data collection often relies on sampling. Statistical inference uses values from samples to estimate values for the population. This is generally based on simple random samples.

---

## Self-assessment questions

**14.1**   What is the purpose of sampling?

**14.2**   What is statistical inference?

# 14.2 | Estimating the population mean

In this section we are going to look at the most widely used analysis of statistical inference. This finds the mean of some variable in a population by looking at the values in a sample. The first thing we have to do, then, is to examine the distribution of values in a sample.

## 14.2.1 | Distribution of sample means

If you take any population and take a series of samples from it, you would expect some variation between samples. Suppose, for example, apples are delivered to a jam factory in boxes with a nominal weight of 10 kg. If you take a sample of ten boxes you would expect the mean weight to be about 10 kg, but would not be surprised by small variations about this. Samples of ten boxes taken over consecutive days might have mean weights of 10.2 kg, 9.8 kg, 10.9 kg, 10.1 kg, 9.4 kg, and so on. If you continued this over some period you would build a distribution of sample means.

Any distribution that is found from samples is called a sampling distribution. When we build a distribution of sample means it is called the **sampling distribution of the mean** (see Figure 14.1).

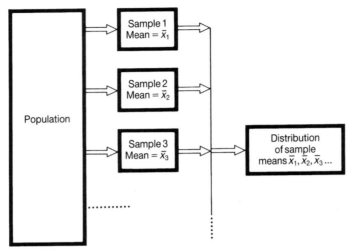

**Figure 14.1** Derivation of the sampling distribution of the mean.

Now we can relate the properties of the sampling distribution of the mean back to the original population. To do this we rely on a general result of the **central limit theorem**. This says that if we take large random samples from a population, the sample means are Normally distributed. This is true regardless of the distribution of the original population.

The central limit theorem gives us some other information, but for this we need to use a standard notation. This has:

- a population with size of $N$, mean of $\mu$ (the Greek letter mu) and standard deviation of $\sigma$ (the Greek letter sigma)
- a sample with size $n$, mean $\bar{x}$ and standard deviation $s$

Then the central limit theorem says:

---

- If a population is Normally distributed, the sampling distribution of the mean is also Normally distributed.
- If the sample size is large (say more than 30) the sampling distribution of the mean is Normally distributed regardless of the population distribution.
- The sampling distribution of the mean has a mean $\mu$ and a standard deviation of $\sigma/\sqrt{n}$.

---

Now you can see that the sampling distribution of the mean has three useful properties (see Figure 14.2):

- It is Normally distributed if a sample size of more than 30 is used or if the population is Normally distributed

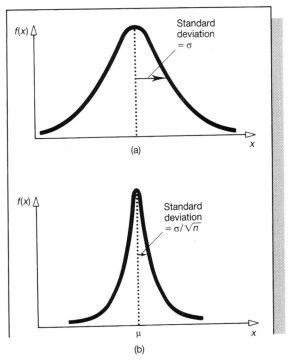

**Figure 14.2** Comparison of distributions for (a) population and (b) sampling distribution of the mean.

● The mean of the sampling distribution of the mean equals the mean of the population, $\mu$

● The standard deviation of the sampling distribution of the mean ($\sigma/\sqrt{n}$) is less than the standard deviation of the population ($\sigma$) and decreases as the sample size increases. This standard deviation is often called the **standard error**.

The third property confirms the result you would expect, that larger samples give more reliable results.

One obvious problem with talking about statistical inference is the clumsy statements needed to describe, for example, 'the mean of the sampling distribution of the mean'. The ideas behind these phrases are fairly simple, but you must keep a clear mind about what they describe. Remember that the basic distribution is the distribution of sample means. This is the sampling distribution of the mean, which has its own mean and standard deviation.

# WORKED EXAMPLE 14.1

A production line makes units with a mean length of 60 cm and standard deviation of 1 cm. What is the probability that a sample of 36 units has a mean length of less than 59.7 cm?

## Solution

Imagine what happens if you take a large number of samples of 36 units. The mean length of each sample is found, and the distribution of these means is:

- Normally distributed
- has mean length $= \mu = 60$ cm
- has standard deviation $= \sigma/\sqrt{n} = 1/\sqrt{36} = 0.167$ cm

Then we can find the probability that one sample has a mean length less than 59.7 cm from the area in the tail of this sampling distribution of the mean. To find this area we use the number of standard deviations the point of interest (59.7) is away from the mean:

$$Z = \frac{59.7 - 60}{0.167} = -1.80$$

As Normal tables are symmetrical, we look up 1.80, which gives the probability of 0.0359, so we expect 3.59% of samples to have a mean length of less than 59.7 cm (see Figure 14.3).

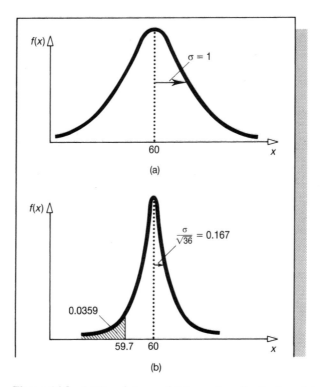

**Figure 14.3**  (a) Population and (b) sampling distribution of the mean for Worked Example 14.1.

## WORKED EXAMPLE 14.2

Soft drinks are put into cans that hold a nominal 200 ml, but the filling machine introduces a standard deviation of 10 ml. These cans are packed into cartons of 25 and exported to a market that insists the mean weight of a carton is at least the quantity specified by the manufacturer. To make sure this happens, the canner sets the machine to fill cans to 205 ml. What is the probability that a carton chosen at random will not pass the quantity test?

### Solution

The mean volume per can is set at 205 ml and has a standard deviation of 10 ml. Taking a random sample of 25 cans gives a sampling distribution of the mean with mean 205 ml and standard deviation of $10/\sqrt{25} = 2$ ml. The case will fail the quantity test if the average quantity per can is less than 200 ml. That is:

$$Z = \frac{200 - 205}{2} = -2.5$$

probability = 0.0062

About six cases in a thousand will fail the test (as shown in Figure 14.4).

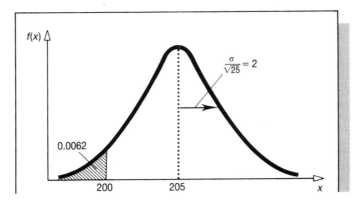

**Figure 14.4**  Sampling distribution of the mean for Worked Example 14.2.

IN SUMMARY

If samples of size $n$ are taken from a large population with mean $\mu$ and standard deviation $\sigma$:

- the mean of sample means is equal to $\mu$
- the standard deviation of sample means is equal to $\sigma/\sqrt{n}$
- if the sample size is large the distribution of sample means is Normal

## 14.2.2 | Confidence intervals

The last two worked examples found the characteristics of a sample from the known characteristics of the population. In general, it is much more useful to work the other way round and find the characteristics of a population from a sample. This is the basis of statistical inference.

Suppose we take a sample of 100 parts and find that the mean length is 30 cm. How can we estimate the mean length of the population of parts? The obvious approach suggests that the sample is representative of the population, in which case we can estimate the population mean at 30 cm. This single value is a **point estimate**. Unfortunately, we know that any point estimate comes from a sample and is unlikely to be exactly right. It should be close to the population mean, but is likely to have some error.

To overcome the problem with point estimates, we can define a range that the population mean is likely to be within. This gives an **interval estimate**. But for an interval estimate to be useful we need two measures:

- the limits of the interval
- the level of confidence that the mean is within the interval

As the limits of the interval get narrower, you would expect your confidence that the mean is within the limits to decrease. If we have a sample of 100 parts with mean length of 30 cm we might be 99% confident that the population mean is in the interval 20 to 40 cm; we might be 95% confident that the mean is between 25 and 35 cm; and we might be 90% confident that the mean is between 27 and 33 cm. This kind of range is called a **confidence interval**, and typically we make a statement like, 'We are 95% confident that the population mean lies within a range ...'.

We can calculate the 95% confidence interval using the following argument. The sample mean $\bar{x}$ is the best point estimate for the population mean $\mu$. But this point estimate is one observation from the sampling distribution of the mean. This sampling distribution is Normal, so 95% of observations lie within 1.96 standard deviations of the mean. The standard deviation of the sampling distribution of the mean is $\sigma/\sqrt{n}$, so 95% of samples are within the range:

$$\mu - 1.96\, \sigma/\sqrt{n} \quad \text{to} \quad \mu + 1.96\, \sigma/\sqrt{n}$$

In other words, the probability that the sample mean is within this range is:

$$P(\mu - 1.96\, \sigma/\sqrt{n} \leqslant \bar{x} \leqslant \mu + 1.96\, \sigma/\sqrt{n}) = 0.95$$

But we can rearrange this to give the confidence interval for the population:

$$P(\bar{x} - 1.96\, \sigma/\sqrt{n} \leqslant \mu \leqslant \bar{x} + 1.96\, \sigma/\sqrt{n}) = 0.95$$

The 95% confidence interval for the population mean is:
$$\bar{x} - 1.96\,\sigma/\sqrt{n} \quad \text{to} \quad \bar{x} + 1.96\,\sigma/\sqrt{n}$$

Similarly, the 90% confidence interval for the population mean is:
$$\bar{x} - 1.645\,\sigma/\sqrt{n} \quad \text{to} \quad \bar{x} + 1.645\,\sigma/\sqrt{n}$$

and the 99% confidence interval is:
$$\bar{x} - 2.58\,\sigma/\sqrt{n} \quad \text{to} \quad \bar{x} + 2.58\,\sigma/\sqrt{n}$$

# WORKED EXAMPLE 14.3

A machine produces parts that have a standard deviation in length of 1.4 cm. A random sample of 100 parts has a mean length of 80 cm. What is the 95% confidence interval for the true mean length of the parts?

## Solution

A sample of 100 has a mean length of 80 cm. So the point estimate for population mean is 80 cm.

The sampling distribution of the mean has a mean of 80 cm and standard deviation of $\sigma/\sqrt{n} = 1.4/\sqrt{100} = 0.14$ cm. 95% of observations are within 1.96 standard deviations of the mean, so we expect 95% of observations to be within the range (see Figure 14.5):

$$\bar{x} - 1.96\,\sigma/\sqrt{n} \quad \text{to} \quad \bar{x} + 1.96\,\sigma/\sqrt{n}$$
$$80 - 1.96 \times 0.14 \quad \text{to} \quad 80 + 1.96 \times 0.14$$

that is:

$$79.73 \text{ cm} \quad \text{to} \quad 80.27 \text{ cm}$$

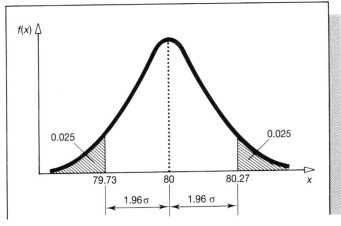

**Figure 14.5**   Confidence limits for Worked Example 14.3.

In the last worked example we estimated the population mean from a sample mean. But we assumed that the standard deviation of the population was known. Although possible, it is unlikely that we would know the standard deviation of a population, but not its mean. It is much more likely that we only have information from the sample and will use this to estimate both the population mean and standard deviation.

The obvious estimator of the population standard deviation is the sample standard deviation $s$. Then the 95% confidence interval becomes:

$$\bar{x} - 1.96\, s/\sqrt{n} \quad \text{to} \quad \bar{x} + 1.96\, s/\sqrt{n}$$

## WORKED EXAMPLE 14.4

Homelock Security employs night-watchmen to patrol warehouses and they want to find the average time to patrol warehouses of a certain size. On a typical night, they recorded the times to patrol 40 similar warehouses. These gave a mean time of 76.4 minutes, with a standard deviation of 17.2 minutes. What are the 95% and 99% confidence intervals on the population mean?

### Solution

The point estimate for the population mean is 76.4 minutes.

The standard deviation of the sample is 17.2 minutes. If we use this as an approximation for the standard deviation of the population, we get a standard error of $\sigma/\sqrt{n} = 17.2/\sqrt{40} = 2.72$ minutes. Then:

- 95% confidence interval:

$$76.4 - 1.96 \times 2.72 \quad \text{to} \quad 76.4 + 1.96 \times 2.72 \quad = \quad 71.07 \quad \text{to} \quad 81.73$$

- 99% confidence interval:

$$76.4 - 2.58 \times 2.72 \quad \text{to} \quad 76.4 + 2.58 \times 2.72 \quad = \quad 69.38 \quad \text{to} \quad 83.42$$

## WORKED EXAMPLE 14.5

A company wants to find the average value of its customer accounts. A large initial sample shows that the standard deviation of the value is £60. What sample size would give a 95% confidence interval for the population mean that is (a) £25 wide, (b) £20 wide, (c) £15 wide?

### Solution

The standard deviation of the initial sample is £60, so we can use this as an approximation for the standard deviation of the population and get a standard error of $60/\sqrt{n}$. Then:

(a) A 95% confidence interval is:

$$\text{mean} - 1.96 \times 60/\sqrt{n} \quad \text{to} \quad \text{mean} + 1.96 \times 60/\sqrt{n}$$

giving a range of:

$$2 \times 1.96 \times 60/\sqrt{n}$$

and we want this range to be £25 wide. So:

$$2 \times 1.96 \times 60/\sqrt{n} = 25 \quad \text{or} \quad \sqrt{n} = 9.41 \quad \text{or} \quad n = 88.5$$

In other words, a sample size of 88.5 (rounded to 89) will give a confidence interval for the population mean that is £25 wide.

(b) Repeating this calculation with a confidence interval of £20 has:

$$2 \times 1.96 \times 60/\sqrt{n} = 20 \quad \text{or} \quad \sqrt{n} = 11.76 \quad \text{or} \quad n = 138.3$$

(c) Repeating the calculation with a confidence interval of £15 has:

$$2 \times 1.96 \times 60/\sqrt{n} = 15 \quad \text{or} \quad \sqrt{n} = 15.68 \quad \text{or} \quad n = 245.9$$

As expected, larger samples give narrower confidence intervals. Decreasing the range from £25 to £20 increased the sample size by (138.3 − 88.5 =) 49.8, while decreasing the range from £20 to £15 increased the sample size by (245.9 − 138.3 = ) 107.6. There are clearly diminishing returns with increasing sample size. As the standard deviation of the sampling distribution is proportional to $1/\sqrt{n}$, reducing the range to a half would need a sample four times as large, reducing the range to a third would need a sample nine times as large, and so on.

Using the sample standard deviation as an approximation for the population standard deviation works well provided the sample size is large. But with smaller samples it tends to underestimate the population standard deviation. Then it introduces a bias, which can be removed by a small adjustment. This involves multiplying the sample standard deviation by $\sqrt{(n/(n-1))}$. Although it seems strange, there is a sound theoretical reason for using this multiplier.

# WORKED EXAMPLE 14.6

MLP Mail-order collects a random sample of 40 customer orders, as shown in the following table. Find the 95% confidence limits on the population mean.

| Size of order | Number of customers |
|---|---|
| £0 – £100 | 4 |
| £100 – £200 | 8 |
| £200 – £300 | 14 |
| £300 – £400 | 8 |
| £400 – £500 | 4 |
| £500 – £600 | 2 |

## Solution

Remember that for grouped data the mean and standard deviation are calculated from:

$$\bar{x} = \frac{\Sigma f x}{\Sigma f}$$

$$s = \sqrt{\frac{\Sigma f (x - \bar{x})^2}{\Sigma f}}$$

where $x$ is the midpoint of each range and $f$ is the number of observations in each range.

Substituting the data for the sample in these equations gives:

$$\bar{x} = 265 \quad \text{and} \quad s = 127.57$$

Now we can use $\bar{x}$ as a point estimator for the population mean and multiply $s$ by $\sqrt{(n/(n-1))}$ to get the unbiased estimator for the population standard deviation, which becomes $127.57 \times \sqrt{(40/39)} = 129.20$. Then the standard error is $129.20/\sqrt{40} = 20.43$.

The 95% confidence interval is 1.96 standard deviations from the mean:

$$265 - 1.96 \times 20.43 \quad \text{to} \quad 265 + 1.96 \times 20.43$$

which is:

$$224.96 \quad \text{to} \quad 305.04$$

This range is relatively wide because of the large variance of the data and the relatively small sample size. This example also shows that the multiplier $\sqrt{(n/(n-1))}$ usually makes very little difference to the result.

---

### IN SUMMARY

Point estimates for the population mean are less useful than interval estimates. The sampling distribution of the mean allows confidence intervals to be found for a population mean. Then the 95% confidence interval for the population mean is:

$$\bar{x} - 1.96\,s/\sqrt{n} \quad \text{to} \quad \bar{x} + 1.96\,s/\sqrt{n}$$

## | 14.2.3 | Estimating population proportions

Sometimes, instead of estimating the value of some variable in a population, we want to estimate the proportion of the population that share some characteristic. For quality assurance we might want the proportion of output that is faulty; for finance we might want the proportion of invoices smaller than some amount; or for personnel records we might want the proportion of people who work overtime. In these circumstances, statistical inference will take a sample, find the proportion of the sample with the required property, and then estimate the proportion of the population with that property.

This is done using another result of the central limit theorem. Suppose that the proportion of a population with a certain characteristic is $\pi$ (the Greek letter pi) and a sample is taken that contains a proportion $p$ with the same characteristic. The central limit theorem says that if the sample size is large (say over 30) the sample proportions are:

- Normally distributed
- with mean $\pi$
- and standard deviation $\sqrt{\left(\dfrac{\pi(1-\pi)}{n}\right)}$

We have a sample with a proportion $p$, and this is the best point estimate for the population proportion $\pi$. But this point estimate is one observation from the sampling distribution, which is Normal. Using exactly the same reasoning as before, we can find the 95% confidence interval for the population as:

$$p - 1.96 \times \sqrt{\left(\frac{\pi(1-\pi)}{n}\right)} \quad \text{to} \quad p + 1.96 \times \sqrt{\left(\frac{\pi(1-\pi)}{n}\right)}$$

Unfortunately, this range contains the term $\pi$, which is the proportion that we are trying to find. As before, though, we can use the sample value $p$ as an estimator for $\pi$.

> The 95% confidence interval for a population proportion is:
>
> $$p - 1.96 \times \sqrt{\left(\frac{p(1-p)}{n}\right)} \quad \text{to} \quad p + 1.96 \times \sqrt{\left(\frac{p(1-p)}{n}\right)}$$

# WORKED EXAMPLE 14.7

Queen Charlotte's Hospital gives a random sample of 50 patients a new treatment for an illness. 60% of these are cured. Calculate the 95% confidence interval for the proportion of all patients who will be cured by the treatment.

## Solution

The proportion of patients in the sample who are cured, $p$, is 0.6. This is the point estimate for the proportion who will be cured in the population, $\pi$.

The 95% confidence interval for the proportion in the population is given by:

$$p - 1.96 \times \sqrt{\left(\frac{p(1-p)}{n}\right)} \quad \text{to} \quad p + 1.96 \times \sqrt{\left(\frac{p(1-p)}{n}\right)}$$

$$0.6 - 1.96 \times \sqrt{\left(\frac{0.6 \times 0.4}{50}\right)} \quad \text{to} \quad 0.6 + 1.96 \times \sqrt{\left(\frac{0.6 \times 0.4}{50}\right)}$$

$$0.6 - 0.136 \quad \text{to} \quad 0.6 + 0.136$$

$$0.464 \quad \text{to} \quad 0.736$$

We would be 95% confident that between 46.4% and 73.6% of patients given the new treatment will be cured. This seems a wide range, but again we are dealing with a small sample.

# WORKED EXAMPLE 14.8

Last month an opinion poll in Helmsburg suggested that 30% of people would vote for the Green party. This month the poll is being rerun. How many people should be interviewed for the poll to be within 2% of actual voting intentions with a 95% level of confidence?

## Solution

In polls the proportion of people voting for the Green party is Normally distributed with mean $p$ and standard deviation $\sqrt{(\pi(1-\pi)/n)}$. For the 95% confidence interval we want the error to be within 1.96 standard deviations of the mean. Then:

$$\text{maximum error} = 1.96 \times \text{standard deviation}$$

$$= 1.96 \times \sqrt{\left(\frac{\pi(1-\pi)}{n}\right)}$$

The best estimate we have for the proportion of people in the poll who will vote for the party is $p = 0.3$, found in last month's poll. This is the point estimate for the proportion in the population, $\pi$. The maximum error is 2%, so we get:

$$0.02 = 1.96 \times \sqrt{\left(\frac{0.3 \times 0.7}{n}\right)}$$

or

$$n = 2017$$

In other words, we need to take a poll of 2017 people to get the accuracy needed.

IN SUMMARY

Point estimates and confidence intervals can be calculated for proportions of the population sharing some characteristic in the same way as point estimates and confidence intervals for the mean.

## 14.2.4 | One-sided confidence intervals

So far we have assumed that the confidence interval is symmetrical about the mean. Then we use both sides of the sampling distribution to find probabilities. But there are many circumstances where we are only interested in one side of the sampling distribution. We might, for example, want to be 95% confident that the mean number of defects is below some maximum, or the weight of goods is above some minimum, or the cost is below some maximum.

One-sided confidence intervals use the same approach as the two-sided intervals discussed previously. A two-sided 95% confidence interval is 1.96 standard deviations away from the mean (with 2.5% of the distribution in each tail); a one-sided 95% confidence interval is 1.645 standard deviations from the mean (with 5% of the distribution in one tail) (Figure 14.6).

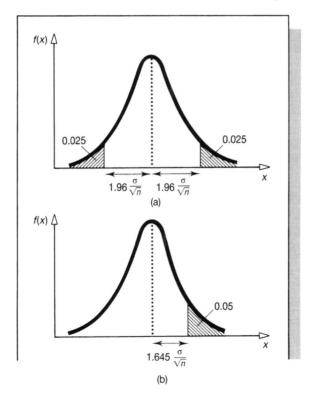

**Figure 14.6** Comparison of (a) two-sided and (b) one-sided 95% confidence intervals.

Now we can use the following rules for finding the one-sided 95% confidence interval:

- to find the value that we are 95% confident the population mean is above, use:

$$\bar{x} - 1.645 \text{ standard errors}$$

- to find the value that we are 95% confident the population mean is below, use:

$$\bar{x} + 1.645 \text{ standard errors}$$

We could, of course, use other levels of confidence, but are using 95% simply because this is convenient and popular.

## WORKED EXAMPLE 14.9

An automated process makes a product, but introduces some variability in the weight of each unit. One day a sample of 60 units is taken and found to have a mean weight of 45 kg and standard deviation of 5 kg.

(a) What weight are we 95% confident the population mean is below?

(b) What weight are we 95% confident the population mean is above?

### Solution

The best estimate of the standard error is $s/\sqrt{n}$:

$$\text{standard error} = 5/\sqrt{60} = 0.65$$

(a) We are 95% confident that the population mean will be less than $\bar{x} + 1.645 \times$ standard error, i.e.:

$$45 + 1.645 \times 0.65 = 46.07 \text{ kg}$$

(b) We are 95% confident that the population mean will be more than $\bar{x} - 1.645 \times$ standard error, i.e.:

$$45 - 1.645 \times 0.65 = 43.93 \text{ kg}$$

## WORKED EXAMPLE 14.10

A quality assurance programme takes a random sample of 40 invoices, and finds that eight have mistakes:

(a) What is the level of mistakes that we are 95% confident the population will fall below?

(b) What is the level of mistakes that we are 95% confident the population will fall above?

(c) How does this compare with the two-sided 90% confidence interval?

(d) What is the 95% two-sided confidence interval?

## Solution

(a) We know that the 95% confidence interval for a one-sided distribution corresponds to 1.645 standard errors.

The proportion of mistakes in the sample, $p$, is $8/40 = 0.2$. The best estimate for the standard error of a proportion is:

$$\sqrt{(p(1-p)/n)} = \sqrt{(0.2 \times 0.8/40)} = 0.063.$$

So we can be 95% confident that the proportion of mistakes in the population is less than:

$$\bar{x} + 1.645 \times \text{standard error} = 0.2 + 1.645 \times 0.063 = 0.304$$

(b) Similarly, we can be 95% confident that the proportion of mistakes in the population is more than:

$$0.2 - 1.645 \times 0.063 = 0.096$$

(c) The two-sided 90% confidence limits are 1.645 standard errors from the mean, giving an interval of:

$$0.2 - 1.645 \times 0.063 \quad \text{to} \quad 0.2 + 1.645 \times 0.063$$
$$0.096 \quad \text{to} \quad 0.304$$

(d) The two-sided 95% confidence limits are 1.96 standard errors from the mean, giving an interval of:

$$0.2 - 1.96 \times 0.063 \quad \text{to} \quad 0.2 + 1.96 \times 0.063$$
$$0.077 \quad \text{to} \quad 0.323$$

---

### IN SUMMARY

Sometimes we are only interested in a confidence interval in one tail of a distribution. In these cases the approach is similar to the method with two-sided confidence intervals.

# Self-assessment questions

**14.3** What is the sampling distribution of the mean?

**14.4** Describe the shape of the sampling distribution of the mean.

**14.5** Why is a point estimate for the mean unlikely to be exactly right?

**14.6** What is the 95% confidence interval for a value?

**14.7** Is a 95% confidence interval wider or narrower than a 90% interval?

**14.8** When would you use a one-sided confidence interval?

**14.9** If a sample of size $n$ produces a confidence interval that is $w$ wide, how big a sample would generally be needed to produce a confidence interval that is $w/5$ wide?

# 14.3  Using small samples

Early in this chapter we described an important result of the central limit theorem, which said that when the population is Normally distributed or the sample size is large, the sampling distribution of the mean is Normally distributed. What happens, though, when these conditions are not met? Suppose we do not know what the population distribution is, and can only take a small sample (where 'small' is below 30). In these circumstances we cannot assume the sampling distribution is Normal.

The problem is that a small sample must be less representative of the population than a large sample. In particular, small samples show less variation than a population, as they include fewer outlying results. What we need is a distribution that looks at a small sample and takes such factors into account. The distribution that does this is called a **_t_-distribution**.

The _t_-distribution looks similar to the Normal, but its shape depends on the **degrees of freedom**. For our purpose, the degrees of freedom are found from the sample size $n$, and are simply defined as $n - 1$. This definition comes about because the degrees of freedom measure the number of independent pieces of information that are used. You might ask, then, 'Why does a sample of size $n$ have $n - 1$ pieces of information rather than $n$?' The answer is that we have a value for the mean, so only $n - 1$ values can vary. Suppose, for example, we have four numbers whose mean is 5. The first three numbers can take any value (3, 5 and 7 perhaps) but then the fourth number is fixed (at 5) to get the correct mean.

When the sample size is close to 30, the _t_-distribution looks the same as a Normal distribution. But as the degrees of freedom get smaller, the distribution gets wider and lower, as shown in Figure 14.7.

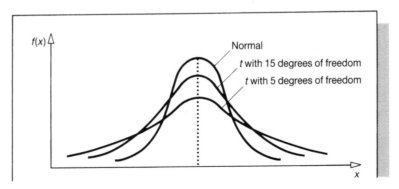

**Figure 14.7**  Comparison of Normal and _t_-distributions.

_t_-distributions are used in the same way as Normal distributions, and can be found by computers or tables, as shown in Appendix G. When using the tables we have to look up values with the correct number of degrees of freedom. For a two-sided 95% confidence interval we look up the significance level of 0.05 (giving a probability of 0.025 as the area in each tail) and this gives a column of entries for different degrees of freedom. The value is 12.706 with one degree of freedom, 4.303 with two degrees of freedom, 3.182 with three degrees of freedom, and so on. This is the number of standard deviations away from the mean. With a large number of degrees of freedom the value decreases to 1.96, which is the same as the Normal value.

# WORKED EXAMPLE 14.11

A survey of ten items in a sales ledger has a mean value of £60 and standard deviation of £8. What is the 95% confidence interval for the population of items?

## Solution

The point estimate for the population mean is £60.

If the sample size was large we could calculate the confidence interval by the method used before. With a small sample we can use a similar approach, but substituting a *t*-distribution for a Normal distribution.

The number of degrees of freedom is $10 - 1 = 9$. Looking up a probability of 0.05 with 9 degrees of freedom in the table in Appendix G gives a value of 2.262. So the confidence limits are 2.262 standard errors from the mean.

The best estimate for the standard error is $s/\sqrt{n} = 10/\sqrt{8} = 3.56$. So the confidence interval is:

$$\bar{x} - 2.262 \times \text{standard error} \quad \text{to} \quad \bar{x} + 2.262 \times \text{standard error}$$

$$60 - 2.262 \times 3.536 \quad \text{to} \quad 60 + 2.262 \times 3.536$$

which is:

$$52 \quad \text{to} \quad 68$$

There is a 95% chance that the population mean is within the range £52 to £68.

# WORKED EXAMPLE 14.12

The time taken for eight people working in an office to travel to work has a mean of 37 minutes and a standard deviation of 12 minutes.

(a) What is the 90% confidence interval for the mean travel time of everyone in the office?

(b) What is the 95% confidence interval?

(c) If the same results had been found from a sample of 20 what would be the 95% confidence interval?

(d) What would the last result be if a Normal distribution had been used?

## Solution

(a) The sample size is 8, so there are 7 degrees of freedom. Looking up the value for a probability of 0.1 (i.e. 5% in each tail) with 7 degrees of freedom in $t$-distribution tables gives a value of 1.895.

The best estimate of the standard error is $s/\sqrt{n} = 12/\sqrt{8} = 4.24$, so the 90% confidence interval is:

$$\bar{x} - 1.895 \times \text{standard error} \quad \text{to} \quad \bar{x} + 1.895 \times \text{standard error}$$
$$37 - 1.895 \times 4.24 \quad \text{to} \quad 37 + 1.895 \times 4.24$$
$$28.97 \quad \text{to} \quad 45.03$$

(b) For the 95% confidence interval we look up a probability of 0.05 with 7 degrees of freedom and get a value of 2.365. Then the 95% confidence interval is:

$$37 - 2.365 \times 4.24 \quad \text{to} \quad 37 + 2.365 \times 4.24$$
$$26.97 \quad \text{to} \quad 47.03$$

(c) With a sample of 20 the standard error becomes $12/\sqrt{20} = 2.68$ and there are 19 degrees of freedom. Then the 95% confidence interval is within 2.093 standard errors of the mean:

$$37 - 2.093 \times 2.68 \quad \text{to} \quad 37 + 2.093 \times 2.68$$
$$31.39 \quad \text{to} \quad 42.61$$

(d) 95% confidence limits with a Normal distribution correspond to 1.96 standard errors. Then the interval is:

$$37 - 1.96 \times 2.68 \quad \text{to} \quad 37 + 1.96 \times 2.68$$
$$31.75 \quad \text{to} \quad 42.25$$

The small sample has not allowed for the full variability of the data, so the Normal distribution has assumed that the data are less spread out than they actually are. This interval, therefore, tends to be too narrow.

---

### IN SUMMARY

Sampling distributions are only Normal if the population follows a Normal distribution, or if large samples are taken. If these conditions are not met, a $t$-distribution should be used. This distribution is similar to the Normal distribution, but its shape is affected by the degrees of freedom, and hence by the sample size.

---

## Self-assessment questions

**14.10** Why are sampling distributions not Normal when samples are small?

**14.11** What are the 'degrees of freedom'?

# 14.4 | QUALITY CONTROL

## 14.4.1 | Acceptance sampling

One of the obvious uses of sampling is in quality control. In particular, **acceptance sampling** takes samples from a batch of products to see if the whole batch reaches an acceptable level of quality, or whether it should be rejected. Acceptance sampling uses a **sampling plan**, which:

- specifies a sample size, $n$
- takes a random sample of this size from a batch
- specifies a maximum allowed number of defects in the sample, $c$
- tests the sample to find the number that are actually defective
- if the number of defects is greater than this allowed maximum number, $c$, rejects the batch
- if the number of defects is less than the allowed maximum number, $c$, accepts the batch

The value of $c$, the maximum allowed number of defects in a sample, is largely a matter of policy – it relies on opinions about the acceptable level of quality. Four important measures related to this decision are:

- **acceptance quality level** (AQL) – which is the overall percentage of defects that is acceptable.
- **lot tolerance per cent defective** (LTPD) – which is the highest percentage of defects that customers will accept in a single batch.
- **producer's risk** ($\alpha$) – which is the probability of rejecting a good batch.
- **consumer's risk** ($\beta$) – which is the probability of accepting a bad batch.

These definitions assume that customers are willing to accept an overall level of quality equal to AQL. As customers are demanding higher quality this figure is inevitably approaching zero. Here we assume that customers are willing to accept an overall proportion of defects given by AQL, and they are willing to accept an occasional batch that is as poor as the LTPD. They will not accept any batches with a higher proportion of defects.

The other two factors are measures of risk. Producers want to minimize $\alpha$ – the probability of rejecting a good batch – while consumers want them to minimize $\beta$ – the probability of accepting a bad batch. Typical sampling plans call for values of $\alpha$ equal to 0.05 and $\beta$ equal to 0.1.

Using these four measures we can find values for $n$, the sample size, and $c$, the maximum number of allowed defects. In practice, these calculations are so common that we will always use standard programs or tables.

## WORKED EXAMPLE 14.13

Juliet Ndalla buys components in batches from a supplier. The supplier uses an acceptance quality level of 2% defective, while Juliet accepts batches with a maximum of 6% defective. What are appropriate values of $n$ and $c$?

### Solution

We are told that:

$$AQL = 0.02$$
$$LTPD = 0.06$$

We can find values for $n$ and $c$ from standard sampling plans. The usual procedure is to calculate the ratio of LTPD/AQL and find the entry in sampling tables that is equal to, or just greater than, this value. Here LTPD/AQL = 0.06/0.02 = 3. The following extract from sampling tables shows the value that is slightly greater than this is 3.21. This corresponds to $c = 6$. Now we can use the third column of the table to find an implied sample size. The corresponding value of $n \times AQL$ is 3.29. We know that AQL = 0.02, so $n \times 0.02 = 3.29$, or $n = 164.5$. This gives the sampling plan:

● take samples of 165 units

● if 6 or less units are defective accept the batch

● if more than 6 units are defective reject the batch

| LTPD/AQL | $c$ | $n \times AQL$ |
|---|---|---|
| 44.89 | 0 | 0.05 |
| 10.95 | 1 | 0.36 |
| 6.51 | 2 | 0.82 |
| 4.89 | 3 | 1.37 |
| 4.06 | 4 | 1.97 |
| 3.55 | 5 | 2.61 |
| 3.21 | 6 | 3.29 |
| 2.96 | 7 | 3.98 |
| 2.77 | 8 | 4.70 |
| 2.62 | 9 | 5.43 |
| 2.50 | 10 | 6.17 |

Many standard programs do this analysis, with a simple example shown in Figure 14.8. Notice that this gives four alternative plans based on slightly different values of $\alpha$ and $\beta$.

****** **QUALITY CONTROL STATISTICS** ******

| Analysis by | attribute |
|---|---|
| Designing | sampling plan |

**DATA ENTERED**

- Acceptance quality level (AQL)     =     0.02
- Lot tolerance percent defective (LTPD)     =     0.06
- Producer's risk (alpha)     =     0.05
- Consumer's risk (beta)     =     0.10

**SUGGESTED PLANS**

| Plan Number | Sample size (N) | Number of failures (c) | Actual alpha | Actual beta |
|---|---|---|---|---|
| 1 | 165 | 6 | 0.051 | 0.137 |
| 2 | 176 | 6 | 0.067 | 0.099 |
| 3 | 200 | 7 | 0.051 | 0.090 |
| 4 | 197 | 7 | 0.048 | 0.098 |

**Figure 14.8** Example of a printout giving alternative sampling plans.

---

> ## IN SUMMARY

Acceptance sampling checks to see whether the quality of a batch of products is acceptable, or whether the batch should be rejected. It uses a sampling plan to specify the maximum number of failures permitted in a sample.

## 14.4.2 | Process control

Acceptance sampling checks the quality of products. A slightly different approach uses **process control** to check that the process making the products is working as planned.

There is always some random variation in a process; process control makes sure that this random variation is within acceptable limits. The way of doing this is to take samples over time to see whether there are any noticeable trends. You can see these trends most clearly in a **process control chart**.

Suppose we take a series of samples over time and plot a graph of the proportion of defective units. This gives a **p-chart**. The proportion of defects is usually around the proportion of defects in the population. Provided it does not vary far from this value, the process is working as planned. If there is a trend, the proportion of defective units moves away from the mean, and when it reaches some specified limit the process is said to be out of control and needs correcting. To show when a process is out of control we need two limits: an **upper control limit** (UCL) and a **lower control limit** (LCL). Provided the output stays between these two limits the process is in control, but if it moves outside the limits it is out of control (as shown in Figure 14.9).

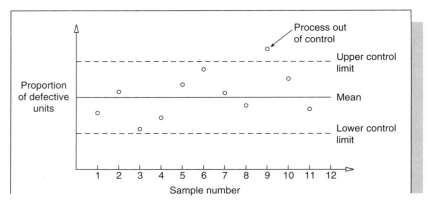

**Figure 14.9** Typical process control chart.

The key decision in process control is the calculation of control limits, and this relies on results that we have already used. If the proportion of defects in a population is $p$, the proportion of defects in a sample of size $n$ is Normally distributed with mean, $p$, and standard deviation of $\sqrt{(p(1-p)/n)}$. Then we can calculate the control limits from:

- upper control limit = UCL = $\mu + Z \times$ standard deviation
- lower control limit = LCL = $\mu - Z \times$ standard deviation

where $Z$ is the number of standard deviations of the specified confidence limit.

## WORKED EXAMPLE 14.14

Jim Springwell collected a sample of 500 units of the output from a process for each of 30 working days when it was known to be working normally. He tested these samples and recorded the number of defects as follows:

| Day | Number of defects | Day | Number of defects | Day | Number of defects |
|-----|-------------------|-----|-------------------|-----|-------------------|
| 1 | 70 | 11 | 45 | 21 | 61 |
| 2 | 48 | 12 | 40 | 22 | 57 |
| 3 | 66 | 13 | 53 | 23 | 65 |
| 4 | 55 | 14 | 51 | 24 | 48 |
| 5 | 50 | 15 | 60 | 25 | 42 |
| 6 | 42 | 16 | 57 | 26 | 40 |
| 7 | 64 | 17 | 55 | 27 | 67 |
| 8 | 47 | 18 | 62 | 28 | 70 |
| 9 | 51 | 19 | 45 | 29 | 63 |
| 10 | 68 | 20 | 48 | 30 | 60 |

Draw a control chart with 95% confidence limits.

## Solution

The average proportion of defects is:

$$p = \frac{\text{total number of defects}}{\text{number of observations}} = \frac{1650}{50 \times 500} = 0.11$$

$$\text{standard deviation} = \sqrt{(p(1-p)/n)} = \sqrt{(0.11 \times 0.89/500)} = 0.014$$

The 95% confidence limits have Z = 1.96, so:

- UCL = $p + Z \times$ standard deviation = 0.11 + 1.96 × 0.014 = 0.137
- LCL = $p - Z \times$ standard deviation = 0.11 − 1.96 × 0.014 = 0.083

If the proportion of defects is between 0.083 and 0.137 we can assume that the process is under control and differences are simply random variations; if the proportion of defects is outside this range the process is out of control and needs adjusting. With samples of 500 the process is under control when the number of defects is between 0.083 × 500 = 42 and 0.137 × 500 = 69.

Notice in the last example that the data for drawing the control charts were collected when the process was known to be working normally. If the process was already out of control when the data were collected, the results would be meaningless.

Process control charts will have some observations that lie outside the control limits purely by chance. With a 95% confidence interval, random variations will leave 5% of samples outside the control limits. So every observation suggesting the process is out of control should be carefully checked to see whether the process is really out of control, or whether it is actually operating normally.

As well as checking the proportion of defects, control charts can also be used to sample the value of a variable. Then the usual approach is to plot two charts, one showing the mean values of the samples and a second showing the ranges (where the range is the difference between the largest and smallest observation in a sample). Suppose, for example, that a telephone company takes samples to monitor the duration of calls. It can plot two control charts, one showing the mean length of calls in each sample and a second showing the range. Provided that future samples keep within control limits for both charts, the process is in control. If a sample moves outside the control limits on either chart the process is out of control and needs further checking.

As before, the calculations for these charts are done so frequently that the easiest way to find the control limits is either in tables or using standard software.

## WORKED EXAMPLE 14.15

Samples of ten units have been taken from a process in each of the past 20 days. Each unit in the sample was weighed, and the mean weight and range were recorded. Draw process control charts for the sample means and ranges.

## Solution

The easiest way of doing this is to use standard software. Figure 14.10 shows the results from one package.

****** QUALITY CONTROL STATISTICS ******

| Analysis by | weight |
| Designing | control charts |

**DATA ENTERED**

Sample size = 10

| Sample | Mean | Range | Sample | Mean | Range |
|--------|------|-------|--------|------|-------|
| 1 | 12.2 | 4.2 | 11 | 12.5 | 3.3 |
| 2 | 13.1 | 4.6 | 12 | 12.3 | 4.0 |
| 3 | 12.5 | 3.0 | 13 | 12.5 | 2.9 |
| 4 | 13.3 | 5.1 | 14 | 12.6 | 2.7 |
| 5 | 12.7 | 2.9 | 15 | 12.8 | 3.9 |
| 6 | 12.6 | 3.1 | 16 | 12.1 | 4.2 |
| 7 | 12.5 | 3.2 | 17 | 13.2 | 4.8 |
| 8 | 13.0 | 4.6 | 18 | 13.0 | 4.6 |
| 9 | 12.2 | 4.3 | 19 | 13.2 | 5.0 |
| 10 | 12.0 | 5.0 | 20 | 12.6 | 3.8 |

**CONTROL LIMITS**

| overall mean value | = | 12.65 |
| overall mean of sample ranges | = | 3.96 |

**Control limits on sample means:**
- Lower control limit     =     11.42
- Centre line     =     12.65
- Upper control limit     =     13.88

**Control limits on sample ranges:**
- Lower control limit     =     0.87
- Centre line     =     3.96
- Upper control limit     =     7.05

**Figure 14.10** Sample of a printout for process control charts and charts of sample means and sample ranges.

---

| IN SUMMARY |

Process control checks that a process is working as planned. It draws control charts to make sure that the performance is within acceptable limits.

---

# Self-assessment questions

**14.12** What is the purpose of acceptance sampling?

**14.13** What does it mean if an observation is outside the control limits in a process control chart?

CHAPTER REVIEW

A lot of data collection relies on sampling. This chapter has described some statistical analyses that can be used with samples. In particular it:

- outlined the purpose of sampling and statistical inference
- discussed the sampling distribution of the mean
- found point estimates and confidence intervals for population means
- estimated population proportions
- used one-sided confidence intervals
- used *t*-distributions for small samples
- introduced the ideas of quality control

# Problems

**14.1** A production line makes units with a mean weight of 80 g and standard deviation of 5 g. What is the probability that a sample of 100 units has a mean weight of less than 79 g?

**14.2** A machine produces parts with a variance of 14.5 cm in length. A random sample of 50 parts is taken and has a mean length of 106.5 cm. What are the 95% and 99% confidence intervals for the length of all parts?

**14.3** A food processor specifies the mean weight of a product as 200 g. The output is Normally distributed with a standard deviation of 15 g. A random sample of 20 has a mean of 195 g. Does this suggest that the mean weight is too low?

**14.4** During an audit, a random sample of 60 invoices is taken from a large population. The mean value of invoices in this sample was £125.50 and the standard deviation was £10.20. Find the 90% and 95% confidence intervals for the mean value of all invoices.

**14.5** Sheila Brown times 60 people doing a task. The mean time is 6.4 minutes, with a standard deviation of 0.5 minutes. How long would it take the population to do this job?

**14.6** Wade (Retail) looked at a random sample of 100 invoices from a large population. Eight of these were found to contain an error. What are the 90% and 95% confidence intervals for the proportion of invoices with faults?

**14.7** A company wants to find the weight of its products. A large initial sample shows that the standard deviation of the weight is 20 g. What size of sample would give a 95% confidence interval of the population that is (a) 10 g wide, (b) 8 g wide, (c) 5 g wide?

**14.8** Last year a trial survey found that 65% of houses in a town had a mobile telephone. This year a follow-up survey wants to find the number of houses with a mobile to within 3% with a 95% confidence interval. How many houses should be surveyed?

**14.9** Henry Lom feels that the quantity of chocolates in a particular type of packet seems to have decreased. To test this feeling he takes a sample of 40 packets and finds that the mean weight is 228 g with a standard deviation of 11 g.
(a) What weight is Henry 95% confident that the mean falls below?
(b) What are the two-sided confidence limits on this weight?

**14.10** BC's assurance programme chooses a random sample of 50 units, and finds that 12 are defective.
(a) What is the number of defectives that BC are 95% sure the population mean will fall below?
(b) What is the number of defectives that BC are 95% confident the population mean will fall above?
(c) How does this compare with the two-sided 90% confidence interval?

**14.11** A survey of 20 items in a sales ledger has a mean value of £100 and standard deviation of £20.
(a) What is the 95% confidence interval for the population of items?
(b) What is the 99% confidence interval?

**14.12** The time taken for a sample of eight pieces of equipment to do a task has a mean of 52 minutes and a standard deviation of 18 minutes.
(a) What is the 90% confidence interval for the mean time of all equipment to do the task?
(b) What is the 95% confidence interval?
(c) If the same results had been found from a sample of 20 pieces of equipment what would be the 95% confidence interval?
(d) What would be the last result if a Normal distribution had been used?

**14.13** Twenty-four samples of 200 units were collected from a process that was known to be working properly. The number of defects was as follows:

| Day | Number of defects | Day | Number of defects | Day | Number of defects |
|-----|-----|-----|-----|-----|-----|
| 1 | 21 | 9 | 15 | 17 | 20 |
| 2 | 32 | 10 | 13 | 18 | 19 |
| 3 | 22 | 11 | 16 | 19 | 25 |
| 4 | 17 | 12 | 17 | 20 | 16 |
| 5 | 16 | 13 | 20 | 21 | 15 |
| 6 | 14 | 14 | 19 | 22 | 13 |
| 7 | 21 | 15 | 17 | 23 | 24 |
| 8 | 17 | 16 | 22 | 24 | 25 |

Draw control charts with 95% and 99% confidence limits on the process.

**14.14** Gunta Hans took 30 samples of size 15 from a process. The average sample range for the 30 samples is 1.025 kg and the average mean is 19.872 kg. Draw suitable control charts for the process.

# Computer exercises

**14.1** Figure 14.11 shows a printout from a statistics package (Minitab) used for sampling. This printout shows a set of 20 numbers put into a column, C1. These are described by the package. Then a set of six numbers is randomly selected from C1, put into the column C2 and described. Make sure you understand what is happening in this printout. Use a suitable package to get equivalent results.

```
MTB  > set c1
DATA > 3 4 1 6 5 4 4 3 2 3
DATA > 5 3 4 2 2 3 1 4 3 5
DATA > end
MTB  > describe c1
```

|     | N  | MEAN  | MEDIAN | TRMEAN | STDEV | SEMEAN |
|-----|----|-------|--------|--------|-------|--------|
| C1  | 20 | 3.350 | 3.000  | 3.333  | 1.348 | 0.302  |

|     | MIN   | MAX   | Q1    | Q3    |
|-----|-------|-------|-------|-------|
| C1  | 1.000 | 6.000 | 2.250 | 4.000 |

```
MTB > sample 6 from c1 put into c2
MTB > print c2
```

```
C2
    4   1   4   4   5   2
```

```
MTB > describe c2
```

|     | N | MEAN  | MEDIAN | TRMEAN | STDEV | SEMEAN |
|-----|---|-------|--------|--------|-------|--------|
| C2  | 6 | 3.333 | 4.000  | 3.333  | 1.506 | 0.615  |

|     | MIN   | MAX   | Q1    | Q3    |
|-----|-------|-------|-------|-------|
| C2  | 1.000 | 5.000 | 1.750 | 4.250 |

**Figure 14.11** Printout from a statistical package used for taking a sample.

**14.2** Use a computer to:
- generate a population of random numbers
- draw a frequency distribution of the numbers and confirm that they follow a uniform distribution (which is one in which each number has the same probability)
- take large samples from this population of numbers, and calculate the mean of each sample
- draw a frequency distribution of these means (that is, the sampling distribution of the mean)
- confirm that the result is Normally distributed

Repeat this process for different sample sizes to see what effect this has.

14.3 Take a large population of people's weights (or any other property that is Normally distributed). Use a computer to take random samples from these data and calculate the means. Confirm that, even for small samples, the mean weight of the samples is Normally distributed. Repeat this analysis using data that follow different distributions.

14.4 Spreadsheets can be used to define samples and then do appropriate analyses. Design a spreadsheet to draw control charts for a process. Use it to get results for a specific process, and write a report about your findings.

14.5 How are computers used for quality control? Illustrate your answer with examples of actual software. Give a demonstration of how this software works with a set of real data.

# Case study

## Kings Fruit Farm

In the 1920s Edward Filbert became the tenant of Kings Farm in Cambridgeshire. In 1978 his grandson James Filbert became the latest manager. But in the intervening years the farm has changed considerably. It has now grown from 195 acres to over 3000 acres and is owned by an agricultural company who own several other farms in the area. Most of Kings Farm is used for growing a variety of vegetables, cereals and fruit. Kings Fruit Farm is a subsidiary of Kings Farm, and manages a range of apple, plum and cherry orchards.

Recently, James has been looking at the sales of plums. These are graded and sold as fruit to local shops and markets, for canning to a local cannery, or for jam to a more distant processor. The plums sold for canning generate about half as much income as those sold for fruit, but twice as much income as those sold for jam.

James is trying to estimate the weight of plums sold each year. He does not know this, as the plums are sold by the basket rather than by weight. Each basket holds about 25 kg of plums. For a pilot study James set up some scales to see if he could weigh the amount of fruit in a sample of baskets. On the first day he weighed ten baskets, six of which were sold as fruit, three for tinning and one for jam. The weights of fruit, in kilogrammes, were as follows:

25.6  20.8  29.4  28.0  22.2  23.1  25.3  26.5  20.7  21.9

This trial seemed to work, so James then weighed a sample of 50 baskets on three consecutive days. The weights of fruit, in kilograms, were as follows:

- Day 1  24.6 23.8 25.1 26.7 22.9 23.6 26.6 25.0 24.6 25.2
         25.7 28.1 23.0 25.9 24.2 21.7 24.9 27.7 24.0 25.6
         26.1 26.0 22.9 21.6 28.2 20.5 25.8 22.6 30.3 28.0
         23.6 25.7 27.1 26.9 24.5 23.9 27.0 26.8 24.3 19.5
         31.2 22.6 29.4 25.3 26.7 25.8 23.5 20.5 18.6 21.5

- Day2   26.5 27.4 23.8 24.8 30.2 28.9 23.6 27.5 19.5 23.6
         25.0 24.3 25.3 23.3 24.0 25.1 22.2 20.1 23.6 25.8
         24.9 23.7 25.0 24.9 27.2 28.3 29.1 22.1 25.0 23.8
         18.8 19.9 27.3 25.6 26.4 28.4 20.8 24.9 25.4 25.6
         24.9 25.0 24.1 25.5 25.2 26.8 27.7 20.6 31.3 29.5

- Day 3  27.2 21.9 30.1 26.9 23.5 20.7 26.4 25.1 25.7 26.3
         18.0 21.0 21.9 25.7 28.0 26.3 25.9 24.7 24.9 24.3
         23.9 23.0 24.1 23.6 21.0 24.6 25.7 24.7 23.3 22.7
         22.9 24.8 22.5 26.8 27.4 28.3 31.0 29.4 25.5 23.9
         29.5 23.3 18.6 20.6 25.0 25.3 26.0 22.2 23.9 25.7

He also recorded the number of each sample sent to each destination:

|       | Fruit | Cans | Jam |
|-------|-------|------|-----|
| Day 1 | 29    | 14   | 7   |
| Day 2 | 25    | 15   | 10  |
| Day 3 | 19    | 15   | 16  |

Pickers are paid by the basket, so the payments book was used to find the number of baskets picked on the three days as 820, 750 and 700 respectively. During a good harvest, around 6000 baskets are picked.

What information can James find from these figures?

# 15 | Testing hypotheses

| | | | |
|---|---|---|---|
| Chapter outline | 452 | Problems | 483 |
| 15.1 Hypotheses about | 453 | Computer exercises | 485 |
|       population means | | Case study: | 487 |
| 15.2 Other tests | 460 |       Willingham Consumer | |
| 15.3 Non-parametric tests | 471 |       Protection Department | |
| Chapter review | 483 | | |

## CHAPTER OUTLINE

The last chapter showed how we can use statistical inference to estimate the value of a variable in a population by looking at the value of the variable in a sample. This chapter extends these ideas by describing hypothesis testing. This starts by making a statement describing some aspect of the population. This is the hypothesis to be tested. A sample is then taken from the population to see if evidence can be found to support the hypothesis.

We will normally use a type of statistical test that is called 'parametric'. In some circumstances we cannot use this and have to use non-parametric tests. We will illustrate these by the chi-squared test, which shows how closely actual observations match expected ones.

After reading this chapter and doing the numerical exercises you should be able to:

- appreciate the objectives of hypothesis testing
- understand the function of a significance level and its link with errors
- test hypotheses about population means using data supplied by samples
- extend these ideas to proportions, one-sided tests, differences between means and small samples
- appreciate the use of non-parametric tests
- use the chi-squared test for goodness of fit

# | 15.1 | Hypotheses about population means

## | 15.1.1 | Approach to hypothesis testing

In the last chapter we saw how statistical inference used data from a sample to estimate values for a population. In this chapter we are going to extend this idea by testing whether a belief about a population is supported by the evidence from a sample. This is the basis of **hypothesis testing**.

Suppose we have some preconceived idea about the value taken by a population variable. We might, for example, believe that domestic telephone bills have fallen by 10% in the past year. This is a hypothesis we want to test. For this test we take a sample from the population and see whether the results support our hypothesis or do not support it. The formal procedure for this is as follows:

---

1　define a simple, precise statement about the situation (the hypothesis)

2　take a sample from the population

3　test this sample to see whether it supports the hypothesis, or whether it makes the hypothesis highly improbable

4　if the hypothesis is highly improbable reject it, otherwise accept it

---

In practice, statisticians are rather more cautious than this, and they do not talk about 'accepting' a hypothesis. Instead they say that a hypothesis 'can be rejected' if it is highly unlikely, or it 'cannot be rejected' if it is more likely.

## WORKED EXAMPLE 15.1

Bottles are filled with a nominal 400 g of fluid. There are small deviations around this nominal amount and the actual weights are Normally distributed with a standard deviation of 20 g. Periodic samples are taken to make sure that the mean weight is still 400 g. A sample bottle is found to contain 446 g. Are the bottles now being overfilled?

### Solution

An initial hypothesis is that the mean weight of bottles is still 400 g. We have a limited sample, which gives data for testing this hypothesis. The distribution of bottle weights should be Normal with mean 400 g and standard deviation 20 g.

Assuming that this is correct, we can find the probability of finding a sample containing 446 g. The number of standard deviations from the mean is:

$$Z = \frac{446 - 400}{20} = 2.3$$

Normal tables show that this has probability = 0.01.

If our hypothesis about the population is true, finding a bottle weighing 446 g is highly improbable (1% of occasions). We can, therefore, reject the initial hypothesis that the mean content is 400 g, as we now believe the bottles are being overfilled.

The original statement is called the **null hypothesis**, which is usually called $H_0$. The name 'null' implies that there has been no change in the value being tested since the hypothesis was formulated. If we reject the null hypothesis then we implicitly accept an alternative. In the worked example above we rejected the hypothesis that the mean weight of bottles is 400 g, so we accept the alternative hypothesis that the mean weight is not 400 g. For each null hypothesis there is always an alternative hypothesis, which is usually called $H_1$. If the null hypothesis, $H_0$, is that domestic telephone bills have fallen by 10% in the last year, the alternative hypothesis, $H_1$, is that they have not fallen by 10%; if the null hypothesis, $H_0$, is that first-class letters take two days to deliver, the alternative hypothesis, $H_1$, is that they do not take two days to deliver, and so on.

Notice that the null hypothesis must be a simple, specific statement, while the alternative hypothesis is more vague and suggests that some statement other than the null hypothesis is true. In practice, this means that the null hypothesis is phrased in terms of one thing equalling another. We might have a null hypothesis that the mean weight is 1.5 kg and an alternative hypothesis that the mean weight is not 1.5 kg; a null hypothesis might be that the average salary in an office is £20,000, while the alternative hypothesis is that the average salary is lower than this.

> ### IN SUMMARY
>
> A null hypothesis is a precise statement about a situation. Hypothesis testing uses a sample to see whether the evidence supports this statement, or whether the hypothesis must be rejected.

## 15.1.2 | Errors in hypothesis testing

Even a good sample may not accurately represent the population, so sampling always contains some uncertainty. When we use a sample to test a null hypothesis about a population, we can never be certain of the result. In Worked Example 15.1

we said the result was unlikely and therefore rejected the null hypothesis – but in 1% of samples the result found would occur by chance, and we would be rejecting a perfectly true hypothesis. In general, there are two ways of getting the wrong answer with hypothesis testing, called Type I and Type II errors:

- we may reject a null hypothesis that is actually true (this is a Type I error)
- we may not reject a null hypothesis that is actually false (this is a Type II error)

| Decision | Null hypothesis is | |
|---|---|---|
| | True | False |
| Not reject | Correct decision | Type II error |
| Reject | Type I error | Correct decision |

Ideally, we should like the probabilities of both Type I and Type II errors to be close to zero. Unfortunately, the only way of doing this is to use a large sample. If we try any other adjustments to reduce the probability of Type I errors, the probability of Type II errors increases, and vice versa. With a limited sample size, we have to accept a compromise between the two errors.

# WORKED EXAMPLE 15.2

Jenny Bishop says that the mean wage of her employees is £300 a week with a standard deviation of £60. A random sample of 36 wages is checked, and it is decided to reject the null hypothesis if the mean is less than £270 or greater than £330. What are the probabilities of making a Type I error?

## Solution

We can start by defining a null hypothesis, $H_0$, that the mean wage is £300, and the alternative hypothesis, $H_1$, that the mean wage is not £300.

Hypothesis tests assume that the null hypothesis is true while the tests are being done. Then we assume that the population has a mean of £300 and a standard deviation of £60. With a sample of 36, the standard error (which is the standard deviation of the sampling distribution of the mean) is $s/\sqrt{n} = 60/\sqrt{36} = 10$.

The probability that a sample of 36 wages is greater than £330 is found from Normal tables with $Z = (330 - 300)/10 = 3$. The probability of this is 0.0013. By symmetry, the probability that a sample has a mean of less than £270 is also 0.0013. The null hypothesis is rejected if the sample value is outside the range £270 to £330, so there is a probability of 0.0013 + 0.0013 = 0.0026 that the hypothesis is rejected even though it is actually true. This is the probability of a Type I error. Unfortunately, it is more difficult to find the probability of a Type II error.

## WORKED EXAMPLE 15.3

Halifax city takes a survey of monthly food and shelter costs for a particular type of family. They think that the mean cost is £160 with a standard deviation of £48.90. A sample of 100 families had an average expenditure of £171.25. Is the suggested value of £160 true?

### Solution

The null hypothesis, $H_o$, is that the monthly cost of food and shelter is £160 while the alternative hypothesis, $H_1$, is that it is not £160.

With a sample of 100 the standard error is $48.90/\sqrt{100} = 4.89$. Then $Z = (171.25 - 160)/4.89 = 2.3$, which corresponds to a probability of 0.0107.

There is a likelihood of 0.0107 that the monthly cost of food and shelter is £171.25, so we would say that the outcome is extremely unlikely, reject the null hypothesis and accept the alternative hypothesis.

So far in the examples we have rejected the null hypothesis if we considered the result from the sample to be extremely unlikely. But the judgement of what is 'unlikely' has been purely subjective. In the following section we show how to measure this using a significance level.

### IN SUMMARY

Results from samples always contain uncertainty. In hypothesis testing this means that there are two types of error:

- Type I error, of rejecting a null hypothesis that is true
- Type II error, of not rejecting a null hypothesis that is false

## 15.1.3 | Significance levels

In the last example we considered a probability of 0.0107 as unlikely, but this was only an opinion. We can formalize such judgements into a **significance level**, which is the minimum acceptable probability that an observation is a random sample from the hypothesized population. If we set a 5% significance level, we do not reject a null hypothesis if there is a probability greater than 5% that an observation comes from a population with the specified value. On the other hand, if there is a probability of less than 5% that the observation came from such a population, we reject the null hypothesis.

If we take a large sample, the value we are testing is Normally distributed. If we are working with a 5% significance level, we are concerned with the range that is within 1.96 standard deviations of the mean. In other words, we shall not reject the null hypothesis if the sample result is within 1.96 standard deviations of the mean, and we shall reject it if it is outside this range (see Figure 15.1).

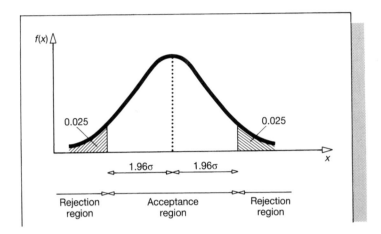

**Figure 15.1** Acceptance and rejection regions for 5% significance level.

With a 5% significance level we reject the null hypothesis when an observation falls outside the 95% acceptance range. But if the null hypothesis is true, 5% of observations will fall outside this range anyway. In other words, we accept that there is a 5% chance of rejecting a true null hypothesis, which is a Type I error. So you can think of the significance level as the probability of a Type I error.

Although significance levels can take any value, the most frequently used in business is 5%, followed by 1% and occasionally 0.1%. If a 1% significance level is used, the null hypothesis is not rejected if the observation is within 2.58 standard deviations of the mean. This is a less stringent test, and shows how smaller significance levels need stronger evidence to reject the null hypothesis. With lower significance levels the probability of a Type I error is reduced, but the probability of a Type II error is increased.

# WORKED EXAMPLE 15.4

The mean value of accounts received by a firm is thought to be £260. An auditor checks this by taking a sample of 36 accounts, which are found to have a mean of £240 and a standard deviation of £45. Use a 5% significance level to test whether the original view is supported by the evidence of the sample.

## Solution

The null hypothesis is that the mean value of all accounts is £260, while the alternative hypothesis is that the mean is not £260. Then:

$$H_o: \quad \mu = 260 \qquad H_1: \quad \mu \neq 260$$

The significance level is 5%, so the null hypothesis is rejected if there is a probability of less than 0.05 that the sample result comes about by chance.

With a sample of 36, the sampling distribution of the mean is Normal with mean 260 and standard deviation $45/\sqrt{36} = 7.5$. For a 5% significance level we look at the points that are within 1.96 standard deviations of the mean. The acceptance range is then:

$$260 - 1.96 \times 7.5 \quad \text{to} \quad 260 + 1.96 \times 7.5$$

or:

$$245.3 \quad \text{to} \quad 274.7$$

The actual observation is outside this range, so we reject the null hypothesis and implicitly accept the alternative hypothesis that the mean value of accounts is not equal to £260.

---

Now we have seen the detailed steps in hypothesis testing and can list them as follows:

1 state the null and alternative hypotheses
2 specify the level of significance
3 calculate the acceptance range for the variable tested
4 find the actual value for the variable tested
5 decide whether to accept or reject the null hypothesis
6 state the conclusion reached

This procedure is used, with slight variations, for all types of hypothesis test, as we shall see in the following sections.

# WORKED EXAMPLE 15.5

The average income per capita in Port Elizabeth is claimed to be £15,000. A sample of 45 people found their mean income to be £14,300 with a standard deviation of £2,000. Use a 5% significance level to check the original claim. What would be the effect of using a 1% significance level?

## Solution

The procedure described above gives the following steps:

1.  State the null and alternative hypotheses
    $$H_o: \quad \mu = 15\,000 \qquad H_1: \quad \mu \neq 15\,000$$

2.  Specify the level of significance
    This is given as 5%.

3.  Calculate the acceptance range for the variable tested
    With a sample of 45, the sampling distribution of the mean is Normal with mean 15 000 and standard deviation $2000/\sqrt{45} = 298.14$. For a 5% significance level we look at the points that are within 1.96 standard deviations of the mean. The acceptance range is then:
    $$15\,000 - 1.96 \times 298.14 \quad \text{to} \quad 15\,000 + 1.96 \times 298.14$$
    or:
    $$14\,416 \quad \text{to} \quad 15\,584$$

4.  Find the actual value for the variable tested
    £14,300

5.  Decide whether to accept or reject the null hypothesis
    The actual value is outside the acceptance range, so we must reject the null hypothesis.

6.  State the conclusion reached
    The evidence from the sample does not support the original claim that the average income per capita in the area is £15,000.

With a 1% significance level, the acceptance range is within 2.58 standard deviations of the mean, or:
$$15\,000 - 2.58 \times 298.14 \quad \text{to} \quad 15\,000 + 2.58 \times 298.14$$
$$14\,231 \quad \text{to} \quad 15\,769$$

The actual observation is £14,300, which is within this range, and we cannot reject the null hypothesis (see Figure 15.2).

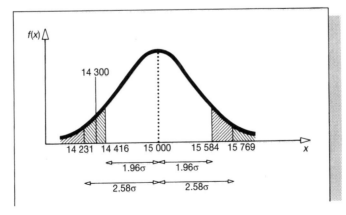

**Figure 15.2**  Acceptance ranges for Worked Example 15.5.

> ### *IN SUMMARY*
>
> A significance level is the minimum acceptable probability that an observation is a random sample from the hypothesized population. It is equivalent to the probability of making a Type I error.

## Self-assessment questions

**15.1** What is the purpose of hypothesis testing?

**15.2** Which is a more precise statement, $H_0$ or $H_1$?

**15.3** What are Type I and Type II errors?

**15.4** What is a significance level?

**15.5** Is the probability of a Type II error lower with a 5% significance level or with a 1% significance level?

**15.6** If a value is in the acceptance range does this prove that the null hypothesis is true?

# 15.2 Other tests

## 15.2.1 Population proportions

In the last chapter we showed how sampling can be used to test the proportion of a population that shares some common characteristic. We used the standard result that if the proportion of the population is $\pi$, the sampling distribution of the proportion has mean of $\pi$ and standard deviation of $\sqrt{(\pi(1 - \pi)/n)}$. Now we can use this to test hypotheses about proportions.

## WORKED EXAMPLE 15.6

Last year it was claimed that high street banks were lending the funds for 20% of all house purchases. To test this, a sample of 100 people with mortgages was interviewed. Eighteen of them arranged their loan with a bank. Does this sample support the original claim?

### Solution

Hypothesis tests always use the same procedure, and the only difference with this problem is that we are interested in a proportion, $\pi$, rather than a mean.

1   State the null and alternative hypotheses
    The null hypothesis is that banks lend 20% of funds for mortgages, so using
    proportions we have:

$$H_o: \quad \pi = 0.2 \qquad H_1: \quad \pi \neq 0.2$$

2   Specify the level of significance
    This is not given, so we shall assume 5%.

3   Calculate the acceptance range for the variable tested
    With a sample of 100, the sampling distribution is Normal with mean 0.2 and
    standard deviation $\sqrt{(\pi (1 - \pi)/n)} = \sqrt{(0.2 \times 0.8/100)} = 0.04$. For a 5%
    significance level we look at the points that are within 1.96 standard deviations
    of the mean. The acceptance range is:

$$0.2 - 1.96 \times 0.04 \quad \text{to} \quad 0.2 + 1.96 \times 0.04$$

    or:

$$0.12 \quad \text{to} \quad 0.28$$

4   Find the actual value for the variable tested
    The sample had a proportion of $18/100 = 0.18$.

5   Decide whether to accept or reject the null hypothesis
    The actual value is within the acceptance range, so we cannot reject the null
    hypothesis.

6   State the conclusion reached
    The evidence from the sample supports the original claim that banks are
    lending money for 20% of mortgages.

---

## IN SUMMARY

The standard method of hypothesis testing can be extended to consider the
proportion of a population sharing some characteristic.

## One-sided tests

**15.2.2**

In all the problems we have examined so far we have stated a null hypothesis of the
form:

$$H_o: \quad \mu = 10$$

and an alternative hypothesis in the form:

$$H_1: \quad \mu \neq 10$$

In practice, we are often concerned that an actual value is above (or sometimes
below) the claimed value. If we buy boxes of chocolates, we only want to make
sure that their weight is not below the specified value; on the other hand, if we are
delivering parcels, we only want to make sure that their weight is not above the

claimed value. We can tackle problems of this type using the standard procedure, but with one adjustment. This adjustment is in the phrasing of the alternative hypothesis and calculation of the acceptance range.

If we are buying boxes of chocolates with a claimed weight of 500 g, and want to make sure that the actual weight is not below this, we can have:

$$\text{null hypothesis, } H_o: \quad \mu = 500 \text{ g}$$

$$\text{alternative hypothesis, } H_1: \quad \mu < 500 \text{ g}$$

If we are delivering parcels with a claimed weight of 25 kg, and want to make sure that the actual weight is not above this, we can have:

$$\text{null hypothesis, } H_o: \quad \mu = 25 \text{ kg}$$

$$\text{alternative hypothesis, } H_1: \quad \mu > 25 \text{ kg}$$

For this kind of test we only use one tail of the sampling distribution, so the acceptance range is altered. In particular, a 5% significance level has the 5% area of rejection in one tail of the distribution. In a Normal distribution this point is 1.645 standard deviations from the mean, as shown in Figure 15.3.

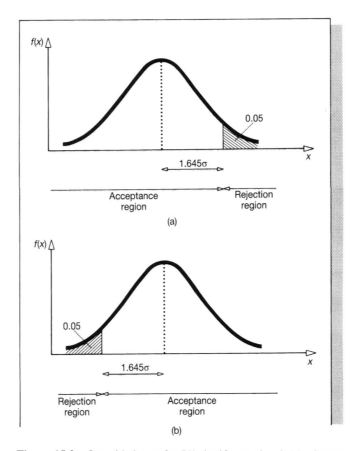

**Figure 15.3** One-sided tests for 5% significance level: (a) when concerned with a maximum value; (b) when concerned with a minimum value.

One-sided tests are said to measure consumers' risk or producers' risk. If a packet of soap powder has a stated weight of 1 kg, consumers will only be concerned if the actual quantity is less than this. Consumer groups will, therefore, sample packets using a null hypothesis that the mean weight is 1 kg and an alternative hypothesis that the weight is less than 1 kg. Producers are concerned if the quantity is significantly more than 1 kg. They will sample packets using a null hypothesis that the mean weight is 1 kg and an alternative hypothesis that the mean weight is above 1 kg. In practice, of course, their testing is much more complicated than this.

# WORKED EXAMPLE 15.7

BookCheck Mail-Order company charges a customer a flat rate for delivery based on a mean weight for packages of 1.75 kg with a standard deviation of 0.5 kg. Postal charges now seem high and it is suggested that the mean weight is greater than 1.75 kg. A random sample of 100 packages has a mean weight of 1.86 kg. Does this support the view that the mean weight is more than 1.75 kg?

## Solution

We can again use the standard procedure.

1    State the null and alternative hypotheses
     This time we want to make sure that the mean weight is not above 1.75 kg, so we have:

$$H_0: \quad \mu = 1.75 \text{ kg} \qquad H_1: \quad \mu > 1.75 \text{ kg}$$

2    Specify the level of significance
     This is not given, so we shall assume 5%.

3    Calculate the acceptance range for the variable tested
     With a sample of 100, the sampling distribution of the mean is Normal with mean of 1.75 kg and standard deviation $0.5/\sqrt{100} = 0.05$ kg. For a 5% significance level and a one-sided test, we look at the points that are more than 1.645 standard deviations above the mean. The acceptance range is then below $1.75 + 1.645 \times 0.05 = 1.83$ kg.

4    Find the actual value for the variable tested
     The observed weight of parcels is 1.86 kg.

5    Decide whether to accept or reject the null hypothesis
     The actual value is outside the acceptance range, so we must reject the null hypothesis.

6    State the conclusion reached
     The evidence from the sample does not support the view that the mean weight of packages is 1.75 kg. The evidence suggests that the mean weight is more than this (see Figure 15.4).

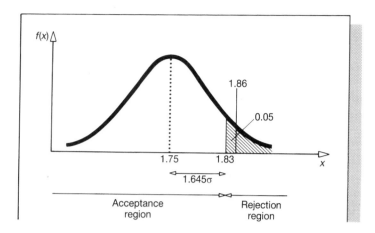

**Figure 15.4**  Acceptance region for Worked Example 15.7.

# WORKED EXAMPLE 15.8

Jenny Brady is a management consultant who has recently introduced new procedures to a reception desk. The receptionist should not do more than 10 minutes of paperwork in each hour, with a standard deviation of 3 minutes. A check is made on 40 random hours of operation and the mean time spent on paperwork is 11.05 minutes. Based on these figures, can the assumption that the new procedures meet specifications be rejected at a 1% level of significance?

## Solution

1 State the null and alternative hypotheses
   This time we are only interested in making sure that the time spent on paperwork is not above 10 minutes in an hour. Then we have

$$H_o: \quad \mu = 10 \text{ minutes} \qquad H_1: \quad \mu > 10 \text{ minutes}$$

2 Specify the level of significance
   This is given as 1%.

3 Calculate the acceptance range for the variable tested
   With a sample of 40, the sampling distribution of the mean is Normal with mean of 10 minutes and standard deviation $3/\sqrt{40} = 0.47$ minutes. For a 1% significance level and a one-sided test, we look at the points that are more than 2.33 standard deviations above the mean. Then the acceptance range is below $10 + 2.33 \times 0.47 = 11.10$ minutes.

4 Find the actual value for the variable tested
   The observed number of minutes spent on paperwork in each hour is 11.05.

5 Decide whether to accept or reject the null hypothesis
   The actual value is inside the acceptance range, so we cannot reject the null hypothesis.

6 State the conclusion reached
   The evidence from the sample supports the view that the mean time spent on paperwork is 10 minutes an hour.

---

### IN SUMMARY

The standard two-sided analysis can be extended to a one-sided analysis when we are only interested in means that are above or below specified levels.

## 15.2.3 | Testing for differences in means

There are many situations in which we have two different populations and want to know whether the means are the same. We might, for example, operate shops in two areas and want to know whether the profitability is the same in each area, or we might have two factories and want to know whether the productivity is the same, or we might want to check sales before and after an advertising campaign.

To see whether the means of two populations are the same, we start by taking a sample from each population. If the sample means are fairly close, we can assume that the population means are the same, but if there is a large difference in the samples we have to assume that the population means are different. Now we need to define how close the sample means must be to make these decisions. For this we take the means of two samples, $\bar{x}_1$ and $\bar{x}_2$, and find the difference, $\bar{x}_1 - \bar{x}_2$. Then we use the standard result that for large samples the sampling distribution of $\bar{x}_1 - \bar{x}_2$ is Normal with mean 0 and standard deviation:

$$standard\ error = \sqrt{\frac{s_1^2}{n_1} + \frac{s_2^2}{n_2}}$$

where:

$n_1$ = sample size from population 1
$n_2$ = sample size from population 2
$s_1$ = standard deviation of sample 1
$s_2$ = standard deviation of sample 2

With these results we can again use the standard procedure. In this case the null hypothesis is phrased to make the means of the two populations the same.

# WORKED EXAMPLE 15.9

A company uses two machines to fill packets of crisps. A sample of 30 packets from the first machine had a mean weight of 180 g and a standard deviation of 14 g. A sample of 40 packets from the second machine had a mean weight of 170 g and a standard deviation of 10 g. Does the evidence from these samples support the view that the two machines produce packets of equal weight?

## Solution

Again we can use the standard approach.

1   State the null and alternative hypotheses
    We want to see whether the two machines put the same mean quantities in packets. So the null hypothesis is that they do put the same mean in, while the alternative hypothesis is that they do not. This gives

    null hypothesis, $H_0$:     $\mu_1 = \mu_2$

    alternative hypothesis, $H_1$:     $\mu_1 \neq \mu_2$

2   Specify the level of significance
    We can use the standard 5%.

3   Calculate the acceptance range for the variable tested
    We are looking at the sampling distribution of $\bar{x}_1 - \bar{x}_2$, with sample sizes $n_1 = 30$ and $n_2 = 40$, and standard deviations $s_1 = 14$ and $s_2 = 10$. This gives a sampling distribution of $\bar{x}_1 - \bar{x}_2$, which is Normal with mean 0 and standard error:

$$standard\ error = \sqrt{\frac{s_1^{\,2}}{n_1} + \frac{s_2^{\,2}}{n_2}} = \sqrt{\frac{14^2}{30} + \frac{10^2}{40}} = 3.01$$

   For a 5% significance level and a two-sided test, the acceptance range is within 1.96 standard deviations of the mean. This defines the range:

$$0 - 1.96 \times 3.01 \quad to \quad 0 + 1.96 \times 3.01$$
$$- 5.90 \quad to \quad + 5.90$$

4   Find the actual value for the variable tested
    The observed difference in samples is $\bar{x}_1 - \bar{x}_2 = 180 - 170 = 10$.

5   Decide whether to accept or reject the null hypothesis
    The actual value is outside the acceptance range, so we reject the null hypothesis and accept the alternative hypothesis.

6   State the conclusion reached
    The evidence from the samples does not support the view that the mean weight put into packets is the same from each machine.

> *IN SUMMARY*

The standard approach to hypothesis testing can be extended to deal with the difference between sample means.

## 15.2.4 | Tests with small samples

When we looked at confidence intervals we noted that sampling distributions were only Normal when the population is Normal or the sample size is more than 30. If this condition is not met the sampling distribution follows a *t*-distribution. You will remember that the shape of the *t*-distribution depends on the sample size: with samples greater than 30 the *t*-distribution is very similar to the Normal, but as the sample size gets smaller the distribution gets lower and wider.

## WORKED EXAMPLE 15.10

A supermarket is getting complaints that its tins of strawberries contain a lot of juice and few strawberries. A team from the supermarket make a surprise visit to the supplier, who is about to deliver another batch. The tins in this batch are claimed to have a minimum of 300 g of fruit in a tin, but a random sample of 15 tins has a mean quantity of only 287 g with a standard deviation of 18 g. What can you say about the tins?

### Solution

Again we can use the standard approach for hypothesis testing.

1  State the null and alternative hypotheses
   The null hypothesis is that the mean weight of the fruit is 300 g, while the alternative hypothesis is that the weight is less than this. Then we have

$$H_0: \quad \mu = 300 \text{ g} \qquad H_1: \quad \mu < 300 \text{ g}$$

2  Specify the level of significance to be used
   We can use the standard 5%.

3  Calculate the acceptance range for the variable tested
   With a sample of size 15, the sampling distribution of the mean follows a *t*-distribution with $n - 1 = 15 - 1 = 14$ degrees of freedom, a mean of 300 g and standard deviation $s/\sqrt{n} = 18/\sqrt{15} = 4.65$ g. For a 5% significance level and a one-sided test, we look up a probability of 0.1 (i.e. 0.05 in each tail) with 14 degrees of freedom in *t*-tables. This gives a value of 1.761. Then the acceptance range is above $300 - 1.761 \times 4.65 = 291.81$ g.

4  Find the actual value for the variable tested
   The actual mean of the sample was 287 g.

5   Decide whether to accept or reject the null hypothesis
    The actual value is outside the acceptance range, so we reject the null hypothesis.

6   State the conclusion reached
    The evidence from the sample does not support the view that the mean weight is 300 g, but it supports the alternative hypothesis that the mean weight of fruit is less than 300 g.

---

IN SUMMARY

With small samples the sampling distribution of the mean follows a *t*-distribution. This can be used in the standard procedure for hypothesis testing.

## 15.2.5 | Paired tests

In the last two sections we have looked at tests to see whether two samples have the same mean, and then how to use the *t*-distribution for small samples. Now we can combine these two ideas into another useful test. This new test is used when the observations can be paired. If, for example, we want to see whether a diet works we can weigh a set of people before the diet, and then weigh them again after the diet. This gives pairs of data – two weights for each person on the diet. Now we can test to see whether there are differences between the first and the second observations – in other words we can see whether people have lost weight on the diet. Another place where you might use paired data is in an advertising campaign, where you can interview people before and after the campaign to see whether they have altered their views. Or we might have two different people interviewing candidates for a job. If the interviewers give each candidate an overall mark, we have paired observations and can check that the two interviewers are using the same criteria to judge candidates.

The easiest way to test for differences between paired observations is to calculate the difference between each pair. If the two sets of observations are similar, we would expect the mean difference to be around zero. But if the mean difference is actually much bigger than this, then we can assume that there are real differences between the two samples. So we are going to test the null hypothesis that the mean difference is zero.

## WORKED EXAMPLE 15.11

Amethyst Interviews counted the number of interviews eight of their staff did in a day. Then they adjusted the way the questions were presented, and again counted the number of interviews the eight staff did. From the following results, can you say whether the adjustments had any effect?

| Interviewer | 1 | 2 | 3 | 4 | 5 | 6 | 7 | 8 |
|---|---|---|---|---|---|---|---|---|
| Original interviews | 10 | 11 | 9 | 6 | 8 | 10 | 7 | 8 |
| Later interviews | 10 | 9 | 11 | 10 | 9 | 12 | 9 | 11 |

## Solution

For this test we are going to look at the differences between samples, so we will subtract the number of original interviews from the number of later interviews:

| Interviewer | 1 | 2 | 3 | 4 | 5 | 6 | 7 | 8 |
|---|---|---|---|---|---|---|---|---|
| Original interviews | 10 | 11 | 9 | 6 | 8 | 10 | 7 | 8 |
| Later interviews | 10 | 9 | 11 | 10 | 9 | 12 | 9 | 11 |
| Difference | 0 | −2 | 2 | 4 | 1 | 2 | 2 | 3 |

Now we can use the standard approach to see whether the differences are small enough to suggest the two samples are the same, or are big enough to suggest they are different.

1   State the null and alternative hypotheses
    We want to look at the differences between the pairs of figures and see how big these are. So we will use the null hypothesis that the mean difference is zero, and the alternative hypothesis that the mean difference is not zero.

$$\text{null hypothesis, } H_0: \quad \mu = 0$$

$$\text{alternative hypothesis, } H_1: \quad \mu \neq 0$$

2   Specify the level of significance to be used
    We will use the standard 5%.

3   Calculate the acceptance range for the variable tested
    We can use the standard formulae to calculate the mean of the differences as $(0-2+2+4+1+2+2+3)/8 = 1.5$, the variance of the differences as $((1.5)^2 + (3.5)^2 + (0.5)^2 + (2.5)^2 + (0.5)^2 + (0.5)^2 + (0.5)^2 + (1.5)^2)/8 = 3.0$ and the standard deviation as $\sqrt{3.0} = 1.732$. With a small sample of eight pairs of observations, the standard error is $1.732/\sqrt{8} = 0.612$, and we shall use a $t$-distribution with $8 - 1 = 7$ degrees of freedom. Appendix G shows that for a two-tail test the $t$-distribution with 7 degrees of freedom and 5% significance level has a value of 2.365. So the acceptance range is:

$$0 - 2.365 \times 0.612 \quad \text{to} \quad 0 + 2.365 \times 0.612$$

$$-1.447 \quad \text{to} \quad +1.447$$

4  Find the actual value for the variable tested
   The mean of the differences is $(0 - 2 + 2 + 4 + 1 + 2 + 2 + 3)/8 = 1.5$.

5  Decide whether to accept or reject the null hypothesis
   The actual value is outside the accepted range, so we can reject the null hypothesis.

6  State the conclusion reached
   The evidence does not support the view that there is no difference between the number of interviews before and after the adjustment. More plainly, you can say that the adjustments have made a significant difference to the number of interviews done.

We could, of course, use a computer for such calculations and Figure 15.5 shows the results from a spreadsheet. Here the data are shown on the left, and the analysis is on the right. The spreadsheet starts by summarizing the data. Then it gives some calculations. You will notice that the computer uses a slightly different way of presenting the results. We have calculated the limits within which we accept the null hypothesis, and then seen whether the actual value lies within these limits. An alternative would state the number of standard errors the acceptable range is from

|    | A | B | C | D | E | F | G |
|----|---|---|---|---|---|---|---|
| 1  | **Paired tests** | | | | | | |
| 2  | | | | | | | |
| 3  | **Amethyst Interviews** | | | | | | |
| 4  | | | | | | | |
| 5  | **Data** | | | | **t-test: Paired two-sample for means** | | |
| 6  | | | | | | | |
| 7  | **Original interviews** | | **Later interviews** | | | *Original* | *Later* |
| 8  | 10 | | 10 | | Mean | 8.6250 | 10.1250 |
| 9  | 11 | | 9 | | Variance | 2.8393 | 1.2679 |
| 10 | 9 | | 11 | | Observations | 8 | 8 |
| 11 | 6 | | 10 | | Hypothesized mean difference | 0 | |
| 12 | 8 | | 9 | | Degrees of freedom | 7 | |
| 13 | 10 | | 12 | | t statistic | 2.4510 | |
| 14 | 7 | | 9 | | P(T<=t) one-tail | 0.0279 | |
| 15 | 8 | | 11 | | t critical one-tail | 1.8946 | |
| 16 | | | | | P(T<=t) two-tail | 0.0557 | |
| 17 | | | | | t critical two-tail | 2.3646 | |

**Figure 15.5**  Spreadsheet calculations for paired tests.

the mean, and then find how many standard errors the actual value is away from the mean. In this example, the acceptable range is within 2.365 standard errors from the mean (this is called the critical *t*-value), while the actual value is 1.5/0.612 = 2.451 standard errors from the mean. If this value is less than the critical value then we accept the null hypothesis, but if – as in this case – the value is more than the critical value we reject the null hypothesis.

---

IN SUMMARY

We can extend the last two types of test we have done by looking at paired observations for small samples. Here we look at the differences between each pair and test whether they are close to zero.

## Self-assessment questions

**15.7**  When is a one-sided hypothesis test used?

**15.8**  Why can we not use the Normal distribution for small samples?

# 15.3 | Non-parametric tests

## 15.3.1 | Introduction

So far in this chapter we have looked at a range of problems where hypothesis testing can be used. In all of these we have proposed a hypothesis about the value of a variable and have then measured the variable in a sample to see if actual observations support the hypothesis. Variables that take a specific value during an investigation are often called parameters, so the hypothesis tests we have described are called **parametric tests**.

There are many situations where we want to test a hypothesis, but there is no variable we can measure. This happens with nominal data such as the type of industry, value for money, quality, and so on. Then we might suggest a hypothesis that one product gives better value for money than another, but we cannot do any measurement to support this view. In these circumstances we cannot use parametric hypothesis tests. Neither should we use them if we do not know the sampling distribution.

When we cannot use parametric tests, **non-parametric** or **distribution-free** tests are useful. These have the major benefit of making no assumptions about the distribution of the population. The most important non-parametric test is the $\chi^2$ test. $\chi$ is the Greek letter chi (pronounced 'ki'); in this context $\chi$ is always squared, and the individual value $\chi$ has no meaning.

There are situations in which parametric tests cannot be used and distribution-free, or non-parametric, tests are needed.

## 15.3.2 | Chi-squared test for goodness of fit

The chi-squared test is a hypothesis test, so the general approach is the same as with parametric tests. But the chi-squared test looks at the frequency of observations and sees if these match the expected frequencies.

Suppose we have a series of observed frequencies $O_1, O_2, O_3, ..., O_n$, and were expecting the frequencies $E_1, E_2, E_3, ..., E_n$. The difference between these tells us how closely the observations match expectations. To be specific, we can define $\chi^2$ as:

$$\chi^2 = \frac{(O_1 - E_1)^2}{E_1} + \frac{(O_2 - E_2)^2}{E_2} + \frac{(O_3 - E_3)^2}{E_3} \cdots \frac{(O_n - E_n)^2}{E_n}$$

or:

$$\chi^2 = \sum \frac{(O - E)^2}{E}$$

Squaring the difference between observed and expected values removes any negative values, and then dividing by $E_i$ gives a distribution with a standard shape.

If the hypothesis is true, the observed frequencies will be close to the expected frequencies, and $\chi^2$ will have a value close to zero. On the other hand, if the original hypothesis is not true the differences will be large and $\chi^2$ will have a larger value. Now we need to define a test value of $\chi^2$ so that an actual value above this test value leads us to reject the hypothesis, but an actual value below this test value means we cannot reject the hypothesis. This test level is called the **critical value** and can be found from standard tables, shown in Appendix H.

The shape of the $\chi^2$ distribution depends on the degrees of freedom, as shown in Figure 15.6. You can also notice that the distribution only has positive values. We met the idea of degrees of freedom when talking about the $t$-distribution and you will remember that they essentially measure the number of pieces of information that are free to take any value. If we know the mean of $n$ values, $n - 1$ values are free to take any value, but the $n$th value must then be fixed to give the correct mean. So there are $n - 1$ degrees of freedom. With the $\chi^2$ distribution we are looking at the frequency of observations in classes. Then the number of degrees of freedom is calculated from:

degrees of freedom = number of classes – number of estimated variables – 1

Now we have all the information we need, and can now start to do the test. Even though the $\chi^2$ test is non-parametric, the approach is the same as for the parametric test. But there are some small differences. In particular, instead of

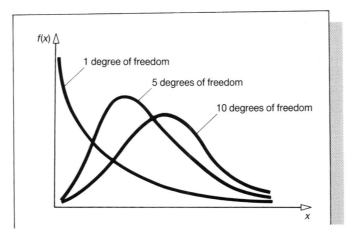

**Figure 15.6**   Chi-squared distribution with varying degrees of freedom.

finding an acceptance range, we find a critical value. If the actual value of $\chi^2$ is above this value we reject the hypothesis, and if it is below this value we accept it. (This is similar to the computer's approach in Worked Example 15.11.)

## WORKED EXAMPLE 15.12

Five factories report the following number of minor accidents in a five-year period:

| Factory | 1 | 2 | 3 | 4 | 5 |
|---|---|---|---|---|---|
| Number of accidents | 31 | 42 | 29 | 35 | 38 |

Does this evidence suggest that some factories have more accidents than others?

### Solution

Now we can use the standard procedure.

1   State the null and alternative hypotheses
    The null hypothesis, $H_0$, is that each factory expects the same number of accidents. Then the alternative hypothesis, $H_1$, is that each factory does not have the same number of accidents.

2   Specify the level of significance
    We can take this as 5%.

3   Calculate the critical value of $\chi^2$
    In this problem there are five classes, and no variables have been estimated, so the degrees of freedom are $5 - 0 - 1 = 4$. With a 5% significance level we look up 0.05 in $\chi^2$ tables and find a critical value of 9.49.

4 Find the actual value of $\chi^2$

For this we calculate:

$$\chi^2 = \Sigma \, \frac{(O - E)^2}{E}$$

There are 175 accidents. If each factory expects the same number, the expected number of accidents in each factory, $E$, is 175/5 = 35. Then the calculations are as shown in Table 15.1. This tells us that the actual value of $\chi^2$ is 3.143.

**Table 15.1**

| Factory | $O$ | $E$ | $(O - E)$ | $(O - E)^2$ | $(O - E)^2/E$ |
|---------|-----|-----|-----------|-------------|----------------|
| 1 | 31 | 35 | $-4$ | 16 | 0.457 |
| 2 | 42 | 35 | 7 | 49 | 1.400 |
| 3 | 29 | 35 | $-6$ | 36 | 1.029 |
| 4 | 35 | 35 | 0 | 0 | 0.000 |
| 5 | 38 | 35 | 3 | 9 | 0.257 |
| Total | 175 | 175 | | | 3.143 |

5 Decide whether to accept or reject the null hypothesis

The actual value (3.143) is less than the critical value (9.49) so we cannot reject the null hypothesis.

6 State the conclusion reached

The evidence suggests that each factory can expect the same number of accidents. Any variation is purely by chance.

The above example effectively tested whether there was a uniform distribution of accidents across factories. In other words, we hypothesized that the accident rate was a uniform distribution and saw whether the data fitted this. We could use the same approach for other distributions, so we could find whether a distribution fits a binomial, Poisson or any other distribution.

# WORKED EXAMPLE 15.13

A quality management department recorded the number of reports that were defective each day. They found the following results:

| Defects | 0 | 1 | 2 | 3 | 4 | 5 |
|---------|---|---|---|---|---|---|
| Days | 26 | 42 | 18 | 10 | 3 | 1 |

Does the number of defects follow a binomial distribution?

## Solution

Using the standard procedure:

1   State the null and alternative hypotheses
    The null hypothesis, $H_0$, is that the distribution is binomial. The alternative hypothesis, $H_1$, is that the distribution is not binomial.

2   Specify the level of significance
    We can take this as 5%.

3   Calculate the critical value of $\chi^2$
    In this problem there is going to be some adjustment of the data, so we shall return to this calculation a little later.

4   Find the actual value of $\chi^2$
    We have 100 days of data, and the total number of defects is:

$$(26 \times 0) + (42 \times 1) + (18 \times 2) + (10 \times 3) + (3 \times 4) + (1 \times 5) = 125$$

The mean number of defects is $125/100 = 1.25$ a day and we want to find the probability of 0, 1, 2, 3, 4 and 5 defects happening in a day. We know from Chapter 13 that the mean of a binomial distribution is $np$, where $n$ is the number of trials and $p$ is the probability of success. In this case the number of trials is the maximum number of defects, so $n = 5$. Then $1.25 = 5 \times p$ or $p = 0.25$.

Now we have the probability of a success and can find the expected distribution from the binomial tables in Appendix D. Multiplying these probabilities by the total number of days gives the expected distribution of defects shown in the following table:

| Number of defects | 0 | 1 | 2 | 3 | 4 | 5 |
|---|---|---|---|---|---|---|
| Probability | 0.2373 | 0.3955 | 0.2637 | 0.0879 | 0.0146 | 0.0010 |
| Expected frequency | 23.73 | 39.55 | 26.37 | 8.79 | 1.46 | 0.10 |

One problem here is that the $\chi^2$ distribution does not work well with expected frequencies of less than 5. When these occur, we have to combine adjacent classes so that the expected number of observations becomes greater than 5. Adding the last three classes gives the modified expected distribution below:

| Number of defects | 0 | 1 | 2 | 3 or more |
|---|---|---|---|---|
| Probability | 0.2373 | 0.3955 | 0.2637 | 0.1035 |
| Frequency | 23.73 | 39.55 | 26.37 | 10.35 |

Now you can see why we delayed the calculation of the critical value. There are now four classes, and we have estimated one parameter (the probability of success), so the number of degrees of freedom is:

number of classes – number of estimated parameters – 1 = 4 – 1 – 1 = 2

Looking up the critical value for a significance level of 5% and two degrees of freedom gives a value of 5.99.

**Table 15.2**

| Frequency | $O$ | $E$ | $(O-E)$ | $(O-E)^2$ | $(O-E)^2/E$ |
|---|---|---|---|---|---|
| 0 | 26 | 23.73 | 2.27 | 5.153 | 0.217 |
| 1 | 42 | 39.55 | 2.45 | 6.003 | 0.152 |
| 2 | 18 | 26.37 | −8.37 | 70.057 | 2.657 |
| 3 or more | 14 | 10.35 | 3.65 | 13.323 | 1.287 |
| Total | 100 | 100 | | | 4.313 |

The actual value of $\chi^2$ is calculated in Table 15.2 as 4.313.

5 Decide whether to accept or reject the null hypothesis
The actual value of $\chi^2$ (4.313) is less than the critical value (5.99) so we cannot reject the null hypothesis.

6 State the conclusion reached
The evidence suggests that the observations follow a binomial distribution.

# WORKED EXAMPLE 15.14

An electrical contractor records the frequency of faults per kilometre of a certain type of cable as follows:

| Number of faults | 0 | 1 | 2 | 3 | 4 | 5 | 6 |
|---|---|---|---|---|---|---|---|
| Number of kilometres | 37 | 51 | 23 | 7 | 4 | 2 | 1 |

Do these data follow a Poisson distribution?

## Solution

1 State the null and alternative hypotheses
The null hypothesis, $H_0$, is that the distribution is Poisson. The alternative hypothesis, $H_1$, is that the distribution is not Poisson.

2 Specify the level of significance
We can assume that this is 5%.

3 Calculate the critical value of $\chi^2$
Again, there is going to be some adjustment of the data, so we shall return to this calculation a little later.

4 Find the actual value of $\chi^2$
We have 125 km of data, and the total number of defects is:

$$(37 \times 0) + (51 \times 1) + (23 \times 2) + (7 \times 3) + (4 \times 4) + (2 \times 5) + (1 \times 6) = 150$$

|  | A | B | C | D | E | F | G |
|---|---|---|---|---|---|---|---|
| 1 | **Chi-squared test** | | | | | | |
| 2 | | | | | | | |
| 3 | | | **Expected** | **Revised** | **Actual** | | |
| 4 | **Number of defects** | **Probability** | **frequency** | **frequency (E)** | **frequency (O)** | **(O – E)** | **(O – E)²/E** |
| 5 | 0 | 0.3012 | 37.6493 | 37.6493 | 37 | –0.6493 | 0.0112 |
| 6 | 1 | 0.3614 | 45.1791 | 45.1791 | 51 | 5.8209 | 0.7500 |
| 7 | 2 | 0.2169 | 27.1075 | 27.1075 | 23 | –4.1075 | 0.6224 |
| 8 | 3 | 0.0867 | 10.8430 | 15.0641 | 14 | –1.0641 | 0.0752 |
| 9 | 4 | 0.0260 | 3.2529 | | | | |
| 10 | 5 | 0.0062 | 0.7807 | | | | |
| 11 | >=6 | 0.0015 | 0.1875 | | | | |
| 12 | **Totals** | **1** | **125** | | | | **1.4587** |

**Figure 15.7**  Calculations for chi-squared test in Worked Example 15.14.

The mean number of defects is $150/125 = 1.2$ per km. This is the mean of the Poisson distribution, so we can find the expected distribution from the tables in Appendix E or we can use a spreadsheet as shown in Figure 15.7. Again, we need to combine adjacent classes so that each class has more than five observations. Adding the last four classes gives the revised values. Now you can see why we delayed the calculation of the critical value. There are now four classes, so the number of degrees of freedom is:

number of classes – number of estimated parameters – $1 = 4 - 1 - 1 = 2$

with the mean being the estimated parameter.

Looking up the critical value for a significance level of 5% and two degrees of freedom gives a value of 5.99. The actual value of $\chi^2$ is 1.4587.

5   Decide whether to accept or reject the null hypothesis

The actual value is less than the critical value, so we cannot reject the null hypothesis.

6   State the conclusion reached

The evidence suggests that the observations follow a Poisson distribution.

# WORKED EXAMPLE 15.15

Humbolt Farm Products is about to do some statistical analyses on the mean weight of a product delivered to it, but these analyses are only valid if the weight is Normally distributed. The product is known to have a mean weight of 45 g and a standard deviation of 15 g. A sample of 500 units was taken, with weights given in the distribution shown in Table 15.3. Can this be considered Normal?

**Table 15.3**

| Weight (g) | Number of observations |
|---|---|
| less than 10 | 9 |
| 10 to 19.99 | 31 |
| 20 to 29.99 | 65 |
| 30 to 39.99 | 97 |
| 40 to 49.99 | 115 |
| 50 to 59.99 | 94 |
| 60 to 69.99 | 49 |
| 70 to 79.99 | 24 |
| 80 to 89.99 | 16 |

## Solution

This is an important question, as many statistical analyses are only valid if there is a Normal distribution.

1   State the null and alternative hypotheses
    The null hypothesis, $H_0$, is that the distribution is Normal. The alternative hypothesis, $H_1$, is that the distribution is not Normal.

2   Specify the level of significance
    We can assume that this is 5%.

3   Calculate the critical value of $\chi^2$
    The number of degrees of freedom is $(9 - 0 - 1 = )$ 8. Appendix H shows that the critical value for $\chi^2$ with 8 degrees of freedom at a 5% significance level is 15.5.

4   Find the actual value of $\chi^2$
    The probability that an observation is in the range 10 to 19.99 is:
    $$P(\text{between 10 and 19.99}) = P(\text{less than 20}) - P(\text{less than 10})$$

   Now:
    20 is $(20 - 45)/15 = -1.67$ standard deviations from the mean, corresponding to a probability of 0.0475

   and
    10 is $(10 - 45)/15 = -2.33$ standard deviations from the mean, corresponding to a probability of 0.0099.

   So:
    $$P(\text{between 10 and 19.99}) = 0.0475 - 0.0099 = 0.0376$$
    The expected number of observations in this range is $0.0376 \times 500 = 19$ (to the nearest integer). Repeating this calculation for the other probabilities gives the results in Table 15.4. Adding the values for $(O - E)^2/E$ gives the actual value of $\chi^2$ as 43.41.

5   Decide whether to accept or reject the null hypothesis

    The actual value (43.41) is greater than the critical value (15.5), so we must reject the hypothesis that the sample is Normally distributed.

6   State the conclusion reached

    The evidence suggests that the observations do not follow a Normal distribution.

**Table 15.4**

| Weight | O | Probability | E | $(O - E)^2/E$ |
|---|---|---|---|---|
| < 10 | 9 | 0.0099 | 4.95 | 3.31 |
| 10 to 19.99 | 31 | 0.0376 | 18.8 | 7.92 |
| 20 to 29.99 | 65 | 0.1112 | 55.6 | 1.59 |
| 30 to 39.99 | 97 | 0.2120 | 106.0 | 0.76 |
| 40 to 49.99 | 115 | 0.2586 | 129.3 | 1.58 |
| 50 to 59.99 | 94 | 0.2120 | 106.0 | 1.36 |
| 60 to 69.99 | 49 | 0.1112 | 55.6 | 0.78 |
| 70 to 79.99 | 24 | 0.0376 | 18.8 | 1.44 |
| 80 to 89.99 | 16 | 0.0099 | 4.95 | 24.67 |

## IN SUMMARY

The $\chi^2$ distribution allows a non-parametric test for hypotheses. It is particularly suited to testing the goodness of fit, to see whether data follow a specified distribution.

## Tests of association

The $\chi^2$ test is also useful for testing association, which is shown in a **contingency table**. Suppose you are analysing the results of a questionnaire about the source of finance for purchasing a house. You might come across two questions that have the number of responses in the following two tables:

| Size of loan | Number of replies |
|---|---|
| Less than £20,000 | 65 |
| £20,000 to £60,000 | 90 |
| More than £60,000 | 45 |
| Total | 200 |

| Source of loan | Number of replies |
|---|---|
| Building society | 125 |
| Bank | 55 |
| Elsewhere | 20 |
| Total | 200 |

Looking at these answers you might ask whether there is any relationship or association between the size of a loan and the organization giving it. When you look more closely at the replies to these questions they may break down into the pattern shown in Table 15.5. This is a contingency table. A $\chi^2$ test can tell whether there is any statistical association between the two sets of answers. Not surprisingly, the method for this is the same one we have been using for all hypothesis tests.

**Table 15.5**

| Source of mortgage | Size of loan | | | Total |
| --- | --- | --- | --- | --- |
| | *less than £20,000* | *£20,000 to £60,000* | *more than £60,000* | |
| Building society | 30 | 55 | 40 | 125 |
| Bank | 23 | 29 | 3 | 55 |
| Elsewhere | 12 | 6 | 2 | 20 |
| Total | 65 | 90 | 45 | 200 |

# WORKED EXAMPLE 15.16

Find whether there is any association between the two answers described in the contingency table above.

## Solution

1  State the null and alternative hypotheses
   The null hypothesis, $H_0$, is that there is no association between the size of the mortgage and its source – so these two are independent. The alternative hypothesis, $H_1$, is that there is an association between the two sets of answers; the two are not independent.

2  Specify the level of significance
   We can assume that this is 5%.

3  Calculate the critical value of $\chi^2$
   For a contingency table the degrees of freedom are calculated from:

   degrees of freedom = (number of rows – 1) × (number of columns – 1)

   Here there are three rows and three columns (ignoring the totals) so there are:

   $(3 - 1) \times (3 - 1) = 4$ degrees of freedom

   Looking up $\chi^2$ tables for a 5% significance level and 4 degrees of freedom gives a critical value of 9.49.

4  Find the actual value of $\chi^2$
   For this we need to calculate the expected number of replies in each element of the matrix. Take the top left-hand cell, which shows the number of people who take a loan of less than £20,000 from a building society. A total of 125 loans come from a building society, so the probability that any particular loan comes

from a building society is 125/200 = 0.625. A total of 65 loans were for less than £20,000, so the probability that any particular loan is for less than £20,000 is 65/200 = 0.325. Then the probability that a loan came from a building society and is for less than £10,000 is 0.625 × 0.325 = 0.203. Since there are 200 loans described in the questionnaire, the expected number of this type is 0.203 × 200 = 40.625.

Repeating this calculation for every other element in the matrix gives the numbers of expected loans shown in Table 15.6.

**Table 15.6**

| Source of mortgage | Size of loan | | | Total |
|---|---|---|---|---|
| | less than £20,000 | £20,000 to £60,000 | more than £60,000 | |
| Building society | 40.625 | 56.250 | 28.125 | 125 |
| Bank | 17.875 | 24.750 | 12.375 | 55 |
| Elsewhere | 6.500 | 9.000 | 4.500 | 20 |
| Total | 65 | 90 | 45 | 200 |

Now we have nine observed frequencies, and a corresponding set of nine expected frequencies. When we calculated the expected frequencies we assumed that there was no connection between the loan size and its source. If there are differences between these expected and observed values, these are caused by an association between the loan size and its source. The closer the association, the larger will be the difference, and the larger the calculated value of $\chi^2$. So now we need to find the actual value of $\chi^2$. This is done in Table 15.7 where the actual value of $\chi^2$ is found to be 24.165.

**Table 15.7**

| | $O$ | $E$ | $(O - E)$ | $(O - E)^2$ | $(O - E)^2/E$ |
|---|---|---|---|---|---|
| | 30 | 40.625 | −10.625 | 112.891 | 2.779 |
| | 55 | 56.250 | −1.25 | 1.563 | 0.028 |
| | 40 | 28.125 | 11.875 | 141.016 | 5.014 |
| | 23 | 17.875 | 5.125 | 26.266 | 1.469 |
| | 29 | 24.750 | 4.25 | 18.063 | 0.730 |
| | 3 | 12.375 | −9.375 | 87.891 | 7.102 |
| | 12 | 6.500 | 5.500 | 30.250 | 4.654 |
| | 6 | 9.000 | −3.000 | 9.000 | 1.000 |
| | 2 | 4.500 | −2.500 | 6.250 | 1.389 |
| Total | 200 | 200 | | | 24.165 |

5   Decide whether to accept or reject the null hypothesis
    The actual value is greater than the critical value, so we reject the null hypothesis and accept the alternative hypothesis.

6   State the conclusion reached

The evidence suggests that there is an association between the answer to the two questions, so the size of a mortgage is related to its source.

You should always be careful when doing $\chi^2$ tests, because they do not work well if the number of expected observations in any class falls below five. In this example one element has an expected frequency of 4.5, so we should really combine this cell with others, perhaps combining the rows for banks and other sources.

Figure 15.8 shows the printout from a statistics package that calculates the value of $\chi^2$ for this problem.

```
001 > read data columns c1–c3
002 > 30   55   40
003 > 23   29    3
004 > 12    6    2
005 > column titles <20, 20-60, >60
006 > row titles building society, bank, elsewhere
007 > end data
008 > chisquare calculate c1–c3
```

Expected counts are printed below observed counts

|  | <20 | 20–60 | >60 | Total |
|---|---|---|---|---|
| building | 30 | 55 | 40 | 125 |
| society | 40.62 | 56.25 | 28.12 | |
| bank | 23 | 29 | 3 | 55 |
| | 17.88 | 24.75 | 12.37 | |
| elsewhere | 12 | 6 | 2 | 20 |
| | 6.50 | 9.00 | 4.50 | |
| Total | 65 | 90 | 45 | 200 |

```
ChiSq =2.779 + 0.028 + 5.014 +
        1.469 + 0.730 + 7.102 +
        4.654 + 1.000 + 1.389 = 24.165
df = 4

* WARNING *
1 cell with expected counts less than 5.0

009 > significance = 0.05
010 > chisquare test c1–c3

Critical value of ChiSq = 9.488
Calculated value of ChiSq = 24.165
Conclusion        = reject null hypothesis
```

**Figure 15.8**   Printout from a statistics package doing a chi-squared test.

---

| IN SUMMARY |

Chi-squared distributions can be used for contingency tables. These typically note the association between the answers in a questionnaire.

# Self-assessment questions

**15.9**  What is the main difference between a parametric and a non-parametric test?

**15.10**  When are non-parametric tests used?

**15.11**  'When a parametric test cannot be used, a non-parametric test can always be used instead.' Is this statement true?

**15.12**  Why does a $\chi^2$ test only have a critical value rather than an acceptance range?

**15.13**  What is $\chi$ (the square root of $\chi^2$) used for?

---

CHAPTER REVIEW

This chapter has discussed hypothesis testing, which is used to see whether a statement about a population is supported by the evidence in a sample. In particular, the chapter:

- described the overall approach of hypothesis testing
- used hypothesis testing on population means
- extended the standard approach to proportions, one-sided tests, differences between means and small samples
- outlined the use of non-parametric tests
- used $\chi^2$ tests for goodness of fit

---

# Problems

**15.1**  The mean wage of people living in a block of flats is said to be £400 a week with a standard deviation of £100. A random sample of 36 people was examined.

(a) What is the acceptance range for a 5% significance level?

(b) What is the acceptance range for a 1% significance level?

**15.2**  The weight of packets of biscuits is claimed to be 500 g. A random sample of 50 packets has a mean weight of 495 g and a standard deviation of 10 g. Use a significance level of 5% to see if the data from the sample support the original claim.

**15.3**  Hamil Coaches says that its long-distance coaches take 5 hours for a particular journey. Last week a consumer group tested these figures by timing a sample of 30 journeys. These had a mean time of 5 hours 10 minutes with a standard deviation of 20 minutes. What report can the consumer group make?

**15.4**  A food processor specifies the mean weight of a product as 200 g. The output is Normally distributed with a standard deviation of 15 g. A random sample of 20 has a mean of 195 g. Does this evidence suggest that the mean weight is too low?

**15.5** A survey suggests that 50% of all people have a mobile phone. A random sample of 100 people were interviewed, and 45 of them had a mobile. Does this sample support the original claim?

**15.6** The quality management function in ScotElecGen plc says that 12% of letters posted contain errors. A sample of 200 letters was checked and 31 of them contained errors. What do these results suggest?

**15.7** Health Service managers say that doctors should not spend more than 2 hours a day doing paperwork. A sample of 40 doctors spent an average of 2 hours 25 minutes a day doing paperwork, with a standard deviation of 55 minutes. Does the sample support the view that doctors only spend 2 hours a day on paperwork?

**15.8** A computer monitor has an advertised life of 30 000 hours. A sample of 50 monitors had a life of 28 500 hours with a standard deviation of 1000 hours. What can you say about the advertisements?

**15.9** A company operates two similar factories. There is some disagreement, because people working in each factory think those in the other factory are getting higher wages. A sample of wages was taken from each factory with the following results:

    Sample 1:   size = 45   mean = £350   standard deviation = £45

    Sample 2:   size = 35   mean = £330   standard deviation = £40

    What can you say about the wages?

**15.10** A car manufacturer says its cars cost £500 a year less to maintain than those of its competitors. To test this, a consumer group found the cost of maintaining ten cars for a year, and the mean saving was £410 with a standard deviation of £100. What can you say about the manufacturer's claim?

**15.11** Five construction sites reported the following numbers of minor accidents in a year:

| Factory | 1 | 2 | 3 | 4 | 5 |
|---|---|---|---|---|---|
| Number of accidents | 23 | 45 | 18 | 34 | 28 |

Does this evidence suggest that some sites have statistically more accidents than others?

**15.12** The following table shows the number of defective components supplied each day by a factory:

| Number of defects | 0 | 1 | 2 | 3 | 4 | 5 |
|---|---|---|---|---|---|---|
| Number of days | 8 | 22 | 33 | 29 | 15 | 3 |

Do these data follow a binomial distribution?

**15.13** The number of road accidents reporting to a hospital emergency ward is shown in the following table. Do these figures follow a Poisson distribution?

| Number of accidents | 0 | 1 | 2 | 3 | 4 | 5 | 6 |
|---|---|---|---|---|---|---|---|
| Number of days | 17 | 43 | 52 | 37 | 20 | 8 | 4 |

**15.14** Do the figures in the following table follow a Normal distribution?

| Weight (g) | Number of observations |
|---|---|
| less than 5 | 5 |
| 5 to 19.99 | 43 |
| 20 to 34.99 | 74 |
| 35 to 49.99 | 103 |
| 50 to 64.99 | 121 |
| 65 to 79.99 | 97 |
| 80 to 94.99 | 43 |
| 95 to 109.99 | 21 |
| 110 and more | 8 |

# Computer exercises

**15.1** It is quite difficult to get statistics packages that automatically do $\chi^2$ goodness of fit tests. Nonetheless, they can give some help. Use a statistics package to see how it tackles these tests. Use it to check the results given in Figure 15.8. How could the package be improved?

**15.2** Figure 15.9 shows a spreadsheet doing some calculations for a $t$-test on the means of two samples. Look at this printout and make sure you know what is happening. See whether you have a spreadsheet that does similar calculations, and find what tests it can do. How could you improve the format?

**15.3** Eight observations were taken and a null hypothesis was proposed that these fit a Poisson distribution. Figure 15.10 shows a computer printout from a statistics package used for doing a $\chi^2$ goodness of fit test with these figures. Make sure you can understand what is happening in this printout. Use a statistics package to check the results. Why do you think only four values were tested?

**15.4** Design a spreadsheet to check the results of Worked Example 15.16. Extend the spreadsheet to deal with larger contingency tables.

**15.5** Supermarkets often claim that they give the lowest prices. Collect some data from competing stores and analyse the results. What can you say about the prices?

| | A | B | C | D | E | F |
|---|---|---|---|---|---|---|
| 1 | **Two samples** | | | | | |
| 2 | | | | | | |
| 3 | **Data** | | | **t-test: Two-sample assuming equal variances** | | |
| 4 | **Variable 1** | **Variable 2** | | | | |
| 5 | 10 | 8 | | | *Variable 1* | *Variable 2* |
| 6 | 16 | 10 | | Mean | 10.600 | 7.786 |
| 7 | 13 | 9 | | Variance | 12.489 | 4.335 |
| 8 | 6 | 6 | | Observations | 10 | 14 |
| 9 | 8 | 4 | | Pooled variance | 7.671 | |
| 10 | 9 | 10 | | Hypothesized mean difference | 0 | |
| 11 | 16 | 9 | | df | 22 | |
| 12 | 9 | 9 | | t stat | 2.454 | |
| 13 | 12 | 7 | | P(T<=t) one-tail | 0.011 | |
| 14 | 7 | 4 | | t critical one-tail | 1.717 | |
| 15 | | 10 | | P(T<=t) two-tail | 0.023 | |
| 16 | | 9 | | t critical two-tail | 2.074 | |
| 17 | | 6 | | | | |
| 18 | | 8 | | | | |

**Figure 15.9** Spreadsheet doing calculations for a *t*-test.

```
001 > name c1 'obs' c2 'expt' c3 'chisqr'

002 > set c1
003 > 34 38 16 7
004 > end

005 > set c2
006 > 36.8 36.8 18.4 8.0
007 > end

008 > let c3=(c1–c2)**2/c2
009 > sum c3 k1
      SUM       =      0.69022

010 > cdf k1 k2;
SUBC > chisquare 3.
011 > let k2=1–k2
012 > print c1–c3 k1 k2
K1          0.690217
K2          0.875502

      ROW         obs       expt       chisqr

        1          34       36.8      0.213043
        2          38       36.8      0.039130
        3          16       18.4      0.313043
        4           7        8.0      0.125000

013 > stop
```

**Figure 15.10** Printout from a statistics package doing a $\chi^2$ test.

# Case study

## Willingham Consumer Protection Department

Willingham Consumer Protection Department (WCPD) is responsible for administering all weights and measures laws in its area. A part of its service makes sure that packages of food and drink contain the quantities stated.

One week, WCPD decided to test containers of milk. Most of these tests were done at dairies, where procedures and historical data were also examined. WCPD also visited local shops and milk roundsmen to buy random samples of products.

On two consecutive days they bought 50 containers with a nominal content of 4 pints or 2.27 litres. The actual contents of these, in litres, are as follows:

| Day 1: | 2.274 | 2.275 | 2.276 | 2.270 | 2.269 | 2.271 | 2.265 | 2.275 | 2.263 | 2.278 |
|--------|-------|-------|-------|-------|-------|-------|-------|-------|-------|-------|
|        | 2.260 | 2.278 | 2.280 | 2.275 | 2.261 | 2.280 | 2.279 | 2.270 | 2.275 | 2.263 |
|        | 2.275 | 2.281 | 2.266 | 2.277 | 2.271 | 2.273 | 2.283 | 2.260 | 2.259 | 2.276 |
|        | 2.286 | 2.275 | 2.271 | 2.273 | 2.291 | 2.271 | 2.269 | 2.265 | 2.258 | 2.283 |
|        | 2.274 | 2.278 | 2.276 | 2.281 | 2.269 | 2.259 | 2.291 | 2.289 | 2.276 | 2.283 |

| Day 2: | 2.270 | 2.276 | 2.258 | 2.259 | 2.281 | 2.265 | 2.278 | 2.270 | 2.294 | 2.255 |
|--------|-------|-------|-------|-------|-------|-------|-------|-------|-------|-------|
|        | 2.271 | 2.284 | 2.276 | 2.293 | 2.261 | 2.270 | 2.271 | 2.276 | 2.269 | 2.268 |
|        | 2.272 | 2.272 | 2.273 | 2.280 | 2.281 | 2.276 | 2.263 | 2.260 | 2.295 | 2.257 |
|        | 2.248 | 2.276 | 2.284 | 2.276 | 2.270 | 2.271 | 2.269 | 2.278 | 2.276 | 2.274 |
|        | 2.291 | 2.257 | 2.281 | 2.276 | 2.274 | 2.273 | 2.273 | 2.270 | 2.272 | 2.278 |

When they were collecting these figures, WCPD inspectors were convinced that there were no problems with the large dairies, but some small operations were not so reliable. This was because large dairies could afford modern, well-designed equipment and employed special quality assurance staff. Smaller operators used older, less reliable equipment, and could not afford to run a quality assurance department. Two companies, in particular, were identified as needing further checks. Random samples of 15 containers were taken from each of these dairies, with the following results:

Company 1: 2.261  2.273  2.250  2.268  2.268  2.262  2.272  2.269  2.268  2.257
           2.260  2.270  2.254  2.249  2.267
Company 2: 2.291  2.265  2.283  2.275  2.248  2.286  2.268  2.271  2.284  2.256
           2.284  2.255  2.283  2.275  2.276

What kind of report could the milk inspectors write about their findings? What follow-up action could they recommend?

# PART FIVE

# Business problems with uncertainty

This book is divided into five parts, each of which covers a different aspect of quantitative methods in business. The first part gave the background and context for the rest of the book. The second part discussed data collection and description. The third part looked at methods of solving specific types of business problem. The fourth part gave an introduction to probability and statistical methods, laying the foundations of business statistics. This is the fifth part, which uses some of the ideas developed so far to tackle specific business problems. These problems contain uncertainty and involve some statistical analysis.

There are four chapters in this part.

Chapter 16 looks at ways of analysing business decisions, particularly those where probabilities can be given to various outcomes. Decisions are often made in an unstructured environment, so it is important to describe problems in a standard format.

Chapter 17 shows how to use quantitative models in the control of stocks. Every organization holds stocks of some kind, and the costs can be surprisingly high. Models can help minimize these costs in a range of circumstances.

Chapter 18 describes the use of network analysis for planning projects. A project consists of any self-contained piece of work. Network analysis divides this into a set of activities and analyses their relationships using a network.

Chapter 19 looks at the management of queues. A system will have queues whenever a customer arrives for a service and finds that the server is busy. There are many analyses for different queuing problems, but the arithmetic can become tedious. Simulation gives another way of tackling such problems.

## Ideas in Practice – Ace Dairies

Ace Dairies gives a home delivery service for milk, dairy products and a range of related goods. Roger Smitheram has run the dairy for the past 12 years.

At the heart of the business is an information system which records full details of the 500 regular customers, including their usual orders, details of special orders, where to deliver, how they pay and so on. Every day the system calculates the sales that Roger can expect in two days' time. He adjusts this to allow for possible variations and to give some safety, and he passes the resulting order to Unigate Dairies in Totnes. This dairy supplies milkmen in Wales and the whole of south-west England. The following day Unigate delivers to a holding depot in Camborne and passes on Roger's order to his cold store in Hayle. At 5.30 the following morning Roger collects the order from his cold store and starts delivering. This normally takes until 1.30 in the afternoon, but on Fridays he collects most money and can finish after 5.00 pm.

There are several specific problems facing Ace Dairies. There is, for example, some variation in demand, so Roger has to carry spare items. He cannot carry too many of these as dairy products have a short life, and anything not delivered quickly is thrown away. Roger aims at keeping his waste down to 2% of sales. There are also problems with maintaining service during holidays and when Unigate has problems delivering from its distant dairy.

Perhaps Roger's main concern is maintaining his sales over the long term. Demand for doorstep deliveries is declining as more people are buying cheap milk in bulk at supermarkets. As a result, the number of milkmen in Hayle has declined from ten to three over the past few years.

Ace Dairies has to make a series of decisions about forecast demand, stocks, amount of waste, delivery times, service levels and so on. In common with most businesses, these decisions have to be made in an uncertain and changing environment.

# 16 | Analysing business decisions

Chapter outline                              490
16.1  Giving structure to                    491
      decisions
16.2  Decision-making under                  493
      certainty
16.3  Decision-making under                  495
      strict uncertainty
16.4  Decision-making                        501
      under risk
16.5  Sequential decisions                   510
      and decision trees
Chapter review                               518
Problems                                     518
Computer exercises                           521
Case study:                                  525
      The Newisham Reservoir

## CHAPTER OUTLINE

This chapter talks about decision analysis. Its purpose is to show a logical approach to decision-making, and to develop ways of making better decisions.

The chapter starts by showing how some structure can be given to decisions. Then it considers decisions with certainty, strict uncertainty (using decision criteria) and risk (using expected values and utilities).

As well as single decisions, the chapter considers series of sequential decisions using decision trees.

After reading this chapter and doing the exercises you should be able to:

- draw a map of a decision situation
- design a payoff matrix
- make decisions under certainty
- describe situations of strict uncertainty and use decision criteria
- describe situations of risk and use expected values
- use Bayes' theorem to update conditional probabilities for decisions under risk
- appreciate the use of utilities
- use decision trees for sequential decisions

# 16.1 | Giving structure to decisions

Everybody has to make decisions: which car is the best buy; should we buy an ISA, where should we eat; should we drive to work or go by train; which play should we go to; should we make tea or coffee; and so on. These decisions come in a steady stream. Most of them are fairly unimportant, and are made using a combination of experience, intuition and subjectivity. But in business, decisions can be important, and managers need a more formal approach to decision-making.

Many business decisions are complicated and involve a lot of different factors. Suppose a company makes a product but finds its profit is too low. Two obvious remedies are to reduce costs or increase the price. But if the price is increased the demand may go down. On the other hand, if costs are reduced the price may be reduced and demand may go up. If demand changes, the factory may have to reschedule production and change marketing strategies. Changed production schedules could affect production of other items, change employment prospects and so on.

We could continue with these more or less random thoughts for some time, but would soon lose track of the main points of our argument. So it is useful to have a simple diagram that shows the interactions. A **problem map** (or relationship diagram) is useful for this, and part of a map for the discussion above is given in Figure 16.1.

As you can see, the map is an informal way of representing a stream of connected ideas. Such maps are useful for sorting out ideas and clearly showing the interactions. But they do not help directly in decision-making, as they do not identify the best choices. If we want to make good decisions, we should start by looking at their structure and listing the different factors that are involved. In any situation where a decision is needed there must be:

- a decision maker who is responsible for making the decisions
- a number of alternatives are available to the decision maker
- the object of the decision maker is to choose the best alternative
- when the decision has been made, events occur over which the decision maker has no control
- each combination of an alternative chosen followed by an event happening leads to an outcome that has some measurable value

To illustrate these, consider a house owner who can buy fire insurance at a cost of £400 a year. The decision maker is the person who owns the house. They have an objective of minimizing costs and must select the best alternative from:

(1) insure the house, or

(2) do not insure the house

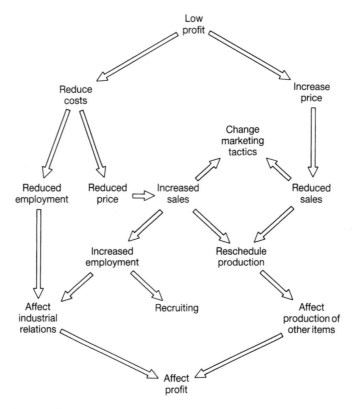

**Figure 16.1** Part of a problem map.

Then an event happens, but the decision maker has no control over whether it is:

(1) the house burns down, or

(2) the house does not burn down

We have obviously simplified this problem, and in reality there are many different insurance companies and policies, the house may be damaged but not destroyed by fire, and so on. If the value of the house is £100,000 and the insurance company pays for all costs and inconvenience if the house burns down, we can summarize the combinations of alternatives, events and outcomes in the following table:

| | | *Events* | |
| --- | --- | --- | --- |
| | | House burns down | House does not burn down |
| *Alternatives* | Insure house | £400 | £400 |
| | Do not insure house | £100,000 | £0 |

This is called a **payoff matrix**; the entries show the cost to the house owner of every combination of alternative and event. It is important to remember that the alternatives (one of which has to be chosen) are listed down the left-hand side; the events (one of which happens and over which the decision maker has no control) are listed across the top. The values of the outcomes given in the body of the matrix are in consistent units and can be either costs or gains.

We now have two formats to describe the circumstances around decisions: maps and payoff matrices. Both of these are useful in adding structure to an otherwise unstructured and complex situation. There are, of course, other formats for describing problems and in the following sections we will show how these can help with decisions in a number of different situations.

---

IN SUMMARY

Managers make decisions in complex situations. Maps and payoff matrices describe such situations and add structure to problems. This structure needs to identify events, alternatives and outcomes.

---

## 16.2  Decision-making under certainty

The main characteristic of decision-making under certainty is that we know, with certainty, which event will occur. So we need only consider one event. Then the method of solution is obvious, as we can list all possible outcomes and choose the alternative which gives the best.

Suppose you have £1,000 to invest for a year. You could list all the alternatives that you want to consider in the following payoff matrix:

|  |  | *Event*<br>Earns interest |
|---|---|---|
| *Alternatives* | Bank | £1,065 |
|  | Building society | £1,075 |
|  | Government stock | £1,085 |
|  | Stock market | £1,100 |
|  | Others | £1,060 |

This is obviously a simplified view of the original problem with 'others' describing a range of alternatives and using forecast returns from investments in the stock market. There is only one event – 'earns interest' – and by looking down the list of outcomes you can identify the best alternative. The highest value at the end of the year comes from investing in the stock market.

In reality, even decisions under certainty can be difficult, particularly in complex situations. Would it be better, for example, for the Health Service to invest money in providing more kidney dialysis machines, giving nurses higher wages, doing open-heart surgery, funding research into cancer, or providing more parking spaces at hospitals?

---

# WORKED EXAMPLE 16.1

The manager of La Pigalle Restaurant has a booking for a large wedding banquet. He has several ways of providing staff, each with different costs. His most convenient alternatives are to pay full-time staff to work overtime (costing £400), hire current part-time staff for the day (£300), hire new temporary staff (£350) or use an agency (£500). Draw a payoff matrix for this decision and identify the best alternative.

## Solution

The payoff matrix for this decision under certainty is shown below. The entries are costs, so we want to identify the lowest. This is £300 for hiring current part-time staff for the day.

|  |  | *Event*<br>Pay staff |
|---|---|---|
| *Alternatives* | Pay full-time staff for overtime | 400 |
|  | Hire current part-time staff | 300 |
|  | Hire new temporary staff | 350 |
|  | Use an agency | 500 |

---

# Self-assessment questions

**16.1** Why are maps and payoff matrices useful for describing decision-making situations?

**16.2** What are the five main parts of a decision process?

**16.3** What is meant by 'decision-making under certainty'?

| # Decision-making under strict uncertainty

With most decisions there are a number of possible events. Sometimes we cannot say which event will actually occur or even give reasonable probabilities. If, for example, you decide to change your job a number of events can happen: you may not like the new job and quickly start looking for another; you may get the sack; you may like the job and stay; you may be moved by the company. These events are essentially outside your control and it is impossible to give reliable probabilities to them.

When we can not give probabilities to events we are dealing with **strict uncertainty**. Then simple rules called **decision criteria** are useful in recommending a solution. There are many different criteria, but we shall describe three common ones.

## 16.3.1 | Laplace decision criterion

As no probabilities can be given to events, Laplace suggests that they should all be treated as equally likely and no more importance given to one event than to others. The method of finding the best alternative is:

1  For each alternative find the mean value of the outcomes (that is, find the average of each row in the payoff matrix).

2  Choose the alternative with the best average outcome (that is, lowest cost or highest gain).

## WORKED EXAMPLE 16.2

A restaurateur is going to set up a cream-tea stall at a local gala. On the morning of the gala she visits the wholesale market and has to decide whether to buy a large, medium or small quantity of strawberries. Her profit depends on the number of people attending the gala and this is largely determined by the weather. The matrix of gains (in thousands of pounds) for different weather conditions is given below. The gains in this matrix are found by subtracting the costs of buying strawberries from the net income. What quantity of strawberries should the restaurateur buy?

|  | | *Event* | |
|  | Weather good | Weather average | Weather poor |
| --- | --- | --- | --- |
| *Alternatives* Large quantity | 10 | 4 | $-2$ |
| Medium quantity | 7 | 6 | 2 |
| Small quantity | 4 | 1 | 4 |

## Solution

1 Taking the average value of outcomes for each alternative:
- large quantity $(10 + 4 - 2)/3 = 4$
- medium quantity $(7 + 6 + 2)/3 = 5$
- small quantity $(4 + 1 + 4)/3 = 3$

2 Choose the best average outcome. As these figures are profits the best is the highest, which is to buy a medium quantity.

---

## IN SUMMARY

Decision criteria are simple rules for helping with decisions under strict uncertainty. The Laplace criterion finds the average outcome for each alternative, and chooses the alternative with the best average outcome.

## 16.3.2 | Wald decision criterion

Most organizations have limited resources and cannot afford to risk a big loss. This is the basis of the Wald decision criterion, which assumes that decision makers are cautious (or even pessimistic) and want to avoid big potential losses. The steps are:

1 For each alternative find the worst outcome.
2 Choose the alternative with the best of these worst outcomes.

With a payoff matrix showing costs, this is sometimes known as the 'minimax cost' criterion, as it looks for the maximum cost of each alternative and then chooses the alternative with the minimum of these (that is, the minimum[maximum cost] or minimax cost). With a gains matrix it becomes the 'maximum gains' criterion.

---

## WORKED EXAMPLE 16.3

Use the Wald decision criterion for the example of a cream-tea stall at a local gala described by the following gains matrix:

|  |  | Event Weather good | Weather average | Weather poor |
|---|---|---|---|---|
| *Alternatives* | Large quantity | 10 | 4 | − 2 |
|  | Medium quantity | 7 | 6 | 2 |
|  | Small quantity | 4 | 1 | 4 |

## Solution

1   Taking the worst value of outcomes for each alternative:
- large quantity = minimum of $[10, 4, -2] = -2$
- medium quantity = minimum of $[7, 6, 2] = 2$
- small quantity = minimum of $[4, 1, 4] = 1$

2   Choose the best of these worst outcomes. As the figures are profits the best is the highest, which comes from buying a medium quantity.

---

### IN SUMMARY

The Wald decision criterion is pessimistic and assumes that the worst outcome will occur. Then it chooses the alternative which gives the best of these worst outcomes.

## 16.3.3 | Savage decision criterion

Sometimes we are judged not by how well we actually did but by how well we could possibly have done. Students who get 70% in an exam might be judged by the fact that they did not get 100%. An investment broker who recommended a client to invest in platinum may be judged not by the fact that platinum rose 15% in value, but by the fact that gold rose 25%. This happens particularly when performance is judged by someone other than the decision maker.

In such cases there is a **regret,** which is the difference between actual outcome and best possible outcome. A student who gets 70% has a regret of $100 - 70 = 30\%$. An investor who gains 15% when they could have gained 25% has a regret of $25 - 15 = 10\%$. The Savage criterion is based on these regrets. It is essentially pessimistic and minimizes the maximum regret. The steps are:

1   For each event find the best possible outcome (that is, find the best entry in each column of the payoff matrix).

2   Find the regret for every other entry in the column, which is the difference between the best in the column and the entry.

3   Put the regrets found in Step 2 into a 'regret matrix'. There should be at least one zero in each column, and regrets are always positive.

4   For each alternative find the highest regret (that is, the largest number in each row).

5   Choose the alternative with the lowest value of these highest regrets.

As you can see, steps 1 to 3 build a regret matrix, and then steps 4 and 5 apply the Wald criterion to this matrix.

## WORKED EXAMPLE 16.4

Use the Savage criterion on the example of the cream-tea stall at a local gala described by the following gains matrix:

|  |  | Event |  |  |
| --- | --- | --- | --- | --- |
|  |  | Weather good | Weather average | Weather poor |
| Alternatives | Large quantity | **10** | 4 | – 2 |
|  | Medium quantity | 7 | **6** | 2 |
|  | Small quantity | 4 | 1 | **4** |

## Solution

1  The best outcome for each event is shown in bold (that is, with good weather a large quantity, with average weather a medium quantity and with poor weather a small quantity).

2  The regret for every other entry in the column is the difference between this bold value and the actual entry. So if the weather is good and a medium quantity has been bought the regret is $10 - 7 = 3$. If the weather is good and a small quantity has been bought the regret is $10 - 4 = 6$, and so on.

3  Form these regret figures into a regret matrix, replacing the original profit figures:

|  |  | Event |  |  |
| --- | --- | --- | --- | --- |
|  |  | Weather good | Weather average | Weather poor |
| Alternatives | Large quantity | 0 | 2 | 6 |
|  | Medium quantity | 3 | 0 | 2 |
|  | Small quantity | 6 | 5 | 0 |

4  For each alternative find the highest regret:
  - large quantity = maximum of [0, 2, 6] = 6
  - medium quantity = maximum of [3, 0, 2] = 3
  - small quantity = maximum of [6, 5, 0] = 6

5  Choose the alternative with the lowest of these maximum regrets. This is the medium quantity.

---

## IN SUMMARY

The Savage criterion considers regret, which is the difference between the best outcome for an event and the actual outcome. Then it finds the highest regret for each alternative and chooses the alternative with the lowest of these highest regrets.

## 16.3.4 | Choosing the criterion to use

Often different criteria recommend the same alternative, but there is no guarantee of this. When different alternatives are recommended you should use the most relevant criterion. If, for example, you are working as a consultant and will be held responsible to others, there may be a case for using the Savage criterion. If the decision is made for a small company that cannot afford to risk high losses, then Wald may be best. If there is really nothing to choose between the different events, then Laplace may be useful.

Although it is difficult to go beyond these general guidelines you should notice one other factor. Both the Wald and Savage criteria effectively recommend their decision based on one outcome (the worst for Wald, and the one that leads to the highest regret for Savage). This means that the choice might be dominated by a few atypical results. The Laplace criterion is the only one that uses all values to make its recommendation.

It could be that none of the criteria we have looked at is suitable. We have only described a few criteria for illustration and there are many others that could be used. An ambitious organization might aim for the highest profit and use a criterion that chooses the alternative which gives the highest return (a 'maximax profit' criterion). Alternatively it may try to balance the best and worst outcomes for each event and use a criterion based on the best value for:

$$\alpha \times \text{best outcome} + (1 - \alpha) \times \text{worst outcome}$$

where $\alpha$ has a value between zero and one.

Different criteria often suggest the same alternative, and this perhaps reduces the importance of selecting the 'right' one for a particular problem. Certainly, a major strength of decision criteria is not their ability to recommend good alternatives, but their use in formalizing the structure of a problem and allowing informed discussion.

# WORKED EXAMPLE 16.5

Lawrence Pang has found the following payoff matrix (showing the costs in consistent units) associated with a decision. Use the Laplace, Wald and Savage decision criteria to select the best alternatives.

|   | 1 | 2 | 3 |
|---|---|---|---|
| A | 14 | 22 | 6 |
| B | 19 | 18 | 12 |
| C | 12 | 17 | 15 |

### Solution

- As the entries are costs, Laplace chooses the alternative with the lowest average costs, which is alternative A:

|   | 1 | 2 | 3 | Mean |
|---|---|---|---|------|
| A | 14 | 22 | 6 | **14.0\*** |
| B | 19 | 18 | 12 | 16.3 |
| C | 12 | 17 | 15 | 14.7 |

- Wald assumes that the highest cost will occur for each alternative, and then chooses the lowest of these. This suggests alternative C:

|   | 1 | 2 | 3 | Highest |
|---|---|---|---|---------|
| A | 14 | 22 | 6 | 22 |
| B | 19 | 18 | 12 | 19 |
| C | 12 | 17 | 15 | **17\*** |

- Savage forms the regret matrix, finds the highest regret for each alternative and chooses the alternative with the lowest of these. This is alternative A:

| Regret | 1 | 2 | 3 | Highest |
|--------|---|---|---|---------|
| A | 2 | 5 | 0 | **5\*** |
| B | 7 | 1 | 6 | 7 |
| C | 0 | 0 | 9 | 9 |

# Self-assessment questions

**16.4** What is meant by decision-making under strict uncertainty?

**16.5** List three useful decision criteria.

**16.6** How many of these criteria take into account all outcomes associated with a particular alternative?

**16.7** Are the listed criteria the only ones available? If not, can you suggest others that might be useful?

# 16.4 | Decision-making under risk

In the last section we considered decision-making under strict uncertainty, where a number of events could occur but we had no idea of the relative likelihood of each. With decision-making under risk there are again a number of events, but now we can give probabilities to each of them. As we should include every possible event, these probabilities should add to one. A simple example of decision-making under risk is a gamble on the outcome of spinning a coin. The events are the coin coming down heads or tails, and we can put probabilities to these (0.5 in each case).

## 16.4.1 | Expected values

Problems with risk are solved by calculating the **expected value** for each alternative and choosing the alternative with the best expected value. The expected value is defined as the sum of the probability times the value of the outcome:

$$\text{expected value} = \Sigma\,(\text{probability} \times \text{value of outcome})$$

The expected value for an alternative is the average gain (or cost) if the decision is repeated a large number of times. It is not the value that is returned *every* time but the average value for a large number of repetitions.

Then for decision-making under risk there are two steps:

1 Calculate the expected value for each alternative.

2 Choose the alternative with the best expected value (that is, highest value for gains and lowest value for costs).

---

## WORKED EXAMPLE 16.6

What is the best alternative for the following matrix of gains?

| | | Events | | | |
|---|---|---|---|---|---|
| | | 1<br>$P = 0.1$ | 2<br>$P = 0.2$ | 3<br>$P = 0.6$ | 4<br>$P = 0.1$ |
| *Alternatives* | A | 10 | 7 | 5 | 9 |
| | B | 3 | 20 | 2 | 10 |
| | C | 3 | 4 | 11 | 1 |
| | D | 8 | 4 | 2 | 16 |

### Solution

Calculating the expected value for each alternative as the sum of the probability times the value of the outcome gives:

- alternative A: $0.1 \times 10 + 0.2 \times 7 + 0.6 \times 5 + 0.1 \times 9 = 6.3$
- alternative B: $0.1 \times 3 + 0.2 \times 20 + 0.6 \times 2 + 0.1 \times 10 = 6.5$

- alternative C:  $0.1 \times 3 + 0.2 \times 4 + 0.6 \times 11 + 0.1 \times 1 = 7.8$
- alternative D:  $0.1 \times 8 + 0.2 \times 4 + 0.6 \times 2 + 0.1 \times 16 = 4.4$

As these are gains, the best alternative is C with an expected value of 7.8. If this decision is made repeatedly the average return in the long run will be 7.8; if the decision is made only once the gain could be any of the four values 3, 4, 11 or 1.

## WORKED EXAMPLE 16.7

H. J. Symonds Haulage Contractors bids for a long-term contract to move newspapers from a printing works to wholesalers. It can submit one of three tenders: a low one that assumes newspaper sales will increase and unit transport costs will go down; a medium one that gives a reasonable return if newspaper sales stay the same; or a high one that assumes newspaper sales will decline and unit transport costs will rise. The probabilities of newspaper sales and profits (in thousands of pounds) for the firm are shown in the following table. Based on this matrix, which tender should it submit?

|  | Newspaper sales | | |
|---|---|---|---|
|  | decrease<br>$P = 0.4$ | stay same<br>$P = 0.3$ | increase<br>$P = 0.3$ |
| Low tender | 10 | 15 | 16 |
| Medium tender | 5 | 20 | 10 |
| High tender | 18 | 10 | − 5 |

### Solution

Calculating the expected value for each alternative:

- low tender:   $0.4 \times 10 + 0.3 \times 15 + 0.3 \times 16 = 13.3$
- medium tender:   $0.4 \times 5 + 0.3 \times 20 + 0.3 \times 10 = 11.0$
- high tender:   $0.4 \times 18 + 0.3 \times 10 - 0.3 \times 5 = 8.7$

As these are profits, the best alternative is the one with the highest expected value, which is the low tender.

---

### IN SUMMARY

Expected values are defined as $\Sigma$(probability × value of outcome). They can be used to suggest the best alternative in situations of risk.

## Using Bayes' theorem to update probabilities

In Chapter 12 we showed how Bayes' theorem could be used to update conditional probabilities:

$$P(a/b) = \frac{P(b/a) \times P(a)}{P(b)}$$

where:

$P(a/b)$ = probability of event $a$ happening given that $b$ has already happened

$P(b/a)$ = probability of $b$ given that $a$ has already happened

$P(a), P(b)$ = probabilities of $a$ and $b$ respectively

Now we can use Bayes' theorem for updating conditional probabilities of events.

## WORKED EXAMPLE 16.8

The crowd for a sports event might be small (with a probability of 0.4) or large. The organizers can analyse advance sales of tickets a week before the event. The advance sales can be classified as high, average or low, with the probability of advance sales conditional on crowd size given by the following table:

|            |       | Advance sales | | |
|            |       | High | Average | Low |
|------------|-------|------|---------|-----|
| Crowd size | Large | 0.7  | 0.3     | 0.0 |
|            | Small | 0.2  | 0.2     | 0.6 |

The organizers must choose one of two plans in running the event, and the table below gives the net profit in thousands of pounds for each combination of plan and crowd size:

|            |       | Plan 1 | Plan 2 |
|------------|-------|--------|--------|
| Crowd size | Large | 10     | 14     |
|            | Small | 9      | 5      |

If the organizers use the information on advance sales, what strategy would maximize their expected profits? How much should they pay for the information on advance sales?

## Solution

We can use the abbreviations:

- CL and CS for crowd size large and crowd size small

- ASH, ASA and ASL for advance sales high, average and low.

If the organizers do not use the information on advance sales, the best they can do is use the probabilities of large and small crowds (0.6 and 0.4 respectively) to calculate expected values for the two plans:

- Plan 1:     $0.6 \times 10 + 0.4 \times 9 = 9.6$

- Plan 2:     $0.6 \times 14 + 0.4 \times 5 = \mathbf{10.4}$   better plan

They would use plan 2 with an expected value of £10,400.

If the organizers do use the information on advance ticket sales they can use the conditional probabilities $P(ASH/CL)$, $P(ASH/CS)$, etc. They would like these the other way around, $P(CL/ASH)$, $P(CS/ASH)$, etc, and can use Bayes' theorem to give these. The calculations are shown in the following table (if you have forgotten the details of these calculations you should look them up in Chapter 12):

|      | ASH  | ASA  | ASL  |      | ASH  | ASA  | ASL  |
|------|------|------|------|------|------|------|------|
| CL   | 0.7  | 0.3  | 0.0  | 0.6  | 0.42 | 0.18 | 0.00 |
| CS   | 0.2  | 0.2  | 0.6  | 0.4  | 0.08 | 0.08 | 0.24 |
|      |      |      |      |      | 0.50 | 0.26 | 0.24 |
|      |      |      |      | CL   | 0.84 | 0.69 | 0.00 |
|      |      |      |      | CS   | 0.16 | 0.31 | 1.00 |

The probability of advance sales being high is 0.5. If this happens, the probability of a large crowd is 0.84 and the probability of a small crowd is 0.16. Then, if the organizers choose plan 1 the expected value is $0.84 \times 10 + 0.16 \times 9 = 9.84$; if the organizers choose plan 2 their expected value is $0.84 \times 14 + 0.16 \times 5 = 12.56$. If advance sales are high they should clearly choose plan 2.

This reasoning can be extended to the other alternatives:

ASH:  Plan 1   $0.84 \times 10 + 0.16 \times 9 = 9.84$
      Plan 2   $0.84 \times 14 + 0.16 \times 5 = \mathbf{12.56}$

ASA:  Plan 1   $0.69 \times 10 + 0.31 \times 9 = 9.69$
      Plan 2   $0.69 \times 14 + 0.31 \times 5 = \mathbf{11.21}$

ASL:  Plan 1   $0.00 \times 10 + 1.00 \times 9 = \mathbf{9.00}$
      Plan 2   $0.00 \times 14 + 1.00 \times 5 = 5.00$

The overall strategy that maximizes the organizer's profit is: if the advance sales are high or average select plan 2; if they are low select plan 1.

We can go a little further with this analysis, as we know the probability of high, average and low advance sales are respectively 0.5, 0.26 and 0.24. So we can calculate the overall expected value of following the recommended strategy as:

$$0.5 \times 12.56 + 0.26 \times 11.21 + 0.24 \times 9 = 11.35$$

This compares with the expected profit of £10,400 when the advance sales information is not used; using the additional information raises expected profits by 11 350 − 10 400 = £950, or over 9%.

## WORKED EXAMPLE 16.9

Humbalt Oil drills an exploratory well in deep water off the Irish coast. The company is uncertain about the amount of recoverable oil it will find, but experience suggests the amount can be minor (with a probability of 0.3), significant (with probability 0.5) or major. The company now has to decide how to develop the find and has a choice of either moving quickly to minimize its long-term debt, or moving slowly to get a continuing income. The profits for every combination of size and development speed are given in the following table, where entries are in millions of dollars:

|  | *Size of find* | | |
|---|---|---|---|
|  | Minor | Significant | Major |
| Develop quickly | 100 | 130 | 180 |
| Develop slowly | 80 | 150 | 210 |

Some geological tests can be done to give a more accurate picture of the size of the find, but these cost $2.5 million and are not entirely accurate. The tests give results classified as A, B and C with conditional probabilities of results given size of find shown in the following table:

|  |  | *Test result* | | |
|---|---|---|---|---|
|  |  | A | B | C |
| *Find size* | Minor | 0.3 | 0.4 | 0.3 |
|  | Significant | 0.5 | 0.0 | 0.5 |
|  | Major | 0.25 | 0.25 | 0.5 |

If Humbalt Oil wants to maximize its profits, should it do the geological tests?

## Solution

Defining the abbreviations:

- MIN, SIG and MAJ for minor, significant and major finds
- QUICK and SLOW for the quick and slow development

then, without using geological tests, the expected values with each speed of development are:

- QUICK $\quad 0.3 \times 100 + 0.5 \times 130 + 0.2 \times 180 = 131$
- SLOW $\quad 0.3 \times 80 + 0.5 \times 150 + 0.2 \times 210 = \mathbf{141}$

The company should develop the find slowly with an expected value of $141 million.

With the geological test the company will want information in the form $P(MIN/A)$, etc, but it is actually presented in the form $P(A/MIN)$. Humbalt must use Bayes' theorem:

|      | A    | B    | C   |     | A    | B    | C    |
|------|------|------|-----|-----|------|------|------|
| MIN  | 0.3  | 0.4  | 0.3 | 0.3 | 0.09 | 0.12 | 0.09 |
| SIG  | 0.5  | 0.0  | 0.5 | 0.5 | 0.25 | 0.00 | 0.25 |
| MAJ  | 0.25 | 0.25 | 0.5 | 0.2 | 0.05 | 0.05 | 0.10 |
|      |      |      |     |     | 0.39 | 0.17 | 0.44 |
|      |      |      |     | MIN | 0.23 | 0.71 | 0.20 |
|      |      |      |     | SIG | 0.64 | 0.00 | 0.57 |
|      |      |      |     | MAJ | 0.13 | 0.29 | 0.23 |

If the test result is A, the probabilities of minor, significant and major finds are 0.23, 0.64 and 0.13 respectively. Developing the well quickly will give a profit, which we can find by multiplying the profits for each size by the probability:

expected profit with test result A and developing quickly

$$= 0.23 \times 100 + 0.64 \times 130 + 0.13 \times 180 = 129.6$$

Repeating this calculation for other results gives the following values:

A: QUICK $\quad 0.23 \times 100 + 0.64 \times 130 + 0.13 \times 180 = 129.6$
    SLOW $\quad 0.23 \times 80 + 0.64 \times 150 + 0.13 \times 210 = \mathbf{141.7}$

B: QUICK $\quad 0.71 \times 100 + 0.00 \times 130 + 0.29 \times 180 = \mathbf{123.2}$
    SLOW $\quad 0.71 \times 80 + 0.00 \times 150 + 0.29 \times 210 = 117.7$

C: QUICK $\quad 0.20 \times 100 + 0.57 \times 130 + 0.23 \times 180 = 135.5$
    SLOW $\quad 0.20 \times 80 + 0.57 \times 150 + 0.23 \times 210 = \mathbf{149.8}$

The best policy is to develop slowly if test results are A or C and quickly if the test results are B. This policy has an expected value of:

$$0.39 \times 141.7 + 0.17 \times 123.2 + 0.44 \times 149.8 = 142.12$$

Profit without doing the tests is $141 million, while doing the test raises it to $142.12 million minus the cost of $2.5 million. In these circumstances it is not worth doing the tests, and would not be worth doing them unless their cost was less than $1.12 million.

We could, of course, use a computer to do these calculations automatically, and Figure 16.2 shows the results on a spreadsheet.

| | A | B | C | D | E | F | G | H |
|---|---|---|---|---|---|---|---|---|
| 1 | **Oil exploration** | | | | | | | |
| 2 | | | | | | | | |
| 3 | **First analysis** | | | | | | | |
| 4 | | | | | | | | |
| 5 | | Size of find | | | | | | |
| 6 | | Minor | Significant | Major | | Expected value | | |
| 7 | Probability | 0.3 | 0.5 | 0.2 | | | | |
| 8 | Quick dev. | 100 | 130 | 180 | | 131 | | |
| 9 | Slow dev. | 80 | 150 | 210 | | 141 | **** | |
| 10 | | | | | | | | |
| 11 | **Bayes' analysis** | | | | | | | |
| 12 | | Conditional | | | Prior | Revised | | |
| 13 | | A | B | C | | A | B | C |
| 14 | Minor | 0.3 | 0.4 | 0.3 | 0.3 | 0.09 | 0.12 | 0.09 |
| 15 | Significant | 0.5 | 0 | 0.5 | 0.5 | 0.25 | 0 | 0.25 |
| 16 | Major | 0.25 | 0.25 | 0.5 | 0.2 | 0.05 | 0.05 | 0.1 |
| 17 | | | | | | 0.39 | 0.17 | 0.44 |
| 18 | | | | Predictions | Minor | 0.23 | 0.71 | 0.20 |
| 19 | | | | | Significant | 0.64 | 0.00 | 0.57 |
| 20 | | | | | Major | 0.13 | 0.29 | 0.23 |
| 21 | | | | | | | | |
| 22 | **Calculations** | | | | | | | |
| 23 | | | | | Probabilities | | Expected value | |
| 24 | A | Quick dev. | 129.6 | | 0.39 | | | |
| 25 | | Slow dev. | 141.7 | **** | 0.39 | | 55.26 | |
| 26 | B | Quick dev. | 123.2 | **** | 0.17 | | 20.94 | |
| 27 | | Slow dev. | 117.7 | | 0.17 | | | |
| 28 | C | Quick dev. | 135.5 | | 0.44 | | | |
| 29 | | Slow dev. | 149.8 | **** | 0.44 | | 65.91 | |
| 30 | | | | | | Total | 142.12 | |
| 31 | | | | | | | | |
| 32 | **Conclusion** | | | | | | | |
| 33 | First analysis | 141.00 | | | | | | |
| 34 | Using Bayes' | 142.12 | **** | | | | | |
| 35 | Extra profit | 1.12 | | | | | | |

**Figure 16.2**  Calculations for decision analysis using Bayes' theorem.

# 16.4.3 | Utilities

Expected values are easy to use but they have some problems. In particular, they do not always reflect real preferences. Have a look at the investment in the payoff matrix below, which has a 90% chance of giving a loss:

|                        |              | *Events* |            |
|                        |              | Gain $P = 0.1$ | Lose $P = 0.9$ |
|------------------------|--------------|----------|------------|
| *Alternatives* | Invest | £500,000 | – £50,000 |
|                | Do not invest | £0 | £0 |

The expected values are:

- invest $\qquad 0.1 \times 500\,000 - 0.9 \times 50\,000 = £5000$
- do not invest $\quad 0.1 \times 0 + 0.9 \times 0 = £0$

Expected values would suggest investing even though there is a 90% chance of losing. The reason is that expected values give the average value in the long run when the decision is repeated a large number of times. If a decision is made only once, expected values can give misleading advice. For this reason **utilities** have been developed, which show the real value of money more accurately.

Expected values assume a linear relationship between the amount of money and its value. So £100 has a value a hundred times as great as £1, and £1,000,000 has a value ten thousand times as great as £100. In practice this strict linear relationship is not accurate. A more realistic utility function is shown in Figure 16.3.

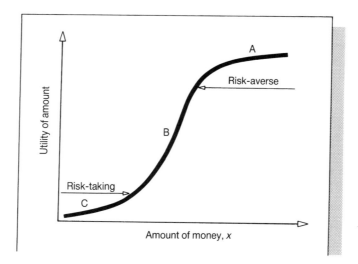

**Figure 16.3**   Utility curve relating amount of money to its value.

This utility function has three distinct regions. At the top, near point A, the utility is rising slowly with the amount of money. A decision maker in this region already has a lot of money and would not put a high value on even more. But the decision maker would certainly not like to lose money and move nearer to point B where the utility falls rapidly. Gaining an amount of money is not very attractive but losing it is very unattractive, so this leads to a conservative decision maker who does not like to take risks.

Region B on the graph has the utility of money almost linear, which is the assumption of expected values. A decision maker at point C does not have much money, so losing any would not really affect the utility. On the other hand, gaining money and moving nearer to B would have a high value. A decision maker here is keen to make a gain and does not unduly mind a loss, which is characteristic of a risk taker.

Although utilities are useful in principle, it is very difficult to define a reasonable function. Each individual and organization has a different view of the value of money and will work on a different utility function. To make things more complicated, the curves will also vary over time. This problem is so difficult to overcome that relatively few organizations use utility theory for real problems. But in principle, once they have defined a utility function, the process of choosing the best alternative is the same as with expected values, but with expected utilities replacing expected values.

## WORKED EXAMPLE 16.10

Suppose a person's utility curve is a reasonable approximation to $\sqrt{x}$. What is their best decision with the following gains matrix?

|  |  | Events | | |
|---|---|---|---|---|
|  |  | X<br>$P = 0.7$ | Y<br>$P = 0.2$ | Z<br>$P = 0.1$ |
| *Alternatives* | A | 14 | 24 | 12 |
|  | B | 6 | 40 | 90 |
|  | C | 1 | 70 | 30 |
|  | D | 12 | 12 | 6 |

### Solution

The calculations are similar to those for expected values, except the amount of money, $x$, is replaced by its utility, which in this case is the square root, $\sqrt{x}$:

- alternative A:  $0.7 \times \sqrt{14} + 0.2 \times \sqrt{24} + 0.1 \times \sqrt{12} = \mathbf{3.95}$
- alternative B:  $0.7 \times \sqrt{6} + 0.2 \times \sqrt{40} + 0.1 \times \sqrt{90} = 3.93$
- alternative C:  $0.7 \times \sqrt{1} + 0.2 \times \sqrt{70} + 0.1 \times \sqrt{30} = 2.92$
- alternative D:  $0.7 \times \sqrt{12} + 0.2 \times \sqrt{12} + 0.1 \times \sqrt{6} = 3.36$

Although the difference is small, the best alternative is A. (If you calculate the results using expected values you will find that alternative B is the best.)

> ### *IN SUMMARY*
>
> Utilities are designed to show the value of different amounts of money. Expected utilities can be used to help decisions in situations of risk, provided a realistic utility function can be defined.

## Self-assessment questions

**16.8**   What is meant by 'decision-making under risk'?

**16.9**   What is the expected value of a course of action?

**16.10**   Could a subjective probability be assigned to events under risk?

**16.11**   When could Bayes' theorem be used to calculate expected values?

**16.12**   Why might expected utilities be a better measure than expected values?

# 16.5 || Sequential decisions and decision trees

So far we have looked at single decisions. In other words, we have solved the problem when we find the best alternative. But there are many situations where one decision leads to a series of other decisions. If, for example, you decide to buy a car your initial decision might be to choose a new or a second-hand one. If you choose a new car, this opens the choice of Japanese, French, German, Italian or others. If the choice here is a Japanese car the choice is Honda, Toyota, Nissan, Mitsubishi and so on. Then if you choose a Nissan you have to make a range of other decisions. At each stage in the decision process the selection of one alternative opens up a series of other choices (or sometimes events). We can describe these problems in a **decision tree**, where the alternatives (or events) are represented by the branches of a horizontal tree.

## WORKED EXAMPLE 16.11

A company goes to a bank manager for a loan to finance an expansion. The bank manager has to decide whether or not to grant the loan. If the bank manager grants the loan the company expansion may be successful or it may not. If the bank manager does not grant the loan, the company may continue banking as before or it may move its account to another bank. Draw a decision tree of this situation.

## Solution

A decision tree shows the sequence of alternatives and events. There is a notional timescale going from left to right with early decisions or events on the left followed by later ones towards the right. There is only one decision in this example followed by events over which the bank manager has no control, so the sequence is:

- the manager makes a decision
- one of several possible events happens

We can represent these by the decision tree in Figure 16.4.

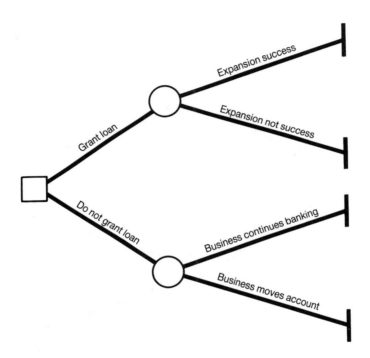

**Figure 16.4** Decision tree for Worked Example 16.11.

We have drawn the alternatives and events as the branches, so each branch represents a different path (decision or event) that may be followed through the tree. There are also three distinct types of node, which are the points from which branches come:

**|** **terminal node.** These are at the right-hand side of the tree and show the ends of all sequences of decisions and events.

**○** **random node.** These are points at which things happen, so that all branches leaving random nodes are events with known probabilities.

**□** **decision node.** These are points at which decisions are made, so that all branches leaving a decision node are alternatives, the best of which is selected.

This is the basic structure of the tree, but we still have to add the probabilities and values. Suppose the bank currently values its business with the company at £2,000 a year. If the manager grants the loan and the expansion succeeds the value to the bank of increased business and interest charges is £3,000 a year. If the expansion does not succeed the bank will still have business valued at £1,000 a year (reduced because of reduced volume and allowance for writing off bad debt). There is a probability of 0.7 that the expansion plan will be successful. If the manager does not grant the loan there is a probability of 0.6 that the company will transfer its account to another bank. We can add these figures to the tree as shown in Figure 16.5.

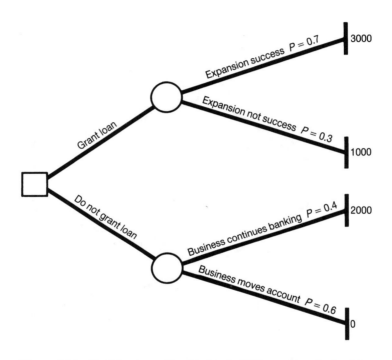

**Figure 16.5** Decision tree with added probabilities and terminal values.

Now we have put probabilities on the event branches (making sure all events are included and the sum of the probabilities from each random node equals one). And we have put values on terminal nodes, giving the total value of moving through the tree and reaching the terminal node. In this case these values are the annual business expected by the bank.

The next stage of the analysis moves from right to left through the tree and assigns a value to each node in turn. This is done by finding the best decision at each decision node and the expected value at each random node.

● At each decision node the alternative branches leaving are connected to following nodes. The values on these following nodes are compared, the best branch is chosen and the node value is transferred.

- At each random node the value is the expected value of the leaving event branches (that is, the sum, for all branches, of the probability of leaving by a branch times the value of the node at the end of the branch).

The value at the left-hand originating node is the overall expected value of following the best policies.

Using this procedure on the tree in Figure 16.5 gives the results shown in Figure 16.6.

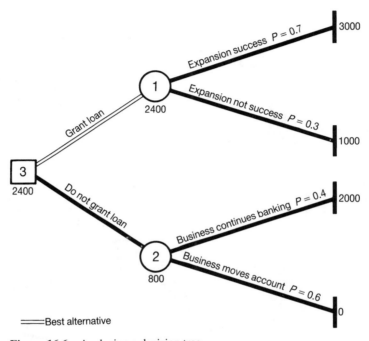

═══Best alternative

**Figure 16.6**   Analysing a decision tree.

The calculations are as follows:

At random node 1 calculate expected value:
$$0.7 \times 3000 + 0.3 \times 1000 = 2400$$

At random node 2 calculate expected value:
$$0.4 \times 2000 + 0.6 \times 0 = 800$$

At decision node 3 choose the best alternative:
$$\text{Maximum of } [2400, 800] = 2400$$

The best policy is to grant the loan, and this has an expected value of £2,400.

## WORKED EXAMPLE 16.12

Draw a decision tree of the problem of planning a sports event described in Worked Example 16.8.

## Solution

This problem has a single decision for which we have already done the calculations. We can draw these on the tree shown in Figure 16.7. Overall, the expected value is confirmed as £11,350 using the advance sales information.

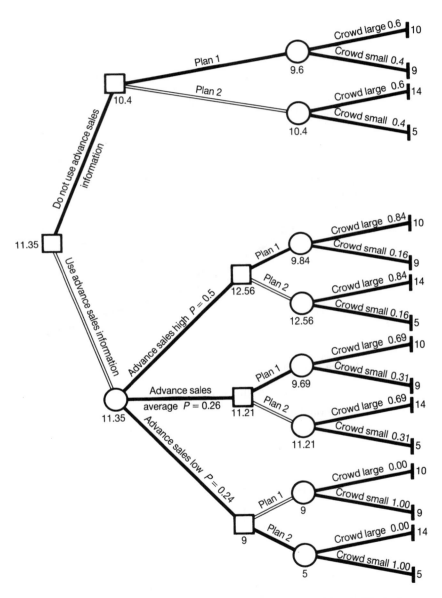

**Figure 16.7** Decision tree for Worked Example 16.12 (for problem in Worked Example 16.8).

# WORKED EXAMPLE 16.13

A workshop is about to install a new machine for stamping parts for domestic appliances. Three suppliers have made bids to supply the machine. The first supplier offers the Basicor machine, which automatically makes parts of acceptable, but not outstanding, quality. The output from the machine is variable (depending on material supplied and a variety of settings) and could be 1000 a week (with probability 0.1), 2000 a week (with probability 0.7) or 3000 a week. The notional profit for this machine is £4 a unit. The second supplier offers a Superstamp machine, which makes higher quality parts. The output from this can be 700 a week (with probability 0.4) or 1000 a week, with a notional profit of £10 a unit. The third supplier offers the Switchover machine, which can be set to make either 1300 high-quality parts a week at a profit of £6 a unit, or 1600 medium-quality parts a week with a profit of £5 a unit.

If the machine makes 2000 or more units a week, it is possible to export all production as a single bulk order. Then there is a 60% chance of selling for 50% more profit, and a 40% chance of selling for 50% less profit.

What would you do to maximize expected profits?

## Solution

The tree for this decision is shown in Figure 16.8. The terminal node values are weekly profit found by multiplying the number made by the profit on each unit. If 1000 are made on the Basicor machine the value is £4,000, and so on. If the output from Basicor is exported, profit may be increased by 50% (that is, to £6 a unit) or reduced by 50% (that is, to £2 a unit).

Calculations at each node are as follows:

1   Expected value at random node
$$= 0.6 \times 12\,000 + 0.4 \times 4000 = 8800$$

2   Expected value at random node
$$= 0.6 \times 18\,000 + 0.4 \times 6000 = 13\,200$$

3   Best alternative at decision node
$$= MAX[8800, 8000] = 8800$$

4   Best alternative at decision node
$$= MAX[13\,200, 12\,000] = 13\,200$$

5   Expected value at random node
$$= 0.1 \times 4000 + 0.7 \times 8800 + 0.2 \times 13\,200 = 9200$$

6   Expected value at random node
$$= 0.4 \times 7000 + 0.6 \times 10\,000 = 8800$$

7    Best alternative at decision node

$$= MAX[7800, 8000] = 8000$$

8    Best alternative at decision node

$$= MAX[9200, 8800, 8000] = 9200$$

The best overall policy is to buy the Basicor machine and, if it makes more than 2000 units, export all production. The expected profit from this is £9,200 a week.

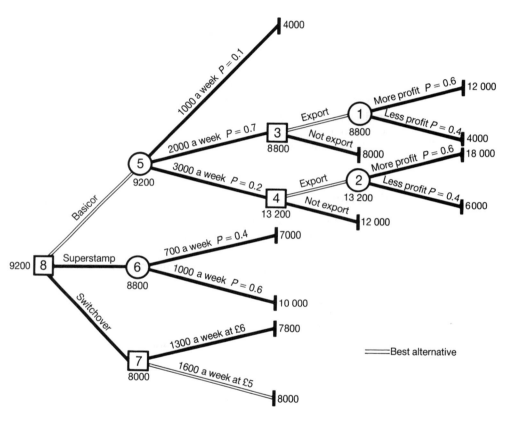

**Figure 16.8**   Decision tree for Worked Example 16.13.

Decision trees can involve a lot of arithmetic, but they are not easy to draw with a computer. Most software lists tables of results without actually drawing a tree. Figure 16.9 shows a typical printout for Worked Example 16.13. This needs all nodes to be numbered as well as branches from decision nodes, so the tree has to be drawn by hand and then the computer calculates node values. (Notice that the computer assigns different node numbers from the ones used in Figure 16.8.)

DECISION TREE MODEL

−=✻=−   INFORMATION ENTERED   −=✻=−

MAXIMIZATION PROBLEM

−=✻=−   DECISION NODES   −=✻=−

| NODE | BRANCHES | ALTERNATIVE NUMBER | ENDING NODE |
|------|----------|--------------------|-------------|
| 0 | 3 | 1 | 1 |
|   |   | 2 | 2 |
|   |   | 3 | 3 |
| 3 | 2 | 4 | 9 |
|   |   | 5 | 10 |
| 5 | 2 | 6 | 11 |
|   |   | 7 | 12 |
| 6 | 2 | 8 | 13 |
|   |   | 9 | 14 |

−=✻=−   CHANCE NODES   −=✻=−

| NODE | BRANCHES | PROBABILITY | ENDING NODE |
|------|----------|-------------|-------------|
| 1 | 3 | 0.1000 | 4 |
|   |   | 0.7000 | 5 |
|   |   | 0.2000 | 6 |
| 2 | 2 | 0.4000 | 7 |
|   |   | 0.6000 | 8 |
| 11 | 2 | 0.6000 | 15 |
|    |   | 0.4000 | 16 |
| 13 | 2 | 0.6000 | 17 |
|    |   | 0.4000 | 18 |

−=✻=−   TERMINAL NODES   −=✻=−

| NODE | PAYOFF |
|------|--------|
| 4 | 4 000.00 |
| 7 | 7 000.00 |
| 8 | 10 000.00 |
| 9 | 7 800.00 |
| 10 | 8 000.00 |
| 12 | 8 000.00 |
| 14 | 12 000.00 |
| 15 | 12 000.00 |
| 16 | 4 000.00 |
| 17 | 18 000.00 |
| 18 | 6 000.00 |

−=✻=−   RESULTS   −=✻=−

MAXIMIZATION PROBLEM

| NODE | EXPECTED PAYOFF | SELECTED ALTERNATIVE |
|------|-----------------|----------------------|
| 0 | 9 200.00 | 1 |
| 1 | 9 200.00 | |
| 2 | 8 800.00 | |
| 3 | 8 000.00 | 5 |
| 4 | 4 000.00 | |
| 5 | 8 800.00 | 6 |
| 6 | 13 200.00 | 8 |
| 7 | 7 000.00 | |
| 8 | 10 000.00 | |
| 9 | 7 800.00 | |
| 10 | 8 000.00 | |
| 11 | 8 800.00 | |
| 12 | 8 000.00 | |
| 13 | 13 200.00 | |
| 14 | 12 000.00 | |
| 15 | 12 000.00 | |
| 16 | 4 000.00 | |
| 17 | 18 000.00 | |
| 18 | 6 000.00 | |

EXPECTED PAYOFF  =  9200

−−−−−−−−−−   END OF ANALYSIS   −−−−−−−−−−

**Figure 16.9**   Printout for Worked Example 16.13.

### IN SUMMARY

Sequential decisions can be shown as a decision tree. For this we:

- find the alternatives, events and their probabilities, outcomes, etc
- draw a tree (moving from left to right) showing the sequences of events and alternatives, and setting the values at terminal nodes
- analyse the tree (moving from right to left) choosing the best alternative at decision nodes and calculating the expected value at random nodes

## Self-assessment questions

**16.13** How is the node value calculated at a terminal node, a decision node and a random node?

**16.14** How do you find the expected value of following the best policy in a decision tree?

### CHAPTER REVIEW

This chapter has described some aspects of decision analysis. In particular it:

- outlined the characteristics of decision-making
- described decision maps and payoff matrices
- mentioned decision-making under certainty
- used decision criteria for decision-making under strict uncertainty
- calculated expected values for decision-making under risk
- mentioned utilities
- discussed sequential decisions and decision trees

## Problems

**16.1** O'Brians Pub on the seafront at Blackpool notices that its profits are falling. The landlord has a number of alternatives for increasing his profits (attracting more customers, increasing prices, getting customers to spend more, etc) but each of these leads to a string of effects. Draw a map showing the interactions for this situation.

**16.2** Choose the best alternatives in the following matrix of gains:

|  |  | Event |
|---|---|---|
| Alternatives | a | 100 |
|  | b | 950 |
|  | c | − 250 |
|  | d | 0 |
|  | e | 950 |
|  | f | 500 |

**16.3** Use the Laplace, Wald and Savage decision criteria to choose alternatives in the following matrices:

(a) Cost matrix

|  |  | Events | | | | |
|---|---|---|---|---|---|---|
|  |  | 1 | 2 | 3 | 4 | 5 |
| Alternatives | a | 100 | 70 | 115 | 95 | 60 |
|  | b | 95 | 120 | 120 | 90 | 150 |
|  | c | 180 | 130 | 60 | 160 | 120 |
|  | d | 80 | 75 | 50 | 100 | 95 |
|  | e | 60 | 140 | 100 | 170 | 160 |

(b) Gains matrix

|  |  | Events | | | |
|---|---|---|---|---|---|
|  |  | 1 | 2 | 3 | 4 |
| Alternatives | a | 1 | 6 | 3 | 7 |
|  | b | 2 | 5 | 1 | 4 |
|  | c | 8 | 1 | 4 | 2 |
|  | d | 5 | 2 | 7 | 8 |

**16.4** (a) Which is the best alternative with the following gains matrix?

|  |  | Events | | |
|---|---|---|---|---|
|  |  | 1 | 2 | 3 |
|  |  | $P = 0.4$ | $P = 0.3$ | $P = 0.3$ |
| Alternatives | a | 100 | 90 | 120 |
|  | b | 80 | 102 | 110 |

(b) Would this decision change if a utility function of $\sqrt{x}$ is used?

**16.5** A company can launch one of three versions of a new product, X, Y or Z. The profit depends on market reaction and there is a 30% chance that this will be good, a 40% chance that it will be medium and a 30% chance that it will be poor. Which version should the company launch with the profits given in the following table?

|  |  | Market reaction | | |
|---|---|---|---|---|
|  |  | Good | Medium | Poor |
| Version | X | 100 | 110 | 80 |
|  | Y | 70 | 90 | 120 |
|  | Z | 130 | 100 | 70 |

A market survey can be done to give more information on market reaction. Experience suggests that these surveys give results A, B or C with probabilities $P(A/Good)$, etc shown in the following table:

|  |  | Result | | |
|---|---|---|---|---|
|  |  | A | B | C |
| Market reaction | Good | 0.2 | 0.2 | 0.6 |
|  | Medium | 0.2 | 0.5 | 0.3 |
|  | Poor | 0.4 | 0.3 | 0.3 |

How much should the company be prepared to pay for this information?

**16.6** A road haulage contractor owns a lorry with a one-year-old engine. He has to decide now, and again in one year's time, whether or not to replace the engine. If he decides to replace it, there is a cost of £500. If he does not replace it there is an increased chance that it will break down during the year, and the cost of replacing an engine then is £800. If an engine is replaced during the year the replacement engine is assumed to be one year old at the time when the next decision is taken. The probability of breakdown of an engine during a year is as follows:

|  | Age of engine in years | | |
|---|---|---|---|
|  | 0 | 1 | 2 |
| Probability of breakdown | 0.0 | 0.2 | 0.7 |

Draw a decision tree for this problem and find the decisions that minimize the total cost over the next two years.

**16.7** Wilshaw Associates is considering launching an entirely new service. If the market reaction to this service is good (which has a probability of 0.2) Wilshaw will make £3,000 a week; if market reaction is medium (with probability 0.5) they will make £1,000 a week; but if reaction is poor (with probability 0.3) they will lose £1,500 a week. Wilshaw could run a survey to test market reaction with results A, B or C. Experience suggests that the reliability of such surveys is described by the following matrix of P(A/good), etc. Use a decision tree to find how much Wilshaw should pay for this survey.

|  |  | Result | | |
|---|---|---|---|---|
|  |  | A | B | C |
| Market reaction | Good | 0.7 | 0.2 | 0.1 |
|  | Medium | 0.2 | 0.6 | 0.2 |
|  | Poor | 0.1 | 0.4 | 0.5 |

**16.8** A television company has an option on a new six-part series. They could sell the rights to this series to the network for £100,000, or they could make the series themselves. If they make the series themselves, advertising profit from each episode is not known exactly but could be £15,000 (with a probability of 0.25), £24,000 (with a probability of 0.45) or £29,000, depending on the success of the series.

A local production company can be hired to run a pilot for the series. For a cost of £30,000 they will give either a favourable or an unfavourable report on the chances of the series being a success. The reliability of their report (phrased in terms of the probability of a favourable report given the likely advertising profit, etc) is given in the following table:

|  | Advertising profit | | |
|---|---|---|---|
|  | £15,000 | £24,000 | £29,000 |
| Unfavourable report | 0.85 | 0.65 | 0.3 |
| Favourable report | 0.15 | 0.35 | 0.7 |

Draw a decision tree of this problem and identify the best course of action and expected profit.

## Computer exercises

**16.1** Figure 16.10 shows a printout of a program that does the calculations for decision criteria. Describe the criteria that are being used. Use a package to check these results. What other criteria are available? What is the biggest problem that you can tackle?

```
        - = * = -      INFORMATION ENTERED      - = * = -
NUMBER OF STATES                            :  5
NUMBER OF ALTERNATIVES                      :  5
HURWICZ COEFFICIENT                         :   .3

                     PAYOFF TABLE
```

| STATES | PAYOFF FROM EACH ALTERNATIVE | | | | |
|---|---|---|---|---|---|
| | 1 | 2 | 3 | 4 | 5 |
| 1 | 1.00 | 5.00 | 9.00 | 2.00 | 6.00 |
| 2 | 3.00 | 7.00 | 3.00 | 5.00 | 1.00 |
| 3 | 6.00 | 4.00 | 4.00 | 6.00 | 8.00 |
| 4 | 8.00 | 2.00 | 7.00 | 5.00 | 6.00 |
| 5 | 6.00 | 9.00 | 4.00 | 1.00 | 2.00 |

DECISION-MAKING UNDER STRICT UNCERTAINTY

- = * = -   RESULTS   - = * = -

| CRITERION | ALTERNATIVE | PAYOFF |
|---|---|---|
| 1. MAXIMAX | A2 | 9.00 |
| 2. MAXIMIN | A3 | 3.00 |
| 3. LIKELIHOOD | A2 | 5.40 |
| 4. MINIMAX REGRET | A3 | 5.00 |
| 5. HURWICZ RULE | A3 | 4.80 |

------------ END OF ANALYSIS ------------

**Figure 16.10** Computer printout for decision criteria.

**16.2** Design a spreadsheet that finds the best alternative when using a variety of decision criteria.

**16.3** Figure 16.11 shows a spreadsheet that does some calculations using Bayes' theorem. Make sure you understand what is happening here. Describe the problem that is being tackled. How could you improve the format of the spreadsheet? Design you own spreadsheet for doing this kind of analysis.

**16.4** Figure 16.12 shows a printout for a program that does the calculations for a decision tree. Look at this printout, and make sure you understand what is happening. Draw the tree being described. Use an equivalent package to check the results.

**16.5** Some decision trees use Bayes' theorem for calculating the probabilities. Devise a problem of this type and use the best software you have to calculate the probabilities and suggest decisions in the tree. Collect some real data to illustrate your findings and write a report on your results.

**16.6** Spreadsheet packages can draw decision trees automatically. What are the benefits of using these packages? Design your own spreadsheet for doing these analyses.

|    | A | B | C | D | E | F | G | H |
|----|---|---|---|---|---|---|---|---|
| 1 | **Decision analysis** | | | | | | | |
| 2 | | | | | | | | |
| 3 | **First analysis** | | | | | | | |
| 4 | | | | | | | | |
| 5 | | Events | | | | | | |
| 6 | | One | Two | Three | | Expected value | | |
| 7 | Probability | 0.2 | 0.4 | 0.4 | | | | |
| 8 | Standard | 1100 | 800 | 700 | | 820 | | |
| 9 | Deluxe | 1400 | 1000 | 500 | | 880 | **** | |
| 10 | | | | | | | | |
| 11 | **Bayes' analysis** | | | | | | | |
| 12 | | Conditional | | | Prior | Revised | | |
| 13 | | A | B | C | | A | B | C |
| 14 | One | 0.1 | 0.3 | 0.6 | 0.2 | 0.02 | 0.06 | 0.12 |
| 15 | Two | 0.4 | 0.2 | 0.4 | 0.4 | 0.16 | 0.08 | 0.16 |
| 16 | Three | 0.3 | 0.6 | 0.1 | 0.4 | 0.12 | 0.24 | 0.04 |
| 17 | | | | | | 0.3 | 0.38 | 0.32 |
| 18 | | | | Predictions | One | 0.07 | 0.16 | 0.38 |
| 19 | | | | | Two | 0.53 | 0.21 | 0.50 |
| 20 | | | | | Three | 0.40 | 0.63 | 0.13 |
| 21 | | | | | | | | |
| 22 | **Calculations** | | | | | | | |
| 23 | | | | | Probabilities | | Expected value | |
| 24 | A | Standard | 774 | | 0.3 | | | |
| 25 | | Deluxe | 828 | **** | 0.3 | | 248.40 | |
| 26 | B | Standard | 769 | **** | 0.38 | | 292.22 | |
| 27 | | Deluxe | 749 | | 0.38 | | | |
| 28 | C | Standard | 871 | | 0.32 | | | |
| 29 | | Deluxe | 1097 | **** | 0.32 | | 351.04 | |
| 30 | | | | | | Total | 891.66 | |
| 31 | | | | | | | | |
| 32 | **Conclusion** | | | | | | | |
| 33 | First analysis | | 880.00 | | | | | |
| 34 | Using Bayes' | | 891.66 | **** | | | | |
| 35 | Extra profit | | 11.66 | | | | | |

**Figure 16.11** Spreadsheet used for decision analysis calculations.

—=＊=— INFORMATION ENTERED —=＊=—

MINIMIZATION PROBLEM

—=＊=— DECISION NODES —=＊=—

| NODE | BRANCHES | ALTERNATIVE NUMBER | ENDING NODE |
|---|---|---|---|
| 0 | 3 | 1 | 1 |
| | | 2 | 2 |
| | | 3 | 3 |
| 7 | 2 | 4 | 9 |
| | | 5 | 10 |
| 8 | 2 | 6 | 11 |
| | | 7 | 12 |

—=＊=— CHANCE NODES —=＊=—

| NODE | BRANCHES | PROBABILITY | ENDING NODE |
|---|---|---|---|
| 2 | 3 | 0.3000 | 4 |
| | | 0.3000 | 5 |
| | | 0.4000 | 6 |
| 3 | 2 | 0.5000 | 7 |
| | | 0.5000 | 8 |
| 10 | 3 | 0.4800 | 13 |
| | | 0.3600 | 14 |
| | | 0.1600 | 15 |
| 12 | 3 | 0.1200 | 16 |
| | | 0.2400 | 17 |
| | | 0.6400 | 18 |

—=＊=— TERMINAL NODES —=＊=—

| NODE | PAYOFF |
|---|---|
| 1 | 22 000.00 |
| 4 | 16 000.00 |
| 5 | 22 000.00 |
| 6 | 28 000.00 |
| 9 | 22 300.00 |
| 11 | 22 300.00 |
| 13 | 16 300.00 |
| 14 | 22 300.00 |
| 15 | 28 300.00 |
| 16 | 16 300.00 |
| 17 | 22 300.00 |
| 18 | 28 300.00 |

—=＊=— RESULTS —=＊=—

MINIMIZATION PROBLEM

| NODE | EXPECTED PAYOFF | SELECTED ALTERNATIVE |
|---|---|---|
| 0 | 21 340.00 | 3 |
| 1 | 22 000.00 | |
| 2 | 22 600.00 | |
| 3 | 21 340.00 | |
| 4 | 16 000.00 | |
| 5 | 22 000.00 | |
| 6 | 28 000.00 | |
| 7 | 20 380.00 | 5 |
| 8 | 22 300.00 | 6 |
| 9 | 22 300.00 | |
| 10 | 20 380.00 | |
| 11 | 22 300.00 | |
| 12 | 25 420.00 | |
| 13 | 16 300.00 | |
| 14 | 22 300.00 | |
| 15 | 28 300.00 | |
| 16 | 16 300.00 | |
| 17 | 22 300.00 | |
| 18 | 28 300.00 | |

EXPECTED PAYOFF = 21 340

———— END OF ANALYSIS ————

**Figure 16.12** Computer printout for a decision tree.

# Case study

## The Newisham Reservoir

Newisham has a population of about 30 000. It had traditionally got its water supply from the nearby River Feltham. Unfortunately, increasing quantities of water were being extracted from the river by industry upstream. When the flow reaching the Newisham water treatment works became too small to supply the town's needs, they decided to build a reservoir by damming the Feltham and diverting tributaries. This work was finished in the early 1990s and gave a guaranteed supply of water to Newisham.

Unfortunately, the dam reduced the amount of water available to farmers downstream. One of these recently found that the water supply to his cattle has effectively dried up. He is faced with the option of either connecting to the local mains water supply at a cost of £44,000 or drilling a new well. The cost of the well is not known with certainty but could be £32,000 (with a probability of 0.3), £44,000 (with a probability of 0.3) or £56,000, depending on the underground rock structure and depth of water.

A local water survey company can be hired to do on-site tests. For a cost of £600 they will give either a favourable or an unfavourable report on the chances of easily finding water. The reliability of this report (phrased in terms of the probability of a favourable report given that the drilling cost will be low, etc.) is given in the following table:

|  | Drilling well cost | | |
|---|---|---|---|
|  | £32,000 | £44,000 | £56,000 |
| Unfavourable report | 0.8 | 0.6 | 0.2 |
| Favourable report | 0.2 | 0.4 | 0.8 |

Draw a decision tree of the farmer's problem and find his best course of action and expected costs.

# 17 Controlling stocks

| | | | |
|---|---|---|---|
| Chapter outline | 526 | 17.5 ABC analysis of stock | 541 |
| 17.1 Background to stock control | 527 | Chapter review | 544 |
| | | Problems | 544 |
| 17.2 The economic order quantity | 530 | Computer exercises | 545 |
| | | Case study: | 546 |
| 17.3 Probabilistic demand | 534 | Templar Manufacturing | |
| 17.4 Periodic review systems | 538 | | |

**CHAPTER OUTLINE**

This chapter describes some models for controlling stocks. It starts by discussing the reasons why stocks are needed, how much they cost and how these costs can be minimized. The 'economic order quantity' defines an order quantity which can, in certain circumstances, minimize the costs of a stock system.

If demand is highly variable, we have to use a probabilistic model. The chapter describes a model where demand is Normally distributed, leading to a policy that ensures a specified level of customer service.

All stock control systems need some effort, and sometimes the costs involved outweigh the benefits. An ABC analysis shows the amount of effort worth spending on different items.

After reading this chapter and doing the exercises you should be able to:

- appreciate the need for stocks and the associated costs
- calculate economic order quantities and reorder levels
- appreciate the need for safety stock when demand varies
- calculate a safety stock when lead time demand is Normally distributed
- describe periodic review systems
- do ABC analyses of inventories

# 17.1 | Background to stock control

## 17.1.1 | Why hold stocks?

**Stocks** are the stores of goods that an organization holds. If you look around any organization, you will find stocks of some kind. These always have associated costs to cover warehouse operations, tied-up capital, deterioration, loss, and so on. So an obvious question is, 'Why do organizations hold stock?' There are several answers to this, but the main one is, 'To allow a buffer between supply and demand'.

Think of a supermarket, which obviously has a large stock of goods on its shelves and in its stockroom. They hold this stock because large deliveries are made relatively infrequently by lorry, while small demands from customers occur almost continuously. There is a mismatch between supply and demand, that can only be overcome by holding stock.

> The main purpose of stocks is to act as a buffer between supply and demand.

The short-term mismatch between supply and demand is only one reason for holding stock, and other reasons include:

- to act as a buffer between different production operations (that is, they 'decouple' operations)
- to allow for demands that are larger than expected, or come at unexpected times
- to allow for deliveries that are delayed or too small
- to take advantage of price discounts on large orders
- to buy items when the price is low and expected to rise
- to buy items that are going out of production or are difficult to find
- to make full loads and reduce transport costs
- to give cover for emergencies

Organizations have dramatically changed their views of stock. Historically, they saw stock as a benefit, with high stocks ensuring continued operations and even giving a measure of wealth. This is the same thinking that encourages countries to keep reserves of gold and individuals to keep stores of food in their freezers. Early in the twentieth century, it became clear that these stocks had costs that could be surprisingly high. Then organizations accepted that stocks were necessary, but looked for ways of controlling them to minimize costs.

More recently, some organizations have gone further in reducing stocks, and try to work with very low levels. Their methods are known by different names, with the most common being **just-in-time** (JIT). The basis of JIT is that organizations co-ordinate the supply of materials to demand, so that there is no accumulation of stock. When it works, this can give considerable savings and speed the flow of materials through its supply chain.

Most organizations still hold stocks, and these have associated costs. Here we will look at some models for **stock control** that try to minimize these costs.

In practice, two common policies are:

- **Fixed order quantity**, where an order of fixed size is placed whenever stock falls to a certain level. A central heating plant, for example, may order 25 000 litres of oil whenever the amount in the tank falls to 1000 litres. Such systems need continuous monitoring of stock levels and are better suited to systems with low, irregular demand for relatively expensive items.

- **Periodic review**, in which orders of varying size are placed at regular intervals to raise the stock level to a specified level. Supermarket shelves, for example, may be refilled every evening to replace whatever was sold during the day. The operating cost of this system is generally lower, so it is better suited to high, regular demand of low-value items.

---

| IN SUMMARY |

The main purpose of stocks is to act as a buffer between supply and demand. The associated costs can be high, so the trend is towards lower stocks. Stock control finds policies that minimize associated costs.

## 17.1.2 | Costs of holding stock

The cost of holding stock is typically around 25% of its value a year. This total cost has four components – unit, reorder, holding and shortage costs.

### Unit cost ($U_c$)

This is the price of an item charged by the supplier, or the cost to the company of acquiring one unit of an item. It may be fairly easy to find values by looking at quotations or recent invoices from suppliers. But sometimes, it is more difficult when there are several suppliers offering alternative products or giving different purchase conditions. If a company makes the item itself, it may be difficult to set a production cost or to calculate a transfer price.

### Reorder cost ($R_c$)

This is the cost of placing a repeat order for an item, and might include allowances for drawing up an order, correspondence and telephone costs, receiving, supervision, use of equipment and follow-up. Sometimes, costs such as quality control, transport charges, sorting and movement of received goods are included in the reorder cost. In practice, you will probably get the best estimate for a reorder cost by dividing the total annual cost of the purchasing department by the number of orders sent out.

There is a special instance of the reorder cost when the company makes the item itself. Then the reorder cost is a batch set-up cost and might include production documentation costs, allowance for production lost while resetting machines, idle time of operators, material spoilt in test runs, time of specialist tool setters, and so on.

## Holding cost ($H_c$)

This is the cost of holding one unit of an item in stock for a period of time (typically a year). The obvious cost is for tied-up money that either is borrowed (with interest payable) or could be put to other use (in which case there are opportunity costs). Other holding costs are due to storage space (supplying a warehouse, rent, local taxes, heat, light, etc.), loss (due to damage, deterioration, obsolescence and theft), handling (including special packaging, refrigeration, putting on pallets, etc.), administration (stock checks, computer updates, etc.) and insurance.

## Shortage cost ($S_c$)

If an item is needed but cannot be supplied from stock, there is usually a cost associated with this shortage. In the simplest case a retailer may lose direct profit from a sale, but the effects of shortages are usually much more widespread. There may be loss of customer goodwill and potential future sales, as well as some loss of reputation. Shortages of raw materials for production could cause disruption and force rescheduling of production, retiming of maintenance, laying off of employees, and so on. There can also be costs for positive action to overcome the shortage, perhaps sending out emergency orders, paying for special deliveries, storing partly finished goods or using alternative, more expensive suppliers.

Shortage costs are always difficult to find. But there is general agreement that they can be very high, particularly if operations are disrupted. Now we can look at the purpose of stocks again and rephrase our earlier statement by saying, 'The cost of shortages can be very high and to avoid this organizations are willing to pay the relatively lower costs of carrying stock'.

---

## IN SUMMARY

Holding stocks is expensive, with typical costs amounting to 25% of unit cost a year. The costs of holding stock can be classified as unit, reorder, holding or shortage.

---

## Self-assessment questions

**17.1** What is the main reason for holding stock?

**17.2** Name two approaches for setting order quantities in stock control systems.

**17.3** List four types of cost associated with stock holdings.

# 17.2 | The economic order quantity

## 17.2.1 | Developing the model

The **economic order quantity** is at the heart of many inventory control systems. This is a fixed order quantity, which minimizes costs when a number of assumptions are made.

The analysis considers a single item whose demand is known to be continuous and constant at $D$ per unit time. It also assumes that unit cost $U_c$, reorder cost $R_c$ and holding cost $H_c$ are all known exactly, while the shortage cost $S_c$ is so large that all demands must be met and no shortages are allowed. Initially, we shall also assume that the lead time between placing an order and having it arrive is zero. This means that there is no point in placing orders until existing stock is completely used up.

We are using a fixed order quantity system, so that orders are always placed for the same quantity, $Q$. Then the stock level alternatively rises with deliveries and falls as units are removed to meet demand, giving the sawtooth pattern shown in Figure 17.1.

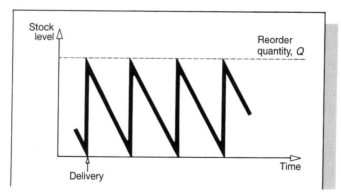

**Figure 17.1** Sawtooth stock level over time.

Consider one cycle of this sawtooth pattern (shown in Figure 17.2). At some point an order is placed for a quantity $Q$, which arrives immediately. This is used at a constant rate $D$ until there is no stock left, at which point another order is placed. The resulting stock cycle has length $T$, and we know:

$$\text{amount entering stock in the cycle} = \text{amount leaving stock in the cycle}$$

$$Q = D \times T$$

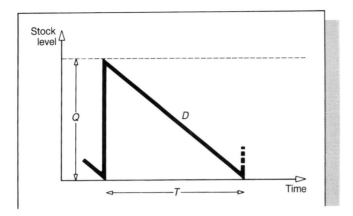

**Figure 17.2**   A single stock cycle.

Now we can do some analysis of the costs over the cycle, but we are really only interested in the result, which is the **economic order quantity**, $Q_o$:

$$\text{economic order quantity} = Q_0 = \sqrt{\frac{2R_c D}{H_c}}$$

Another useful result we could derive is that the equation for minimum total cost contains a 'fixed' element, $U_c D$, which does not vary with order quantity, and a 'variable' element, $VC_o$, which does. Optimal values for these are:

$$\text{total cost} = TC_0 = U_c D + VC_0$$

$$\text{variable cost} = VC_0 = \sqrt{2R_c H_c D}$$

# WORKED EXAMPLE 17.1

The demand for an item is constant at 20 units a month. The unit cost is £50, cost of processing an order and arranging delivery is £60, and the holding cost is £18 a unit a year. What are the economic order quantity, corresponding cycle length and costs?

### Solution

Listing the values we know in consistent units:

$$D = 20 \times 12 = 240 \text{ units a year}$$

$$U_c = £50 \text{ a unit}$$

$$R_c = £60 \text{ an order}$$

$$H_c = £18 \text{ a unit a year}$$

Then substitution gives:

$$Q_o = \sqrt{\frac{2R_c D}{H_c}} = \sqrt{\frac{2 \times 60 \times 240}{18}} = 40 \text{ units}$$

$$VC_o = \sqrt{2R_c H_c D} = \sqrt{2 \times 60 \times 18 \times 240} = £720 \text{ a year}$$

$$TC_o = U_c D + VC_o = 50 \times 240 + 720 = £12,720 \text{ a year}$$

We can find the cycle length $T_o$ from $Q_o = DT_o$, so $40 = 240T_o$ or $T_o = 1/6$ years or 2 months.

The optimal policy (with total costs of £12,720 a year) is to order 40 units every 2 months.

---

*IN SUMMARY*

An economic order quantity can be calculated from:

$$Q_o = \sqrt{\frac{2R_c D}{H_c}}$$

This minimizes the total cost of stocking an item and allows several related measures to be found.

## 17.2.2 | Reorder levels with fixed lead times

The economic order quantity shows how much to order, but we still need to know when to place an order. This decision is based on the lead time $L$ between placing an order and having it arrive in stock. For simplicity, we shall assume that this is fixed. The stock level follows the sawtooth pattern shown in Figure 17.3, with stock rising when a delivery is made and falling slowly back to zero. To make sure that a delivery arrives just as stock is running out, we must place another time $L$ earlier. The easiest way of finding this point is to look at the current stock and place an order when there is just enough left to last the lead time. With

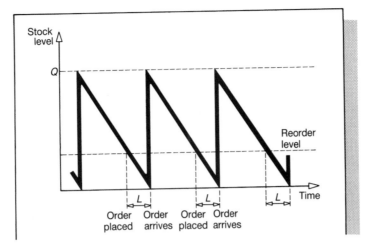

**Figure 17.3** Stock level with a fixed lead time, $L$.

constant demand of $D$, we place an order when the stock level falls to lead time×demand, and this point is called the reorder level:

$$\text{reorder level} = \text{lead time demand}$$

$$= LD$$

One way of timing orders in practice is called the 'two-bin system'. In this, stock is kept in two bins, one of which holds an amount equal to the reorder level while the second holds all remaining stock. Demand is met from the second bin until this is empty. At this point the stock level has fallen to the reorder level and it is time to place an order.

# WORKED EXAMPLE 17.2

Demand for an item is constant at 20 units a week, reorder cost is £125 an order and holding cost is £2 a unit a week. If suppliers guarantee delivery within two weeks, what is the best ordering policy for the item?

## Solution

Listing the variables in consistent units:

$$D = 20 \text{ units a week}$$
$$R_c = £125 \text{ an order}$$
$$H_c = £2 \text{ a unit a week}$$
$$L = 2 \text{ weeks}$$

Then substitution gives:

- economic order quantity:

$$Q_o = \sqrt{\frac{2R_cD}{H_c}} = \sqrt{\frac{2 \times 125 \times 20}{2}} = 50 \text{ units}$$

- reorder level:

$$\text{reorder level} = LD = 2 \times 20 = 40 \text{ units}$$

The optimal policy is to place an order for 50 units whenever stock falls to 40 units. This will happen when:

$$Q_o = DT_o \qquad \text{so} \qquad T_o = 50/20 = 2.5 \text{ weeks}$$

The variable costs are:

$$VC_o = \sqrt{2R_cH_cD} = \sqrt{2 \times 125 \times 2 \times 20} = £100 \text{ a week}$$

---

### IN SUMMARY

A convenient way of finding the time to place an order is to define a reorder level. For constant lead time and demand the reorder level equals lead time demand.

---

## Self-assessment questions

**17.4** What is the economic order quantity?

**17.5** If small orders are placed frequently (rather than placing large orders infrequently) does this: (a) reduce total costs, (b) increase total costs, (c) either increase or decrease total costs?

**17.6** What is the reorder level?

**17.7** How would you calculate a reorder level?

# 17.3 | Probabilistic demand

The economic order quantity assumes that demand is constant and known exactly. In practice this is rarely true and the demand for almost any item is uncertain and varies over time. Fortunately, these effects are generally small and the economic order quantity is widely used in practice. Sometimes, however, the variations are too large and we have to choose another approach.

A useful alternative looks for a balance between shortage costs and holding costs. Shortage costs are usually high in relation to holding costs, so organizations are willing to hold additional stocks, above their likely needs, to add a margin of safety and avoid the risk of shortages. These **safety stocks** are available if the normal working stock runs out (see Figure 17.4).

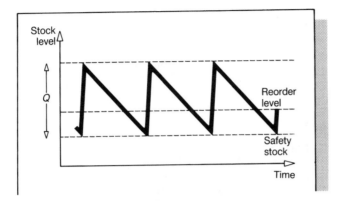

**Figure 17.4** Stock levels when a safety stock is added.

In principle, we could calculate the cost of shortages and balance them with the cost of holding stock. Unfortunately, this is rarely possible, as shortage costs are so difficult to find that they are little more than informed guesses.

An alternative approach relies more directly on the judgement of managers and uses a **service level**. This needs a positive decision to specify the desired probability that a demand is met directly from stock (or, conversely, the maximum acceptable probability that a demand cannot be met from stock). Typically, a company will specify a service level of 95%, giving a probability of 0.05 that a demand is not met.

There are several ways of defining service level, but here we shall use the probability of not running out of stock in a stock cycle. This is sometimes called the **cycle service level**.

Consider an item whose demand is Normally distributed with a mean of $D$ per unit time and standard deviation of $\sigma$. If the lead time is constant at $L$, the lead time demand is Normally distributed with mean of $LD$, variance of $\sigma^2 L$ and standard deviation of $\sigma\sqrt{L}$. This result comes from the fact that variances can be added but standard deviations cannot.

So:

- demand in a single period has mean $D$ and variance $\sigma^2$
- demand in two periods has mean $2D$ and variance $2\sigma^2$
- demand in three periods has mean $3D$ and variance $3\sigma^2$
- and so on, so that
- demand in $L$ periods has mean $LD$ and variance $L\sigma^2$.

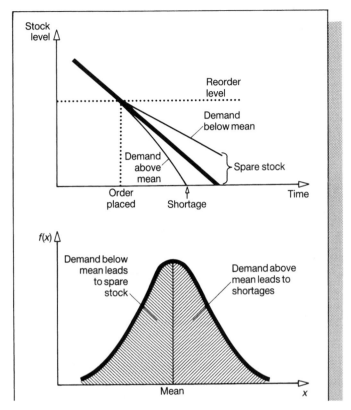

**Figure 17.5** When demand is Normally distributed, the probability of a shortage is 0.5.

With constant demand we used lead time demand (= $LD$) as a reorder level. But if lead time demand is Normally distributed, it will be greater than the mean value in half the stock cycles. This means that there will be shortages in 50% of cycles. Conversely, the lead time demand will be less than the mean in 50% of stock cycles, and this will give spare stock (as shown in Figure 17.5).

To give a cycle service level that is greater than 0.5 we need to add a safety stock, so the reorder level becomes:

> reorder level = mean lead time demand + safety stock

When managers specify a service level, they implicitly set the size of the safety stock. If they specify a high service level, the safety stock must also be high. In particular, when lead time demand is Normally distributed the safety stock becomes:

$$\text{safety stock} = Z \times \text{standard deviation of lead time demand}$$
$$= Z\sigma\sqrt{L}$$

Here $Z$ is the number of standard deviations the safety stock is away from the mean, with corresponding probabilities found in Normal tables. To give some examples:

- if $Z = 1$ a shortage will occur in 15.9% of stock cycles
- $Z = 2$ gives shortages in 2.3% of stock cycles
- $Z = 3$ gives shortages in 0.1% of stock cycles

If demand varies widely, the standard deviation of lead time demand will be high and lead to very high safety stocks for a service level near to 100%. This may be too expensive and companies will usually set a lower level, typically around 95%. Sometimes it is convenient to give items different service levels depending on their importance. Very important items may have levels close to 100%, while less important ones are set around 85%.

# WORKED EXAMPLE 17.3

Demand for an item is Normally distributed with a mean of 200 units a week and a standard deviation of 40 units. Reorder cost (including delivery) is £200, holding cost is £6 a unit a year and lead time is fixed at 3 weeks.

(a) Describe an ordering policy that will give a 95% cycle service level.
(b) What is the cost of holding the safety stock in this case?
(c) How much would the costs rise if the service level is raised to 97%?

## Solution

Listing the values we know:

$$D = 200 \text{ units a week}$$
$$\sigma = 40 \text{ units}$$
$$R_c = £200 \text{ an order}$$
$$H_c = £6 \text{ a unit a year}$$
$$L = 3 \text{ weeks}$$

(a) Substituting these gives:

$$\text{order quantity } Q_o = \sqrt{\frac{2R_cD}{H_c}} = \frac{\sqrt{2 \times 200 \times 200 \times 52}}{6}$$

$$= 833 \text{ (rounded to the nearest integer)}$$

$$\text{reorder level} = LD + \text{safety stock} = 3 \times 200 + \text{safety stock}$$

$$= 600 + \text{safety stock}$$

For a 95% service level:

$$Z = 1.645 \text{ standard deviations from the mean.}$$

Then:

$$\text{safety stock} = Z\sigma\sqrt{L} = 1.645 \times 40 \times \sqrt{3}$$
$$= 114 \text{ (to the nearest integer)}$$

The best policy is to order 833 units whenever stock falls to $600 + 114 = 714$ units. On average, orders should arrive when there are 114 units left.

(b) The expected cost of the safety stock is:

$$\text{safety stock} \times \text{holding cost} = 114 \times 6$$
$$= £684 \text{ a year}$$

(c) If the service level is raised to 97%, $Z$ becomes 1.88 and:

$$\text{safety stock} = Z\sigma\sqrt{L} = 1.88 \times 40 \times \sqrt{3} = 130$$

The cost of holding this is:

$$\text{safety stock} \times \text{holding cost} = 130 \times 6 = £780 \text{ a year}$$

---

### IN SUMMARY

The assumption that demand is constant gives reasonable results as long as actual variations are small. If the variations are large a different model must be used. When the lead time demand is Normally distributed:

$$\text{reorder level} = \text{mean lead time demand} + \text{safety stock}$$

## Self-assessment questions

**17.8** What is meant by service level and why is it used?

**17.9** What is the purpose of safety stock?

**17.10** How might the service level be improved?

# 17.4 Periodic review systems

At the beginning of the chapter we said that there were two different ordering policies:

- **fixed order quantity system**, where an order of fixed size is placed whenever stock falls to a certain level
- **periodic review system**, where orders of varying size are placed at regular intervals to raise the stock to a specified level (the target stock level)

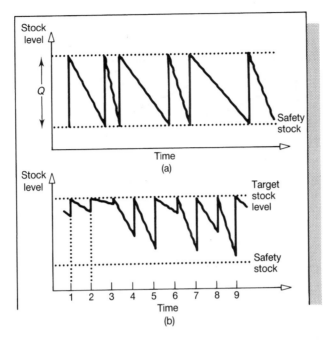

**Figure 17.6** Different ways of dealing with varying demand: (a) fixed order quantity; (b) periodic review.

If the demand is constant these two systems are identical, so differences only appear when the demand varies, as shown in Figure 17.6.

We can extend the last analysis by considering a periodic review system, in which demand is Normally distributed. Then we look for answers to two basic questions:

● How long should the interval between orders be?
● What should the target stock level be?

The order interval $T$ can really be any convenient period. It might, for example, be easiest to place an order at the end of every week, or every morning, or at the end of a month. If there is no obvious cycle we might aim for a certain number of orders a year or some average order size. We might calculate an economic order quantity, and then find the period that gives orders of about this size. The final decision is largely a matter for managers' judgement.

Whatever interval is chosen, we need to find a suitable target stock level. The system then works by examining the amount of stock on hand when an order is placed and ordering the amount that brings this up to the target stock level:

order quantity = target stock level − stock on hand

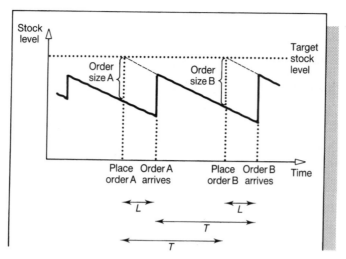

**Figure 17.7**   Calculating the target stock level.

Suppose the lead time is constant at $L$. When an order is placed, the stock on hand plus this order must be enough to last until the next order arrives, which is $T + L$ away (as shown in Figure 17.7).

The target stock level should be high enough to cover mean demand over this period, so it must be at least $(T + L)D$. As demand is Normally distributed, there must be some safety stock to allow for the 50% of cycles when demand is above average. Assuming that both the cycle length and lead time are constant, the demand over $T + L$ is Normally distributed with mean of $(T + L)D$, variance of $\sigma^2(T + L)$ and standard deviation of $\sigma\sqrt{(T + L)}$. We can then define a safety as:

$$\text{safety stock} = Z \times \text{standard deviation of demand over } T + L$$
$$= Z\sigma\sqrt{(T + L)}$$

Then:

$$\text{target stock level} = \text{mean demand over } (T + L) + \text{safety stock}$$
$$= D(T + L) + Z\sigma\sqrt{(T + L)}$$

# WORKED EXAMPLE 17.4

Demand for an item has a mean of 200 units a week and standard deviation of 40 units. Stock is checked every four weeks and lead time is constant at two weeks. Describe a policy that gives a 95% service level. If the holding cost is £2 a unit a week, what is the cost of the safety stock with this policy? What is the effect of a 98% service level?

### Solution

The variables are:

$$D = 200 \text{ units}$$
$$\sigma = 40 \text{ units}$$
$$H_c = £2 \text{ a unit a week}$$
$$T = 4 \text{ weeks}$$
$$L = 2 \text{ weeks}$$

For a 95% safety stock $Z$ is 1.645. Then:

- safety stock = $Z\sigma\sqrt{(T + L)} = 1.645 \times 40 \times \sqrt{6} = 161$
  (rounded to the nearest integer)
- target stock level = $D(T + L)$ + safety stock = $200 \times (4+2) + 161 = 1361$

When it is time to place an order, the policy is to find the stock on hand, and place an order for:

$$\text{order size} = 1361 - \text{stock on hand}$$

If, for example, there are 200 units in stock we order 1161 units.
The cost of holding the safety stock is $161 \times 2 = £322$ a week.
If the service level is increased to 98%, $Z = 2.05$:

$$\text{safety stock} = 2.05 \times 40 \times \sqrt{6} = 201$$

The target stock level is then $1200 + 201 = 1401$ units and the cost of the safety stock is $201 \times 2 = £402$ a week.

---

| IN SUMMARY |

A periodic review system places orders of variable size at regular intervals. The quantity ordered is enough to raise stock on hand to a target level:

$$\text{target stock level} = D(T + L) + Z\sigma\sqrt{(T + L)}$$

---

## Self-assessment questions

**17.11** How is the order size calculated for a periodic review system?

**17.12** Will the safety stock be higher for a fixed order quantity system or a periodic review system?

## | 17.5 || ABC analysis of stock

All stock control systems are computerized, but they still need some effort to input data, check values, update supplier details, confirm orders and so on. For some items, especially cheap ones, this effort is not worth while. Very few organizations, for example, include routine stationery in their computerized stock system. At the other end of the scale are very expensive items, which need special care above the routine calculations.

An ABC analysis is one way of putting items into categories that reflect the amount of effort worth spending on stock control. This kind of analysis is sometimes called a Pareto analysis or the 'rule of 80/20' (suggesting that 80% of stock items need 20% of the attention, while the remaining 20% of items need 80% of the attention). ABC analyses define:

- A items as expensive and needing special care
- B items as ordinary ones needing standard care
- C items as cheap and needing little care

Typically, an organization might use an automated system to deal with all B items. The computer system might make some suggestions for A items, but final decisions are made by managers who are familiar with all the circumstances. C items may be left out of the system, with any control left to *ad hoc* procedures.

An ABC analysis starts by calculating the total annual use of each item in terms of value, by multiplying the number of units used in a year by the unit cost. Usually, a few expensive items account for a lot of use, while many cheap ones account for little use. If we list the items in order of decreasing annual use by value, A items are at the top of the list and C items are at the bottom. We might typically find:

| Category | % of items | Cumulative % of items | % of use by value | Cumulative % of use by value |
|----------|-----------|----------------------|-------------------|------------------------------|
| A | 10 | 10 | 70 | 70 |
| B | 30 | 40 | 20 | 90 |
| C | 60 | 100 | 10 | 100 |

Plotting the cumulative percentage of use by value against the cumulative percentage of items gives the graph shown in Figure 17.8.

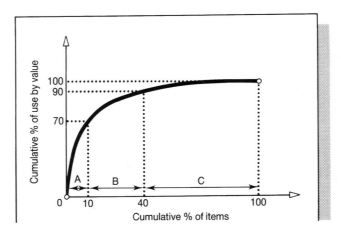

**Figure 17.8** ABC analysis of stocks.

# WORKED EXAMPLE 17.5

A small store has ten categories of product with the following costs and annual demands:

| Product | P1 | P2 | P3 | P4 | P5 | P6 | P7 | P8 | P9 | P0 |
|---|---|---|---|---|---|---|---|---|---|---|
| Unit Cost (£) | 20 | 10 | 20 | 50 | 10 | 50 | 5 | 20 | 100 | 1 |
| Annual demand ('00s) | 2.5 | 50 | 20 | 66 | 15 | 6 | 10 | 5 | 1 | 50 |

Do an ABC analysis of these items. If resources for stock control are limited, which items should be given least attention?

## Solution

The annual use of P1 in terms of value is $20 \times 250 = £5,000$. Repeating this calculation for the other items sorting them into order of decreasing annual use by value gives the results shown in Table 17.1. The boundaries between categories of items are sometimes unclear, but in this case P4 is clearly an A item, P2, P3 and P6 are B items and the rest are C items.

**Table 17.1**

| Product | P4 | P2 | P3 | P6 | P5 | P8 | P9 | P1 | P7 | P0 |
|---|---|---|---|---|---|---|---|---|---|---|
| Cumulative % of items | 10 | 20 | 30 | 40 | 50 | 60 | 70 | 80 | 90 | 100 |
| Annual use (£'000s) | 330 | 50 | 40 | 30 | 15 | 10 | 10 | 5 | 5 | 5 |
| Cumulative annual use | 330 | 380 | 420 | 450 | 465 | 475 | 485 | 490 | 495 | 500 |
| Cumulative % annual use | 66 | 76 | 84 | 90 | 93 | 95 | 97 | 98 | 99 | 100 |
| Category | ◄─A─► | ◄─── | B ─── | ──►◄─ | ─────── | ─────── | C ───── | ─────── | ───► | |

The C items account for only 10% of annual use by value and these should be given least attention if resources are limited.

---

## IN SUMMARY

ABC analyses allow items to be categorized according to importance, so that available effort can be shared out appropriately. Typically, 20% of items account for 80% of use by value (A items) while the bulk of items account for very little use by value (C items).

## Self-assessment questions

**17.13** What is the purpose of doing an ABC analysis of inventories?

**17.14** Which items can best be dealt with by routine, automated control procedures?

---

| CHAPTER REVIEW |

This chapter described some quantitative models for controlling stocks. In particular, the chapter

- discussed the purpose of holding stocks and the associated costs
- outlined the aims of inventory control
- described the economic order quantity
- discussed service levels and safety stocks
- described periodic review systems
- described ABC analyses

---

## Problems

**17.1** The demand for an item is constant at 100 units a year. Unit cost is £50, cost of processing an order is £20 and holding cost is estimated at £10 per unit per annum. What are the economic order quantity, corresponding cycle length and costs?

**17.2** Beograd Inc. works 50 weeks a year and has demand for an item that is constant at 100 units a week. The cost of each unit is £20 and Beograd aims for a return of 20% on capital invested. Annual warehouse costs are 5% of the value of goods stored. The purchasing department of the company costs £45,000 a year and sends out an average of 2000 orders. Find the optimal order quantity for the item, the optimal time between orders and the minimum cost of stocking the item.

**17.3** Demand for an item is steady at 20 units a week and the economic order quantity has been calculated at 50 units. What is the reorder level when the lead time is (a) 1 week, (b) 2 weeks?

**17.4** H.R. Prewett Limited forecasts its demand for one component to average 18 a day over a 200-day working year. If there are any shortages, production will be disrupted, with very high costs. The holding cost for the component is £40 a unit a year and the cost of placing an order is £80 an order. Find:

(a) the economic order quantity

(b) the optimal number of orders a year

(c) the total annual cost of operating the system (including the cost of purchases) if the real interest rate is 25% a year.

**17.5** A company advertises a 95% cycle service level for all stock items. Stock is replenished from a single supplier who guarantees a lead time of four weeks.

(a) What reorder level should the company adopt for an item that has a Normally distributed demand with mean of 1000 units a week and standard deviation of 100 units?

(b) What would the reorder level be if a 98% cycle service level is used?

**17.6** An item of stock has a unit cost of $400, reorder cost of $500 and holding cost of $10 a unit a week. Demand for the item has a mean of 100 a week with standard deviation 10. Lead time is constant at three weeks. Design a stock policy for the item to give a service level of 95%. How would this change for a 90% service level? What are the costs of these two policies?

**17.7** Describe a periodic review system with interval of two weeks for the company described in Problem 17.5.

**17.8** A small store has ten categories of product with the following costs and annual demands:

| Product | X1 | X2 | X3 | Y1 | Y2 | Y3 | Z1 | Z2 | Z3 | Z4 |
|---------|----|----|----|----|----|----|----|----|----|----|
| Unit cost (£) | 20 | 25 | 30 | 1 | 4 | 6 | 10 | 15 | 20 | 22 |
| Annual demand ('00s) | 3 | 2 | 2 | 10 | 8 | 7 | 30 | 20 | 6 | 4 |

Do an ABC analysis of these items.

**17.9** Annual demand for an item is 2000 units; each order costs £10 to place and the annual holding cost is 40% of the unit cost. The unit cost depends on the quantity ordered as follows:

- for quantities less than 500, unit cost is £1
- for quantities between 500 and 1000, unit cost is £0.80
- for quantities of 1000 or more, unit cost is £0.60

What is the best ordering policy for the item?

# Computer exercises

**17.1** Figure 17.9 shows the printout from a computer program with some calculations for an item held in stock. Examine this printout and make sure you understand what is happening. What software do you have for inventory control? Use a suitable program to check these results.

**17.2** Most stocks are controlled by computer. Describe the functions that you would expect to find in a computerized stock control system.

+++---===  ECONOMIC ORDER QUANTITY CALCULATION  ===---+++

Results for Component

EOQ Input Data:

Demand per year (D)                                       = 400
Order or setup cost per order (Co)                        = 650
Holding cost per unit per year (Ch)                       = 20
Shortage cost per unit per year (Cs)                      = 1000
Shortage cost per unit, independent of time ($\pi$)       = 100
Replenishment or production rate per year (P)             = 500
Lead time for a new order in year (LT)                    = .25
Unit cost (C)                                             = 120

EOQ Output:

EOQ                                  =        360.555
Maximum inventory                    =         72.111
Maximum backorder                    =          0.000
Order interval                       =          0.901 year
Reorder point                        =        100.000
        Ordering cost                =        721.110
        Holding cost                 =        721.110
        Shortage cost                =          0.000
Subtotal of inventory cost per year  =       1442.220
Material cost per year               =      48000.000
Total cost per year                  =      49442.219

**Figure 17.9**  Printout from inventory control package.

**17.3** A small company wants to control the stocks of 50 items. It seems extravagant to buy an inventory control system for this number of items, and there is no one in the company to write their own software. It has been suggested that a spreadsheet can be used to record weekly sales and do associated calculations. Design a spreadsheet that the company can use.

**17.4** Recent developments, such as lean manufacturing, JIT and e-commerce, have changed the way that organizations manage their stocks. Show how, giving suitable examples, technology has affected stock control.

# Case study

## Templar Manufacturing

Mr Templar founded his own manufacturing company when he was 21 years old. He has continued to run it for the past 35 years and through steady expansion it now employs over 200 people.

A management consultant has recently suggested improving the stock control system, but Mr Templar is not sure that this is really necessary. He was talking to a meeting of managers and said: 'I don't know how much the present stock control system costs, if it works as well as it could, or if the proposals would save money or not. I know that we have the things we need in stock, and if we have a shortage enough people complain to make sure we don't have any more. What I want is someone to show me if the proposals are worth looking at'.

When the management consultant asked what kind of demonstration Mr Templar would like, he got the following reply: 'I know you wanted to run a pilot scheme before starting work on a revised stock control system. I still need convincing that it is even worth going ahead with the pilot scheme. I don't want anything fancy. Let me give you an example of one of the components we make and see what you can do.

'This component is basically a flanged orbital hub contact that costs us about £15 to make. We use about 2000 a year. At the moment we can make them at a rate of 70 a week, but only plan one batch every quarter. Each time we set up the production it costs £345 to change the production line and £85 for preparation and scheduling costs. Other stock-holding costs are related to the unit costs, including insurance (1% a year), deterioration (2%) and capital (13%). I think that we could make them a bit faster, say up to 90 a week, and the unit cost could even fall a few per cent. Of course, we could make them a bit slower, but this would raise the cost by a few per cent'.

If you were the management consultant, how would you demonstrate the benefit of a new stock control system to Mr Templar?

# 18 | Planning projects with networks

Chapter outline                     548
18.1 Project network analysis       549
18.2 Networks for projects          550
18.3 Timing of projects             557
18.4 Resource planning              563

Chapter review                      568
Problems                            568
Computer exercises                  571
Case study:                         575
    Westin Contractors

## CHAPTER OUTLINE

A project consists of a set of activities, with a clear start and finish, and with an aim of making a distinct product. In business, projects need detailed planning. This chapter describes the most widely used method of doing this planning.

The first part of the chapter introduces the need for project management. Then it describes how to draw a network for the project. Having drawn a network, the next stage is to analyse the timing of individual events and activities, and hence the overall duration of the project.

Gantt charts give an alternative view of a project, emphasizing its timing and finding the resources used at any time.

After reading this chapter and doing the exercises you should be able to:

- appreciate the need for planning complex projects
- represent projects by networks of connected activities and events
- calculate the timing of events and activities
- identify critical paths and hence overall project duration
- change the times of activities to achieve stated objectives
- draw Gantt charts
- find the resources needed during a project

# 18.1 | Project network analysis

This chapter describes how to use networks for managing projects, so we should start by defining a **project**:

> A project is a self-contained piece of work with a clear start and finish. It consists of a series of activities that result in a distinct product.

With this broad definition you can see that each of us does a number of small projects every day, such as preparing a meal, writing a report, building a fence, or organizing a party. Each of these projects needs planning, and in particular we have to identify:

- the activities that make up the project
- the order in which these activities must be done
- the timing of each activity
- the resources needed at each stage

We can do small projects with almost no formal planning, and a little thought is usually enough to make sure they run smoothly. But business projects can be very large and involve a lot of money. The installation of a new computer system, building a nuclear power station, organizing the Olympic Games and building a rail tunnel under the English Channel are examples of large projects, and we should only expect them to run smoothly if there had been a lot of planning. **Project network analysis** is the most widely used technique for helping organize complex projects.

### IN SUMMARY

A project is a coherent piece of work that has a clear start and finish, and an aim of making a distinct product. Projects are often very large and rely on detailed planning. Project network analysis is the most widely used technique for doing this planning.

## Self-assessment questions

**18.1** What is a project?

**18.2** What is the purpose of project management?

**18.3** 'Project management is only concerned with major capital projects.' Do you think this is true?

# 18.2 | Networks for projects

## 18.2.1 | Drawing networks

A project network consists of a series of nodes connected by arrows. We shall use the convention that each **activity** in a project is represented by an arrow and each node represents a point in time at which activities begin and end. The nodes are called **events**, and a network consists of alternating activities and events.

Figure 18.1 shows part of a project network. This has two activities, A followed by B, and three events. Event 1 is the start of activity A, event 2 is the finish of activity A and the start of activity B, and event 3 is the finish of activity B. We can develop this basic idea to give larger and more complex networks.

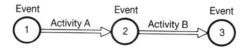

**Figure 18.1** Part of a project network.

# WORKED EXAMPLE 18.1

Imagine that you want to build a greenhouse from a kit. The instructions make it clear that this is a project with three parts:

- A, preparing the base (which takes 3 days)
- B, building the frame (which takes 2 days)
- C, fixing the glass (which takes 1 day)

Draw a network for the project.

## Solution

The project is made up of three activities, which must be done in a fixed order; building the frame must be done after preparing the base and before fixing the glass. We can describe this order by a precedence or **dependence table**, in which each activity is listed along with those activities that immediately precede it:

| Activity | Duration (days) | Description | Immediate predecessor |
|----------|-----------------|-------------|-----------------------|
| A | 3 | prepare base | - |
| B | 2 | build frame | A |
| C | 1 | fix glass | B |

Labelling the activities A, B and C is a convenient shorthand and allows us to refer to activity B having activity A as immediate predecessor, which is normally stated as 'B depends on A'. In this table we only list immediate predecessors, so we do not have to add that activity C (fixing the glass) depends on activity A as well as B but can infer this from other dependences. Activity A has no immediate predecessors and can be started whenever convenient.

Now we can draw a network from the dependence table, as shown in Figure 18.2.

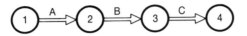

**Figure 18.2**  Network for Worked Example 18.1.

The directions of arrows in a project network show precedence. Each preceding activity must be finished before the following one starts, and following activities can start as soon as preceding ones finish. In Worked Example 18.1, preparing the base must be done first, and as soon as this is finished the frame can be built. The glass can then be fixed as soon as the frame is built.

After drawing the basic network for the project we can consider its timing. It is convenient to work with a notional starting time of 0, and then we can find the start and finish times of each activity.

# WORKED EXAMPLE 18.2

For the project described in Worked Example 18.1, find the times for each activity. What happens if preparing the base takes more than three days, or building the frame takes less than two days?

## Solution

If we take a starting time of 0, preparing the base can be finished by the end of day 3. Then building the frame can start, and as it takes two days it can be finished by the end of day 5. Then fixing the glass can start, and as it takes one day it can be finished by the end of day 6.

If the base takes more than three days the project will be delayed. If the frame take less than two days the project can be finished early.

We now have a timetable for the project showing when each activity starts and finishes. We can use this timetable to schedule resources, so we can list the major steps in project planning as:

- define the separate activities and their durations
- find the dependence of activities
- draw a network
- analyse the timing of the project
- schedule resources

---

*IN SUMMARY*

Project network analysis starts by dividing the whole project into a number of separate activities. The relationship between these is shown by arrows in a network of alternating activities and events. After the network has been drawn, calculations can be done for timing and resource allocation.

## 18.2.2 | Larger networks

Now that we have seen the principles, we can draw larger networks from a dependence table, and you will find that this becomes much easier with practice. A useful approach is to start drawing the network on the left-hand side with those activities that do not depend on any other. Then you can add those activities that only depend on these first activities, then those that only depend on the latest activities, and so on. You systematically expand the network, working generally from left to right, until all activities have been added and the network is complete.

This procedure relies on some implicit rules, and before continuing, we should state these more formally. The two main rules are:

- before an activity can start all preceding activities must be finished
- the arrows representing activities only show precedence and neither the length nor orientation is significant

By convention, there are also two other rules:

- a network has only one starting and one finishing event
- any two events can only be connected by one activity

This last rule is for convenience so that we can refer to 'the activity between events $i$ and $j$' and know exactly which one we are talking about. Using these rules, we can draw networks of almost any size.

# WORKED EXAMPLE 18.3

A company is opening a new office and identifies the main activities and dependences as follows:

| Activity | Description | Depends on |
|----------|-------------|------------|
| A | find office location | – |
| B | recruit new staff | – |
| C | make office alterations | A |
| D | order equipment | A |
| E | install new equipment | D |
| F | train staff | B |
| G | start operations | C, E, F |

Draw a network of this project.

## Solution

Activities A and B have no predecessors and can start as soon as convenient. As soon as activity A is finished both C and D can start; E can start as soon as D is finished and F can start as soon as B is finished. G can only start when C, E and F have all finished. This gives the network shown in Figure 18.3. The network does not break any of the rules above, and in particular has a single starting and finishing event, and only one activity between any pair of events.

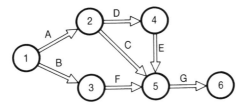

**Figure 18.3**   Network for Worked Example 18.3.

The network shows the project starting with activities A and B, but this does not mean that these must start at the same time, only that they can start as soon as convenient and must be finished before any following activity can start. Similarly, event 2 marks the point at which both C and D can start, but this does not mean that they must start at the same time. Event 5 is the point at which C, E and F are finished, but this does not mean that they must finish at the same time, only that they must all be finished before G can start.

---

| *IN SUMMARY* |

Networks of almost any size can be drawn from a dependence table. The general approach is to draw the first activities, and then systematically add all following ones.

## 18.2.3 | Dummy activities

There are two circumstances that make networks more complicated. We can illustrate the first of these by the following dependence table:

| Activity | Depends on |
|----------|------------|
| A | - |
| B | A |
| C | A |
| D | B, C |

You may be tempted to draw this as shown in Figure 18.4(a), but this breaks one of the rules above, which says, 'Any two events can only be connected by one activity'. The conventional way round this is to define a **dummy activity**. This is not a part of the project, has zero duration and needs no resources, but is simply there to allow a sensible network. In this case the dummy makes sure that only one activity goes between two events and is called a **uniqueness dummy**. In Figure 18.4(b) the dummy activity is shown as the broken line, X.

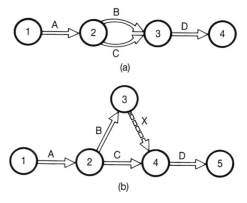

**Figure 18.4** Network with a uniqueness dummy: (a) incorrect network; (b) correct network using dummy activity X.

A second situation that needs a dummy activity is illustrated by the part of a dependence table shown below:

| Activity | Depends on |
|----------|------------|
| D | not given |
| E | not given |
| F | D, E |
| G | D |

You may be tempted to draw this part of the network as shown in Figure 18.5(a), but the dependence is clearly wrong. Activity F is shown as depending on D and E, which is correct, but G is shown as having the same dependence. The dependence table shows that G can start as soon as D is finished but the network shows it waiting for E to finish as well. The way to avoid this relies on separating the dependences by introducing a dummy activity, as shown in Figure 18.5(b). The dependence of F on D is shown through the dummy activity X. In effect, the dummy cannot start until D has finished, and then F cannot start until the dummy and E are finished. As the dummy activity has zero duration this does not add any time to the project. This type of dummy is called a **logical dummy**.

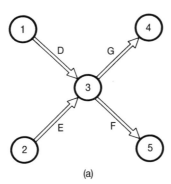

(a)

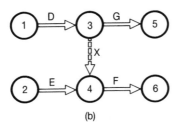

(b)

**Figure 18.5** Network with a logical dummy: (a) incorrect network; (b) correct network using dummy activity X.

These are the only two circumstances (making sure that only one activity goes between two events and making sure the logic is correct) where dummies are used.

## WORKED EXAMPLE 18.4

A project is described by the following dependence table. Draw a network of the project.

| Activity | Depends on | Activity | Depends on |
|----------|------------|----------|------------|
| A | J | I | J |
| B | C, G | J | - |
| C | A | K | B |
| D | F, K, N | L | I |
| E | J | M | I |
| F | B, H, L | N | M |
| G | A, E, I | O | M |
| H | G | P | O |

### Solution

This seems a difficult network, but the steps are fairly straightforward. Activity J is the only one that does not depend on anything else, so this starts the network. Then we can add activities A, E and I, which only depend on J. Then we can add activities that depend on A, E and I. Continuing this systematic addition of activities leads to the network shown in Figure 18.6, which includes four dummy activities: W, X, Y and Z.

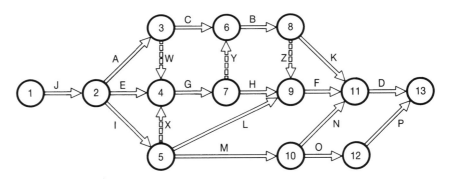

**Figure 18.6** Network for Worked Example 18.4.

---

### IN SUMMARY

Two types of dummy activity may be needed to draw a network. Uniqueness dummies make sure that only one activity starts and finishes with the same events, and logical dummies make sure that the logic of the network is accurate.

## Self-assessment questions

**18.4** In the networks we have drawn, what are represented by: (a) nodes, (b) arrows?

**18.5** What information is needed to draw a project network?

**18.6** What are the main rules for drawing a project network?

**18.7** When are dummy activities used?

# 18.3 Timing of projects

The timing of events and activities is a major part of project planning. In particular, it is important to find the earliest time that an activity can start and the latest time by which it must be finished.

## 18.3.1 Event analysis

Suppose a project is represented by the following dependence table, where a duration (in weeks) has been added:

| Activity | Duration | Depends on |
|----------|----------|------------|
| A | 3 | - |
| B | 2 | - |
| C | 2 | A |
| D | 4 | A |
| E | 1 | C |
| F | 3 | D |
| G | 3 | B |
| H | 4 | G |
| I | 5 | E, F |

The network for this project is shown in Figure 18.7, where durations are noted under the activities.

The analysis of times starts by finding the earliest possible time for each event, assuming a start time of zero for the project as a whole. The earliest time for event 1 is clearly 0. The earliest time for event 2 is when A finishes, which is three weeks after its earliest start at 0 (week 3); the earliest time for event 4 is the time when C finishes, which is two weeks after its earliest start at 3 (week 5). Similarly, the earliest time for event 5 is 4 + 3 = 7, for event 3 is 2 and for event 7 is 2 + 3 = 5 (as shown in Figure 18.8).

When several activities have to finish before an event, the earliest time for the event is the earliest time by which **all** preceding activities can be finished. The earliest time for event 6 is when both E and F are finished. E can finish one week after its earliest start at 5 (week 6), F can finish three weeks after its earliest start at 7

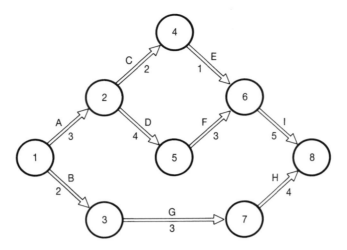

**Figure 18.7** Network for event timing.

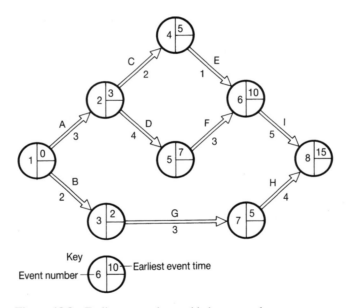

Key

Event number —⌀ 6 | 10 ⌀— Earliest event time

**Figure 18.8** Earliest event times added to network.

(week 10). Then the earliest time when both of these can be finished is week 10. Similarly, event 8 must wait until both activities H and I are finished. Activity H can be finished by week $5 + 4 = 9$ while activity I can be finished by week $10 + 5 = 15$. The earliest time for event 8 is the later of these which is week 15. This gives the overall duration of the project as 15 weeks. Figure 18.8 shows the earliest times for each event noted on the network.

Having gone through the network and found the earliest time for each event we can do a similar analysis to find the latest time for each. For this we use almost the reverse of the procedure to find the earliest times. Starting at the end of the project with event 8, this has a latest time for completion of week 15. To allow activity I to be finished by week 15 it must be started five weeks before this, so the latest time for event 6 is week $15 - 5 = 10$. The latest that H can finish is week 15, so the latest time it can start is 4 weeks before this, so the latest time for event 7 is week $15 - 4 = 11$. Similarly, the latest time for event 3 is $11 - 3 = 8$, for event 5 is $10 - 3 = 7$ and for event 4 is $10 - 1 = 9$ (as shown in Figure 18.9).

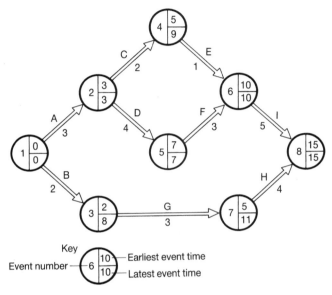

**Figure 18.9** Latest event times added to network.

For events that have more than one following activity, the latest time must allow all following activities to be finished on time. Event 2 is followed by activities C and D; C must be finished by week 9 so it must be started 2 weeks before this (week 7), while D must be finished by week 7 so it must be started 4 weeks before this (week 3). The latest time for event 2 that allows both C and D to start on time is the earlier of these, which is week 3.

Similarly, the latest time for event 1 must allow both A and B to finish on time. The latest start time for B is $8 - 2 = 6$ and the latest start time for A is $3 - 3 = 0$. The latest time for event 1 must allow both of these to start on time and this means a latest time of 0. Figure 18.9 shows the network with latest times noted on each event.

---

**IN SUMMARY**

Finding the times for events and activities is an important part of project planning. An earliest and latest time can be found for each event.

## 18.3.2 | Activity analysis

We can now extend the analysis of project times to activities, by finding the earliest and latest start times (and corresponding earliest and latest finish times).

The earliest start time for an activity is the earliest time of the preceding event; the earliest finish time is the earliest start time plus the duration. Looking at one activity in Figure 18.9, say G, the earliest start time is week 2, so the earliest finish time is week $2 + 3 = 5$.

We can find the latest start and finish time for an activity using similar reasoning, but working backwards. The latest finish time for each activity is the latest time of the following event; the latest start time is the latest finish time minus the duration. For activity G the latest finish is week 11, so the latest start is week $11 - 3 = 8$ (see Figure 18.10).

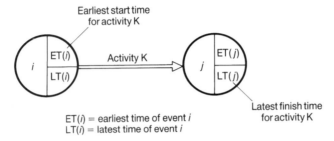

ET($i$) = earliest time of event $i$
LT($i$) = latest time of event $i$

**Figure 18.10** Earliest and latest activity times.

**Table 18.1**

| Activity | Duration | Earliest start | Earliest finish | Latest start | Latest finish |
|---|---|---|---|---|---|
| A | 3 | 0 | 3 | 0 | 3 |
| B | 2 | 0 | 2 | 6 | 8 |
| C | 2 | 3 | 5 | 7 | 9 |
| D | 4 | 3 | 7 | 3 | 7 |
| E | 1 | 5 | 6 | 9 | 10 |
| F | 3 | 7 | 10 | 7 | 10 |
| G | 3 | 2 | 5 | 8 | 11 |
| H | 4 | 5 | 9 | 11 | 15 |
| I | 5 | 10 | 15 | 10 | 15 |

Repeating these calculations for all activities in the project gives the results in Table 18.1. In this table there are some activities that have flexibility in time: activity G, as we have seen, can start as early as week 2 or as late as week 8, while activity C can start as early as week 3 or as late as week 7. On the other hand there are some activities that have no flexibility at all: activities A, D, F, and I have no freedom and their latest start time is the same as their earliest start time. The activities that have to be done at fixed times are called the **critical activities**, and they form a continuous path through the network, called the **critical path**. The length of this path sets the overall project duration. If one of the critical activities is extended by a certain amount the overall project duration is also extended by this amount; if one of the critical activities is delayed by some time the overall project duration is extended by the time of the delay. But if one of the critical activities is reduced in duration the overall project duration may be reduced by this amount.

Those activities that have some flexibility in timing are the **non-critical activities**, and these may be delayed or extended without necessarily affecting the overall project duration. But there is a limit to the possible expansion, and this is measured by the **float**. The total float of an activity is defined as the difference between the maximum amount of time available for it and the time actually used. It follows that critical activities have zero total float, while non-critical activities have some positive amount:

---

total float = latest finish – earliest start – duration

---

Calculating the total float for activity G in the example above has:

latest finish = latest time of following event (7) = 11

earliest start = earliest time of preceding event (3) = 2

duration of activity G = 3

So:

total float = latest finish – earliest start – duration

= 11 – 2 – 3 = 6

Repeating the calculations for other activities in the example gives the results in Table 18.2.

The total float measures the amount an activity can expand without affecting the duration of the project. Activity E, for example, can expand by up to four weeks without affecting the duration of the project, as can activity C. But these expansions are not independent, and only one of them can occur without delaying the project.

**Table 18.2**

| Activity | Duration | Earliest | | Latest | | Total float |
|---|---|---|---|---|---|---|
| | | start | finish | start | finish | |
| A | 3 | 0 | 3 | 0 | 3 | 0 * |
| B | 2 | 0 | 2 | 6 | 8 | 6 |
| C | 2 | 3 | 5 | 7 | 9 | 4 |
| D | 4 | 3 | 7 | 3 | 7 | 0 * |
| E | 1 | 5 | 6 | 9 | 10 | 4 |
| F | 3 | 7 | 10 | 7 | 10 | 0 * |
| G | 3 | 2 | 5 | 8 | 11 | 6 |
| H | 4 | 5 | 9 | 11 | 15 | 6 |
| I | 5 | 10 | 15 | 10 | 15 | 0 * |

Note: * identifies the critical activities

# WORKED EXAMPLE 18.5

Building a small telephone exchange is planned as a project with ten main activities. Estimated durations (in weeks) and dependences are shown in Table 18.3. Draw the network for this project, find its duration and calculate the total float of each activity.

**Table 18.3**

| Activity | Description | Duration | Depends on |
|----------|-------------|----------|------------|
| A | design internal equipment | 10 | – |
| B | design exchange building | 5 | A |
| C | order parts for equipment | 3 | A |
| D | order material for building | 2 | B |
| E | wait for equipment parts | 15 | C |
| F | wait for building material | 10 | D |
| G | employ equipment assemblers | 5 | A |
| H | employ building workers | 4 | B |
| I | install equipment | 20 | E, G, J |
| J | complete building | 30 | F, H |

## Solution

The network for this is shown in Figure 18.11; repeating the calculations described above gives the results listed in Table 18.4. The duration of the project is 77 days, defined by the critical path A, B, D, F, J and I.

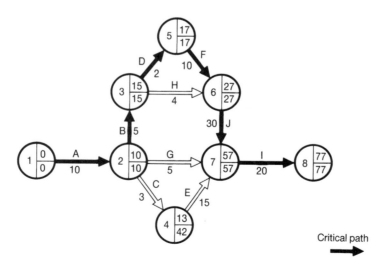

**Figure 18.11**   Network for Worked Example 18.5.

**Table 18.4**

| Activity | Duration | Earliest start | Earliest finish | Latest start | Latest finish | Total float |
|----------|----------|-------|--------|-------|--------|-------------|
| A | 10 | 0 | 10 | 0 | 10 | 0 * |
| B | 5 | 10 | 15 | 10 | 15 | 0 * |
| C | 3 | 10 | 13 | 39 | 42 | 29 |
| D | 2 | 15 | 17 | 15 | 17 | 0 * |
| E | 15 | 13 | 28 | 42 | 57 | 29 |
| F | 10 | 17 | 27 | 17 | 27 | 0 * |
| G | 5 | 10 | 15 | 52 | 57 | 42 |
| H | 4 | 15 | 19 | 23 | 27 | 8 |
| I | 20 | 57 | 77 | 57 | 77 | 0 * |
| J | 30 | 27 | 57 | 27 | 57 | 0 * |

---

### IN SUMMARY

An earliest and latest start and finish time can be found for each activity. The amount of flexibility can be measured by the total float. Critical activities have no float and form the critical path, which determines the overall project duration.

## Self-assessment questions

**18.8** How would you calculate the earliest and latest times for an event?

**18.9** What is meant by the total float of an activity?

**18.10** How big is the total float of a critical activity?

**18.11** What is the significance of the critical path?

# 18.4 Resource planning

## 18.4.1 Changing project durations

There are two main reasons why project durations may need changing:

- when a network is analysed the timing is found to be unacceptable – it may, for example, take longer than the organization has available
- during the execution of a project an activity might take a different time from that originally planned

Taking the first of these, the initial length of a project may be too long and need reducing. We know that the duration of a project is set by the critical path, so we can only reduce the overall duration by reducing the durations of critical activities. Reducing the duration of non-critical activities has no effect on the overall project duration.

We must also consider what happens when a critical path is shortened. Small reductions may have little effect, but if we keep reducing the time of the critical path there must come a point when some other path through the network becomes critical. We can find this point from the total float on paths parallel to the critical path. Each activity on a parallel path has the same total float, and when the critical path is reduced by more than this, the parallel path becomes critical.

# WORKED EXAMPLE 18.6

The project network shown in Figure 18.12 has a duration of 14 with A, B and C as the critical path. If each activity can be reduced by up to 50% of the original duration, how would you reduce the overall duration to: (a) 13 weeks, (b) 11 weeks, (c) 9 weeks? If reductions cost an average of £1,000 per week what is the cost of finishing the project by week 9?

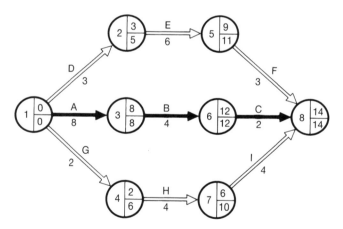

**Figure 18.12**   Network for Worked Example 18.6.

# Solution

The analysis of activity times for this project is shown in Table 18.5. We can find the amount the critical path can be reduced without affecting any parallel path from the total float in parallel paths. In this network there are three parallel paths: A–B–C, D–E–F and G–H–I. The total floats of activities on these paths are 0, 2 and 4 respectively. This means that the critical path A–B–C can be reduced by up to 2, but if it is reduced by more than this the path D–E–F becomes critical. If the critical path is reduced by more than 4, the path G–H–I also becomes critical.

**Table 18.5**

| Activity | Duration | Earliest | | Latest | | Total float |
| | | start | finish | start | finish | |
|---|---|---|---|---|---|---|
| A | 8 | 0 | 8 | 0 | 8 | 0 * |
| B | 4 | 8 | 12 | 8 | 12 | 0 * |
| C | 2 | 12 | 14 | 12 | 14 | 0 * |
| D | 3 | 0 | 3 | 2 | 5 | 2 |
| E | 6 | 3 | 9 | 5 | 11 | 2 |
| F | 3 | 9 | 12 | 11 | 14 | 2 |
| G | 2 | 0 | 2 | 4 | 6 | 4 |
| H | 4 | 2 | 6 | 6 | 10 | 4 |
| I | 4 | 6 | 10 | 10 | 14 | 4 |

(a) We need a reduction of 1 week in the critical path, so reducing the longest activity (as it is usually easier to find savings in longer activities) gives activity A a duration of 7 weeks and the project is finished by week 13.

(b) To finish in 11 weeks needs a further reduction of 2 weeks in the critical path, and we can again remove this from A. Unfortunately, the path D–E–F now becomes critical with a duration of 12 weeks, and we must remove a week from E (again chosen as the longest activity in the critical path).

(c) To finish in 9 weeks needs 5 weeks removing from the path A–B–C (say 4 from A and 1 from B), 3 weeks removed from the path D–E–F (say from E) and 1 week removed from the path G–H–I (say from H).

To achieve a 5-week reduction in project duration we have needed a total reduction of 5 + 3 + 1 = 9 weeks from individual activities, at a total cost of £9,000.

---

IN SUMMARY

A critical path can only be reduced by a certain amount before another path becomes critical. This limit is the total float of each activity on the parallel path.

## 18.4.2 | Gantt charts and resource levelling

When a project is actually being done, we have to keep a continuous check on progress to make sure that activities are performed at the right times. But it is difficult to check these times on a network. A **Gantt chart** shows them much more clearly. A Gantt chart is simply another way of representing a project, which emphasizes the timing of activities. The chart has a timescale across the bottom; activities are listed down the left-hand side, and times when activities should be done are blocked off in the body of the chart.

# WORKED EXAMPLE 18.7

Draw a Gantt chart for the original data in Worked Example 18.6, assuming that each activity starts as early as possible.

## Solution

The activity analysis for this example was listed in Table 18.5. If each activity starts as early as possible, we can show the times needed by the blocked-off areas in Figure 18.13. The total float of each activity is added afterwards as a broken line. The total float is the maximum expansion that can still allow the project to finish on time, so provided an activity is completed before the end of the broken line there should be no problem keeping to the planned project duration.

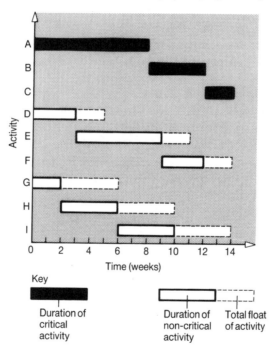

**Figure 18.13**   Gantt chart for Worked Example 18.7.

The main benefit of Gantt charts is that they show clearly the state of each activity at any point in the project. They show which activities should be in hand, as well as those that should be finished, and those about to start. Gantt charts are also useful for planning the allocation of resources.

Look at the Gantt chart shown in Figure 18.14 and assume, for simplicity, that each activity uses one unit of a particular resource (perhaps one team of workers). If all activities start as soon as possible, we can draw a vertical bar chart to show the resources in use at any time. The project starts with activities A, D and G so three teams are needed. At the end of week 2 one team can move from G to H, but three teams are still needed. Continuing this allocation gives the graph of resources shown at the bottom of Figure 18.14.

In this example, the use of resources is steady for most of the project and only begins to fall near the end. It is rare to get such a smooth pattern of resource use, and usually there are a series of peaks and troughs, which should be levelled. As critical activities are at fixed times, we have to do this levelling by rescheduling non-critical activities, and in particular by delaying those activities with relatively large total floats.

Adjusting and monitoring schedules, workloads, times and costs are best done using a computer. Unfortunately, the quality of software for project network analysis is variable. Some programs need details of the network to be specified as input data and simply do the timing calculations.

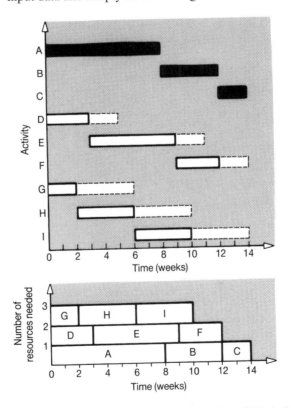

**Figure 18.14**  Resources used during project of Worked Example 18.7.

IN SUMMARY

Gantt charts give another representation of projects, emphasizing the timing. They are used in the planning of resources, and to monitor progress through the execution of a project.

## Self-assessment questions

**18.12** Which activities must be shortened to reduce the overall duration of a project?

**18.13** By how much can a critical path usefully be shortened?

**18.14** What are the main benefits of Gantt charts?

**18.15** How can the use of resources be smoothed during a project?

---

## CHAPTER REVIEW

A project is a coherent piece of work with a clear start and finish. It consists of the activities needed to make a distinct product. This chapter has described the way in which project network analysis can help with the planning and control of projects. In particular it:

- showed how the relationship between activities in a project can be shown in a dependence table
- showed how a project can be represented by a network of alternating activities and events
- calculated the timing of events and activities
- found the critical path
- changed the duration of a project
- used Gantt charts to monitor progress and plan resources.

---

## Problems

**18.1** A project consists of the activities described by the following dependence table. Draw the network for this project.

| Activity | Depends on | Activity | Depends on |
|----------|------------|----------|------------|
| A | - | G | B |
| B | - | H | G |
| C | A | I | E, F |
| D | A | J | H, I |
| E | C | K | E, F |
| F | B, D | L | K |

**18.2** (a) An amateur dramatic society is planning its annual production and is interested in using a network to coordinate the various activities. What activities do you think should be included in the network?

(b) If discussions lead to the following activities, what would the network look like?

- assess resources and select play
- select actors and cast parts
- design and organize advertisements
- prepare stage, lights and sound
- final arrangements for opening
- prepare scripts
- rehearse
- build scenery
- sell tickets

**18.3** Draw a network for the dependence table shown in Table 18.6.

**Table 18.6**

| Activity | Depends on | Activity | Depends on |
|----------|-----------|----------|-----------|
| A | H | I | F |
| B | H | J | I |
| C | K | K | L |
| D | I, M, N | L | F |
| E | F | M | O |
| F | - | N | H |
| G | E, L | O | A, B |
| H | E | P | N |

**18.4** If each activity in Problem 18.3 has a duration of one week, find the earliest and latest times for each event. Calculate the earliest and latest start and finish times for each activity and the corresponding total floats.

**18.5** Draw the network represented by the dependence table given in Table 18.7, and calculate the total float for each activity. If each activity can be reduced by up to two weeks, what is the shortest duration of the project and which activities are reduced?

**Table 18.7**

| Activity | Duration (weeks) | Depends on |
|----------|-----------------|-----------|
| A | 5 | - |
| B | 3 | - |
| C | 3 | B |
| D | 7 | A |
| E | 10 | B |
| F | 14 | A, C |
| G | 7 | D, E |
| H | 4 | E |
| I | 5 | D |

**18.6** A project consists of ten activities with estimated durations (in weeks) and dependences shown in Table 18.8.

(a) What are the estimated duration of the project and the earliest and latest times for activities?

(b) If activity B needs special equipment to be hired, when should this be scheduled?

(c) A check on the project at week 12 shows that activity F is running 2 weeks late, that activity J will now take 6 weeks, and that the equipment for B will not arrive until week 18. What affect does this have on the overall project duration?

**Table 18.8**

| Activity | Depends on | Duration | Activity | Depends on | Duration |
|----------|-----------|----------|----------|-----------|----------|
| A | - | 8 | F | C, D | 10 |
| B | A | 6 | G | B, E, F | 5 |
| C | - | 10 | H | F | 8 |
| D | - | 6 | I | G, H, J | 6 |
| E | C | 2 | J | A | 4 |

**18.7** Draw a Gantt chart for the project described in Problem 18.6. If each activity uses one team of people, draw a graph of staffing needs assuming each activity starts as soon as possible. How might these requirements be smoothed?

**18.8** Analyse the times and resources needed by the project described by the following data:

| Activity | Depends on | Duration | Resources |
|----------|-----------|----------|-----------|
| A | - | 4 | 1 |
| B | A | 4 | 2 |
| C | A | 3 | 4 |
| D | B | 5 | 4 |
| E | C | 2 | 2 |
| F | D, E | 6 | 3 |
| G | - | 3 | 3 |
| H | G | 7 | 1 |
| I | G | 6 | 5 |
| J | H | 2 | 3 |
| K | I | 4 | 4 |
| L | J, K | 8 | 2 |

**18.9** In the project described in Problem 18.8 it costs £1,000 to reduce the duration of an activity by 1. If there is £12,000 available to reduce the overall duration of the project, how should this be allocated and what is the shortest time in which the project can be completed? What are the minimum resources needed by the revised schedule?

# Computer exercises

18.1 Figure 18.15 shows a spreadsheet doing some calculations for a project network. Make sure you understand what this is doing. Draw the network and check the calculations. How could you improve the format of the spreadsheet? Design your own spreadsheet for doing the calculations for network analysis.

|   | A | B | C | D | E | F | G | H | I |
|---|---|---|---|---|---|---|---|---|---|
| 1 | **Network analysis** | | | | | | | | |
| 2 | | | | | | | | | |
| 3 | **Activity analysis** | | | | | | | | |
| 4 | | | | **Earliest** | | **Latest** | | **Total float** | **Critical** |
| 5 | **Activity** | **Depends on** | **Duration** | **Start** | **Finish** | **Start** | **Finish** | | |
| 6 | A | - | 4 | 0 | 4 | 0 | 4 | 0 | Yes |
| 7 | B | - | 2 | 0 | 2 | 2 | 4 | 2 | |
| 8 | C | A | 3 | 4 | 7 | 5 | 8 | 1 | |
| 9 | D | A | 6 | 4 | 10 | 4 | 10 | 0 | Yes |
| 10 | E | B | 2 | 2 | 4 | 4 | 6 | 2 | |
| 11 | F | D | 1 | 10 | 11 | 10 | 11 | 0 | Yes |
| 12 | G | E | 5 | 4 | 9 | 6 | 11 | 2 | |
| 13 | H | C | 4 | 7 | 11 | 8 | 12 | 1 | |
| 14 | I | H | 6 | 11 | 17 | 12 | 18 | 1 | |
| 15 | J | F AND G | 7 | 11 | 18 | 11 | 18 | 0 | Yes |
| 16 | K | B | 4 | 2 | 6 | 6 | 10 | 4 | |
| 17 | L | K | 5 | 6 | 11 | 10 | 15 | 4 | |
| 18 | M | L | 3 | 11 | 14 | 15 | 18 | 4 | |
| 19 | | | | | | | | | |
| 20 | **Event analysis** | | | | | | | | |
| 21 | **Event** | **Earliest** | **Latest** | **Slack** | | | | | |
| 22 | 1 | 0 | 0 | 0 | | | | | |
| 23 | 2 | 4 | 4 | 0 | | | | | |
| 24 | 3 | 2 | 4 | 2 | | | | | |
| 25 | 4 | 7 | 8 | 1 | | | | | |
| 26 | 5 | 10 | 10 | 0 | | | | | |
| 27 | 6 | 4 | 6 | 2 | | | | | |
| 28 | 7 | 6 | 10 | 4 | | | | | |
| 29 | 8 | 11 | 12 | 1 | | | | | |
| 30 | 9 | 11 | 11 | 0 | | | | | |
| 31 | 10 | 11 | 15 | 4 | | | | | |
| 32 | 11 | 18 | 18 | 0 | | | | | |

**Figure 18.15** Spreadsheet doing calculations for network analysis.

18.2 Sometimes we do not know the duration of an activity exactly, as there is some uncertainty. The most common way of tackling problems with uncertain durations is to give three estimates – an optimistic duration, a most likely and a pessimistic. From these three estimates the computer will calculate the expected duration, and can then do some statistical analyses. Figure 18.16 shows a printout from a program that does these calculations. Make sure you understand what the computer is doing and draw the network described. Use some suitable software to check the results.

18.3 The duration of an activity can often be reduced by using more resources. This is called 'crashing'. Then an activity has a normal duration with a normal cost, and a shorter crashed duration with a higher crashed cost. Figure 18.17 shows a printout from a program that crashes networks. Make sure you understand what is happening. Draw a network of the problem. Use some software to check the calculations and give a full analysis of results.

18.4 Find a project with which you are familiar and break it into about 50 activities. Draw the network for the project, and do the relevant analyses. Write a detailed report on your findings. How useful did you find available software?

### PROJECT PLANNING AND CONTROL
#### Three Time Estimates
#### DATA ENTERED

| Activity | Times | | # pred | <– –predecessor activities –> | |
|---|---|---|---|---|---|
| 1 Plan | Optimistic | 12 | 0 | | |
| | Modal | 14 | | | |
| | Pessimistic | 18 | | | |
| 2 Searc | Optimistic | 2 | 0 | | |
| | Modal | 3 | | | |
| | Pessimistic | 5 | | | |
| 3 Order | Optimistic | 10 | 1 | 1-Plan | |
| | Modal | 12 | | | |
| | Pessimistic | 14 | | | |
| 4 Emplo | Optimistic | 2 | 1 | 2-Searc | |
| | Modal | 5 | | | |
| | Pessimistic | 8 | | | |
| 5 Buy | Optimistic | 3 | 1 | 1-Plan | |
| | Modal | 4 | | | |
| | Pessimistic | 4 | | | |
| 6 Cost | Optimistic | 3 | 1 | 2-Searc | |
| | Modal | 5 | | | |
| | Pessimistic | 6 | | | |
| 7 Build | Optimistic | 12 | 2 | 4-Emplo | 5-Buy |
| | Modal | 15 | | | |
| | Pessimistic | 20 | | | |
| 8 Setup | Optimistic | 2 | 2 | 4-Emplo | 5-Buy |
| | Modal | 5 | | | |
| | Pessimistic | 8 | | | |
| 9 Check | Optimistic | 2 | 2 | 3-Order | 8-Setup |
| | Modal | 5 | | | |
| | Pessimistic | 8 | | | |
| 10 Contr | Optimistic | 6 | 1 | 6-Cost | |
| | Modal | 7 | | | |
| | Pessimistic | 9 | | | |

**Figure 18.16**   Printout for network analysis.

## SOLUTION

| Activity | | Start | Finish | Expected Duration | Total Float | Critical Path |
|---|---|---|---|---|---|---|
| 1 Plan | Earliest: | 0 | 14.333 | 14.333 | 0 | yes |
| | Latest: | 0 | 14.333 | | | |
| 2 Searc | Earliest: | 0 | 3.167 | 3.167 | 10 | no |
| | Latest: | 10 | 13.167 | | | |
| 3 Order | Earliest: | 14.333 | 26.333 | 12 | 2.167 | no |
| | Latest: | 16.500 | 28.500 | | | |
| 4 Emplo | Earliest: | 3.167 | 8.167 | 5 | 10 | no |
| | Latest: | 13.167 | 18.167 | | | |
| 5 Buy | Earliest: | 14.333 | 18.167 | 3.833 | 0 | yes |
| | Latest: | 14.333 | 18.167 | | | |
| 6 Cost | Earliest: | 3.167 | 8 | 4.833 | 18.333 | no |
| | Latest: | 21.500 | 26.333 | | | |
| 7 Build | Earliest: | 18.167 | 33.500 | 15.333 | 0 | yes |
| | Latest: | 18.167 | 33.500 | | | |
| 8 Setup | Earliest: | 18.167 | 23.167 | 5 | 5.333 | no |
| | Latest: | 23.500 | 28.500 | | | |
| 9 Check | Earliest: | 26.333 | 31.333 | 5 | 2.167 | no |
| | Latest: | 28.500 | 33.500 | | | |
| 10 Contr | Earliest: | 8 | 15.167 | 7.167 | 18.333 | no |
| | Latest: | 26.333 | 33.500 | | | |

## Project Summary

Expected Completion Time : 33.500
Variance on Critical Path : 2.806
Standard Deviation : 1.675
Critical Path = 1-Plan 5-Buy 7-Build

## PROBABILITY ANALYSIS

| | | |
|---|---|---|
| Project Due Date | : | 30 |
| Expected Completion Time | : | 33.500 |
| Variance on Critical Path | : | 2.806 |
| Standard Deviation | : | 1.675 |

| | | |
|---|---|---|
| Z (number of standard deviations) | : | −2.090 |
| Probability of Completion by Due Date | : | 0.018 |

| | | |
|---|---|---|
| Revised Due Date | : | 31 |
| Expected Completion time | : | 33.500 |
| Variance on Critical Path | : | 2.806 |
| Standard Deviation | : | 1.675 |

| | | |
|---|---|---|
| Z (number of standard deviations) | : | −1.493 |
| Probability of Completion by Due Date | : | 0.068 |

**Figure 18.16**   (cont.)

Input Data for the Problem – CPM Demonstration

| Activity number | Activity name | Start event | End event | Normal duration | Crash duration | Normal cost | Crash cost |
|---|---|---|---|---|---|---|---|
| 1 | Start 1 | 1 | 2 | 15.000 | 12.000 | 4500 | 5500 |
| 2 | Start 2 | 1 | 3 | 10.000 | 8.000 | 3000 | 4500 |
| 3 | Check | 2 | 3 | 7.000 | 5.000 | 1500 | 1800 |
| 4 | Build | 2 | 4 | 8.000 | 6.000 | 800 | 1200 |
| 5 | Employ | 3 | 4 | 15.000 | 10.000 | 4000 | 5000 |
| 6 | Purchase | 3 | 5 | 12.000 | 10.000 | 3500 | 4000 |
| 7 | Install | 4 | 6 | 16.000 | 12.000 | 6000 | 8000 |
| 8 | Operate | 5 | 6 | 12.000 | 8.000 | 6000 | 8000 |

CPM Analysis for the problem – CPM Demonstration

| Activity number | Activity name | Earliest Start | Latest Start | Earliest Finish | Latest Finish | Slack LS–ES |
|---|---|---|---|---|---|---|
| 1 | Start 1 | 0 | 0 | 15.000 | 15.000 | Critical |
| 2 | Start 2 | 0 | 12.000 | 10.000 | 22.000 | 12.000 |
| 3 | Check | 15.000 | 15.000 | 22.000 | 22.000 | Critical |
| 4 | Build | 15.000 | 29.000 | 23.000 | 37.000 | 14.000 |
| 5 | Employ | 22.000 | 22.000 | 37.000 | 37.000 | Critical |
| 6 | Purchase | 22.000 | 29.000 | 34.000 | 41.000 | 7.000 |
| 7 | Install | 37.000 | 37.000 | 53.000 | 53.000 | Critical |
| 8 | Operate | 34.000 | 41.000 | 46.000 | 53.000 | 7.000 |

Completion time  =  53      Total cost  =  29 300

Critical paths for CPM Analysis for the problem – CPM Demonstration

Critical Path Number 1   :
| Activities | Start 1 | | Check | | Employ | | Install | |
|---|---|---|---|---|---|---|---|---|
| Events | 1 | =====> | 2 | =====> | 3 | ======> | 4 | ======> 6 |

Crash Analysis for the Problem – CPM Demonstration

Target Crashed Duration is 40

| Activity number | Activity name | Earliest Start | Latest Start | Earliest Finish | Latest Finish | Slack LS–ES |
|---|---|---|---|---|---|---|
| 1 | Start 1 | 0 | 0 | 12.000 | 12.000 | Critical |
| 2 | Start 2 | 0 | 7.000 | 10.000 | 17.000 | 7.000 |
| 3 | Check | 12.000 | 12.000 | 17.000 | 17.000 | Critical |
| 4 | Build | 12.000 | 19.000 | 20.000 | 27.000 | 7.000 |
| 5 | Employ | 17.000 | 17.000 | 27.000 | 27.000 | Critical |
| 6 | Purchase | 17.000 | 17.000 | 28.000 | 28.000 | Critical |
| 7 | Install | 27.000 | 27.000 | 40.000 | 40.000 | Critical |
| 8 | Operate | 28.000 | 28.000 | 40.000 | 40.000 | Critical |

Completion time  =  40      Total cost  =  33 350

Critical Paths for CPM Analysis for the Problem – CPM Demonstration

Critical Path Number 1  :
| Activities | Start 1 | | Check | | Employ | | Install | |
|---|---|---|---|---|---|---|---|---|
| Events | 1 | ======> | 2 | ======> | 3 | ======> | 4 | ======> 6 |

Critical Path Number 2   :
| Activities | Start 1 | | Check | | Purchase | | Operate | |
|---|---|---|---|---|---|---|---|---|
| Events | 1 | ======> | 2 | ======> | 3 | ======> | 5 | ======> 6 |

**Figure 18.17**  Printout for an analysis of crashed costs.

Analysis of Crashed Activities for the Problem – CPM Demonstration

Crash activity Start 1
    by 3 time units:   new duration = 12:  incremental cost = 1000
Crash activity Check
    by 2 time units:   new duration = 5:  incremental cost = 300;
Crash activity Employ
    by 5 time units:   new duration = 10:  incremental cost = 1000
Crash activity Purchase
    by 1 time unit:   new duration = 11:  incremental cost = 250
Crash activity Install
    by 3 time units:   new duration = 13:  incremental cost = 1500

Crashed duration = 40:  new duration = 4050:  Crashed cost = 33 350

**Figure 18.17**  (cont.)

# Case study

## Westin Contractors

William Purvis looked across his desk at the company's latest recruit and said: 'Welcome to Westin Contractors. This is a good company to work for, and I hope you settle in and will be very happy here. Everyone working for Westin has to be familiar with our basic tools, so you should start by looking at network analysis. Here is a small project that we have just costed, and I have to give the customer some details about times, workloads and costs by the end of the week. I would like a couple of alternative views, with your recommendation of the best. Everything you need is available in the office, so don't be afraid to ask for help and advice'.

William Purvis supplied the data listed in Table 18.9. There is a penalty cost of £3,500 for every week the project finished after week 28. Your job is to prepare a suitable report for the company.

**Table 18.9**

| Activity | Depends on | Normal time | Normal cost | Crashed time | Crashed cost | Number of teams |
|----------|------------|------|------|------|------|-----------|
| A | – | 3 | 13 | 2 | 15 | 3 |
| B | A | 7 | 25 | 4 | 28 | 4 |
| C | B, E | 5 | 16 | 4 | 19 | 4 |
| D | C | 5 | 12 | 3 | 24 | 2 |
| E | – | 8 | 32 | 5 | 38 | 6 |
| F | E | 6 | 20 | 4 | 30 | 1 |
| G | F | 8 | 30 | 6 | 35 | 5 |
| H | – | 12 | 41 | 7 | 45 | 6 |
| I | H | 6 | 25 | 3 | 30 | 4 |
| J | E | 4 | 18 | 3 | 26 | 6 |
| K | I, J | 12 | 52 | 10 | 60 | 4 |
| L | I, J | 6 | 20 | 3 | 30 | 1 |
| M | D, G, I | 2 | 7 | 1 | 14 | 1 |
| N | B, E | 6 | 18 | 5 | 24 | 5 |

# 19 Queues and simulation

Chapter outline 576
19.1 Background to queuing 577
19.2 Single-server queues 578
19.3 Simulation models 583
Chapter review 590

Problems 590
Computer exercises 590
Case study: 593
The Palmer Centre for
Alternative Therapy

## CHAPTER OUTLINE

This chapter looks at the management of queues. We are all familiar with queues of people, but there are many other types of queue, such as programs queuing to be processed in a computer, faulty machines queuing to be repaired and aeroplanes queuing to land.

Models of queuing systems often have the objective of balancing the number of servers with the length of the queue. Unfortunately, we can only find analytical solutions for small problems.

Simulation offers a more useful method of tackling queuing problems by imitating the operations of the system over a typical period. It can tackle problems that are too complex to be solved by other means. The models involve large amounts of arithmetic, so computers are always used for real simulations.

After reading this chapter and doing the exercises you should be able to:

- appreciate the scope of queuing problems
- calculate the characteristics of queues at a single server
- describe the characteristic approach of simulation
- do manual simulations of queuing systems

# 19.1 | Background to queuing

Queues form when customers want a particular service but must wait to be served. This situation is familiar to us all; it happens when we buy a ticket for a train, get money from a bank, join the line at a supermarket checkout, wait for traffic lights to change, and in many other circumstances. Not all queues involve people, so we may also have a queue of jobs waiting to be processed on a computer, items waiting to move along an assembly line, telephone calls waiting for equipment to become free, faulty equipment waiting to be repaired, or ships waiting for a berth.

All queues have features in common, so we can describe some general characteristics. By convention a **customer** is anyone or anything wanting a service and a **server** is the person or thing giving that service. Then queues are formed when a customer wants a service, but arrives to find that the server is busy. The customer may decide not to use the service, particularly if other customers are already waiting, but more usually they decide to wait and line up in the queue (Figure 19.1).

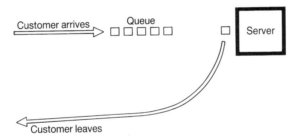

**Figure 19.1**  A single-server queuing system.

The queue can take many forms:

- customers may form a single queue or they may form separate queues for each server
- customers may arrive singly or in batches (when, for example, a train arrives)
- arrivals may be at random or spread out by an appointment system
- customers may be served individually or in batches (at a bus stop, for example)
- servers may be in parallel (where each does the same job) or in series (where each gives part of the service and then passes the customer on to the next stage)
- service time may be constant or variable
- customers may be served in order of arrival or some other order (hospitals admit patients in order of urgency, and so on)

As you know from experience, the service provided is, in part, judged by the time that customers have to wait. And the length of the queue depends on three factors:

- the rate at which customers arrive to be served
- the time taken for a server to deal with a customer
- the number of servers available

In any given situation, providing a lot of servers gives a short queue, but the cost of giving the service is high; providing a few servers reduces the cost of the service, but potential customers might see the length of the queues and go somewhere else. A balance is needed that seems reasonable to all parties. This will differ according to circumstances. When you visit a doctor's surgery you often have to wait a long time. This is because doctors' time is considered expensive while patients' time is cheap. To make sure that the doctor does not wait for patients, appointments are made close together and patients are expected to wait. On the other hand, in petrol stations the cost of servers (petrol pumps) is low and customers will drive to a competitor if there is a queue. Then a large number of servers is provided and, although the utilization of each server is low, customers wait a short time in any queue.

---

**IN SUMMARY**

Queues arise in many situations, not all of which involve people. When managing queues, a balance is needed between large numbers of servers and reasonable costs.

---

## Self-assessment questions

**19.1** What causes a queue?

**19.2** 'Customers should not have to wait, so enough servers should be provided to eliminate queues.' Is this statement true?

# | 19.2 | | Single-server queues

The simplest type of queue consists of:

- a single server dealing with a queue of customers
- random arrivals of customers
- random service times

In Chapter 13 we said that random occurrences could be described by a Poisson distribution. Now we can use this to describe customer arrivals. If the average number of customers arriving per unit time is $\lambda$ the probability of $r$ arrivals in unit time is:

$$P(r) = \frac{e^{-\lambda}\lambda^r}{r!}$$

where:

$$r = \text{number of arrivals}$$

$$\lambda = \text{mean number of arrivals}$$

$$e = \text{exponential constant } (2.71828...)$$

Service time is a continuous variable, which experience shows to follow a negative exponential distribution (Figure 19.2). This is related to the Poisson distribution and has the useful property that the probability of service being completed within some specified value $T$ is given by:

$$P(t \leqslant T) = 1 - e^{-\mu T}$$

where:

$$\mu = \text{mean service rate}$$

$$= \text{the average number of customers served per unit of time}$$

So the probability that service is not completed by time $T$ is:

$$P(t > T) = 1 - P(t \leqslant T) = e^{-\mu T}$$

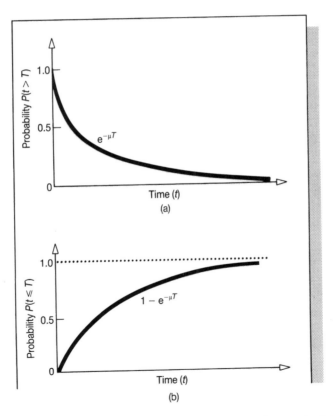

**Figure 19.2** Random service times follow a negative expotential distribution: (a) probability that service is not completed within a time $T$; (b) probability that service is completed within a time $T$.

We have now described a random arrival rate of customers in terms of $\lambda$ (the mean arrival rate) and a random service time in terms of $\mu$ (the mean service rate). If the mean arrival rate is greater than the mean service rate, the system will never settle down to a steady state but the queue will increase in length continuously. So any analysis of queues must assume that a steady state has been reached and that $\mu$ is greater than $\lambda$.

The following set of results describe the **operating characteristics** of a single-server queue. Some of these results are not obvious, and we are simply stating them as standard results.

On average, the system is busy for a proportion of time $\lambda/\mu$. Here 'busy' is defined as having at least one customer either being served or in the queue. This is also the average number of customers being served at any time. If, for example, the mean arrival rate is two an hour and the mean service rate is four an hour, we have $\lambda/\mu = 2/4 = 0.5$. This means that the system is busy for half the time or there is an average of half a customer in the system.

The probability that there is no customer in the system is:

$$P_0 = 1 - \lambda/\mu$$

This is the probability that a new customer can be served without any wait.

The probability that there are $n$ customers in the system is given by:

$$P_n = P_0(\lambda/\mu)^n$$

Using this result we can calculate some other characteristics of the queue. To start with, the average number of customers in the system is given by:

$$L = \sum_{n=0}^{\infty} nP_n = \frac{\lambda}{\mu - \lambda}$$

The average number of customers in the queue is equal to the average number in the system minus the average number being served:

$$L_q = L - \frac{\lambda}{\mu} = \frac{\lambda}{\mu - \lambda} - \frac{\lambda}{\mu} = \frac{\lambda^2}{\mu(\mu - \lambda)}$$

If $L$ is the average number of customers in the system and $\lambda$ is the mean arrival rate, the average time that any arriving customer has to spend in the system is:

$$W = \frac{L}{\lambda} = \frac{1}{\mu - \lambda}$$

The average time spent in the queue is the average time in the system minus the average service time:

$$W_q = W - \frac{1}{\mu} = \frac{\lambda}{\mu(\mu - \lambda)}$$

## WORKED EXAMPLE 19.1

People arrive randomly at a bank teller at an average rate of 30 an hour. What is the average number of customers in the queue if the teller takes an average of 0.5 minutes to serve each customer? What is the average time in the queue?

### Solution

The average arrival rate is $\lambda = 30$. If the teller takes an average of 0.5 minutes to serve each customer, this is equivalent to a service rate of 120 an hour. Then the average number of customers in the queue (excluding anyone being served) is:

$$L_q = \frac{\lambda^2}{\mu(\mu - \lambda)} = \frac{30^2}{120 \times (120 - 30)} = 0.083$$

The average time in the queue is:

$$W_q = \frac{\lambda}{\mu(\mu - \lambda)} = \frac{30}{120 \times (120 - 30)} = 0.003 \text{ hours}$$
$$= 0.167 \text{ minutes}$$

## WORKED EXAMPLE 19.2

Customers arrive randomly at a railway information desk at a mean rate of 20 an hour. The single server manning the desk takes an average of two minutes with each customer. Calculate the characteristics of the queuing system.

### Solution

The mean arrival rate $\lambda$ is 20 an hour and the mean service rate $\mu$ is 30 an hour.

The probability that there is no one in the system is:
$$P_0 = 1 - \lambda/\mu = 1 - 20/30 = 0.33$$
So, there is a probability of 0.67 that a customer has to wait to be served.

The probability of $n$ customers in the system is:
$$P_n = P_0 \times (\lambda/\mu)^n = 0.33 \times (0.67)^n$$
That is, $P_1 = 0.22$, $P_2 = 0.15$, $P_3 = 0.10$, $P_4 = 0.07$, etc

The average number of customers in the system is:
$$L = \frac{\lambda}{\mu - \lambda} = \frac{20}{30 - 20} = 2$$

The average number of customers in the queue is:
$$L_q = \frac{\lambda^2}{\mu(\mu - \lambda)} = \frac{20^2}{30 \times 10} = 1.33$$

The average time that a customer spends in the system is:

$$W = \frac{1}{\mu - \lambda} = \frac{1}{30 - 20} = 0.1 \text{ hours} = 6 \text{ minutes}$$

The average time that a customer spends in the queue is:

$$W_q = \frac{\lambda}{\mu(\mu - \lambda)} = \frac{20}{30 \times 10} = 0.0667 \text{ hours} = 4 \text{ minutes}$$

We could now go on to describe multiserver or other types of queue, but the calculations for these become even more complicated. We could, of course, use a computer to do the arithmetic. Figure 19.3 shows a printout from a package working with (a) a single-server queue and (b) multiservers. This package, like most others, finds the operating characteristics and then calculates some cost figures.

```
SUMMARY OF A 1 CHANNEL WAITING LINE WITH
*************************************************
        MEAN NUMBER OF ARRIVALS = 25
        MEAN NUMBER OF SERVICES = 30
        COST FOR UNITS IN THE SYSTEM = £ 20 PER TIME PERIOD
        COST FOR A CHANNEL = £ 35 PER TIME PERIOD

THE PROBABILITY THAT THE CHANNEL IS IDLE                    0.1667
THE AVERAGE NUMBER OF UNITS WAITING FOR SERVICE            4.1667
THE AVERAGE NUMBER OF UNITS IN THE SYSTEM                  5.0000
THE AVERAGE TIME A UNIT SPENDS WAITING FOR SERVICE         0.1667
THE AVERAGE TIME A UNIT SPENDS IN THE SYSTEM               0.2000
THE PROBABILITY THAT AN ARRIVING UNIT HAS TO WAIT          0.8333
THE TOTAL COST PER TIME PERIOD                            £135.00
```
(a)

```
SUMMARY OF A 4 CHANNEL WAITING LINE WITH
*************************************************
        MEAN NUMBER OF ARRIVALS = 100
        MEAN NUMBER OF SERVICES PER CHANNEL = 30
        COST FOR UNITS IN THE SYSTEM = £ 20 PER TIME PERIOD
        COST FOR A CHANNEL = £ 35 PER TIME PERIOD

THE PROBABILITY THAT ALL 4 CHANNELS ARE IDLE               0.0213
THE AVERAGE NUMBER OF UNITS WAITING FOR SERVICE           3.2886
THE AVERAGE NUMBER OF UNITS IN THE SYSTEM                 6.6219
THE AVERAGE TIME A UNIT SPENDS WAITING FOR SERVICE        0.0329
THE AVERAGE TIME A UNIT SPENDS IN THE SYSTEM              0.0662
THE PROBABILITY THAT AN ARRIVING UNIT HAS TO WAIT         0.6577
THE TOTAL COST PER TIME PERIOD                           £272.44
```
(b)

**Figure 19.3**  Printout from a package for analysing queues.

After making a number of assumptions, the operating characteristics of a single-server queue can be calculated. The arithmetic with more complex queuing problems becomes very tedious.

## Self-assessment questions

**19.3** Define the variables $\lambda$ and $\mu$ in a queuing system.

**19.4** What happens in a queue if $\lambda \geqslant \mu$?

**19.5** What are the assumptions of the single-server queue model?

# 19.3 Simulation models

## 19.3.1 Overall approach

In this section we are going to describe an alternative way of solving problems. This does not rely on finding the solution to an equation, but on simulating the operations.

The term **simulate** is used quite widely (simulated anger, simulated leather, etc). Here we are going to use it in the same general sense, but specifically referring to the way quantitative models can imitate real situations. Then the essential characteristic of simulation is that it is dynamic and duplicates the continuous operation of a system. An ordinary model for, say, stock control looks at the system, collects data for some fixed point of time and draws conclusions: a simulation follows the operations of the system and sees exactly what happens over time. A simple analogy would be an ordinary model giving a snapshot of the system at some fixed point, while a simulation model takes a movie of the system.

We can demonstrate this approach with a simple example. An item is made on a production line at a rate of one every two minutes. At some point there is an inspection, which takes virtually no time. At this inspection 50% of units are rejected and the remaining 50% continue along the line to the next process which takes three minutes per unit (as shown in Figure 19.4).

We might be interested in answering a number of questions about this system, such as:

- How much space should we leave for the queue between the inspection and the next process?
- How long does each unit stay in the system?
- What is the utilization of the processor?
- Are there any bottlenecks?

**Figure 19.4** An illustration of a simulation.

The system is essentially a single-server queue in which all data are known, so we could use a queuing theory model. An alternative is to stand and watch the system operating over a typical period and see what happens. We could follow a few units through the system and record information, perhaps using a table like that shown in Table 19.1.

**Table 19.1**

| Unit no. | Arrival time | Accept or reject | Time joins queue | No. in queue | Time process starts | Time in queue | Time process finishes | Time in system |
|---|---|---|---|---|---|---|---|---|
| 1 | 0 | A | 0 | 0 | 0 | 0 | 3 | 3 |
| 2 | 2 | A | 2 | 0 | 3 | 1 | 6 | 4 |
| 3 | 4 | A | 4 | 0 | 6 | 2 | 9 | 5 |
| 4 | 6 | R | - | - | - | - | - | - |
| 5 | 8 | R | - | - | - | - | - | - |
| 6 | 10 | A | 10 | 0 | 10 | 0 | 13 | 3 |

Here the first unit arrived for inspection at some time, which we arbitrarily set to 0. The unit was accepted and moved straight to processing which took 3 minutes. The total time the unit was in the system (consisting of inspection, queue and processing) was 3 minutes.

The second unit arrived at time 2 from the arbitrary start time, was accepted and joined the queue (the fifth column shows the number already in the queue when the next customer joins it). Processing could only start on unit 2 when unit 1 finished at time 3. This processing then took 3 minutes and unit 2 left the system at time 6.

We could stand and watch the operation for as long as we needed to get a reliable view of its operation. Then we could analyse the figures collected to give the information we need. But if we know all the characteristics of the process, we do not actually need to watch it to get a set of figures like those in Table 19.1. We could make up a set of typical figures. Provided these made-up figures accurately describe the process, and could reasonably be expected in a typical period, we have a simulation of the process. So we could now get

Table 19.1 without having to take detailed observations of the actual process. The problem, of course, is making sure that our made-up figures could really have come from a typical period.

In this example there is one element of uncertainty in the system: whether a unit is accepted or rejected. We need some method of randomly assigning these decisions to a unit, giving a 50% chance of acceptance and a 50% chance of rejection. An obvious way of doing this is to spin a coin. If it comes down heads we reject the unit and if it comes down tails we accept it (or vice versa). A more formal way of doing the same thing is to use random numbers, as described in Chapter 3. Given the following string of random digits:

$$5284778016941356756454793017714943179046825$$

we could use even digits (including 0) for acceptance and odd digits for rejection. So the first unit is rejected (based on 5), the second is accepted (based on 2), the third accepted (based on 8), and so on. We can now develop a typical set of results for the process without actually watching it. Table 19.2 shows one set of results using the random numbers above. We know that one unit arrives for inspection every 2 minutes, so we can complete column 2. Column 3 shows the sequence of random numbers and the corresponding decision is given in column 4.

**Table 19.2**

| 1 | 2 | 3 | 4 | 5 | 6 | 7 | 8 | 9 | 10 |
|---|---|---|---|---|---|---|---|---|---|
| Unit no. | Arrival time | Random number | Accept or reject | Time joins queue | No. in queue | Time process starts | Time in queue | Time process finishes | Time in system |
| 1 | 0 | 5 | R | - | - | - | - | - | 0 |
| 2 | 2 | 2 | A | 2 | 0 | 2 | 0 | 5 | 3 |
| 3 | 4 | 8 | A | 4 | 0 | 5 | 1 | 8 | 4 |
| 4 | 6 | 4 | A | 6 | 0 | 8 | 2 | 11 | 5 |
| 5 | 8 | 7 | R | - | - | - | - | - | 0 |
| 6 | 10 | 7 | R | - | - | - | - | - | 0 |
| 7 | 12 | 8 | A | 12 | 0 | 12 | 0 | 15 | 3 |
| 8 | 14 | 0 | A | 14 | 0 | 15 | 1 | 18 | 4 |
| 9 | 16 | 1 | R | - | - | - | - | - | 0 |
| 10 | 18 | 6 | A | 18 | 0 | 18 | 0 | 21 | 3 |

Units that are rejected leave the system, while those that are accepted join the queue at their arrival time (assuming that the inspection takes no time). This completes column 5. Column 6 shows the number already in the queue, while column 7 shows the time at which processing starts. If there is already a unit being processed, a queue is formed until the processor becomes free (shown in column 9); if there is no unit being processed, work can start immediately (at the time shown in column 5).

Processing finishes three minutes after it starts (shown in column 9) and the time spent in the queue (column 8) is the difference between arrival time and the time that processing starts. Column 10 shows the total time in the system, which is the difference between arrival time and the time that processing is finished.

This gives the rules for calculating each column in the table as:

- column 1: number increases by 1 for each unit entering
- column 2: arrival time increases by 2 for each unit entering
- column 3: from the given string of random numbers
- column 4: a unit is accepted if the corresponding random number is even and is rejected if it is odd
- column 5: accepted units join the queue straight away (that is, at arrival time) while rejected ones leave the system
- column 6: the number already in the queue is 1 more than it was for the last arrival, minus the number that have left since the last arrival
- column 7: processing starts at the arrival time if the equipment is already free, or when the equipment next becomes free (the previous entry in column 9)
- column 8: the time in the queue is the difference between the arrival time in the queue and the time that processing starts (column 7 − column 5)
- column 9: processing finishes three minutes after it starts (column 7 + 3)
- column 10: the time in the system is the difference between the arrival time and the finish of the processing (column 9 − column 2)

The simulation has been run for ten units arriving, and the figures obtained can give a number of results. We can, for example, note that there was at most one unit in the queue for the processor. We could also find:

- number accepted = 6 (in the long run this would be 50% of units)
- number rejected = 4 (again this would be 50% in the long run)
- maximum time in queue = 2 minutes
- average time in queue = 4/6 minutes = 40 seconds
- maximum time in system = 5 minutes
- average time in system = 22/6 = 3.67 minutes
- average time in system including rejects = 22/10 = 2.2 minutes
- processor was busy for 18 minutes
- utilization of processor = 18/21 = 86%

It is important to ask how reliable these figures are. The simulation certainly follows the working of the system through a typical period of 10 units, but this is a very small number of observations. So the next step would be to extend this simulation for a much larger number of observations. When information has been collected about several hundred arrivals we can be fairly confident that the results are reliable. As the process includes a random element, we can never be sure that the results are absolutely accurate, but with large numbers of repetitions we should get a reasonable picture. To repeat the simulation so many times needs a lot of simple, repetitive arithmetic, so real simulations are always done by computer.

---

### IN SUMMARY

Simulation gives a way of dynamically modelling problems. The purpose of simulation is to reproduce a typical set of results from operations without actually running the operation. It produces realistic, but artificial results.

## 19.3.2 | Random sampling

In the last section we used random numbers in simulation, but only looked at situations where a variable could take two values, each with a probability of 0.5. With more complex problems we need better ways of giving values to variables. How, for example, could we deal with a probability of acceptance of 0.6? In practice, we could do this by using random digits 0 to 5 to represent acceptance and 6 to 9 to represent rejection. Then the string:

$$52847780169413567564547930177149431790465825$$

represents accept, accept, reject, accept, reject and so on. We can extend this approach to sampling from more complex patterns. If 50% of units are accepted, 15% sent for reworking, 20% for reinspection and 15% rejected we might use the following approach.

Split the stream of random digits into pairs:

$$52\ 84\ 77\ 80\ 16\ 94\ 13\ 56\ 75\ 64\ 54\ 79\ 30\ 17\ 71\ \text{etc}$$

Then let:

$$00 \text{ to } 49 \text{ (i.e. 50% of pairs) represent acceptance}$$

$$50 \text{ to } 64 \text{ (i.e. 15% of pairs) represent reworking}$$

$$65 \text{ to } 84 \text{ (i.e. 20% of pairs) represent reinspection}$$

and:

$$85 \text{ to } 99 \text{ (i.e. 15% of pairs) represent rejection}$$

The stream of random digits would then represent rework, reinspect, reinspect, reinspect, accept and so on. In the long term the proportion of outcomes will be accurate, but in the short term there will be some random variations. Here three units out of the first four need reinspecting, and while you may be tempted to 'adjust' such figures you should not do so. Simulation needs a large number of repetitions to show typical figures and these will include fairly unlikely occurrences from time to time.

# WORKED EXAMPLE 19.3

Peter checks the stock of an item at the beginning of each month and places an order so that:

$$\text{order size} = 100 - \text{initial stock}$$

The order is equally likely to arrive at the end of the month in which it is placed or one month later. Demand follows the pattern:

| Monthly demand | 10 | 20 | 30 | 40 | 50 | 60 | 70 |
|---|---|---|---|---|---|---|---|
| Probability | 0.1 | 0.15 | 0.25 | 0.25 | 0.15 | 0.05 | 0.05 |

Assuming that there are 40 units in stock at the beginning of the first month, simulate the system for 10 months and say what information Peter can find from the results.

## Solution

The variables are delivery time and demand. Peter can take samples for these using the following schemes.

Delivery time:

- even random number means delivery in current month
- odd random number means delivery in next month

Demand:

| Demand | 10 | 20 | 30 | 40 | 50 | 60 | 70 |
|---|---|---|---|---|---|---|---|
| Probability | 0.1 | 0.15 | 0.25 | 0.25 | 0.15 | 0.05 | 0.05 |
| Random number | 00–09 | 10–24 | 25–49 | 50–74 | 75–89 | 90–94 | 95–99 |

Two streams of random digits were generated by computer:

delivery time:      2 5 9 1 0 7 3 8 7 6

demand:      83 50 56 49 37 15 84 52 66 41

Following the system through ten months gives the results in the spreadsheet in Figure 19.5. In this, the stock at the end of a month is found from the initial stock plus arrivals minus demand. In month 1 the initial stock is 40, so 60 are ordered. The arrival random number determines that this arrives in the same month. The demand random number determines a demand of 50 in the month, so the closing stock is:

$$\text{closing stock} = \text{initial stock} + \text{arrivals} - \text{demand}$$

$$= 40 + 60 - 50 = 50$$

| | A | B | C | D | E | F | G | H | I | J | K |
|---|---|---|---|---|---|---|---|---|---|---|---|
| 1 | **Simulation of stocks** | | | | | | | | | | |
| 2 | | | | | | | | | | | |
| 3 | **Month** | 1 | 2 | 3 | 4 | 5 | 6 | 7 | 8 | 9 | 10 |
| 4 | | | | | | | | | | | |
| 5 | **Initial stock** | 40 | 50 | 10 | 20 | 80 | 150 | 130 | 80 | 60 | 20 |
| 6 | **Order** | 60 | 50 | 90 | 80 | 20 | 0 | 0 | 20 | 40 | 80 |
| 7 | **Arrival RN** | 2 | 5 | 9 | 1 | 0 | 7 | 3 | 8 | 7 | 6 |
| 8 | **Arrival month** | 1 | 3 | 4 | 5 | 5 | 7 | 8 | 8 | 10 | 10 |
| 9 | | | | | | | | | | | |
| 10 | **Demand RN** | 83 | 50 | 56 | 49 | 37 | 15 | 84 | 52 | 66 | 41 |
| 11 | **Demand size** | 50 | 40 | 40 | 30 | 30 | 20 | 50 | 40 | 40 | 30 |
| 12 | **Arrival** | 60 | 0 | 50 | 90 | 100 | 0 | 0 | 20 | 0 | 120 |
| 13 | **Closing stock** | 50 | 10 | 20 | 80 | 150 | 130 | 80 | 60 | 20 | 110 |
| 14 | **Shortages** | 0 | 0 | 0 | 0 | 0 | 0 | 0 | 0 | 0 | 0 |

**Figure 19.5** Simulation of stock system for Worked Example 19.3.

There are no shortages and the closing stock is transferred to the opening stock for month 2. These calculations are repeated for the following ten months.

The conclusions from this very limited simulation are not at all reliable. But if the simulation is continued for longer, reliable figures could be found for measures such as distribution of opening and closing stock levels (including mean, maximum and minimum), distribution of orders (mean, minimum and maximum), mean demand, shortages and mean lead time.

IN SUMMARY

Random numbers can be used to generate samples with a range of characteristics. These can then be used in more sophisticated simulation models.

## Self-assessment questions

**19.6** What is meant when simulation is described as a 'dynamic' representation?

**19.7** 'Simulation can be used to model complex situations.' Is this statement true?

**19.8** Why are random numbers used in simulation?

Queues occur in a number of circumstances. This chapter described some aspects of the management of queues. In particular it:

- discussed the characteristics of queues and the need to balance the quality of service offered with its cost
- developed a model for a single-server queue where both arrivals and service times were random
- mentioned the difficulty of solving realistic queuing problems
- described the general approach of simulation
- illustrated the use of simulation in queuing problems

# Problems

**19.1** Describe the operating characteristics of a single-server queue where arrivals are random at an average rate of 100 an hour and service time is random at an average rate of 120 an hour.

**19.2** A single-server queue has random arrivals at a rate of 30 an hour and random service time at a rate of 40 an hour. If it costs £20 for each hour a customer spends in the system and £40 for each hour of service time, how much does the queue cost?

**19.3** A self-employed plumber offers a 24-hour emergency service to deal with burst pipes. For most of the year, calls arrive randomly at a rate of six a day. The time he takes to travel to a call and do the repair is randomly distributed with a mean of 90 minutes. Forecasts for February suggest that the weather will be cold; the last time this happened, emergency calls came in at a rate of 18 a day. Because of repeat business, the plumber is anxious not to lose a customer and wants average waiting time to be no longer in February than during a normal month. How many assistants should he employ to achieve this?

# Computer exercises

**19.1** Figure 19.6 shows the printout from a program that analyses queues. The title 'M/M/3' is an abbreviation that shows the queue has random arrivals, random service time and three servers. Make sure you understand what is happening here. Use a suitable package to check these results.

**19.2** Figure 19.7 shows the printout from a program that analyses the cost of queues. Make sure you can understand what is happening. Check the results with your own software.

Input Data of the Problem Queueing

M/M/3

| | | |
|---|---|---|
| Customer arrival rate (lambda) | = | 20.000 |
| Distribution | : | Poisson |
| Number of servers | = | 3 |
| Service rate per server | = | 8.000 |
| Distribution | : | Poisson |
| Mean service time | = | 0.125   hour |
| Standard deviation | = | 0.125   hour |
| Queue limit | = | Infinity |
| Customer population | = | Infinity |

Final Solution for The Problem Queueing

M/M/3

With lamda = 20 customers per hour      and $\mu$ = 8 customers per hour

| | | |
|---|---|---|
| Utilization factor (p) | = | .8333333 |
| Average number of customers in the system (L) | = | 6.011236 |
| Average number of customers in the queue (Lq) | = | 3.511236 |
| Average time a customer in the system (W) | = | .3005618 |
| Average time a customer in the queue (Wq) | = | .1755618 |
| The probability that all servers are idle (Po) | = | 4.494328E$-$02 |
| The probability an arriving customer waits (Pw) | = | .7022472 |

P(1) = 0.11236     P(2) = 0.14045     P(3) = 0.11704     P(4) = 0.09753
P(5) = 0.08128     P(6) = 0.06773     P(7) = 0.05644     P(8) = 0.04704
P(9) = 0.03920     P(10) = 0.03266

$$\sum_{i=1}^{10} P(i) = 0.791736$$

**Figure 19.6**   Printout from a queue analysis program.

**19.3**  Figure 19.8 shows the printout from a statistical program (Minitab) that is generating a sample of ten random numbers from a Normal distribution with mean 10 and standard deviation 2. See what programs you have to get equivalent results.

**19.4**  Customers arrive at a server at a rate of 100 an hour and each server can serve at a rate of 15 an hour. If customer time is valued at £20 an hour and server time costs £50 an hour, use a suitable program to find the best number of servers.

**19.5**  There are many specialised programs for simulation. Some of these are very sophisticated, including three-dimensional animation and a range of other features. What features would you expect to see in a major simulation package? Illustrate your answer with references to real packages.

**19.6**  Spreadsheets can be used for some types of simulation. Look at a specific queuing problem and build a simple model on a spreadsheet. Run the simulation and write a report of your findings. How could you expand your model to deal with more complex situations?

MULTIPLE SERVER QUEUES

−=✷=−    INFORMATION ENTERED    −=✷=−

ALTERNATIVE CHOSEN    :    MULTIPLE SERVER – FINITE QUEUE

| | | |
|---|---|---|
| Arrival Rate | : | 30.000 |
| Service Rate | : | 12.000 |
| | | |
| Number of Servers | : | 1  –  5 |
| Maximum in System | : | 20 |
| | | |
| Service Cost Rate | : | 150.000 |
| Waiting Cost Rate | : | 25.000 |

−=✷=−    RESULTS – NUMBER OF SERVERS    −=✷=−

| NUMBER OF SERVERS | SYSTEMS WAIT | SYSTEMS LENGTH | TOTAL COSTS |
|---|---|---|---|
| 1 | arrival rate exceeds system capacity | | |
| 2 | arrival rate exceeds system capacity | | |
| 3 | 0.183 | 5.470 | 586.743 |
| 4 | 0.101 | 3.031 | 675.774 |
| 5 | 0.088 | 2.630 | 815.758 |

OPTIMAL NUMBER OF SERVERS IS 3

−=✷=−    RESULTS – WITH 3 SERVERS    −=✷=−

| | | |
|---|---|---|
| BALKING RATE (PERCENT) | : | 0.542 |
| SERVER IDLE (PERCENT) | : | 17.118 |
| EXPECTED NUMBER IN SYSTEM | : | 5.470 |
| EXPECTED NUMBER IN QUEUE | : | 2.983 |
| EXPECTED TIME IN SYSTEM | : | 0.183 |
| EXPECTED TIME IN QUEUE | : | 0.100 |
| COST OF SERVICE | : | 450.000 |
| COST OF WAITING | : | 136.743 |
| TOTAL COST | : | 586.743 |

−=✷=−    END OF ANALYSIS    −=✷=−

**Figure 19.7**    Analysis of a queue with costs.

```
MTB  > random  10  c1;
SUBC > normal mean 10 standev 2.
MTB  > print c1

C1
 11.3160     9.3408     8.7069    10.1302     9.4253
 10.8556    10.5541    11.2570     8.9433    11.9657

MTB > stop
```

**Figure 19.8**    Using a computer to generate random numbers.

# Case Study

## The Palmer Centre for Alternative Therapy

Jane and Andrew Palmer own an 'alternative therapy centre' which offers a range of services to people suffering from long-term back problems. Their treatments range from fairly traditional ones such as osteopathy to more experimental ones that work with the body's 'energy pathways'.

The Palmer Centre employs a receptionist who deals with around 20 customers an hour. Seventy per cent of these only ask for information and the receptionist can deal with them in a couple of minutes. The remainder are actual patients.

Each patient takes about 3 minutes to give the receptionist information before moving on to consultations with either Jane or Andrew. Roughly two-thirds of patients see Andrew, who spends around 15 minutes with each one. The rest see Jane, who spends around 20 minutes with each. After they have finished treatment, the patients return to the receptionist, who takes two minutes to collect information, prepare bills and arrange follow-up appointments.

This arrangement seems to work well, but some patients complain of having to wait. This is particularly important, as the clinic is thinking of expanding and employing another therapist. They will have to do some marketing to attract new customers, but feel that alternative treatments are becoming more popular so finding new business should not be too difficult.

One problem is that they will have to make some changes to their centre and build another office and waiting area for the new therapist. If the expansion is a success, they might be tempted to get even bigger in the future. This raises the question of how many offices the centre will need for varying levels of demand and how big the waiting areas should be.

Suppose that the Palmers have asked for your advice. How would you judge the current performance of the centre? What resources would be needed to give at least the same level of service to increasing numbers of patients?

# Appendix A

# References for further reading

Many books describe quantitative methods for business. Some of these are general and cover a range of topics, while others are more specialized. Unfortunately, the books are of variable quality and use. The following list shows a number that you might find useful.

### Books giving a general overview

Anderson D., Sweeney D. and Williams T. (1997)
*Quantitative Methods for Business* 6th edn. St Paul, MN: South Western.
Bancroft G. and O'Sullivan G. (2000)
*Foundations of Quantitative Business Techniques*. Maidenhead: McGraw-Hill.
Burton G., Carrol G. and Wall S. (1998)
*Quantitative Methods for Business and Economics*. Harlow: Longman.
Curwin J. and Slater R. (1996)
*Quantitative Methods for Business Decisions* 4th edn. London: Thomson International.
Hesse R. (1996)
*Managerial Spreadsheet Modeling and Analysis*. Homewood, IL: Irwin.
Johnson D. (1986)
*Quantitative Business Analysis*. London: Butterworth.
Morris C. (1996)
*Quantitative Approaches in Business Studies* 4th edn. London: Pitman.
Oakshot L. (1998)
*Essential Quantitative Methods for Business Management and Finance*. London: Macmillan.
Slater R. and Ashcroft P. (1990)
*Quantitative Techniques in a Business Context*. London: Chapman and Hall.
Thomas R. (1997)
*Quantitative Methods for Business Studies*. London: Prentice Hall.
Vazsonyi A., Weida N. and Richardson R. (1999)
*Quantitative Management Using Microsoft Excel*. Cincinnati, OH: Duxbury Press.
Waters D. (1998)
*Essential Quantitative Methods*. Harlow: Addison-Wesley.
Waters D. (1998)
*A Practical Introduction to Management Science* 2nd edn. Harlow: Addison Wesley.
Watsham T. and Parramore K. (1998)
*Quantitative Methods in Finance*. London: International Thomson.

Whigham D, (1998)
  *Quantitative Business Methods Using Excel*. Oxford: Oxford University Press.
Wisniewski M. (1996)
  *Foundations of Quantitative Methods for Business*. London: Financial Times
  Prentice Hall.


## Regression and forecasting

Brockwell P. and Davis R. (1996)
  *Introduction to Time Series and Forecasting*. New York: Springer-Verlag.
Gaynor P. and Kirkpatrick R. (1994)
  *An Introduction to Time Series Modeling and Forecasting for Business and
  Economics*. New York: McGraw-Hill.
Hanke J. and Reitsch A. (1999)
  *Business Forecasting* 5th edn. Englewood Cliffs, NJ: Prentice Hall.
Makridakis S., Wheelwright S. and Hyndman R. (1998)
  *Forecasting: Methods and Applications* 4th edn. New York: Wiley.
Pecar B. (1994)
  *Business Forecasting for Management*. New York: McGraw-Hill.
Willis R.E. (1987)
  *A Guide to Forecasting for Planners and Managers*. Englewood Cliffs, NJ:
  Prentice Hall.
Yaffee R. and McGee M. (2000)
  *Introduction to Time Series Analysis and Forecasting*. New York: Academic.


## Linear programming

Bunday B. (1984)
  *Basic Linear Programming*. London: Edward Arnold.
Darst R. (1991)
  *Introduction to Linear Programming*. New York: Dekker.
Gass S. (1990)
  *An Illustrated Guide to Linear Programming*. New York: Dover Publications.
Inston W. (1996)
  *Introduction to Mathematical Programming with Windows Lindo*. New York:
  Wadsworth.
Kolman B. and Beck R. (1995)
  *Elementary Linear Programming with Applications* 3rd edn. New York:
  Academic.
Pannell D. (1996)
  *Introduction to Practical Linear Programming*. New York: Wiley.
Schrage L. (1991)
  *LINDO: an Optimization Modeling System* 4th edn. San Francisco, CA:
  Scientific Press.

## Calculus

Adams R. (1995)
*Single Variable Calculus*. Reading, MA: Addison-Wesley.
Mendelson E. (1985)
*Beginning Calculus*. New York: McGraw-Hill.
Pearson J.M. (1982)
*Mathematics for Economists*. London: Longman.
Praserk C. (1987)
*Calculus with Applications to Management, Economics and the Social and Natural Sciences*. New York: Merrill.


## Statistics

Anderson D., Sweeney D. and Williams T. (1999)
*Essentials of Statistics for Business and Economics*. St Paul, MN: South Western.
Berenson M. (1998)
*Basic Business Statistics*. Englewood Cliffs, NJ: Prentice Hall.
Berenson M. and Levin D. (1998)
*Business Statistics*. Englewood Cliffs, NJ: Prentice Hall.
Fleming M. and Nellis J. (1996)
*The Essence of Statistics for Business*. Englewood Cliffs, NJ: Prentice Hall.
Gerbing D. (1998)
*Relevant Business Statistics Using Excel*. St Paul, MN: South Western.
Levin R. and Rubin D. (1996)
*Statistics for Management*. Englewood Cliffs, NJ: Prentice Hall.
McClave J. and Benson P. (1998)
*A First Course in Business Statistics*. Englewood Cliffs, NJ: Prentice Hall.
Mendenhall W. and Beaver R. (1995)
*Brief Course in Business Statistics*. Cincinnati, OH: Duxbury Press.
Rowntree D. (1981)
*Statistics Without Tears: a Primer for Non-Mathematicians*. Harmondsworth: Penguin.
Silver M. (1997)
*Business Statistics*. New York: McGraw-Hill.
Triola M. and Franklin L. (1993)
*Business Statistics*. Reading, MA: Addison Wesley Longman.
Weiers R. (1998)
*Introduction to Business Statistics* 3rd edn. Cincinnati, OH: Duxbury Press.


## Sampling

Cryer J. and Miller R. (1995)
*Statistics for Business* 2nd edn. Cincinnati, OH: Duxbury Press.
Farnum N. (1993)
*Modern Statistical Quality Control and Improvement*. Cincinnati, OH: Duxbury Press.

Hague P. and Harris P.
   *Sampling and Statistics*. London: Kogan Page.
Lohr S. (1999)
   *Sampling*. Cincinnati, OH: Duxbury Press,
Montgomery D. (1996)
   *Introduction to Statistical Quality Control*. Chichester: Wiley,
Thompson S. (1992)
   *Sampling*. Chichester: Wiley.

## Decision analysis

Albright S., Winston W. and Zappe C. (1999)
   *Data Analysis and Decision Making with Microsoft Excel*. Cincinnati, OH:
   Thomson International.
Bunn D. (1984)
   *Applied Decision Analysis*. New York: McGraw-Hill.
Clemen R. (1996)
   *Making Hard Decisions*. Cincinnati, OH: Duxbury Press.
Cooke S. and Slack N. (1991)
   *Making Management Decisions* 2nd edn. London: Prentice Hall.
Daellenbach H. (1994)
   *Systems and Decision Making*. Chichester: Wiley.
Golub A. (1997)
   Decision Analysis. New York: Wiley.
Goodwin P. and Wright G. (1998)
   *Decision Analysis for Management Judgement*. Chichester: Wiley.
Lindley D. (1985)
   *Making Decisions* 2nd edn. Chichester: Wiley.
Moore P. and Thomas H. (1988)
   *The Anatomy of Decisions* 2nd edn. Harmondsworth: Penguin.
Samson D. (1988)
   *Managerial Decision Analysis*. Homewood, IL: Irwin.

## Inventory control

Arnold J. (1996)
   *Introduction to Materials Management*. London: Prentice Hall.
Lewis C. (1998)
   Demand Forecasting and Inventory Control. Chichester: Wiley.
Mecimore C. and Weeks J. (1987)
   *Techniques of Inventory Management and Control*. London: Institute of
   Management Accountants.
Tersine R.J. (1994)
   *Principles of Inventory and Materials Management* 4th edn. London: Prentice
   Hall.
Waters C.D.J. (1992)
   *Inventory Control and Management*. Chichester: Wiley.

## Project network analysis

Burke R. (1999)
*Project management.* Chichester: Wiley.
Kerzner H. (1997)
*Project Management.* New York: Wiley.
Lock D. (2000)
*The Essentials of Project Management* 2nd edn. Aldershot: Gower.
Lockyer K. and Gordon J. (1995)
*Project Management and Project Network Techniques.* London: Financial Times Prentice Hall.
Maylor H. (1996)
*Project Management.* London: Pitman.
Meredith J. and Mantel S. (1999)
*Project Management: a Managerial Approach.* New York: Wiley.
Ralph K. (2000)
*Project Management.* New York: Macmillan.
Shtub A., Bard J. and Globerson S. (1994)
Project Management. Englewood Cliffs, NJ: Prentice Hall.
Verzuh E. (1999)
*The Fast Forward MBA in Project Management.* Chichester: Wiley.
Young T. (1997)
*30 Minutes to Plan a Project.* London: Kogan Page.

## Queues and simulation

Banks J. and Carson J.S. (1984)
*Discrete-Event Simulation.* Englewood Cliffs, NJ: Prentice Hall.
Gross D. and Harris C. (1997)
*Fundamentals of Queueing Theory.* Chichester: Wiley.
Kleijnen J. (1992)
*Simulation.* Chichester: Wiley.
Oakshott L. (1996)
*Business Modelling and Simulation.* London: Financial Times Prentice Hall.
Pidd M. (1997)
*Computer Simulation in Management Science* 4th edn. Chichester: Wiley.
Solomon S.L. (1983)
*Simulation of Waiting-Line Systems.* Englewood Cliffs, NJ: Prentice-Hall.

# Appendix B

# Solutions to self-assessment questions

## Chapter 1
## Numbers and managers

**1.1** They allow rational analyses of problems, measurement of various factors, and decisions based on a sound, logical footing.

**1.2** No, but most analyses include quantitative elements.

**1.3** No; managers make decisions.

**1.4** There are several reasons for this, including increased availability of computers, fiercer competition needing better decisions, development of new quantitative methods, good experiences with earlier analyses encouraging managers to expand their use, and better education of managers making available techniques more widely known.

**1.5** A simplified representation of reality.

**1.6** They are used to develop solutions for real problems, allow experimentation without risk to actual operations, allow experiments that would not be possible in reality, assess the consequences of decisions, see how sensitive operations are to change, and so on.

**1.7** Symbolic models.

**1.8** Observation, modelling, experimentation and implementation.

**1.9** No. Any approach that efficiently gets a good answer can be used.

## Chapter 2
## Tools for quantitative methods

**2.1** Yes.

**2.2** (a) 4, (b) 168/15 or 11.2, (c) 3.

**2.3** There is no difference. None is always the best, so the choice depends on circumstances.

**2.4** 1 745 800.362 and 1 750 000.

**2.5** Because it gives a precise method of describing and solving quantitative problems.

**2.6** Yes.

**2.7** No. Two equations are needed to find two unknowns.

**2.8** There is no best format for all occasions. You should use the format that is best suited to your needs.

**2.9** 0.

**2.10** By rearranging them to (a) $x = 11 - 8pr/3q$ and (b) $x = q/4 - 7pq/2r$.

**2.11** 7.

**2.12** 27/32 = 0.84.

**2.13** 1.

**2.14** $1.23 \times 10^9$ and $2.53 \times 10^{-7}$.

**2.15** They are imaginary.

**2.16** Because (with odd exceptions) there are no other formulae.

**2.17** One whose value is set by the value taken by the independent variable.

**2.18** (0,0).

**2.19** It is a straight line that crosses the $y$ axis at 4 and has a gradient of 2.

**2.20** (a) 0, (b) 1, (c) infinite.

**2.21** At the points where the curve crosses the $x$ axis.

**2.22** A point where the gradient changes from positive to negative (or vice versa), often corresponding to a maximum or minimum value.

**2.23** Because graphs are difficult to draw exactly and it is difficult to read accurate results from them.

**2.24** At the point where the graphs cross, equations for both lines are true.

# Chapter 3
# Collecting data

**3.1** Data are the raw numbers, measurements, opinions, etc that are processed to give useful information.

**3.2** Because managers need reliable information to make their decisions, and this is provided by data collection (and subsequent analysis).

**3.3** No – you can collect too much data.

**3.4** Because data of different types are collected, analysed and presented in different ways.

**3.5** There are several ways, including quantitative/qualitative, nominal/ordinal/ cardinal, discrete/continuous, primary/secondary.

**3.6** Discrete data can only take integer values, while continuous data can take any values.

**3.7** There are many possible examples, such as: nominal – industrial sectors of companies; ordinal – social class; cardinal – weight of products.

**3.8** Because it would be too expensive, time-consuming or impractical to collect data from the population.

**3.9** Because the wrong population would give misleading survey results.

**3.10** One classification has census, random, systematic, quota, stratified, multi-stage and cluster samples.

**3.11** Every member of the population has an equal chance of being chosen.

**3.12** Stratified sampling is random and ensures that all groups within the population are represented; quota sampling is not truly random but it ensures that the sample has the same properties as the population.

**3.13** Relevant figures are published by the government and by international organizations such as the United Nations. They should be available in any reasonable library.

**3.14** Different views are valid, but suggestions are: (a) telephone interview, (b) personal interview, (c) longitudinal survey, (d) observation.

**3.15** (a) Leading question. (b) Vague – what is 'too much'? (c) Several questions in one. (d) Speculative.

**3.16** They should be contacted and encouraged to reply. If this gets no response they should be examined for common characteristics to ensure that no bias is introduced.

**3.17** Because interviewers will keep asking people until they fill the required quotas.

**3.18** No – it needs careful planning.

# Chapter 4
# Using diagrams to present data

**4.1** Data are the raw numbers, measurements, opinions, etc that are processed to give useful information.

**4.2** Many of these can be found in advertisements, political campaigns, company reports, newspapers, etc.

**4.3** To simplify raw data, remove the detail, and show underlying patterns.

**4.4** Unfortunately not.

**4.5** Graphical and numerical methods.

**4.6** They can show lots of information, show varying attributes and highlight specific results.

**4.7** Graphs show patterns well, but if the axes are not scaled properly they can give a misleading impression. Labelling the axes shows that they are properly drawn and the meaning is clear.

**4.8** Probably tables.

**4.9** No. There are many variations in bar charts and the best is largely a matter of choice. This is also true of other presentation methods.

**4.10** They are not very accurate and can be misleading.

**4.11** A diagram showing the number of observations in a set of data falling into each class.

**4.12** A frequency distribution shows the number of observations in each class; a percentage frequency distribution shows the percentage of observations in each class; a cumulative frequency distribution shows the total number of observations up to (and including) the class; the cumulative percentage frequency distribution shows the percentage of observations up to (and including) the class.

**4.13** No. It is true for bar charts, but in histograms the area shows the number of observations.

**4.14** The average height of the two separate bars.

**4.15** To show the cumulative frequency against class.

**4.16** Not really. The diagonal line shows an equally distributed population, but this may not be fair.

# Chapter 5
## Using numbers to describe data

**5.1** They give an overall impression of data, but are not so good at giving objective measures.

**5.2** Where the centre of the data is (when drawn on a frequency diagram). This is generally some form of average.

**5.3** No. These only partially describe a set of data.

**5.4** No.

**5.5** The most common measures are: arithmetic mean = $(\Sigma x)/n$; median = middle observation; mode = most frequent observation.

**5.6** There are a number of reasons, including its ease of calculation, use in further analysis, and general acceptance.

**5.7** $(10 \times 34 + 5 \times 37)/15 = 35$.

**5.8** Because the calculations will usually be done by a computer.

**5.9** Range, mean absolute deviation, variance, standard deviation. Yes.

**5.10** Because positive and negative deviations cancel each other.

**5.11** Metres$^2$.

**5.12** Because it is very useful in other analyses.

**5.13** The coefficients of variation are 0.203 and 0.128 respectively, which suggests that the first set of data is more widely dispersed than the second.

# Chapter 6
## Describing changes with index numbers

**6.1** To measure the changes in a variable over time.

**6.2** No. Any suitable base value can be used, but 100 is the most common.

**6.3** When circumstances change significantly or when the old index gets too high.

**6.4** A percentage rise of 10% increases the value by 10% of the previous value; a percentage point rise of 10 increases the value by 10% of the base value.

**6.5** 364.32.

**6.6** Mean price relative index for period $n$
$$= \frac{\text{sum of all price relatives for period } n}{\text{number of indices}} \times 100$$
Simple aggregate index for period $n$
$$= \frac{\text{sum of prices in period } n}{\text{sum of prices in base period}} \times 100$$

**6.7** They are sensitive to the units used and do not take into account the relative importance of variables.

**6.8** Base-period weighting assumes that the basket of items used in the base period is always used; current-period weighting considers price changes based on the current basket of items.

**6.9** Because the basket of items actually used will be affected by prices. In particular, any items with rapidly rising prices are replaced by ones with lower price rises.

**6.10** Yes.

**6.11** Not really. The RPI considers only purchases by a 'typical' family, it omits expenses that may be significant (such as income tax and life insurance), it does not mention the quality of goods, and so on.

# Chapter 7
## Calculations with money

**7.1** No.

**7.2** Return on assets $= \dfrac{\text{income}}{\text{assets}}$

**7.3** The number of units made.

**7.4** The number of units that must be sold before a profit is made.

**7.5** The product is making a loss, as revenue does not cover all costs.

**7.6** No – there may also be diseconomies of scale.

**7.7** (a) More than £1000 in five years' time.

**7.8** No. £100 invested for a year at 12% will have a value of $100 \times (1+0.12) = £112$; £100 invested for 12 months at 1% will have a value of $100 \times (1+0.01)^{12} = £112.68$.

**7.9** By reducing all costs and revenues to present values, and calculating the net present value for each project.

**7.10** An estimate of the proportional increase or decrease in the value of money in each time period.

**7.11** Straight-line depreciation reduces the value by a fixed amount each period; the reducing-balance method reduces the value by a fixed percentage each period.

**7.12** A fund that receives regular payments so that a specified sum is available at some time in the future.

**7.13** By using the equation $A_n = A_0 \times (1 + i)^n + [F \times (1 + i)^n - F]/i$, to find $A_0$ when $A_n = 0$ and $F$ is the regular payment received.

**7.14** No; other factors can be included.

# Chapter 8
# Relating variables by regression

**8.1** The errors, or deviations from expected values.

**8.2** Mathematical relationships look at underlying patterns, but they cannot deal with short-term, random noise. Errors are introduced by noise, identifying the wrong underlying pattern and changes in the system being modelled.

**8.3** The mean error is defined as $1/n \times \Sigma E_i$. Positive and negative errors cancel each other, so the mean error should have a value around zero unless there is bias.

**8.4** Mean absolute deviation = $1/n \times \Sigma |E_i|$ and mean squared error = $1/n \times \Sigma (E_i)^2$.

**8.5** By using each equation to calculate values for the dependent variable for a range of values of the independent variable. These give the individual errors, which we can use to give mean errors, mean absolute deviations, and mean squared errors. The stronger relationship is the one with smaller errors.

**8.6** To find the line of best fit relating a dependent variable to an independent one, and predict values for the dependent variable.

**8.7** $x_i$ and $y_i$ are the $i$th values of independent and dependent variables respectively; $a$ is the point where the line crosses the $y$ axis, $b$ is the gradient of the line; $E_i$ is the error introduced by random noise.

**8.8** The time period (e.g. week or month number).

**8.9** The proportion of the total sum of squared error that is explained by the regression.

**8.10** −1 to +1. The coefficient of determination is the square of the coefficient of correlation.

**8.11** They are essentially the same, but Pearson's coefficient is used for cardinal data, while Spearman's is used for ordinal data.

**8.12** No. Variation in the dependent variable is explained by, but not necessarily caused by, variation in the independent variable.

**8.13** Non-linear and multiple linear regression.

**8.14** Not really.

**8.15** By comparing the coefficients of determination – or better, the adjusted values.

**8.16** A linear relationship between the 'independent variables'.

# Chapter 9
# Business forecasting

**9.1** All decisions become effective at some point in the future, so they should take into account future circumstances, and these must be forecast.

**9.2** No.

**9.3** Judgemental, projective and causal forecasting.

**9.4** Relevant factors include: What is to be forecast? Why is this being forecast? Are quantitative data available? How does the forecast affect other parts of the organization? How far into the future are forecasts needed? Are reliable data available and how frequently are they updated? What external factors are relevant? How much will the forecast cost and how much will errors cost? How much detail is required? How much time is available?

**9.5** Forecasts that are subjective views based on opinions and intuition rather than quantitative analysis.

**9.6** Personal insight, panel consensus, market surveys, historical analogy and the Delphi method.

**9.7** They can be unreliable, experts may give conflicting views, cost of data collection is high, there may be no available expertise, and so on.

**9.8** No.

**9.9** Because observations contain random noise, which cannot be forecast.

**9.10** By using both methods over a typical period of time and comparing the errors.

**9.11** Because older data tend to swamp more recent (and more relevant) data.

**9.12** By using a lower value of $n$.

**9.13** It can be influenced by random fluctuations.

**9.14** By using a moving average with *n* equal to the length of the season.

**9.15** Because the weight given to the data declines exponentially with age, and the method smooths the effects of noise.

**9.16** By using a higher value for the smoothing constant α.

**9.17** An additive model adds separate numbers for *T*, *S* and *C* to give a value. A multiplicative model uses a number, *T*, and multiplies this by ratios for *S* and *C*.

**9.18** Because it is very difficult to get reliable data for long-term cycles.

**9.19** No; only when there is an even number of periods in a season.

**9.20** Regression is generally preferred.

# Chapter 10
# Planning with linear programming

**10.1** A problem where an optimal solution is needed, but there are constraints that limit the solution.

**10.2** A method of tackling problems of constrained optimization.

**10.3** The problem is constrained optimization, both constraints and objective function are linear with respect to decision variables, proportionality and additivity assumptions are valid, problem variables are non-negative and reliable data are available.

**10.4** Formulation involves putting a problem in a standard form.

**10.5** Decision variables, constraints (including non-negativity) and an objective function.

**10.6** The area representing solutions that satisfy all constraints, including the non-negativity conditions.

**10.7** To give the measure by which solutions are judged and find the optimal solution.

**10.8** The feasible region is always surrounded by straight lines; the corners of the feasible region are the extreme points. An optimal solution is always at an extreme point.

**10.9** As the objective function line moves away from the origin its value increases and the maximum value is at the last point that it passes through in the feasible region. As the line moves in towards the origin its value decreases and the minimum value is at the last point that it passes through in the feasible region.

**10.10** The solution needs a lot of simple arithmetic which can be done easily by computers.

**10.11** Many kinds of information can be given, but the most usual are: a copy of the problem solved; details of the optimal solution; limiting constraints and unused resources; shadow prices and ranges over which these are valid; variations in the objective function that will not change the position of the optimal solution.

**10.12** This looks at the way that an optimal solution varies with changes to the constraints and objective function.

**10.13** These measure the rate of change of the objective function with changes in resource levels; they are equivalent to the marginal values of resources.

**10.14** Until so many resources become available that the constraint is no longer limiting (or resources are reduced until a new constraint becomes limiting).

# Chapter 11
# Using calculus to describe changes

**11.1** It finds the instantaneous rate of change (or gradient) of a function at any point.

**11.2** This is the notation used to describe the derivative of *y* with respect to *x*. It is the equation of the gradient at any point.

**11.3** The function is continuous in the region considered, $dy/dx = 0$ and $d^2y/dx^2 > 0$.

**11.4** The variable names have no significance, so $dp/dc = dq/dc + dr/dc$.

**11.5** The gradient of a function is found from $dy/dx$. This gradient itself changes with *x*, and the rate of change is given by $d^2y/dx^2$.

**11.6** The additional cost of producing one more unit of a product.

**11.7** The average revenue is the total revenue divided by the number produced, while the marginal revenue is found by differentiating the total revenue function.

**11.8** It is the ratio of change in demand over change in price.

**11.9** Demand would rise with increasing price.

# Chapter 12
## Uncertainty and probabilities

**12.1**   A measure of its likelihood or its relative frequency.

**12.2**   Events where the probability of one occurring is not affected by whether or not the other occurs.

**12.3**   Events which cannot both occur.

**12.4**   Using the rule 'OR means ADD' and adding the separate probabilities.

**12.5**   Using the rule 'AND means MULTIPLY' and multiplying the separate probabilities.

**12.6**   $P(A) = 1 - P(B) - P(C)$.

**12.7**   Events are dependent if they are not independent. This obvious statement means that $P(a) \neq P(a/b) \neq P(a/\underline{b})$.

**12.8**   Conditional probabilities take the form $P(a/b)$ and are the probability of event $a$ occurring given that event $b$ has already occurred.

**12.9**   Bayes' theorem is used for calculating conditional probabilities. It states:

$$P(a/b) = \frac{P(b/a) \times P(a)}{P(b)}$$

**12.10**  It gives a diagrammatic view of a problem and organizes some calculations.

# Chapter 13
## Probability distributions

**13.1**   To describe the probability or relative frequencies of events or classes of observations.

**13.2**   Empirical data show historical values that actually happened; *a priori* data are found from theoretical reasoning.

**13.3**   1.

**13.4**   $n!$.

**13.5**   The order of selection is not important for a combination, but it is important for a permutation.

**13.6**   There are more permutations.

**13.7**   When there is a series of trials; each trial has two possible outcomes; the two outcomes are mutually exclusive; there is a constant probability of success, $p$, and failure, $q = 1 - p$; the outcomes of successive trials are independent.

**13.8**   $P(r)$ is the probability of $r$ successes, $n$ is the number of trials, $p$ is the probability of success in each trial, $q$ is the probability of failure in each trial, $^nC_r$ is the number of ways of combining $r$ items from $n$.

**13.9**   Mean $= np$; variance $= npq$; standard deviation $= \sqrt{npq}$.

**13.10**  0.2753.

**13.11**  When events occur infrequently and at random. Other requirements include: independent events; the probability of an event happening in an interval is proportional to the length of the interval; an infinite number of events should be possible in an interval.

**13.12**  Mean $=$ variance $= np$.

**13.13**  0.1438.

**13.14**  When the number of events, $n$, in the binomial process is large and the probability of success is small, so $np$ is less than 5.

**13.15**  In many applications when there is a large number of observations.

**13.16**  Binomial and Poisson distributions describe discrete data, while the Normal distribution describes continuous data.

**13.17**  The mean determines the location of the distribution and the standard deviation determines its spread.

**13.18**  When the number of events $n$ is large and the probability of success is relatively large (with $np$ greater than 5).

**13.19**  About 68% of observations are within one standard deviation of the mean.

**13.20**  The Normal distribution describes continuous data, so a small continuity correction can be used for discrete data. This correction is usually small.

# Chapter 14
## Using samples in business

**14.1**   To take a sample of observations that fairly represent the whole population.

**14.2**   A process in which the value of a property in a sample is used to estimate the value of the property in the population.

**14.3**   If a series of samples are taken from a population and a mean value of some variable is found for each sample, these means form the sampling distribution of the mean.

**14.4**   If the sample size is greater than about 30, or the population is Normally distributed, the sampling distribution of the mean is Normally distributed with mean $\mu$ and standard deviation $\sigma/\sqrt{n}$.

**14.5** Because it comes from a sample that is unlikely to be perfectly representative of the population.

**14.6** The range within which we are 95% confident the actual value lies.

**14.7** Wider.

**14.8** When you want to be confident that a value is either above or below a certain point.

**14.9** $25n$.

**14.10** Because the samples are not representative of the population, and tend to underestimate variability.

**14.11** The number of independent pieces of data.

**14.12** It checks whether a batch of units is acceptable or whether it should be rejected.

**14.13** The process may need adjusting.

# Chapter 15
## Testing hypotheses

**15.1** To test whether a statement about a population is supported by the evidence collected in a sample.

**15.2** The null hypothesis, $H_0$.

**15.3** Type I error rejects a true hypothesis; type II error does not reject a false hypothesis.

**15.4** The minimum acceptable probability that an observation is a random sample from the hypothesized population.

**15.5** 5% significance.

**15.6** No; but the evidence does support the null hypothesis and means it cannot be rejected.

**15.7** When we want to make sure that a variable is above or below a specified value.

**15.8** Because a small sample is not truly representative of the population, and it underestimates the variability.

**15.9** A parametric test makes assumptions about the distribution of variables, and only works with quantitative data.

**15.10** When the conditions needed by parametric tests are not met.

**15.11** No; there may be no suitable test.

**15.12** Because the distribution only takes positive values, so the acceptance range is 0 to the critical value.

**15.13** Nothing.

# Chapter 16
## Analysing business decisions

**16.1** Because they give structure to the situation and clearly show alternatives, events and consequences.

**16.2** A decision maker, a number of alternatives, a number of events, a set of measurable outcomes, and an objective of choosing the best alternative.

**16.3** There is only one event.

**16.4** One of several events can occur, but there is no way of telling which events are more likely. Probabilities cannot be given to events.

**16.5** The three criteria described are due to Laplace, Wald and Savage.

**16.6** Only the Laplace criterion.

**16.7** No. There are many criteria, and ones mentioned are maximax profit and $\alpha \times$ best outcome $+ (1 - \alpha) \times$ worst outcome.

**16.8** There are several events that may occur and probabilities can be given to each of them.

**16.9** The sum of the probabilities multiplied by the values of the outcomes: expected value $= \Sigma P \times V$.

**16.10** Yes, but the results may be unreliable.

**16.11** When the conditional probabilities are available in situations of risk.

**16.12** Expected values assume that the value of money rises linearly with the amount. A utility function describes a more realistic relationship.

**16.13** The value of a terminal node is the total cost or gain of reaching that node. The value of a decision node is the best value of nodes reached by leaving alternative branches. The value of a random node is the expected value of the leaving branches.

**16.14** The value given at the left-hand, originating node is the overall expected value of following the best policy.

# Chapter 17
## Controlling stocks

**17.1** To act as a buffer between supply and demand.

**17.2** Fixed order quantity and periodic review system.

**17.3** Unit cost, reorder cost, holding cost and shortage cost.

**17.4** The fixed order quantity that minimizes costs (with the assumptions made).

**17.5** (c) Either increase or decrease total costs, depending on the economic order quantity.

**17.6** The amount of an item that is in stock when an order for replenishment is made.

**17.7** From the lead time demand.

**17.8** The service level gives the probability that a demand can be satisfied. We have used cycle service level, which is the probability that an item remains in stock during a cycle. It is used because alternative analyses are based on shortage costs, which are very difficult to find.

**17.9** Without safety stock there would be shortages in 50% of cycles. Safety stock reduces the probability of shortages and increases service levels.

**17.10** By increasing the amount of safety stock.

**17.11** Order size is equal to the difference between current stock and target stock level.

**17.12** A periodic review system.

**17.13** To find the importance of items so that appropriate effort can be spent on controlling their stocks.

**17.14** B items.

# Chapter 18
# Planning projects with networks

**18.1** A coherent piece of work with a clear start and finish, consisting of the set of activities that make a distinct product.

**18.2** To plan, schedule and control the activities in a project and hence the resources used.

**18.3** No.

**18.4** (a) Events (that is, the start and finish of activities), (b) activities.

**18.5** A list of all activities in the project and the immediate predecessors of each activity.

**18.6** Before an activity can begin all preceding activities must be finished. The arrows representing activities show precedence only and neither the length nor orientation is significant.

**18.7** Uniqueness dummies make sure that only one activity is directly between any two events. Logical dummies make sure that the logic of the dependence table is maintained in the network.

**18.8** The earliest time of an event is the earliest time by which **all** preceding activities can be finished. The latest time of an event is the latest time that allows **all** following activities to be started on time.

**18.9** Total float is the difference between the maximum amount of time available for an activity and the time actually used.

**18.10** Zero.

**18.11** The critical path is the chain of activities that determine the project duration. If any critical activity is extended or delayed the whole project is delayed.

**18.12** The critical activities.

**18.13** By the amount of total float of activities on a parallel path.

**18.14** They show what stage each activity in a project should have reached at any time.

**18.15** By delaying non-critical activities to times when fewer resources are needed.

# Chapter 19
# Queues and simulation

**19.1** Customers who want a service but find the server is busy, so they have to wait.

**19.2** No. A balance is needed between large numbers of servers and high costs.

**19.3** $\lambda$ is the average arrival rate and $\mu$ is the average service rate.

**19.4** Customers arrive faster than they are served and the queue continues to grow.

**19.5** Assumptions include: a single server; random arrivals; random service time; first come first served service discipline; the system has reached its steady state; there is no limit to the number of customers allowed in the queue; there is no limit on the number of customers who use the service and all customers wait until they are served.

**19.6** Ordinary quantitative analyses describe a problem at some point of time and build a model accordingly. Simulation models follow the process over time.

**19.7** Yes.

**19.8** To give typical values to variables.

# Appendix C

# Solutions to numerical problems

This Appendix lists the answers to the numerical problems at the end of each chapter.

## Chapter 1
## Numbers and managers

**1.1**   1946
**1.2**   $5.84, £30.62
**1.3**   30 minutes
**1.4**   £40

## Chapter 2
## Tools for quantitative methods

**2.1**   (a) −96, (b) 5, (c) 144, (d) 2, (e) −10
**2.2**   (a) 11/10, (b) 1/8, (c) 5/8, (d) −15, (e) 35/96
**2.3**   (a) 1.1, (b) 0.125, (c) 0.625, (d) −15, (e) 0.365
**2.4**   (a) 57.5%, (b) 65/100 = 13/20, (c) 0.17
**2.5**   (a) 74.071, (b) 74.1, (c) 74, (d) 70

**2.6**   The first exam
**2.7**   60 miles/hour      speed = distance/time
**2.8**   $n \times$ (selling price − purchase price)
**2.9**   15 match balls and 45 practice balls
**2.10**  Direct labour costs £7500, raw materials cost £16,000 and overheads cost £1500
**2.11**  (a) $a = 4$, $b = −1$; (b) $x = 3$, $y = 7$; (c) $x = 3$, $y = −1$, $z = 2$; (d) $r = −1$, $s = −2$, $t = 4$
**2.12**  $n = 3$, $e = 5$
**2.13**  (a) $x^{3/4}$, (b) $x$, (c) 3, (d) 32, (e) 506.19, (f) 288
**2.14**  (a) 2, 4; (b) 10/6, −1; (c) roots are imaginary
**2.15**  6.18
**2.17**  53
**2.20**  $y = 300,000$ when $x = 250$
**2.21**  cost = 1600 when $x = 40$
**2.22**  (−0.557,3.86) and (12.557,266.14)

## Chapter 3
## Collecting data

**3.6**

|        |      | 16–25 | 26–35 | 36–45 | 46–55 | 56–65 | 66–75 | ≥76 |
|--------|------|-------|-------|-------|-------|-------|-------|-----|
| Female | A    | 22    | 40    | 44    | 33    | 22    | 15    | 7   |
|        | B    | 33    | 60    | 66    | 49    | 33    | 22    | 11  |
|        | C1   | 22    | 40    | 44    | 33    | 22    | 15    | 7   |
|        | C2   | 11    | 20    | 22    | 16    | 11    | 7     | 4   |
|        | D    | 4     | 7     | 7     | 5     | 4     | 2     | 1   |
| Male   | A    | 36    | 65    | 71    | 54    | 36    | 24    | 12  |
|        | B    | 54    | 98    | 107   | 80    | 54    | 36    | 18  |
|        | C1   | 36    | 65    | 71    | 54    | 36    | 24    | 12  |
|        | C2   | 18    | 33    | 36    | 27    | 18    | 12    | 6   |
|        | D    | 6     | 11    | 12    | 9     | 6     | 4     | 2   |

## Chapter 4
## Using diagrams to present data

**4.7**

|  | Frequency | Cumulative frequency | Percentage |
|---|---|---|---|
| less than 100 | 3 | 3 | 6.67 |
| 100–149 | 4 | 7 | 8.89 |
| 150–199 | 3 | 10 | 6.67 |
| 200–249 | 5 | 15 | 11.11 |
| 250–299 | 7 | 22 | 15.56 |
| 300–349 | 5 | 27 | 11.11 |
| 350–399 | 8 | 35 | 17.78 |
| 400–449 | 4 | 39 | 8.89 |
| 450 or greater | 6 | 45 | 13.33 |

## Chapter 5
## Using numbers to describe data

**5.1**  3, 2, 1
**5.2**  24.77, 24.50, 24
**5.3**  13.94, 14, 13.86
**5.4**  7.57, 7.73, 7.82
**5.5**  39.93, 38.28, 34.13
**5.6**  2.67, 8.67, 2.94
**5.7**  624.72, 24.99
**5.8**  ● range = 6, variance = 5.2, standard deviation = 2.28
       ● range = 8, variance = 3.54, standard deviation = 1.88
**5.9**  ● variance = 23.54, standard deviation = 4.85
       ● variance = 5.39, standard deviation = 2.32
       ● variance = 297.85, standard deviation = 17.26
**5.10**  mean = 150, standard deviation = 32.13
**5.11**  mean = 3.36, standard deviation = 1.54

## Chapter 6
## Describing changes with index numbers

**6.1**  100, 101.9, 104.7, 105.7, 111.3, 117.9, 122.6, 124.5
       80.3, 81.8, 84.1, 84.8, 89.4, 94.7, 98.5, 100
**6.2**  100, 98.8, 97.2, 90.5, 80.9, 74.2, 60.6, 45.5, 31.4, 21.5
       464.3, 458.6, 451.4, 420.0, 375.7, 344.3, 281.4, 211.4, 145.7, 100.0

**6.3**  100, 95.0, 80.2, 92.6, 105, 111.6, 125.6, 128.1, 133.1, 121.5, 109.9, 108.3
**6.4**  19 080, 23 850, 29 192, 31 864, 34 731, 39 830, 44 609, 52 575; 25%, 22%, 9%, 9%, 15%, 12%, 18%
**6.5**  261, 291, 353, 397; 45.9, 55.8, 66.7, 74.9, 84.4; 395, 481, 574, 645, 727, 861, 973, 1085, 1318, 1481
**6.6**  Base weighted indices = 106.1, 114.2; current-period weighted indices = 106.5, 114.8
**6.7**  100, 109, 115, 124; 100, 109, 116, 126
**6.8**  106.65, 106.78
**6.9**  110.6, 126.7, 144.8
**6.10**  1.85%, 0.21%

## Chapter 7
## Calculations with money

**7.1**  45 000, £48,000, £11,500
**7.2**  300; No (greater than plane capacity)
**7.3**  Probably C
**7.4**  £4661
**7.5**  £20,000 now
**7.6**  A 6133, B 18 540, C 29 856
**7.7**  A 24.95%, B 27.24%, C 37.52%
**7.8**  −5.39%
**7.9**  £2167, £2670, 49.2%
**7.10**  £15,741
**7.11**  £263.31
**7.12**  10% loan, £1288

## Chapter 8
## Relating variables by regression

**8.1**  Production manager's forecast: mean error = −1.0, MAD = 2.0, MSE = 5.6
       Foreman's forecast: mean error = −2.0, MAD = 2.0, MSE = 5.6
       Management services' forecast: mean error = 0, MAD = 1.0, MSE = 1.4
**8.2**  $y = 16.59 + 4.98x$, $r = 0.9976$
**8.3**  £493
**8.4**  $2.16 + 2.96 \times$ bonus. Coefficient of determination = 0.99
**8.5**  265.9, 293.0, 320.1, 347.2, 374.3, 401.4
**8.7**  $r_s = 0.741$
**8.8**  $r_s = 0.952$
**8.9**  $y = -158 + 13.2a + 38.8b + 4.9c + 3.1d$
**8.10**  $y = 6.47 \times 1.45^x$

# Chapter 9
# Business forecasting

**9.1** 215.5, 224.8, 234.1
**9.2** 164.4
**9.3** $F_{11} = 193$
**9.4** 2 period: MAD = 83.33, MSE = 8366.67
3 period: MAD = 76, MSE = 7422.22
4 period: MAD = 73.75, MSE = 7043.75
**9.5** 280, 276, 284.4, 290, 291, 283.9, 275.5, 283.9
280, 272, 289.6, 299.7, 299.7, 283.8, 267, 285.6
**9.6** 208.4, 209.2, 230.6, 256.2, 251.8, 247.4, 243.5
208.8, 210.2, 253, 299.6, 282.1, 267.3, 255.4
209.2, 211.2, 275.1, 338.4, 300.4, 272.7, 253.3
209.6, 212.2, 296.9, 372.5, 308.3, 268.2, 244.1
**9.7** $y = 50.6 + 1.75t$
**9.8** 36.3, 63.0, 106.4, 39.1, 67.6, 114.0
**9.9** 127.9, 192.9, 140.1
**9.10** 207.8, 238.0, 224.6, 204.2, 250.5, 284.4,
266.4, 240.5
**9.11** 133.0, 186.4, 147.0
203.9, 195.4, 228.5, 251.2, 246.1, 237.6,
270.8, 293.4

# Chapter 10
# Planning with linear programming

**10.2** X1 = 0.167, X2 = 0.167, cost = £11.67
**10.4** X = 40, Y = 20, profit = £14,000
**10.5** (b) E = 200, G = 1200, income = £116,000,
annual profit = £2.8m;
(c) spare capacity in forming (400), machine
shop (400), market for E (600) and market
for G (50);
(d) shadow prices for assembly (£10) and
testing (£20);
(e) £20 for up to 33.34 hours a week;
(f) £268
**10.6** (b) S = 20, N = 30, profit = 3,600,000Zl;
(c) spare capacity in wiring (60);
(d) shadow prices for pressing (10,000Zl)
and assembly (10,000Zl); (e) 80,000Zl;
(f) £10,000Zl
**10.7** No feasible solution

# Chapter 11
# Using calculus to describe changes

**11.1** $84x^6$
**11.2** $24.8x^3 + 9.9x^2 - 14.2x - 11.9$
Easiest to find is minimum when $x = 0.9$
**11.3** $4y - 3$

**11.4** $30, -x^2 + 30x - 30, x = 15$
**11.5** Minimum of 19.4 when $x = 1.25$
Minimum of $-8$ when $x = 1$, maximum of
100 when $x = -5$
**11.6** (a) 3, (b) 6.67, (c) 6

# Chapter 12
# Uncertainty and probabilities

**12.1** (a) 0.15, (b) 0.08, (c) 0.48, (d) 0.56, (e) 0.44,
(f) 0.22
**12.2** (a) 0.2, (b) 0.6, (c) 0.6
**12.3** (a) 0, (b) 0.3, (c) 0.7, (d) 0, (e) 0.6, (f) 0.4
**12.4** (a) 1/13, (b) 1/4, (c) 1/52, (d) 16/52
**12.5** (a) 0.125, (b) 0.5, (c) 0.125
**12.6** 0.589
**12.7** 0.12, 0.2
**12.8**

|   | A | B | C |
|---|---|---|---|
| X | 0.18 | 0.77 | 0.4 |
| Y | 0.82 | 0.23 | 0.6 |

**12.9**

|   | G | A | P |
|---|---|---|---|
| X | 0.38 | 0.34 | 0.40 |
| Y | 0.41 | 0.22 | 0.15 |
| Z | 0.22 | 0.44 | 0.45 |

**12.11** 0.57
**12.12** 0.67
**12.13** 248, 49

# Chapter 13
# Probability distributions

**13.1**

| 10 | 11 | 12 | 13 | 14 | 15 | 16 | 17 |
|---|---|---|---|---|---|---|---|
| 0.025 | 0.075 | 0.125 | 0.175 | 0.275 | 0.175 | 0.125 | 0.025 |

**13.2** 0.5, 0.2
**13.3** (a) 3003, 360 360, (b) 45, 90,
(c) 45, 1 814 400
**13.4** 3 628 800, 1 814 400
**13.5** 479 001 600, 495, 19 958 400
**13.6** 1.2, 1.01 (a) 0.2376, (b) 0, (c) 0.0002
**13.7** 0.1672, 0
**13.8** $0.1 \times 10^{-11}$, 0.2824, 0.3766, 0.1109
**13.9** 2, 1.414 (a) 0.2707, (b) 0.0034, (c) 0.0165
**13.10** 1.08, $P(0) = 0.3329$, $P(1) = 0.3662$,
$P(2) = 0.2014$, $P(3) = 0.0738$,
$P(4) = 0.0203$, $P(5) = 0.0045$, etc

**13.11** 0.0778
**13.12** 0.642, 0.564
**13.13** (a) 0.0668, (b) 0.0668, (c) 0.8664,
(d) 0.8351, (e) 0.1865
**13.14** (a) 0.0228, (b) 0.1587, (c) 0.8185,
(d) 0.1359, (e) 0.6247
**13.15** (a) 0.0475, (b) 0.0062, (c) 0.5934, (d) 5232
**13.16** Mean = 15 minutes, variance = 5 minutes
(reasonably); 0.0901, 0.0125

# Chapter 14
# Using samples in business

**14.1** 0.0228
**14.2** 105.44–107.56, 105.11–107.89
**14.3** Yes, the probability equals 0.0681
**14.4** 123.33–127.67, 122.92–128.08
**14.5** Mean = 6.4 minutes, standard
deviation = 3.87 minutes
**14.6** 0.035–0.125, 0.027–0.133
**14.7** (a) 61.5, (b) 96.0, (c) 245.9
**14.8** 971
**14.9** (a) 230.86, (b) 224.59–231.41
**14.10** (a) 0.339, (b) 0.141, (c) 0.141–0.339
**14.11** (a) 90.64–109.36, (b) 87.21–112.79
**14.12** (a) 39.94–64.06, (b) 36.95–67.05,
(c) 43.58–60.42, (d) 44.11–59.89
**14.13** 0.0544 – 0.1356, 0.0416 – 0.1484

# Chapter 15
# Testing hypotheses

**15.1** (a) 367.33 – 432.67, (b) 357 – 443
**15.2** No
**15.3** The claim can be rejected
**15.4** No
**15.5** Yes
**15.6** The claim cannot be rejected
**15.7** No
**15.8** The claim can be rejected
**15.9** The claim cannot be rejected at 1%
significance level
**15.10** Reject the manufacturer's claim
**15.11** Yes
**15.12** Cannot reject hypothesis
**15.13** Cannot reject hypothesis
**15.14** Can reject hypothesis

# Chapter 16
# Analysing business decisions

**16.2** b or e
**16.3** (a) d, d, d, (b) d, d, d

**16.4** (a) a, (b) a
**16.5** Z, 2.66
**16.6** £592
**16.7** £70.35
**16.8** £139,500

# Chapter 17
# Controlling stocks

**17.1** 20, 0.2, £5200
**17.2** 212, 0.042, £101,060
**17.3** (a) 20, (b) 40
**17.4** (a) 120, (b) 30, (c) £580,800
**17.5** (a) 4328, (b) 4410
**17.6** $Q = 100$, ROL = 328.4, cost = £41,284 a
week, ROL = 322.2, cost = £41,222 a week
**17.7** TSLs = 6402, 6502
**17.9** $Q = 1000$

# Chapter 18
# Planning projects with networks

**18.4**

| Activity | Duration | Earliest start | Earliest finish | Latest start | Latest finish | Total float |
|---|---|---|---|---|---|---|
| A | 1 | 3 | 4 | 3 | 4 | 0 |
| B | 1 | 3 | 4 | 3 | 4 | 0 |
| C | 1 | 3 | 4 | 6 | 7 | 3 |
| D | 1 | 6 | 7 | 6 | 7 | 0 |
| E | 1 | 1 | 2 | 1 | 2 | 0 |
| F | 1 | 0 | 1 | 0 | 1 | 0 |
| G | 1 | 2 | 3 | 6 | 7 | 4 |
| H | 1 | 2 | 3 | 2 | 3 | 0 |
| I | 1 | 1 | 2 | 5 | 6 | 4 |
| J | 1 | 2 | 3 | 6 | 7 | 4 |
| K | 1 | 2 | 3 | 5 | 6 | 3 |
| L | 1 | 1 | 2 | 4 | 5 | 3 |
| M | 1 | 5 | 6 | 5 | 6 | 0 |
| N | 1 | 3 | 4 | 5 | 6 | 2 |
| O | 1 | 4 | 5 | 4 | 5 | 0 |
| P | 1 | 4 | 5 | 6 | 7 | 2 |

**18.5** 14 weeks, A, B, C, D, E, F
**18.6** (a) 34 weeks, (b) any convenient time starting
between weeks 8 and 17,
(c) 2 weeks delay
**18.9** 14

# Chapter 19
# Queues and simulation

**19.1** $P(0) = 0.167$, $P(n) = 0.167 \times (0.833)^n$,
$L = 5$, $L_q = 4.167$, $W = 0.05$, $W_q = 0.04$
**19.2** £100 an hour
**19.3** 2

# Appendix D

# Probabilities for the binomial distribution

|       |     |       |       |       |       | $p$   |       |       |       |       |       |
|-------|-----|-------|-------|-------|-------|-------|-------|-------|-------|-------|-------|
| $n$   | $r$ | .05   | .10   | .15   | .20   | .25   | .30   | .35   | .40   | .45   | .50   |
| 1     | 0   | .9500 | .9000 | .8500 | .8000 | .7500 | .7000 | .6500 | .6000 | .5500 | .5000 |
|       | 1   | .0500 | .1000 | .1500 | .2000 | .2500 | .3000 | .3500 | .4000 | .4500 | .5000 |
| 2     | 0   | .9025 | .8100 | .7225 | .6400 | .5625 | .4900 | .4225 | .3600 | .3025 | .2500 |
|       | 1   | .0950 | .1800 | .2550 | .3200 | .3750 | .4200 | .4550 | .4800 | .4950 | .5000 |
|       | 2   | .0025 | .0100 | .0225 | .0400 | .0625 | .0900 | .1225 | .1600 | .2025 | .2500 |
| 3     | 0   | .8574 | .7290 | .6141 | .5120 | .4219 | .3430 | .2746 | .2160 | .1664 | .1250 |
|       | 1   | .1354 | .2430 | .3251 | .3840 | .4219 | .4410 | .4436 | .4320 | .4084 | .3750 |
|       | 2   | .0071 | .0270 | .0574 | .0960 | .1406 | .1890 | .2389 | .2880 | .3341 | .3750 |
|       | 3   | .0001 | .0010 | .0034 | .0080 | .0156 | .0270 | .0429 | .0640 | .0911 | .1250 |
| 4     | 0   | .8145 | .6561 | .5220 | .4096 | .3164 | .2401 | .1785 | .1296 | .0915 | .0625 |
|       | 1   | .1715 | .2916 | .3685 | .4096 | .4219 | .4116 | .3845 | .3456 | .2995 | .2500 |
|       | 2   | .0135 | .0486 | .0975 | .1536 | .2109 | .2646 | .3105 | .3456 | .3675 | .3750 |
|       | 3   | .0005 | .0036 | .0115 | .0256 | .0469 | .0756 | .1115 | .1536 | .2005 | .2500 |
|       | 4   | .0000 | .0001 | .0005 | .0016 | .0039 | .0081 | .0150 | .0256 | .0410 | .0625 |
| 5     | 0   | .7738 | .5905 | .4437 | .3277 | .2373 | .1681 | .1160 | .0778 | .0503 | .0312 |
|       | 1   | .2036 | .3280 | .3915 | .4096 | .3955 | .3602 | .3124 | .2592 | .2059 | .1562 |
|       | 2   | .0214 | .0729 | .1382 | .2048 | .2637 | .3087 | .3364 | .3456 | .3369 | .3125 |
|       | 3   | .0011 | .0081 | .0244 | .0512 | .0879 | .1323 | .1811 | .2304 | .2757 | .3125 |
|       | 4   | .0000 | .0004 | .0022 | .0064 | .0146 | .0284 | .0488 | .0768 | .1128 | .1562 |
|       | 5   | .0000 | .0000 | .0001 | .0003 | .0010 | .0024 | .0053 | .0102 | .0185 | .0312 |
| 6     | 0   | .7351 | .5314 | .3771 | .2621 | .1780 | .1176 | .0754 | .0467 | .0277 | .0156 |
|       | 1   | .2321 | .3543 | .3993 | .3932 | .3560 | .3025 | .2437 | .1866 | .1359 | .0938 |
|       | 2   | .0305 | .0984 | .1762 | .2458 | .2966 | .3241 | .3280 | .3110 | .2780 | .2344 |
|       | 3   | .0021 | .0146 | .0415 | .0819 | .1318 | .1852 | .2355 | .2765 | .3032 | .3125 |
|       | 4   | .0001 | .0012 | .0055 | .0154 | .0330 | .0595 | .0951 | .1382 | .1861 | .2344 |
|       | 5   | .0000 | .0001 | .0004 | .0015 | .0044 | .0102 | .0205 | .0369 | .0609 | .0938 |
|       | 6   | .0000 | .0000 | .0000 | .0001 | .0002 | .0007 | .0018 | .0041 | .0083 | .0516 |

|  |  |  |  |  |  | *p* |  |  |  |  |  |
| --- | --- | --- | --- | --- | --- | --- | --- | --- | --- | --- | --- |
| *n* | *r* | .05 | .10 | .15 | .20 | .25 | .30 | .35 | .40 | .45 | .50 |
| 7 | 0 | .6983 | .4783 | .3206 | .2097 | .1335 | .0824 | .0490 | .0280 | .0152 | .0078 |
|  | 1 | .2573 | .3720 | .3960 | .3670 | .3115 | .2471 | .1848 | .1306 | .0872 | .0547 |
|  | 2 | .0406 | .1240 | .2097 | .2753 | .3115 | .3177 | .2985 | .2613 | .2140 | .1641 |
|  | 3 | .0036 | .0230 | .0617 | .1147 | .1730 | .2269 | .2679 | .2903 | .2918 | .2734 |
|  | 4 | .0002 | .0026 | .0109 | .0287 | .0577 | .0972 | .1442 | .1935 | .2388 | .2734 |
|  | 5 | .0009 | .0002 | .0012 | .0043 | .0115 | .0250 | .0466 | .0774 | .1172 | .1641 |
|  | 6 | .0000 | .0000 | .0001 | .0004 | .0013 | .0036 | .0084 | .0172 | .0320 | .0547 |
|  | 7 | .0000 | .0000 | .0000 | .0000 | .0001 | .0002 | .0006 | .0016 | .0037 | .0078 |
| 8 | 0 | .6634 | .4305 | .2725 | .1678 | .1001 | .0576 | .0319 | .0168 | .0084 | .0039 |
|  | 1 | .2793 | .3826 | .3847 | .3355 | .2670 | .1977 | .1373 | .0896 | .0548 | .0312 |
|  | 2 | .0515 | .1488 | .2376 | .2936 | .3115 | .2965 | .2587 | .2090 | .1569 | .1094 |
|  | 3 | .0054 | .0331 | .0839 | .1468 | .2076 | .2541 | .2786 | .2787 | .2568 | .2188 |
|  | 4 | .0004 | .0046 | .0185 | .0459 | .0865 | .1361 | .1875 | .2322 | .2627 | .2734 |
|  | 5 | .0000 | .0004 | .0026 | .0092 | .0231 | .0467 | .0808 | .1239 | .1719 | .2188 |
|  | 6 | .0000 | .0000 | .0002 | .0011 | .0038 | .0100 | .0217 | .0413 | .0703 | .1094 |
|  | 7 | .0000 | .0000 | .0000 | .0001 | .0004 | .0012 | .0033 | .0079 | .0164 | .0312 |
|  | 8 | .0000 | .0000 | .0000 | .0000 | .0000 | .0001 | .0002 | .0007 | .0017 | .0039 |
| 9 | 0 | .6302 | .3874 | .2316 | .1342 | .0751 | .0404 | .0207 | .0101 | .0046 | .0020 |
|  | 1 | .2985 | .3874 | .3679 | .3020 | .2253 | .1556 | .1004 | .0605 | .0339 | .0176 |
|  | 2 | .0629 | .1722 | .2597 | .3020 | .3003 | .2668 | .2162 | .1612 | .1110 | .0703 |
|  | 3 | .0077 | .0446 | .1069 | .1762 | .2336 | .2668 | .2716 | .2508 | .2119 | .1641 |
|  | 4 | .0006 | .0074 | .0283 | .0661 | .1168 | .1715 | .2194 | .2508 | .2600 | .2461 |
|  | 5 | .0000 | .0008 | .0050 | .0165 | .0389 | .0735 | .1181 | .1672 | .2128 | .2461 |
|  | 6 | .0000 | .0001 | .0006 | .0028 | .0087 | .0210 | .0424 | .0743 | .1160 | .1641 |
|  | 7 | .0000 | .0000 | .0000 | .0003 | .0012 | .0039 | .0098 | .0212 | .0407 | .0703 |
|  | 8 | .0000 | .0000 | .0000 | .0000 | .0001 | .0004 | .0013 | .0035 | .0083 | .0716 |
|  | 9 | .0000 | .0000 | .0000 | .0000 | .0000 | .0000 | .0001 | .0003 | .0008 | .0020 |
| 10 | 0 | .5987 | .3487 | .1969 | .1074 | .0563 | .0282 | .0135 | .0060 | .0025 | .0010 |
|  | 1 | .3151 | .3874 | .3474 | .2684 | .1877 | .1211 | .0725 | .0403 | .0207 | .0098 |
|  | 2 | .0746 | .1937 | .2759 | .3020 | .2816 | .2335 | .1757 | .1209 | .0763 | .0439 |
|  | 3 | .0105 | .0574 | .1298 | .2013 | .2503 | .2668 | .2522 | .2150 | .1665 | .1172 |
|  | 4 | .0010 | .0112 | .0401 | .0881 | .1460 | .2001 | .2377 | .2508 | .2384 | .2051 |
|  | 5 | .0001 | .0015 | .0085 | .0264 | .0584 | .1029 | .1563 | .2007 | .2340 | .2461 |
|  | 6 | .0000 | .0001 | .0012 | .0055 | .0162 | .0368 | .0689 | .1115 | .1596 | .2051 |
|  | 7 | .0000 | .0000 | .0001 | .0008 | .0031 | .0090 | .0212 | .0425 | .0746 | .1172 |
|  | 8 | .0000 | .0000 | .0000 | .0001 | .0004 | .0014 | .0043 | .0106 | .0229 | .0439 |
|  | 9 | .0000 | .0000 | .0000 | .0000 | .0000 | .0001 | .0005 | .0016 | .0042 | .0098 |
|  | 10 | .0000 | .0000 | .0000 | .0000 | .0000 | .0000 | .0000 | .0001 | .0003 | .0010 |

|   |   | | | | | $p$ | | | | | |
| $n$ | $r$ | .05 | .10 | .15 | .20 | .25 | .30 | .35 | .40 | .45 | .50 |
|---|---|---|---|---|---|---|---|---|---|---|---|
| 11 | 0 | .5688 | .3138 | .1673 | .0859 | .0422 | .0198 | .0088 | .0036 | .0014 | .0005 |
|   | 1 | .3293 | .3835 | .3248 | .2362 | .1549 | .0932 | .0518 | .0266 | .0125 | .0054 |
|   | 2 | .0867 | .2131 | .2866 | .2953 | .2581 | .1998 | .1395 | .0887 | .0513 | .0269 |
|   | 3 | .0137 | .0710 | .1517 | .2215 | .2581 | .2568 | .2254 | .1774 | .1259 | .0806 |
|   | 4 | .0014 | .0158 | .0536 | .1107 | .1721 | .2201 | .2428 | .2365 | .2060 | .1611 |
|   | 5 | .0001 | .0025 | .0132 | .0388 | .0803 | .1321 | .1830 | .2207 | .2360 | .2256 |
|   | 6 | .0000 | .0003 | .0023 | .0097 | .0268 | .0566 | .0985 | .1471 | .1931 | .2256 |
|   | 7 | .0000 | .0000 | .0003 | .0017 | .0064 | .0173 | .0379 | .0701 | .1128 | .1611 |
|   | 8 | .0000 | .0000 | .0000 | .0002 | .0011 | .0037 | .0102 | .0234 | .0462 | .0806 |
|   | 9 | .0000 | .0000 | .0000 | .0000 | .0001 | .0005 | .0018 | .0052 | .0126 | .0269 |
|   | 10 | .0000 | .0000 | .0000 | .0000 | .0000 | .0000 | .0002 | .0007 | .0021 | .0054 |
|   | 11 | .0000 | .0000 | .0000 | .0000 | .0000 | .0000 | .0000 | .0000 | .0002 | .0005 |
| 12 | 0 | .5404 | .2824 | .1422 | .0687 | .0317 | .0138 | .0057 | .0022 | .0008 | .0002 |
|   | 1 | .3413 | .3766 | .3012 | .2062 | .1267 | .0712 | .0368 | .0174 | .0075 | .0029 |
|   | 2 | .0988 | .2301 | .2924 | .2835 | .2323 | .1678 | .1088 | .0639 | .0339 | .0161 |
|   | 3 | .0173 | .0852 | .1720 | .2362 | .2581 | .2397 | .1954 | .1419 | .0923 | .0537 |
|   | 4 | .0021 | .0213 | .0683 | .1329 | .1936 | .2311 | .2367 | .2128 | .1700 | .1208 |
|   | 5 | .0002 | .0038 | .0193 | .0532 | .1032 | .1585 | .2039 | .2270 | .2225 | .1934 |
|   | 6 | .0000 | .0005 | .0040 | .0155 | .0401 | .0792 | .1281 | .1766 | .2124 | .2256 |
|   | 7 | .0000 | .0000 | .0006 | .0033 | .0115 | .0291 | .0591 | .1009 | .1489 | .1934 |
|   | 8 | .0000 | .0000 | .0001 | .0005 | .0024 | .0078 | .0199 | .0420 | .0762 | .1208 |
|   | 9 | .0000 | .0000 | .0000 | .0001 | .0004 | .0015 | .0048 | .0125 | .0277 | .0537 |
|   | 10 | .0000 | .0000 | .0000 | .0000 | .0000 | .0002 | .0008 | .0025 | .0068 | .0161 |
|   | 11 | .0000 | .0000 | .0000 | .0000 | .0000 | .0000 | .0001 | .0003 | .0010 | .0029 |
|   | 12 | .0000 | .0000 | .0000 | .0000 | .0000 | .0000 | .0000 | .0000 | .0001 | .0002 |
| 13 | 0 | .5133 | .2542 | .1209 | .0550 | .0238 | .0097 | .0037 | .0013 | .0004 | .0001 |
|   | 1 | .3512 | .3672 | .2774 | .1787 | .1029 | .0540 | .0259 | .0113 | .0045 | .0016 |
|   | 2 | .1109 | .2448 | .2937 | .2680 | .2059 | .1388 | .0836 | .0453 | .0220 | .0095 |
|   | 3 | .0214 | .0997 | .1900 | .2457 | .2517 | .2181 | .1651 | .1107 | .0660 | .0349 |
|   | 4 | .0028 | .0277 | .0838 | .1535 | .2097 | .2337 | .2222 | .1845 | .1350 | .0873 |
|   | 5 | .0003 | .0055 | .0266 | .0691 | .1258 | .1803 | .2154 | .2214 | .1989 | .1571 |
|   | 6 | .0000 | .0008 | .0063 | .0230 | .0559 | .1030 | .1546 | .1968 | .2169 | .2095 |
|   | 7 | .0000 | .0001 | .0011 | .0058 | .0186 | .0442 | .0833 | .1312 | .1775 | .2095 |
|   | 8 | .0000 | .0000 | .0001 | .0011 | .0047 | .0142 | .0336 | .0656 | .1089 | .1571 |
|   | 9 | .0000 | .0000 | .0000 | .0001 | .0009 | .0034 | .0101 | .0243 | .0495 | .0873 |
|   | 10 | .0000 | .0000 | .0000 | .0000 | .0001 | .0006 | .0022 | .0065 | .0162 | .0349 |
|   | 11 | .0000 | .0000 | .0000 | .0000 | .0000 | .0001 | .0003 | .0012 | .0036 | .0095 |
|   | 12 | .0000 | .0000 | .0000 | .0000 | .0000 | .0000 | .0000 | .0001 | .0005 | .0016 |
|   | 13 | .0000 | .0000 | .0000 | .0000 | .0000 | .0000 | .0000 | .0000 | .0000 | .0001 |

| $n$ | $r$ | .05 | .10 | .15 | .20 | $p$ .25 | .30 | .35 | .40 | .45 | .50 |
|---|---|---|---|---|---|---|---|---|---|---|---|
| 14 | 0 | .4877 | .2288 | .1028 | .0440 | .0178 | .0068 | .0024 | .0008 | .0002 | .0001 |
|  | 1 | .3593 | .3559 | .2539 | .1539 | .0832 | .0407 | .0181 | .0073 | .0027 | .0009 |
|  | 2 | .1229 | .2570 | .2912 | .2501 | .1802 | .1134 | .0634 | .0317 | .0141 | .0056 |
|  | 3 | .0259 | .1142 | .2056 | .2501 | .2402 | .1943 | .1366 | .0845 | .0462 | .0222 |
|  | 4 | .0037 | .0348 | .0998 | .1720 | .2202 | .2290 | .2022 | .1549 | .1040 | .0611 |
|  | 5 | .0004 | .0078 | .0352 | .0860 | .1468 | .1963 | .2178 | .2066 | .1701 | .1222 |
|  | 6 | .0000 | .0013 | .0093 | .0322 | .0734 | .1262 | .1759 | .2066 | .2088 | .1833 |
|  | 7 | .0000 | .0002 | .0019 | .0092 | .0280 | .0618 | .1082 | .1574 | .1952 | .2095 |
|  | 8 | .0000 | .0000 | .0003 | .0020 | .0082 | .0232 | .0510 | .0918 | .1398 | .1833 |
|  | 9 | .0000 | .0000 | .0000 | .0003 | .0018 | .0066 | .0183 | .0408 | .0762 | .1222 |
|  | 10 | .0000 | .0000 | .0000 | .0000 | .0003 | .0014 | .0049 | .0136 | .0312 | .0611 |
|  | 11 | .0000 | .0000 | .0000 | .0000 | .0000 | .0002 | .0010 | .0033 | .0093 | .0222 |
|  | 12 | .0000 | .0000 | .0000 | .0000 | .0000 | .0000 | .0001 | .0005 | .0019 | .0056 |
|  | 13 | .0000 | .0000 | .0000 | .0000 | .0000 | .0000 | .0000 | .0001 | .0002 | .0009 |
|  | 14 | .0000 | .0000 | .0000 | .0000 | .0000 | .0000 | .0000 | .0000 | .0000 | .0001 |
| 15 | 0 | .4633 | .2059 | .0874 | .0352 | .0134 | .0047 | .0016 | .0005 | .0001 | .0000 |
|  | 1 | .3658 | .3432 | .2312 | .1319 | .0668 | .0305 | .0126 | .0047 | .0016 | .0005 |
|  | 2 | .1348 | .2669 | .2856 | .2309 | .1559 | .0916 | .0476 | .0219 | .0090 | .0032 |
|  | 3 | .0307 | .1285 | .2184 | .2501 | .2252 | .1700 | .1110 | .0634 | .0318 | .0139 |
|  | 4 | .0049 | .0428 | .1156 | .1876 | .2252 | .2186 | .1792 | .1268 | .0780 | .0417 |
|  | 5 | .0006 | .0105 | .0449 | .1032 | .1651 | .2061 | .2123 | .1859 | .1404 | .0916 |
|  | 6 | .0000 | .0019 | .0132 | .0430 | .0917 | .1472 | .1906 | .2066 | .1914 | .1527 |
|  | 7 | .0000 | .0003 | .0030 | .0138 | .0393 | .0811 | .1319 | .1771 | .2013 | .1964 |
|  | 8 | .0000 | .0000 | .0005 | .0035 | .0131 | .0348 | .0710 | .1181 | .1647 | .1964 |
|  | 9 | .0000 | .0000 | .0001 | .0007 | .0034 | .0116 | .0298 | .0612 | .1048 | .1527 |
|  | 10 | .0000 | .0000 | .0000 | .0001 | .0007 | .0030 | .0096 | .0245 | .0515 | .0916 |
|  | 11 | .0000 | .0000 | .0000 | .0000 | .0001 | .0006 | .0024 | .0074 | .0191 | .0417 |
|  | 12 | .0000 | .0000 | .0000 | .0000 | .0000 | .0001 | .0004 | .0016 | .0052 | .0139 |
|  | 13 | .0000 | .0000 | .0000 | .0000 | .0000 | .0000 | .0001 | .0003 | .0010 | .0032 |
|  | 14 | .0000 | .0000 | .0000 | .0000 | .0000 | .0000 | .0000 | .0000 | .0001 | .0005 |
|  | 15 | .0000 | .0000 | .0000 | .0000 | .0000 | .0000 | .0000 | .0000 | .0000 | .0000 |

|   |   |   |   |   | | $p$ | | | | | |
| n | r | .05 | .10 | .15 | .20 | .25 | .30 | .35 | .40 | .45 | .50 |
|---|---|-----|-----|-----|-----|-----|-----|-----|-----|-----|-----|
| 16 | 0 | .4401 | .1853 | .0743 | .0281 | .0100 | .0033 | .0010 | .0003 | .0001 | .0000 |
|    | 1 | .3706 | .3294 | .2097 | .1126 | .0535 | .0228 | .0087 | .0030 | .0009 | .0002 |
|    | 2 | .1463 | .2745 | .2775 | .2111 | .1336 | .0732 | .0353 | .0150 | .0056 | .0018 |
|    | 3 | .0359 | .1423 | .2285 | .2463 | .2079 | .1465 | .0888 | .0468 | .0215 | .0085 |
|    | 4 | .0061 | .0514 | .1311 | .2001 | .2252 | .2040 | .1553 | .1014 | .0572 | .0278 |
|    | 5 | .0008 | .0137 | .0555 | .1201 | .1802 | .2099 | .2008 | .1623 | .1123 | .0667 |
|    | 6 | .0001 | .0028 | .0180 | .0550 | .1101 | .1649 | .1982 | .1983 | .1684 | .1222 |
|    | 7 | .0000 | .0004 | .0045 | .0197 | .0524 | .1010 | .1524 | .1889 | .1969 | .1746 |
|    | 8 | .0000 | .0001 | .0009 | .0055 | .0197 | .0487 | .0923 | .1417 | .1812 | .1964 |
|    | 9 | .0000 | .0000 | .0001 | .0012 | .0058 | .0185 | .0442 | .0840 | .1318 | .1746 |
|    | 10 | .0000 | .0000 | .0000 | .0002 | .0014 | .0056 | .0167 | .0392 | .0755 | .1222 |
|    | 11 | .0000 | .0000 | .0000 | .0000 | .0002 | .0013 | .0049 | .0142 | .0337 | .0667 |
|    | 12 | .0000 | .0000 | .0000 | .0000 | .0000 | .0002 | .0011 | .0040 | .0115 | .0278 |
|    | 13 | .0000 | .0000 | .0000 | .0000 | .0000 | .0000 | .0002 | .0008 | .0029 | .0085 |
|    | 14 | .0000 | .0000 | .0000 | .0000 | .0000 | .0000 | .0000 | .0001 | .0005 | .0018 |
|    | 15 | .0000 | .0000 | .0000 | .0000 | .0000 | .0000 | .0000 | .0000 | .0001 | .0002 |
|    | 16 | .0000 | .0000 | .0000 | .0000 | .0000 | .0000 | .0000 | .0000 | .0000 | .0000 |
| 17 | 0 | .4181 | .1668 | .0631 | .0225 | .0075 | .0023 | .0007 | .0002 | .0000 | .0000 |
|    | 1 | .3741 | .3150 | .1893 | .0957 | .0426 | .0169 | .0060 | .0019 | .0005 | .0001 |
|    | 2 | .1575 | .2800 | .2673 | .1914 | .1136 | .0581 | .0260 | .0102 | .0035 | .0010 |
|    | 3 | .0415 | .1556 | .2359 | .2393 | .1893 | .1245 | .0701 | .0341 | .0144 | .0052 |
|    | 4 | .0076 | .0605 | .1457 | .2093 | .2209 | .1868 | .1320 | .0796 | .0411 | .0182 |
|    | 5 | .0010 | .0175 | .0668 | .1361 | .1914 | .2081 | .1849 | .1379 | .0875 | .0472 |
|    | 6 | .0001 | .0039 | .0236 | .0680 | .1276 | .1784 | .1991 | .1839 | .1432 | .0944 |
|    | 7 | .0000 | .0007 | .0065 | .0267 | .0668 | .1201 | .1685 | .1927 | .1841 | .1484 |
|    | 8 | .0000 | .0001 | .0014 | .0084 | .0279 | .0644 | .1134 | .1606 | .1883 | .1855 |
|    | 9 | .0000 | .0000 | .0003 | .0021 | .0093 | .0276 | .0611 | .1070 | .1540 | .1855 |
|    | 10 | .0000 | .0000 | .0000 | .0004 | .0025 | .0095 | .0263 | .0571 | .1008 | .1484 |
|    | 11 | .0000 | .0000 | .0000 | .0001 | .0005 | .0026 | .0090 | .0242 | .0525 | .0944 |
|    | 12 | .0000 | .0000 | .0000 | .0000 | .0001 | .0006 | .0024 | .0081 | .0215 | .0472 |
|    | 13 | .0000 | .0000 | .0000 | .0000 | .0000 | .0001 | .0005 | .0021 | .0068 | .0182 |
|    | 14 | .0000 | .0000 | .0000 | .0000 | .0000 | .0000 | .0001 | .0004 | .0016 | .0052 |
|    | 15 | .0000 | .0000 | .0000 | .0000 | .0000 | .0000 | .0000 | .0001 | .0003 | .0010 |
|    | 16 | .0000 | .0000 | .0000 | .0000 | .0000 | .0000 | .0000 | .0000 | .0000 | .0001 |
|    | 17 | .0000 | .0000 | .0000 | .0000 | .0000 | .0000 | .0000 | .0000 | .0000 | .0000 |

# Appendix E

# Probabilities for the Poisson distribution

| | | | | | $\mu$ | | | | | |
|---|---|---|---|---|---|---|---|---|---|---|
| r | .005 | .01 | .02 | .03 | .04 | .05 | .06 | .07 | .08 | .09 |
| 0 | .9950 | .9900 | .9802 | .9704 | .9608 | .9512 | .9418 | .9324 | .9231 | .9139 |
| 1 | .0050 | .0099 | .0192 | .0291 | .0384 | .0476 | .0565 | .0653 | .0738 | .0823 |
| 2 | .0000 | .0000 | .0002 | .0004 | .0008 | .0012 | .0017 | .0023 | .0030 | .0037 |
| 3 | .0000 | .0000 | .0000 | .0000 | .0000 | .0000 | .0000 | .0001 | .0001 | .0001 |

| | | | | | $\mu$ | | | | | |
|---|---|---|---|---|---|---|---|---|---|---|
| r | 0.1 | 0.2 | 0.3 | 0.4 | 0.5 | 0.6 | 0.7 | 0.8 | 0.9 | 1.0 |
| 0 | .9048 | .8187 | .7408 | .6703 | .6065 | .5488 | .4966 | .4493 | .4066 | .3679 |
| 1 | .0905 | .1637 | .2222 | .2681 | .3033 | .3293 | .3476 | .3595 | .3659 | .3679 |
| 2 | .0045 | .0164 | .0333 | .0536 | .0758 | .0988 | .1217 | .1438 | .1647 | .1839 |
| 3 | .0002 | .0011 | .0033 | .0072 | .0126 | .0198 | .0284 | .0383 | .0494 | .0613 |
| 4 | .0000 | .0001 | .0002 | .0007 | .0016 | .0030 | .0050 | .0077 | .0111 | .0153 |
| 5 | .0000 | .0000 | .0000 | .0001 | .0002 | .0004 | .0007 | .0012 | .0020 | .0031 |
| 6 | .0000 | .0000 | .0000 | .0000 | .0000 | .0000 | .0001 | .0002 | .0003 | .0005 |
| 7 | .0000 | .0000 | .0000 | .0000 | .0000 | .0000 | .0000 | .0000 | .0000 | .0001 |

| | | | | | $\mu$ | | | | | |
|---|---|---|---|---|---|---|---|---|---|---|
| r | 1.1 | 1.2 | 1.3 | 1.4 | 1.5 | 1.6 | 1.7 | 1.8 | 1.9 | 2.0 |
| 0 | .3329 | .3012 | .2725 | .2466 | .2231 | .2019 | .1827 | .1653 | .1496 | .1353 |
| 1 | .3662 | .3614 | .3543 | .3452 | .3347 | .3230 | .3106 | .2975 | .2842 | .2707 |
| 2 | .2014 | .2169 | .2303 | .2417 | .2510 | .2584 | .2640 | .2678 | .2700 | .2707 |
| 3 | .0738 | .0867 | .0998 | .1128 | .1255 | .1378 | .1496 | .1607 | .1710 | .1804 |
| 4 | .0203 | .0260 | .0324 | .0395 | .0471 | .0551 | .0636 | .0723 | .0812 | .0902 |
| 5 | .0045 | .0062 | .0084 | .0111 | .0141 | .0176 | .0216 | .0260 | .0309 | .0361 |
| 6 | .0008 | .0012 | .0018 | .0026 | .0035 | .0047 | .0061 | .0078 | .0098 | .0120 |
| 7 | .0001 | .0002 | .0003 | .0005 | .0008 | .0011 | .0015 | .0020 | .0027 | .0034 |
| 8 | .0000 | .0000 | .0001 | .0001 | .0001 | .0002 | .0003 | .0005 | .0006 | .0009 |
| 9 | .0000 | .0000 | .0000 | .0000 | .0000 | .0000 | .0001 | .0001 | .0001 | .0002 |

| $r$ | 2.1 | 2.2 | 2.3 | 2.4 | $\mu$ 2.5 | 2.6 | 2.7 | 2.8 | 2.9 | 3.0 |
|---|---|---|---|---|---|---|---|---|---|---|
| 0 | .1225 | .1108 | .1003 | .0907 | .0821 | .0743 | .0672 | .0608 | .0550 | .0498 |
| 1 | .2527 | .2438 | .2306 | .2177 | .2052 | .1931 | .1815 | .1703 | .1596 | .1494 |
| 2 | .2700 | .2681 | .2652 | .2613 | .2565 | .2510 | .2450 | .2384 | .2314 | .2240 |
| 3 | .1890 | .1966 | .2033 | .2090 | .2138 | .2176 | .2205 | .2225 | .2237 | .2240 |
| 4 | .0992 | .1082 | .1196 | .1254 | .1336 | .1414 | .1488 | .1557 | .1662 | .1680 |
| 5 | .0417 | .0476 | .0538 | .0602 | .0668 | .0735 | .0804 | .0872 | .0940 | .1008 |
| 6 | .0146 | .0174 | .0206 | .0241 | .0278 | .0319 | .0362 | .0407 | .0455 | .0504 |
| 7 | .0044 | .0055 | .0068 | .0083 | .0099 | .0118 | .0139 | .0163 | .0188 | .0216 |
| 8 | .0011 | .0015 | .0019 | .0025 | .0031 | .0038 | .0047 | .0057 | .0068 | .0081 |
| 9 | .0003 | .0004 | .0005 | .0007 | .0009 | .0011 | .0014 | .0018 | .0022 | .0027 |
| 10 | .0001 | .0001 | .0001 | .0002 | .0002 | .0003 | .0004 | .0005 | .0006 | .0008 |
| 11 | .0000 | .0000 | .0000 | .0000 | .0000 | .0001 | .0001 | .0001 | .0002 | .0002 |
| 12 | .0000 | .0000 | .0000 | .0000 | .0000 | .0000 | .0000 | .0000 | .0000 | .0001 |

| $\mu$ $r$ | 3.1 | 3.2 | 3.3 | 3.4 | 3.5 | 3.6 | 3.7 | 3.8 | 3.9 | 4.0 |
|---|---|---|---|---|---|---|---|---|---|---|
| 0 | .0450 | .0408 | .0369 | .0334 | .0302 | .0273 | .0247 | .0224 | .0202 | .0183 |
| 1 | .1397 | .1304 | .1217 | .1135 | .1057 | .0984 | .0915 | .0850 | .0789 | .0733 |
| 2 | .2165 | .2087 | .2008 | .1929 | .1850 | .1771 | .1692 | .1615 | .1539 | .1465 |
| 3 | .2237 | .2226 | .2209 | .2186 | .2158 | .2125 | .2087 | .2046 | .2001 | .1954 |
| 4 | .1734 | .1781 | .1823 | .1858 | .1888 | .1912 | .1931 | .1944 | .1951 | .1954 |
| 5 | .1075 | .1140 | .1203 | .1264 | .1322 | .1377 | .1429 | .1477 | .1522 | .1563 |
| 6 | .0555 | .0608 | .0662 | .0716 | .0771 | .0826 | .0881 | .0936 | .0989 | .1042 |
| 7 | .0246 | .0278 | .0312 | .0348 | .0385 | .0425 | .0466 | .0508 | .0551 | .0595 |
| 8 | .0095 | .0111 | .0129 | .0148 | .0169 | .0191 | .0215 | .0241 | .0269 | .0298 |
| 9 | .0033 | .0040 | .0047 | .0056 | .0066 | .0076 | .0089 | .0102 | .0116 | .0132 |
| 10 | .0010 | .0013 | .0016 | .0019 | .0023 | .0028 | .0033 | .0039 | .0045 | .0053 |
| 11 | .0003 | .0004 | .0005 | .0006 | .0007 | .0009 | .0011 | .0013 | .0016 | .0019 |
| 12 | .0001 | .0001 | .0001 | .0002 | .0002 | .0003 | .0003 | .0004 | .0005 | .0006 |
| 13 | .0000 | .0000 | .0000 | .0000 | .0001 | .0001 | .0001 | .0001 | .0002 | .0002 |
| 14 | .0000 | .0000 | .0000 | .0000 | .0000 | .0000 | .0000 | .0000 | .0000 | .0001 |

| $\mu$ $r$ | 4.1 | 4.2 | 4.3 | 4.4 | 4.5 | 4.6 | 4.7 | 4.8 | 4.9 | 5.0 |
|---|---|---|---|---|---|---|---|---|---|---|
| 0 | .0166 | .0150 | .0136 | .0123 | .0111 | .0101 | .0091 | .0082 | .0074 | .0067 |
| 1 | .0679 | .0630 | .0583 | .0540 | .0500 | .0462 | .0427 | .0395 | .0365 | .0337 |
| 2 | .1393 | .1323 | .1254 | .1188 | .1125 | .1063 | .1005 | .0948 | .0894 | .0842 |
| 3 | .1904 | .1852 | .1798 | .1743 | .1687 | .1631 | .1574 | .1517 | .1460 | .1404 |
| 4 | .1951 | .1944 | .1933 | .1917 | .1898 | .1875 | .1849 | .1820 | .1789 | .1755 |
| 5 | .1600 | .1633 | .1662 | .1687 | .1708 | .1725 | .1738 | .1747 | .1753 | .1755 |
| 6 | .1093 | .1143 | .1191 | .1237 | .1281 | .1323 | .1362 | .1398 | .1432 | .1462 |
| 7 | .0640 | .0686 | .0732 | .0778 | .0824 | .0869 | .0914 | .0959 | .1002 | .1044 |
| 8 | .0328 | .0360 | .0393 | .0428 | .0463 | .0500 | .0537 | .0575 | .0614 | .0653 |
| 9 | .0150 | .0168 | .0188 | .0209 | .0232 | .0255 | .0280 | .0307 | .0334 | .0363 |
| 10 | .0061 | .0071 | .0081 | .0092 | .0104 | .0118 | .0132 | .0147 | .0164 | .0181 |
| 11 | .0023 | .0027 | .0032 | .0037 | .0043 | .0049 | .0056 | .0064 | .0073 | .0082 |
| 12 | .0008 | .0009 | .0011 | .0014 | .0016 | .0019 | .0022 | .0026 | .0030 | .0034 |
| 13 | .0002 | .0003 | .0004 | .0005 | .0006 | .0007 | .0008 | .0009 | .0011 | .0013 |
| 14 | .0001 | .0001 | .0001 | .0001 | .0002 | .0002 | .0003 | .0004 | .0004 | .0005 |
| 15 | .0000 | .0000 | .0000 | .0000 | .0001 | .0001 | .0001 | .0001 | .0001 | .0002 |

| r | 5.1 | 5.2 | 5.3 | 5.4 | 5.5 | 5.6 | 5.7 | 5.8 | 5.9 | 6.0 |
|---|---|---|---|---|---|---|---|---|---|---|
| 0 | .0061 | .0055 | .0050 | .0045 | .0041 | .0037 | .0033 | .0030 | .0027 | .0025 |
| 1 | .0311 | .0287 | .0265 | .0244 | .0225 | .0207 | .0191 | .0176 | .0162 | .0149 |
| 2 | .0793 | .0746 | .0701 | .0659 | .0618 | .0580 | .0544 | .0509 | .0477 | .0446 |
| 3 | .1348 | .1293 | .1239 | .1185 | .1133 | .1082 | .1033 | .0985 | .0938 | .0892 |
| 4 | .1719 | .1681 | .1641 | .1600 | .1558 | .1515 | .1472 | .1428 | .1383 | .1339 |
| 5 | .1753 | .1748 | .1740 | .1728 | .1714 | .1697 | .1678 | .1656 | .1632 | .1606 |
| 6 | .1490 | .1515 | .1537 | .1555 | .1571 | .1584 | .1594 | .1601 | .1605 | .1606 |
| 7 | .1086 | .1125 | .1163 | .1200 | .1234 | .1267 | .1298 | .1326 | .1353 | .1377 |
| 8 | .0692 | .0731 | .0771 | .0810 | .0849 | .0887 | .0925 | .0962 | .0998 | .1033 |
| 9 | .0392 | .0423 | .0454 | .0486 | .0519 | .0552 | .0586 | .0620 | .0654 | .0688 |
| 10 | .0200 | .0220 | .0241 | .0262 | .0285 | .0309 | .0334 | .0359 | .0386 | .0413 |
| 11 | .0093 | .0104 | .0116 | .0129 | .0143 | .0157 | .0173 | .0190 | .0207 | .0225 |
| 12 | .0039 | .0045 | .0051 | .0058 | .0065 | .0073 | .0082 | .0092 | .0102 | .0113 |
| 13 | .0015 | .0018 | .0021 | .0024 | .0028 | .0032 | .0036 | .0041 | .0046 | .0052 |
| 14 | .0006 | .0007 | .0008 | .0009 | .0011 | .0013 | .0015 | .0017 | .0019 | .0022 |
| 15 | .0002 | .0002 | .0003 | .0003 | .0004 | .0005 | .0006 | .0007 | .0008 | .0009 |
| 16 | .0001 | .0001 | .0001 | .0001 | .0001 | .0002 | .0002 | .0002 | .0003 | .0003 |
| 17 | .0000 | .0000 | .0000 | .0000 | .0000 | .0001 | .0001 | .0001 | .0001 | .0001 |

$\mu$

| r | 6.1 | 6.2 | 6.3 | 6.4 | 6.5 | 6.6 | 6.7 | 6.8 | 6.9 | 7.0 |
|---|---|---|---|---|---|---|---|---|---|---|
| 0 | .0022 | .0020 | .0018 | .0017 | .0015 | .0014 | .0012 | .0011 | .0010 | .0009 |
| 1 | .0137 | .0126 | .0116 | .0106 | .0098 | .0090 | .0082 | .0076 | .0070 | .0064 |
| 2 | .0417 | .0390 | .0364 | .0340 | .0318 | .0296 | .0276 | .0258 | .0240 | .0223 |
| 3 | .0848 | .0806 | .0765 | .0726 | .0688 | .0652 | .0617 | .0584 | .0552 | .0521 |
| 4 | .1294 | .1249 | .1205 | .1162 | .1118 | .1076 | .1034 | .0992 | .0952 | .0912 |
| 5 | .1579 | .1549 | .1519 | .1487 | .1454 | .1420 | .1385 | .1349 | .1314 | .1277 |
| 6 | .1605 | .1601 | .1595 | .1586 | .1575 | .1562 | .1546 | .1529 | .1511 | .1490 |
| 7 | .1399 | .1418 | .1435 | .1450 | .1462 | .1472 | .1480 | .1486 | .1489 | .1490 |
| 8 | .1066 | .1099 | .1130 | .1160 | .1188 | .1215 | .1240 | .1263 | .1284 | .1304 |
| 9 | .0723 | .0757 | .0791 | .0825 | .0858 | .0891 | .0923 | .0954 | .0985 | .1014 |
| 10 | .0441 | .0469 | .0498 | .0528 | .0558 | .0588 | .0618 | .0649 | .0679 | .0710 |
| 11 | .0245 | .0265 | .0285 | .0307 | .0330 | .0353 | .0377 | .0401 | .0426 | .0452 |
| 12 | .0124 | .0137 | .0150 | .0164 | .0179 | .0194 | .0210 | .0227 | .0245 | .0264 |
| 13 | .0058 | .0065 | .0073 | .0081 | .0089 | .0098 | .0108 | .0119 | .0130 | .0142 |
| 14 | .0025 | .0029 | .0033 | .0037 | .0041 | .0046 | .0052 | .0058 | .0064 | .0071 |
| 15 | .0010 | .0012 | .0014 | .0016 | .0018 | .0020 | .0023 | .0026 | .0029 | .0033 |
| 16 | .0004 | .0005 | .0005 | .0006 | .0007 | .0008 | .0010 | .0011 | .0013 | .0014 |
| 17 | .0001 | .0002 | .0002 | .0002 | .0003 | .0003 | .0004 | .0004 | .0005 | .0006 |
| 18 | .0000 | .0001 | .0001 | .0001 | .0001 | .0001 | .0001 | .0002 | .0002 | .0002 |
| 19 | .0000 | .0000 | .0000 | .0000 | .0000 | .0000 | .0000 | .0001 | .0001 | .0001 |

# Appendix F

# Probabilities for the Normal distribution

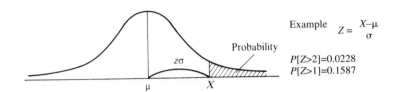

Example $Z = \dfrac{X-\mu}{\sigma}$

$P[Z>2]=0.0228$
$P[Z>1]=0.1587$

| Normal Deviate $z$ | .00 | .01 | .02 | .03 | .04 | .05 | .06 | .07 | .08 | .09 |
|---|---|---|---|---|---|---|---|---|---|---|
| 0.0 | .5000 | .4960 | .4920 | .4880 | .4840 | .4801 | .4761 | .4721 | .4681 | .4641 |
| 0.1 | .4602 | .4562 | .4522 | .4483 | .4443 | .4404 | .4364 | .4325 | .4286 | .4247 |
| 0.2 | .4207 | .4168 | .4129 | .4090 | .4052 | .4013 | .3974 | .3936 | .3897 | .3859 |
| 0.3 | .3821 | .3783 | .3745 | .3707 | .3669 | .3632 | .3594 | .3557 | .3520 | .3483 |
| 0.4 | .3446 | .3409 | .3372 | .3336 | .3300 | .3264 | .3228 | .3192 | .3156 | .3121 |
| 0.5 | .3085 | .3050 | .3015 | .2981 | .2946 | .2912 | .2877 | .2843 | .2810 | .2776 |
| 0.6 | .2743 | .2709 | .2676 | .2643 | .2611 | .2578 | .2546 | .2514 | .2483 | .2451 |
| 0.7 | .2420 | .2389 | .2358 | .2327 | .2296 | .2266 | .2236 | .2206 | .2177 | .2148 |
| 0.8 | .2119 | .2090 | .2061 | .2033 | .2005 | .1977 | .1949 | .1922 | .1894 | .1867 |
| 0.9 | .1841 | .1814 | .1788 | .1762 | .1736 | .1711 | .1685 | .1660 | .1635 | .1611 |
| 1.0 | .1587 | .1562 | .1539 | .1515 | .1492 | .1469 | .1446 | .1423 | .1401 | .1379 |
| 1.1 | .1357 | .1335 | .1314 | .1292 | .1271 | .1251 | .1230 | .1210 | .1190 | .1170 |
| 1.2 | .1151 | .1131 | .1112 | .1093 | .1075 | .1056 | .1038 | .1020 | .1003 | .0985 |
| 1.3 | .0968 | .0951 | .0934 | .0918 | .0901 | .0885 | .0869 | .0853 | .0838 | .0823 |
| 1.4 | .0808 | .0793 | .0778 | .0764 | .0749 | .0735 | .0721 | .0708 | .0694 | .0681 |
| 1.5 | .0668 | .0655 | .0643 | .0630 | .0618 | .0606 | .0594 | .0582 | .0571 | .0559 |
| 1.6 | .0548 | .0537 | .0526 | .0516 | .0505 | .0495 | .0485 | .0475 | .0465 | .0455 |
| 1.7 | .0446 | .0436 | .0427 | .0418 | .0409 | .0401 | .0392 | .0384 | .0375 | .0367 |
| 1.8 | .0359 | .0351 | .0344 | .0336 | .0329 | .0322 | .0314 | .0307 | .0301 | .0294 |
| 1.9 | .0287 | .0281 | .0274 | .0268 | .0262 | .0256 | .0250 | .0244 | .0239 | .0233 |
| 2.0 | .0228 | .0222 | .0217 | .0212 | .0207 | .0202 | .0197 | .0192 | .0188 | .0183 |
| 2.1 | .0179 | .0174 | .0170 | .0166 | .0162 | .0158 | .0154 | .0150 | .0146 | .0143 |
| 2.2 | .0139 | .0136 | .0132 | .0129 | .0125 | .0122 | .0119 | .0116 | .0113 | .0110 |
| 2.3 | .0107 | .0104 | .0102 | .0099 | .0096 | .0094 | .0091 | .0089 | .0087 | .0084 |
| 2.4 | .0082 | .0080 | .0078 | .0075 | .0073 | .0072 | .0069 | .0068 | .0066 | .0064 |
| 2.5 | .0062 | .0060 | .0059 | .0057 | .0055 | .0054 | .0052 | .0051 | .0049 | .0048 |
| 2.6 | .0047 | .0045 | .0044 | .0043 | .0041 | .0040 | .0039 | .0038 | .0037 | .0036 |
| 2.7 | .0035 | .0034 | .0033 | .0032 | .0031 | .0030 | .0029 | .0028 | .0027 | .0026 |
| 2.8 | .0026 | .0025 | .0024 | .0023 | .0023 | .0022 | .0021 | .0021 | .0020 | .0019 |
| 2.9 | .0019 | .0018 | .0018 | .0017 | .0016 | .0016 | .0015 | .0015 | .0014 | .0014 |
| 3.0 | .0013 | .0013 | .0013 | .0012 | .0012 | .0011 | .0011 | .0011 | .0010 | .0010 |

# Appendix G

# Probabilities for the *t*-distribution (two-tail)

| Degree of freedom | Student's t-distribution | | | | | | | | | | | | |
|---|---|---|---|---|---|---|---|---|---|---|---|---|---|
| | Level of significance (α) | | | | | | | | | | | | |
| | .9 | .8 | .7 | .6 | .5 | .4 | .3 | .2 | .1 | .05 | .02 | .01 | .001 |
| 1 | .158 | .325 | .510 | .727 | 1.000 | 1.376 | 1.963 | 3.078 | 6.314 | 12.706 | 31.821 | 63.657 | 636.619 |
| 2 | .142 | .289 | .445 | .617 | .816 | 1.061 | 1.386 | 1.886 | 2.910 | 4.303 | 6.965 | 9.925 | 31.598 |
| 3 | .137 | .277 | .424 | .584 | .765 | .978 | 1.250 | 1.638 | 2.353 | 3.182 | 4.541 | 5.841 | 12.941 |
| 4 | .134 | .271 | .414 | .569 | .741 | .941 | 1.190 | 1.533 | 2.132 | 2.776 | 3.747 | 4.604 | 8.610 |
| 5 | .132 | .267 | .408 | .559 | .727 | .920 | 1.156 | 1.476 | 2.015 | 2.571 | 3.365 | 4.032 | 6.859 |
| 6 | .131 | .265 | .404 | .553 | .718 | .906 | 1.134 | 1.440 | 1.943 | 2.447 | 3.143 | 3.707 | 5.959 |
| 7 | .130 | .263 | .402 | .549 | .711 | .896 | 1.119 | 1.415 | 1.895 | 2.365 | 2.998 | 3.499 | 5.405 |
| 8 | .130 | .262 | .399 | .546 | .706 | .889 | 1.108 | 1.397 | 1.860 | 2.306 | 2.896 | 3.355 | 5.041 |
| 9 | .129 | .261 | .398 | .543 | .703 | .883 | 1.100 | 1.383 | 1.833 | 2.262 | 2.821 | 3.250 | 4.781 |
| 10 | .129 | .260 | .397 | .542 | .700 | .879 | 1.093 | 1.372 | 1.812 | 2.228 | 2.764 | 3.169 | 4.587 |
| 11 | .129 | .260 | .396 | .540 | .697 | .876 | 1.088 | 1.363 | 1.796 | 2.201 | 2.718 | 3.106 | 4.437 |
| 12 | .128 | .259 | .395 | .539 | .695 | .873 | 1.083 | 1.356 | 1.782 | 2.179 | 2.681 | 3.055 | 4.318 |
| 13 | .128 | .259 | .394 | .538 | .694 | .870 | 1.079 | 1.350 | 1.771 | 2.160 | 2.650 | 3.012 | 4.221 |
| 14 | .128 | .258 | .393 | .537 | .692 | .868 | 1.076 | 1.345 | 1.761 | 2.145 | 2.624 | 2.977 | 4.140 |
| 15 | .128 | .258 | .393 | .536 | .691 | .866 | 1.074 | 1.341 | 1.753 | 2.131 | 2.602 | 2.947 | 4.073 |
| 16 | .128 | .258 | .392 | .535 | .690 | .865 | 1.071 | 1.337 | 1.746 | 2.120 | 2.583 | 2.921 | 4.015 |
| 17 | .128 | .257 | .392 | .534 | .689 | .863 | 1.069 | 1.333 | 1.740 | 2.110 | 2.567 | 2.898 | 3.965 |
| 18 | .127 | .257 | .392 | .534 | .688 | .862 | 1.067 | 1.330 | 1.734 | 2.101 | 2.552 | 2.878 | 3.922 |
| 19 | .127 | .257 | .391 | .533 | .688 | .861 | 1.066 | 1.328 | 1.729 | 2.093 | 2.539 | 2.861 | 3.883 |
| 20 | .127 | .257 | .391 | .533 | .687 | .860 | 1.064 | 1.325 | 1.725 | 2.086 | 2.528 | 2.845 | 3.850 |
| 21 | .127 | .257 | .391 | .532 | .686 | .859 | 1.063 | 1.323 | 1.721 | 2.080 | 2.518 | 2.831 | 3.819 |
| 22 | .127 | .256 | .390 | .532 | .686 | .858 | 1.061 | 1.321 | 1.717 | 2.074 | 2.508 | 2.819 | 3.792 |
| 23 | .127 | .256 | .390 | .532 | .685 | .858 | 1.060 | 1.319 | 1.714 | 2.069 | 2.500 | 2.807 | 3.767 |
| 24 | .127 | .256 | .390 | .531 | .685 | .857 | 1.059 | 1.318 | 1.711 | 2.064 | 2.492 | 2.797 | 3.745 |
| 25 | .127 | .256 | .390 | .531 | .684 | .856 | 1.058 | 1.316 | 1.708 | 2.060 | 2.485 | 2.787 | 3.725 |
| 26 | .127 | .256 | .390 | .531 | .684 | .856 | 1.058 | 1.315 | 1.706 | 2.056 | 2.479 | 2.779 | 3.707 |
| 27 | .127 | .256 | .389 | .531 | .684 | .855 | 1.057 | 1.314 | 1.703 | 2.052 | 2.473 | 2.771 | 3.690 |
| 28 | .127 | .256 | .389 | .530 | .683 | .855 | 1.056 | 1.313 | 1.701 | 2.048 | 2.467 | 2.763 | 3.674 |
| 29 | .127 | .256 | .389 | .530 | .683 | .854 | 1.055 | 1.311 | 1.699 | 2.045 | 2.462 | 2.756 | 3.659 |
| 30 | .127 | .256 | .389 | .530 | .683 | .854 | 1.055 | 1.310 | 1.697 | 2.042 | 2.457 | 2.750 | 3.646 |
| 40 | .126 | .255 | .388 | .529 | .681 | .851 | 1.050 | 1.303 | 1.684 | 2.021 | 2.423 | 2.704 | 3.551 |
| 60 | .126 | .254 | .367 | .527 | .679 | .848 | 1.046 | 1.296 | 1.671 | 2.000 | 2.390 | 2.660 | 3.460 |
| 120 | .126 | .254 | .386 | .526 | .677 | .845 | 1.041 | 1.289 | 1.658 | 1.980 | 2.358 | 2.617 | 3.373 |
| ∞ | .126 | .253 | .385 | .524 | .674 | .842 | 1.036 | 1.282 | 1.645 | 1.960 | 2.326 | 2.576 | 3.291 |

# Appendix H

# Critical values for the $\chi^2$ distribution

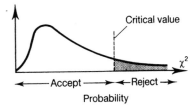

| Degree of freedom | 0.250 | 0.100 | 0.050 | 0.025 | 0.010 | 0.005 | 0.001 |
|---|---|---|---|---|---|---|---|
| 1 | 1.32 | 2.71 | 3.84 | 5.02 | 6.63 | 7.88 | 10.8 |
| 2 | 2.77 | 4.61 | 5.99 | 7.38 | 9.21 | 10.6 | 13.8 |
| 3 | 4.11 | 6.25 | 7.81 | 9.35 | 11.3 | 12.8 | 16.3 |
| 4 | 5.39 | 7.78 | 9.49 | 11.1 | 13.3 | 14.9 | 18.5 |
| 5 | 6.63 | 9.24 | 11.1 | 12.8 | 15.1 | 16.7 | 20.5 |
| 6 | 7.84 | 10.6 | 12.6 | 14.4 | 16.8 | 18.5 | 22.5 |
| 7 | 9.04 | 12.0 | 14.1 | 16.0 | 18.5 | 20.3 | 24.3 |
| 8 | 10.2 | 13.4 | 15.5 | 17.5 | 20.3 | 22.0 | 26.1 |
| 9 | 11.4 | 14.7 | 16.9 | 19.0 | 21.7 | 23.6 | 27.9 |
| 10 | 12.5 | 16.0 | 18.3 | 20.5 | 23.2 | 25.2 | 29.6 |
| 11 | 13.7 | 17.3 | 19.7 | 21.9 | 24.7 | 26.8 | 31.3 |
| 12 | 14.8 | 18.5 | 21.0 | 23.3 | 26.2 | 28.3 | 32.9 |
| 13 | 16.0 | 19.8 | 22.4 | 24.7 | 27.7 | 29.8 | 34.5 |
| 14 | 17.1 | 21.1 | 23.7 | 26.1 | 29.1 | 31.3 | 36.1 |
| 15 | 18.2 | 22.3 | 25.0 | 27.5 | 30.6 | 32.8 | 37.7 |
| 16 | 19.4 | 23.5 | 26.3 | 28.8 | 32.0 | 34.3 | 39.3 |
| 17 | 20.5 | 24.8 | 27.6 | 30.2 | 33.4 | 35.7 | 40.8 |
| 18 | 21.6 | 26.0 | 28.9 | 31.5 | 34.8 | 37.2 | 42.3 |
| 19 | 22.7 | 27.2 | 30.1 | 32.9 | 36.2 | 38.6 | 43.8 |
| 20 | 23.8 | 28.4 | 31.4 | 34.2 | 37.6 | 40.0 | 45.3 |
| 21 | 24.9 | 29.6 | 32.7 | 35.5 | 38.9 | 41.4 | 46.8 |
| 22 | 26.0 | 30.8 | 33.9 | 36.8 | 40.3 | 42.8 | 48.3 |
| 23 | 27.1 | 32.0 | 35.2 | 38.1 | 41.6 | 44.2 | 49.7 |
| 24 | 28.2 | 33.2 | 36.4 | 39.4 | 43.0 | 45.6 | 51.2 |
| 25 | 29.3 | 34.4 | 37.7 | 40.6 | 44.3 | 46.9 | 52.6 |
| 26 | 30.4 | 35.6 | 38.9 | 41.9 | 45.6 | 48.3 | 54.1 |
| 27 | 31.5 | 36.7 | 40.1 | 43.2 | 47.0 | 49.6 | 55.5 |
| 28 | 32.6 | 37.9 | 41.3 | 44.5 | 48.3 | 51.0 | 56.9 |
| 29 | 33.7 | 39.1 | 42.6 | 45.7 | 49.6 | 52.3 | 58.3 |

| Degree of freedom | 0.250 | 0.100 | 0.050 | 0.025 | 0.010 | 0.005 | 0.001 |
|---|---|---|---|---|---|---|---|
| 30 | 34.8 | 40.3 | 43.8 | 47.0 | 50.9 | 53.7 | 59.7 |
| 40 | 45.6 | 51.8 | 55.8 | 59.3 | 63.7 | 66.8 | 73.4 |
| 50 | 56.3 | 63.2 | 67.5 | 71.4 | 76.2 | 79.5 | 86.7 |
| 60 | 67.0 | 74.4 | 79.1 | 83.3 | 88.4 | 92.0 | 99.6 |
| 70 | 77.6 | 85.5 | 90.5 | 95.0 | 100 | 104 | 112 |
| 80 | 88.1 | 96.6 | 102 | 107 | 112 | 116 | 125 |
| 90 | 98.6 | 108 | 113 | 118 | 123 | 128 | 137 |
| 100 | 109 | 118 | 124 | 130 | 136 | 140 | 149 |

# Index

*a priori* probability   359
ABC analysis of stock   541–4
acceptance quality level   441
acceptance sampling   441–3
acid test   191
activity (in project)   550
  analysis of   560–3
  dummy   554–5
additive model for forecasting   283–4
aggregate index   172–3
algebra   21–39
alternative hypothesis   454
annual percentage rate   203
annuities   216–17
APR (annual percentage rate)   203
approach to problems   81–2
AQL (acceptance quality level)   441
arithmetic   14–17
  algebra   22–3
  order of   15–16
  with fractions   17–19
  with percentages   17–19
  with powers   32–6
  with probabilities   359–65
arithmetic mean – *see* mean
autocorrelation   250
average   128–43
  arithmetic mean   129–36
  alternative measures   128–9, 141–3
  of grouped data   132–5
  mean   129–36
  median   136–7
  mode   139–41
  moving average   274–8
  weighted mean   131–2
axes   40–3, 96–102

bar charts   103–6
base period   164
  changing   169–71
  for index   165–8
  weighting   174–5
base value   164
Bayes' theorem
  conditional probabilities   365–72
  in decisions   503–7
bias   70, 145–6
binomial distribution   388–95
  definition   388–9
  mean, etc   292–4
  shape   389–92

  tables   611–15
break even point   193–8

calculus   335–50
  differentiation   335–45
  economic applications   346–50
cardinal data   64–5
Cartesian co-ordinates   40–3, 96–102
case study
  Consumer advice office   161–2
  Crown and Anchor, The   56
  Elemental Electronics   332–3
  Gamblers' Press, The   379–80
  Hammerson and Sons   11–12
  High Acclaim Importers   123–4
  Kings Fruit Farm   450–1
  Lundquist Transport   351–2
  machined components
  Macleod Engines   184–5
  Mrs Hamilton's retirement savings   222–3
  Natural Biscuits   86–7
  Newisham Reservoir, The   525
  Northern Feedstuffs   57–8
  Retail sales in Europe   185–6
  Templar Manufacturing   546–7
  Western General Hospital   259–60
  Westin Contractors   575
  Willingham Consumer Protection Department
    487
  workload planning   298–9
causal forecast   234–8, 264
causal relationship   230
census   67, 69, 422
central limit theorem   424–5, 433
certainty, decisions under   493–4
change
  index numbers   164–80
  rate of   46–6, 335–50
charts – *see* diagrams
Chebyshev   10
Chi-squared distribution   472–82
  critical values   473–3, 621–2
  definition   472
  goodness of fit   472–9
  shape   473
  tests of association   479–82
class   93, 108–9
cluster sample   74
coefficient of
  correlation   241–6
  determination   238–40

**623**

coefficient of (*continued*)
    rank correlation 244–6
    skewness 154–6
    variation 154
collecting data 61–82
combinations 384–7
composite index 172–3
common fraction 17–19
compound interest 202–3
conditional probability 365–72, 503–7
confidence interval 428–40
    one sided 435–7
    for means 428–32
    for proportion 432–5
    small samples 438–40
constant 23–6
constant series 268
constrained optimisation 301
constraints 302–3
    in LP graphs 308–11
consumer's risk 441–3
contingency table 479–82
continuity correction 411–12
continuous data 66
    in frequency distribution 109–10
    probability distributions 404–5
control limit 443–6
controlling stock – *see* stock control
co-ordinates 40–3, 96–102
correlation
    coefficient 241–6
    rank 244–6
costs
    break even analysis 193–8
    data collection 62–3
    economies of scale 198–200
    in projects 563–5
    in queues 577–82
    in stock control 528–9
    marginal 346–9
covariance 153
crashing project time 563–5
criteria for decisions 495–500
critical chi-squared values 472–3
    table 621–2
critical path 560–3
cubic equations 48–9
cumulative frequency distribution 110–12
cumulative percentage frequency distribution
    110–12
current period weighting 175–7
curve fitting 252–4
cycle service level 353
cyclical factors 283–4

data
    cardinal 64–5
    classes 93

collection 61–82
definition 61–2
description 126–57
diagrams 88–118
measures of 126–56
ordinal 64–5
presentation 89–118
reduction 90–1, 126
sampling 422–47
spread 26, 143–53
types 64–7
use 81–2
value of 62–3
decimal fraction 17–19
decimal places 19–20
decision
    analysis 491–518
    criteria 495–500
        choice 499–500
        Laplace 495–6
        Savage 497–8
        Wald 496–7
    features 491
    map 491–2
    node 511
    payoff matrix 492
    tree 510–17
    variable ( for LP) 302
decision making
    analysing problems 491–518
    giving structure 491–3
    quantitative view 4–6
    sequential decisions 510–17
    under certainty 493–4
    under risk 501–510
    under strict uncertainty 495–500
degrees of freedom
    in chi-squared 472
    in t distribution 438–9
Delphi method 266–7
demand
    Normally distributed 534–8
    price elasticity of 349–50
    in stock control 527
denominator 17
dependence table 550–1
dependent events 365–72
dependent variable 40, 96, 230
depreciation 209–12
describing data
    by diagrams 89–118
    by numbers 126–57
deseasonalising data 277–8, 285–8
determination, coefficient of 238–40
deviation 145
diagrams 88–118
    bar charts 103–6
    frequency distribution 108–12

diagrams (*continued*)
  histogram  112–5
  Gantt chart  565–7
  graphs  40–52, 96–101
  Lorenz curve  116–8
  network  550–2
  ogive  115, 137–8, 144–5
  p-chart  443–6
  pictograms  106–8
  pie charts  102–3
  scatter diagrams  96–7
  tables  92–6
  tree
    decision  510–17
    probability  373–5
differentiation  335–45
  definition  335–7
  economic applications  346–50
  maxima and minima  340–5
  rules for  338–40
discounting to present value  204–7
discrete data  66
diseconomies of scale  199–200
dispersion – *see* spread
distribution free test – *see* non-parametric test
distributions, probability  382–416
  binomial  388–95, 611–15
  chi-squared  471–82
  definition  382–3
  empirical  383
  negative exponential  578–9
  Normal  404–15, 619
  Poison  396–404, 616–18
  t  438–40
distribution of sample means  423–40
dummy activity  554–5

e (exponential constant)  49–50
economic order quantity  530–2
economics  346–50
economies of scale  198–200
elasticity of demand  349–50
empirical probability  359
equations
  graphs of  40–52, 96–102
  solving
    quadratic  36–9, 47–8
    simultaneous  27–31, 51–2
    simple  23–6
error
  in forecasts  269–70
  in hypothesis testing  454–6
  in regression  225–234
  in time series  269–71
  measures
    mean error  145–6, 227–9, 270
    mean absolute deviation  145–9, 228–9, 271

    mean squared error  149–53, 228–9, 271
estimating
  population means  423–32
  population proportions  432–5
event
  dependent  365–6
  in project  550
  independent  362–3
  mutually exclusive  359–60
  random  396–7
event analysis (project)  557–9
expected value  501–2
experimentation  8–9, 81–2
exponential constant  49–50
  graphs of  49–50
exponential smoothing  279–82
extrapolation  237

feasible region  310–11
feedback  9
finance models  189–217
  annuities  216–17
  break even point  193–8
  depreciation  209–12
  discounting  204–9
  economies of scale  192–200
  interest  201–3
  internal rate of return  207–9
  mortgages  215–16
  net present value  205–7
  sinking fund  214–15
financial ratios  190–2
fit
  goodness of  472–9
  line of best  230–4
fixed costs
  break even point  193–8
  in economies of scale  192–200
fixed order quantity  528
float  561–3
forecasting  263–94
  causal  264, 234–8
  exponential smoothing  279–82
  judgemental  264, 265–7
  linear regression  234–8
  methods  263–4
  moving averages  274–8
  projective  267–94
  seasonality and trend  283–94
  sensitivity  275–6, 281–2
  simple averages  272–4
  smoothing constant  279
  time series  268–72
  time horizon  263
formulation
  linear programming  301, 302–8
  models  8–10, 81–2

fractions 17–19
freedom, degrees of
 in chi-squared 472
 in t distribution 438–9
frequency distributions 108–12
 cumulative 110–12
 definition 108–12
 measures of
  median 137–8
  mean 132–5
  mean absolute deviation 147
  mode 140
  skewness 154–6
  standard deviation 152–3
  variance 152–3
 percentage 110–12
 relative 110–12, 382
frequency tables 93, 108–12
further reading 594–8

Gantt chart 565–7
Gaussian distribution – *see* Normal distribution
gearing 191
goodness of fit test 472–82
gradient 45–6
 from differentiation 335–7
 instantaneous 336
 turning points 340–45
 straight line 45–6
graphs 40–52, 96–102
 Cartesian co-ordinates 40–3, 96–102
 drawing 40–2
 exponential 49–50
 for linear programmes 308–15
 gradient 45–6, 336–7
 polynomials 48–9
 quadratic equations 47–8
 simultaneous equations 51–2
 straight line 43–6, 96–102
grouped data
 median 137–8
 mean 132–5
 mean absolute deviation 147
 mode 140
 standard deviation 152–3
 variance 152–3

histograms 112–5
historical analogy 266
horizon, forecasting 263
hypothesis testing 453–83
 alternative hypothesis 454
 association 479–82
 chi-squared test 472–82
 differences in means 465–7
 errors 454–6
 goodness of fit 472–9
 method 453–4, 458

non-parametric tests 471–82
null hypothesis 454
one-sided 461–5
paired tests 468–71
parametric tests 435–71
population means 453–60
population proportions 460–1
significance level 456–60
small samples 467–8

ideas in practice
 Ace Dairies 488–9
 CIS personal pensions
 Mareco/Gallup International 58–9
 RPF Global 1–2
 Survey into the use of quantitative methods 188
implementation 8–9, 81–2
independent equations 29
independent events 362–4
independent variable 40, 96, 230
index number 164–80
 aggregate 172–3
 average 172–3
 base period 164–71
 base period weighting 174–5
 changing base period 169–71
 composite 172–3
 current period weighting 175–8
 definition 164
 mean price relative 172–3
 price 165–8, 178–80
 weighted 174–80
indices – *see* index
infeasible solution 326
information 61
integers 17
intercept 45–6
interest 201–3
 annual percentage rate 203
 compound 202–3
 simple 201–2
internal rate of return 207–9
interpolation 237
interval estimate 428
interviews 76
inventory control – *see* stock control
inverse matrix 29–31
investment 201–3
IRR (internal rate of return) 207–9

judgemental forecast 264, 265–7

kurtosis 156

Laplace decision criterion 495–6
Laspeyre index 174–8
lead time 532–4
line graph 40

line of best fit    230–4
linear programming    301–27
    computer solutions    315–18
    constraints    302–3
    decision variables    302
    definition    301
    formulation    302–8
    graphical solutions    308–15
    non-negativity constraint    303
    objective function    304
    sensitivity analysis    301, 319–26
linear regression    230–46, 85–6
    for forecasting    234–8
    line of best fit    230–4
    linear relationship    225–7
    measuring errors    227–9
    multiple    247–51
    noise    225–7
    non-linear data    252–4
    strength of relationship    238–46
loans    213–17
location of data – *see* mean
logical dummy    554–5
long term forecast    263
longitudinal survey    77
Lorenz curve    116–18
lot tolerance percent defective (LTPD)    441–3
LP – *see* linear programming

MAD – *see* mean absolute deviation
map, problem    291–2
marginal analysis    346–9
market survey    266
matrix    29–31
maximum    340–45
mean    128–43
    arithmetic mean    129–36
    choice of measure    141–3
    estimating population    423–40
    median    128, 136–8
    mode    128, 139–41
    of binomial distribution    392
    of grouped data    132–5
    of Poison distribution    398
    sampling distribution of    423–7
    weighted    131–2
mean absolute deviation    145–9, 228–9, 271
    of grouped data    147–8
mean deviation    145–6
mean error    227–9, 270
mean price relative index    172–3
mean squared error    149–53, 228–9, 271
measures
    financial    190–2
    of change    164–80
    of data    126–56
        location    128–43
        spread    126, 143–56

of error    225–9
of relationship    241–6
median    128, 136–8
    for grouped data    137–8
minimum    340–45
mode    128, 139–41
    grouped data    140
model    7–10, 24
model building    8–10, 24, 81–2
money, time value of    204–9
mortgages    215–6
moving average    274–8, 284
MSE – *see* mean squared error
multi-stage sample    73
multicollinearity    249
multiple (linear) regression    247–51
multiplicative model    283–4
mutually exclusive events    359–61

negative exponential distribution    578–9
net present value    205–7
    internal rate of return    207–9
network analysis – *see* project network analysis
node
    in decision trees    511
    in networks    550–1
    in probability trees    373–5
noise
    in time series    269–72
    in regression    225–34
nominal data    64–5
non-critical activities    560–1
non-linear regression    252–4
non-negativity constraint    303
non-parametric tests    471–82
    chi-squared    472–82
    definition    471
non-response to surveys    80–1
Normal distribution    404–15
    approximation to binomial    403–4
    definition    404–6
    shape    406–8
    tables    619
    use    408–15
notation, scientific    36
notional interest rate    203
null hypothesis    454
numbers
    arithmetic    14–17
    changing to letters    21–39
    index numbers    164–80
    working with    4–6, 14–20
numerator    17
numerical problems, solutions    607–610
numerical views    126–8

objective function    304
    in graph    311–12

observation
   for data collection   75
   in problem solving   8–9, 81–2
ogive   115, 137–8, 144–5
one-sided
   confidence intervals   435–7
   hypothesis test   461–5
operating characteristics   580–2
optimal
   solution to linear programme   311–15
   value at turning points   340–5
ordinal data   64–5
origin   40

p-chart   443–6
Paasche index   175
panel consensus   265–6
panel survey   77
parametric tests   453–471
Pareto analysis   541–4
payoff matrix   492–3
Pearson
   coefficient of correlation   241–6
   coefficient of skewness   154–6
percentage   18–19
percentage frequency distribution   110–11
percentage points   166–7
percentile   145
periodic review   528, 538–41
permutations   385–7
personal insight   265
personal interview   76
pictograms   106–8
pie charts   102–3
planning
   projects   549–68
   with linear programming   301–27
point estimate   428
Poison distribution   396–404
   approximation to binomial   394–5
   definition   396–7
   for queues   578–9
   mean etc   398
   shape   398–400
   tables   616–18
polynomials   48–9
population
   definition   67–8, 422–3
   estimating mean   423–32
   estimating proportions   432–5
postal survey   76–7
powers, raising to   32–6
present value of money   204–7
presentation of data   89
price elasticity of demand   349–50
price index   165–8
price relative   172–3
primary data   66

principal   201
probability
   Bayes theorem   365–72
   calculations with   359–64
   conditional   365–72
   definitions   356–9
   distributions   382–416
   independent events   362–4
   mutually exclusive events   359–61
   tree   373–5
probability distributions   382–416
   binomial   388–95, 611–15
   chi-squared   471–82
   definition   382–3
   empirical 383
   negative exponential   578–9
   Normal   404–15, 619
   Poison   396–404, 616–18
   t   438–40
problem map   491–2
problem solving   8–10
   stages in   8–10, 81–2
process control   443–6
producer's risk   441–3
profit   190, 193
project   549
project network analysis   549–68
   activity   550
   changing duration   563–5
   crashing   563–5
   critical path   560–3
   definition   549
   dependence table   550–1
   drawing networks   550–2
   dummy   554–5
   event   550
   float   561–3
   Gantt chart   565–7
   timing   557–63
project planning   549–568
   activity analysis   560–3
   changing duration   563–5
   changing resources   565–7
   crashing   563–5
   event analysis   557–9
   scheduling resources   563–7
   steps in   452
projective forecast   263, 267–94
   approach   263, 267
   exponential smoothing   279–82
   moving averages   274–8
   seasonality and trend   283–94
   simple averages   272–4
   time series   268–72

quadratic equations   36–9, 47–8
   graphs   47–8

quality control 441–3
    acceptance sampling 441–3
    process control 443–6
quantitative measures 4–6
quartile 144
    deviation 144
queues 577–90
    definition 577–8
    multiserver 582
    operating characteristics 580–2
    simulation 583–9
    single server 578–82
questionnaire 77–80
quota sample 71–3

random events 396–7
random node 511
random numbers 69–70
random sample 69–70, 587–9
range 143
rank correlation 244–6
ratios for finance 190–2
rectangular axes 40–3, 96–102
reducing balance depreciation 210–2
reduction of data 90–1
references 594–8
regression – *see* linear regression
relative frequency distribution 110–12, 382
reorder level
    constant demand 532–4
    variable demand 534–8
residual 227, 270
resources
    linear programming 319–20
    projects 563–7
retail price index 172, 178–80
return on equity 191
return on total assets 190
risk 501–9
    expected value 501–2
    updating probabilities 503–7
    utility 508–9
roots
    of numbers 32–6
    of quadratic equations 37–9
    square and cube 32
rounding 19–20, 24

safety stock 535–8, 540–1
sample
    choosing 67–74
    definition 67, 422–3
    purpose 67, 422
    random 67–70, 587–9
    small 438–40
    types 69–74
sampling 422–47

acceptance 441–3
confidence interval 428–37
distribution of sample mean 423–40
frame 68
plan 441–3
for population mean 423–32
for population proportions 432–5
for quality control 441–6
for simulation 587–9
one-sided interval 435–40
process control 443–6
purpose 67–8, 422–3
questionnaire 77
random 587–9
survey 74–7
t distribution 438–40
Savage decision criterion 497–8
scatter diagram 96–7
scheduling
    combinations and permutations 384–7
    number of sequences 384
    projects 549–68
scientific notation 36
seasonal index 288–90
seasonal series 268, 283, 288–90
secondary data 66
self assessment questions, solutions 599–606
semi-interquartile range 144–5
sensitivity analysis (in LP) 301, 319–26
    changing resources 319–20
    changing profits 320–1
sensitivity of forecasts 275
sequencing 384
sequential decisions 510–21
service level 535–8, 540–1
shadow price 319–20
significance level 456–60
significant figures 19–21
simple aggregate index 172–3
simple average forecast 272, 274
simulation 583–9
    approach 583–7
    random sampling 587–9
simultaneous equations 27–31, 51–2
single server queue 578–82
sinking funds 214–5
skewness 154–6
solutions
    numerical problems 607–10
    self assessment questions 599–606
solving
    linear programmes 308–15
    quadratic equations 36–9, 47–8
    simultaneous equations 27–31
    simple equations 23–7
Spearman's coefficient 244–6
spread of data 143–53
    mean absolute deviation 145–9

spread of data (*continued*)
    mean deviation   145–6
    mean squared deviation   149–53
    quartile deviation   144
    range   143
    semi-interquartile range   145–5
    standard deviation   149–53
    variance   149–53
square roots   32–6
stages in solving problems   8–10
standard deviation   149–53
    grouped data   152–3
    of binomial distribution   392
    of Normal distribution   406–8
    of Poison distribution   398
standard error   425
statistical inference   422–47
statistical tables   611–20
statistics
    probability   356–72
    probability distributions   382–416
    sampling   422–47
    testing   453–71
stochastic problems   356
stock control   527–44
    ABC analysis   541–4
    background   527–8
    costs   528–9
    economic order quantity   530–2
    periodic review   538–41
    probabilistic demand   534–8
    reorder level   532–6
    service level   535
straight line depreciation   210–12
straight line graphs   43–6
stratified sample   73
strict uncertainty   485–500
subjective forecast   265–7
survey
    non-responses   80–1
    purpose   74–5
    questionnaires   77–80
    types   74–7
symbolic models   7–10
systematic sample   71

t-distribution   438–40
tables of data   92–6
    binomial distribution   611–15
    chi-squared distribution   621–2
    frequency tables   93, 108–12
    Normal distribution   619
    Poison   616–18
    t distribution   620
telephone survey   76
terminal node   511
testing hypotheses – *see* hypothesis testing
time series   268–72
tools, mathematical   14–52
tree
    decision   510–17
    probability   373–5
trend   97–8, 268, 283
    finding   285–8
turning points   340–5

unbound solution   326
uncertainty
    decisions under   495–500
    measuring   356–9
    risk   501–9
utility   508–10

value
    of data   62–3
    of money over time   204–9

variable   23–6
    in linear regression   225–54
variable cost   193–8
variance   149–53
    grouped data   152–3
    of binomial distribution   392
    of Normal distribution   406–8
    of Poison distribution   398
variation, coefficient of   154
Venn diagrams   361–2

Wald decision criterion   496–7
weighted index   174–80
weighted mean   131–2